DESTROYER LEADER

Books by the same Author:

TASK FORCE 57 *(Foreword by Admiral of the Fleet, Lord Fraser of North Cape)*
PEDESTAL *(Foreword by Admiral of the Fleet, The Lord Lewin)*
STUKA AT WAR *(Foreword by Hans-Ulrich Rudel)*
HARD LYING
BRITISH BATTLE-CRUISERS
WAR IN THE AEGEAN
THE STORY OF THE TORPEDO BOMBER
HERITAGE OF THE SEA
ROYAL NAVY SHIPS' BADGES
R.A.F. SQUADRON BADGES
BATTLES OF THE MALTA STRIKING FORCES
PER MARE, PER TERRAM *(Foreword by The Earl Mountbatten of Burma)*
FIGHTING FLOTILLA *(Foreword by Mrs R.M.J. Hutton)*
ARCTIC VICTORY
DESTROYER ACTION *(Foreword by Admiral Sir Gresham Nicholson)*
THE BATTLE OF MIDWAY
THE GREAT SHIPS PASS
HIT FIRST, HIT HARD *(Foreword by Vice-Admiral B.C.B. Brooke)*
IMPACT!
ACTION IMMINENT
CRUISERS IN ACTION
DIVE BOMBER!
HOLD THE NARROW SEA
H.M.S. *WILD SWAN (Foreword by Bob Burns)*
INTO THE ASSAULT
VENGEANCE!
JUNGLE DIVE BOMBERS AT WAR
VICTORIA'S VICTORIES *(Foreword by David Chandler)*
CLOSE AIR SUPPORT
THE ROYAL MARINES – A PICTORIAL HISTORY *(Foreword by Lieutenant-General Sir Steuart Pringle)*
MASSACRE AT TOBRUK
DIVE BOMBERS IN ACTION
BATTLESHIP ROYAL SOVEREIGN
STUKA SQUADRON
SHIP STRIKE!
EAGLE'S WAR
T-6; THE HARVARD, TEXAN AND WIRRAWAY.
DOUGLAS SBD DAUNTLESS
CURTISS SBZC HELLOIVER
JUNKERS Ju87 STUKA
AICHI D3A1/2 VAL
DOUGLAS AD SKYRAIDER
STRAIGHT DOWN!
FAIRCHILD-REPUBLIC A-10 THUNDERBOLT-II
NORTH AMERICAN T-6, SNJ, HARVARD 7 CAC WIRRAWAY
LOCKHEED C-130 HERCULES
PETLYAKOV Pe-2 PESHKA

See all Peter C. Smith's books at www.dive-bombers.co.uk

DESTROYER LEADER

The Story of HMS *Faulknor* 1935–46

'The hardest-worked destroyer in the Fleet'

Peter C. Smith

Pen & Sword

MARITIME

Dedication

To the memory of the late Bill Silltow, *Faulknor* veteran and a great man.

This 3rd expanded and revised edition first published in
Great Britain in 2004
By Pen & Sword Maritime
An imprint of Pen and Sword Books Ltd
47 Church Street
Barnsley
South Yorkshire
S70 2AS
England

ISBN 1 84415 121 2

Typeset in the UK by Mac Style Ltd, Scarborough, N. Yorkshire.
Printed and bound in the UK by CPI UK.

Pen & Sword Books Ltd incorporates the imprints of Pen & Sword Aviation, Pen & Sword Maritime, Pen & Sword Military, Wharncliffe Local History, Pen & Sword Select, Pen & Sword Military Classics and Leo Cooper.

For a complete list of Pen & Sword titles please contact
Pen & Sword Books Limited
47 Church Street, Barnsley, South Yorkshire, S70 2AS, England
E-mail: enquiries@pen-and-sword.co.uk
Website: www.pen-and-sword.co.uk

Contents

	Tables and Diagrams	vi
	Acknowledgements, First edition	vii
	Acknowledgements, Third edition	viii
	Introduction	1
CHAPTER ONE	*Birth of a Greyhound*	3
CHAPTER TWO	*Grey Seas and Sky*	19
CHAPTER THREE	*The Club*	58
CHAPTER FOUR	*'Twixt Malta and the Bay*	86
CHAPTER FIVE	*Arctic Battleground*	114
CHAPTER SIX	*The Fight Avails*	168
CHAPTER SEVEN	*D-Day to End Game*	233
Appendix I	Statistical Details	278
Appendix II	Wartime Alterations	280
Appendix III	Battle Honours	281
Appendix IV	Commanding Officers	282
Appendix V	Distinguished Personages aboard HMS *Faulknor*	283
Appendix VI	Those Who Did Not Return	284
Appendix VII	Prime Sources, References and Secondary Material	285
	Notes	288
	Index	293

Tables and Diagrams

Tables

1. Original Composition of the 6th Flotilla – May, 1935   15
2. Oiling at Sea – May, 1943   174
3. Disposition of Royal Navy Ships during the Aegean Campaign   221

Diagrams

1. Typical Depth-Charge Pattern for Destroyers Pre- and early War   7
2. Battle of Spartivento 27th November 1940. British Fleet Dispositions   74
3. U-Boat attacks on Convoy SL.67 – 8th March 1941   83
4. First Air Attack on 8th Flotilla in Sicilian Channel – 10th May 1941   94
5. Second Air Attack on 8th Flotilla in Sicilian Channel – 10th May 1941   95
6. German Mass Torpedo-Bomber Attack on Convoy PQ.18 – 13th September 1942 138
7. Planned Day Cruising Diagram for Convoy QP.15 – 20th November 1942   145
8. Surrender of Italian Fleet – 10th September 1943   191
9. The Action off Stampalia – 18th September 1943   194
10. Night air attacks on HMS *Faulknor* off Leros – 0145 to 0230 21st October 1943   208
11. Allied aircraft's aerial depth-charge attack on HMS Faulknor, 19th/20th March, 1944   232
12. Operation 'Neptune' – Juno Beach bombarding ship – 6th June 1944   237

Acknowledgements
(First Edition)

I have been very fortunate during the writing of this book in securing the unselfish assistance of a great many people, the majority of whom were complete strangers, but who nevertheless gave up a great deal of their time to talk and write to me. Truly, without them there would not have been a book. In particular, I would like to thank the following.

Lord Justice Danckwerts – in addition to valuable reminiscences his unique photographs add much to my knowledge of the ship. Admiral Sir Deric Holland-Martin, GCB, DSO, DSC; Captain A. F. De Salis; Commander W. K. Cornish-Bowden, R.N.; Mr C. Watson; Mr S. Hollett and Mr H. Vivash – all of them veterans of *Faulknor's* ships company who presented me with eye-witness accounts and memoirs. Commander T. D. Manning for early inspiration and encouragement and also many other individuals and organisations, in particular Messrs. Yarrow and Company, Scotstoun, and others who wish to remain anonymous.

Much of the original basic outline for this work owed it origins to Mr Douglas Kinghorn and the now defunct Warship Records Club, a small group of enthusiasts dedicated to recording the wartime histories of all fighting ships; here again in particular to Mr W. Scrivener for pre-war research and to Mr John Dominy for the outstanding drawings which so enhance the book, and to Mr Edwin Walker for his assistance, advice and encouragement in the face of adversity. I would also like to thank Commander H. Lovegrove for his memories of the pre-war China Station and my late brother, David, for his assistance in the indexing of the original book.

To all these and many others, my sincere thanks.

Peter C. Smith
London, 1967

Acknowledgements
(Third Edition)

When the first edition of this book was written, anything appertaining to World War II was still regarded as 'Secret' and 'Restricted'. One had to beaver away with the minimum of official help or assistance to find out every basic fact. It was very hard work indeed. One notable exception to the relentless obstruction by Officialdom was the then Head of the Naval Historical Branch, Rear-Admiral Peter Buckley, who was kindness itself within permissible parameters. Alas, on his departure a very different attitude was encountered and remains.

Nowadays of course, every Report of Proceeding, the various Naval War Diaries of all the commands, the Pink List of Movements and much, much more is freely available at the Public Record Office. Today modern historians following the same route are spoilt for choice, indeed often the problem is what to omit when earlier it was finding anything at all. Against these advantages, in the intervening years, somewhere between the famine and the feast, the Civil Service has done its mindless work and in the process they term 'weeding' much very valuable and irreplaceable documentation has been confirmed to the bonfire. So, of the Log Books of Faulknor, which I was able to view in 1967, most have since been so destroyed and only a few remain thirty years later. Such official vandalism almost defies belief, but is, alas, par for the course.

It is essential to add eyewitness documentation to the dry factual bones, and in this I have been handsomely provided. Since the book was first published the HMS Faulknor Association has been formed and flourishes. More than fifty ex-serving members meet annually and they have adopted me and made available to me their memories and photographs. I would like to acknowledge herewith my gratitude to those following gallant gentlemen of that organisation, who have helped me with their memoirs, diaries and photographs: Carl G. Huer; Raymond Johnson; Jack Banner;

Eric H. Prigmore; Laurie 'Tom' Piper; Peter A.G. Heeley; Bill L. Silltow; Griffith E. Fanthorpe; Alfie Pavey; Robby Robinson; Rosie G. Budd; Ken Timson; Curlie Lee; Ronald Smith; T ed Slinger; Larry V. Chandler; Bob Parham (like myself, a life-long West Ham United supporter!); Ellis Clarke; Rowland Fairweather; Harry Pine; Vernon Coles, D.S.M.; also to Mrs Jessica Newman, Mrs Diane Rust and Mrs Christine Wheeler, for permission to quote extracts from Ted Newmans personal diary kept aboard, and also Jack Barrett for permission to quote passage from his personal diary kept aboard; Doctor 1. D. M. Nelson, former Surgeon-Lieutenant of the Faulknor at D-Day, for permission to quote from his extensive notes and for his very special photographs of her final days; others who deserve my thanks in full are Guy Robbins, Bob Todd and David Hodge of the National Maritime Museum Annexe at the Brass Foundry, Woolwich Arsenal, London; Hugh G. Owen for so generously sharing his unrivalled knowledge of destroyer photograph sources; Lady Winfred Scott Moncrieff; Harry Stapleton, Harleston; Chaz Bowyer, Mulbarton; Sarah Bowen, Dyfed County Council Archivist Office, Haverfordwest, Dr H. Tomlinson, Priaulx Library, Guernsey; Eric G H Moody, Stourbridge; Mrs Joan M. Braithwaite, Milfordon-Sea; H. Jack Haden, Historian and Author, Stourbridge; Dave Weaver, Stourbridge Royal Naval Association; Mr David Hickman and his staff at Stourbridge Library; Roger Dodsworth, Dudley Metropolitan Borough; Mrs K H Atkins, Dudley Library; Laverick Breeze, formerly of T. W. Wards, Milford Haven; Terry Bevan, The Milford Haven Museum; Vernon Scott, Author and Historian, Pembroke Dock; Tim Hart, owner of the cottage Faulknor at Little Haven; P. F. Lisle-Taylor, Milford Haven Port Authority; David G. Rye, Milford Haven Port Health Authority, Martin Rowland; Dr. I. R. Buxton, Department of Marine Technology, University of Newcastle-upon-Tyne; Raymond Harding; Lieutenant M. D. Evans, R.N., HMS Tamar, Hong Kong; Steve Harris, Directorate of History, National Defence HQ, Ottawa; Vernon R. Smith,

Archives II Reference Branch, Textual Reference Section, National Archives, Washington D.C; Francis de Salis, for his faith in commissioning Destroyer Leader originally Lieutenant Commander G. B. Mason, for encouragement and wise counsel; Captain John Wells, R.N., for wise discourse on gunnery and technical matters; Stephen Harvey, Mildenhall, for the log book of his father, Sub-Lieutenant (A) 'Jack' F. Harvey, 815 Squadron, FAA; The Chief Design Engineer and also to Sharon Bremner, both of Yarrow Shipbuilders Limited, Scotstoun7 Glasgow, for supplying original photographs of the launch and trials as well as original documentation, Herrn Döringhoff, Bundesarchiv Militarachiv, Freiburg; and again to my old friend and fellow researcher, Edwin R. Walker, for continual help, advice and assistance down the years. Edwin Walker probably knows more about the movements and war records of British destroyers in World War II than any other person alive, and much more than many self-appointed 'experts' who continually proclaim their limited knowledge in that field at wearisome length.

Peter C. Smith
Riseley, Beds. February 2004

'If I were to die tomorrow, want of Frigates would be engraved on my heart'
Admiral Lord Nelson

'Our destroyers were greatly over worked and under-rested'
Admiral Andrew B. Cunningham

Introduction

My original reason for writing this book in the 1960s I set out at the time. It was a determination to set the record straight as far as destroyer men were concerned in the accounts of their achievements in the Second World War. The destroyer played a dominant role in Britain's last great struggle for control of the sea. The life and death of every single inhabitant of this nation then depended on keeping open the sea-lanes, without the oil and food and munitions thus brought in starvation was certain, as was defeat. All the other claimants on the winning of the war were as nothing compared with the issue of sea-power successfully applied. On land, without the Royal Navy, the defeated British armies could not have been brought home from Norway, France, Greece and Crete to fight another day. Nor supplied and rebuilt, nor taken back to the enemy shores to finish the job. In the air neither the Battle of Britain nor the bomber offensive could have taken place, had the Royal Navy not got the oil fuel through to keep the aircraft airborne. The fate of Germany in World War One, as a result of the British Naval blockade, is an often ignored example of Britain's own fate had the Royal Navy failed.

The destroyer paid a leading part in this six-year struggle. By their very nature destroyers were, in those fateful years, the very symbol of Britain's sea power. They were small, numerous, fast, beautiful, powerful and brilliantly manned and commanded, despite the sneering denigration of some post-war 'historians'. They were highly adaptable to a degree to which no other warship has aspired before or since. They guarded the huge battleships and aircraft carriers, being at once both their screen against submarine attack and their aggressive counter-punch as torpedo craft. They performed the same function for the mercantile convoys, defending them against surface attack, submarine attack and air attack. They laid mines in the enemy's minefields; they swept enemy mines. They acted as improvised troop transports for both evacuations as at Dunkirk and Crete and landings as in the Aegean; They formed striking forces with cruisers or on their own against German and Italian battleships or convoys. They closed-in to enemy shores to bombard coastal defences as at Salerno, Anzio and Normandy, or duelled with German tanks over open sights as at Boulogne. They were ubiquitous.

All this is a fact but, looking through the numerous histories of the naval war published over the last sixty years, official and unofficial, of the hundreds of such books, only a dozen or so will *really* tell you about the destroyers. In official accounts they are too often dismissed as anonymous escorts, only mentioned when sunk. In popular books their names are often spelt incorrectly[1], their actions incorrectly recounted from other secondary sources, 'facts' are repeated, falsely, with no attempt at checking. Little improvement has been seen since the first edition of this book, indeed some 'reference' books on British destroyers published since then are an absolute disgrace. Attempts to give a fuller, truer accounts have been scorned by some 'pundits' as not worth the effort, as if any history which is researched and presented properly, being beyond the reviewers themselves, is therefore deemed without merit. Not so; while the eyewitnesses still remain who served in these vessels, and the records are finally opened to the public at long, long last; here is as full an account of a British destroyer's war career as has yet been presented. As I wrote forty years ago, I have chosen one typical destroyer of that period, one which served before the war, and right through the war, in the front line. In many ways HMS *Faulknor's* war service was unique, but she represents all the destroyers of the Royal Navy of that era. Her breed should *not* to be casually dismissed as, '… obsolete when built', as one worthy has done. Nor am I in any doubt of whether, a destroyer's war career, '… is worth a book', as in the eyes of one dreary list compiler, or if it, '… merits full treatment', as another dull critic would have it. Such people would dismiss six years of unique war service and achievement as not worth retaining. On the contrary, I regard the recounting of such facts as a proud and integral part of our naval heritage, which has to be preserved in print as it has not been preserved in actuality. I am proud to 'Chronicle' such history and regard that label as an honour.

So here are the achievements of HM destroyer *Faulknor* in full. She typifies all the other British destroyers, her story is their story, and, in this book the men who manned 'the boats', are *not* forgotten.

Peter C. Smith
Riseley, Bedford – February 2004

CHAPTER I

Birth of a Greyhound

HMS *Faulknor* was a hybrid type of warship, now extinct in the world's navies, the Flotilla Leader – a type of warship, which originated in this country because of ever-increasing speeds obtained by the successive destroyer classes from 1911 onwards. Prior to that date the larger staff required to control the average flotilla of twenty boats was accommodated in small cruisers. The first *Faulknor* and her sisters, although not laid down as Leaders, were large enough to be used as such and were completed early in the First World War.

From 1921, flotillas of eight destroyers, plus a Leader, were introduced. Each was subdivided into three divisions, each of three ships, for attacking purposes, the Leader and two destroyers in one division, a divisional leader and two destroyers in the others. Flotilla Leaders were always distinguished by a broad black band around the rim of the fore-funnel, the two divisional leaders having a similar, but thinner ring. These funnel markings should not be confused with the flotilla identity markings consisting of one, two or three red, white or black rings on the *after* funnel, each flotilla having its own combination. Nor with the Pendant Number, a destroyer's individual identity code, usually a letter and two numbers, painted on the ships' hulls either side of the bridge. Until the 1950s, only smaller vessels actually painted them up, and Flotilla Leaders normally did not.

The flotilla system soon tended to break down under confused operational conditions, especially in the muddled fighting off Norway and the Low Countries in spring 1940; the flotillas becoming hopelessly mixed. In 1940-41, very heavy losses in destroyers ended attempts at homogeneity. *Faulknor's* wartime flotilla, the 8th, retained its identity longer than most, but after the *Fame* ran aground in October 1940, never again regained its peacetime composition.

Following the experimental prototype destroyers *Amazon* and *Ambuscade* of 1925, Admiralty policy with regard to destroyers was for a class of eight to be laid down annually, each succeeding class incorporating some small improvement over the previous one. In addition, complementary to these programmes, a Flotilla Leader was built for each class, thus providing a continuous flow of modern flotillas to replace the steadily ageing 'V' and 'Ws'. For the 'Echo' class of 1934 the size of the Leader was increased to 1,475 tons and a fifth 4.7-inch gun was reinstated in *Exmouth,* this design being closely followed for *Faulknor.*

The Admiralty invited tenders from interested shipbuilders on 8 November 1932, the letter itself from W. S. D. Jenkins, Director for Naval Contracts, going out 15 November, with replies due 19 December. The Yarrow Company's tender was written on 19 December, received the next day at the Admiralty. On 25 January 1933 the Board decision was made and Yarrow's tender was chosen. The contract was placed on 22 February and the design specification promulgated 17 March 1933.[1]

Yarrow's figures were £118,300 for the Hull; £145, 351 for Main and Auxiliary Machinery with Boilers and £8,235 for further auxiliary machinery. When the tender was accepted certain information appertaining to the Portsmouth Dockyard-built *Exmouth* was made available to the company, including the Scheme of Welding, and a print was taken personally by Sir Harold Yarrow himself, as well as one sheet of offsets.

The only modifications initially to *Exmouth's* specification were that first the Engineer in Chief decided that 'Refrigerator Plant' should read 'Cooling Plant'. Second, the DSD modified the W/T equipment so that *Faulknor* was to be equipped with the Type 49Y as the main set; the Type 52 as the Fire Control set and the Type 44 as the second set. Finally, a VC/VF outfit was to be fitted. On 23 October, DTM decreed that a 32-cwt TSDS winch was installed instead of the 20-cwt winch in *Exmouth*.

The heroine of this story – ordered 17 March 1933, from the yard of Messrs. Yarrow and Company of Scotstoun, Glasgow and built to this well-tested design – followed a long line of famous warships constructed by that company over the previous forty years, when the name Yarrow had become synonymous with destroyers. Indeed, in 1893 they built the world's *first* destroyer, the little *Havock*.

Faulknor, coming in a direct line from such as these, was sure of inheriting the qualities of sound design, capable draughtsmanship and skilled construction, which had made her many predecessors such successful warships.

The destroyers of the thirties were graceful, pleasing-looking ships; this, coupled with a seaworthy hull and a high standard of training and seamanship among their crews made them superior to all types of foreign destroyers, save in two respects. First, lack of endurance; ships of the 'F' class carried 490 tons of oil fuel which gave a range of 6,350 nautical miles at 15 knots, 4,290 nautical miles at 20 knots and only 1,285 nautical miles at full power. At $36\frac{1}{2}$ knots, her trial speed (maintained for six hours), she steamed three miles for each ton of oil, the hourly consumption being 11.86 tons.

Then designed motive power was the standard destroyer outfit of Parsons I.R. single reduction turbines giving an SHP of 35,800, 360 RPM with an official speed of $31\frac{1}{2}$ knots in deep loaded condition, her displacement then being recorded as 1,651 tons. The Destroyer Section New Construction designer, Mr A. P. Cole, made a report on 28 June 1935 that, when inclined, *Faulknor* was 36 tons lighter than *Exmouth*. These inclining experiments had been conducted on the afternoon of Saturday 23 March. *Faulknor* was placed in Messrs. Barclay Curles Dock, the wind being about Force 2, about two points off her stern on the starboard side. This wind dropped afterwards and so did not affect the figures over-much. The sea was smooth. The ship's hawsers were slackened during each reading of the pendulums.

The figures revealed the Inclining Displacement was 1,316 tons, and the Inclining G.M. was 3.01 feet. The net weight to be added for deep condition was 695 tons. The estimated deep displacement was 2,011 tons as against a designed 2,066 tons, and the Deep G.M. (Solid) was 2.89 feet. The machinery was about 30 tons less than the designed figure of 540 tons, the remainder of the difference being spread over hull, equipment etc. The decision not to fit either *Exmouth* or *Faulknor* with the TSDS saved 12 tons.

Her boilers were of standard Admiralty 3-drum type with 300-lb per square inch pressure at 620° F. Specific weight in boilers and machinery had been reduced to 540 tons. The temperature in *Faulknor's* engine room on trials reached 91° F, on the floors of her boiler rooms 81° F and back on boilers 170° F.

The second weakness was the lack of useful dual-purposed capability in their main 4.7-inch armament. These guns had a maximum elevation of 40°, being principally a surface weapon. Thus new British destroyers carried only the quadruple 0.5-inch machine gun against aircraft, which had neither the range nor the weight of shell to stop determined dive-bombing.

Initially in *Exmouth's* design, which *Faulknor* followed, a single, or even a pair, of 3-inch High Angle (HA) guns were actively considered, but, ultimately, the Director of Naval Construction, rejected this, and also adoption of a 4.7-inch gun with 60° elevation, then under trial. This decision was disastrous. At this time, 1931/32, both the United States Navy and the Imperial Japanese Navy were adopting dual-purpose 5-inch guns for the main armament of their destroyers, and the failure of the Admiralty to follow suit came home to roost eight years later.

Apologists for such pusillanimity give as reason the lack of stability of destroyers for Anti-Aircraft (AA) fire, and a variety of technical production problems[2]. Captain Roskill, a gunnery expert, gives a different explanation, 'The truth was that as long ago as the late 1920s the Admiralty had gone for the wrong sort of control system', while even the Admiralty themselves admitted, through the ABE Committee, in January, 1939, that British destroyers, 'were virtually defenceless against air attack.' The Naval Ordnance Department themselves proclaimed, 'eye-shooting weapons are sufficient.' However, none of these excuses explain *why* the Royal Navy found it impossible to fit their destroyers with such a weapon when the Japanese and Americans had, with no great difficulties, *ten* years before!

Every warship design is based on a compromise and *Faulknor* carried within her slim hull the typical inter-war period answer. Her armament was based on the massed torpedo attack on the enemy fleet's battle-line, which formed the principal destroyer tactic. She was therefore equipped with two quadruple QR Mk VI torpedo-tube mountings, carrying the standard Mark IX 21-inch torpedo, each of which weighed 3,510 lb, giving her a powerful offensive punch of eight. These were ordered 1 February 1933. Unlike Japanese destroyers, she carried no reloads.

Speculation that an improved torpedo might be carried, was noted on 31 March 1932:

> As DTM has proposed the torpedo outfits for the 1932 Programme vessels to be the same as for 1931, it is presumed the proposal to fit larger and heavier torpedoes has been dropped. Increase in length of ship of five feet would be necessary, displacement up by ten tons or after deckhouse reduced and cabin space for two officers given up.

Finally, she was equipped with two sets of the 21-inch QR torpedo tubes. 'Generally design similar to 1931 but modified to have combined (Electro Percussion) firing, external depth setting gear and 'W' gear and a new type of rear door.'

The need for such a strong emphasis on the torpedo had already been questioned;[3] the argument being that there was no longer any potential enemy (excluding Japan and the United States of course) with a large enough battleship force to justify it. This was a shortsighted argument, and here the Admiralty made the absolutely correct decision. Their Lordships were convinced that the torpedo would play a leading part in any future sea conflict, and it was just as well that they did, as often it was the mere *threat* of torpedo attack by British destroyers that discouraged superior enemy forces from pressing home attacks on inferior British forces. Many larger enemy ships were sunk or badly damaged by torpedoes from our destroyers. The other principal duty that destroyers had was in resisting similar attacks from enemy torpedo craft, reflected in *Faulknor's* main gun armament of five 4-7-inch low-angled guns.

The Gun Mountings for *Faulknor* had been ordered on 1 December 1932, and were of the newly-introduced 4.7-inch Mark IX guns on a CP Mark XVII type and differed from earlier models of the same calibre weapon in that removable deck-plates were featured around each gun's training base. These, as their name implied, were portable plates, which could be removed prior to action to reveal deck wells of 14 feet in diameter and fourteen inches deep. The trunnion height was increased by $4\frac{1}{2}$ inches and this, combined with the well, gave 51 inches for LA working. This enabled the gun to elevate to 40°, slightly better than the 30° of earlier types. The guns weighed 10 tons and fired a 50 lb shell with a 30 lb brass cartridge with a $26\frac{1}{2}$-inch recoil. The destroyers carried 200 rounds per gun, but NO HA ammunition was provided!

This was confirmed in a memo, dated 2 June, 1932, on the proposed increase in elevation of 4.7-inch CP XIV Gun Mounting for *Eclipse* class destroyers and *Exmouth*, which read:

> In accordance with Controllers verbal directions, arrangements are being made in the tender drawings and specifications of the 1931 destroyers to provide for 4.7-inch guns to give 40° elevation. The mountings are being arranged in wells about 14 feet diameter and 14 inches deep.

This weapon was a Quick-Firer featuring a sliding breechblock. The guns were controlled for surface action by a Destroyer Director Control Tower mounted on the ship's bridge, which worked in association with the Mark I Admiralty Fire Control Clock as a Surface calculator. No High Angle Fire Control was installed so that for work against low-flying aircraft, like torpedo-bombers, only barrage fire was possible. It was later admitted by the DNAD in October, 1938, that, '… an attack by six torpedo aircraft would have a 90 per cent chance of sinking an "F" class steaming at 25 knots …' Despite this the incredible conclusion reached by the DTD was that, '… a fully HA main armament is not a destroyer requirement …'

Her secondary armament consisted of two 0.5-inch Mk I 4-barrel multiple machine-guns with 2,500 rounds-per-gun carried, and four Lewis machine-guns, with 2,000 rounds-per-gun plus 500 tracer, on Field mountings and one Vickers .303 machine gun.

The biggest impact on naval warfare for many years was the appearance and rapid development of the submarine. The only real safeguard was found to be the age-old system of convoy and escort, the ideal vessel to act as escort obviously being the destroyer, fast, agile and manoeuvrable. Later, when depth-charges were added to their armoury, this fresh duty was added to the destroyers' many chores. The Asdic detection device was another step forward in the control of the underwater danger, and by a decision of 17 June 1932, was standard equipment for all new destroyers.[4]

The principle behind the Asdic device was that an alternating electric current was applied to the Oscillator, a quartz crystal suspended in a dome. This dome was carried raised within the ship's lower hull in a special compartment and was lowered below the ship during use. As the quartz crystal expanded and contracted, the vibrations set up within it are emitted as pulses of sound through the water. When these sound waves struck a submerged object they would be reflected back and this 'echo' received on the crystal, which transmitted them originally. Thus the direction of such an object could be ascertained and also the approximate range according to the delay of the return signal. Unfortunately, the depth of the object so detected was not revealed and had to be guessed at until much later developments.

A special control position, the 'Asdic hut' was built into destroyers' bridges and here a specialist operator sat with a headset on, directed by a trained anti-submarine Control Officer. The returning echo (the 'Ping') was enhanced aurally over loudspeakers and skilled operators could distinguish between submarines, whales, wrecks and other 'red-herrings'. The ship's course was automatically plotted on a chart and the echoes could be read-off to give direction and distance. Pre-war practice had led to a large number of detections and the efficiency of Asdic sets was much over-rated before 1939.

The Asdic equipment itself increased a destroyer's displacement by some sixteen tons, five being for the gear itself, five for depth-charges and throwers and six for the hull weight. An extra three feet of hull length was required to house the dome in which the equipment was seated and which could be raised or lowered. Because of this, destroyers adopted the three boiler-room arrangement, which became standard. Each set cost £1,700 plus installation and the sets were manufactured in the Royal Dockyards to ensure secrecy.

The weak points of the Asdic device were that it was useless against U-boats operating on the surface, which most wolf-packs did in the event; U-boats were shielded in 'layered' water, like the Straits of Gibraltar for example; it was highly unreliable in heavy weather (optimum speed for use was twenty knots) and it was vulnerable to damage, as *Faulknor* herself was to prove on several occasions! Finally, in the last stages of an Asdic approach the Asdic beam would lose the target, depending on how deep the submarine was. There was thus always a 'blind' spot in any attack approach. However, against a submerged enemy and in the hands of a skilled operator, they did bring about many victories.

Once the submarine had been detected, it had to be destroyed, and the standard 1934 weapon for this was the Mark VII depth-charge fitted with Mk VII firing pistol and a primer. The pistol was hydrostatically triggered at its pre-set depth, upon which the 3-ft long, 18-inch diameter steel drum, filled with more than 300 lb of TNT high explosives, detonated. The standard pre-war depth-charge pattern was for five charges to be dropped from Asdic equipped ships, set to explode at varying depths, three from the trap over the stern of the ship and two from depth-charge throwers, mortars with a range of 120 yards on either beam of the ship. Before twenty depth-charges were carried on deck but in wartime the number stowed rapidly increased. In 1939 *Faulknor* was carrying thirty Mark D.3 charges, by 1942 this number of the more powerful Mark D.11s had more than doubled and the new Mark X Minol 'super-charges', which were fired from the destroyers torpedo-tubes, had entered service. The ideal attacking speed was twenty knots. A diamond pattern was thus laid down over the approximate position of the U-boat (See Diagram).

'Prevention is better than cure' became the Government's excuse for funding as little as possible. The use of submarines to attack merchant shipping was solemnly declared illegal, and politicians patted themselves on the back for thus solving the problem while saving the cost of building sufficient destroyers. How much was actually saved in the twenties and thirties thus is hard to calculate: what is certain is that any saving was more than offset by the millions of tons of merchant shipping sunk by U-boats between 1939 and 1945, even without adding the lives of all the seamen killed. Destroyer men put their faith in intensive training, rather than in trumpeted promises.

While the Royal Navy has been much criticised (in retrospect) for concentrating on anti-submarine training to protect the battle-fleet, rather than slow convoys, any destroyer that could protect a 30-knot fleet was more than capable of protecting a nine-knot convoy. Indeed, when the Germans developed U-boats with underwater speeds in excess of twenty-five knots, the only escorts that could catch, let alone sink, such predators were high-speed destroyers.

All the ships of the F Class were originally designed to carry the Two Speed Destroyer Sweep gear, designed to be used to sweep mines ahead of the fleet. All the destroyers were fitted with this

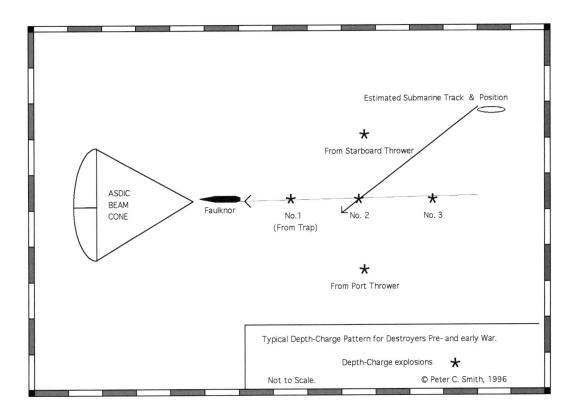

equipment, [TSDS] but the requirement for *Faulknor* to carry it was cancelled on 15 February 1934, four months before she was launched.

The Director of Engineering had noted on 1 February, that the fitting of this gear in Leaders, '… restricts space far more than in the destroyers, for in the Leaders the after superstructure is wider to provide cabin space for additional officers. The narrow gangway between the winches and the ships side had to be accepted.' However, the size of the winches grew and a representative from the DNC inspected a mock-up of the intended arrangement at Portsmouth. He noted the gangway was less than ten inches wide. Among the many solutions was the shifting of the depth charges aft to the quarterdeck. This was unacceptable as it was, '.. already congested in these ships as the after-gun-well is 16 feet in diameter.' The after deck-house could be recessed but this led to further complications and N. V. Grace of the DTD recommended that *Exmouth* and *Faulknor*, '.. should not be fitted with TSDS' in a Memo dated 2 February 1934.

Finally, air power gradually increased in prominence. The Royal Navy tackled this problem less successfully than it did others, perhaps because there was no real experience to back the claims of either side; bombing stationary obsolete battleships or shooting at towed targets was no substitute for combat experience. Generally, the airmen vastly over-estimated their ability to hit moving ships (other than by dive-bombing) while the sailors over-estimated their ability to destroy modern aircraft.

At the time *Faulknor's* armament was considered well-balanced, and despite hindsight disparagement by post-war 'experts', proved well-built and outstandingly sea-worthy destroyers, which gave sterling service in most weather and combat conditions.

For navigation *Faulknor* was fitted with the Chernikeef depth-sounding logs, purchased for her on 6 September 1933. On 10 October *Faulknor's* W/T was confirmed as Type 49, against Type 37M in the destroyers of her flotilla.

Faulknor was built of riveted mild steel plates, although her Longitudinals were of 'D' Quality steel. Galvanised steel was used for her shell decks, longitudinal frames, deck girders (except for the 12 inch channels), beams, floors, E & B seats, Water Tank and Oil Tank bulkheads, except between Oil Fuel Tanks, anchor and cable gear, stanchions and deck fittings. She carried two 32-cwt and one 5-cwt close stowing anchors. Her cable equipment included one $112^1/_2$ fathom and one $62^1/_2$ fathom sets of $1^7/_{16}$-inch diameter and 150 fathoms of $3^1/_2$-inch ESFSWR galvanised cable.

Her masts and yards were part steel and part Norway Spruce. Her foremast had the lower mast constructed of 7-inch diameter steel, 53 feet long, but the top mast of 18 feet $6^5/_8$-inch was wood which tapered from 7-inches to $3^3/_4$-inches, with the Fore Top Lower Yard 24 feet in length of 6-inch diameter tapering at the ends to 3-inch diameter and W/T Yard 18 feet long of 4-inch diameter tapering to 3-inch diameter, with the Housing of the Topmast being 2 feet long of $6^1/_2$-inch diameter tapering to 4-inch. The Main Mast showed the same construction, the Lower Mast being 42 feet 6-inches of $7^1/_2$-inch steel tapering to 6-inch diameter, but the Top Mast of just over 11 feet, the Main Mast at 18 feet and the Housing at 2 feet was of Norway Spar, as was the 8 feet long Ensign Gaff of $2^3/_4$-inch diameter tapering to $2^1/_4$-inch diameter.

Other wooden fittings included a Coaling Derrick, Jack Staff, Ensign Staff, two Lower Booms, a Sounding Boom, Stern Boom and twenty-four Side-screen Booms, for a total masting weight of 1,716 tons. The highest fixed part of the Foremast, the Weather Vane, was 90 feet 11-inches, the highest part of the Topmast being 89 feet. The highest fixed part of the Main Mast was 71 feet 5-inches. The reason for the high Main Masts was due to an International Ruling on the height of Navigation Lights, but this did not long last the onset of war, when it was soon drastically cut down.

With regard to upper deck coverings, on 16 March 1934, a memorandum stated:

> Naval brass securing strips for linoleum are to be fitted only on the quarter-deck, and below the upper deck. On the upper deck, except the quarter deck, and on the forecastle

deck, other weather decks, galvanised steel securing strips are to be fitted and the steel strips aboard to be galvanised *after* the holes for securing are drilled in it.

Coir matting is *not* to be fitted but rubber matting with $12^1/_2$ – oz cotton backing, and overall thickness of 0.11-inch and approximate weight of $5^1/_2$ lb per square yard is to be supplied and fitted where Coir matting is indicated on the approved tracing of deck coverings. The rubber matting is to be obtained from The India Rubber Gutta Percha & Telegraph Works Co. Ltd, Silvertown, London, E.16

Her building was swift and, less than a year after her first plates were laid; her hull was gliding smoothly down the slipway. The date, 12 June, 1934, was a major milestone; on that day she ceased to be a mere job number, 1640, and became HMS *Faulknor*, heir to a famous name and tradition, launched by Mrs. Henderson, wife of Rear-Admiral Sir Reginald E.H. Henderson, Third Sea Lord and Controller of the Navy, who broke the traditional bottle of champagne against her knife-edge bows. As the tugs fussed about her, towing her away to the fitting-out basin, the subtle change from 'it', an inert mass of steel, to 'she', a thing of grace and beauty to a sailor's eye, took place. It is probably 'Politically Incorrect' in this self-obsessed and pretentious age, with female sailors crewing warships, but it is still a fact that every ship was 'she' to the sailors of those days, from rowing-boat to battleship, from *Saucy Sue* to *Iron Duke*. [Our hideous modern TV and press media charmingly refer to a ship as 'it' of course, and even the hitherto sensible *Lloyds List* has recently succumbed to the same madness, sad to relate] Graceful she was as she took shape in the experienced hands of the Yarrow workmen. Complementing her slender hull were the two slim raking funnels and the frail pole masts, which typified our warships of this period.

Down the slip! The launch of the third HMS Faulknor *by Mrs Henderson, wife of the Third Sea Lord who was Controller of the Navy, at the Scotstoun Yard of Yarrow on 12 June 1934.* (Yarrow.)

HMS Faulknor *is secured alongside at the Scotstoun Yard of Yarrow on 12 June 1934 after the launching ceremony, in readiness to be completed and fully 'fitted out' for the Royal Navy.* (A.T. Kelly, Glasgow, via Yarrow & Co.)

As the months sped by, the guns and torpedo tubes, depth-charge rails, traps and throwers, the thousand-and-one fittings, were lowered into place, bolted down, wired-up and tested. She had extra accommodation for the Staff, fifteen officers. The multi-barrelled machine-guns were emplaced on their sponsons at signal-deck level. On its platform between two pairs of torpedo mountings, the powerful 24-inch searchlight was fixed into position, while on the bridge the big, ten-foot range finder and the Director Control Tower, with their myriad of delicate instruments, without which all the armament was half-deaf and blind, were fixed. The W/T equipment was initially to have been of the Type 49Y, but this was later changed and she received instead, the Type 37M. Also unique to her was the fitting of an echo-sounder. Gradually the noise and clamour faded away and the ship was made ready; ready for her trials; ready to show that she could measure up to the best that Yarrow's had produced; ready to get away to the sea where she belonged.

The small complement of naval personnel joined the ship, merging with the dwindling numbers of painters, carpenters and bowler-hatted supervisors. On Tuesday 14 May 1935, Final Gunnery Trials were conducted and the report read:

> The gunnery equipment was generally in a very satisfactory state.

One slightly humorous anachronism from the days of sail was revealed when the report continued:

> The overhead stowage for cutlasses in the after superstructure fouls the block of the ammunition whip from the after magazine. This will be moved as necessary to clear the whip.

HMS Faulknor *running her speed trials on 'The Arran Mile' in the Clyde, in the spring of 1935, prior to being handed over to the Royal Navy.* (A. T. Kelly, Glasgow, via Yarrow & Co.)

At last, to the hoots of sirens from nearby ships and the cheers of the men who had built her, she slipped down the Clyde to show her paces. On the measured course, the Arran Mile, her turbines and boilers working full out for the first time, she sped through the water, pushing it disdainfully aside, piling up a foamy white wake astern. The duration of the trial was a full six hours, and she ran them with a Mean draft of 9 ft $4^3/_8$ in, a Forward draft of 8 ft $10^3/_8$ in and Aft draft of 9 ft $10^3/_8$ in, with an actual trial displacement of 1661.65 tons. Her coefficiency of Fineness was 54.1 and she developed 35,783 SHP, with 360.093 revolutions.

All on board could tell that she was a winner, at 36.648 knots at 35,841 S.H.P. with 361.281 revolutions, exceeding her designed speed by over a knot-and-a-half, and answering her helm perfectly. The fuel consumption trial for HMS *Faulknor* at 5000 SHP read as follows: 12 Hours at 20.76 knots. Oil burnt = 24.93 tons = 0.929 lbs/SHP/hour. SHP 5004. Radius of action on 430.6 tons of oil, i.e 85% full capacity, at that speed was 4304 nautical miles. The coursed was over the Arran Mile for six hours, and a top speed of 36.648 knots was attained on 35841 SHP., with 361.281 revolutions. Oil per SHP, per Hour Full Speed was 0.75 lb. Knots per Ton Oil (Full Speed) was 3.049. The Radius of Action, Full Speed was 1313 nautical miles – on 430.6 of or 85% total oil fuel capacity. Knots *Achieved per each Ton of oil fuel used* (Cruising) was 11.72 at 16.60 knots speed and 9.994 at 20.76 knots speed.[5]

Her trials completed, she returned to the dockyard where, on 24 May, a receipt was signed for 'One Flotilla Leader'. A handshake followed, and she became part of the Royal Navy. Portsmouth was assigned as her home, or manning, port and here, three days later, the commissioning ceremony took place with the crew of *Campbell* whom she was relieving. Her commanding officer, and, as Captain (D), the man in control of all the new destroyers of the 'Fearless' class she was to lead, in the 6th

HMS Faulknor *running her Navy speed trials in the Solent, May 1936. Midships detail, showing both sets of torpedo tubes (right) with their hoisting davit (left) and dan buoy and whaler, and looking forward past both funnels, with 6th Flotilla markings on after and Flotilla Lead band on former, to the bridge, with semaphore arm on bridge wing.* (Sir Harold Danckwerts.)

HMS Faulknor *running her Navy speed trials in the solent in 1936. Originally comissioned by Captain M. L. Clarke, DSC, RN, as Flotilla Leader of the 6th Destroyer Flotilla, Home Fleet, in March 1936, Captain Victor H. Danckwerts, CMG, RN (seen here on her bridge), assumed command. His brother, an Army officer who later became a very famous legal figure, was invited to attend with fellow officers as a guest of the new CO.* (Sir Harold Danckwerts.)

Destroyer Flotilla, was Captain Marshall L. Clarke, DSC RN. Most of these ships were already in service or working up in readiness: *Fame, Fearless, Foresight, Forester, Fortune* and *Fury*. The remaining two, *Firedrake* and *Foxhound*, joined by the end of June.

Just four months before, Hitler tore up the Versailles Treaty, thus ending any secrecy about his massive rearmament programme; the international picture was darkening. During the few remaining years of peace left to them, the men of the 6th Flotilla flexed their muscles and carefully learnt their trade. However the country as a whole reacted, the crisis would not find them unprepared.

* * *

Robert Faulknor[6], after whom HMS *Faulknor* was named, was a famous frigate captain of the Napoleonic wars. The ship which bore his name bravely between 1934 and 1946 had as her motto, the inscription 'Love of Fatherland Leads', and a more fitting description of the life of Robert Faulknor would be hard to find.

Two earlier warships had carried the name and added lustre to it, the first a Flotilla Leader which served in the First World War at Jutland and Zeebrugge; and the second a tiny river launch which had served at Hong Kong and on the anti-piracy patrols on the West River in China in the 1920s.

The third HMS *Faulknor* spent the years since June 1935, as leader of the 6th Destroyer Flotilla, Home Fleet and she remained a Flotilla Leader from this date until October 1944, [except for a three-week period in February, 1944] the longest period of any of her type.

A Flotilla Leader, of course, apart from her normal duties as a fleet destroyer, carried a large number of additional officers and men to administer control of the flotilla as a whole. 'The Staff', as they were generally derisively referred to by the other destroyers' crews, were the most senior officers of their trades in the flotilla, top specialists in a specialist field, and ultimate responsibility fell on them for the smooth application of the many facets of the flotilla's work. The staff had to be better than the best, for a slip by the flotilla leader attracted more adverse comment than if it had occurred in one of the other destroyers, this being human nature! In the period between the wars the Leaders

Captain Robert Faulknor, 1763–94, after whom all three Royal Navy warships were named. Typical of the young frigate captains of the Napoleonic Wars, he came from a distinguished naval family going back three generations. He entered the Royal Naval College, Portsmouth, at the age of eleven, and first went to sea in 1777, serving in the West Indies and taking part in three naval battles by the time he was eighteen. By 1788 he was in command of the sloop Zebra *and earned high praise at the capture of Fort Royale, Martinique, in 1794. As captain of the* Rose *he was again to the forefront in the seizure of St Lucia and the fight in Barrington Bay, and was given command of the frigate* Blanche. *He fought at the capture of Fort d'Epée on Guadeloupe, but his final battle was against the French frigate* Pique *off Pointe a' Pitre. Here he was killed while trying to secure the enemy vessel's bowsprit to his own ship's capstan so that she could not escape. Like Nelson, he was shot down and killed at the height of his success. A memorial was erected to his gallant memory, and can still be seen in St Paul's Cathedral, a rare and fitting tribute to a young man who had served his nation so well. 'Love to Fatherland Leads' was to be the ship's motto of HMS* Faulknor, *reflecting this bravery.* (National Maritime Museum, Greenwich.)

The first HMS Faulknor, *a flotilla leader, formerly the Chilean destroyer* Almirante Simpson, *built at Vickers Armstrongs and taken over by the Royal Navy at the start of the First World War. She had a very distinguished war record, serving with both the Grand Fleet and the Dover patrol. At the Battle of Jutland in 1916, she became the only British destroyer to ever sink an enemy battleship single-handed when, in the night action, she torpedoed the German* Pommern, *which blew up without survivors.* Faulknor *herself survived being damaged by a mine in the English Channel in 1918, and this view shows her returning to Dover down by the bow after that incident. She continued to serve until 1930, when she was sold back to Chile and renamed* Almirante Riveros, *her third and final name. As such she survived until the mid-1940s.* (Crown Copyright.)

were not large enough to carry all the extra officers and therefore various of the staff were accommodated in some of the other 'boats' (as destroyer men always irreverently called their craft) of the flotilla, whenever possible in one of the two Divisional Leaders. While the flotilla system proved workable, this arrangement worked very well; but, as we shall see, the stress of war complicated things.

The second HMS Faulknor, *the former chinese river steam launch* Po-On. *During the emergency of 1925, when the Communist adviser Borodin started to stir up anti-Western hatred with Sun Yat-sen of the Kuomintang, she was purchased for river patrol service by the Hong Kong Government to protect British shipping on the West River. Manned by a Royal Navy crew as a tender to HMS* Tamar, *and named* Faulknor *by the Senior Officer, who had served in her predecessor at Jutland, she was fitted with a single 3-pounder gun, three Lewis guns and a Maxim, and was commanded by Lieutenant P.A. Berry. For three years she patrolled the West River up to Canton, and in one incident landed a force which defeated a group of river pirates decisively. Later commanded by Lieutenant S.A.M. Thomas, she was finally returned to her original owners in March 1929, after the Hong Kong authorities refused to pay for her upkeep any longer. She is shown here as fitted out and armed and flying the White Ensign.* (World Ship Society via Brian Hargreaves.)

The 6th Destroyer Flotilla had originally been organised thus:

Fame (Divisional Leader – S.O.)	} 21st (20th) }	
Foresight	} Sub-Division }	
		} 11th (15th) Division)
Fearless (S.O.)	} 22nd (30th) }	
Foxhound	} Sub-Division}	
Fortune (Divisional Leader – S.O.)	} 23rd (31st) }	
Forester	} Sub-Division }	
		} 12th (16th) Division
Fury (S.O.)	} 24th (32nd)}	
Firedrake	} Sub-Division}[7]	

Faulknor had spent the next few years on the fringes of war, including taking part in the Nyon patrols during the Spanish Civil War, surviving a collision with a merchant ship in thick fog and the

HMS Faulknor *arriving at Portsmouth in August 1937. Clearly seen is the long damage scar along her bow to her amidships hull plating, just above the lower line of scuttles, and the damage amidships just below 'Q' gun, after her collision with the liner* Clan MacFadyen *in thick fog in the Bay of Biscay. There was no loss of life, but repairs took three months.* (Vernon Coles.)

Spanish refugees taken on board HMS Faulknor *at Valencia in 1937, while she was operating off the east coast of Spain during the Spanish Civil War. This is the only known photograph of the ship to show the ship's crest on her gun tampions.* (William English.)

HMS Faulknor *in January 1938, dressed overall and secured alongside at a French port during a courtesy visit. She is painted in Mediterranean Fleet colours, white overall, with the Red/White/Blue 'Neutrality' markings painted on 'B' gun shield, while serving with the Nyon Patrol off Spain during the Spanish Civil War. These markings did not prevent the Italian Air Force bombing her on occasions, fortunately without any damage.* (Charles W. Cownden.)

numerous alerts caused by Munich and similar crisis points. By 1939, her flotilla had been re-numbered as the 8th, and were still part of the Home Fleet.

As the last days of peace ran steadily out, the 8th Flotilla sailed from Portsmouth on 29 July and sailed up the North Sea, east-about, to Rosyth, where the destroyers arrived on 30 July. After a week's exercises out of that port, they sailed to Scapa Flow on 11 August, joining the other units of Admiral Sir Charles Forbes Home Fleet. At this critical juncture in the nation's history this fleet consisted of battleships *Nelson* (Flag), *Rodney*, *Ramillies*, *Royal Oak* and *Royal Sovereign*, battle-cruisers *Hood* and *Repulse*, aircraft-carrier *Ark Royal*, three cruiser squadrons totalling twelve ships in all, and two destroyer flotillas, the eight 'Tribals' of the new 6th Flotilla and the nine ships of the 8th Flotilla.

Between 12 August and 3 September, the whole of this fleet was engaged in a series of sweeps across the North Sea between the Shetland Islands and Norway. This was to prevent any breakout by German heavy units before the declaration of war, but in fact, two of their pocket battleships had already sailed and were on station deep in the Atlantic. *Faulknor* was refuelling at Scapa Flow at the end of one of these sweeps at 1100 on 3 September, when the signal 'Commence hostilities with Germany' was received.

During the troubled years since she was first commissioned, *Faulknor* had been on the fringes of war almost continually, had searched for hostile submarines with her Asdic, been bombed by the Italians, and had constantly practised her role for when the opportunity to strike back should arrive. The 8th Flotilla was now a well-tested unit, they were confident of their ships and of their skills, the die was now cast and before long they were to show the enemy their worth.

Above: Eve of war. HMS Faulknor *anchored in Portland harbour in April 1939, with awnings rigged and ship's launch moored from her stern boom. Note the canvas tops on her after funnel, with her flotilla mate's after funnel just visible behind it.* (Richard Perkins Collection.)

Left: Captain C.S. Daniel, CB, CBE, RN. He led the Faulknor *and the 8th Flotilla from the last days of peace into war in September 1939, and the first sinking of a Nazi submarine was achieved under his command.* (Imperial War Museum.)

CHAPTER II

Grey Seas and Sky

At 1530, 3 September 1939, *Faulknor* and her division left Scapa to rejoin the fleet at sea, and, at 1310/4th, sighted first destroyer *Punjabi* then *Fearless* of her own flotilla. By midday, the fleet was patrolling in 59°30′ N, 55° 7′ W. They turned north again at 1200 to intercept the German liner *Bremen*, pride of the Nazi Merchant Fleet, but she had already reached the safe haven of Hitler's new-found Soviet ally, Murmansk.

At 2300, the fleet received news of the torpedoing of the unarmed liner *Athenia* without any warning. *Fame* was sent to the stricken ships assistance. This set the pattern of their work for those first bleak weeks of the Second World War.

Griff Fanthorpe remembered:

> When war was declared *Faulknor* was already a veteran of that complex period of history that embraced the prelude to the real war that followed and of course from the word go *Faulknor* was instantly into action. In 1940 a close-knit crew which remained substantially unchanged for the first two years of combat, served under the wise command of our Captain (D).

He also recalled the next Captain (D) who took over in February, Captain De Salis,

> … not a young man, but was brilliant as a destroyer commander, with experience from World War I and great coolness in action, of which there was to be a great deal, watched with admiration by those who stood near him on the bridge, altering course with great calmness in the face of high-level bombing.

The Home Fleet continued to patrol east of the Shetlands but this was a largely unproductive beating of empty seas, and, for a time, was encompassed in thick fog. The fleet returned to Scapa at 0700/6 September, *Faulknor* taking on board 168 tons of fuel from oiler *War Diwan*. *Faulknor* was not to enjoy a long stay in harbour, sailing at 0554 next day with *Nelson, Rodney, Repulse, Ark Royal*, light cruisers *Aurora* and *Sheffield* and destroyers *Foresight, Firedrake, Fortune, Fury, Bedouin, Mashona, Punjabi, Somali* and *Tartar*. The fleet headed for the vicinity of the Norwegian coast at 61°, with the object of intercepting enemy vessels and of exercising contraband control.

In Pentland Firth evidence of enemy submarines manifested themselves. While leading the fleet SSE of Fair Isle, in 59° 21′ N, 00° 55′ W, *Faulknor* obtained her first Asdic contact. At 1116, she dropped a single depth-charge, set at 150 ft, in 65 fathoms of water, but contact was immediately lost and was later thought to have been a 'non-sub'.

Faulknor was close ahead of *Nelson* ENE of Sumburgh Head, when, at 1815, two officers on the bridge and the Chief Yeoman of Signals saw what appeared to be the track of a torpedo. Following up, *Faulknor* almost immediately got a firm contact. Five depth-charges were dropped in position 60° 19′ N, 00° 58′ E, two with settings of 100 ft and three with 250 ft but after this contact was lost. No oil was seen.

The fleet spent the 8th and 9th off the Norwegian coast as far north as 63°, Stadlandet headland, searching for German merchant vessels. The weather remained poor and they left empty-handed; any enemy ships making good use of Norwegian territorial waters.

Return to Scapa at 1930/10th, and another refuelling followed. At 1900/11th, *Faulknor* slipped pass Hoxa Gate at 2025 with *Fortune, Firedrake* and *Foxhound*, screening *Ark Royal*. The use of valuable fleet carriers for anti-submarine patrols was a routine operation early in the war, until the loss of *Courageous* showed how dangerous this was. On this occasion it led to the near loss of *Ark*, but the first of many successes for *Faulknor* and her flotilla.

U-boats were known to be operating off Rockall, and, after leaving the Western swept channel, the force shaped course towards 59° 40′ N, 13° 50′ W, where steamer *Kirby* had been sunk by *U-48*. In order that a Direction Finding guard could be kept on 488 kc/s, *Eskimo* replaced *Fortune* at 2100. The four ships then proceeded in leisurely sweeps down the north-west coast of Ireland, westward of the Hebrides throughout the next three days. As the weather cleared the carrier's aircraft searched ahead and around the hunting group.

At dawn on Tuesday 12 September, an all-round air search was launched to a depth of sixty miles and, at 0700; one aircraft reported a submarine on the surface 39 miles away. The aircraft then attacked, dropping six 100-lb anti-submarine bombs, all of which missed and the submarine dived. *Faulknor* and *Firedrake* were immediately detached to hunt, while the carrier continued westward to land – on her aircraft escorted by *Eskimo*. At the time the weather was fine and clear, but the barometer fell rapidly and, by 1100, there was a strong south-westerly wind blowing, unsuitable for further flying. The two destroyers made no contacts, aircraft had been unable to direct them, while the rapidly worsening weather made Asdic conditions difficult, Captain Daniel therefore rejoined the carrier at 1300, course being set ten minutes later for 55° 00′ N, 15° 00′ W, following an Admiralty signal.

At 0741/13th, one of the carrier's aircraft sighted a U-Boat south of Rockall, and attacked with bombs. Three further Swordfish were flown off, and *Foxhound* and *Eskimo* joined the hunt, but found no trace of the enemy. At 0857, still in the same area, with poor weather, a strong north-westerly wind and a heavy swell running, *Ark Royal,* with her remaining two destroyers, ran into a large oil patch, and, soon after, *Firedrake* dropped back from the screen to investigate an Asdic contact which she gained to starboard. At 0907, *Faulknor* was also detached to join the hunt, but, being unable to confirm the intermittent contact, Captain Daniel moved his ship around to a position approximately at right-angles to the bearing of *Firedrake's* last contact, and one mile off, to get a cross-fix echo if he could. He was immediately rewarded with a firm contact, but in a position quite different to that of *Firedrake's*. This contact remained on a steady bearing on the port beam, although *Faulknor* was doing revolutions for ten knots and steaming head-on to the wind and sea, so only making eight knots actual headway.

Captain Daniel decided that *Faulknor* should attack as she was in firm contact, but, as soon as *Faulknor* turned, contact was lost again in the noise. The attack was temporarily abandoned, speed reduced and efforts made to regain the echo again, which was achieved at 0948 with a range of 800 yards. *Faulknor* attacked at twelve knots because, in the prevailing conditions, any higher speed would lose the echo. Contact was again lost at 500 yards but Captain Daniel continued using the Chernikeef depth-sounder, and, at 0948, dropped a full pattern of five depth-charges, with deep settings, in 56° 54′ N, 13° 30′ W.

No results were observed because there was already substantial oil on the surface. It was decided that both contacts should be classified as 'non-sub' and that the echoes were possibly emitting from the wreck of *Athenia*, but later intelligence confirmed two enemy were present, *U-23* and *U-39,* and that *Firedrake's* initial charge had detonated close to the latter. The destroyers rejoined *Ark Royal* and continued patrolling.

By 0635, destroyers, *Bedouin, Punjabi* and *Tartar* reinforced the screen and, with *Eskimo*, stationed twenty miles from the carrier in a wide circle so that any D/F bearings could be cross-plotted. At 1240, a call for help was received from SS *Fanad Head*, reporting herself under attack and torpedoed in 56° 45′ N, 15° 21′ W, two-hundred miles to the south-west. The carrier recalled her airborne patrols and set course for the stricken merchant ship; the four 'Tribals' being sent ahead to give assistance. *Faulknor*, *Firedrake* and *Foxhound* closed the ring around the carrier and also turned, steering a course 225° at 24 knots.

At 1432, the distance had reduced to 180 miles and *Ark* flew off three Skua dive-bombers to locate and attack the submarine. Grave risks were run in their comparative ignorance. In order for the aircraft to be flown off into the wind, *Ark* needed to turn about 180° off course. In order to 'save time' the carrier's captain decided not to readjust the destroyer screen, and Captain Daniel was ordered to maintain his flotilla's course and speed, *Ark* relying solely on her speed of 26 knots to safeguard against a torpedo attack.

The Director of Anti-Submarine Warfare later wrote that *Ark Royal* had, '… slipped her destroyer screen whilst turning into the wind to fly-off. Whilst the value of Asdics during such alterations of course is not likely to be high, it is considered advisable to keep the screen with an aircraft carrier in these circumstances, as the physical obstruction of destroyers moving at high speed to their new positions is large.'

Ark's high vulnerability was immediately apparent to the watching enemy beneath the waves. At 1507, when the carrier was rejoining her destroyers, still some four miles ahead of her, and about to fly off another patrol, an alert lookout sighted the tracks of torpedoes speeding towards her. Two torpedoes had been fired at *Ark Royal;* only a prompt turn to port saved her and both exploded in her wake. The carrier sped away, transmitting to Captain Daniel the course of the torpedoes, he later reported:

> … HMS *Ark Royal* was seen to alter course rapidly to port, and shortly afterwards a high white splash appeared on her port side, followed by a flash and black smoke to starboard. At the same time the signal to close was made.

The wake created by HMS Faulknor *at thirty knots.* (Sir Harold Danckwerts.)

War – First Kill! The Nazi U-boat U-39 falls victim to the 8th Destroyer Flotilla on 14 September 1939 as the first confirmed destruction of an enemy submarine in the Second World War. Here a sailor aboard the destroyer Foxhound *prepares to throw a line to two German survivors in the water, while another can be seen getting ready to jump from the stricken submarine's conning tower. In the background,* Faulknor *is silhouetted standing guard and preparing to save further crew members.* (Crown Copyright.)

The destroyers took up the hunt, spreading to 2,000 yards apart in line abreast with *Foxhound* to port of *Faulknor* and *Firedrake* to starboard. They reduced speed to fifteen knots on reaching the carriers wake, and both *Faulknor* and *Foxhound* made contact to port at 1525. This position agreed with the expected position of the submarine, based on the course of the torpedo of 140° as signalled to them by the carrier. They were immediately rewarded, *Foxhound* gaining a contact at 1525 and dropping a two-charge pattern set to 250 and 300 feet respectively. Amidst the great disturbance caused by these explosions, *Faulknor* also gained a firm Asdic contact at 1527 and held it, dropping a full pattern of five depth-charges four minutes later. Contact remained firm, the Asdic operator reporting that the target was moving fast, but this time there was no escape.

Firedrake, in turn, gained contact at 1540, and attacked with depth-charges set to explode at 250 ft and 500 ft, which, six minutes later, blew the evil shape of the submarine to the surface in a welter of spray as she blew her tanks. *Faulknor*, *Firedrake* and *Foxhound* all opened fire at 1549, one hit being observed on the fore part of her hull. Fire was ceased fire two minutes later as the fore hatch was opened and men were seen exiting the conning tower. *Foxhound* dug her stern in and came racing

U-boat survivors from U-39. (Harry Robinson.)

up to ram the stricken vessel. This was too much for the Germans, who began throwing themselves into the sea. *Faulknor* lowered her whaler as *Foxhound* slowed down and turned away, and soon picked up most of the 43 survivors. As they did so, their victim, *U-39*, sank, stern-first, at 1607, in 58°29′ N, 11°50′ W.

This textbook attack by the 8th Flotilla had produced what was later confirmed to be the first U-boat kill of the Second World War. The survivors told them that the submarine had tried to torpedo them during their attack but their swiftness had made this impossible. They also told their captors that all the depth-charge attacks had taken effect, the third one bursting the submarine's foremost tanks.

There was not time to rest on their laurels; they had made a brilliant debut.

However, the war had hardly begun. *Ark Royal* was now far away on the horizon and after rejoining her, they took close station, while *Bedouin* and *Eskimo*, also recalled, took station at 1645 and 1806 respectively, the whole force continuing to steer towards the last known position of *Fanad Head.*

The Skuas flown off the carrier just before this brief little battle, had attacked another enemy, *U-30*, while she was firing into the ship as her crew attempted to abandon her. The aircrew were eager and inexperienced and flew too low before releasing their bombs, two of them being blown into the sea by the ensuing explosions. Once the remaining Skua had flown off, the U-boat resurfaced and took the surviving aircrew prisoner. Meanwhile *Ark Royal* erroneously considered the submarine damaged or even, 'probably destroyed', but detached *Bedouin*, *Eskimo* and *Tartar*, to join *Punjabi* and make certain. They found nothing although they continued to search all through that night. There was little they could do except to rescue the seamen who were picked up by *Tartar* and later landed at Mallaig.

At dawn on Friday 15th, nine more Swordfish were flown off to search the area where *Fanad Head* had gone down, 56° 20′ N, 15° 21′ W, while the carrier and her three escorts steered eastward to meet *Fearless*, *Forester*, *Fortune* and *Fury,* which had sailed from Loch Ewe to take over screening.

At 1732, a further air search was conducted, without result and, at 1800; *Faulknor*, *Firedrake* and *Eskimo* were detached to Loch Ewe, while *Foxhound* was sent into Kirkwall to land the German prisoners. *Faulknor* and *Firedrake* duly arrived in Loch Ewe at 0900 next morning and found *Eskimo* refuelling from alongside the tanker *Broomdale*. Securing outboard, *Faulknor* in turn received 318 tons oil fuel, remaining until 1220/19th when she left for the Hebrides for another anti-submarine search.

While aboard *Faulknor* the First Lieutenant of *U-39*, J. S. von Goertzke, had talked quite a lot and Captain Daniel submitted his remarks for study. Goertzke had revealed that the U-Boat had watched *Ark Royal* and her destroyers for some time before they attacked. Only one torpedo was fired, and, although it was obviously fitted with a magnetic head, von Goertzke would not admit it. He did admit that every one of the depth-charge attacks made had been effective, and that the submarine had started to surface before the final attack was made as she was leaking badly forward. The concussion of the depth-charges had extinguished all lights and the crew had to use hand torches. Most of the survivors suffered from severe headaches for up to five hours after they had been rescued.

Meanwhile, at 0630/19 September, reports of another U-boat intercepting and sinking fishing vessels off the Butt of Lewis came in and destroyers were despatched from Loch Ewe to hunt her: *Fearless*, *Firedrake*, *Forester*, *Fortune*, *Fury* of the 8th Flotilla and *Eskimo*, *Matabele*, *Punjabi* and *Somali* of the 6th Flotilla under Captain (D 6), Captain R.S.G. Nicholson, DSC, in the latter ship. At 1130 it was decided to send Captain Daniel in *Faulknor* from Loch Ewe to take charge of the hunt as the senior officer. The U-boat had sunk two trawlers off the Hebrides before the destroyers arrived on the scene.

At 1330, Captain Gresham Nicholson reported that he was conducting an organised sweep twenty miles north-east of the Butt of Lewis with *Firedrake*, *Matabele*, *Punjabi* and *Somali*. Captain Daniel decided not to join him there, nor to interrupt him in this sweep but to proceed on a course of 220°, which was the course the U-Boat had been last reported on by the Admiralty at 0730. *Faulknor* had meanwhile been joined by *Tartar* off the entrance to Loch Ewe and, at 1445, while these two ships were proceeding thus at 30 knots, Captain Daniel received a signal from *Fearless* leading the other group, *Fortune*, *Fury* and *Eskimo*, that she was hunting in the same direction.

Captain Daniel overtook this latter group an hour later and instructed them to carry out an Asdic search towards St. Kilda, while *Faulknor* and *Tartar* proceeded ahead at 30 knots hoping to cross the U-boat's estimated 'furthest on' position at her best estimated surface speed. All seven destroyers met off the island at 1800 and then swept to the north towards St. Kilda in line abreast, their Asdics probing the sunlit waters ahead of them. Circling St. Kilda they then turned north-east and a further search was organised, initially without luck. At 2030, the destroyers formed into two groups in single line-ahead a mile apart, *Faulknor*, *Fearless* and *Fury* in one and *Tartar*, *Eskimo*, *Forester* and *Fortune* in the other. Captain Daniel then ordered them to patrol through the night along the parallel of the Butt of Lewis.

Visibility was excellent, the Aurora Borealis being very bright after nightfall. At 2333, *Fortune*, not keeping Asdic watch, as she was rear ship, visibly sighted a U-Boat on the surface off her starboard beam and immediately altered course to attack. The enemy dived as *Fortune* turned, and two torpedo tracks were seen and almost at once these missiles exploded, one deep and one shallow, in the wake of one of the 'Tribals'. Later it was ascertained that the submarine commander had fired *three* torpedoes at this larger ship believing her to be a light cruiser. He soon discovered his mistake. *Fortune*, nearest to the line of attack, dropped a single line of five depth-charges, firing 'by eye', and signalling her contact report to *Faulknor*. *Fortune*, turning again, regained her contact and dropped a second five-charge pattern, but at once lost it again. It transpired that this attack caught the U-Boat at 270-feet depth and caused considerable damage to one propeller and shaft and also put her depth gauge out of action. Meanwhile Captain Daniel took *Faulknor* over to join in but *Fortune* had now lost the contact and so the flotilla was formed up again into line-abreast of search on the last reported bearings. *Fortune* rejoined the line at 0100/20th and they settled down for a determined hunt.

At 0115, firm Asdic contact was made about three miles from the first attack, and, twelve minutes later, *Forester* dropped a pattern of depth-charges, which shook the enemy submarine considerably. The hunt continued and *Fortune* making deliberate attacks between 0217 to 0214 with great accuracy. The first caused severe flooding to the U-Boat, considerably shook her crew, and forced her closer to the surface. At 0239 a second deep pattern was fired which had less effect and, at 0248, their target, *U-27*, was seen surfacing astern. *Fortune* opened fire, getting off four salvoes at 0241 and turning in a tight circle to ram. The U-boat was seen moving quickly ahead, illuminated by the northern lights and the beams of the destroyer's searchlights, under gunfire by other ships. The submarine crew came tumbling out of her conning-tower and signalled 'Save us'. The submarine skipper ordered her engines to be stopped and told his men to abandon ship as *Fortune* put her helm over just in time to miss her, then slowed down. The enemy eventually stopped at 0315, more than a mile from where she had surfaced, being slightly down by the stern with a dozen of the crew still on deck, the rest having leapt off earlier. *Fortune* organised a boarding party but remained ready to ram if there were any tricks. Their job was no sinecure, knowing the German passion for scuttling, but they did manage to get aboard and get below although she was quickly settling. The living spaces were found to be full of chlorine gas but some valuable documents were retrieved before they had to make a hasty exit.

Meanwhile, on sighting gunfire flashes, *Faulknor*, turned to close and, at 0320, sighted a flashing light about one mile to the northward. She turned towards it and found five officer and fifteen German ratings from the U-boat in their escape apparatus swimming in the sea, one of them flashing a torch. In Captain Daniel's dry words: – 'There was considerable noise.'

The bulk of these survivors were picked up by *Fortune's* whaler, *Faulknor* picking up twenty others who had jumped overboard when the firing started. Ultimately these latter were also transferred to *Fearless* and later landed at Kirkwall. Meanwhile, at 0350, *U-27* sank vertically, in the glare of the searchlights, stern first in position 58° 30' N, 09° 06' W.

Larry Chandler wrote:

> I well remember *U-27*, the German engineer hanging on to the guard rail as she went down; you see, with submarines it's the engineer that goes down with the ship, NOT the Captain. I still 'see' the engineer every night in my prayers, standing behind the conning tower on the starboard side.

One interesting sidelight of this action should be recorded. It came in the form of a letter written by the commander of *U-27*.

> May the seamen and officers of our valiant submarine *U-27* sunk by British destroyer *Faulknor,* never in word or deed denounce the Captain, commander as my friends. Who treated us with all respect and courtesy in our hour of distress. May I on behalf of myself and crew, thank them and the Lord.
>
> Signed: Johannes Franz,
> Kapitan-Leutnant
> Commander *U-27*
> 20 September 1939.

Johannes Franz died on October 25th, 1986, but Ron Smith stated:

> This is an example of comradeship amongst navies of the world and one bestowed upon *Faulknor* with honour.

Captain Daniel submitted a detailed report compiled by members of the submarine's crew, which made interesting reading. They told him the submarine had been stationed off southern Ireland for over three weeks and that their orders were to attack Merchant Shipping only. This was in strict contrast to the official German line of the time [and of the present day also!] that attacks on Merchant ships were banned at that time. They knew of the sinking of *Courageous*. They had mistaken the 1,850-ton 'Tribal' class destroyers for 6,000-ton light cruisers and had fired torpedoes set at 15-ft depths against the rear three ships of the line at about 2,000 yards range.

Three times they had been attacked and after each they had surfaced and been forced to dive again. Although the first depth-charges had been ineffective, all the subsequent ones told and in the final attack, the submarine had gone down to 120 metres, their normal limit being 100. By that time they were leaking so badly that they had no alternative but to surface. When attacked by *Fortune* the commanding officer had been the first to abandon ship, '… and this created a very bad impression on the crew.' All the officers, save one, and fifteen ratings, had been picked up by *Faulknor* about a mile from the position in which she finally sank.

Captain Daniel reported:

> The Engineering Officer was most expansive, and beside some of the information referred to above, volunteered the information that their torpedoes are fitted with magnetic heads, which are set to explode on passing under a ship. They are not set to explode at the end of their run, and should sink without exploding if they fail to find a target. He admitted that they are very unreliable and this is borne out by experience in encounters with both *U-27* and *U-39*. The officers believed that if they had been able to lie on the bottom with engines stopped out A/S would have been unable to locate them.

The flotilla proceeded at 18 knots at 0418, well satisfied with the nights work. At 0930, *Faulknor* transferred her prisoners to *Fearless* and continued to patrol, finally entered harbour at midday and refuelled from oiler *Prestol*. In the afternoon *Faulknor* shifted berth to transfer provisions from battleship *Nelson* in Loch Ewe, weighing anchor at 1910 and passing the Boom Defence Gate at 1930, screening *Hood* to Scapa arriving at 0805 next day.

Faulknor then left with the Fleet to cover a projected raid by 2nd Cruiser Squadron into the Skagerrak, carrying out an anti-submarine sweep ahead of the big ships at 1030/22nd. This sortie was cancelled due to a collision between two of the 7th flotillas destroyers and, 1930/23rd, they returned, *Faulknor* refuelling from the *War Diwan*.

On 25 September, news was received that British submarine *Spearfish* was badly damaged off Horn Reef and unable to submerge. Immediately 2nd Cruiser Squadron and 7th Destroyer Flotilla were sailed to meet and escort her home. In case the enemy decided to intervene, Admiral Forbes sailed battle-cruisers *Hood* and *Repulse,* light cruisers *Aurora* and *Sheffield*, with *Faulknor, Fearless, Forester* and *Foxhound* as screen, at 0900/25th. The C-in-C followed at 1020, with *Nelson, Rodney, Ark Royal* and destroyers *Fame, Firedrake, Foresight, Fortune, Bedouin* and *Punjabi.*

Submarine alarms were numerous with *Fearless, Forester* and *Foxhound* and *Faulknor* all carrying out frequent searches. They sighted *Nelson* and the main force at 1235, but were continuing to screen *Hood* at 1415 when the first dive-bombing commenced. There were four Junkers Ju.88s from I/KG 30 who attacked both forces, and from *Faulknor's* bridge, they had a grandstand view of this first air/sea encounter. The fleet's barrage proved ineffective in deterring the enemy and in a dive from 6,000 feet, one aircraft scored a direct hit on *Hood*. This bomb hit her port side torpedo bulge aft, but glanced off without exploding. Some minor damage and flooding took place but it was an early example of the accuracy of this form of attack.

It was also an early example of the impotence of the destroyers to participate in such a contest, their main armament was useless against dive-bombing, nor could it be controlled very well, while the multiple machine-guns had neither the range, weight of fire or accuracy to play any meaningful part.

Ark Royal was near-missed, leading to the first of many enemy claims to have sunk her. High-level attacks later by Heinkel He.111s were less impressive and caused no damage, this was also to be the pattern for future events. *Spearfish* was safely escorted into Rosyth while the Home Fleet returned to Scapa, encountering thick fog as they did so.

During the return, *Hood* reported a torpedo track, and *Faulknor* took *Firedrake, Fortune* and *Foxhound* back along the sighting track to hunt for the enemy. After about an hour *Fortune* and *Firedrake* both gained Asdic contacts and made a long series of depth-charge attacks. They were rewarded by diesel oil coming to the surface, which, by dusk, stretched away for two or three miles. They were convinced they had sunk a U-boat but post-war records show that this was not so.

The division then set course back to Scapa Flow but while still some distance away, there was another interruption. *Faulknor*, as a Leader, was one of the few destroyers at that time fitted with a simple MF/DF (Medium Frequency/Direction Finder) coil fitted on a pole at the top of her fore mast. This enabled enemy signals on that frequency to be picked up but it required at least one other source from another ship on another bearing to obtain a 'fix' (the position in which two signals crossed) to locate the source and therefore the enemy target. As none of the other destroyers of the flotilla had this coil as part of their standard equipment Captain Daniel had no choice but to cover both options.

Faulknor's direction-finding wireless apparatus had detected what was taken to be very strong German *telefunken,* either due north or due south of them. Therefore while *Faulknor* and *Foxhound* turned north to investigate, *Fortune* and *Firedrake* were sent in the opposite direction. The latter pair gained visual contact of a warship target, bows-on, within fifteen minutes and prepared to attack. Both guns and torpedoes were trained and ready to open fire when the 'enemy' identified herself as the *Eskimo,* on her way south with turbine trouble for repair. It had been a very close thing to a tragic outcome and was a good example of the strain destroyer captains operated under in those pre-radar

Anthony Fane De Salis, Captain (D) 8th Destoyer Flotilla, HMS Faulknor, *1940–2. From Narvik to the Battle of Spartivento, Malta convoys and Bay of Biscay patrols, Captain De Salis led the* Faulknor *in the face of heavy odds.* (Harry Robinson.)

days. *Faulknor* had meanwhile come upon the actual originator of the mysterious signals, a captured German freighter proceeding to Rosyth under armed guard. The flotilla had not been informed of the movement of either ship.

Location of the enemy by direction finding had been employed in the First World War by means of D/F stations ashore, but U-boats transmitted on High Frequency wavelengths. Their convoy sighting report, the most important of a range of standard brief format signals, had the prefix of the Greek 'Beta' sent twice, and this distinctive opening corresponded to the English Morse Code as 'B-Bar'. Thus, on picking up this prefix to any U-Boat operating signal which the Germans sent to their HQ to alert them they had a sighting report to transmit, the listening convoy escorts like *Faulknor* were immediately alerted, but the transmissions were of very brief duration, no more than fifteen seconds, and so homing in on them required a skilled operator and interpreter. *Faulknor's* specialist team was one of the best. The resultant 'sky-wave' signals went out in a straight line tangential to the earth's curvature and were 'bounced' back to their destination by the ionosphere. The 'ground-wave' signals along the surface only had a life of fifteen miles or so and thus indicated a U-Boat was transmitting from close by and was a good indication of an imminent threat to the convoy.

Two types of HF/DF (known as 'Huff-Duff') receiving equipment were developed, the prototype being approved by the Admiralty in March, 1940 and put into production. It consisted of a non-revolving aerial, which achieved directional sensitivity by measuring the signal strength received by several loops. It was so good that it could differentiate between sky and ground waves, while, in the hands (or ears) of a good operator *individual* submarines could be identified. *Faulknor* was not fitted with this apparatus until late in 1941, when the pylon appeared on the fore edge of 'X' gun deckhouse, while the MF/DF aerial was moved to the front of the bridge. The FH3, an aural null type, was later replaced by the improved FH4, which utilised a twin-channel receiver, which began to be fitted in 1943. Aural only reception was finally replaced by the much more accurate cathode ray display on a circular screen, marked off in degrees, which she received in 1942.

As for Radar (known then as RDF or Reflection Direction Finding), this was developed initially as an air-warning apparatus in Great Britain but as a surface-warning by Germany, and was not fitted to destroyers at this stage of the war. The later arrival of radar sets, for both air- and surface search, tended to overshadow the success of HF/DF but many years after the war it received its due from our former enemies, German historian Rohwer writing that a detailed analysis of the Atlantic convoy battles of the period June 1942 to May 1943 revealed that, '… the remarkable fact is that the outcome depended decisively on the efficient use of HF/DF'. Similar examination of the true facts led a British expert in electronics warfare, Dr. David Kiely, to proclaim that, '… it made a great contribution when the opportunity was there to do so, and it served the Royal Navy as the first true application of electronic warfare.'[1]

Faulknor finally arrived back at Scapa Flow on the afternoon of the 27th, fuelling from oiler *Belgol.* The 29th saw them heading out to sea again when a submarine sighting report was received at 0741, from an aircraft ten miles south of Fair Isles. *Faulknor* sailed at 1100 to take charge of the hunt, in company with *Fame, Fearless, Firedrake* and *Eskimo,* arriving on the scene at 1315. Captain

Daniel found that Captain Nicholson with *Somali, Ashanti, Bedouin, Foresight, Forester, Foxhound, Fury, Mashona* and *Matabele,* had already swept an area within a radius of eight miles of that position and were extending the search to the south-west.

Faulknor continued to search off Fair Isle until 1730; the radius of the area searched was around seventeen miles. Contact was obtained on two occasions but lost each time before an attack could be made. The first Asdic contact was obtained by *Foresight* at 1030, near the last reported position of the U-Boat, and the second by *Fearless* at 1635, six miles farther north-east. By 1845, the searching destroyers were some 13 miles north of Dennis Head and *Somali* took four companions to patrol in the Fair Isle Channel during the night, while *Faulknor* and five destroyers [the remainder having been detached to refuel] steamed westward for seventy miles in order to search back along the U-boats estimated 'furthest on' position, allowing for a course of between 260° and 280°. Nothing further was found during the night.

On the 30th, they searched the area south of Fair Isle again, and, at 1130, *Faulknor* obtained an Asdic contact in 59° 18.5′ N, 01° 28′ W, the same location as *Firedrake's* of the previous day. *Faulknor* dropped five depth-charges, set to explode on the sea bottom, the depth being about 50 fathoms at this point. Disappointingly there were no visible results from this attack and the search was finally abandoned at midday, the ships returning to Scapa.

Captain Daniel commented:

> Although this contact was classified as doubtful, it may well be that the aircraft inflicted considerable damage on the submarine and that it dived in a leaking condition, subsequently moving with the help of the tide to a position five or six miles to the south eastward before coming to rest on the bottom. It is understood that a flooded submarine will give little or no echo.

To which Captain A. Madden of HMS *Osprey,* the anti-submarine school at Portland, was to comment wryly:

> The theory that flooded submarines will give little or no echo is unfortunately not true. A large number of non-sub echoes would be eliminated if flooded wrecks gave no echoes.

On 1 October destroyer *Matabele* secured alongside and later *Punjabi* secured outside her. At 0832, *Faulknor* slipped and proceeded to No.14 buoy and, at 0832 on 3 October, she sailed in company with *Punjabi* to investigate a submarine report off Ronaldshay. At 1050, the two destroyers made contact in 59° 00′ N, 2° 08′ W. This position was fixed accurately by sextant angles to avoid further attacks in this position. They obtained a very strong echo at 1,800 yards range in 46 fathoms of water and, with *Punjabi* acting as the directing ship, at 1125 *Faulknor* dropped a single Mark D.11 depth charge [which had replaced the Mark D.3s] from her trap set to explode at 350 feet, but with no obvious result. She entered Ronaldshay later that evening but was at sea again early next morning and investigated several merchant ships in the area. Patrolling continued and half an hour before midnight, another full depth-charge pattern was dropped on a firm contact.

On 4 October, in position 58° 52′ N, 01° 31′ W the SS *Glen Farg* was torpedoed by a U-boat. She broke in half and the submarine surfaced and finished her by shelling. This, according to a post-war German account was done, 'in mercantile warfare and according to prize regulations'. Scraps of her alarm signal were intercepted and *Faulknor* put to sea to search for her attacker. There was a howling gale raging at the time, but despite the almost impossible conditions, while carrying out an anti-submarine sweep in the Fair Isle Channel *Faulknor* obtained a submarine contact at 2235 hours, in 59° 35′ N, 02° 31′ W. The echo appeared to move left fairly rapidly and was lost with the range down to 200 yards. *Faulknor* was on her own so there was no directing ship but she carried out a depth-charge attack, firing a full pattern of five charges set to explode at 100 and 200 feet, but contact was not maintained after the attack, and no results could be seen in the darkness. The attack was classified as a 'doubtful'.

The hunt continued next day, *Faulknor* being joined by *Firedrake,* and right through the next night, when she, in turn, was relieved by *Fortune. Firedrake* found *Glen Farg's* boats and rescued survivors. *Faulknor* arrived back in the Flow at 1248/6th.

There was little respite, for, at 1505, *Faulknor* weighed anchor again, and passed through the gate to escort *Aurora* to Scapa Flow, passing the Switha Gate at 1835 and anchoring at No. 7 berth, being joined by *Fame, Foresight* and *Fury.* It was at this time that HM King George visited his fleet in the Orkneys and at 1030/7th, *Faulknor* landed some of her crew for review by the Sovereign. These men returned aboard at 1250, normal work continued. *Faulknor* weighed at 1400 and secured outboard *Fame* alongside oiler *Prestol.* She also took on extra depth-charges from drifter *Little Orme* and, at 1740, slipped and proceeded to No.14 buoy.

Faulknor was back at sea again on 8 October. Intelligence reported the German battle-cruiser *Gneisenau*, escorted by light cruiser *Köln* and nine destroyers, had put to sea with orders to trail their coat as far as the south coast of Norway in order to attack any British shipping they found there. Avoiding battle, they were to lure any British warships encountered into the Skagerrak, for attack by submarines and bombing. Confirmation that this squadron had been sighted steering north off the Lister Light was received at 1320 and the Home Fleet raised steam. Assuming the heavy units might be trying to break out into the Atlantic, Admiral Forbes sailed Force 'E', battle-cruisers *Hood* and *Repulse*, with light cruisers *Aurora* and *Sheffield* escorted by *Fame, Foresight, Forester* and *Fury,* to patrol fifty miles north-west of Stadtlandet, and rendezvous with the Humber Force, and *Faulknor* conducted an anti-submarine sweep ahead of this squadron as they left the Flow.

At 1840 that day, Force 'F', *Nelson, Rodney,* carrier *Furious* and light cruiser *Newcastle* also sailed, with *Faulknor* as Senior Officer of the screen, leading *Firedrake, Ashanti, Bedouin, Eskimo, Mashona, Punjabi* and *Somali,* steering for a position north-east of the Shetland Islands. The plan was for the two halves of the trap to spring shut on the German squadron.

They sailed north-east into increasingly worsening weather. Next day they turned further northwards, convinced the enemy was heading out into the open sea. The fleet maintained their search between the 8th and 12th, but to no avail. On the 9th, bombers of both sides were despatched, with results that were to become all too predictable over the coming years; the Luftwaffe found their targets, the cruisers of the Humber Force and carried out attacks, unsuccessfully; the RAF failed to find their targets at all. For *Faulknor* and the battle-fleet this day was one of searching empty seas, the fleet moving up to the area between the Faeroe Islands and Iceland to block the route out into the North Atlantic, but they were beating the wrong way for the German ships had long since reversed course for home. They were not finally sighted steering south through the Great Belt until early on the 10th and were in Kiel at 0100 that day.

But by then the men of *Faulknor* were contending with a different enemy. In the cold water between the Faroes and Iceland the ships rolled and plunged as the great seas swept inboard and the wind tore through the signal halyards. *Faulknor* herself had been taking it green continuously as they clawed northwards, until she ran slap into the mother and father of all waves, crashing down into the trough with a roar and a shudder. Tons of angry water thudded aboard and her forecastle sagged and bent like a tin box. Throwing this mass of water sluggishly to one side, *Faulknor* righted herself again, but she had been badly hurt.

At 1638/8th then C-in-C, Home Fleet signalled:

> *Faulknor* has sustained damage, request instructions.

The Admiralty responded at 1842:

> Approved for *Faulknor* to proceed when convenient to be taken in hand by Barclay Curle for repairs to weather damage and other urgent defects. *Faulknor* is to report date and time of arrival.

Fortunately, Admiral Forbes had recalled his units, the battle-fleet sailing for Loch Ewe with *Nelson*, *Rodney* and *Hood*, escorted by *Faulknor*, *Firedrake*, *Forester, Fury*, *Bedouin* and *Punjabi,* while the rest of the fleet returned to Scapa Flow. On 11th, they were off the Butt of Lewis and, by 0539, off the Mull of Kintyre. In the calmer waters of the Minches it was found that *Faulknor's* forecastle was too badly damaged to be repaired at the fleet base, so she was detached and steered a course for Greenock, anchoring off there at 0859/12th, before embarking a pilot and proceeding up the Clyde to the shipyard of Barclay Curle, Scotstoun at 1425.

Admiral Forbes signalled at 1904/12th:

> While *Faulknor* is in hand request they be given 14 days to refit including docking, coating of bottom and boiler cleaning.

Captain D8 signalled at 1141/13 October:

> *Faulknor* is de-ammunitioned in anticipation. If approved will be taken in hand on Sunday 16 October.

Faulknor had de-ammunitioned ship on the 13th and, on the 15th, DoD was reporting that she had been, 'Taken in hand 15/10 for Docking and repairs.'

Opportunity was also taken to undertake necessary work on her armament. On the 18 October No. 5 4.7-inch gun was hoisted out and her foremost quadruple 21-inch torpedo tube mounting was also hoisted out. Both were replaced, the gun mounting the next day, the torpedo tubes the day after. On 21st tugs towed *Faulknor* to dry dock at 0910, where she remained until the 0725/26th when the dock was flooded to float her out, all work having been completed. Jobs included fitting a degaussing cable, which reduced the ships permanent magnetic field as protection against magnetic mines. In compensation for the extra five tons of added weight, two 21-inch torpedoes each weighing 4,222-lb, were landed. Then it was found that the fore store room was flooded and the dock gates had to be closed for a while. At 0816, the draining of the dock was resumed and by late forenoon, *Faulknor* pronounced a seaworthy vessel once more, securing alongside *Fortune*. On 27th she refuelled and next day the tugs towed her back to dock again.

At 1545, both *Faulknor* and *Fortune* undocked, while *Forester* replaced them for refitting. On 30th she proceeded up river to turn ship, later returning down the Clyde to anchor off Greenock to ammunition ship. Next day *Faulknor* slipped from the jetty and swung her compasses, then anchored off Tail 'O the Bank with *Firedrake*.

On 2 November, *Faulknor* finally sailed leading *Foresight, Fortune, Icarus, Intrepid, Impulsive, Ivanhoe* and *Punjabi*, escorting *Nelson*, passing Flannan Islands on the 3rd. That evening *Faulknor*, *Fortune* and *Intrepid*, took station two miles ahead of *Nelson* and, at 1930, they were detached to refuel at Sullum Voe in the Shetlands. Here they found *War Diwan* and, at 1030, secured alongside her to replenish.

At 1631, *Faulknor* proceeded up Yell Sound with *Fortune* and *Intrepid* to Muckla Flugga. They sailed 6 November, forming screen on *Nelson* again, passing an anti-submarine valve to *Intrepid* during the day by heaving line. On 8th destroyers *Foresight* and *Ivanhoe* joined the screen, while

Hood, Imperial, Ivanhoe and *Kingston* parted company. *Faulknor* continued as leader of the fleet ahead of the Flagship as the rest of the squadron continued its patrol.

They returned to Rosyth on 9 November, securing at 'U' berth with *Fortune* alongside and later anchored. The fleet, with *Nelson* and *Rodney*, sailed again on 12 November, to cover the second convoy of iron-ore ships from Norway; *Faulknor* leading *Fame, Foresight, Fortune, Foxhound, Icarus, Imogen* and *Impulsive*. They passed through Pentland Firth on 13th and that evening the three 'I' class destroyers left. The fleet passed the Butt of Lewis in the early hours of 17th and entering Loch Ewe (now known as 'Port 'A' – a totally vain attempt to hoodwink the Germans) later that morning. *Faulknor* refuelled from *War Pindari* with *Foresight,* and the new ships 'Doc', Commander David Rendall, joined, as Flotilla Surgeon.

They left at 0730/20th, *Faulknor, Fame, Firedrake, Fortune, Foxhound, Somali* and *Tartar* escorting *Nelson* and *Rodney* back into the Clyde. They anchored on the 21st, but, at 1551, the C-in-C had received a signal from the Armed Merchant Cruiser *Rawlpindi* saying she had sighted the enemy, which she incorrectly reported as pocket-battleship *Deutschland*. In fact, she was quickly sunk by *two* battle-cruisers, *Scharnhorst* and *Gneisenau*. The fleet raised steam with all despatch and proceeded to Greenock, *Faulknor* passing the gate at 1001 and oiling from *Montenol* with *Fame*, both later anchoring.

At 1920, *Nelson* and *Rodney*, sailed with heavy cruiser *Devonshire* and screening destroyers *Faulknor, Fame, Firedrake, Foresight, Fortune, Forester* and *Fury*. Admiral Forbes' intention was to proceed through the Minches and round the top of Scotland via the Pentland Firth to 58° 36′ N, 03° 00′ E, east of the Fair Isle Channel, to intercept the enemy. This required a whole days hard steaming from Loch Ewe. Off the Mull of Kintyre destroyers *Ashanti, Mashona, Punjabi* and *Somali*, joined. Their passage through the Minches in a severe gale was appalling and, in endeavouring to maintain the battleships' speed, they being less affected by the storm, the flotilla took a heavy pounding.

On the afternoon of the 24th Cape Wrath was passed, and *Fame, Foresight* and *Fortune* parted company, all having suffered severe weather damage the night before. *Faulknor* and the fleet continued north though the Pentland Skerries that night. Next day they swept up past the Shetlands to cover the cruiser patrol lines off southern Norway. By 1600/25th the fleet reached their intercepting position 60 miles off the Norwegian coast, patiently tracking up and down in a box, the destroyers being refuelled in relays. At 0950/26th *Faulknor, Forester* and *Fury* were relieved by *Bedouin* and *Firedrake,* entering Sullum Voe and refuelling from *War Diwan*, rejoining the fleet at 1530/27th. The weather remained appalling and next day caused their first war casualty, when *Faulknor* lost a man overboard. The unfortunate was Leading Seaman John W. Spanner (P/JX 129498) and there was never a hope of recovering his body. Vernon Coles remembered:

> Our first death was that of Leading Seaman Spanner. We were in very heavy seas right up near the North Cape early in 1940 and poor Spanner was an LTO on board and he had just been relieved of his watch he was one of the depth-charge party. He tried to get forward in very heavy weather, with the upper deck being continually washed down. We who were in Nos. 2 & 3 boiler rooms and the engine room were also changing watches and, although life lines had been rigged, it was hell's own job getting for'ard as, of course, in destroyers there was no companionway below decks. On his attempting to come for'ard along the upper deck, we were 'pooped' and a huge wave caught him, carrying him right over the ship and he was never seen again.

This tragedy was part-and-parcel of Home Fleet operations in the northern oceans during the first winter of the war. Tragically, the German heavy ships had already slipped through the net, evading light cruiser *Newcastle* and passing undetected though other patrol lines established off Norway, back to Wilhelmshaven by 1300/27 November. The Home Fleet continued to hunt the grim northern wastes for three more days. Finally, at 0800/29th, the fleet swept the north-east. *Rodney* developed rudder defects and had to return to the Clyde. *Faulknor* and her consorts continued screening *Nelson* and *Devonshire* throughout the 29th and 30th, being in 64° 19′ N, 0° 56′ E at 2000 that night, before turning south again on 30th.

Next day they returned to the Clyde. Refuelling at sea could not be conducted properly as insufficient fast tankers existed; the destroyers' tanks were now dangerously low, so they steered for Loch Ewe on 4 December, and it was while entering that anchorage at thirteen knots that *Nelson* was badly damaged by a magnetic mine, lain earlier by *U-31*. At the entrance to the Loch the destroyers fell astern to conduct the customary anti-submarine sweeps outside while the flagship passed through them and it was then *Nelson* detonated the mine. Vernon Coles witnessed this:

> I recall *Nelson* being mined as we led the fleet in. The mine detonated for'rard under *Nelson's* side right under the ratings heads and the only reported casualty was that a rating who was sat on the heads ended up with a rather battered and sore rear end!

The explosion forced in the outer bottom plating on the starboard side for a length of seventy feet and flooded the ship, she heeling three degrees over to starboard. The 16-inch gun main-armament loading equipment was damaged by shock, but the machinery remained intact.

Initially it was thought the flagship might have been torpedoed and the destroyers intensified their Asdic searches, dropping random depth-charges to ward off further attacks, until the truth was realised. Not only was *Nelson* put out of commission for many months, it effectively trapped her, and other warships, inside the Loch for a time, until improvised magnetic sweeping could be conducted.

While this was being organised, *Faulknor, Forester* and *Fury*, remained at the Loch with the cripple, in order, as Doctor Rendall recalls, to maintain continuous anti-submarine patrols off the entrance to ensure no further submarine minelaying was carried out. Thus *Faulknor* missed the next big convoy operation. She had been due to lead the inward escort of destroyers to meet the First Canadian Troop Convoy, TC1, but now her place had to be taken by Captain D6 in *Somali*. Only temporary repairs could be done to *Nelson* during this period and, belatedly, a degaussing coil was fitted. The anti-aircraft cruiser *Calcutta* arrived next day in case the enemy tried to capitalise on the flagships immobility with an air raid, but none took place. Rudimentary attempts were made to explode any other mines that might be present by the use of drifters containing a large electro-magnet, and counter-mining was conducted by the destroyers dropping depth-charges.

Faulknor thus spent most of December at 'Port A'; and during this period awards for the actions against the U-boats were received, Captain Daniel being awarded the DSO, the flotilla anti-submarine and navigation officers, Lieutenant-Commanders Carss and Akerton, each receiving the DSC.

Faulknor went alongside *Nelson* at 1130/28th but cast off at 1315 when news was received of yet another setback. The battleship *Barham* was torpedoed by *U-30*, ten miles off the Butt of Lewis. The explosion in the ship's port side, abreast the forward 15-inch shellroom tore open her bilges and flooded her compartments and she took on a 7-degree list to port, later righted. *Repulse* and five destroyers were in company and *Faulknor, Foxhound* and *Mashona* were immediately sailed from Loch Ewe to stand by the cripple, reaching her at 2324.

An error in *Barham's* signals had prevented an effective hunt being made for her assailant by her escorts, however next day *Faulknor* carried out a comprehensive search, but, because of the time lag, this proved unsuccessful and they finally escorted *Barham* into Liverpool, where she was docked for three months. Combined with the sinking of *Royal Oak* and *Courageous*, plus severe damage to *Nelson,* this was a heavy blow. On 30 December *Faulknor* and *Foxhound* returned to Loch Ewe.

As the old year died, the men of the 8th Flotilla looked back on four months of hard, weary steaming; indeed the whole Home Fleet had set new records in sea-keeping time, made more remarkable by the appalling conditions in which they had worked. Some destroyers had spent over a hundred days at sea during those months, steaming from 25,000 to 30,000 miles, according to an official statement, and despite the weather damage we have already recorded, the little ships had stood the test fairly well. The C-in-C reported:

> All classes of ships have kept the sea for a greater number of days per month than ever before since the advent of steam. The average has been in the region of 23 days per month. The weather experienced in northern waters from October onwards can only be described as foul; one gale has followed another with monotonous frequency. On the whole, the machinery and boilers have stood the strain remarkably well and great credit is due to the engine room complements for this. It can also be said that the hulls of ships have come through the test well, with the following exceptions ...

The C-in-C then enumerated those examples that did not come up to his hopes. He had no criticism of the 'F' Class destroyers at all, but was scathing in his description of later [so-called superior] classes:

> The 'Tribal' class destroyers have been a great disappointment: as many as 12 out of the 16 were out of action at one time ... The 'K' class destroyers have also been a great disappointment ...

The views of the wartime C-in-C contrast strangely with the post-war adulation heaped on these destroyers by 'experts', indeed *Faulknor* and her sisters were to prove their superior sea-keeping qualities over these vaunted types repeatedly in the years ahead.

Added responsibilities for the Home Fleet's limited destroyers commenced early in October 1939, with the Norwegian convoys. These ran from Methil, in the Firth of Forth, across to Bergen (ON = Outward-Norwegian) and back again (H.N. = Homeward-Norwegian). The route was exposed to U-boat assault, and they were within range of the Luftwaffe, so strong destroyer escort had to be given, a further drain on Forbes' meagre resources. Escorts could not be given for the entire journey, procedure being for the destroyers to take one convoy to about 90° north and then return with the homeward one.

Early in January an intensive counter-mining operation was conducted at Loch Ewe where damaged *Nelson* still lay trapped, an improvised mine-sweeping force of requisitioned trawlers and drifters fitted with Oropesa magnetic sweeps spent two days clearing a passage to the open sea. Five further mines had been exploded in the Loch but how many others remained undetected was unknown. The large prize merchant ship, *Ilsenstein*, in ballast, was brought into Loch Ewe as a 'mine-detonator'.

On 4 January 1940, *Faulknor* led the destroyer escort to sea as *Ilsenstein* came out first, closely followed by *Nelson*, the idea being that any mines still in the channel would be detonated by the big merchant man whose draught was about the same as that of the damaged battleship. No further mines were exploded and *Nelson* sailed under the escort of *Faulknor, Fame, Foresight, Foxhound, Impulsive* and *Isis,* and setting course south through the Irish Sea at her best speed of 14 knots. The squadron reached at Portsmouth 1050 Monday 8th; *Nelson's* repairs took six months.

Faulknor left Portsmouth at 0800/10 January, with *Foxhound* and *Impulsive* being joined by *Fame, Foresight* and *Isis* as they passed Plymouth on their way to rejoin the Home Fleet. As usual, their passage was not to be without incident. The steamer *Holyhead* reported sighting a U-Boat off Point of Ayr, Isle of Man and, at 1000, *Faulknor* and *Foxhound* were diverted to investigate. Further confirmation of submarine activity was given when tanker *El Oro*, homeward-bound in a convoy, suffered an internal explosion and sank about six miles west of the Bar Light Vessel at 1100. Two the convoy's escorting destroyers, *Vimy* and *Walker*, carried out an anti-submarine search which *Faulknor* and *Foxhound* duly joined.

The tanker had been mined [lain by *U-30* 6 January] and this fact being appreciated by Captain Daniel, he took his two destroyers to search for the minelaying submarine north of the Isle of Man, while the other four destroyers maintained a patrol across the North Channel until 1747, when the whole force was ordered to search to the north.

Faulknor and her companions finally anchored in the Clyde at 1150/14th. *Faulknor* went alongside depot ship *Woolwich* in the James Watt dock for a short refit until 19 January. She then remained in the Clyde, the Home Fleet's new temporary base now that Scapa Flow *and* Loch Ewe had both been denied them. During the first two months of the year the weather was severe, with icy winds, very low temperatures and Arctic conditions adding to the usual wartime problems of naval operations in northern waters.

These terrible conditions did not mean that the warships remained at anchor, on the contrary, in February 1940 Home Fleet ships were at sea for twenty-three days out of thirty-one, more sea time in fact, 'since the advent of steam.' Despite the constant strain and stress on their crews, the ships themselves, especially the fragile and delicate destroyers, had to endure much heavy weather damage.

On 24 January 1940, *Faulknor* sailed at 1935 with destroyer *Kelvin* and sloop *Scott* to conduct an anti-submarine sweep in the approaches to the Clyde which lasted all night, returning at 1450 next day. On 27 January, *Rodney* and *Repulse*, escorted by *Faulknor, Fame, Fearless, Foresight, Fortune, Foxhound* and *Fury,* left the Clyde at 1030 to cover a Norwegian convoy, returning 1500/31st, anchoring off Greenock.

Early in 1940, there was an influenza epidemic in the fleet, with many officers and men being affected. On 2 February 1940, for example, as the bulk of her own officers were incapacitated, *Faulknor* was taken to sea by the senior Divisional Officer of the flotilla, Commander P. N. Walter, this being the trip when the destroyers met and escorted safely home the third Canadian Troop Convoy, TC3. *Faulknor* led *Fame, Fearless, Firedrake, Foresight, Forester, Fortune, Foxhound, Fury, Daring, Delight, Diana* and *Kelvin* to rendezvous with the five large liners, *Aquitania, Chrobry, Empress of Australia, Empress of Britain* and *Monarch of Bermuda*, guarded by battleships *Malaya* and *Valiant*, light cruiser *Enterprise* and destroyer *Hunter*; *Delight* had to abort the sortie so *Kingston* replaced her, all twelve destroyers sailing from the Clyde at 1100/2 February. The flotilla met the convoy at 0825/5th, in 55° 25′ N, 23° 10′ W, and escorted them back towards the Clyde.

The convoy was not to escape problems completely. Just before dusk on 6th the Senior Office, aboard *Malaya*, in order to simplify the manoeuvring and signalling in the narrow waters and the bad weather as they passed through the swept channel, formed the convoy into two separate groups, the First Division, *Malaya, Aquitania* and *Empress of Britain* screened by *Faulknor, Fearless, Firedrake, Foresight, Forester* and *Foxhound*, and the Second Division, one mile astern and manoeuvring independently at 16 knots, *Valiant, Chroby, Monarch of Bermuda* and *Empress of Australia*, screened by *Daring, Diana, Fortune, Fury, Hunter* and *Kingston*, while *Fame* and *Kelvin* further supplemented the escort off Ailsa Craig.

As the two groups approached Inistrahull, the visibility deteriorated rapidly. The Inistrahull Light could be seen, but there was no sign of the Rathlin Island Light through the murk and the huge ships and their little escorts passed within two miles of the island without sighting a glimpse of it.

From that time until their arrival in the Clyde the visibility varied from between three miles and 100 yards, and, not surprisingly the two divisions lost contact with each other soon after 2200 when *Valiant* judged the First Division had altered course to the northward. Some idea of the conditions prevailing at this time can be gleaned from the words of *Valiant's* skipper:

> The signal reports in HMS *Valiant* for this period are not reliable as the wind and rain made it impossible to write down signals on the bridge, and the noise of the wind made the CCO. multiphones useless.

If these were the conditions on the bridge of a 30,000-ton battleship the conditions aboard *Faulknor* and the other destroyers trying to keep station on these battleships and the 'Monster' liners without being trampled underfoot, can only be imagined. It is hardly surprising that strict and immaculate formation was not adhered to, but the guiltiest proved to be the liners themselves.

Meanwhile *Faulknor* arrived in the Clyde during the morning with the First Division. They had experienced great difficulties station-keeping but had remained in company, arriving safely with no incidents, and *Faulknor* had anchored at midday on 7th.

At 1050/9 February, *Faulknor* led *Fame, Firedrake, Foresight, Forester, Fortune, Foxhound* and *Fury* screening *Warspite* and *Hood* covering the Norwegian convoys ON11 and HN11. They proceeded north to the westward of the Hebrides on the 10th, detaching *Fame* and *Forester* at 1900 to refuel at Sullom Voe. Throughout the 11th/13th, the squadron patrolled to the north-west of the Shetlands. At 0600/12th, *Fame* and *Forester* rejoined and *Faulknor, Fortune* and *Foxhound* were detached to refuel at Sullom Voe. *En route Faulknor* rescued ten survivors from the Swedish *Orania* torpedoed by *U-50*, on 11 February 60 miles north-east of the Shetlands. They arrived at 1650, replenished from *War Diwan*, leaving at 0800 and rejoining the flag at 1427, when it was the turn of *Firedrake, Foresight* and *Fury* to refuel. *Forester* was detached at 1750/13th and before the fleet was recalled to Scapa.

At this time the heavy ships had only *Faulknor, Fame, Fortune* and *Foxhound* as screen and so it was decided not to set course for the Clyde's dangerous waters until *Firedrake, Foresight* and *Fury* had rejoined. They remained north-west of the Shetlands throughout the 14th, *Hood* carrying out an inclination exercise with *Warspite* early that day.

The three refuelled destroyers hove in sight four hours later and course was then set for the Clyde, with *Warspite* carrying out practice firings of her 4-inch HA guns. At 1830, the C-in-C instructed the squadron to alter course for the Pentland Firth in case heavy support was required by the destroyers intercepting the German prison ship *Altmark* in Norwegian territorial waters. Once this operation had been brought to its successful conclusion, the fleet steered for the Clyde at 0520/17th, *Faulknor* anchoring at 0945/18th.

Next day there were several changes of officers, with Captain C. S. Daniel being relieved by Captain A. F. De Salis, also reliefs arrived for the flotilla engineering, gunnery, signal and pay officers in the forms of Lieutenant-Commander L. H. Stileman and Lieutenants R. L. Moss, J. S. Daglish, and P. D. G. Mather. The new secretary was Lieutenant W. G. Jack. Captain Daniel, after an eventful two years in command of the 8th Flotilla, went on to command battle-cruiser *Renown* in 1942. Later, as Vice-Admiral, he was in charge of all administration for the huge British Pacific Fleet during the final drive on Okinawa and Japan, attaining the rank of Admiral before his retirement after the war.

As a young Acting Sub-Lieutenant, Captain De Salis had fought in destroyers in the First World War. At Jutland his ship, *Moresby*, had been mistaken for a German destroyer and was fired on by battle-cruiser *Tiger* during that battle. She survived and in the night action, Petty-Officer Brummage fired a torpedo, which sank German destroyer *V-4*. In 1936 De Salis had written a detailed narrative of those events from his own eyewitness viewpoint. With roots such as this in the destroyer service he proved to be the ideal man for the job and his time with *Faulknor* was a memorable period.

They sailed at 1410 on 19 February, *Faulknor, Fearless, Firedrake, Foresight, Fortune, Foxhound, Fury* and *Hardy* escorting *Rodney* and *Hood* to cover Norwegian convoy ON14 of 24 ships, a duty which lasted until 1040/24th, when they returned to the Clyde. Although two heavy ships, a battleship and a battle-cruiser, alternated in these continuous patrols up in the Arctic Circle, there were only enough destroyers to provide one good anti-submarine screen, so that when each squadron returned to harbour almost always the same few destroyers sailed with the next.

At 1150/27th, *Faulknor* again left the Clyde, leading *Fame, Forester, Fury, Kandahar* and *Mohawk*, escorting battleship *Malaya*, which was carrying 42 tons of Gold Bullion from the British

Treasury for safe-keeping in Canada, along with AMC *Ascania* for Hvalfjord, Iceland. They took the two big ships part of the way on their journey north, parting company at 2000/28th.

Vernon Coles related:

> We sped at high speed with other units of our flotilla and we anchored at 'Tail 'o the Bank', Greenock during the dog watches. We all took on fuel and, during the night, the great liner *Queen Elizabeth* arrived down the Clyde during the hours of darkness.

To cover both the next Norwegian convoy and the Northern Cruiser Patrols, the Home Fleet again sortied from the Clyde, at 1600 on that same Saturday, with *Hood* and *Valiant,* escorted by destroyers *Faulknor, Fame, Forester, Kelly, Kandahar* and *Sikh*.

At 1130 Sunday 3 March, while passing through the Minches at 16 knots, in 58° 27' N, 5° 46' W, *Forester* obtained an Asdic contact, '… that had every indication of being a U-boat', and carried out a depth-charge attack. Captain De Salis ordered *Fame* to join her and together the two carried out eight attacks over a period of 24 hours. They were rewarded by the sight of small patches of oil and bubbles before having to leave and rejoin the screen.

The fleet's patrol was extended up beyond the Arctic Circle and met vicious weather. For the next two days the squadron continued to patrol north and then turned south, the weather remained poor and no enemy sightings were made. *Faulknor* and *Forester* were sent into Scapa to refuel being followed at 1800 on Thursday 7th by the rest of the First Battle-Cruiser squadron. This was the first time the Home Fleet had returned to its main base since *Royal Oak's* loss. For *Faulknor* the stay was a brief one.

At 2340, the C-in-C signalled *Hood,* repeated Vice Admiral Commanding, Orkney and Shetlands, requesting that *Faulknor* and *Forester* be sailed again to rendezvous with him off Cape Wrath at 1230/8th.

The Commander-in-Chief had the First Lord, Sir Winston Churchill, embarked in his flagship, leaving the Clyde at 1600/7th with battleship *Rodney* and battle-cruisers *Renown* and *Repulse,* screened by destroyers *Hardy, Hostile, Inglefield, Imogen, Fortune, Foxhound, Firedrake, Punjabi* and *Kimberley*.

At 2340 on Friday 8 March, *Faulknor* and *Forester* were sailed to reinforce the fleet's escort, and duly rendezvoused with the C-in-C, 270°, Cape Wrath 7 miles, at 1230. It was as well they did so because the Germans knew all about their movements *and* the return of the fleet to Scapa. No fewer than nine U-boats were concentrated off the Orkneys and Shetlands. Although they had no success against the Home Fleet, this concentration did torpedo six merchant ships in the area.

On arrival back off the Orkneys at 1730 on 8 March, the fleet found the Hoxa entrance to the Flow closed because it was thought that German aircraft had dropped magnetic mines earlier in the afternoon, about one mile 055° from the north-east end of the Calf of Flotta. As a result most of the ships were obliged to remain outside for the night whilst the passage to the anchorage was swept. At 1748, *Rodney* stopped off the entrance to the Switha boom and transferred the First Lord, along with Captain R. D. Olliver and Rear-Admiral A. L. St. G. Lyster, the men responsible for the new Scapa Flow defences under Plan 'R', to destroyer *Kimberley*. She then proceeded on ahead, escorted by *Faulknor,* and Churchill was transferred to *Hood* at anchor inside Scapa Flow. The rest of the fleet eventually entered Scapa Flow at 1045/9th, watched by Churchill, Oliver and Lyster from a ships motor launch off Hoxa Sound before presiding over a meeting aboard *Rodney*.

On 12 March, *Faulknor* and *Fortune* sailed at 0730 to escort twelve merchant ships from Kirkwall to join the Norwegian convoy ON19, which had left Methil at 1500 the previous day with twenty-eight merchantmen bound for Bergen and one for Aberdeen, escorted by destroyers *Cossack, Nubian, Gurkha* and *Ilex*. Once the 'Fs' joined they took command of the Kirkwall section of the convoy relieving *Ilex*. There were no attacks and they transferred to returning convoy HN19 at Point 'E' at

1400 on Thursday 14th. This followed a signal from Rear Admiral (D) Home Fleet, timed 1221/14th:

> *Faulknor* and *Fortune* to escort west ships and return to Scapa.

The average speed of these convoys was deliberately set at just seven knots, even so, many of the freighters proved incapable of achieving or maintaining even this crawl, averaging only 5.3 knots. The weather continued bleak, and, during the morning of the 15th, a south-easterly gale had blown up bringing with it thick snowstorms, forcing the convoy to heave-to. *Faulknor* and *Fortune* were detached with the sixteen ships of the westbound group in 60° 44′ N, 01° 14′ E, at 0720. On the first day, *Faulknor* was in the van with *Fortune* to the rear of the Scandinavians, but subsequently they took up positions on each bow and beam, zigzagging independently day and night. This group was thus able to resume its progress at seven knots to Muckle Flugga despite the strong south-easterly wind and with the visibility falling to half-a-mile in the snow flurries. There was a brief period of calm that same afternoon but, by evening, it was blowing a full gale from the north-west.

Their speed for the next twelve hours was five knots and the course varied from that steered by 20. This gale gradually moderated during the night of 15th/16th and speed was increased to seven knots again, but morning found the convoy scattered with many stragglers, so speed had to be reduced again for them to catch up. Captain De Salis recorded that the Convoy guide, *North Devon*, '... did not appear to realise the need to maintain the revolutions for the speed ordered, or to inform the escort if an alteration was made. Such alterations were made on several occasions without notice, and rendered the navigation of the Convoy (and the responsibility of the Escort) unnecessarily difficult.'

They were kept employed rounding the ships up and re-forming them. This was eventually done and the convoy proceeded at eight knots from the vicinity of Foula Island to the usual dispersal position off Cape Wrath, where *Faulknor* and *Forester* left it, anchoring at Longhope, Scapa at

HMS Faulknor *(extreme right) leads two of her flotilla and the battleship HMS* Nelson, *Flagship of the Home Fleet, to sea from Scapa Flow on one of the many sweeps across northern waters in the winter of 1939–40.* (Crown Copyright.)

0700/17th, pending the clearance of mines from their normal anchorage of Gutter Sound, which was not done until 1116.

Faulknor later went alongside depot ship *Woolwich* for temporary weather-damage repairs, to complete by 22nd. While she lay there inactive on 19 March 1940, the Admiralty, believing more air attacks were imminent, ordered the fleet to sea at 1445, and they cruised to the north of the Shetlands and Faeroes and between the Norwegian coast and Iceland, until 27th. Whilst at sea they provided cover for the Scandinavian convoys and also to the 2nd Cruiser Squadron, which carried out sweeps into the Skagerrak on the nights of 21/22 and 22/23 March: Operation 'DU'.

On completion of her running repairs *Faulknor* herself conducted Anti-submarine exercises with submarine *Swordfish* on 23 March, but had to curtail these at 1500, when she was sailed from Scapa to reinforce a real anti-submarine hunt which had been underway since the previous morning. At 1050 the previous day an aircraft had reported a U-boat in 50° 12′ N, 4° 36′ W near Fule Skerry and destroyers *Electra* and *Encounter* had been diverted from east of the Orkneys to conduct a search. At 1850 another aircraft reported the U-boat again, in 59° 26′ N, 3° 54′ W and the two destroyers reached this spot at 2000 to start hunting.

When Captain De Salis arrived to take charge of the operations during the afternoon of 23 March, the trail was cold but, at 1705, a third aircraft made an attack, dropping bombs ahead of a long oil patch she had sighted in 60° 16′ N, 3° 22′ W. The three destroyers continued to search in this area throughout the night, but to no avail.

At 0600, Captain De Salis was instructed to leave the search and to proceed to Kirkwall to pick up and escort the Kirkwall contingent of Norwegian convoy ON 22. In company with these, *Faulknor* then steered to join the rest of the convoy, twenty freighters screened by destroyers *Escapade*, *Kashmir*, *Kimberley* and *Zulu*, the whole force steering northward, before the five destroyers left to join the escort of the homeward Norwegian convoy HN22. This convoy sailed from Hovden at 0900 on 27 March, into a rising north-easterly wind that, by the following night, had reached gale force and which continued to blow at Force 8 to 9 until 1000/28th. This caused the merchant ships great discomfiture; for example, at 0130 the Convoy Leader, *Breda,* signalled she was hove-to but did not require assistance. Her skipper might have thought otherwise had he known that Captain De Salis had received a signal from the Admiralty informing him that a German naval squadron of two cruisers and two destroyers had been reported leaving the Freisian Islands at 1330 on the 27 March and could be making a raid on the Scandinavian convoy routes.

In fact this was the preliminary movements of the German invasion of Norway, Operation 'Weser Exercise' and the ships reported were light cruisers *Königsberg* and *Köln* with the torpedo-boats *Leopard* and *Wolf* assembling before sailing to occupy Bergen. However, Captain De Salis reasoned that, should this be a raid, then this squadron could only reach his convoy by steaming at a constant speed of twenty knots. 'As this was obviously impossible in the sea then running no further anxiety was felt on this score, and W/T silence was not broken to inform Cover of the amended dawn position by star fix.'

By the forenoon of 28th, the convoy had been re-formed satisfactorily and *Kashmir* and *Kimberley* were able to collect the Westbound Section, ready to part company at 1900. At 1245, two Dornier Do.17 bombers were sighted on the northern flank of the fore, which were engaged by *Kashmir*. *Faulknor* transmitted a 'Help' signal, but the bombers did not press their luck and satisfied themselves by circling at a distance and observing.

In response to their alarm, light cruisers *Aurora* and *Sheffield* and AA cruiser *Cairo* arrived at 1400 to add their firepower to the convoy's protection. No air attack materialised, however, until 1900, when a solitary Heinkel He.111 bomber dropped five bombs in among the merchant ships, all of which missed. She was engaged by all the cruisers and destroyers in turn as she came within range, but vanished unscathed into the dusk. Captain De Salis then dispersed the westbound part of the convoy off Cape Wrath as normal, while *Faulknor*, *Escapade* and *Zulu*, reinforced by *Tartar*, continued with the rest of the convoy.

Another aircraft was heard in the vicinity and she strafed the convoy with tracer bullets before retiring at 2045. There was no further enemy activity and, by 0230/29th, the convoy was abreast Scapa Flow. Every ship was then illuminated and clearly silhouetted by a searchlight from the defences ashore at a distance of 35 miles. Fortunately the Luftwaffe had gone home or else this indiscretion could have had serious repercussions.

Faulknor, *Escapade*, *Tartar* and *Zulu* finally entered Rosyth on the morning of Saturday the 30th, for refuelling. At midday on 31st, they sailed from Methil as screen for the eighteen ships of convoy ON24. The Kirkwall contingent, with three more ships, left at 1030 Monday 1 April, with destroyers *Somali*, *Mashona* and *Matabele,* who were to escort them most of the way to Bergen before picking up the homeward-bound HN 23A. However, this winter was an endless one and, although it was officially spring, the weather had not done with them yet.

During the night of the 1/2 April a strong easterly gale blew up and in the mountainous seas and poor conditions the two convoys and the Kirkwall contingent were unable to meet as intended. The two groups of merchantmen became scattered eastward of the Orkney Islands, with what the official report described as, '… resultant confusion and risk of collision owing to the restricted sea room.' It was indeed a wild night and not for the faint-hearted.

Despite the conditions prevailing, the course and speed at the time was afterwards found to have been accurate, despite the fact that the last 'Fix' they had been able to take had been at 0500 and conditions had subsequently become extremely bad. Subsequently the East-North-Easterly gale backed to the North, and the convoy was able to make good a greater speed but drifted 20° to leeward, being in 105° 15'. By 1730 on the evening of the 1st, Captain De Salis had abandoned any hope of effecting a safe rendezvous with the Kirkwall section until next day. His own main section was getting closer to the shore and D/F bearings from *Somali* gave it as only five miles south-east of Copinsay at 1600. Although Captain De Salis thought this was a pessimistic estimate, he was faced with the fact that the course steered by the convoy guide, who was being overhauled by other ships who could not steer at the guide's speed made good, was uncertain; the visual signalling visibility was one cable at the most, and speed was problematical. As Captain De Salis stated:

> To alter course under such circumstances is a matter of difficulty, and would have become impossible after dark. It appeared to be wise to stand out from the land for the night and accept the risk of an encounter with HN 23A. In fact the ships in convoy were already becoming nervous and steering well to starboard of ordered course. The decision to heave to on course 060° was accordingly taken …

The positions of the HN convoys were plotted on the heaving table on *Faulknor's* bridge as far as possible using information from the signals received and it appeared probable that even if the wind did not back and therefore continued to delay ON24 there would be little chance of a collision before the half light of dawn. Captain De Salis added:

> In any case it was realised from own previous experience that the estimated and true positions of HN23A would probably differ widely so that it would have been unwise to pin any faith on them as far as making plans for avoidance went. To avoid stranding of the unwieldy mass of ships, mostly out of touch with each other, was more important.

At 1846, Captain De Salis advised C-in-C, Rosyth:

> ON 24 estimated position 1800 is 230 LKBP 21U. Course and speed made good 060° 2 knots or less. Intend to pass East of Shetland.

The convoy's speed was 8 knots throughout the night but the actual speed made good up to midnight was only about one knot and subsequently about two knots up to 0500, the wind dropping to Force 5 and the weather was fair from then on, but the ships had become very scattered by 0800/2nd. At 2123/1st Captain De Salis informed Captain D6 in *Somali,* repeated to the C-in-C ashore:

> Suggest rendezvous in approximate position 140 LKBP 7 at 0800 tomorrow Tuesday or to ENE of this if wind backs. Will recommence transmissions for D/F half-hourly from 0500.

At 2304/1 April C-in-C, Rosyth, signalled to Captain D8 and Captain D4:

> ON 24 in approximate position JSW/S/4839 at 2000 is steering to the East of Shetlands. Route for ON 24 is to be amended to MWE. HN 23 A should steer from present position for Buchan Ness.

But this was too late to affect the real situation, indeed it was not received in *Faulknor's* coding office until 0045/2nd, '… by which time it was not possible to alter the convoy's course to comply with it, even by the emergency method, nor was it considered prudent to make a further W/T signal until dawn … in view of proximity of submarines.'

The C-in-C admitted:

> Both Captain (D) 4th Destroyer Flotilla and Captain (D) 8th Destroyer Flotilla had difficult jobs to perform. Both found themselves unable to comply with Commander-in-Chief, Rosyth's Message timed 2308 of 1 April, but neither said so; it is considered they should have reported the fact although, in this case, it would have made little difference.

By the morning of 2 April, the weather began to moderate, and, after heaving to for the night, the two portions finally made contact with each other in 58° 58′ N, 01° 23′ W at 0900 on Tuesday 2 April. After the convoy had been reorganised and marshalled, *Faulknor, Escapade* and *Zulu* returned to Scapa at 1300.

This convoy marked the end of the first period of *Faulknor's* war service. So far, the work of the Home Fleet destroyers had been much like those of their counterparts of the Grand Fleet during the First World War, with the weather, Norwegian convoys and the U-boats presenting much the same threats. Air attacks had added another dimension but had proved remarkably ineffective. However, the tempo was to abruptly change; the war shifted up several gears and, if the destroyers felt themselves over-worked between September 1939 and April 1940, then the next few months were to prove they had not seen anything yet!

* * *

Hitler had determined to occupy both Denmark (for her airfields) and Norway (for her ports and iron-ore). The British were concerned by the regular abuse of Norwegian territorial waters by the enemy to pass their supplies of iron-ore and blockade-runners to feed the Nazi war machine, and the complete spinelessness of the Norwegians themselves to resist it, witness their disgraceful conduct regarding British prisoners during the *Altmark* affair.

At the repeated urgings of the First Lord of the Admiralty, Winston Churchill, a decision was made to lay extensive minefields in the 'Inner Leads', the coastal waterways off the Norwegian coast, to force German shipping out into International Waters where it could be intercepted. As it was expected that this minelaying would provoke strong German reaction, further plans were put in hand to occupy the strategic Norwegian ports and forestall the enemy. A military force was made ready and troopships were loaded ready to sail.

The minelaying, code-named Operation 'Wilfred', was put into effect on 6 April, 1940. Hitler had already been persuaded by Grand-Admiral Raeder that swift occupation of Norway would not only protect vital iron-ore supplies and harbours, but secure Germany's northern flank at minimal effort prior to the main European offensive in the spring. It would also, as a by-product, give his navy easy access to the North Atlantic and his air force more bases with which to outflank the British Isles. With the promised help of the Norwegian Fascist leader Vidkun Quisling, Hitler sanctioned the occupation to be put into effect during the first week of April. In the face of overwhelming British Naval superiority the German scheme, 'Operation 'Weser Exercise', was very bold. It called for the seizure of all the main Norwegian ports and cities by simultaneous landings from the sea by naval task forces with rapid following up operations by land and air. Just about every ship that could steam in the German Navy was committed. Hitler was convinced of the inability of the British to react with speed to any surprise move and events were to prove his judgement sound.

Both nations' plans were set in motion on the same fateful day. Although alert and on their guard, neither side had any precise knowledge of what their opponent intended; when they initially clashed, it was in a series of confused skirmishes and naval battles up and down the whole length of the rugged Norwegian coast.

The Germans succeeded in their audacious plan, occupying most of the main towns and airfields and flying in fighters, bombers and dive-bombers, which were soon to dominate the fighting on both land and sea to an extent hitherto not seen before in warfare.

Faulknor sailed from Scapa on 2 April, reaching the Clyde at 1800 next day. They were to lead the escort for the Polish troopship *Chroby* to occupy Trondheim and Narvik under the original Plan 'R4'. Between the 4th and 7th *Faulknor* remained in the Clyde with light cruiser *Aurora*, flying the flag of Admiral Evans, and destroyers *Foxhound*, *Forester* and *Delight*, preparing for the sailing of the troop convoy, but this plan was abandoned when the preliminary movements of the German's own Norwegian invasion forces were assumed to be the German fleet breaking into the North Atlantic.

At 1307/8th, *Faulknor* returned to Scapa with light cruiser *Aurora* and destroyers *Fortune*, *Forester*, *Foxhound*, *Delight*, *Ashanti* and *Maori*. On the way they again ran into heavy weather, *Delight* was so damaged that she had to return to the Clyde to effect repairs. *Ashanti*, *Maori* and *Fortune* were also sent back to the Clyde in order to screen the aircraft carrier *Furious*, and thus only *Faulknor*, *Forester* and *Foxhound* finally arrived at Scapa Flow at 0555 next day. The Home Fleet, *Rodney* and *Valiant*, battle-cruiser *Repulse*, light-cruisers *Penelope* and *Sheffield*, destroyers *Bedouin*, *Eskimo*, *Jupiter*, *Kashmir*, *Kelvin*, *Kimberley*, *Matabele*, *Mashona*, *Punjabi* and *Somali*, had sailed evening 7th. Various cruiser squadrons were also already at sea.

While these forces were casting about for the enemy fleet, the first clashes at sea and ashore were taking place at Norway, generating confused reports. Reinforcements continued to arrive, battleship *Warspite* escorted by destroyers *Havant* and *Hesperus;* and also *Furious*, escorted by *Fortune*, *Ashanti* and *Maori*. It was obvious that Admiral Forbes' heavy ships would require fresh escorts and, at 1500/ 9th, *Faulknor, Forester* and *Foxhound* sailed at 0700/10 April and took their places on the C-in-C's screen.

The damaged German heavy cruiser *Admiral Hipper* was thought to be sheltering at Trondheim and a strike force of Swordfish torpedo planes from the carrier was sent in after her, but the bird had flown. The fleet then continued north under sporadic air attack, destroyer *Eclipse* being badly damaged.

Meanwhile other events and decisions were deciding *Faulknor's* fate: her own imminent involvement in the Narvik affair. Following the second battle of Narvik Vice-Admiral Whitworth in *Warspite*, with the surviving undamaged destroyers, moved to Vestifjord to support any moves by the Allies to occupy Narvik itself following Admiral Forbes' signal of 1410/14th, which stated that his intention was to retain *Warspite* in the Narvik area until the army was established ashore. At 1327 Flag Officer, Narvik, Admiral of the Fleet, Lord Cork and Orrery, signalled:

> Following for General. In view of successful naval action at Narvik yesterday 13 April, and as enemy appears thoroughly frightened, suggest we take every advantage of this before enemy has recovered.

However, the Military Commander, Major-General P. J. Mackesy, was not convinced that a hastily mounted operation by ships boats through deep snow and in the face of machine-gun fire, would succeed, no matter how demoralised the enemy appeared. Lord Cork was forced to postpone his assault, at least until 16 April.

Admiral Forbes signalled Vice Admiral Whitworth at 1729, that destroyers, *Esk, Ivanhoe, Icarus, Punjabi, Hostile* and *Hero*, were to sail from Vestifjord and rendezvous with the Home Fleet on the afternoon of the 15 April, being replaced by *Faulknor* (Captain D.8), *Foxhound, Forester, Bedouin, Zulu, Kimberley, Escapade* and *Electra*. Although not all these movements actually took place, most were completed and the first was the detaching of *Faulknor* with Captain De Salis who, as Senior Destroyer Officer, was to assume command of all the Narvik area destroyers.

At 2000 on Saturday 13 April, in 68° 06′ N, 11° 48′ E, *Faulknor* and *Zulu* proceeded to Skjelfjord, Norway, arriving at 0614/14th and oiling from the tanker *British Lady*. Fuelling complete, they anchored in Skjelfjord with light cruiser *Penelope* and destroyers *Esk, Express* and *Hostile* and *Punjabi*. At 1945, *Faulknor* sailed to conduct an anti-submarine patrol, which lasted until 0720. At 0835, *Faulknor* proceeded to reconnoitre Narvik harbour, being joined by *Zulu* at 1130.

In London it was finally understood that a full-scale German invasion of Norway was underway and troops embarked in the liners *Batory, Reina del Pacifico* and *Monarch of Bermuda*, as troop convoy NP1, and sailed for Harstad where a British base was to be set up for the land advance to retake Narvik.

Meanwhile, Captain De Salis had assumed command as Senior Officer, Narvik Patrol, and *Faulknor* and *Zulu* were sent to search along the approaches to Narvik and report on the state of the German defences. Captain De Salis listed the following as the main duties of the Destroyer patrols in the confined inland-waters around Narvik.

> (a) Submarine defence and hunting.
> (b) Obtaining visual information of the state of Narvik defences.
> (c) Obtaining local information of the same by landings.
> (d) Bombardment of military objectives.

He went on to list the problems involved, stating that although destroyers were suitable for all these duties there were limitations, these being, '… a marked disadvantage against submarines, particularly at night. The latter can lie up close against the land, on the surface, and be absolutely indistinguishable from it at 500 yards. Submarines cannot be detected by A/S in that position. They can back down a narrow fjord so as to command any ship passing in the main channel and be unapproachable by a destroyer who cannot drop a depth charge, even if she could reach the submarine after the latter had fired.'

He continued:

> For these reasons, destroyers should always work in pairs. This would deter the submarine from attacking one of them since there is a certainty of reprisal. To work a single destroyer in these narrow waters, out of V/S touch with a second, would be to court losses sooner or later. A single destroyer hit at night can offer no reprisal, missed she remains without knowledge of her risk.

> Navigational difficulties, while not insuperable in fine weather and light nights, would become continuous in real darkness or fog. Anchorage's are very rare, there is a stream (which will increase when the snows melt), and there are many outlying rocks, some, but not all of which are marked with spars, and none lit. Submarines can reach positions in the archipelago which are quite unapproachable to destroyers.

Wise words, but politics demanded they got on with the job with the resources they were given. At 1230 on Monday 15 April, *Faulknor* entered Fuglefjord alone to investigate a reported enemy submarine. She lowered a dinghy for a close inshore search but found nothing, although, at 1610, they observed a German flying boat taking off. Therefore Captain De Salis took *Faulknor* into Narvik harbour and reconnoitred. One of the wrecked German merchant ships appeared to still be in good condition, so *Faulknor* pumped a few rounds of 4.7-inch shell into her at 1635 and fifteen minutes later they switched target to a gun emplacement. Satisfied they had demolished both targets Captain De Salis took *Faulknor* into Rombaksfjord to see what the state of play was here. Five German torpedoes were seen lying on the beach there, presumably salvaged from one of the stricken German destroyers, which littered the scene, and *Faulknor* landed her Torpedo Officer with a party to investigate them. When they returned they brought with them a Norwegian interpreter. All was quiet and so, at 2200, the two destroyers established an endless chain patrol off the Baroy Light.

While awaiting developments ashore, *Faulknor* operated in Ofotfjord, Rombaksfjord and Herjangsfjord over the next few days on anti-submarine patrols and carried out several bombardments of shore positions. At 0820/16th, *Zulu* was detached to Narvik and at 0950 *Faulknor* proceeded to Ofotsfjord to examine the wreck of HMS *Hardy*. They joined *Zulu* at 1125 and a party was sent on board *Hardy* to make sure no vital documentation remained and to see if she was in a salvageable condition, which did not prove to be the case. At noon Captain De Salis ordered *Zulu* to proceed to Ballangen and obtain information about *Hardy's* wounded, who were being cared for ashore there. While thus respectively employed the two destroyers observed a Junkers Ju.88 at 2,000 feet, which circled *Zulu* and was engaged by her main armament at 8,000 yards range. She did not like this treatment, dived, hid behind a hill and, when next seen, was heading off to the north. This aircraft whistled up his companions and the two destroyers were soon subjected to more unwelcome attentions from the Luftwaffe.

At 1445 a single Junkers Ju.88 carried out a bombing attack on *Zulu* from 12,000 feet, a solitary bomb missing the ship by 150 yards, and for the next hour-and-a-half they were subjected to repeated attacks, being bombed at intervals by eight German aircraft. Although 30 bombs were dropped no hits were obtained on the British destroyers, but splinters caused one dead and one wounded in *Zulu*. The attacks followed each other in quick succession and from all directions. Here the first bitter limitations of the British destroyers pre-war main armament designs were revealed. Owing to the height of the aircraft and the high angle of sight at which sightings took place, it was impossible to engage them with the 40-degree elevation 4.7 inch guns. *Zulu* used her 2-pdr pom-pom against some attacks, for, although it could not reach the height the Junkers were operating at, it was hoped the shell bursts would keep them high and lessen their accuracy. *Faulknor* did not even have this option; her multiple 0.5-inch machine-guns being almost useless on this, and many subsequent occasions.

Captain De Salis was to record that the destroyers were:

> … easily recognisable from the air as warships and a fair proportion of them have no long-range AA armament.

At 1800, the attacks having tailed off, the two destroyers proceeded back to Narvik and carried out a close reconnaissance of the port with the aid of the Norwegian they had embarked, who pointed out significant locations. After two hours of note-taking they proceeded down Herjangfjord and a landing party from *Faulknor* was sent aboard the wreck of the German destroyer *Hermann Kunne* at 69° 31.5′ N, 17° 26′ E.

It was decided to make quite certain the German destroyer was fully inoperational, and also to look for any codes or secret papers that might have been left aboard her. Accordingly, a party was sent out in *Faulknor's* whaler. But German soldiers ashore were still active and this proved a dangerous undertaking. The party came under accurate sniper fire and it was here that they lost another of their crew, AB Thomas Robert Broadbent (P/SSX 26783) from Ashton-under-Lyme, Lancashire. He was hit by a single bullet and slightly wounded, but cheerfully alive. Haste was made to get him back aboard *Faulknor* where his wound could be attended to urgently, but, later, as the whaler rowed back across the fjord to the ship, the marksman ashore opened fire again, and, by a cruel chance or fate, his shot struck home on poor Broadbent once more, killing him this time.

Vernon Coles described the incident:

> Soon after we entered Narvik waters we went roving round the inner fjords, we left Narvik itself to starboard and came across a German destroyer which had been damaged and run aground. Captain De Salis decided to send our whaler in to examine her as the German crew were seen ashore and watching our movements from behind trees and so on. The Germans, it appeared, were removing ammunition and stacking it on the Quarterdeck.
>
> I happened to have been on the ammunition supply to our No. 5 gun on the quarter deck at this time. I wasn't a member of the gun's crew, but being a member of the engine room department my Action Station was 'After damage repair party and ammunition supply to No. 5 gun.' This meant that we carried shells and cordite to the gun when she was in action and if the ship got damaged aft, we broke off, effected the repairs and when this was complete, returned to ammunition humping. We mustered in the Officers' Galley and cabin flat. Thank goodness we were never damaged aft so I had a front-line view of the action.
>
> We were closed up at Action Stations when the whaler was sent in to investigate and the captain of No. 5 gun was a three-badge 'Killick' who happened also to have been *Faulknor's* postman. When the Germans started dodging about between the trees we all tried to persuade 'Postie' to open fire on them, which he finally did, the 4.7-inch shell landing right amongst them, doing untold harm.
>
> However, our First Lieutenant phoned down from the bridge for the person who fired the gun to be put in his report for doing so without orders. Within seconds, however, Captain De Salis phoned down, praising 'Postie' for his initiative, so the previous charge was dropped!
>
> The coxswain of the whaler was Leading Seaman Joe Siggins. On going ashore a sniper started firing at the boat's crew and wounded one of them. On the return trip to *Faulknor* Joe ordered the wounded seaman to lie down in the boat but the poor fellow sat up to look around and got a bullet right through the head.
>
> We buried him at sea after *Faulknor* had withdrawn down the fjord. We returned at dusk and opened fire on the enemy ship and, in so doing, hit the stack of ammunition and also a magazine which exploded nicely.

Rodney Budd recalls Thomas Broadbent thus:

> He was a friend of mine and we used to have runs ashore together in Glasgow. He was in the boat's crew, which went to board the German destroyer. He was hit in the leg first and told to remain in the boat while the others went aboard the destroyer. When the

boarding party returned to the boat he sat up to help row then he was hit again and killed outright. We buried him at sea off Narvik.

At 2150, *Faulknor* proceeded down Ofotfjord and then set course back to Herjangfjord where she bombarded both the pier and *Kunne*. *Faulknor* commenced firing on the pier at 0010/17th and setting fire to both ammunition and stores lying there. Then they switched target to the destroyer and by the time they had ceased firing she was well ablaze. *Zulu* opened fire after *Faulknor* had finished to make certain of the job.

Rodney 'Rosie' Budd describes the events thus:

> When we first saw the ship it didn't look to be a wreck, but it must have been put out of action. It was nearly dark when we arrived at Narvik, and each gun was allocated four rounds and each gun had to fire individually, first 'A' gun, then 'B' gun and so forth. I was captain of 'X' gun and the firing caused quite a bit of structural damage. I can't say how close we were to the destroyer but it was quite close. 'Cease Fire' was called before we had fired a round.

Having made his detailed reconnaissance and gained vital information from Norwegians, Captain De Salis was able, in a signal timed at 2343/16th, to transmit to Their Lordships, a further detailed list of the German defences at Narvik on which to base their estimates for its occupation.

> Plan Chart 37 53 516 Framnes Point, Norwegian railway guns, also one pillbox partly demolished by HMS *Zulu*. Ground mines on shore abreast of Littlevik, Kvitevik and Kviteberget. Five small AA guns on hill, only one said to work, about 300 yards inshore. Above guns said to be from German destroyers, base of pier by Vogterboig, of limited training arc. Ammunition dump in air raid shelter under unfinished house immediately in rear of this, with machine gun in Fjellheim restaurant, about 1.5 cables west of Oscarsborg and 4000 feet up hill. Ammo dump in Hotel Royal. At Fagernes, certainly one machine gun in old Norwegian blockhouse and believed to be one British merchant ship's gun. Merchant ships have certainly lost guns. No civilian allowed near foreshore or near Fagernes. One machine gun at car-ferry pier at Vasvika. Germans also hold car pier at Oydeyord opposite end of Rombokifjord. Germans have guns or machine guns at Cape 1.5 miles east of Taralsvik and some moveable machine guns on railway line up Rombokifjord and patrols of Austrian ski troops on mountains between that and Beisfjord. There are also various machine guns on slope above town. Since my reconnaissance yesterday when HMS *Faulknor* entered harbour, Norwegians have seen aircraft dropping parachute mines across entrance. Norwegians are being conscripted, presumably for labour. Detailed position of some guns can be signalled if required.

Early on 17 April *Faulknor* and *Zulu* bombarded a destroyer and the pier in Herjangfjord, setting fire to both targets. Later in the day a gun emplacement at Narvik was bombarded and ammunition set on fire. This done the two destroyers set up another continuous patrol off the Baroy light all night and, at 1000, they conducted a burial service for AB Broadbent (088°, Baroy Light 1.7′) This sad duty done they received yet another submarine sighting report and, at 1045, *Faulknor* proceeded at 25 knots to Fuglefjord to investigate, once more lowering the ship's whaler to help inshore. Again nothing was found and, at 1215, they left Fuglefjord for Hundholm and again lowered the whaler for a diligent search which was also unrewarded. They left Hundholm at 1330 and, at 1515 the Norwegian patrol boat *Nordland* came alongside to give Captain De Salis more local information.

As a result of what they told him Captain De Salis took *Faulknor* back to Narvik harbour and, at 1650, opened fire on the gun emplacement there, again setting ammunition on fire. After ten minutes they proceeded down Herjangfjord once more to investigate the wreck of the German destroyer but all seemed undisturbed from their last check. At 1725 a third all-night patrol off Baroy Light with *Zulu* was commenced.

Early 18th, *Zulu* was detached to Skjelfjord and her place taken by *Encounter*, which joined at 0655. At midday *Faulknor* arrived at Ballanger and landed two officers to visit again the hospital and check on the condition of *Hardy's* wounded. On their return at 1400 the whaler was hoisted and they sailed to Narvik. At 1637 that day Captain De Salis signalled:

> Am continuing Ofotfjord patrol with *Encounter*. Exploded a small dump apparently ammunition. 12-pdr gun on Faornes Point 17/4.

Three-quarters of an hour later *Encounter* reported seeing enemy paratroops being dropped at the top of Herjangfjord and *Faulknor* left Narvik and steered westward. They returned at 1700, re-entered Ballanger and dropped extra medical supplies for the hospital. At 1745 they patrolled off Bogenfjord and then, with *Encounter,* the usual all-night beat off Baroy Light was undertaken.

At 1145 three enemy bombers were overhead but no attacks were made. There was another alert at 1250 when four ships were sighted in Tjeldsundetfjord, *Faulknor* went to action stations but they turned out to be the four trawlers of the rather grandly named 12th Anti-Submarine Striking Force of whose presence they had not been advised. Early in the afternoon they joined light cruiser *Aurora* and *Encounter* and at 1700 *Escapade* relieved the latter and destroyer *Jupiter* joined. At 1945, *Faulknor* circled *Aurora* and transferred mail in her boat to *Jupiter*. A continuous patrol was mounted to cover the seaward approaches to Narvik and to prevent any seaborn reinforcements reaching the German garrison. *Faulknor, Escapade* and *Jupiter,* spent most of that day on these duties, screening light cruisers *Aurora* and *Effingham*. Frequent snowstorms added to their navigational difficulties in these restricted and congested water, while in between times, the Luftwaffe was growing increasingly more menacing. They remained closed-up at actions stations until 0200 while patrolling off the Tranoy Light and, at 2315, met and challenged *Effingham*. At 0640 on Sunday 20th *Jupiter* was relieved by destroyer *Grenade* and the two cruisers and three destroyers continued to patrol until 0750 when *Effingham* was detached.

Grenade relieved *Jupiter* in the morning and soon after this, *Enterprise* took *Effingham's* place, as the latter was in urgent need of refuelling. At 0800, there was an air raid alarm, which turned out to be a lone Norwegian machine, a rare sight.

Meanwhile discussions at high level were deciding the fate of the expedition. General Mackesy met Admiral Lord Cork as the liners *Batory*, *Monarch of Bermuda* and *Reina del Pacifico* arrived at Bygden, twelve miles from Vaagsfjord. The troops and their equipment then had to be laboriously transferred to Harstad, another task for the destroyers. All this took an inordinate amount of time and the assault date was continually postponed.

At their first meeting Lord Cork and General Mackesy studied Captain De Salis's detailed reconnaissance report. The main thrust of it was that he considered a landing from Rombaksfjord, north of Narvik, would not be opposed by any fixed enemy defences and could be covered by gunfire from the supporting warships. Lord Cork therefore pressed for an immediate landing to take advantage of this situation and before the Germans could consolidate. General Mackesy had to tell him his orders specifically forebade him to make any such landings, '… in the face of opposition.' He had been told that: – 'You may have a chance of taking advantage of naval action and you should do so if you can. Boldness is required.' However, the General had no landing craft, no tanks, and no artillery and considered the terrain favoured the enemy. The German General Dietl had two thousand men trained for just such conditions and their morale was rising with each day's delay. Unwilling, as he saw it, for, '.. the snow of Narvik being turned into another version of the mud of Passchendaele', General Mackesy proposed limited action at Rombaksfjord and the Ankenes peninsula, and then to await the thaw. Lord Cork had no choice but to accept his decision. After further discussion it was provisionally agreed that a bombardment be carried out by *Warspite* and supporting ships, with troops embarked ready to be landed if the results of the attack seemed to justify it.

It was decided that the General himself with Lord Cork should embark in *Aurora* and make a close inspection of the area and, accordingly, Captain De Salis transferred from *Faulknor* to the cruiser to act as their guide and both ships proceeded up towards Narvik. At 1030, while on the way up they were attacked by a single German bomber, which dropped six small bombs, none of which hit. The attack was repeated at 1215, again by just a solitary aircraft, this time four heavy bombs were dropped, which shook the ships up but which, again, were all misses. *Faulknor* was unable to reply, but *Aurora's* 4-inch anti-aircraft battery barked hopefully away as the plane droned away out of range at high altitude.

'The bombers came in over the mountains', recalls Rodney Budd, 'and were over you more or less as soon as you saw them. The Quartermaster got the order 'Full Ahead', 'Port or Starboard 20° to dodge the bombs. I don't know how near we were to copping it, but we had a few close calls.'

Between 1230 and 1430 *Faulknor* carried out anti-submarine sweeps around *Aurora* while the various officers aboard her studied the area. *Faulknor's* ships doctor, David Rendall, recalled that *Aurora* used one of her 4-inch HA guns to 'remove' the Nazi flag that was flying from atop a neighbouring mountain, '… but I understand it was back up again the next day!' Once their army passengers were satisfied, the British naval force then withdrew down the fjord and, at 1520, Captain De Salis re-embarked. The result of this further reconnaissance was not as Lord Cork had hoped because General Mackesy told the Chief of the Imperial General Staff, Lord Ironside, that:

> Owing to the nature of the ground, flat trajectory of naval guns, and the impossibility of locating the concealed machine guns, I am convinced that the naval bombardment cannot be militarily effective, and that a landing from open boats in the above conditions must be ruled out absolutely. Any attempt of the sort would involve not the neutralisation but the destruction of the 24th (Guards) Brigade.

Only if the planned bombardment induced the enemy to surrender would he agree to his troops going ashore. The long-awaited thaw eventually set in and Lord Cork was again thinking of direct action, but a plan put forward by the French General Bethouart, commander of the Chasseurs-Alpins, was rejected by the British General. Meantime *Faulknor* returned to Skjelfjord, oiled from *Aldersdale* while *Bedouin* took her place on watch, going out again with *Aurora* and Polish destroyer *Grom* just before midnight to anchor early next day off Bögen once more. Here they remained while other warships covered the troop movements across the fjord. During the afternoon there was an air raid warning, but no attack came, and soon after this destroyers *Codrington* and *Ardent* left for Skjelford, *Faulknor* sailing early on the 20th to Ballanger where she embarked a company of the South Wales Borderers who were to make a landing farther along the southern coast towards Ankenes.

At 0515 they weighed and proceeded along Ofotfjord, pausing *en route* to take in tow the 'puffer' – a small local fishing craft – the *Solbin*, with more troops aboard. Off Skjelfjord they transferred the soldiers to a Norwegian fishing vessel to be landed before herself rejoining *Bedouin* off Narvik. The British troops thus conveyed made a toehold landing west of Haavik, four miles from Ankenes, from where they slowly advanced.

While preparations were in hand for the naval attack *Faulknor* continued her routine protection patrols around *Aurora*, being joined by *Enterprise* and destroyers *Encounter* and *Grenade* for the routine all-night patrol off the Tranoy Light.

At 0230 on Sunday 21st *Faulknor* was detached from this force and proceeded along to Skjelfjord, passing the net gate at 0715. At 0740/21st, *Faulknor* secured on the repair ship *Vindictive* which was anchored there acting as a floating mother hen to the warships operating from there, and refuelled.

At 1500, they steered to again meet *Aurora* off Narvik, whereupon that ship took over the duties of Senior Officer, Narvik Patrol from Captain De Salis. Further patrolling followed and then they once more returned to refuel.

On 23rd, *Faulknor* returned to the Narvik area again, and spent the rest of that day patrolling up and down their appointed sector, the scudding snow making watch on the bleak coastline very difficult. In the evening three dim shapes joined them from the north; destroyer *Escort* with Polish *Blyskawica* and *Grom*. Just before midnight, *Faulknor* took the Polish vessels under her command, returning once more to Skjelsfjord to refuel from oiler *Aldersdale*. For the moment the snow had ceased and the Aurora Borealis gave them its usual breath-taking display to divert their minds temporarily from the war.

The next day was spent in comparative peace and quiet, awaiting their turn to refuel from a fleet oiler, which had just arrived. *Faulknor* went alongside last of all. Following a request from Admiral Forbes the Flag Officer, Narvik, sent a signal timed at 1209/24th concerning his requirements for destroyers.

> Your 1151 22 April, am retaining HMS *Faulknor*, HMS *Codrington*, HMS *Electra*, HMS *Escapade*, HMS *Ardent*, HMS *Acasta*, HMS *Zulu*, HMS *Bedouin* and one Polish Destroyer. Remainder will be sailed for Scapa p.m. Wednesday 24 April.

Oiling completed, *Faulknor* was left to her own devices until just after midnight when they cast off from *Blyskawica,* returning to their familiar patrol area off the fjord where they again joined *Bedouin*, *Escort* and *Grom*. Towards midday, in company with *Escort,* they swept down Rombaksfjord to keep the German troops ashore under surveillance, the other destroyers doing the same off Narvik harbour itself.

In preparation for the bombardment, *Faulknor* and these three destroyers were ordered to carry out intensive anti-submarine searches throughout all the side fjords to ensure no new U-boats had slipped in under cover of the continuous snowstorms and lay lurking there. *Faulknor* thus nosed into various inlets like a fox around a rabbit warren, but no submarines were found. Soon after 2200, they stopped a small steamer, which was crawling cautiously seaward, examining her in the glare of their searchlight, but she proved to be merely the Norwegian *Nova*, carrying German prisoners from Ballanger to Harstad. *Faulknor* refuelled and left again at 2240 to return to Narvik.

On 24 April they met the bombarding force, battleship *Warspite,* light cruisers *Aurora*, *Enterprise* and *Effingham* escorted by destroyers *Encounter*, *Escort*, *Foxhound*, *Havock*, *Hero*, *Hostile* and *Zulu*. Nearby was the old *Vindictive* with the Irish Guards embarked, ready to be put ashore if required; alas, they were not to be called upon that day. At 0370, the guns of the assembled warships crashed out against enemy positions. *Faulknor* did not join in this cannonade for, with most of the other destroyers, she was detailed to maintain a tight anti-submarine patrol to protect the heavy ships, and so, while the huge shells smashed up and down the coast, whenever frequent snow storms lifted, they plodded around to seaward, their Asdic pinging away unavailing. In spite of the weight of shell flung ashore, little useful destruction of the enemy positions was achieved, as it proved very difficult to locate precise targets on the bleak snow-clad hills above Narvik town. Soon after 1300 the dispirited bombardment force withdrew to Harstad, leaving *Faulknor* and *Encounter* to continue their lonely vigil off the port

As the afternoon wore on the trawler *Northern Spray*, which arrived suddenly out of a snowstorm, joined them. From time to time, Captain De Salis took *Faulknor* closer to the Narvik foreshore but it was impossible to find any worthwhile targets. As evening drew on it grew very cold and they patrolled the north shore of Ofotfjord at slow speed, pushing up into Rombaksfjord on another reconnaissance before it became too murky, and then returned to their beat off Narvik itself.

The following day repeated the pattern of the last. At 0730 *Enterprise* and *Blyskawica* joined them and *Faulknor* and the Polish ship destroyed a railway bridge with a few salvoes from their main armaments. The Germans showed a marked reluctance to reveal themselves; understandably so, for any movement of theirs was quickly followed with a 4.7-inch shell from the patrolling destroyers.

The target the destroyers did manage to destroy on the 25th was a railway engine on the line to the north of Narvik itself. Charles Graves gave an account of this little operation. He was forced by facile Ministry of Information censorship to disguise the identities of the two destroyers, even though the book did not appear in print until more than a year after the events described. Thus, destroyer *Bedouin* he gives the name 'Street Arab', and *Faulknor*, under an even more convoluted strain of thought, was given the *nom-de-plume* of 'Rosey Fingers' [presumably a play on Falconer for *Faulknor*, and the Red Gauntlet worn on the birds perching hand of the former!]

Graves typically describes this incident as, 'One of the strangest encounters of the whole war'. The captain of *Bedouin,* Commander J. A. McCoy, was described as becoming, '... incensed with a German armoured train which would appear from behind a railway cutting, shoot off impertinent rounds at almost point-blank range, and then disappear into the heart of the mountain side. This went on for three weeks'. The account continues in the same vein, with Captain De Salis and Commander McCoy going, '... into a huddle'. It was quite clear to the second captain that his colleague had the armoured train on his brain. After all, he had been bushwhacking it for nearly a month.

'The decision was reached that, on the next occasion the armoured train, '... stuck its head out', *Bedouin* would fire with her main armament at the entrance to one end of a quarter-mile long rail tunnel, while *Faulknor* would do the same to the entrance of the other cutting. In this way the pom-poms and lesser armament of the two destroyers would be able to take the armoured train to pieces where it stood exposed between its two bolt-holes.'[2] This plan was crystallised in a signal, reportedly sent by Captain De Salis to Commander McCoy at the time, which read:

> Orders for Operation 'Let's Play Trains'. The 11.30 from Narvik is almost due. *Bedouin* will take station to southward and hasten train into tunnel with H.E. After second salvo *Faulknor* is to commence greeting train in a similar manner at northern end of tunnel.[3]

When the plan was put into action, according to Graves hyperbole, '... unfortunately, in their enthusiasm next day, the main armaments of both destroyers were fired at the same cutting when the armoured train reappeared shortly afterwards, and it promptly bolted back into safety.'

Vernon Coles remembers it very differently:

> I remember the railway gun very well. We were doing one of our routine patrols and were in the middle of the junction of Ofotfjord, Rombakfjord and Herjangsfjord when a huge spume of water went up about a hundred yards astern. No one knew where it came from. It was thought at the time that perhaps a howitzer was firing over the hilltops. After about the third water spout one of our lookouts on the bridge sighted this gun backing out of the tunnel, letting a couple of rounds go and dashing back in again. We never saw the engine because the gun only came to the tunnel entrance. Both *Faulknor* and *Bedouin* fired on the entrance, but did no damage at all.
>
> The railway line ran out of Narvik around Rombaks and into the tunnel carved through the mountain. The tunnel I would suggest would be some quarter to half a mile in length so there would be no point in the gun train dashing in one end and exposing itself by coming out the other. Had the engine come out we would certainly have destroyed it.
>
> However, it is true that *Faulknor* did indeed bowl a railway engine over, but this was a stationary one, although under steam and she was heading for what appeared to be an iron ore train in the marshalling yard. We also knocked a few trucks over at the same time.

Rodney Budd remembered:

> There was a railway just above Narvik and a tunnel, but I'm sorry that I cannot remember shelling trains as they came out of it. I was under the impression that the Germans had a

gun mounted on the rail and every so often they came out and fired a couple of rounds and then withdrew. That may also be a yarn, as I did not see it. We were at 'Defence Stations' most of the time we were up the fjord. I was Chief Quartermaster so my defence station was on the wheel.

Charles Graves account continued:

> Another conference was clearly necessary between the two captains, and they decided that they would lull the armoured train into a sense of false security.

He then describes how for the next three days *Bedouin,* '… metaphorically cruised around with her hands in her pockets and looking at nothing, and allowed the armoured train to have several ineffective pops at her..,' as if HM destroyers had nothing better to do at Narvik at this time! He wrote:

> On the fourth day the armoured train grew bolder and came right out into the open.

Promptly both *Bedouin* and *Faulknor*, '… loosed off everything they had at the two cuttings. The armoured train was trapped in the open and was taken apart according to plan.'

Reverting to the known facts, Doctor David Rendall and Nobby Clarke both recalled that a battleship [probably *Warspite]* was called in to finish off the train, because, as Nobby put it very succinctly, '… they had bigger pea-shooters than us!' Robby Robinson recalls:

> I can vouch that *Faulknor* had one or two rounds at the Narvik end of the tunnel, *Bedouin* was in company, but she was out of sight at the other end. It was all finally sorted out the next day as *Warspite* took over, and no more was then heard from that particular gun again!

Early in the same afternoon there was another distraction when observers aboard *Faulknor* spotted a Junkers Ju.52 transport plane dropping troops and ammunition at the head of Herjangsfjord, close to Bjervik. This small town was soon to be assaulted by French troops in their drive on Narvik, and the Germans were building up their strength there. *Faulknor* steamed up the fjord to investigate the landing spot, but could find nothing hostile, so, after sniffing aggressively about for a short time, they steamed back along the southern shore. In the evening they closed Narvik harbour before pushing up Rombaksfjord, rounding off the day by further shelling north of the port. They remained off Narvik until 0800 the following morning, when they joined *Aurora* off Bjervik to transfer charts.

On 26 April, operations by British forces at Ballanger finally began, but heavy snow and deep drifts soon held up progress on all the fronts. Captain De Salis signalled at 0927:

> HMS *Bedouin* sails 1500 today Saturday so as to arrive Harstad by 0900 tomorrow Sunday. You will transport Brigade Headquarters to Bogen. HMS *Southampton* in Lavang Fjord has pilot for Tjeld Sundet. On completion HMS *Bedouin* is to relieve HMS *Zulu*.

At 1940 on the 27 April, the *Penelope* signalled:

> *Faulknor* leaves Skelfjord in accordance with *Aurora's* order.

On 27th and 28th *Faulknor* was off Bogen and next day covered the further movement of 2nd Battalion South Wales Borderers. Destroyers *Ardent* and *Fortune* had each embarked 400 troops from

Flandre and they started to land these at Skaanland at 0300 that morning. However, they had to laboriously re-embark them due to a change of plan and took them to Bogen arriving at 0935. They anchored off Bergvik and began once more to land the soldiers, this time at Bergvik pier in their ships' boats. At 1000, they shifted berths to a position opposite Lenvik and continued the landing at Lenvik Pier, but this latter proved to be in very bad condition. As *Fame's* captain recorded, '… it was a slow business, in spite of assistance from *Faulknor's* boats.'

Next day *Fame* embarked a German torpedo, which had been towed from Ofotsfjord by trawler *Loch Shin* and this torpedo was afterwards transferred aboard *Faulknor* for passage back to the U.K. for detailed examination by the boffins at home. Vernon Coles remembered:

> Our Gunner (T) and his staff emptied the explosive head to make it safe to transport and we then brought it back to the UK to be studied properly.

Faulknor herself returned to Bogen on 30th. On 1 May, *Faulknor* was at Bjervik where she remained next day and then was back in the Narvik area between 3rd and 6th.

All night the two destroyers remained on patrol off Rombaksfjord, *Faulknor* extinguishing a suspicious light off Narvik Point with one round of 4.7-inch shell, and early next morning they headed into the neighbourhood of Herjangsfjord, bombarding enemy positions, which were holding up the French advance. They then closed *Aurora* and embarked her two army liaison officers whom they put ashore in the whaler at Emmenes Point. While transferring signalmen to the cruiser off Narvik that same afternoon they came under fire from the German artillery, up to then mute, two shells exploding only 150 yards from the two ships. They went to Action Stations and replied in kind with three quick rounds of 4.7-inch from 'B' gun, then hauled out of range, stopping off Baatberget where they lowered the whaler once more, took off the two soldiers from ashore and conveyed them back to Bjervik again.

Next morning they were employed in towing small craft across to Skjamenfjord where the army HQ was building up its supplies before continuing its slow progress along the coast. In the afternoon, they embarked stores from fleet auxiliary *Balteaks* at Bjervik, working hard until evening when they once again embarked the two army officers and sailed with them to Beisfjord where they went aboard the waiting *Aurora*. The Germans had begun to attack our troops moving towards Ankenes but were soon stopped by gunfire from the warships, including salvoes from *Faulknor's* main armament. By 0920 firing ceased for lack of suitable targets, and they were again despatched to return the two army officers to Bjervik, on conclusion of which they had a few hours relaxation before returning to Baatberget at first light to continue their close support of the army, relieving *Zulu*. During the afternoon they fired when required at enemy concentrations ashore, regrettably demolishing several delightful little Norwegian houses in the process. About 2200, some enemy activity was observed in Narvik harbour, so they closed and pumped twelve rounds of 4.7-inch HE into some small boats there, sinking three of them. They then returned to Baatberget where the night was spent offshore, repeatedly firing into the thick woods where the Germans were concentrated.

By midday on 3 May, the German counter-attacks had been halted and the Allied troops prepared to move on again to recover the lost ground. The Polish destroyer *Grom* joined *Faulknor* in shelling the woods at close range, but, by evening, again little progress had been made ashore. The Luftwaffe then intervened and made a concentrated effort to drive the two destroyers away by continued bombing attacks from high level, but the destroyers initially managed to avoid damage by violent manoeuvring into Ofotfjord where they had more leeway, returning, undaunted, to continue their close support role after the attacks. The German bombers returned in force, and this time the ships' luck finally ran out.

At 0830/4th one of the Polish destroyers working off Narvik with them, ORP *Grom*, was hit during a high-level air attack by a Heinkel He.111.

Norway. HMS Faulknor *with her boats lowered, picking up survivors from the Polish destroyer* Grom, *bombed and sunk off Narvik, April 1940. Note the early dazzle camouflage scheme, but she still retains the high pre-war mainmast at this period and is light in the water.* (Crown Copyright.)

Rodney Budd again:

> I remember when the Polish destroyer *Grom* got sunk. She was hit by a bomb amidships and sank almost at once, some say the bomb went down the funnel and exploded in the boiler-room. I don't think there were many survivors, as you couldn't last long in those waters. I think that we picked up a few, but I can't remember seeing their transfer to another ship.

A Polish eyewitness told how:

> On the surface our men were struggling in the water. From the shore the Germans were firing at us with machine-guns, while away in the distance, from the end of Rombaksfjord, appeared the tiny outlines of British ships hastening to our rescue.

These were *Faulknor, Bedouin* and *Aurora,* and *Faulknor* soon had her whaler in the water busy about its mercy work. The Polish account continued:

> … the groans of the wounded could also be heard, though both of us, wounded and unhurt, all believed in the brotherhood-in-arms which united us with the British Navy. And the

53

whole world knows that no British ship has ever left sinking comrades on the sea of battle.

It wasn't an easy matter. The engines had to stop in order that the boats could be launched. The whole work of rescue takes a long time, and the rescuing ship gives up its most important anti-air-raid defence; rapidity of manoeuvre. From the sunlit skies bombs might have hit them as they had hit us.

Faulknor, ignoring the remaining bombers overhead, raced up and managed to haul fifty-two survivors aboard, but sixty more died. *Faulknor* then proceeded to Skjamenfjord where the rescued sailors were transferred to battleship *Resolution*, then she again returned to continue to give the army close-fire support.

In *Faulknor's* log the Officer of the Watch made a brief pencilled entry. 'Poor old *Grom.*'

On patrol in Ofotfjord with destroyer *Bedouin, Faulknor* was the target for several heavy attacks the following day, 5 May, the first being especially vicious: four heavy bombs exploded around her, one close alongside. During the forenoon five more attacks took place and German reconnaissance aircraft were continually circling round out of range, freely watching and reporting on every Allied movement afloat or ashore, and completely unmolested by the RAF which, (so the BBC continually assured everyone), was giving 'magnificent protection!'

Later that afternoon *Faulknor* re-entered Rombaksfjord with the intention of destroying German patrols spotted on the southern shore there. Isolated as she then became from her companions, she was singled out by the bombers, but Captain De Salis by skilful ship-handling and keeping his command continually on the move, avoided all these attacks. No ship could remain unscathed forever of course, and while later conducting yet a further shore bombardment of enemy positions at Rombakfjord, in 68° 27' N, 17° 38' E, there came a grinding, wrenching sound and *Faulknor* shuddered to a halt. It was lucky indeed that the Luftwaffe chose that moment to turn their attentions elsewhere and thus they could evaluate their damage undisturbed. It was found that the ship had fouled some obstruction close to Straumein Point – possibly the wreck of one of the German destroyers – and the Asdic dome, along with its directing gear, was severely knocked about and was, for all practical purposes, useless. The ship's hull was damaged and a proper evaluation of the extent of this was to be conducted by *Vindictive,* but for now, they carried on.

Captain De Salis signalled the news at 1714/5th:

> *Faulknor* has struck in Rombaksfjord in position 068° 27.1' N, 017° 38.7' E. No damage except A/S dome and directing gear out of action. Ship requires docking.

Off Narvik, they sighted a small, solitary boat, which they drew alongside and picked up its only occupant, a Norwegian of questionable loyalties. They deposited him with the military authorities at Bogen before continuing to patrol off the anchorage with *Bedouin* and *Blyskawica* during the late evening.

Several more air attacks took place against Bjervik itself and the warships moved in closer to the northern shore for cover; by midnight they were on patrol off Beisfjord, supporting the army' s left wing, *Faulknor* herself coming unscathed again through a rain of heavy bombs, six of them detonating just off her starboard bow and which showered her decks with shrapnel. Norway was the first time that the Royal Navy had been exposed to continuous air attack with absolutely no air protection at all and it proved an eye-opener.

Ashore, reinforcements had arrived for General Mackesy and his plan for a new offensive against Narvik was almost ready, but *Faulknor* was to play no further part in its execution.

At 1145/7th, Rear Admiral (D), Home Fleet signalled:

Propose *Faulknor* be taken in hand for refit and A/S repairs. *Faulknor* should be available about 11/5.

The C-in-C replied at 1521:

Concur.

Next day a further signal, timed 1027, confirmed:

Faulknor can be taken in hand for refit by Messrs Doig at Grimsby.

So their part in the Narvik operation came to an end. Indeed the operation had been so long delayed that events further south made it irrelevant long before it reached its culmination for, once taken after so much effort, Narvik immediately had to be abandoned again! For *Faulknor* sixteen days of almost continuous action with no opportunity to rest or relax ended when they were ordered home. It had been a frustrating period, coming to Narvik as part of the 'Third Wave' after all the battles and euphoria of the first two naval victories, left *Faulknor* with all the chores and none of the glory. But, with her Asdic and hull damaged, she could no longer play an effective role.

On the 6 May, the Commanding Officer of destroyer *Fame* was informed by *Aurora* that he was to take over from Captain (D) 8 as Senior Officer, Vestifjord Destroyers. As *Faulknor* was still off Narvik at that time, he commenced the fuelling of destroyers from the oiler *British Lord* forthwith. Captain De Salis arrived back from Narvik in *Faulknor* at 1500 and Lieutenant H. N. C. Willmott and his staff were transferred to *Fame* to act as Staff Officers. A homeward-bound convoy was assembling with *Faulknor* SO of the escort.

Rodney Budd recollects the later period at Narvik thus:

All seemed quiet except for the occasional air raid, when, one day, we were carrying out an anti-submarine patrol in one of the fjords when the Asdic dome struck a submerged wreck and was badly damaged. We were sent back to the UK and docked at Grimsby to repair it.

At 1342, Captain De Salis signalled FOIC Narvik:

HM Ships *Faulknor, Hesperus* and *Wren* are sailing United Kingdom p.m. today Monday 6 May.

This signal was later cancelled and a reorganisation of available destroyer strength was made as the last job Captain De Salis carried out at Narvik. The result was encapsulated in another signal, timed 1620:

… following destroyers are detailed as escort HMS *Faulknor*, HMS *Amazon,* HMS *Imogen*. HMS *Whirlwind* will accompany convoy as far as 40 miles west of Lofoten Island. Intend to retain HMS *Hesperus* as she has more boiler hours than HMS *Amazon* or HMS *Imogen*.

The C-in-C later commended the work of *Faulknor* and praised Captain De Salis's: '… courage and resource while in command of the destroyer force in Vestifjord from April 12th to May 8th under very arduous conditions. During the latter part of April, frequent gales and snow blizzards occurred but day and night patrols were maintained in the narrow waters around Narvik. Captain (D) 8 displayed courage and imagination in engaging shore targets.'

At 1930/7th, *Faulknor* sailed from Bjervik for the last time, forming the escort along with destroyers *Amazon*, *Imogen* and *Whirlwind*, for a homeward-bound convoy of empty troopships, *Monarch of Bermuda*, *Empress of Australia,* and *Ville D'Alger*. By 0500/8th they reached 66° 30′ N, 1° 00' W, and were then routed direct to Scapa.

Their voyage back across the North Sea was uneventful, and for two days, they kept station as the troopships slowly zigzagged their way westward. The main hazard they encountered was floating mines, broken adrift in the winter storms from our own defensive barrages. *Faulknor* was forced to make several emergency turns to avoid the wicked horns of these ugly black monsters slipping sluggishly by. On the second night of their passage, they ran into thick fog, which did not make mine-spotting any easier, although it effectively hid them from searching German aircraft. *Faulknor*, *Amazon* and *Imogen* finally arrived back in Scapa Flow at 1400/9th, with the three transports, securing to No 13 Buoy in the familiar haven of Gutter Sound at 1510.

The need for a proper refit was obvious for, as well as the grounding damage, the ship had been continuously at sea, often in wicked weather, and this, together with the many near-miss bomb explosions in the confined waters of the fjords around Narvik, had severely strained her hull and peppered her upper-works. Some of her main guns also needed renewing and all this indicated a dockyard job, which, to her weary crew, meant just one thing – leave. *Faulknor* sailed from Scapa at 0001/10 May, bound for the Royal Dock, Grimsby, steaming down the eastern coast of Scotland past familiar, friendly, landmarks, Rattray Head, Girdle Ness, Bell Rock. At 1645, they were steering up the estuary of the Humber after an uneventful passage. Next day, at 1000, she was moved into the Royal Dock at Grimsby. The company which carried out the work was J. S. Doig and Co. and *Faulknor* was their Job Number ER.6522 (ER= Emergency Repair). They prepared for the refit, and members of the crew, including Captain De Salis, went on leave, some never to see *Faulknor* again. It was a strange time to be on leave, a strange time for a warship to be lying motionless alongside a bleak east-coast wall.

On the very day that *Faulknor* reached Grimsby the German army had launched its great offensive on the Western Front, the French, Dutch and Belgian armies breaking as quickly as had the Polish and Norwegian's before them. People at home were stunned, the newspapers and BBC, told little of the real truth of the fighting, relating only aerial victories when there were none, and counter-attacks which never took place. The British army fought its way through the disintegration of all its Allies until it reached the sea, and here it found its only effective ally, the Royal Navy, waiting to come to its aid. Then came the wonderful epic of Dunkirk when a third of a million men were snatched from the very jaws of the German army and brought home safely to re-equip and fight another day.

Days sped by, with shock following shock, but aboard *Faulknor* the only excitement during this incredible debacle was the discovery of a 'lady' in the ERA's mess at 0400 one morning! It is doubtful whether she was a spy, although apparently she was very active! Subsequently the Royal Dock was guarded by police sentries stern in their resolve to prevent any further such infiltration!

On 12 May, Flag Officer, Humber, signalled:

Faulknor taken in hand for refit at Grimsby by J. S. Doig 11/5. Completes 8/6.

This was modified in a further signal dated 1731/8 June.

Faulknor ready for sea 13/6.

However, at 1740 on 12 June the Base Captain, Grimsby signalled:

Faulknor completed 12/6.

With Europe collapsing like a pack of cards, and with very heavy losses being inflicted on the British destroyer flotillas engaged in the series of evacuations all down the French coast to the Bay of Biscay, *Faulknor* and her sisters suddenly became doubly valuable and her refit was hastily terminated.

On 12th, *Faulknor* was manoeuvred out of the dock itself by tugs and moved through the locks into the outer harbour. Here she re-ammunitioned and fuelled before anchoring in the Humber and dropping-off the pilot.

At 1500/13th, *Faulknor* weighed anchor and proceeded down the estuary to the sea, leaving the Humber at 2000 bound for Rosyth to face the enemy once more. On their way out they were informed by the SS *Broughty*, that she had sighted a loose mine, so they hunted for it and blew it up with a satisfactory explosion. Again, this mine had probably broken adrift from our own East Coast mine barrage, which extended right up the coast from Harwich to Aberdeen. *Faulknor* then sailed northward, leaving Flamborough Head astern, and pushing on to retrace their earlier track.

They called in at Rosyth on Saturday, 14 June, leaving the same day. Off the Firth of Forth, they picked up oiler *War Pindari* from Methil, escorting her to Scapa. At 1132 they gained an Asdic contact of a 'possible' submarine, but quickly lost it again. Tempted by the sight of a slow target with just a solitary escort, the U-boat trailed them, trying to get herself into attack position. Twice more *Faulknor* obtained his echo and drove him away, the third time holding him for an hour and dropping a pattern of depth-charges, before he gave up.

They entered the Hoxa Gate 0846/15th and secured alongside oiler *Aldersdale.* Later that morning a launch from depot ship *Woolwich* came alongside with a welcome present – a Hotchkiss gun and spare ammunition. Anti-aircraft weapons were in short supply and they accepted the gift gladly enough. They had already been fitted with a 3-inch HA gun in place of their after set of quadruple torpedo tubes, so that if the depot ship supplied them with another, albeit small, addition, they assumed they were heading for an area where they would need it. In fact, *Faulknor* arrived back at the Home Fleet base to find that she was to lead the 8th DF in a new squadron to be formed to work out of Gibraltar under Admiral Sir James Somerville, Force 'H'.

Italy had declared war on the Allies five days earlier, Mussolini being eager to grab his share of the loot in what he thought were the final days of the conflict. With German armies and air forces massing across the Channel, little could be spared. Any warships, tanks, aircraft and men that could be found – pitifully few – were scraped together and sent to the Mediterranean. A squadron commanded by Vice-Admiral Sir James Somerville was formed and despatched to Gibraltar, including the battle-cruiser *Hood* and the 8th Flotilla. Code-named 'Force H' it was soon to become world-famous.

Faulknor carried out a sub-calibre shoot of her main armament at targets in the Flow on 17 June with *Escapade* and *Fearless,* and, at 1545, escorted *Ark Royal* from Scapa at twenty knots, to the Clyde, being joined by *Foxhound* at 2115. The squadron passed Cape Wrath and by 0530 next morning was well south. The Faulknor met *Hood,* at 2000, 250 miles west of Malin Head and, after her six escorting destroyers returned, set course for Gibraltar.

That evening the ships of the squadron ran into thick fog that shrouded them until midnight. They slipped unseen in a wide sweep through the empty wastes and steamed south across the Bay of Biscay. On the following day *Ark's* aircraft made dummy dive-bombing runs to exercise the ships' gunners, while on 20 June, between 1832 and 2017, *Faulknor* refuelled from *Hood,* a tricky process requiring a great deal of patience and skill. Oiling completed they again worked up to twenty knots.

On the 22nd they sighted a homeward bound convoy escorted by destroyer *Vidette*, the first ships seen for four days. Next morning the towering heights of The Rock hove up on the horizon, seeming to symbolise Britain's determination to fight on against all odds.

At 0700 the four destroyers formed into single line ahead to enter harbour, and, at 0826, *Faulknor* secured alongside oiler *Denbydale.* Force H was in business.

CHAPTER III

The Club

During the succeeding days, *Faulknor* and her companions with Force 'H' were gradually joined by other warships of the new squadron: battleship *Resolution* and light cruiser *Enterprise*. On the 26 June battleship *Valiant* left Scapa escorted by *Escort*, *Foresight* and *Forester*, and three days later *Fame* and *Fury* with Canadian destroyers *Skeena* and *St. Laurent* sailed from Scapa escorting battleship *Nelson,* also bound for Gibraltar, but, in the event, *Nelson* and the two Canadian ships were diverted elsewhere. The additional destroyers brought the flotilla's initial strength to seven, still hardly an adequate screen. Until reinforcements could join the 8th Flotilla they drew on the strength of the Local Defence Flotilla, the 13th, under Captain Francis De Winton with Flotilla Leader *Keppel* and destroyers *Active*, *Douglas, Velox, Vidette, Vortigern, Watchman, Wishart* and *Wrestler*. These ships were to prove welcome additions to Force 'Hs' slender screen from time to time, and indeed without them the squadron would occasionally have been immobilised for want of escorts. Finally, light cruiser *Arethusa* flying the flag of Vice-Admiral Sir James Somerville arrived on 28 June.

Details of the first operation to be carried out by this force had already been revealed. Naval power in 1940 was still based on battleships: Great Britain had 14 with five building; Germany had five with two building, Italy had four with four building. If France's eight with two building was added to the Axis total, the Royal Navy, already at full stretch, just could not cope. It came down to simple mathematics. To ensure that the Vichy-French, Mers-el-Kebir squadron was neutralised Somerville was instructed that, should all else fail, he must sink them.

Faulknor sailed at 1630/26th with *Hood* and *Ark Royal* to shadow the new Vichy battleship *Richelieu,* that had left Brest for Dakar, returning at 1945/27th. *Faulknor* sailed again at 0545, steering toward the Canary Islands to patrol, watching another Vichy battleship, *Jean Bart,* towed from St. Nazaire to Casablanca; *Faulknor* returning at 1343 the same afternoon. She remained alongside throughout 29 June, but sailed in company with *Fearless* at 0800 next day to patrol 30 miles off Oran, returning to Gibraltar at 0700/2 July.

At Mers-el-Kebir, near Oran in Algiers, lay the modern Vichy battle-cruisers *Dunkerque* and *Strasbourg*, old battleships *Bretagne* and *Provence*, seaplane carrier *Commandant Teste* and destroyers *Kersaint, Le Terrible, Mogador, Lynx, Tigre* and *Volta,* commanded by Admiral Gensoul. On surrender, the French Navy was placed under Axis *controle*. The War Cabinet, not trusting the collaborators Petain, Laval and Darlan, instructed Somerville to force this powerful squadron be disarmed.

At 1600/2 July, 1940, Force 'H' sailed for Operation 'Catapault', *Hood, Resolution, Valiant, Ark Royal*, and light cruisers *Arethusa* and *Enterprise*, screened by *Faulknor, Fearless, Foresight, Forester, Foxhound, Escort, Keppel, Active, Wrestler, Vortigern* and *Vidette*.

Captain De Winton told me:

> When Force 'H' arrived at the end of June 1940 and Somerville assumed command, he brought with him (from the Home Fleet) about six or seven destroyers of the E and F classes, led by *Faulknor.* Captain A.F. De Salis and I had been term mates and knew each

other very well. It was agreed between Admirals North and Somerville that the latter would take as many of my destroyers that he needed for an operation and that Admiral North could spare. We never, in my time, had the slightest difficulty about this. For the operation at Mers-el-Kebir on 3 July I embarked in *Keppel* taking with me four destroyers and De Salis had six of his 8th Flotilla, so the force had a quite adequate screen of eleven destroyers. And so it was for subsequent operations and 'Club Runs' as the passing of reinforcements through to Malta were called.

Four destroyers were detached to escort *Ark Royal*, while the remainder took station on the 'waggons', setting course south and zigzagging at 15 knots.

They found the enemy alert and waiting for them. Late on 2nd *Vortigern* sighted a torpedo track in 36° 20′N, 03° 46′W. *Faulknor* followed up and, early on the 3rd, obtained a firm contact. *Keppel* and *Foxhound* confirmed this and four depth-charge attacks resulted in a large patch of oil. This submarine, the Italian *Guglielmo Marconi,* escaped unscathed.

They arrived off Mers-el-Kebir on 3 July, and, at 0805, *Foxhound* anchored at the harbour entrance, outside the torpedo nets. She had Captain C.S. Holland aboard as emissary charged with presenting Gensoul with the various options available to him.

Force 'H'. HMS Faulknor *sailing from Gibraltar harbour as Flotilla Leader, 8th Destroyer Flotilla, Force 'H', in 1940. Note stripped-down early war appearance with 3-inch HA gun in place of after torpedo tubes, mainmast replaced by stump mast on midships bandstand to give this weapon some sort of sky arc, also the Force 'H' livery of dark hull and light upperworks.* (National Maritime Museum, Greenwich, Richard Perkins Collection.)

Gensoul flatly refused to accept *any* alternative, and deliberately delayed negotiations to enable his squadron to raise steam for battle. Hours passed and it required urgent instruction from London before Somerville opened fire, by which time the Vichy ships were almost ready to escape.

Not until 1755 did the British heavy ships finally open fire; French warships and land batteries replying three minutes later. Within a quarter-of-an-hour, thirty-six 15-inch salvoes had blown up *Bretagne* and badly damaged *Dunkerque* and *Provence*. The destroyer *Mogador* had her stern blown off. The *Strasbourg* took full advantage of the delays and the inadequate measures taken to bar the harbour entrance. With five destroyers, she won clear, setting a high-speed course for Toulon.

Somerville, in *Hood* set off on a hopeless stern-chase at 1843, soon working up to full power with cruisers *Arethusa* and *Enterprise* and the destroyers, led by *Faulknor*, in the van. Between 1933 and 1945 a French destroyer was engaged at ranges of 12,000 to 18,000 yards by two light cruisers, *Hood* and, later, *Valiant,* firing a few main armament salvoes. At least three hits were observed before this destroyer turned back towards Oran having fired torpedoes at Force 'H'. By 1950, *Strasbourg* and destroyers were reported to be twenty-five miles ahead of *Hood* and it was calculated that another Vichy squadron from Algiers, which included several 8-inch and 6-inch cruisers and destroyers, would probably meet *Strasbourg* shortly after 2100. Admiral Somerville abandoned the chase at 2020.

Nor could *Ark Royal's* torpedo-bombers stop the French making good their escape. Force 'H' therefore altered course to cruise to the west of Mers-el-Kebir that night and to conduct air attacks on the ships in harbour at dawn on 4 July. At 0603, *Ark Royal* reported that the proposed air attack could not be carried out because of the weather conditions, and *Faulknor* led the squadron back into Gibraltar at 1800. She refuelled and was ready to sail to deal with the *Richelieu* at Dakar, but the Admiralty wanted the job at Mers-el-Kebir finished first. The whole squadron (other than *Resolution* and one destroyer) therefore sailed again at 0800/5 July. to carry out Operation 'Lever'.

When within ninety miles of Oran, an air striking force was launched from *Ark Royal* at 1715/6th. One torpedo sank the auxiliary vessel *Terre Neuve* lying not far from the *Dunkerque* and, subsequently another torpedo detonated her cargo of 44 depth-charges. The seven tons of TNT ignited, ripping open *Dunkerque's* hull, rendering her inoperational. Admiral Somerville considered the job now completed so Force 'H' returned to Gibraltar at 1830.

Neither Hitler's nor the Vichy Government's oft-repeated pledges of the Vichy Navy's neutrality held much water; indeed over thirty warships – cruisers, destroyers, minesweepers, even submarines – were given to Italy during the war by France, and many were used by them and the Germans, indeed *Faulknor* was to fight such ships three years later.[1]

Because of its strategic position astride the main Italian supply lines to Africa, the reinforcing of Malta was vital, and the island base was to become a permanent thorn in the flesh of the Italians, and later Rommel's *Afrika Korps*. Time and time again British convoys escorted by Force 'H', ran the gauntlet to keep Malta on her feet. Thus sustained, British submarines, torpedo-bombers and surface striking-force sortied to hit hard at Axis supply routes to North Africa, sinking troop liners and vital oil tanker alike and thus preventing Rommel reaching the Suez Canal, linking up with the Russia front and threatening Middle East oil sources. One of the most bizarre revisionist hypotheses of recent times is that the retention of Malta in the Second World War was based on sentimental rather than strategical grounds.[2]

The role the island played in the defeat of the Axis in the Mediterranean and the limiting of their expansion is fully admitted to by German and Italian sources. Contemporary Axis testimonies are full of rueful admittance that it was Malta's striking power that prevented their ambitions regarding the Middle East and beyond being attained. It was the Royal Navy's task to keep Malta fighting, it was a hard task but one that they stuck to and were finally triumphant in, and *Faulknor* played her full part in this proud epic.

Faulknor's first sortie eastward took place early in July 1940. In conjunction with various large-scale operations being conducted by Admiral Cunningham's main Mediterranean Fleet in the eastern basin, Force 'H' was to enter the western basin as a diversion and launch an air attack on Cagliari. Accordingly they sailed at 0700/8 July, *Hood*, *Valiant*, *Resolution*, *Ark Royal*, light cruisers *Arethusa*, *Delhi* and *Enterprise*, screened by *Faulknor*, *Fearless*, *Foresight*, *Forester*, *Foxhound*, *Escort*, *Active*, *Douglas*, *Wrestler, Velox*, and *Vortigern*. All that day and the next the squadron pushed on unmolested into enemy waters and soon were on the edge of Mussolini's 'Triangle of Fire'.

From 1545 to 1840, on 9 July, Force 'H' was attacked by wave after wave of Sm.79 high-level bombers, which approached in rigid formation and pattern-bombed the ships, way above the height of their AA defence, although two bombers were destroyed by it. *Ark Royal's* fighters shot down two more; many ships were near-missed but none hit.

The futility of the altitude attacks finally dawned on the enemy and, towards dusk, several of Savoia Sm.79s changed their mode of attack to make shallow dives against the destroyer screen. At 1810, one such singled out *Faulknor*, in her usual place out ahead of the formation, acting as Guide to the Fleet, and came roaring down at mast-head height. The Italian pilot was determined, but he found his match in Captain De Salis, who, after Norway, was by now an old hand at avoiding air attacks, and he manoeuvred *Faulknor* untouched and unharmed through the towering bomb splashes. Force H held on eastward and, with nightfall, the air raids petered out. The persistent bombing was ineffective, but Admiral Somerville reversed course at 2215, and steered back toward Gibraltar at twenty knots. Even so the squadron did not return completely unscathed.

At 0215/11th *Faulknor*, still out ahead and steering west at 18 knots, suddenly sighted a gun flash astern of her, as a destroyer opened fire, followed by a second, much larger flash and the explosion of a torpedo striking home. The Italian submarine *Guglielmo Marconi* had made a cautious approach and, at 0213, fired from well outside the screen. One torpedo hit destroyer *Escort*, tearing a hole 20 feet in her hull from four feet below her upper deck to beyond the keel. The explosion knocked one of her funnels overboard and also blew a large hole in the upper deck above the forward boiler rooms. Further bulkheads burst and flooding steadily spread. *Forester* commenced firing and attempted to ram as her depth-charges were set to safe and could not be released in time. While *Forester* was attacking, the submarine crash-dived firing a torpedo from her stern tube.

At 0325 *Forester* reported that she was standing by *Escort*, and *Faulknor* closed her to find out the extent of the damage. They found *Escort* under control, but listing heavily. Apparently *Forester* had sighted the torpedo's track seconds before it struck her consort, and had attempted, unsuccessfully, to detonate it prematurely.

Despite the great hole amidships and the cockeyed appearance of her after funnel, Captain De Salis was told that there was a good chance of getting her safely into Gibraltar if her remaining bulkheads held. Captain De Salis had a quick consultation with the Commander-in-Chief aboard *Hood* and was given permission to attempt the salvage. The bulk of the crew of the stricken *Escort* were taken aboard *Forester*, leaving twenty officers and men aboard her, and then efforts were made to get her under tow. This was made difficult by the fact her rudder was jammed. Attempts were then made to tow her stern first by 0400, while *Faulknor* circled them. Hopes were still high that she could be saved but as the night wore on the water levels increased and the pumps lost the battle. By 0630, the list had increased and the angle of heel reached 30°. All the crew, save three volunteers, were then taken off. By 0830 she was still afloat and her remaining bulkheads were holding firm, but flooding continued and her list was increasing. By 1100, the water started pouring into her W/T Room on the port side and she went over on her beam-ends. The hull began to bend, her bow and stern came up until they were standing vertically out of the water, her stern broke off and sank, but *Escort's* bows continued to float for another thirty minutes. This was the 8th Flotilla's first loss and it was sad she should sink in sight of safety.

Faulknor and *Forester*, with the survivors aboard, at once increased speed before the expected air attacks developed. At midday they were met by *Keppel*, *Foresight* and *Foxhound* sent back to assist in *Escort's* salvage. Taking station astern, the destroyers then continued at high speed towards safety but barely an hour later, *Faulknor* gained an Asdic contact and all thoughts of flight were forgotten, instead revenge became the theme.

Leaving *Forester* to proceed to Gibraltar with the survivors, the rest of the flotilla took up the hunt. Contact was lost and regained throughout the afternoon and no doubt they made things unpleasant for the Italians below, but they did not get the satisfaction of fully avenging their consort, for the expected air attacks duly materialised. At 1322 two Italian bombers attacked the destroyers and they had to take avoiding action, the bombs falling around *Foxhound*. Asdic contact was finally lost for good and, although searching was continued throughout the rest of the day and night and on through the 12th, they were not rewarded. The four destroyers arrived at Gibraltar early next day.

The crew of *Faulknor* therefore spent three days in comparative idleness painting the ship, the drab 'crabfat' of the Home Fleet being covered over with the dark hull and light upperworks of Gibraltar based units.

Between 13 and 21 July, Captain De Salis spent time working up the flotilla to a fine pitch for the operations that lay ahead. The destroyers sailed regularly for practice shoots, both individually and together and conducted numerous anti-submarine exercises using the British submarines *Pandora* and *Proteus*, based at Gibraltar, for their underwater targets. These exercises were soon to pay off in action. Of course the Straits patrols continued unabated also.

The fo'c'sle party at work aboard HMS Faulknor, *seen here in Gilbraltar dockyard in 1940.* (Glenise Wightman.)

The old aircraft-carrier *Argus* with a cargo of Hurricane fighter aircraft was bound for Malta and required escort across the Bay. The Admiralty also wanted to intercept some suspicious neutral merchant ships proceeding to Spanish and Portuguese ports. Opportunity was to be taken to launch an air striking force to attack merchant shipping in the Le Verdon Roads and at Bordeaux at dawn 27 July. *Ark Royal* sailed from Gibraltar on Tuesday 23 July, escorted by light cruiser *Enterprise* and destroyers *Faulknor, Foresight, Forester* and *Escapade*. Next day, *Escapade* obtained a submarine contact and dropped a depth-charge, but this was subsequently reported as 'non-sub'. At 0100 on Thursday 25 July, a signal was received from the Admiralty cancelling the air attack operation, and they altered course to carry out an all-round air search to locate merchant vessels, but none were sighted, nor on 26th. *Faulknor* acted as target ship for *Enterprise* as she limbered up her 6-inch guns' crews, keeping their fingers crossed in case she decided to make it more interesting by using a few live rounds. The afternoon was spent in fending off dummy dive-bombing attacks by the *Ark's* Swordfish. They returned to the destroyer pens at 1115/27 July.

At 0630/30 July, *Argus*, with twelve Hawker Hurricanes, two Blackburn Skuas and RAF personnel plus stores for Malta, escorted by destroyers *Encounter, Gallant, Greyhound* and *Hotspur,* arrived at Gibraltar. The RAF men and stores were transferred to *Pandora* and *Proteus* for onward passage.

Force 'H' was to escort *Argus* as far as the southern tip of Sardinia where she would fly these aircraft off to reinforce Malta's defences, the operation being code-named 'Hurry'. Malta had been fending-off daily air attacks with four Gloster Sea Gladiator biplanes, hopelessly obsolete; now more substantial help was on the way. Opportunity was now taken to dock *Faulknor* briefly between 28 and 30 July, and on completion of this at 1730, she oiled and secured alongside.

Force 'H' sailed at 0800/31 July with *Hood, Valiant, Resolution, Ark Royal, Argus, Arethusa* and *Enterprise* escorted by *Faulknor, Fearless, Foresight, Forester, Foxhound, Escapade, Encounter, Hotspur, Greyhound, Gallant* and *Velox*. They proceeded on a course of 080° at seventeen knots.

Next day the fleet was subjected to air attacks, and some eighty bombs were dropped, near-misses being made on *Ark Royal* and *Forester*. At 2045 the force split into two groups. Group I, *Hood, Ark Royal, Enterprise, Faulknor, Foxhound, Foresight* and *Forester*, proceeded towards a position for flying-off aircraft for a diversionary attack on Cagliari. Group II proceeded to the eastward to fly-off the Hurricanes at dawn next day. At 2130, *Enterprise* was detached to carry out another diversionary ruse, broadcasting false signals, Operation 'Spark'. Then a signal from the Admiralty ordered the interception of a French ship, which left Algiers for Marseilles with M. Daladier on board.

Force II, *Valiant, Resolution, Argus, Arethusa, Gallant, Greyhound, Encounter, Escapade* and *Velox,* proceeded to the eastward and, at 0515 on 2 August, one Skua led six Hurricanes off her decks, followed, at 0600, by a second group of the same composition, all of which arrived safely at Malta. Also, on the night of 1/2 August, at 0230, the *Ark Royal* launched twelve Swordfish, which attacked Cagliari, Sardinia. The two Groups rejoined at 0520, the combined force being shadowed by Italian aircraft throughout that day. At 0930, *Arethusa* was detached to search for the Vichy French ship and, at 1000, *Enterprise,* operating unsupported to the north of Minorca looking for the same vessel, reported two enemy aircraft overhead. She was told to steer for Gibraltar, passing east of the Balearics, her diversionary mission having obviously succeeded. Neither of the two British cruisers sighted their quarry, nor did air searches by *Ark's* aircraft bring any results, although the Skuas of 800 Squadron shot down a Cant Z506 shadower at 1250.

No further bombing attacks developed. Instead, *Faulknor* obtained a submarine on her Asdic, but, despite a long hunt and dropping two depth-charge patterns, was unrewarded. They reached Gibraltar at daylight on 4 August.

Now came plans to alter the composition of Force 'H' that entailed a return to the U.K. Accordingly, at 0600/4 August, *Hood, Valiant, Arethusa* and *Argus* sailed escorted by *Faulknor, Foresight, Forester, Foxhound* and *Escapade,* joined next day by *Fearless,* steered north across the Bay of Biscay. They were instructed by the Admiralty to search for neutral merchants ships thought to be breaking the British blockade, and, in order to increase the effectiveness of the search, *Ark Royal, Enterprise, Hotspur, Encounter, Gallant* and *Greyhound*, accompanied the force to sea as far north as about 43°.

During the next three days they conducted exercises; during the night of the 6th/7th the flotilla made torpedo attacks against the heavy ships, dashing in at high speed and illuminating the towering bulks of *Hood* and *Valiant* with their searchlights to register hits. Sub-calibre shoots in company with the other ships took place the next day. *Enterprise* intercepted a Brazilian merchant ship on the 5th and examined her papers and next day *Arethusa* intercepted a Greek ship bound for Cork in the same way. On 6th *Ark Royal, Enterprise* and their escorts left them at 1050 and returned to Gibraltar

At 0700/9 August they were met west of Ireland by destroyers *Punjabi, Tartar* and *Zulu,* which took *Hood* into Scapa Flow, arriving at 0500/10th. *Valiant, Argus, Faulknor, Fearless, Forester* and *Foresight* proceeded up the Irish Sea towards the Mersey. Just after midnight on the 10th *Fearless* collided with drifter *Flying Wing*, which blundered into the path of the squadron. Neither vessel was badly damaged, and, after standing by both for an hour or so, *Faulknor* rejoined the rest of the force at dawn. Four hours later *Foresight* was detached with *Argus*, and, at 0530 *Faulknor* herself secured alongside the Queen's Dock at Liverpool.

Faulknor remained docked between the 11th, when DoD reported she was taken in hand for repairs, and 19 August, when these were completed. Meanwhile, Somerville travelled to London to consult with the Admiralty and returned on 13th to raise his flag aboard *Renown*, and, at 1630, she sailed with destroyers *Bedouin, Punjabi, Mashona* and *Tartar,* reaching Gibraltar on the 20th. Over the same ten-day period at Liverpool most of *Faulknor's* crew went on leave.

She was due to leave Liverpool at 1400/21 August, but sailing was delayed by very bad weather and it was the following day that she sailed with *Foresight, Forester* and *Fury*, joining battleship *Valiant,* carrier *Argus* and light cruiser *Ajax*. steering south to arrive at Gibraltar 29 August.

At 1042/20 August aircraft carrier *Illustrious,* heavy cruiser *York*, anti-aircraft cruisers *Calcutta* and *Coventry* (all of which were to reinforce Admiral Sir Andrew Cunningham's main Mediterranean Fleet at Alexandria) and destroyers *Foresight, Forester, Firedrake, Fortune, Fury* and *Greyhound* (to join Force 'H') had left Scapa Flow and the combined force sailed without incident through the Bay of Biscay towards the Straits of Gibraltar. On 27 August, *Renown*, escorted by destroyers *Encounter, Greyhound, Velox* and *Vidette,* rendezvoused with them and the whole force reached Gibraltar to prepare for the complicated operation known as 'Hats'.

As well as passing the reinforcements through to the eastern basin, *Ark Royal* was to fly-off Hurricane fighters to boost Malta's air defences, while her own aircraft were to create one diversion with air attacks on the Sardinian airfields, while destroyers *Velox* and *Wishart* conducted another by broadcasting fake wireless signals north of the Balearic islands.

Renown, Valiant, Ark Royal, Illustrious, light cruiser *Sheffield*, AA cruisers *Calcutta* and *Coventry,* and destroyers *Faulknor, Firedrake, Foresight, Fortune, Forester, Fury, Gallant, Greyhound, Griffin, Encounter, Hotspur, Nubian, Mohawk, Janus, Velox* and *Wishart* sailed at 0845/30 August. The whole operation proceeded like a peacetime exercise, apart from a few shadowing aircraft and a few submarine alarms no opposition was offered by the Italian Navy, and the Italian Air Force lost some snoopers to the combined fighters of the two carriers.

Force 'H' then proceeded northward for a quarter-of-an-hour, altered course to the westward and increased speed to 24 knots to reach a suitable position for the second air attack on Cagliari, which was made on 2 September. Although they remained within range of Italian air bases for 48 hours no attacks developed. Force H returned to the Rock at 1100/3 September without having fired a shot!

Faulknor remained in harbour for the next two days, but on 6th, sailed to battle once more. Their next task was to be the abortive attempt by the Free French forces, with the aid of the Royal Navy, to take over the West African colony of Senegal from the Vichy Government, Operation 'Menace'. The

British naval forces allocated to help General Charles De Gaulle achieve this dream were made up from many different squadrons.

Convoy M.S. comprised the transport *Ocean Coast* (Commodore), with the French, *Nevada, Fort Lamy, Casanance* and *Anadyrm* escorted by Free-French sloop *Savorgnan de Brazza* and trawler *President Houduce*, which left Liverpool on 26 August in company with convoy OB 204 for Sierra Leone. From the Home Fleet came battleship *Barham* and destroyers *Inglefield, Echo, Eclipse* and *Escapade* which sailed from Scapa 28 August for Gibraltar; Convoy MP sailed in three sections on 31 August, from Liverpool; the British troopers *Karanja, Westernland* and *Pennland* (with General de Gaulle embarked) and food ship *Belgravian*; from the Clyde heavy cruiser *Devonshire* (Flag, Force 'M'), Free-French sloops *Commandant Domine,* and *Commandant Duboc*; from Scapa Flow again, British troopships *Sobieski, Kenya* and *Ettrick,* escorted by light cruiser *Fiji*. From the South Atlantic Command heavy cruisers *Cornwall* and *Cumberland,* light cruiser *Delhi* and sloops *Bridgewater* and *Milford*, while Force 'H' contributed battleship *Resolution,* carrier *Ark Royal* and destroyers *Faulknor* (to take command of the combined screen), *Foresight, Forester, Fortune, Fury* and *Greyhound*.

On 1 September *Fiji* was hit and damaged by a U-boat torpedo on the way south and her place was taken by heavy cruiser *Australia* from the Home Fleet. *Barham* and her destroyers arrived at Gibraltar on 2 September and *Faulknor* found them there on her return from 'Hats'.

Barham's group had sailed to carry out this operation in company with the Force 'H' contingent on 6th, *Faulknor* and the other destroyers oiling from the battleships two days later. They conducted exercises near the Canary Islands and Cape Bianco, the destroyers making sub-calibre shoots and a night attack. Aircraft from *Ark Royal* made contact with the convoy at 1145/12th. At 0820/13th, *Faulknor, Foresight, Forester* and *Fury* were detached and reinforced the convoys screen at 1700.

They also received news that a Vichy-French naval squadron from Toulon and bound for Dakar, had been allowed to pass through the Straits of Gibraltar unhindered[3]. Initially, they could not believe it; then incredulity gave way to anger. Captain J. O. H. Gairdner, *Faulknor's* Engineering Officer told me:

> We at Dakar were horrified to find that the ships had passed through unmolested and were on their way to augment an already sizeable enemy force. At a stroke the whole balance of power shifted against us and we thought pretty poorly of Dudley North who had not laid a finger on the ships from his commanding position. We could hardly believe it, coming so soon after Oran.

He went on, '… we were amazed, perplexed, horrified and incredulous that 'they' had allowed the opposition to the Dakar operation to be so significantly augmented without a shot being fired!'

The convoy was sent on to Freetown while *Faulknor,* with Force 'M', hastily reversed course in an attempt to intercept the Vichy force. But, although two Vichy cruisers, *Gloire* and *Primauguet* (from Libreville) were stopped, and ammunition ship *Poitiers* sunk, the rest of the French warships escaped unharmed.

Meantime, *Faulknor, Foresight, Forester* and *Greyhound* escorted *Barham* into Freetown, Sierra Leone, for the battleship to get water, and she and the two 'Fs' sailed again at 0515/15th, leaving *Greyhound* to follow. Course was steered to place themselves some 75 nautical miles west of north from Dakar, but they were too late to be effective so returned to Freetown at 2300. Here *Faulknor* remained until 20 September while Operation 'Menace' was reconsidered at high level over the ether between there and London. That morning Force 'M' and the troopships sailed for Dakar, the decision having been taken to proceed.

The invasion force sailed in groups, *Faulknor* leaving Freetown at 0645/21st, with *Devonshire, Forester, Foresight* and *Echo*, sloops *Milford, Commandant Domine, Commandant Duboc* and

Savorgnan de Brazza, with convoy MP. The destroyers met *Ark Royal* and *Resolution,* as Group 2, with *Fortune* and *Fury* joining after refuelling. At dawn, they rendezvoused with Group 1, *Barham, Devonshire, Inglefield, Escapade* and *Greyhound.* Conditions on board all the warships during the long voyage south were far from pleasant, the temperature of was very hot and sticky; the heat intense both by day and night.

The Allies planned for two eventualities, a welcome reception and an opposed landing, and British warships had been assigned specific roles in both. Both *Faulknor* and *Foresight* carried a Free-French 'Broadcaster' sent aboard at Freetown. Both destroyers had to be prepared to lower their ship's motor-boats (flying the French Ensign) when transports anchored off Dakar, *Foresight's* to proceed to approach Rufisque and broadcast the, 'we come in peace' message. *Faulknor* was to stand by to lower her motorboat at Hann Bay. If an 'unfriendly' response was received, i.e. the motorboat was fired upon, their orders were to retire and proceed to *Ettrick.*

In the event of a hostile reception, and force being required, the heavy ships were allocated their targets, the forts and *Richelieu;* while *Faulknor* and *Forester* were to provide close-in support fire for Landing II at Hann Bay by the First Battalion. It was appreciated that the two ships' movements were likely to be restricted by the shallowness of the water and lack of sea-room inside the boom. One destroyer was to be placed on a front stretching from Tiaroy to just outside Hann, the other from the southern flank of the landing beach, including Belair Point. They were to engage observed targets and, should additional supporting fire be required, they would be called upon by the firing of a succession of Red Very lights from the leading flight of ALC. The two destroyers were to fire on the defences for ten minutes and then switch to targets of opportunity, which 'would not endanger our own troops.' This second stage was to last just five minutes.

Compare this destroyer close-support role for 'Menace'; in many ways a prototype for future allied amphibious assaults, with the ultimate perfection of the concept at Normandy four years on. *Faulknor* took part in both and the development and increased precision of such close-support by destroyers can be seen by comparing her two instructions and fire plans. *Faulknor* helped pioneer this concept, just as she was later to help pioneer another, completely different but war-winning concept, the Support Group in the North Atlantic.

Shallow waters called for precise soundings but only *Faulknor, Inglefield, Greyhound, Echo* and *Escapade* were fitted with Echo Sounding Gear. To shield the transports (and possibly the battle squadron) from the 15-inch shells of *Richelieu* and the shore batteries, the laying of a smoke-screen was a strong possibility, but, again, of the assembled destroyers, only *Foresight, Forester, Fury, Eclipse* and *Greyhound* carried CSA smoke-making apparatus.

The Anglo-French expedition arrived off Dakar at 0500/23 September, when the two battleships and heavy cruisers *Australia, Cumberland* and *Devonshire,* formed into single line ahead, screened by six destroyers, steering to within 30,000 yards of the coast at fifteen knots. They were out of range of the Vichy shore batteries' 9.4-inch guns, but not of *Richelieu's* eight 15-inch weapons. Parleying began, in forlorn hope of an unopposed landing. Meanwhile *Faulknor* remained with the transports, ready to carry out her 'Broadcast' mission, but events soon showed that this would *not* be required!

Closing to 4,000 yards of the forts, Cunningham's fleet commenced firing at 1104, cease-firing half-an-hour later because of poor visibility. *Barham, Resolution, Australia* and *Devonshire* resumed the attack at 0700 next day but visibility was equally as murky as the day before.

On 25 September the fleet returned for one more try, but again, light cruiser *Dragon* and *Faulknor* and *Fury* took no part, remaining with the troop convoy as their protection.

The British squadron opened fire at 0905, *Barham* hitting *Richelieu* at 0915, but was hit by her in return four minutes later, as was *Australia,* twice. Firing ceased, for the final time, at 0921 as *Barham* withdrew to cover *Resolution,* damaged by a submarine torpedo, and this marked the end of the operation.

Meantime, at 1041, both *Dragon* and *Faulknor* separately reported that the troop convoy was being bombed by Vichy-French Glenn Martin aircraft, fortunately without casualties. The Vichy aircraft soon switched their attentions to the Battle Squadron, despite the best efforts of *Ark's* Skuas, and at 1056 a bomb fell two cables to starboard of *Resolution*. At 1108 the C-in-C decided he needed a stronger screen and instructed *Dragon* to send him the destroyer with the most fuel, which was *Faulknor*.

By noon, *Resolution*, with a fire in 'A' Boiler Room and some adjacent compartments, was steering 210° at ten knots escorted by *Barham, Devonshire, Australia, Faulknor, Foresight, Forester* and *Inglefield*. The fuel situation in some of the destroyers was, as always, acute which necessitated their being sent in turn to fuel during the Squadron's long passage back to Freetown. At 1235, *Resolution* had to stop for four minutes to fight fires, and could only continue at five knots. The troopships were sent ahead to Freetown escorted by *Dragon* and destroyer *Fury*. At 1700, *Ark Royal* reported *Escapade*, one of her two screening destroyers, with *Greyhound*, was short of fuel so *Faulknor* and *Forester* were detached from the battleship group to relieve them. *Faulknor* finally arrived at Freetown at 1800/29th.

General de Gaulle and London decided an alternative strategy. The French Cameroons had declared for de Gaulle and the Free-French forces proceeded to Duala, escorted by *Devonshire, Faulknor, Forester, Fury* and *Escapade*. Established there, they could extend their influence to other West African colonies. On 2 October this expedition left Freetown with the same transports and escorts, supported by *Devonshire*.

Faulknor's future employment was being discussed even while this operation was underway. On Saturday 4 October the Admiralty signalled:

> Unless there are good reasons, *Faulknor* is to accompany *Barham* when she proceeds to Gibraltar.

Meanwhile, on 7 October, the force arrived at Ambos Bay, Cameroon River, and between 1020 and 1455 *Faulknor* oiled from *Devonshire*. The following day *Faulknor* conducted anti-submarine patrols across the bay and next day the expedition resumed course for Douala at 0745, *Forester* and *Fury* as close escorts and *Devonshire, Faulknor* and *Escapade* as the covering force. After a few hours all arrived at Douala, where, to everyone's relief, de Gaulle received an enthusiastic welcome.

Their job done, the three destroyers sailed for Freetown at 1105, arriving at 0800/13th. Here they found *Foresight* and, after refuelling, all four sailed for Gibraltar at 1815 to resume their duties with Force 'H', arriving at 1235/19 October.

Until early November *Faulknor* was mainly engaged in routine anti-submarine patrols in the Straits. She was thus employed between 21/23 October and between 26/27 October. On the former date they had sailed to relieve *Greyhound* on patrol off the Island of Alboran in the Straits and next day conducted target practice. Two days in harbour then out again to take over patrol from *Wrestler*; the same lonely beat to and fro between the Pillars of Hercules, relieved on the 27th by a dummy torpedo attack on *Gallant,* then back to harbour again. This became the accepted routine as October gave way to November.

On 31 October *Renown* and *Barham* sailed from Gibraltar at 0815 escorted by *Faulknor, Forester, Fortune, Firedrake, Gallant, Greyhound* and *Griffin* and patrolled along the western coast of Morocco after receiving reports of more suspicious moves by the Vichy Navy. Four destroyers left Toulon and passed through the Straits of Gibraltar *en route* to either Dakar or Casablanca. Force 'H' tracked this force from Cape Spartel southward but did not intercept them. Only a suspected submarine contact preoccupied them during this trip. During the late afternoon the heavy ships carried out a practice shoot of their main armaments and from 2000 a night-encounter exercise was held with destroyers making mock torpedo attacks on the big ships in the light of defending starshells. The whole force was back at the Rock 1030/1 November.

Another Straits patrol followed on 1/3 November, *Faulknor* participating in a Night Encounter exercise with *Wishart* and, early on 2nd, they ran into a concentration of Spanish fishing vessels which they illuminated with their searchlight. The day passed in slow sweeps across the sunlit water. They exercised steam breakdown and repair parties, tried out a new short-range anti-e-boat barrage, with every gun firing flat out on a fixed bearing, scaring every seagull in the area and shattering the sea into a wall of boiling spray. They also carried out a depth-charge attack on a 'doubtful' contact on 2 November. A little bored, they returned to Gibraltar, but as they secured alongside the destroyer pens once more and cast expert eyes around the harbour, they saw that strange ships were present, which could only mean trouble; the brief siesta period was about to terminate. They oiled and they prepared themselves for more serious work. The next sortie east into the Mediterranean was imminent.

A whole series of operations were planned for November 1940. The first of these, Operation 'Coat' was now put into operation; the sailing of *Barham*, heavy cruiser *Berwick*, light cruiser *Glasgow* and destroyers *Encounter, Gallant, Greyhound* and *Griffin* to join Admiral Cunningham's Mediterranean Fleet at Alexandria. The opportunity was taken to reinforce Malta's garrison with 2,000 troops conveyed there by the warships.

On 7 November Force H sailed with *Ark Royal*, light cruiser *Sheffield* and destroyers *Faulknor, Firedrake, Forester, Fortune, Fury* and *Duncan* to cover their passage as far as the south of Sardinia. Because of the presence of the *Admiral Scheer* on the Atlantic convoy routes, *Renown* had been called home temporarily. They sailed steadily eastwards during the night and most of the following day before being sighted by the usual Italian reconnaissance plane, but night fell before any air attack could be mounted.

On 9th, *Ark Royal's* Swordfish attacked Elmas airfield in Sardinia, rejoining the fleet just in time for her Fulmar fighters to knock another Italian Cant into the sea. Shortly afterward, the Italian air force made the expected high-level bombing attacks, to no avail.

Early next morning Force 'F' was detached and *Faulknor, Fortune* and *Fury* were sent with them right through to Malta because of the dangers of the extensive Italian minefields in the Sicilian Channel. The 'Fs' deployed their TSDS (Two Speed Destroyer Sweep) equipment to good effect. Many so-called 'experts' claim that British destroyers equipped with this gear *never* used them in action, but this is palpable nonsense. Certainly the 'F' and 'I' Classes used them on this, and many subsequent occasions, when taking warships and convoys through to Malta. As the name indicated the equipment could be used at 12 knots for slow work, or at 25 knots when operating with the fleet. It took about twenty minutes to 'stream' the twin half-ton paravanes from the stern davits. The two $^3/_4$-inch diameter galvanised steel wires of the tow ropes were kept out from the side and stern of the destroyers by means of the paravanes and tadpoles, which kept the wire at a selected depth. Any mine mooring wire caught by the tow wire was steered along it and into the paravane and held so that the wires sawed through it or it slid back to cutters, which sliced through it. The mine then floated to the surface were it could be seen and avoided, or, if there was time, destroyed by gun or rifle fire. Of course these weapons were only good against the conventional moored type mines but the Italians did not at this stage of the war have access to the German magnetic or acoustic mines. It was no sinecure for the destroyers thus employed, for the gear was heavy and complicated, easily snarled while on deck, and tended to carry away at the higher speeds or if the weather was rough. The destroyers had to steer a straight, true and steady course, (which is why *Faulknor* with the Flotilla Navigation Officer embarked went with them) and could not take avoiding action if attacked.

In the event, the passage of Force 'F' was uneventful and the three Force 'H' destroyers refuelled at Sliema Creek, Malta during 10 November, before sailing again that night for the return passage. While the other warships had been landing their contingent of troops, *Faulknor* had taken on board twenty naval ratings and two RAF officers, all bound for home.

After guiding them back out to sea again, the 'Fs' left the reinforcements to rendezvous with Admiral Cunningham's fleet to the east, and the 8th Flotilla destroyers cleared the channel next evening and sped towards the Sicilian 'Narrows'. Force H was already back at Gibraltar when the three little boats steamed on towards those hostile waters in the gathering dusk but, alone though they were, on this occasion they were not molested, finally securing alongside in the destroyer pens at the Rock just before midnight 14th.

The officers and men of HMS *Faulknor* did not spend long congratulating themselves on their luck, for, after hastily oiling during a day in harbour, they were off to the east again on the 15th for the second operation of the series.

Operation 'White', was the next mission, another aircraft reinforcement mission to fly twelve Hurricane fighters from *Argus* to Malta led by Skua dive-bombers from *Ark Royal*. *Argus* arrived at Gibraltar with light cruiser *Despatch* on 14 November and *Renown* was back on station. At 0400 *Renown* sailed, *Argus* and *Ark Royal* astern of her, cruisers *Despatch* and *Sheffield* formed up ahead and astern of the column. On their starboard flanks were *Faulknor*, *Fortune*, *Fury* and *Wishart*, with *Forester*, *Firedrake*, *Duncan* and *Foxhound* to port.

The speed of the fleet was restricted by the old *Argus* to a maximum of twenty knots so progress was slow. There was no interruption from the enemy and, at 0615 and at 0715 the Hurricanes were duly launched in two separate flights from a position south-west of Sardinia. Unfortunately the range of launching had been too finely calculated to allow for much margin of error and strong headwinds caused all but four of the Hurricanes to run out of fuel and ditch into the sea, along with one of the Skuas who had stayed with them to the end. A planned Swordfish attack on Alghero airfield in Sardinia was abandoned as the weather worsened and the squadron faced a gruelling battle against the elements. Even at slow speed the destroyers took a pounding – less typical Mediterranean weather it was hard to imagine. It was a very weary bunch of men who conned *Faulknor* finally into Gibraltar on the 19th.

On 21 November 1940, *Faulknor* and *Forester*, supported by light cruiser *Despatch,* left Gibraltar to intercept the Vichy blockade-runner *Charles Plumier*. This modern diesel-engined vessel was attempting to reach Marseilles with much-needed supplies for the Petain regime. Admiralty intelligence reported her mission and the fact that *Charles Plumier* was hugging the African coast to avoid interception and that she would then try to reach Spanish territorial waters to reach France.

As a ruse, *Faulknor* and her two companions steered east until just after nightfall until they were in position to carry out an interception. Next day *Charles Plumier* was duly sighted and *Faulknor* and *Forester* intercepted the vessel 110 miles east of Gibraltar in 35° 32′ N, 03° 05′ W. She offered no resistance and an armed guard was put aboard to prevent scuttling. She was then escorted into Gibraltar at 0800/23rd. The Vichy crew vehemently refused to sail to the UK so were repatriated and the Red Ensign hoisted. Their prize was sailed to England with convoy HG52 on 27 January 1941. Here she was converted into an armed boarding vessel fitted with two 6-inch guns, and renamed HMS *Largs*. In 1942, she was again refitted with extensive communication equipment and became an HQ ship for landing craft, (LSH(L) or Landing Ship, Headquarters, Large). She served as Combined Operations Headquarters ship at the invasion of Sicily (Operation 'Husky'), at the invasion of South France in 1944 (Operation 'Dragoon') and in the liberation of Rangoon (Operation 'Dracula'). Thus *Faulknor's* interception had excellent long-term rewards for the war effort.

On 25 November Force 'H' sailed on Operation 'Collar', third of the series of operations, and this led to the Battle of Spartivento. I have given the fullest account of this operation in other books[4] so here will restrict myself to just *Faulknor's* part in this battle.

The Italians had three operational battleships, plus eight heavy and twelve light cruisers and scores of destroyers. Admiral Somerville had therefore to protect his convoy of three fast transports, *Clan Forbes*, *Clan Fraser* and *New Zealand Star,* laden with tanks and vital equipment for the Middle East army, against air, submarine and superior surface attack, with very frugal strength.

Force 'H' comprised *Renown* (with a split in her hull and engine problems), *Ark Royal* (whose squadrons had a high proportion of young and inexperienced pilots and observers), light cruisers *Despatch* and *Sheffield*, and destroyers *Faulknor*, *Firedrake*, *Forester*, *Fury*, *Duncan*, *Wishart*, *Encounter* and *Hotspur*, (the latter on her way to be docked at Malta because of various defects, her speed limited to under twenty knots and having no Asdic) and *Kelvin* and *Jaguar*, fresh out from the UK with Vice-Admiral Holland's two cruisers.

There were also four of the new corvettes, *Gloxinia*, *Hyacinth*, *Peony* and *Salvia*, but their best speed was only fourteen knots. This made them just about OK for Atlantic and other slow convoys, but useless for the fast convoys and fleet actions common with Force 'H'. They fell steadily behind the convoy as the operation developed and, by the time the battle commenced, were ten miles astern and still losing ground.

A squadron from the eastern basin, (Force 'D') battleship *Ramillies*, heavy cruiser *Berwick*, light cruiser *Newcastle*, all with defects, were to join forces with him to return home via Gibraltar, and with them were AA cruiser *Coventry* and destroyers *Defender*, *Greyhound*, *Griffin* and *Hereward* to take the convoy through the Straits and rendezvous with Cunningham's main force. Also going through to the east from Gibraltar, packed with RAF and army personnel, which hampered their fighting capabilities, were light cruisers *Manchester* and *Southampton*.

Against these forces the Italians deployed six submarines, (which proved to be completely ineffectual), their considerable air force (likewise) and a powerful surface fleet, including battleships *Vittorio Veneto* and *Giulio Cesare*, five heavy cruisers and fourteen destroyers, commanded by Admiral Campioni.

Force H sailed eastward late on 25 November. 'Third time unlucky', the old hands muttered to the new recruits, with the usual blend of cheerful pessimism, and indeed it seemed unthinkable that the Italians should again ignore their passage.

The first two days were uneventful. The weather was good, temperatures moderate and spirits high. By 0800/27 November the convoy was steering east with *Despatch*, *Manchester* and *Southampton*, escorted by *Duncan*, *Wishart*, *Jaguar* and *Kelvin*, while Somerville had *Renown*, *Ark Royal*, *Sheffield*, *Faulknor*, *Firedrake*, *Forester*, *Fury* and *Encounter*, ten miles ahead and to the north-east of the convoy, placing himself between it and any enemy threat. They were in 36° 37' N, 06° 54' E steaming at an economical sixteen knots. Force 'D' from the east, had passed unchallenged through the Sicilian Channel and was northeast of Galitia Island, on course and time to affect the rendezvous.

An hour later, having no reports from *Ark Royal's* reconnaissance flights, Force 'H' closed the convoy, placing themselves south, but up-sun, at 0920. Sixteen minutes later a sighting report arrived of five cruisers and five destroyers closing fast. Initially, this was thought to be Force 'D' and *not* the enemy; but amplification was requested. At 0912, *Sheffield* and *Firedrake* were sent to join the close escort because Somerville was initially wrong-footed.

However, further Swordfish sightings left no doubts that they was facing the full Italian fleet, with the British forces still separated. At 1015, two battleships and seven destroyers were sighted, in addition to six cruisers and eight destroyers. While *Ark Royal* prepared a torpedo striking force, *Renown* worked up to 28 knots and steered 075° to interpose herself between the enemy and the convoy, also closing the gap between herself and *Ramillies*.

Renown increased to full speed and, at 1017, Captain De Salis on *Faulknor's* bridge was instructed to detach two destroyers to screen *Ark*, leave a further two with the convoy, and concentrate the remainder in readiness for surface action!

This was done, not without some confusion caused by the scattered positioning of the destroyers. At least one of the newer destroyers was required to screen *Ark*, and *Jaguar* was so assigned, along with *Forester*. However, as the carrier turned away to starboard, *Kelvin*, observing this, and that *Jaguar* was hauling out, did the same. This left *Forester* astern, with some distance to catch them. Captain De Salis decided to make the best of this and, considering that the AA fire of the two new destroyers would help support *Ark*, and also that those two ships were used to working together, allowed *Kelvin* to proceed and recalled *Forester* to join his striking force.

Similar confusion followed the second signal from Somerville, who, at 1026, instructed Captain De Salis to detail two of the remaining destroyers to join the convoy while the rest joined the flag. Captain De Salis chose the crippled *Hotspur* for this duty, along with *Duncan*, as he was aware that the latter ships machinery was not very reliable. Directions were therefore given to call all destroyers by V/S (Visual Signal via Signal Lamp), and this was done. This was a slow process and open to errors, one of which was that *Duncan,* on the far side of the convoy from *Faulknor,* was erroneously given the order to join. The error was compounded by the fact that both Somerville, via Captain De Salis in *Faulknor*, and CS18 in *Manchester*, were signalling the same ships with contradictory instructions. Thus, Captain D (13), Captain A.B.D. James, aboard *Duncan* received the following signals in quick succession within the space of ten minutes:

Time of Receipt	Originator	Signal	Time of Origin
1048 by V/S	D(8)	'Join me'	1048
1050 by W/T	D(8)	'Join FO (H)'	1050
1053 by V/S	D(8)	'*Duncan* and *Hotspur* remain with convoy.'	1051
1058 by W/T	CS (18)	'Join *Manchester*'	1053

Captain James's original movements had been for *Duncan* to commence moving out at 25 knots (increasing to full speed) in anticipation of being told to leave the convoy and join Somerville. It was his intention to take *Encounter* with him, leaving *Hotspur* and *Wishart* with the convoy and to detach *Fury* to join her rightful flotilla. But, because of the signals shown above, '… a somewhat confused situation occurred during the next half an hour.' *Duncan* turned to rejoin the convoy on receipt of the 1051 signal and again altered course for Group One on receiving CS18's 1053. However, *Duncan* herself resolved the dilemma, for, as Captain De Salis had already predicted, on being asked for full power *Duncan's* engines lost steam in two of her three boilers due to trouble with automatic feeds, so that, at 1130 her position was midway between *Ark Royal* and *Renown* with speed varying from 10 to 28 knots. Captain James persisted with telegraphs at 'full speed' until noon, but then his Engineering Officer reported that the most he could expect was 26 knots, and it was decided that in such condition *Duncan* would be more of a liability than an asset and *Duncan* rejoined the convoy at 1320. Captain James concluded:

> Under action conditions, confusing and contradictory signals are likely to be received, and since one cannot obey them all, it is wiser, not necessarily to 'obey the last signal', but to use one's own judgement and stick to it until the situation clears.

Meanwhile Captain De Salis finally obtained permission from Admiral Somerville to continue his round-up via W/T and *Encounter* and *Wishart* finally received their orders. In fact, both ships were already reacting to Captain James's original instructions, *Encounter* to join F/O/(H) and *Wishart* to remain with convoy. Therefore, in the end, *Duncan*, *Hotspur* and *Wishart* took no further part in the action.

At 1055, Admiral Somerville signalled cruisers and destroyers to take station from *Renown* on a bearing 050°, distance five miles and *Faulknor* led out accordingly. By 1106, being uncertain as to the relative position of cruisers and destroyers, Captain De Salis asked CS18 where he would like the destroyers placed, receiving the reply 040°, five miles from the *Renown*. This positioned the cruisers on *Faulknor's* starboard bow, leaving their arcs of fire clear. Captain De Salis subsequently manoeuvred in accordance with Somerville's signal as to bearing from *Renown*.

Quickly working up to more than thirty knots, vibrating, lithe and eager, *Faulknor* cut a narrow swathe through the sunlit sea. Behind her, the rest of the force swung round toward the distant, and as yet unseen enemy, guardrails down, battle ensigns flying. The three cruisers soon crashed past and formed a skirmish line far ahead in line abreast, while two miles away on either flank of *Faulknor,* the other destroyers fell into formation, five cables' length apart, torpedo tubes ready, guns at high elevation, bow waves piled high. Behind them, a picture of strength and power, *Renown* also pounded northward, her twenty-five year old hull being driven forward at the maximum power of her engines to maintain her position in the attack.

This was the kind of warfare that *Faulknor* had trained and was ready for. Over and over again since she had first been commissioned both peacetime and wartime exercises had included practising the fleet action, and Captain De Salis had a finely tuned, perfectly-adjusted weapon under his command with which to carry out the long-awaited task. *Faulknor, Firedrake, Forester* and *Fury* had fought and trained together as a unit for five years, but *Encounter* who was with them, and *Defender, Greyhound, Griffin* and *Hereward,* soon to join, had all undertaken the same training. Indeed some had already taken part in such battles at Narvik, Cape Spada and Calabria. They formed a homogenous flotilla, all of similar design, tonnage and armament, commanded by aggressive and totally-dedicated captains who were masters of their trade and reinforced by the nebulous but so-important factor, the tradition of attack! *No* such training, no such motivation, no such sense of history, of the *automatic* reaction of steering *toward*s, not away, from the enemy, inspired their opposite numbers in the Italian fleet. No matter how brave they were individually, they lacked the moral momentum and basic instinct.

Faulknor's signal halyards became busy with bunting as Captain De Salis organised his destroyers. There was no lack of confidence among the officers and men that they would thrash the Italians, outnumbered or not! David Divine, a journalist embarked in *Firedrake,* caught the *essence* of this moment perfectly:[5]

> We fell into line astern of *Faulknor,* racing straight into the broad tumult of her wake. For a little while we were the van itself – two small ships racing towards the north.
>
> They had stacked the kit away and the hatches were open. The whips trailed down to the magazines, the men of the supply parties, hooded in their white asbestos flash-gear, fantastic as monks of some strange order of battle, were ready at winch and slide. The men above the guns were hooded, their tin hats over all. The torpedo party fussed about their duties. The after supply part was ready. The hoses were laid along the decks.

Captain J. O. H. Gairdner, *Faulknor's* Engineering Officer, told me: -

> I can still recall the excitement when the buzz reached the engine room that we were now between the Italian heavies and their bases.

By 1030, the three light cruisers were concentrating in the 'A–K' line in the van and *Faulknor* was collecting her scattered flotilla, some of which had to steam hard from their screening positions with the convoy to join him. The flotilla gradually came together in *Faulknor's* wake. First to join was *Firedrake,* Lieutenant Commander Stephen H. Norris, receiving the signal to join *Faulknor* at 1044, and *Firedrake* remained in company throughout the action. No difficulty was experienced in keeping station at thirty knots. Next up was *Fury,* Lieutenant Commander T. C. Robinson, receiving the signal to join at 1047, and remaining there throughout the action. As related, *Forester* had lost ground on being ordered to join *Ark Royal* initially at 1028, and it was not until 1035 that Lieutenant Commander E. B. Tancock, DSC, received fresh instructions to join his flotilla leader. *Forester* was then four miles astern of the main body, and speed was increased to 31 knots for a long stern chase. Not until 1150 did *Forester* finally take station astern of *Fury* to become the fourth ship on the line of the 8th Flotilla, who were at that time on a line of bearing 070° on the engaged bow of *Renown* and a distance of three miles. Last to join was *Encounter* and her captain, Lieutenant Commander E. V. St. J. Morgan, recorded that she finally passed *Renown* at noon and continued to chase *Faulknor* and her companions, then stationed three miles from the Admiral. Not until 1216 was *Encounter* finally able to form astern and prolong the line. From then until 1319, *Encounter* adjusted her course and speed to maintain station on *Faulknor*.

With his flotilla assembled Captain De Salis considered the best role for them in what looked like being a long stern chase after a very reluctant opponent. He recorded:

> Although from the form of the action it became evident that destroyers would be unable to help much, it appeared that to form a line of bearing across the line of sight to the enemy would conform to the general intentions of the battle instructions, and would also form a physical obstruction to submarine attack and torpedo bomber attack on the *Renown*, and this disposition was accordingly assumed, and when the smoke of the enemy ships was sighted, the 8th Destroyer Flotilla was spread on a line of bearing of 250° at intervals of five cables, and the destroyers of the Mediterranean Fleet were stationed three miles, 270° from the *Faulknor*. Both groups were then manoeuvred to conform approximately with the movements of the *Renown*.

He listed his reasons for adopting this formation:

> Spreading my destroyers at intervals of five cables confirmed my previous opinion that this was more suitable than close order in an action of this type. It has the advantages that:
>
> (i) Destroyers do not offer a massed target to gunfire, and misses at one ship do not necessarily endanger the rest.
>
> (ii) Commanding Officers are not tied by close station keeping at high speed, but are free to give attention to fighting their ships.
>
> (iii) Should a destroyer suffer steering gear damage, she is not a danger to her neighbours.
>
> (iv) In the event of signals not getting through, this distance allows confirming action to be sufficiently rapid to avoid collisions.
>
> (v) Provided the unit controlled is not above five ships, they may at five cables be considered to be in close support of each other for Gunnery, Torpedo and V/S purposes.

As a newcomer to the 8th Flotilla, *Encounter's* Captain endorsed the tactics of Captain De Salis, Lieutenant Commander Morgan recording that the formation, '… adopted by Captain (D), i.e. ships on a line of bearing, five cables apart, was most successful, giving Commanding Officers freedom of movement and plenty of time to concentrate on other things than station-keeping. It is considered that more than five ships in this formation would be unhandy and also make the reading of flag signals direct from the Leader difficult.'

The flotilla was kept on Fleet Waveband throughout the action, as Captain De Salis considered that little congestion would arise in such a small force, and it seemed desirable to him that all destroyers should receive the enemy sighting reports direct. He also considered that with destroyers spread at five cables as they were, W/T was essential for rapid manoeuvring, and it would have been preferable to put all his ships on the Destroyer Waveband, and for *Faulknor* to pass on any signals affecting the whole flotilla, which she received on the Fleet Wave. The difficulties collecting the destroyers at the start of the action emphasised this point.

Once assembled, her flotilla was stationed 050°, five miles ahead of *Renown* on the estimated plot bearing of the main enemy force. They continued to run north and, about an hour later, the welcome sight of Force 'D' meant that their concentration had been safely made. Four fresh destroyers now joined *Faulknor* from the east, and were eventually placed two miles astern of the cruisers, three miles 270° from *Faulknor* (See Diagram).

With *Greyhound*, *Griffin*, *Hereward* and *Defender* positioned to starboard, Captain De Salis had his full strength deployed. The cruisers were in action ahead and the two capital ships firing from astern, and the destroyer men awaited the chance to show their mettle. The only doubt, (fully justified it transpired), was whether the Italians would stay to fight. Five swift cruisers, ten lithe destroyers and

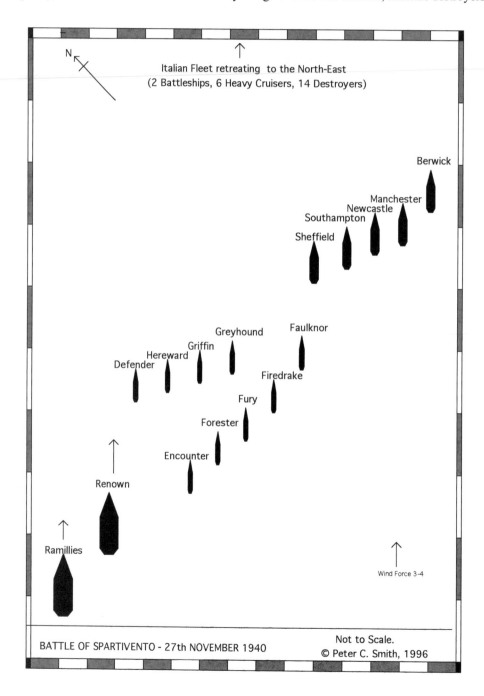

N

Italian Fleet retreating to the North-East
(2 Battleships, 6 Heavy Cruisers, 14 Destroyers)

Berwick

Manchester
Newcastle
Southampton
Sheffield

Greyhound   Faulknor
Griffin
Hereward
Defender   Firedrake

Fury
Forester
Encounter

Renown

Wind Force 3-4

Ramillies

BATTLE OF SPARTIVENTO - 27th NOVEMBER 1940

Not to Scale.
© Peter C. Smith, 1996

two First World War capital ships raced pell-mell toward the Italian fleet, eager to give battle. With the odds heavily in their favour, the superior Italian fleet made their usual decision- it must have been standard training in their pre-war manuals – they turned for home!

Admiral Campioni, '… decided not to become involved in a battle …', turning his ships 180° and heading at top speed for home. But, in order to reach the safety of his own minefields, the Italians had to cross the path of Somerville's squadron; and thus, just after mid-day *Faulknor* sighted the masts of the fleeing enemy dead ahead. Soon our cruisers had opened fire at extreme range and the Italians replied. Both salvoes were accurate; from the destroyer's bridge the splashes from the enemy shells could be seen bursting and, off *Faulknor's* port bow, *Manchester* was straddled.

All still depended on whether the Swordfish striking force could slow them down. While waiting, the British squadron, battle ensigns unfurled and bow waves high, hoped to cut the corner and head them off. At 1207, at extreme range, the fleeing enemy was sighted and excitement increased.

At this juncture *Faulknor* had her eight destroyers formed up five miles 040° from *Renown* and thus perfectly placed by Captain De Salis to counter-attack any move by their Italian opposite numbers against the British heavy ships. No such move was made, or even contemplated by the enemy, who continued to put their trust in their high-speed. While the British cruisers and heavy ships opened fire at very long range *Faulknor* and her companions were, perforce, merely spectators to the long-range duelling.

The Swordfish failed, but in the long-range gunnery duel, *Faulknor* reported seeing at least one hit scored on an enemy ship at 1227. Captain De Salis wrote:

> … a very large cloud of smoke of mushroom form was observed to come from one of the left-hand ships. This was considered to have been a 15-inch hit, and was not associated with the smoke screen the vessel was then emitting.

Lieutenant Commander Robinson of *Fury* reported, also at 1227:

> Ordered by D.8 to concentrate on ships bearing 008°. Range finder reported extreme difficulty in obtaining ranges – one cut of 23,000 yards being obtained. 1223. Observed an enemy salvo to fall about 1,000 yards on port bow, bearing 110°.

The enemy also hit *Berwick* on 'Y' turret, cremating its occupants. These exchanges took place well beyond the range of *Faulknor's* 4.7-inch guns. Ranging shots were made which proved this. Unless the enemy accepted battle or was slowed, there was no chance of emulating her forebear at Jutland and delivering a classic torpedo attack on enemy battleships. Itching for a fight, *Faulknor* had to watch five British cruisers chase the Italian fleet to within thirty miles of their own coast. A few heavy shells, overs from the main duel, landed near *Faulknor* at 1242.

The Italian destroyers disdained battle, confining themselves to laying a smoke-screen to cover the withdrawal.

There was no possibility of *Faulknor's* own 4.7-inch guns playing a part unless the enemy changed his tactics. Lieutenant Commander Norris of *Firedrake* recorded at 1247 that he was ordered by *Faulknor,* '… to engage enemy bearing 350°. Fire was not opened as enemy was considerably outside gun range. Range of 19,000 yards was obtained at 1230, after which range slowly opened.'

The British destroyers were therefore forced to leave it to the heavy ships to decide the issue. It was soon very apparent that the Italian Navy had no more taste for *Renown's* 15-inch salvoes off Spartivento than they had shown for *Warspite's* similar greetings off Calabria five months earlier. The best the British destroyers could do was give the battle-cruiser her chance.

When the British cruisers made their two large alterations of course away from the enemy towards the end of the action, *Faulknor* and her brood conformed with them to avoid fouling their line of fire, and to give them freedom of movement.

The only practice that the British destroyer gunners had was a few ranging shots at a pair of Vichy-French liners which passed like some spectral apparitions through the scene of the naval battle. By 1308 Admiral Somerville signalled his vanguard, 'Is there any chance of catching cruisers?' to which he received the disappointing reply, 'No'.

It was difficult to observe the results of our gunfire at such ranges, although on the British side *Berwick* was hit twice, which reduced her effective main armament by half, but she kept in line. It is now known that on the Italian side heavy cruiser *Fiume* was hit, and destroyer *Lanciere* badly damaged.

It was with a feeling of anti-climax that *Faulknor* now steered back south-east again, although they had the satisfaction of seeing the enemy run from them and their tails were high. Next time *Faulknor* saw the Italian fleet, three years later, they were on their way to Malta to surrender, undamaged but dishonoured. The *Regia Aeronautica* sought to redress the balance with two air attacks out of the sun in V-formation but a heavy barrage and a combined turn by the fleet threw their aim out and there were no hits.

The planes droned off with the loss of two of their number and the convoy continued unharmed. Two further bombing attacks took place in the late afternoon, after Force H had rejoined the convoy, two formations of five planes each, vainly attacking *Ark Royal*.

By 1700, *Faulknor* had the convoy in sight and, at dusk, Force 'H' turned back to the west. They reached Gibraltar unopposed on 29th, having been cheered in by the ships at the Rock.

Faulknor had several days alongside, bows towards the harbour entrance, and watched *Royal Sovereign* and *Newcastle* leave for the UK, 'Home for Christmas, the lucky blanks!', before sailing again on 5 December with *Forester, Eclipse* and *Isis* escorting *Ramillies* for gunnery exercises. The battleship returned to harbour at 1800, but *Faulknor* and *Forester* met submarine *Triumph*, transferring from Home waters to Malta, during the daylight on 7 December and escorted her safely to Gibraltar, all three vessels arriving safely at 1715.

Between 9th and 11 December *Ark Royal* put to sea to conduct intensive flying operations to work up her aircrew, escorted by *Faulknor, Forester, Fury* and *Isis*. Many of these young pilots and observers had only joined the carrier before the triple Malta operations and thus this quiet period was put to good use. Inexperience soon showed itself when a Fulmar and two Swordfish were lost in accidents, the crews of the fighter and one of the bombers being rescued but the four destroyers searched in vain for survivors from the second 'Stringbag'.

About this time *Faulknor* was issued with a Kite, and Surgeon-Lieutenant David Rendall was made 'Kite Officer'. Vernon Coles wryly mused:

> It wasn't a Kite Balloon, it was more like a large Box Kite. What we were supposed to do with it, goodness knows. We were in the Med when it was shipped on board but it was an abject failure!

They returned to Gibraltar briefly and, on 12 December, sailed to carry out one of a series of interceptions of Vichy convoys, Operation 'Ration', returning hastily the following day when this was postponed.

The next big Mediterranean operation was to be the passage of another Malta convoy and transfer west of battleship *Malaya*, but in the interim there were alarms and excursions aplenty to keep the destroyers fully occupied. The first was intelligence reports of a German move against the Azores, which caused 'Ration' to be aborted before it began. Force 'H' sailed at 1040/14 December to patrol north of that group of islands. The squadron was *Renown* and *Ark Royal*, screened by *Faulknor, Forester, Fury, Encounter, Duncan* and *Isis*. The weather was unkind, with strong seas running, but apart from the investigation of suspicious merchant vessels and gunnery and torpedo exercises, nothing untoward interrupted their voyage and, after three days of chasing shadows, the whole force returned to Gibraltar on 19 December.

They sailed again at 1716/20th with *Renown*, *Ark Royal*, *Sheffield*, *Faulknor*, *Firedrake*, *Forester*, *Fortune, Foxhound* and *Fury,* to carry out Operation 'Hide'. The destroyers *Duncan*, *Encounter*, *Isis*, *Wishart* and *Jaguar* went on ahead to carry out Operation 'Seek', rendezvousing with the empty merchant ships, *Clan Forbes* and *Clan Fraser* from Malta and the home-coming *Malaya,* off the Skerki Channel. Force 'H' met the complete 'Seek' party south of Sardinia and returned without opposition to Gibraltar Christmas Eve.

Faulknor secured on 24 December, 1940, and most on board felt pretty sure that Christmas might be observed in the peace and relative calmness of the dockyard. The wardroom and the various officers' and mess decks were vividly, perhaps amateurishly, decorated, and a large stock of 'Christmas Spirits' was stored up in readiness, a general air of festive cheer pervading the whole squadron. This spirit was not even dampened by the heavy and prolonged rain, which poured down all day on 25th. The weather could not spoil their Christmas dinner – but the Germans did!

Hopes of a peaceful Christmas evaporated when a signal was received from the Admiralty ordering Force H to, 'raise steam with all despatch.' The German heavy cruiser *Admiral Hipper* attacked the troop convoy WS5A at dawn in a position 700 miles off Cape Finisterre. The German vessel was presented with an irresistible target including aircraft-carriers *Argus* and *Furious*, their decks full of fighters for Takoradi and five laden freighters destined for the Middle East. In such a state the carriers could no more defend themselves than *Glorious* had off Norway, and again the vulnerability of carriers was exposed. Fortunately, the convoy was protected by heavy cruiser *Berwick* and light cruisers *Bonaventure* and *Dunedin* and the German ship soon found she had bit off more than she could chew. After a brisk exchange at long range during which SS *Empire Trooper* and *Berwick* were both hit by 8-inch shells, *Admiral Hipper* abandoned the attack and fled to Brest.

Less than three hours after receiving the message, the destroyers were putting to sea, followed by the big ships. Admiral Somerville rushed his squadron out in an attempt to head the enemy raider off, sailing at 1400 Christmas Day with *Renown*, *Ark Royal*, *Sheffield*, *Faulknor*, *Firedrake*, *Fortune, Foxhound*, *Duncan*, *Hero, Hereward* and *Wishart*. The fact that several of the small ships' bridges' paper hats had replaced the more conventional headgear, or that toy trumpets were reputed to have been used in place of bosons' whistles, did not go unnoticed by Admiral Somerville. He, more than any other man, had wanted his command to enjoy a brief respite from continual operations, and it was with an understanding gleam in his eye that the sent the destroyers the signal: 'The number of ships which blew off when raising steam showed a great keenness on the part of the force to go to sea – or was it just Christmas Day in the boiler room?'

With such a man to lead them, even sea time on 25 December was almost acceptable. 'Never mind, Nobby, only another 364 days to the next one!'

But it was not all humour that day, tragedy also played a part. The sea was running high as *Faulknor* sailed at top speed out of harbour. Vernon Coles recalled:

> We sailed out of Gibraltar so fast on Christmas Day, 1940, that *Faulknor* heeled right over and our 32 year-old 'Jack Dusty' [Petty Officer, Supply] Idris Wiliam Wirtz, rolled off his desk in his little cubby hole, where he had been sleeping and broke his neck. Eric Welby, who at that time had just joined the ship as a young supply assistant, discovered him on the deck in the supply office. His body was taken to the Captain's Day Cabin back aft, where it was sewn into a hammock ready for burial by the ships 'Buffer', Petty Officer Bacon. We buried him at sea that night.

Force H was soon reeling westward into the teeth of a vicious gale. As the men who had started celebrating early and finished late began to regret it – for rough weather in the Bay of Biscay has a remarkably sobering effect – the 'Temperance men' aboard *Faulknor* became convinced of their wisdom.

The situation was chaotic, *Admiral Hipper* had vanished in stormy weather, sinking an independently-routed steamer as she went, the convoy was scattered and *Berwick* was damaged. Various moves were made to bring all the ships together once more while Force 'H' ploughed the angry ocean to provide cover. Apart from taking a pasting from the elements, which led to *Renown* and other ships to require docking, and the delay of the next operation, their patrolling was unrewarded. By midnight the little destroyers could no longer keep up in the prevailing storm conditions, even at reduced speed. *Sheffield* and some of the destroyers rode the storm out while the big ships pushed on. Other flotilla craft, including *Faulknor,* had to be sent back to refuel, and she arrived back at Gibraltar at 1512/28th.

Next morning the gale had moderated sufficiently to enable them to make a search for the scattered ships of the attacked convoy. *Faulknor* refuelled and sailed again with *Firedrake, Hasty* and *Jaguar* at 2015. She personally managed to round up three of the freighters and shepherded them back towards the Straits, later joining up with carriers *Argus* and *Furious* and then going on ahead with *Firedrake* to escort them in, arriving back at the Rock early next morning. Another quick turn at the oiler and then out again to meet *Renown* and *Ark Royal*, the flagship having suffered heavy weather damage, and the whole force was back at the Rock at 0830/30 December.

Admiral Somerville, was already planning the passing of the next sortie, Operation 'Excess'. Five large and fast merchant ships were to be taken through the Mediterranean despite all the risks involved, *Clan Cumming, Clan McDonald, Northern Prince* and *Empire Song* for Piraeus, Greece and *Essex* for Malta. The remaining ships from the WS5A convoy were routed via the Cape of Good Hope. Accompanying the convoy were reinforcements for Admiral Cunningham, light cruiser *Bonaventure* and destroyers *Hasty, Hero, Hereward* and *Jaguar*, (Force 'F') and meeting the convoy in the 'Narrows' would be light cruisers *Gloucester* and *Southampton* with destroyers *Ilex* and *Janus*.

To provide the usual cover and heavy fire-power Force 'H' sailed at 0800/7 January with *Renown, Malaya, Ark Royal, Sheffield, Faulknor, Firedrake, Forester, Fortune, Foxhound, Fury* and *Duncan,* while the four merchant ships (*Northern Prince* having gone ashore in a gale and being omitted from the operation), *Bonaventure* and Force 'F' which had sailed west the day before, then turned back through the Straits. *Bonaventure* joined Somerville and the main body positioned themselves north-east of the convoy during the initial stages of the journey eastward.

For *Faulknor* the first two days proved quiet as usual on these 'Club Runs'. At 1018 the two cruisers and two destroyers of Force 'B' joined, but it was not until 1300 that the first Italian air opposition was encountered, ten SM.79 bombers, in three ragged formations, bombing from 8,000 feet.

The four merchant ships of the convoy were steaming in two columns in line ahead. The columns were led by *Malaya* and *Gloucester* respectively, and at the rear of the columns were *Bonaventure* and *Southampton*. Seven destroyers provided the screen ahead, while *Faulknor* and her six consorts screened *Renown, Ark Royal* and *Sheffield*, the whole force being in close support on the port quarter of the convoy. All ships were zigzagging at fourteen knots.

At 1346, the attack commenced and all ships opened fire. Most of the bombs were directed against *Malaya*, (mistaken for *King George V*). No bombs hit her, although she and *Gloucester* were near-missed. *Bonaventure's* 5.25's knocked down one of the enemy, *Ark Royal's* fighters shot down two more, their crews being rescued by *Forester* and *Foxhound*. This proved to be the sole Italian air effort against the convoy.

There was still the threat from below the waves. That same afternoon *Faulknor* took part in a submarine hunt, without success. On reaching their pre-arranged position at dusk, Force 'H' turned back some 30 miles west of the Narrows. The weather proved tougher than the enemy for they ran into a gale but, by 12 January 1941, they were safely back at Gibraltar.

Meantime, south of Malta, German Ju.87 dive-bombers crippled carrier *Illustrious* and sank light cruiser *Southampton,* heralding a new era in the Mediterranean war. For Force H the lesson was clear, convoys to Malta would no longer be easy.

For *Faulknor* this was academic, for when she sailed again next day it was to the west, meeting and escorting troop convoy WS. 5B bound for the Cape. The twenty-one troopships had 40,000 soldiers embarked and had a strong escort, battleship *Ramillies*, heavy cruiser *Australia,* light cruisers *Naiad* and *Phoebe* and twelve destroyers, relieved for part of the journey by Force 'H' destroyers, of which *Faulknor* was one. Two troopships, *Cape Town Castle* and *Monarch of Bermuda*, entered Gibraltar, leaving again 19 January, escorted by *Faulknor, Fearless, Forester, Fury* and *Duncan*.

FOCNA signalled at 1816 that day:

> *Faulknor* parts company with *Monarch of Bermuda* and escorts 20/1 and returns to Gibraltar.

However, on 21st, was signalling:

> *Faulknor* is now escorting *Monarch of Bermuda* and *Cape Town Castle* to Freetown.

This proved slow and uneventful. It was not until the morning of 26th that *Faulknor* and *Forester* arrived at Freetown with the troopships, while the other destroyers took *Furious* back to Gibraltar.

They were now temporarily attached to the Freetown Escort Force.

* * *

Sierra Leone lies almost on the equator, and Freetown itself lay some distance up a swift-flowing river, with a wide anchorage suitable for the largest ships. Surrounded by dense forests and steamy swamps it was not an ideal naval base, and *Faulknor's* crew, so recently grumbling at the cold spray off Cape Spartel, soon longed heartily to return.

An enormous flow of convoys from all over the Empire called at Freetown on their way to or from the UK or Middle East. Attracted by the ever-growing volume of valuable convoys, U-boats soon began to gather in search of easier pickings than found farther north.

There were also German surface raiders loose in the Atlantic, so valuable WS convoys were given battleship escorts southward, before handing-over to East Indies fleet cruisers. To temporarily fill the escort shortage until more destroyers could be found, a division of the 8th Flotilla from Gibraltar was provided, under overall command of Captain De Salis in *Faulknor*.

They spent 27 and 28 January at Freetown before WS. 5B sailed on the next leg of its journey at 0630/29 January with heavy cruiser *Australia,* destroyers *Faulknor* and *Forester*, sloop *Milford* and corvettes *Cyclamen* and *Clematis*. The two destroyers remained with the convoy until 1800/1 February and then returned to Freetown.

At 0945 3 February, in 04° 33′ N, 10° 33′ W, when 22 hours away from Freetown, *Faulknor* sighted a small boat containing four men from the tanker *British Premier*, torpedoed on 20 December, 1940. Vernon Cole recalled:

> While on passage we were carrying out the usual exercises with *Forester,* who was hull-down on our Port side. A signalman, Jack Bresnan, was flashing a signal to *Forester* with the large Aldis lamp when he saw a speck carry over a wave top, the sea being quite rough. He immediately reported seeing an object to the Officer of the Watch and we altered course to investigate. When we closed it, we found a ship's lifeboat with four people in it who we thought were dead. As we went alongside one of the four lifted his head so we quickly got them on board. They were all alive but only just and were terribly emaciated. They looked worse than any Belsen inmate.

The four men had spent 41 days in the open boat, without water until the eleventh day when rain fell, and without food, save for one seagull, since the 31st day when their biscuits gave out. *Faulknor* arrived back at Freetown at 0810 next day and landed the survivors. 'A few weeks later these survivors came back aboard *Faulknor* to thank us and they were almost back to normal condition again. A welcome result from Jack Bresnan's incredible chance sighting.'

While at Freetown another visitor met a rather more severe fate. Again Vernon Cole:

> It was whilst we were at Freetown that Ordinary Seaman Cole brought a monkey on board and it got loose when we were at sea. It ran up the funnel guys and, attempting to get over the funnel top, was believed to have been cremated!

On 7 February, the C-in-C South Atlantic ordered *Faulknor* and *Forester* to sail from Freetown at 0800 next day and rendezvous with Force 'Z' (freighters *Alsey*, *Bullfinch* and *Kirriemoor*, with supplies for the Middle East army, going the long, but safer, route via Freetown and the Cape) at 0900/9th, in 12° 35′ N, 18° 10′ W and escort them back to Freetown. This they complied with and, at 1641, they received another signal to act as local escort for the convoy and heavy cruiser *Dorsetshire*. They reached Freetown at 1000/10 February and sailed with the same ships at 0555/11th, remaining with Force 'Z' until 0600/13th, when the two destroyers were instructed to return to

HMS Faulknor *(centre) with a convoy and a 'Colony' class cruiser (right) while working with the Freetown Escort Force, spring 1941.* (Crown Copyright.)

Freetown, adjusting their speed to arrive at 0600/15 February. Admiralty signal timed at 2125/12 February, confirmed they were to rejoin Force 'H' at Gibraltar as soon as available, and that two older destroyers, *Vidette* and *Wishart*, (themselves replaced later by *Velox* and *Wrestler* as being 'more suitable' for the South Atlantic), would be sailed from the Rock in time to escort convoy WS. 6 into Freetown instead.

Further planning confirmed their return to Somerville's control, Admiral Raikes stating *Faulknor* and *Forester* would probably sail from Freetown on the afternoon of 16th or the morning of 17 February. He asked that their replacements should be sailed to arrive at Freetown by 21 February. Further arrangements followed, with the Admiralty signal of 1727/16th stating that it was intended that SL.67 would be escorted by battleship *Malaya* from Freetown to the latitude of the Azores when light cruiser *Kenya* would take over for the rest of the journey to the UK. *Malaya* herself was to be brought ahead of WS.6 and sailed to overtake SL. 67 escorted by *Faulknor* and *Forester*, who were later to be released to proceed to Gibraltar while *Malaya* returned to the UK.

Accordingly, *Faulknor* and *Forester* left Freetown at 1800/22 February and proceeded to rendezvous with WS. 6 in 17° 20′ N, 27° 45′ W, at 0800/25 February. Their stay was brief for, at 1815/28 February, they were ordered to leave the convoy with *Malaya*, and increase speed to pass the Freetown boom at 1600/1 March.

After refuelling, they sailed with *Malaya* at 1705 to overtake and escort convoy SL.67. *Malaya* was to remain with the convoy until relieved by light cruiser *Arethusa* in 37° 51′ N, 22° 34′ W at 1200/14 March, but the two destroyers were to be detached in latitude 20° W, proceeding to Gibraltar, steering east of the Canary Islands to arrive on 0800/10 March.

So much for the plans; but it was *not* to work out quite like that.

* * *

The three warships joined the convoy at 1500/3 March in 10° 20′ N, 18° W, and escorted them onward. Convoy SL.67 (SL = Sierre Leone) consisted of fifty-five heavily-laden freighters disposed in eleven columns of five ships each with the Convoy Commodore, Commodore Illingworth, embarked in *City of Nagpur* leading column six in the centre. The whole mass of shipping covered many square miles of ocean. (See Diagram p. 83).

On the night of the 6/7 March the Admiralty signalled that the convoy's route was to be altered to the eastward and that the two destroyers were to be kept in company to the limit of their endurance. This was to avoid an enemy submarine reported to be west of the Canary Islands. At dawn on 7th, course was altered to 016°. During the afternoon of the 7 March *Malaya* refuelled *Faulknor* and *Forester* in the centre of the convoy, on a course of 346° and the convoy maintained this course to facilitate the operation until 1700, when they altered course 40° to starboard to get back to starboard of the mean line of advance. The battleship also had to give corvette *Asphodel* eighty tons of oil fuel to enable her to reach Gibraltar with two of the convoy later on.

At 2000 the convoy altered course 30° to port, and at midnight altered course 30° to starboard, resuming the mean line of advance. If this zigzag was meant to throw any shadowing U-boats off the scent, then it failed completely. The fuelling course and other alterations placed the convoy twenty-five miles to the westward of the Admiralty's recommended amended route. A further signal from London timed at 1409, which placed a U-boat in 22° N, 21° W, steering south, was not received in the *Malaya* until 0717/8th when it was all over.

The night was dark and clear, with a slight sea and no swell. The visibility was unfortunately good and the wind northeast 2–3. The moon had set just before 0200 on the 8th. *Malaya* was stationed in her usual position in the heart of the convoy between the 6th and 7th columns. Armed Merchant cruiser *Cilicia* was stationed between the 5th and 6th columns. She proceeded ahead of the convoy each dawn, while corvette *Asphodel,* whose Asdic set was inoperational, was positioned ahead of the centre of the convoy by day, and astern the rear of the convoy by night. *Faulknor* and *Forester* were stationed abeam the wing columns during the day, dropping back to cover both quarters, six cables between columns 6 and 7, at night. Course was 355° and speed 6³/₄ knots. It was then that the U-boats *U-105* and *U-124* struck, in 20° 51' North, 20° 32 West.

Between 0251 and 0256 five ships were torpedoed and sunk, *Hindapool, Harmodius, Tielbank, Nardana* and *Lahore*. Commodore Illingworth heard two or three subdued explosions abaft the port beam of the convoy, mistaken for depth charges. Four rockets, each about three minutes apart, went up on the convoy's port wing. The destroyers were seen using their searchlights on the port wing but no red lights from any of the torpedoed ships were observed, although this was mandatory.

At 0258 the convoy made an emergency turn 40° to starboard but, at 0304, *Lahore,* then on the starboard side of *City of Nagdapur*, burst into flames just forward of her bridge. This was followed at 0321 by a W/T transmission from *Lahore* consisting of the single word, 'Explosion' and was taken by Commodore Illingworth to confirm his own theory that an internal explosion had taken place. *Faulknor, Forester* and SS *Guido* all picked up *Lahore's* survivors. Commodore Illingworth reasoned that, if two U-boats were present (which was in fact so) then one would continue on the convoy's original course whilst the other would cut across the convoy's rear and so he continued to steer a course of 035° until 0630 when the original course was resumed again.

We now turn from how the Commodore saw the attack to the view from the warships' bridges. *Forester,* on the port quarter of the convoy, heard two explosions and increased speed at once to take up a position on the port bow. They immediately sighted the wake of a U-boat apparently retiring to the westward, and soon afterwards they glimpsed the submarine itself altering its course to the northward and submerging in a position 260°, four miles from the convoy. *Forester* illuminated the U-boat with her searchlight and fired three salvoes of 4.7-inch, following these shells up with two depth-charge patterns over the position where the enemy was seen to have submerged. *Forester's* skipper thought the charges were close enough to have damaged the U-boat. It transpired that *U-105* was forced to stay submerged by these depth-charge attacks until the afternoon of the 8 March and *U-124* was driven off.

Asphodel saw one torpedo track pass down her starboard side. It was assumed therefore that the U-boat had made an attack on the surface and had fired a salvo of six torpedoes from broad on the port bow of the convoy as a 'browning shot' and incredibly had been rewarded with five hits and five kills out of six, with one near-miss.

On *Malaya's* bridge in the centre of the convoy no explosions had been felt, and the first indication of problems she had was at 0251 when a white rocket was fired on the port beam, followed five minutes later by two more. She complied with an emergency turn to starboard and held that course until 0630. At 0303 *Lahore* was seen to be on fire forward but the fate of the other vessels was not known in the battleship. *Forester* reported at 0332 that she was hunting 260°, five miles from the burning ship. At 0527 Captain De Salis in *Faulknor* reported that both destroyers were searching in the vicinity and would pick up survivors at dawn. He had ordered *Asphodel,* whose Asdic set was still out of order, to remain with the convoy.

Vernon Cole remembers that eventful night:

> In the tropics it was so hot below deck that we were permitted to sleep on the upper deck providing we didn't impede the ships fighting integrity. That night we had an alarm to starboard and, as our guns were swung in that direction, it was found that a hammock had been slung on No. 3 gun barrel. The gun had to train fore and aft for the body to be abruptly tipped out, I believe it was Stoker Oram.

Both *Faulknor* and *Forester* rejoined the convoy at 1130 and Captain De Salis reported the names of the ships sunk in the attack and that the destroyers had rescued 68 Europeans and 245 Lascar

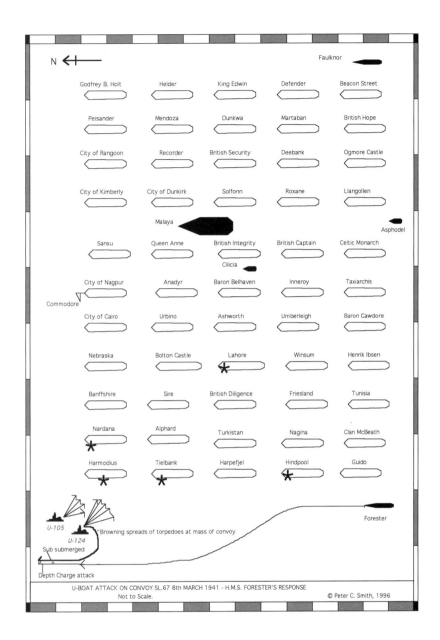

N ←┼—

Faulknor

Godfrey B. Holt	Helder	King Edwin	Defender	Beacon Street
Peisander	Mendoza	Dunkwa	Martaban	British Hope
City of Rangoon	Recorder	British Security	Deebank	Ogmore Castle
City of Kimberly	City of Dunkirk	Solfonn	Roxane	Llangollen

Malaya

Asphodel

| Sansu | Queen Anne | British Integrity | British Captain | Celtic Monarch |

Cilicia

| City of Nagpur | Anadyr | Baron Belhaven | Inneroy | Taxiarchis |

Commodore

City of Cairo	Urbino	Ashworth	Umberleigh	Baron Cawdore
Nebraska	Bolton Castle	Lahore	Winsum	Henrik Ibsen
Banffshire	Sire	British Diligence	Friesland	Tunisia
Nardana	Alphard	Turkistan	Nagina	Clan McBeath
Harmodius	Tielbank	Harpefjel	Hindpool	Guido

U-105

U-124

Sub submerged

'Browning spreads of torpedoes at mass of convoy'

Forester

Depth Charge attack

U-BOAT ATTACK ON CONVOY SL.67 8th MARCH 1941 - H.M.S. FORESTER'S RESPONSE
Not to Scale.

© Peter C. Smith, 1996

survivors from these ships. The destroyers were ordered to modify the escort pattern and drop astern at dusk to put down any submarines possibly shadowing, then to take station on either beam of the wing columns, working up and down between the leading and rear ships. The undersea enemy had struck suddenly and hard, but the convoy now had to face a potentially far worse threat.

During the same afternoon *Forester* was carrying out an anti-submarine search ten miles to the west of the convoy, when, in 21° 50′ N, 19° 40′ W, about 130 miles W.N.W. of Cape Blanco, West Africa, she sighted a large warship, hull down, bearing 290°. At 1331 *Forester*, on reporting this to *Malaya*, was ordered to investigate and unhesitatingly steered to close the ominous contact. She had not closed much of the distance between them before it became very clear indeed to those on *Forester's* bridge that the ship they were steaming at high speed towards was a 26,500-ton German battle-cruiser. She signalled at 1410 via W/T, 'One sighting top and one funnel' and at 1442, 'Possibly *Gneisenau*'. All on the British warships knew that if one *Scharnhorst* class battle-cruiser was present, her sister would not be far away. Suddenly the fifty surviving merchants ships of SL.67 looked very vulnerable indeed.

Ordering Commodore Illingworth to steer the convoy 046° away from the sighting, *Malaya* and *Faulknor* turned westward to intercept the enemy and, at 1645, *Gneisenau* was sighted, bearing 263° steaming directly towards them. Three minutes later, however, the enemy turned away and retired to the south-west at high speed. *Malaya* and *Faulknor* continued to close the enemy whom *Forester* reported was altering course at high speed and, at 1515, *Malaya* catapulted her spotter aircraft ready for a gunnery duel.

Aboard *Faulknor* the same tense feeling of exhilaration mixed with fear that had uplifted them off Cape Spartivento four months earlier pervaded the ship as they raced on; now, as then, the odds were heavily stacked against them – one old, unmodernised battleship and two little destroyers against Germany's two most powerful warships.

At 1645, *Scharnhorst* was in sight from *Malaya's* fighting top at fifteen miles range and the old veteran's eight 15-inch guns rose to full elevation waiting for the range to come down, her twenty-five year old hull straining as she churned onwards at the best speed of twenty knots. *Forester* took station ahead with *Faulknor* on either bow, their lean hulls also thrusting swiftly forward, torpedo tubes trained outward in anticipation; while down in the engine room they prepared to make a smoke screen which would shelter them should *Malaya* be unable to cope with *both* enemy ships at the same time and they were called upon to make a suicidal dash into the enemy's guns.

However, three minutes later the enemy was again seen to alter course to the south-west and increase speed. All the German ship's turrets remained trained fore-and-aft and it was clear that they were not going to get involved in a fight. In fact the German Admiral, Lutjen's, had no stomach for mixing it. He disengaged rapidly and later signalled its position to the waiting U-boat pack. Once again the incredible had happened – with the odds high in his favour the enemy, German this time and not Italian, was once again refusing combat. The *Malaya* was at the very least ten knots slower than the German battle-cruisers, so, after a brief pursuit, all three British ships turned back towards the convoy in case the enemy should decide to use that superiority in speed to work round behind them and annihilate it. Lutjens had *no* such intention; well aware that he had been sighted and his position given away, his chief aim now was to get as far away from the area as he could. Signalling the latest position of the convoy to two U-boats in the vicinity, he sped northwards. He had missed a golden opportunity. One of his two ships could have engaged *Malaya,* her greater speed and range of her modern guns enabling her to keep out of trouble and damage, or even sink the old warrior, while his other battle-cruiser could have attacked the convoy unhindered. No such plan of action seems to have occurred to the Germans: perhaps they had no wish to be entangled with British destroyers again, just one of those eight 21-inch torpedoes that remained to the two British ships would have meant a battle-cruiser crippled and helpless and miles from the nearest safe haven. As a deterrent the British destroyer's 'Sunday Punch' had again proved its worth.

When, during the previous June, these same two German ships had sunk aircraft-carrier *Glorious* off Norway, the torpedo-hit escorting destroyer *Acasta* had scored on *Scharnhorst* had put her out of the war for six months. A similar blow here, in the wastes of the South Atlantic, would be the equivalent of a lost ship, for Lutjens knew he would stand no chance of getting such a lame duck back to Brest.

Malaya and *Faulknor* were by this time twenty-five miles from the convoy, steaming away from it fast. The chance of bringing a ship of the enemy's speed to action in the remaining hour-and-a-half of daylight did not seem to *Malaya's* captain to justify further separation of the escort from the convoy and he decided to return to the convoy at once. At 1651, therefore, they altered course to 070° and *Forester* was ordered to close. At 1704, *Malaya's* aircraft reported two enemy battle-cruisers retiring to the westward at twenty knots, and she confirmed this later. This aircraft was ordered to stay in contact with the enemy squadron as long as possible and return to *Malaya* by 1800, half-an-hour before sunset, but, in the event was unable to locate convoy or *Malaya* and force-landed in the dark at 2004.

The German battle-cruisers later reported *Faulknor* as a 'light cruiser', even though the smallest cruiser that the Royal Navy possessed was *three times Faulknor's* size and tonnage! Once again, the bold face automatically adopted by the Royal Navy had saved the lives of many merchant seamen, and, by 1900, they had their convoy in sight.

The three British warships rejoined at 1900, half-an-hour after sunset. They expected the enemy to return to the attack after dark and tension therefore remained high during that night. Meanwhile both *U-105* and *U-124* were reporting to *Gruppe West*, that they had sighted the convoy. The Admiralty duly informed *Malaya* that at 1828 *Scharnhorst* had made a signal on the U-boat frequency, evidently reporting the position of the convoy and they further signalled at 1416 on Sunday 9 March that signals on the U-boat frequency indicated a U-boat was in contact with SL.67. *Malaya* reported at 1829Z that the German battle-cruisers were last seen at 1829Z steering 245° at twenty knots. The Admiralty confirmed at 1416 on the 9th that it was intended that battleship cover would be provided for the SL.67 convoys and that *Renown* and *Ark Royal*, would take over the escort of SL.67 on the afternoon of the 10th, while the extra bout of steaming at high speed had encroached on the two destroyers oil fuel reserves and both ships were therefore given 50 tons by *Malaya*, sufficient for them to remain with the convoy until the afternoon 12 March.

At 1500/10 March, in 26° 15′ N, 19° 35′ W, Force 'H' was sighted, *Renown* and *Ark Royal* therefore relieved *Malaya* as Ocean Escort for SL.67 and she shaped course for Freetown at 18$\frac{1}{2}$ knots. A dusk reconnaissance flight by Swordfish to a depth of 45 miles revealed no sign of the enemy squadron and after dark course was altered 30° to port and back to 347° four hours later. The two big ships took station in the centre of the convoy with *Asphodel* ahead and *Faulknor* and *Forester* on either wing.

On 11 March *Asphodel* parted company with *British Hope* and *Beacon Street* for Gibraltar as arranged, the rest of the convoy continued northward at 7$\frac{1}{2}$ knots and this continued throughout the following day, an attempt by Somerville to increase the convoy's speed by half a knot resulted in *Taxiarchis* straggling and they had to resume the original speed again. On 13 March *Faulknor* and *Forester* closed with *Renown* and *Ark Royal* respectively and transferred mails to *City of Nagpur* for transfer to the UK. On completion of this operation the two destroyers were detached to Gibraltar and a range and inclination exercise was carried out until they were out of sight. Both destroyers finally docked alongside the Mole on 16 March.

* * *

Nine months of strenuous steaming had taken the expected toll and *Faulknor* was now well over-due for a boiler-clean and general refit; her weather-strained hull also needed examination. The Admiral Superintendent, Gibraltar Dockyard signalled at 1948 on the 16th:

> *Faulknor* docks M.3 for repairs to rudder and stern bushes, estimated ten days.

On the 17th they unloaded all ammunition into lighters alongside and conned the ship into the dockyard. Leave was granted to all watches and, for ten days *Faulknor* was 'out of it'. They remained so until 27 March. She was now one of the surviving senior members of the Force H 'Club', that generally happy band to which warships that had served a certain length of time with Somerville were entitled to join. It was a very select group, with a mythical club tie, 'raspberries on a field of Mediterranean grey', symbolising their defiant attitude towards adversity.

With *Scharnhorst*, *Gneisenau* and *Admiral Hipper* at Brest, a constant watch had to be kept lest they slip away to sea again. The Home Fleet and Force H took turns at watching patrols.

CHAPTER IV

'Twixt Malta and the Bay

Towards the end of March 1941, *Faulknor* rejoined Force H. The Admiralty was still concerned about Vichy French convoys carrying vital war material for the Nazi war machine and intelligence occasionally got wind of 'special' cargoes. The Admiralty instructed Somerville to intercept certain ships, using our belligerent legal right of search and contraband control.

On 29 March *Faulknor*, *Fearless*, *Forester* and *Fury* sailed at 2200 with light cruiser *Sheffield*, to intercept one such convoy of six freighters escorted by two destroyers sailing from Casablanca via the Straits to Marseilles. One ship, *Bangkok* from Indo-China carrying 3,000 tons of rubber destined for the *Wehrmacht, was* intercepted off Nemours. *Sheffield* signalled the convoy to stop and Captain De Salis instructed *Fearless* to go in and 'cut out' *Bangkok* in the 'old-fashioned style', but she was driven off by fire from the 6-inch guns from a shore battery. The issue could have been forced but, because the British warships were required for more important jobs, after an exchange of salvoes between the fortress and *Sheffield* and *Fearless*, the latter backed off. (The rubber was unloaded at Casablanca and still reached the Germans).

On 31st, Force 'H', *Renown* and *Ark Royal*, screened by destroyers *Napier*, *Nizam* and *Fortune*, arrived at Gibraltar after another fruitless patrol in the south-west Bay of Biscay hunting the elusive German battle-cruisers, which, on 28th, were located docked at Brest. The carrier embarked twelve Hurricane fighters for Malta ready for the next planned ferry flight, Operation 'Winch'.

At 0200/2 April following another storm the destroyers were able to carry out A/S sweeps in the Bay preparatory to the heavy ships leaving at 0240. By 0330, *Renown* and *Ark Royal,* screened by *Faulknor*, *Fearless, Foresight*, *Fortune* and *Fury,* were proceeding on course 082° at seventeen knots. *Sheffield* was delayed and did not catch up until daylight. The weather steadily deteriorated during the day and the wind increased, the force remaining undetected.

At 0600 next day, in 37° 42' N, 06° 52' E, some 400 nautical miles from Malta, two Skua dive-bombers were flown off and led the Hurricanes safely to that island. The aircraft launched, Force 'H' withdrew westward at 27 knots, the weather now becoming fair with good visibility, and the squadron returned to Gibraltar at 1230/4 April.

On return, all ships fuelled, then remained at short notice for steaming for Operation 'Principal', the transfer of Fulmar and Skua squadrons stores between *Ark Royal* and *Furious* having been completed. Meanwhile Vichy battle-cruiser *Dunkerque* was reported as preparing to leave Oran for Toulon, and Somerville was ordered to prevent this happening.

At 1915/8 April, *Renown*, *Ark Royal*, *Furious* and *Sheffield* screened by *Faulknor*, *Fearless, Foresight* and *Fortune* sailed. They proceeded eastward at eighteen knots until 2200, when course was reversed and speed increased to twenty knots. However, at 0157 'Principal' was cancelled until further notice. *Renown* and *Ark Royal* were ordered to carry out four-day refits instead. At 0330, the force met light cruiser *Fiji* on her way south-east from Cape St. Vincent and, at 0710 they sighted *Repulse* hull-down, bearing 230°. *Furious* and *Ark Royal* exchanged aircraft at sea (Operation 'Fender') four Swordfish fitted with ASV and ten Fulmars transferring to *Ark*, four Swordfish and nine Skuas to *Furious*. At 1045, *Furious*, screened by *Faulknor* and *Fortune,* was detached to join *Repulse*.

After transferring *Furious* to *Repulse's* force the two 'Fs' rejoined Force 'H' returning to Gibraltar. At 1530, Somerville ordered *Faulknor* to conduct a brief search for a reported sailing vessel containing Danish seamen from Casablanca anxious to join the allied forces, but no trace of them was found and they entered harbour at 2230. As *Faulknor* secured alongside, a message was received ordering Force 'H' and *Fiji* to raise steam! While awaiting amplification, all the ships hastily refuelled. At 0230, *Faulknor* and the two other available destroyers proceeded at twelve knots to carry out the usual anti-submarine sweep while the big ships of Force 'H' slid past. Somerville had been ordered out into the Bay of Biscay and placed under the orders of C-in-C, Home Fleet to help maintain the blockade of *Scharnhorst* and the *Gneisenau* at Brest. There were intelligence indications (again false) that this elusive pair might be preparing to sail back into the Atlantic.

By 0300/6 April *Faulknor* was leading *Renown*, *Ark Royal*, light cruisers *Fiji* and *Sheffield*, and destroyers *Fearless* and *Foresight* to sea for another fruitless pounding in the restless waters of the Bay of Biscay. Soon after daybreak they had to alter course to avoid a group of Spanish fishing vessels, thus dashing any hope they may have had of remaining unobserved. They received warning of five Italian submarines passing through the Straits at this time, so the destroyer screen was somewhat slender, but all that was immediately available. They steamed north, Force 'H' conducting exercises using *Fiji's* new Type 284 radar to pass range and bearings to *Renown's* guns, using *Sheffield* as the target vessel.

Soon after midnight news came in that the enemy had *not* sailed and a watching patrol was adopted. To keep the destroyers on station during this long period on the afternoon of the 7th, *Faulknor* and the other destroyers each proceeded alongside *Renown* and received 105 tons of oil, the time alongside averaging an hour and fourteen minutes. This was a particularly vulnerable period for both parties, with the active screen reduced to just two ships. Further reconnaissance reports still had the enemy at anchor, which photographs confirmed.

Visibility throughout the 8th was variable but from *Faulknor's* bridge flashes were observed on the horizon, bearing 130°. A Swordfish was sent to investigate but found nothing. If it had been surfaced U-boats signalling each other, they had dived. Thick fog enveloped the squadron between 1600 and 1845 with visibility reduced at times to only a few hundred yards. Later that evening *King George V* returned to Scapa Flow and *Repulse* to Gibraltar, so Somerville assumed control of *Hood* and *Queen Elizabeth* which remained on watch in the Bay.

At 0830, a plain language signal from RAF's 19 Group HQ was intercepted instructing aircraft to, '… patrol to maximum prudent limit of endurance. Battle-cruisers may have left 0830'. Admiral Somerville expressed surprise that such a message should have been sent uncoded. Course was altered to 320° to enable each destroyer to once more top up with 107-tons of oil fuel from *Renown*. At 1140, another warning was received from light cruiser *Dunedin* on passage to Gibraltar, to the effect that a large vessel, possibly a warship, escorted by three destroyers, was leaving Brest. This later turned out to be a freighter and *not* one of the battle-cruisers but such alerts helped screw up the tension. Other than a Portuguese fruit boat, investigated by *Faulknor*, nothing was sighted throughout the day.

At 0230/10th, *Scharnhorst* and her sister were again photographed snug at the moorings in Brest but the watch continued in the face of a rising sea whipped up by a north-east wind that rapidly escalated into a gale. At 0740, the speed of the squadron was reduced to fourteen knots, and course was altered to 340° to bring the sea on the beam and improve conditions for the destroyers. By 1300, the weather had continued to worsen and course was altered to 120° to keep as much to windward as possible 'without punishing the destroyers.' *Fiji* parted company that night for Gibraltar and by that time the wind and sea, 'had risen considerably and a speed of twelve knots could not be exceeded without the destroyers bumping excessively.'

The seas were by now throwing the destroyers about like toy boats in a millrace. Admiral Somerville was particularly concerned about the lack of rest; some of Force H's ships had not given their crews leave for months and no matter how high morale is in a front-line unit, all work and no play, if not making Jack Tar a dull boy, at least took the edge off his enthusiasm. There were also outstanding defects in some of his ships caused by the protracted operations with no opportunities for repairs. Somerville himself later recorded in his annual summary that *Faulknor* had spent 266 days at sea and run 84,000 miles in 230 days, more than any other ship in his command[1]

Every two days the escorting destroyers closed the flagship to refuel, a slow, delicate operation which involved slowing down and then taking inboard the large hose-pipe over from *Renown's* quarter-deck, sometimes in conditions that made it almost impossible to manhandle it. Once the hose was securely connected, *Renown* would pump across the oil fuel while the destroyer tried to maintain a steady course. Sometimes when conditions were really rough and life aboard the little ships became one long physical pounding, it was impossible to keep dry or warm, and on occasions such as fuelling *Renown* would take the opportunity to send over pounds and pounds of hot, freshly-baked bread from her kitchens to help provide decent meals for her faithful companions.

While the weather was as rough the destroyer screen would be closed in on the big ships; *Ark Royal* would recall her searching aircraft and batten them down; and the whole force would change course to take advantage of the best conditions of wind and sea to ride it out. On one such day, 10 April, *Faulknor* was almost submerged by a wicked green sea and lost five Dan Buoys from her deck equipment as it crashed over them, swirling away from the 'islands' of the bridge and after deckhouse in an angry white cataract. Other days would pass calmly, with brief glimpses of the sun, and the

... Renown *would pass over hot baked-bread to her companions ...* (Crown Copyright.)

destroyers would then open up the screen, taking station around the big ships like porpoises in the long, lazy swell. The ungainly old Swordfish would lumber into the air from the carrier, disappearing over the horizon, busy with their own affairs. The rest of the fleet would carry out gun and practice exercises with one destroyer acting as target for the rest of the fleet and *Ark's* planes. But on *this* trip such days were almost non-existent!

The 11 April followed much the same pattern as the previous days. At 0904, *Ark Royal* flew off twelve reconnaissance aircraft to conduct searches for the enemy in case they had sailed during the night, but an hour later confirmation was again received that both battle-cruisers were still at Brest. Again the weather was not kind to the three smaller warships, Somerville again recording that, 'Speed had to be reduced to 15 knots at 1130 as the destroyers had again started to bump.'

Queen Elizabeth refuelled at Gibraltar and Force 'H' moved north to cover her patrol area. The British submarine patrols had been withdrawn but the German U-boats were still in evidence, however. At 2130, *Fearless* gained an A/S contact in 44° 24' N, 17° 02' W, and investigated. *Faulknor* joined her, but the echo was not good. After dropping a pattern of depth-charges, the two destroyers rejoined the flag.

From 1030/12th, *Faulknor* and her two companions again had to refuel from *Renown*, course being altered to 140° and speed being reduced to ten knots for this purpose, each destroyer taking on 77-tons. The only sign of life was an empty lifeboat investigated in the forenoon, belonging to either *Bianca* or *San Casimiro*, German supply ships scuttled in those waters on March 20th. No reconnaissance reports from Brest were received and course was maintained to the eastward.

Somerville was told early on the 13th that no aerial survey of Brest would be conducted by the RAF, so flew off his own searches in case the two battle-cruisers had slipped away, Force 'H' turning north-eastward. At 1400, *Faulknor* gained a 'doubtful' submarine contact on her Asdic in 44° 48' N, 14° 06' W. Quickly altering course, she steamed over the spot, dropping a couple of depth-charges, but the twin explosions and resulting mounds of water only wounded the dignity of a whale, which surfaced immediately afterward.

The only ship seen by *Ark Royal's* twelve Swordfish was a three-masted brigantine 120 miles north and heading west. As it would have been dark before a destroyer could reach her position, no steps were taken to investigate her. No aerial reconnaissance was possible over Brest for the third successive day.

At 0800/14th, eight Swordfish searched 120 miles to the north-west but again the Bay was empty. During the day *Renown* and *Ark* carried out 4.5-inch sub-calibre shoots at a splash target towed by one of the screening destroyers and dummy dive-bombing practices were carried out on the destroyers by Fulmars. At 1245, Somerville was informed that one enemy battle-cruiser had been sighted at Brest, and at 1630, he was told that C-in-C, Home Fleet was again assuming command of the Bay patrols and that *Repulse* was on her way back from Gibraltar to relieve them. Force 'H' then steered to return to the Rock, while they covered minelayer *Abdiel* busy laying 300 mines off Brest. They reached Gibraltar at 1245/16 April.

On 20 April, *Faulknor* sailed at 1800 with *Sheffield*, and destroyers *Fortune* and *Wrestler*, to meet carrier *Argus* with more Hurricanes embarked. Next morning the destroyers spread to the extreme visible distance from the cruiser and proceeded northwards. At 0855 /22nd, *Faulknor* investigated a contact to port, which turned out to be merely another small Portuguese motor vessel. At midday first a Walrus amphibian, and then a London float-plane joined, and they sighted the unmistakable shape of the old 'Flat Iron' and they escorted her back to the Rock, arriving at 0700 /24th. Aboard the *Argus* were several replacements for *Faulknor's* ship's company. One was Coder Ted Newman, who kept a very detailed diary of his four-and-a-half years aboard. He recalled:

> We were not expected and, as next day we were taking a convoy to Malta, there was no time to discharge the five people we had relieved, for a time we were put in different

messes and were made quite welcome, everybody wanting to know what England was looking like. Next day we sailed, leading a large convoy containing planes and supplies for besieged Malta. Weather was grand and we didn't expect any enemy activity for a couple of days, so I quite enjoyed the brilliant sunshine.

Another new telegraphist was Griff Fanthorpe:

> I was nineteen years of age – all my friends in the large communications staff that was part of being Captain (D) were in the same age group – all were more experienced than I was personally. I did have the distinction of probably being the first rating that was not 21 years old or 7 and 5 long-term serviceman. The flood of Hostilities Only ratings had not yet appeared, this happened on the ship's later return to the UK for a refit in August. A great proportion of the seasoned and experienced men of the *Faulknor's* professional team were, at that time, drafted to the many new destroyers being commissioned. I had been from 1938 a member of the RNVR at Aberdovey. To serve in the real navy at that time seemed a remote possibility. We were highly impressionable young men, all very conscious of being part of a very elite outfit, Force 'H' of that period under Admiral Sir James Somerville.
>
> The 'F-boats' were a remarkable screen and later Malta convoys suffered from lack of such experienced U-boat killers. The over-rated 'Tribals', like *Cossack,* which replaced *Faulknor* in August, were regarded with some disdain by the old *Faulknor* hands.

The carrier transferred another twenty Hurricanes to *Ark Royal* to be flown off in the usual manner to Malta in Operation 'Dunlop', and light cruiser *Dido* and minelayer *Abdiel* to the eastern Mediterranean plus 5th Destroyer Flotilla, *Kelly, Kashmir, Kelvin, Kipling, Jackal* and *Jersey*, to Malta to form a striking force. The reinforcement transfer was code-named Operation 'Salient'. As usual Force 'H' provided the covering squadron, *Renown, Sheffield, Fiji, Faulknor, Fearless, Foresight, Fortune* and *Fury* sailing 24 April.

Next day they reached the 'flying-off' position, but, as Malta reported bad weather, the operation was delayed and the squadron turned north, hoping to throw enemy snoopers off the scent; however, they were duly reported on Vichy radio that day. On 27th Malta signalled 'all clear' and the twenty Hurricanes were flown off, guided by Fulmars. Before dawn *Dido* and her companions also parted company, both groups eventually reaching Malta safely. Force H was sighted by a German patrol plane while returning to Gibraltar, but not attacked. Dummy raids by the carrier aircraft to exercise the ships' A.A. guns were conducted on 28th, followed by flotilla torpedo attacks and fleet manoeuvres to test a new form of 'blind barrage'. No time was ever wasted in Somerville's command, and Force 'H' docked 28 April.

Vital reinforcements for the British forces in Libya and Greece were normally routed via Freetown and the Cape, but it was estimated that sending tanks in a fast convoy straight through the Mediterranean would save forty days. With the Luftwaffe firmly established on the flanks of the convoy route, both Cunningham and Somerville warned of the dangers, but Churchill decreed planning for Operation 'Tiger' to commence immediately.

A week of intensive preparation followed as the various warships and transports gathered. For *Faulknor* these seven days provided a welcome period of training, and on 1 May she sailed in company with Dutch submarine *O-21* for anti-submarine exercises in the bay.

Faulknor made a series of high-speed runs up the range while the submerged submarine fired dummy torpedoes at her from varying angles. The Dutchmen were uncomfortably accurate, and the destroyer's crew were thankful that the warheads were of the collapsible variety and not high-explosive. While the submarine altered course and manoeuvred to make *Faulknor* lose the scent, they stopped and recovered the still floating 'fish'; then they increased speed to the submarine's last position and began to hunt. She proved elusive, but eventually they found her and, after holding her for a while, she surfaced, signalling her congratulations. *Faulknor* finished with a full-calibre shoot of her main armament. Such exercises were invaluable for keeping the highly-trained teams of the warships at their best. Both ships benefited, for *Faulknor* was soon to add to her tally of U-boat kills, while *O-21* sank *U-95* in these same waters.

Another brush with Vichy followed, *Faulknor* sailing with Force 'H' at 0430/2 May to prevent the recapture of the French liner *Cap Contin,* being brought in by *Foresight.* They returned at 2048 next day, the destroyer and her prize docking early next morning. The Rock was filling up with ships and, between 5 and 12 May *Faulknor* participated in Operation 'Tiger'. Carrying the vital tanks, ammunition and other war cargo were fast motor ships *Clan Chattan, Clan Lamont, Clan Campbell* and *Empire Song* plus *New Zealand Star,* now seaworthy once more. Reinforcements for Admiral Cunningham's fleet acted as escorts for the passage of the convoy, battleship *Queen Elizabeth* and light cruisers *Fiji* and *Naiad*, as did light cruiser *Gloucester* and destroyers *Kashmir* and *Kipling*, locked out of Malta when destroyer *Jersey* had been mined in the harbour entrance and who had been forced to returned to Gibraltar *pro tem.*

To get this mass of ships through the mine-strewn waters and into Grand harbour, *Faulknor*, *Fearless, Foresight, Forester, Fortune* and *Fury* were allocated as both escorts and minesweepers. They were to be met in the narrows by a detachment of four cruisers from the east, *Calcutta, Carlisle, Coventry* and *Phoebe,* for anti-aircraft protection.

Somerville commanded the whole operation up to the narrows. The Admiralty had offered him battle-cruiser *Repulse* and destroyers *Harvester, Havelock* and *Hesperus,* all due to arrive at Gibraltar from a Bay patrol, but Somerville refused the former because of her poor armour protection and weak AA armament. He accepted the three destroyers, (which were almost totally devoid of both), using them to supplement his own slender resources, *Renown, Ark Royal, Sheffield* and *Wrestler.*

In an attempt to keep any knowledge of the convoy from the enemy for as long as possible, the various forces sailed in groups on the 5th and 6th, passing the Straits at night, while Force H also made a deliberate feint into the Atlantic before reversing course back into the Mediterranean.

Only *Faulknor, Forester* and *Fury* remained in the destroyer pens after both the main groups had departed. At 1710, the dim bulk of *Repulse* and her escorting destroyers slid past the gate. The battle-cruiser transferred several ratings due to join *Queen Elizabeth* or to take passage to Malta in *Faulknor*, together with some supplies. That done the 'Hs' refuelled and with the 'Fs' slipped at 0300/6th, and hurried after the convoy.

The six destroyers joined Force 'H' before dawn and took their appointed screening stations. The 7th found the convoy, with Force 'H' ahead of them and to the north, interposing itself between the merchantmen and enemy bases, but they remained undetected. By dawn on 8 May they expected to be spotted and attacked. Anxious eyes scanned the sky continuously, while four Swordfish from the carrier stuttered off to search the approaches to the Italian naval bases. By 0800, they returned with no sign of the Italian fleet

The sky was dull and overcast, but, at 0830, an enemy sighting broadcast was intercepted giving the convoy's speed, course, composition and position. Accordingly, new dispositions were made to prepare for the inevitable bombing. The cruisers took station ahead of each of the merchant ship columns and the heavy ships formed a separate line of battle to the starboard, while the thirteen destroyers fanned out in a wide outer circle. The Fulmar's fighters drove off numerous reconnaissance aircraft, which popped in and out of large cloud formations. Lunch came and went undisturbed as they proceeded sedately in calm seas past the southern tip of Sardinia.

The air attacks finally commenced at 1345, eight Sm.79 torpedo-bombers approaching the fleet from the starboard at wave-top height. They were soon visible from the *Faulknor's* bridge and were engaged at long-range, this gunfire destroyed one and kept the remainder at a distance. The survivors split up into groups of two or three and returned to the attack, launching against the most tempting targets, *Renown*, *Ark Royal* and *Queen Elizabeth,* but these ships met them with a barrage which accounted for two more. Now only five remained and these launched their torpedoes from outside the destroyer screen, without success.

At fourteen knots the convoy drew steadily closer to the Skerki narrows and air attacks resumed. The next wave, at 1630, comprised five Sm.79s who pattern-bombed the destroyers on the outer screen, to no effect. Another altitude attack by three more Sm.79s followed at 1800, against the *Ark,* twelve heavy bombs exploding ahead of her, but none hitting. At 1730, five Sm.79s went for the transports, but once more the heavy barrage forced the aircraft to drop their bombs prematurely, most of these missiles exploding near the destroyers on the outer screen. Half-an-hour later another three bombers, escorted by fighters, approached – but again the defensive fire worried them into jettisoning their bombs over the destroyers.

Another long pause followed, until, at 1910, with *Ark Royal* down to seven defending fighters, the heaviest attack was plotted on the fleet's radar screens. These were the real thing, German Junkers Ju.87 dive-bombers in two groups of twelve and sixteen aircraft, escorted by six twin-engined Me.110 fighters. The ships' gunners stood ready with fresh attention to meet this new, to them, form of attack. The Fulmars flung themselves on the enemy formations, forcing them to break up into small groups, which lost contact with each other. Kept at a distance until their fuel grew low, they were forced to jettison their bombs; not one of the feared Stukas got through.

The major danger past and the Skerki Channel being reached without loss, at 2015 Force 'H' turned back, being attacked at dusk by three Sm.79 torpedo-bombers who achieved surprise, *Renown* being fortunate to avoid being hit. The convoy and close escort pressed on towards Malta at 13½ knots, in thick mist. They had precise co-ordinates to follow what was considered the safest route through the deadly mine-strewn Skerki and Sicilian Channels thus:

Position 'W' 37° 24′ North, 10° 49′ East
Position 'X' 37° 22′ North, 11° 23′ East
Position 'Y' 36° 58′ North, 11° 49′ East
Position 'Z' 36° 52′ North, 12° 09′ East
Position 'A' 36° 15′ North, 12° 40′ East

Force 'F' was to reach Position 'A' at 0800 on Day Four and was then to steer 130° until met by the Mediterranean Fleet escort, while all 'F' Class destroyers, and probably *Naiad*, were to proceed to Malta. All the merchant ships were also to be led into Grand Harbour by the corvette *Gloxinia* (fitted with minesweeps) and a local minesweeping drifter.

At 2317, in 37° 28′ N, 11° 11′ E, 'ripple', which bore a strong resemblance to those which could be heard from mines, was detected by *Faulknor's* Asdic. At 2359 *New Zealand Star*, second-in-line of the Military Transport Ships, detonated a mine in 37° 24′ N, 11° 21′ E. At 0002/9 May, another mine exploded abreast the fourth MTS, *Empire Song,* immediately followed by the detonation of a third mine a short distance ahead of her, countermined by the second explosion.

New Zealand Star hauled out of line and turned 360° *into* the minefield, somehow avoiding further explosions. She soon picked up speed again and resumed her station in the convoy, signalling Captain De Salis that she had no material damage. *Empire Song* maintained her course and speed for a considerable time, but the internal damage to her engines proved fatal. A fire broke out below which got out of hand and eventually she dropped astern of the convoy, *Foresight* and *Fortune* standing by her.

Foresight went alongside the crippled ammunition ship and proceeded to disembark the entire crew, a remarkable act of courage, regarded as 'routine' by the destroyer men. Even braver was the decision reached to re-board the transport with volunteers from *Foresight's* and *Empire Song's* officers in an attempt to bring the fire under control and perhaps save the ship and her invaluable cargo. The destroyer lowered her whaler with these men aboard and they had just got alongside the burning vessel at 0410 when *Empire Song* blew up with a huge explosion, completely vanishing within two and a half minutes. As Captain De Salis recalled:

> The air was filled with flying tanks and projectiles and *Foresight* suffered considerable superficial damage, and casualties. The whaler was sunk but all but one of the crew was rescued by *Fortune.*

In fact, *Foresight* had suffered internal injuries, but these did not become immediately apparent. While this tragedy was enacting itself, enemy aircraft were heard circling overhead and, at 0030, radar revealed ten torpedo-bombers approaching. *Queen Elizabeth* and the cruisers opened fire by radar on these attackers, the battleship having to alter course sharply to avoid torpedoes as the aircraft attacked from astern; *Fearless* herself had four pass close by her at this time but no ships were hit.

Dawn broke revealing the convoy plodding on to the south-east, the warships clustered around them, *Faulknor* in her normal cruising position leading the squadron with, astern of her, the comforting bulk of *Queen Elizabeth*. *Foresight* closed and reported her damage to Captain De Salis and then proceeded with all despatch to Malta, while *Fortune* rejoined the screen at 0730. At this time, away to the south, dim shapes were made out closing fast and *Faulknor* promptly challenged. The newcomers were the light cruisers *Dido* and *Phoebe* joining them from Cunningham's main force and were followed within the hour by *Calcutta*, *Carlisle* and *Coventry*. Between 1000 and 1040 *Faulknor* observed a few floating mines and, at 1040, five Beaufighters arrived overhead. Half-an-hour later a Dornier bomber appeared out of the clouds with one engine stopped and crashed between the screen and the main body, dropping a torpedo as she did so. At 1400 that afternoon the 5th Destroyer Flotilla arrived and *Faulknor* led her consorts to Malta at 24 knots, arriving off Grand Harbour at 1630.

At 1700, the flotilla received permission to enter harbour and *Faulknor* led in by the latest Q.B.B. message route (Q.B.B., followed by the appropriate number, was the code group used for the various minefields around Malta and the Sicilian Straits which were added to almost daily). This was an operation, which called for delicate and precise ship-handling, as Captain De Salis recorded:

> In order to avoid known positions of magnetic mines, it was necessary to reverse the inner screw on two occasions.

The risk from mining as they approached Valetta harbour was great, despite use of TSDS equipment, all crew had to wear their lifebelts, while, as a further precaution, all those who were not on duty had to muster on the upper deck.

The men of the *Queen Elizabeth* draft and those for billets ashore at Malta, were hastily disembarked, as was *Faulknor's* uncomfortable deck-load of ammunition and aviation spirit. The survivors from the mined *Jersey* were embarked; her broken hull still being visible at the mouth of the harbour.

The flotilla completed oiling by 2000, and was clear of Grand Harbour by dark. The plan was to traverse the dangerous Narrows by night and be well to the westward by dawn. The rest of the journey would be made at high speed until out of range of the enemy air bases and the rendezvous with Somerville's squadron south of Sardinia.

Once clear, course was set for Pantellaria and speed increased to 22 knots and, after ten minutes, to 30 knots but at 2145, *Foresight's* hidden damage finally manifested itself. She hauled out of line signalling to *Faulknor* that her starboard engine was out of action, reducing her best speed to twenty knots. Captain De Salis had to weigh the safety of the other five ships of his command against leaving one ship alone in such dangerous waters. He made his choice and the whole flotilla reduced speed to keep *Foresight* company. It was not long, however, before she reported that her faults were too extensive without dockyard assistance. She was therefore sent back to the dubious sanctuary of Malta. The rest of the flotilla increased speed once more but were restricted to 29 knots, the maximum speed of *Fearless*, later reduced to 28 knots when *Fearless* reported that she still had 'nothing in hand'. Fortunately, their passage through the 'Narrows' was uneventful, save sighting the submarine *Taku* five miles north of Pantellaria. She was expected and, when challenged by *Faulknor*, she replied before the challenge was completed. *Faulknor* then used her low-power W/T to inform the rest of the flotilla that the submarine was friendly and they pushed on westward.

Before dawn, all ships went to Action Stations and prepared for an air attack as they passed northwest of Cape Bon. An Italian Cant Z.506b sighted them at 0850 south of Galita Island. Captain De Salis ordered the destroyers to 'stagger and snake' the line from 1000 and prepare for the arrival of the bombers. The first shadower was fired at by the flotilla at 0910 and, again at 1110, when in range. Another Cant Z.506b relieved her at 1100, but this snooper left without relief at 1230. At 1252 it became necessary to reduce speed to 25 knots on account of the weather, further reduced to 18 knots at 1330.

The five destroyers were disposed in 'loose formation' with ships three to four cables apart, with *Faulknor* ahead and between the two columns. *Fearless* was leading *Forester* to port and astern and *Fortune* and *Fury* to starboard. This was a good formation for bringing a concentration of fire against any low-flying attacker, but, when the attack came, it was from high-level bombers against whom only limited AA fire could be brought. *Faulknor* herself only had time to get off two rounds of medium barrage at 4,000 yards from her 3-inch HA gun before this weapon jammed. The time was 1330, in 37° 25′ N, 6° 16′ E, the sea was 43, wind force 6 and there was 4/10th cover with cumulus cloud.

In Captain De Salis's words the attacking Sm.79 bombers made a 'Clever approach, behind clouds and aircraft were first sighted two minutes before bomb release.' Their attack formation was 'a pair in front, one astern of them and one a long way astern. (See Diagram)

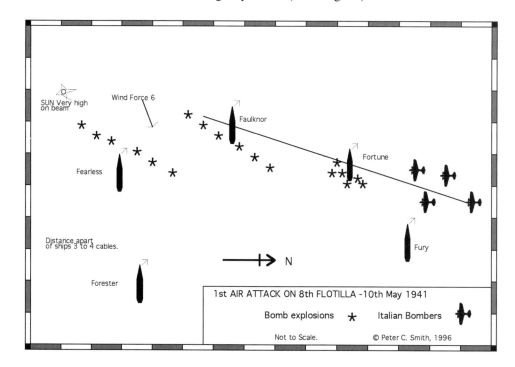

SUN Very high on beam

Wind Force 6

Faulknor

Fearless

Fortune

Distance apart of ships 3 to 4 cables.

Fury

N

Forester

1st AIR ATTACK ON 8th FLOTILLA -10th May 1941

Bomb explosions ✱ Italian Bombers

Not to Scale. © Peter C. Smith, 1996

The bombs dropped were estimated at eighteen 100-kilo, with delay fuses and two 250-kilo bombs with impact fuses and one stick fell across *Faulknor's* stern; one stick across the bows of *Fearless* while the third stick, dropped by the rearmost of the first three bombers, detonated all around *Fortune's* stern. The two larger bombs fell far over to and wide of the port bow which were thought to have been dropped by a lone bomber that had been sighted shadowing at 1100 had tacked itself onto the rear of the standard three-plane formation. The enemy aircraft remained in the vicinity for fifteen minutes apparently homing in the next wave, before departing.

Fortune took the brunt and was badly shaken by several near-misses, which immediately reduced her speed to eight knots. This controlled the speed of the remainder of the flotilla as they zigzagged independently on her while *Fury* prepared to take her in tow if necessary.

The second bombing attack took place at 1545. By this time *Fortune* had worked up to fourteen knots but the sky was much clearer with bright sunlight fine on the port bow of the flotilla. The destroyers were boxed around *Fortune*, with *Fearless* leading *Forester* to port and *Faulknor* ahead of *Fury* to starboard. Wind was force 7 from the port bow and sea 54. When first seen the formation of ten BR.20 High Level Bombers were off the flotilla's starboard quarter, approaching from the northward in two flights of five aircraft each, at about 10,000 feet (See Diagram)

The flights circled around behind the flotilla and came in from astern concentrating on the crippled *Fortune* in the centre, the two flights taking slightly converging courses dropping about thirty 250-kilo bombs with impact fuses. All ships engaged the aircraft, *Faulknor* getting off sixteen rounds Medium Barrage at 4,000 yards from her 3-inch gun, four rounds of 4.7-inch Barrage at 3,500 yards and twenty-three rounds of 4.7-inch Barrage at 1,500 yards.

On the flotilla opening fire two bombs were dropped short, possibly as sighting shots. As the majority of aircraft released their bombs *Fortune*, who had been on a straight and steady course while the others were weaving, made a very hard turn to port and this served to avoid the concentration of

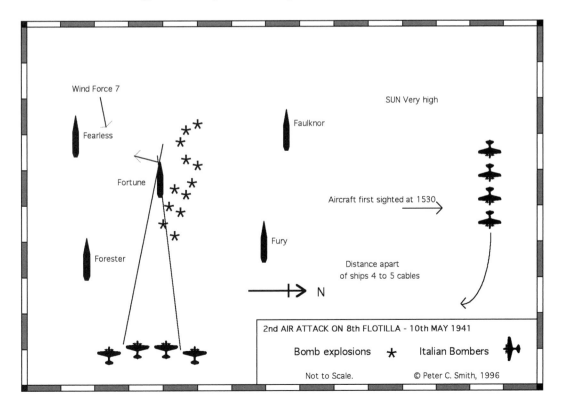

Wind Force 7

SUN Very high

Fearless

Faulknor

Fortune

Aircraft first sighted at 1530

Fury

Forester

Distance apart
of ships 4 to 5 cables

N

2nd AIR ATTACK ON 8th FLOTILLA - 10th MAY 1941

Bomb explosions ★ Italian Bombers

Not to Scale. © Peter C. Smith, 1996

both attacks, which detonated all along her starboard side, ahead, abreast and astern of her. There was no damage caused to either ships or aircraft from this attack. This did not stop German post-war accounts claiming that *Fortune* received 'a heavy hit', which is just pure fiction for no bomb actually struck her!

The Italian aircraft broke up into smaller formations and flew away up-sun, not being seen again and, even as they vanished, two of *Ark Royal's* Swordfish were seen approaching, which meant that help was not too far away. Somerville had brought Force 'H' west to support them. Such a gesture was much appreciated by the crews of the destroyers and is why Sir James Somerville was very well liked by the men of *Faulknor,* who would have followed him anywhere. They waited for a third attack, but it never came, and, at 1759, the remainder of Force 'H' was sighted, the flotilla forming on *Renown* at 1814. On the 12 May, *Renown, Ark Royal, Faulknor, Fearless, Forester, Fury* and *Havelock,* entered harbour at 1800, being followed by the cruiser *Sheffield,* with *Harvester* and *Hesperus,* escorting the damaged *Fortune,* at 2030. While the *Renown* went into dock to remove a damaged 4.5-inch gun turret, organising immediately began for the next sortie eastward.

Of the convoy, the four surviving ships arrived safely at their destinations, protected by the Mediterranean Fleet, and a total of more than 230 tanks were delivered to the Desert Army intact.

Three more 'Club Runs' were now planned to further boost Malta's fighter defences under the overall designation Operation 'Jaguar'. Three sorties were to be made, Operations 'Splice', 'Rocket' and 'Tracer', to fly off further batches of Hurricanes. Admiral Cunningham proposed to Admiral Somerville that *Foresight*, detained at Malta for repairs to her engine bearings, should return to Gibraltar under the cover of Operation 'Splice', but the latter was luke-warm.

> I was averse to this, since the latter operation involved two aircraft-carriers, and it was unlikely with the limited fighter protection available in *Ark Royal*, that I should be able to afford *Foresight* adequate support in the event of enemy air attacks. Apart from this, the provision of cover to *Foresight* would have entailed keeping the carriers for an extended period in the probable bombing area.

Of course, this is what he had just done for *Fortune*!

> I proposed instead that *Foresight* should remain at Malta until other forces were passing from east to west, or that she should wait the determination of the swept channel through the enemy minefields of the Narrows and return independently during a period of low visibility. The best solution of all, however, appeared to be that she should join the Mediterranean Fleet, in which case a relief would be required.
>
> I was informed by the Admiralty that no destroyers were available to reinforce the 8th Destroyer Flotilla, now reduced from eight to five ships,[2] but that *Brilliant* might be used for Operation 'Splice'. In the circumstances, and as it appeared that no other movements from east to west would be taking place, I considered the only alternative was that *Foresight* should make the passage of the Narrows independently, taking advantage of the next moonless period and selecting a calm day with low visibility.

While awaiting the arrival of *Furious* with her 48 Hurricanes, *Faulknor* lay snugly alongside the Mole. Ammunition was embarked, and, on 18th the flotilla's commanding officers came aboard to confer with Captain De Salis. *Furious* transferred some aircraft to *Ark Royal*, and it did not need a crystal ball for the lower deck, anymore than the legendary man on the Spanish border with his Zeiss binoculars, to forcast the destination of the next sortie accurately.

Force 'H' comprising *Renown, Ark Royal, Sheffield* screened by destroyers *Harvester, Havelock* and *Hesperus* sailed 0330/19 May to the westward, followed at 1500 by *Furious* and heavy cruiser

London screened by *Faulknor, Forester*, *Foxhound* and *Fury* which had slipped at 1330 and preceded them to sea. After dusk the two forces rendezvoused, *London, Harvester* and *Havelock* being detached at 1920, while the rest steered east, the five remaining destroyers formed a screen around the heavy ships and were joined by destroyer *Brilliant* from Gibraltar at 0720.

By 0900/20 May, the force was steering east, but at 1215, some 70 miles north of Oran, they passed through a northbound convoy of Vichy-French ships, which extended for at least ten miles, and so could not be avoided. On 21st Italian sighting signals were intercepted and a Vichy aircraft was picked up by radar. *Ark Royal* and *Furious* despatched 48 fighters guided by Fulmars to Malta, and most of them arrived safely. Although the Italian submarines *Corallo* and *Diaspro* were in position south of Sardinia to intercept the force, neither attacked. Meanwhile *Foresight* had departed Malta at 2030, and her estimated time of arrival at Gibraltar was 1600/23rd.

At 0800/22nd, *Furious* entered Gibraltar escorted by *Brilliant* and *Hesperus*. At 1038, Force 'H' intercepted an Italian signal indicating *Foresight* was being shadowed by enemy aircraft, her estimated position being midway between Galita Island and Bougie. Putting aside earlier reservations, Somerville altered course to the eastward, and instructed *Foresight* to report immediately if she was attacked by enemy bombers and the results of such attacks. Somerville also requested FOIC Gibraltar to refuel *Brilliant* and *Hesperus* by 1600, but he couldn't prevent *London*, *Harvester* and *Havelock* sailing for the UK.

Finally, at 1600, not having heard from *Foresight* and assuming that she was by then out of bombing range, Force 'H' reversed course westward, entering harbour at 2245/22 May. *Foresight* had an uneventful, if lonely, passage. Visibility had been good when passing Panterellia with a clear sky but this soon deteriorated. *Foresight* had no idea that she was being shadowed from the air until receipt of Somerville's warning, but she arrived safely at Gibraltar on the 23rd.

Before they could conduct 'Rocket', another dramatic intervention took place. Force 'H' had already received the signals concerning the sortie of German battleship *Bismarck* and heavy cruiser *Prinz Eugen,* but assumed the Home Fleet would deal with them. When heavy cruiser *Norfolk* transmitted a sighting report at 2100/23rd Force 'H' went to two hours notice to steam as a precaution.

In the early hours of the following day the Admiralty ordered Force 'H' to join convoy WS.8B on the morning of 26 May and, at 0200, *Renown, Ark Royal* and *Sheffield*, screened by *Faulknor, Foresight, Forester, Foxhound, Fury* and *Hesperus* sailed westward at 25 knots to rendezvous with the convoy in 47° 20′ N, 26° 05′ W. The squadron ploughed north at 26 knots into the teeth of a north-west gale and, as the day wore on the weather worsened. Their passage remained uneventful save for the sighting of the Portuguese freighter *Madierense,* but, at 1245/25th, *Foresight, Foxhound* and *Fury,* which had not had time to refuel before leaving Gibraltar, had to be sent back as oiling from *Renown* at sea in those conditions was out of the question.

Faulknor, Forester and *Hesperus* kept going, the speed of the squadron being progressively reduced to twenty knots. U-boats were not thought to be able to operate in such conditions, but there was always the chance and also, the destroyers' torpedoes would have proved valuable should Force 'H' have become involved in a surface action with *Bismarck*.

During the night sleep was almost impossible aboard the little ships and station-keeping a matter of guesswork as they battled against the appalling conditions. Speed was reduced again and again, but it took every effort of the racing screws and the strong-armed helmsman to hold *Faulknor* on course. First light brought a hazy, overcast sky, but no further news of their quarry. The weather remained terrible and by dawn on 26th the battered squadron had reached the latitude of Brest and the fuel was also running low in the remaining three destroyers.

Force 'H' was placed under direct control of the Admiralty, so serious did the situation become with the sinking of *Hood*, damage to the *Prince of Wales* and subsequent loss of contact. *Bismarck* could either be steering for Brest or out into the mid-Atlantic to refuel from waiting tankers, Somerville guessed the former, but the Admiralty thought differently and ordered him to steer north-west.

These orders were changed five hours later, when Force 'H' was instructed to steer a more northerly course to cover the French Atlantic ports. Throughout 25 May, *Faulknor* and her consorts were forced to punch and slam their way into a northwesterly gale. Before long the conditions were such that the destroyers were having the utmost difficulty in keeping station and had to reduce speed several times to prevent damage.

At 0330/25th, the Admiralty instructed Force 'H' to steer to intercept *Bismarck* from the southward, and they maintained their existing course of 310° at 24 knots. The Admiralty later instructed Somerville to detach the remaining three destroyers to Gibraltar before it became necessary to fuel them at sea, as Force 'H' might be required for extended operations. However, not until 0900 were *Faulknor*, *Forester* and *Hesperus* finally detached. From *Renown's* bridge, an island of steel in the midst of swirling water, the winking light of a signal lamp could be made out. Captain De Salis was instructed by Somerville to proceed to alter course to the east at the destroyers' best speed, spread to twice visibility distance with the object of locating *Scharnhorst* and the *Gneisenau* should they have broken out of Brest to join *Bismarck*, for nothing had been heard of these two ships since the afternoon of 23rd. Captain De Salis was also ordered, (when some 150 miles clear of Force 'H' in order not to compromise their security), to signal to the Admiralty Somerville's position at 0730 and also request Plymouth for the results of air searches to the north of Force 'H'. De Salis duly complied, but Plymouth had no news to pass back to *Renown* from any air patrols. The three destroyers then steered for Gibraltar to refuel and then sail once more.

With the wind astern they felt the relief from the violent motion of the previous thirty-six hours and some semblance of order began to emerge out of the waterlogged messdecks. The destroyers were soon able to work up to a speed of twenty-one knots.

With one, possibly three or even four (for *Prinz Eugen* had also been lost) large enemy ships on the loose, those in the know on *Faulknor's* bridge spent a few very tense hours as they headed back southward across the Bay. The other two destroyers joined again and all three ships now set course back to the Rock, where they duly arrived early on the 26th. Here they hastily refuelled and sailed again, but were denied the chance to be in on the 'kill'.

In their absence *Ark Royal's* Swordfish, after almost sinking *Sheffield* (in whose close company they had been operating for months) scored a damaging torpedo hit on *Bismarck* which enabled battleships *King George V* and *Rodney* to come up and pound her to junk and heavy cruiser *Dorsetshire* to put her on the bottom with torpedoes. Just how big a risk Somerville had run was shown when *U-556* claimed to have had *Renown* and *Ark Royal* in his sights without a protective destroyer screen. *Faulknor, Forester, Fury* and *Wishart* finally rejoined *Renown* at 0800/29th in 36° 20′ N, 09° 35′ W. The four destroyers formed line-ahead and steamed past their big brothers, cheering them to the echo, before settling down into their screening positions at 24 knots. Exercises were conducted during the 29th, *Wishart* picking up the dead body of an airman from *Sheffield's* Walrus, which crashed close to the flagship, while *Forester* and *Fury* were sent to join a U-boat hunt 180 miles west of the Force. *Faulknor* and *Wishart* escorted the triumphant heavy ships into Gibraltar at 1840 to the cheers of the waiting crowds.

* * *

Force 'H' could now resume its other main business – sustaining Malta. Planning for 'Rocket' was pressed ahead and carriers were soon on their way with forty-four Hurricane fighters for Malta. *Faulknor's* next job was to go to the assistance of the convoy containing carrier *Argus* with more fighters embarked, which had come under U-boat attack. While helping escort *Argus* into Gibraltar at 0600/30 May, *Foresight* sighted a U-boat on the surface in 36° 03′N, 10° 30′ W and attacked, but without success and half an hour later *Faulknor* sailed from the Rock to assist in the hunt.

The waters in the approaches to the Straits were alive with the undersea enemy and the freighter *British Yeoman* reported herself under attack from another submarine in 35° 28′ N, 03° 11′ W, *Forester, Fury* and four Fairmile Motor Launches being sent to search, again with no luck. Their old adversary, Italian submarine *Guglielmo Marconi,* sank R.F.A. tanker *Cairndale* at 0818, 170 miles WSW of Cape Trafalgar. Escorted at the time only by corvette *Fleur de Lys,* she went down in 5° 19′ N, 08° 33′ W.

At 1145 FOCNA signalled:

Faulknor hunting U-boat which sank *Cairndale.*

The other escorts, destroyers *Forester* and *Fury*, and corvettes *Coreopsis* and *Fleur-de-Lys*, had gained a strong Asdic contact and were depth-charging the echo with great gusto, while overhead a baffled Catalina float plane was trying to muscle in on the action. *Faulknor* roared up at thirty knots and, passing inshore of the convoy, soon had a contact of her own and away went the depth-charge pattern. No U-boat surfaced astern – instead contact was lost. Captain De Salis then organised a proper search and the five anti-submarine vessels, spread out in line abreast, swept down the last reported bearing of the enemy at fifteen knots. The enemy captain was no fool and time passed with further contact being obtained; night fell and still the hunt continued, De Salis trying, by thinking like his opponent, to catch him out. Course was altered several times and speed was varied from ten to twelve knots.

At 0600/31st, *Alysse,* a Free French corvette, joined in the search and prolonged the line to starboard. Contact was found, then lost again as the submarine twisted, dived and turned to escape the relentless probes of the pinging Asdic beams. At 0715 they were joined by anti-submarine trawler *Imperialist,* followed an hour later by the sloop *Bideford* and destroyer *Wrestler.* The search went on without success and, toward mid-day the three 'F' Class destroyers returned to Gibraltar leaving the others to continue the hunt.

There were always routine jobs to occupy them when not running convoys, hunting battle-cruisers or searching for submarines. For example, on 3 June *Faulknor* and *Forester* sailed at 2100 to conduct exercises with the Fortress defences. Admiral Somerville supervised from an OP ashore. He later recorded:

It appears that the illumination of distant targets by vessels on patrol using star-shell fired so as to silhouette the target to the guns is a possibility which is worth developing.

Whether it was worth a lost night's sleep for the destroyers or not, they were off again at 1150 to carry out Operation 'Rocket', *Renown, Ark Royal* and *Furious* being screened by *Faulknor, Fearless, Foresight, Forester* and *Fury* who were proceeding eastward and being joined by *Sheffield* later. The weather was fine and calm, with fair visibility. By 1742 the radar picked up a shadowing Vichy-French aircraft and it was assumed that once again Force 'H' was plotted on charts in Rome.

At 0900, the Force split, *Renown, Furious, Faulknor, Foresight* and *Forester* as Group I, while *Ark Royal, Sheffield, Fearless* and *Fury* as Group II, acted independently to the south to aid forming-up by the inexperienced RAF pilots. Ten Blenheim bombers were despatched from Gibraltar to Malta and were picked up on the fleet's radar at 22 miles distance at 0930. In all, 35 Hurricanes were successfully flown off the two carriers. The opportunity was taken to fly an aerial survey over Mers-el-Keibir to ascertain the condition of *Dunkerque,* the two Groups returning to harbour at 0845/7 June.

All ships were ordered to keep steam for one hour's notice and commence refuelling, in readiness for Operation 'Tracer', which planned to utilise Home Fleet carrier *Victorious* instead of *Furious.* Force 'H' sailed at 2230, *Renown, Ark Royal, Furious* and *Sheffield,* screened by *Faulknor, Fearless, Foresight, Forester, Foxhound, Hesperus* and *Wishart,* clearing harbour and heading west at seventeen knots to economise on the destroyers' fuel and ensure efficient Asdic operating conditions while they passed through the U-boat concentrations. On 8 June there were submarine alerts and alarms by patrolling aircraft but no attack materialised, and at 0650 they rendezvoused with *Victorious,* screened by destroyers *Vansittart, Wild Swan, Wivern* and *Wrestler,* detaching *Furious, Sheffield* and *Fury* to join her to form Group II, the remaining ships forming Group I. *Wivern* reported a leaking fuel tank and, at 1030, was sent into Gibraltar.

The transfer of some of the 75 personnel and aircraft then took place before *Furious* and *Sheffield* were sent to overtake *Argus* in 47° N, 24° W for the passage back to the UK, *Sheffield* leaving them and returning to Gibraltar later. The three remaining 'V' & 'Ws' were sent to Gibraltar while *Renown,* the two carriers and the six 'F' class destroyers steered to the south-west at sixteen knots keeping clear of the Straits until the Vichy situation had clarified. At 0100/10 June instructions were received that 'Tracer' was to proceed without delay and the force increased speed to 20, then 26 knots, and steered east. As they re-entered the U-boat area one was sighted and attacked by the Swordfish, to no avail. As the destroyers were needed for protection for the rest of the journey and also had to refuel on arrival, they were not unleashed to join in the hunt. They returned to Gibraltar on 11 June.

Two days later they left for 'Tracer' in which *Ark Royal* and *Victorious,* protected by *Renown, Faulknor, Forester, Foxhound, Hesperus* and *Wishart,* flew off 47 Hurricanes to Malta from a position south of the Balearics on 14 June. Four Hudson bombers acted as their guides but four fighters failed to complete the journey. There was again no interference by the enemy and the force returned to base at 1030 next day. Again ships kept steam for one hour's notice and refuelled. The *Faulknors* heard, almost with disbelief, that two unidentified ships had been sighted sailing from Brest. Could they be the two elusive German battle-cruisers? No one knew, but no chances could be taken. Without waiting to catch their breath, at 1800, they were off into the Bay of Biscay again on another Bay patrol to watch Brest, and protect a WS convoy. *Renown, Ark Royal, Victorious, Faulknor, Fearless, Foresight, Forester, Foxhound* and *Hesperus,* with all available aircraft ranged on the carrier's decks to mislead enemy observers, steered east at eighteen knots. At 2050, course was altered to westward and the force passed through the Straits that night. At 0200 Somerville got an intelligence report that two unidentified ships had been seen leaving Brest at 2100, however, photographs revealed these two vessels as freighters and so they steered to provide aerial anti-submarine protection for the convoy.

On 17 June they ran into fog for two hours before *Hesperus* refuelled from *Renown* with some difficulty. While this always dangerous operation was underway, *Faulknor* obtained an Asdic contact, and delivered a pattern of depth-charges, but this was considered a 'doubtful' and then down-graded to 'non-sub'. At 1140 in 38° 22′ N, 15° 22′ W, the five 'Fs' were detached to return to Gibraltar to refuel and then rejoin the patrol. *Faulknor* led her flotilla eastward and they conducted night-encounter exercises.

At 0440, Cape St.Vincent was abeam and at daybreak *Fearless, Forester, Foresight* and *Foxhound* spread out on either beam of *Faulknor* to carry out an Asdic anti-submarine sweeping exercise. The weather, as they ran down towards the Straits, was perfect, a force 5 wind from the east with eight miles visibility. A hot sun blazed out of a cloudless sky, and in the gentle swell it was easy for the men aboard the destroyers to forget the war and the recent vile weather. As they cantered towards Gibraltar feeling calm and contented, this rare period of peace was suddenly shattered.

At 0920/18th, in 36° 04′ N, 07° 29′ W, about seventy miles west of Cape Trafalgar, *Faulknor* obtained a very firm Asdic contact at a range of 1,400 yards. The contact was quickly classified as a U-boat echo, the inclination was closing, but there was no hydrophone effect. The depth of water here was 600 fathoms. Captain De Salis at once deployed the flotilla starboard by divisions while *Faulknor* herself raced in and made an immediate attack. At 0928 *Faulknor* dropped a single pattern of six depth charges, set to explode at depths of 100, 150 and 250 feet.

U-138 had sailed from L'Orient on the 12 June with sealed orders. She was to sail to the area of Gibraltar, hitherto reserved for Italian submarine operations, with specific instructions to attack the heavy ships of Force 'H'. Earlier the 'Spanish Agency' had been intercepted reporting *Renown* with *Furious* and another aircraft-carrier were at Gibraltar and it is probable that *U-138's* mission was to attempt a Prien-type attack, entering the harbour at night from the north via the Bay of Algeciras. Nothing smaller than a cruiser was to be attacked. That morning while proceeding on the surface, the lookout sighted a dark shape astern, which they misidentified as a cruiser and the submarine crash-dived. They had reached a depth of 40 metres and Captain Gramitsky was ordering the crew to put on their escape apparatus, when *Faulknor's* initial depth-charge pattern detonated.

The results were devastating:

> … there was broken glass and wrecked gear; water came pouring in; a bottle containing compressed air burst and caused an excess of pressure; the pumps were all put out of action and water got into the same exhaust which had already been repaired once before. The port electric motor failed …

Twice the U-boat sank to about 650 ft, but there was enough compressed air left to bring her up to about 100 ft again. The water rushed from one end of the boat to the other and, after 'see-sawing' for some time, she finally went down markedly by the bow. Water continued to pour in and chlorine gas began to fill the living spaces, within half-an-hour *U-138* was forced to surface in a froth of boiling

Seen from HMS Faulknor, *the destroyers HMS* Foresight *(right) and HMS* Forester, *circling U-138's position after depth-charge attacks on 18 June 1941.* (Bill Silltow.)

spray. The internal pressure was so great that her captain was ejected from his command as soon as the conning-tower hatch was thrown open.

Forester sighted the submarine on the surface bearing 135° at three miles range and, increasing speed to 22 knots, opened fire, *Foresight* and *Fearless* following suit shortly afterward. As the 4.7-inch shells exploded around the enemy vessel, to *Forester,* it appeared as if the submarine was preparing to dive again at 1006, and she reduced speed to 18 knots to establish Asdic contact. At 1,700 yards an echo was picked up and held down to 150 yards. The U-boat was seen end-on, with its bow projecting vertically above the waves. At 1009, *Forester* carried out a visual attack, dropping a pattern of six depth-charges set to explode at depths of 100 and 150 ft. As she approached the rest of the U-boat's crew came tumbling up out of her conning tower and began throwing themselves overboard. This depth-charge pattern detonated alongside the submarine, which sank stern first less than of an hour from first contact, in a position 1,700 yards from *Faulknor's* initial attack. A total of 28 survivors were picked up from the sunken enemy craft.

Jack Banner recalled:

> When we picked up the survivors from this U-boat one of the German officers [this was the First Lieutenant, Fricke, described by his own fellow prisoner colleagues as, '... an ardent Nazi, a somewhat unpleasant person ...' stepped aboard and gave the Nazi salute and spat on *Faulknor's* deck. He was immediately hurled back into the sea by Able-Seaman Crisp (known as 'Crippo') who said he did not so much mind the salute but he strongly objected to him spitting on the deck which he had washed down that morning!

U-138 was the only enemy submarine deployed off the Straits at that time, and the ease with which she had been despatched was in sharp contrast to the prolonged hunt that had taken place unsuccessfully a few days earlier in these self-same waters. Their Lordships were fulsome in their praise:

> It is considered that the extreme accuracy of *Faulknor's* attack and the speed with which it was delivered reflects credit on the A/S efficiency of that ship.

As if to celebrate their victory they were allowed to spend the whole of 19th in dock, but the time was not wasted as they re-ammunitioned ship and refuelled. At 0905/20th they sailed to meet and escort Force 'H' back. On conclusion of the Bay operations, Somerville had handed over *Victorious* and *Hesperus* to the care of destroyers *Cossack, Sikh* and *St. Albans*, for return to the UK, while he steered eastward. At 0800/21 June, in 36° 05′ N, 12° 58′ W, *Faulknor, Fearless, Forester, Foxhound* and *Fury* joined *Renown* and *Ark Royal* and course was set for Gibraltar, arriving the morning of 21 June. *Renown* entered harbour but *Ark Royal* with the five 'Fs' continued eastward conducting further exercises and did not secure until 1000.

The following day there was another flap when, at 0900, the Ocean Boarding Vessel *Marsdale,* reported sighting a suspicious vessel resembling the German supply ship *Alstertor* in 35° 52′ N, 18° 42′ W. *Marsdale* lacked sufficient speed to give chase and that fleeting glimpse was the last of her involvement, but two Catalina aircraft were sent from Gibraltar to search further and the available ships of the 8th Destroyer Flotilla were ordered to raise steam with all despatch in readiness to intercept. At 1430, *Faulknor* led *Fearless, Forester, Foxhound* and *Fury* back to sea, steering west, spread to five cables' lengths abeam and speeding into the Atlantic after their distant quarry.

Hour after hour, they raced northwest, constantly checking with the Coastal Command aircraft, which were shadowing. The sun set in a golden blaze and the destroyers closed up for night cruising. As they sped towards the last reported position of the enemy *Faulknor* received update reports from the Catalina aircraft, which confirmed their target was an enemy supply ship. Their bombing attacks

As HMS Faulknor *circles the German supply ship* Alstertor *as she settles by the stern, the crew await rescue in the ship's boats and rafts.* (Bill Silltow.)

had proved totally unsuccessful in persuading her to heave-to. By midnight Cape St. Vincent was left astern but, as the flotilla raced across the Bay of Biscay, an air pump broke down, forcing *Faulknor* to slow down to a mere six knots for quick repairs, an unpleasant reminder of how much the machinery had been overworked. Even worse was the news that both aircraft lost contact at 0030/23rd. From their last reports this vessel was apparently trying to sneak into Bordeaux and was off Cape Finisterre. All now depended on the destroyers.

Dawn broke and the day wore on without any further news but, at 1442, *Fury* reported sighting a merchant ship and Captain De Salis ordered the rest of the flotilla to concentrate on her. At 1543, *Fury* reported that the ship had given her name as *Alstertor* and had signalled that she had British prisoners aboard. She also stated she had a letter and requested a boat might be sent to collect them.

At 1550, *Fury* was joined first by *Fearless* and *Faulknor* and, at 1610 Captain De Salis ordered *Fury* to go alongside and board. Much frantic activity was seen to be taking place on the German vessel, lifeboats and rafts were being lowered. Whilst approaching the enemy ship at 1633, scuttling charges were seen to explode amidships and *Fury* lay off as further charges were fired and *Alstertor* took on a heavy list to port; finally sinking at 1729. The destroyers then picked up all the survivors, 78 British and Lascar prisoners and the German captain, officers, crew and armed guard alike.

Alstertor had acted as a support ship for the disguised raiders *Pinquin*, *Atlantis* and *Kormoran* and she had aboard seventy-eight British seamen from *Rabaul* and *Trafalgar*, sunk earlier by these vessels. They were brought aboard *Faulknor*, very relieved by their rescue, although, unlike *Altmark's* prisoners earlier in the war, had been very well treated by their German captors. The German captain, an elderly man, was also brought aboard, confiding to Captain De Salis that, '… he was getting too

The last seconds of the Nazi supply ship Alstertor *as witnessed by HMS* Faulknor, *23 June 1941.* (Bill Silltow.)

A boatload of survivors from the scuttled German supply ship Alstertor *drifts towards HMS* Faulknor, *awaiting rescue.* (Bill Silltow.)

old for this sort of thing'. The German seamen were prepared for interception, having their personal belongings already packed and they seemed resigned to captivity.

Bill Silltow gave me this memoir of the *Alstertor* affair:

> The numbers of German prisoners was so large, for a small ship, that they were divided amongst all the messes and we were told not to fraternise in any way, even the feeding was to be of the bread and water kind, but later, after Captain De Salis had been informed that the British merchant seamen aboard her had been well treated, all such restrictions on the Germans were relaxed.
>
> We all got on very well with the Germans who now had their roles of captors and prisoners suddenly reversed, after the first feelings of animosity had died away. I still have one of their badges.

Griff Fanthorpe retained contact for many years with one of the German crew, Hans Bantemps from Hamburg.

> We have formed a close friendship over the years – he has visited my home. They spent a peaceful war as POWs in Canada but Hans lost his home and family in the Hamburg bomber raids. He was an interpreter at the Nuremberg trials. *Alstertor* was bringing back British prisoners from the South Atlantic off the notoriously successful German raider *Atlantis* and many of the

Prisoners from the scuttled German supply ship Alstertor *marshalled aboard HMS* Faulknor *after their rescue.* (Bill Silltow.)

Germans who came aboard *Faulknor* were members of the crew of that vessel. So successful had that raider been that the British prisoners were put aboard their supply ship for passage to one of the friendly Vichy French ports. Hans was a gunner from *Atlantis* and joined *Alstertor* as one of the guards. However, he and his companions look back on their brief period aboard *Faulknor* with great pleasure. They were well treated by us, probably helped by the fact that our British prisoners on *Alstertor* were well-cared for.

Ted Newman recorded:

> We had quite a crowd aboard us and six in our Mess, one of whom could speak English. They were mostly raider relief crews and had been looking forward to a spot of leave in France. They idolised Hitler and would not believe they were at war with Russia. We reached port a couple of days later and all ships in harbour cleared lower deck and gave us a cheer, while we circled the harbour with the Jerries on deck. We gave them over to the care of the Army.

While returning to Gibraltar, *Faulknor* and her companions met *Furious*, with yet more Hurricanes embarked, escorted by light cruiser *Hermione* and destroyers *Lance* and *Legion,* the combined squadron reaching the Rock at 1815/25 June. On securing alongside, *Fearless, Foxhound* and *Fury* all reported defects, *Fearless* had serious problems and *Foxhound* had only two boilers in action, which ruled them out of the next flying-off operation then being planned. Admiral Somerville therefore requested the Admiralty that he could retain and utilise the two 'Ls' and this the Admiralty approved.

On 26 June some of *Furious's* fighters were transferred to *Ark Royal*. At 0400 *Renown, Ark Royal, Hermione, Faulknor, Forester, Fury, Lance* and *Legion* left Gibraltar for Operation 'Railway-I'. The force did not encounter the enemy but it did meet with very bad weather, however *Ark* flew off two flights of eleven Hurricane Mark IICs each at 0500/27th from a position off the North African coast, the ships themselves returning to harbour at 0930/28th. Force 'H' therefore spent its First Birthday in harbour refuelling.

This day also saw the transfer of another batch of 26 Hurricane IICs, by ramp from *Furious* to *Ark Royal*. Again, as only five destroyers of the 8th Flotilla were available to screen Force 'H' for the forthcoming operation, during which it would be necessary for the two carriers to operate some miles apart for about two hours, Admiral Somerville again requested permission to use the two 'Ls', and this was again approved.

They left next day at 0110 for Operation 'Railway-II' to the same well-tried pattern. This time *Furious* (with sixteen assembled Hurricanes stowed in her hangar), *Hermione, Fearless, Foxhound*

and *Legion* sailed westward at 1830 during daylight hours to fool the patient watchers in Spain, reversing course after dark as Force 'A'. *Renown, Ark Royal, Faulknor, Forester, Fury* and *Lance* sailed at 0110, passing Europa Point at 0215 and Force 'B' and joining company at 0700. During the afternoon both *Foxhound* and *Forester* investigated submarine contacts but these were later thought to be fish shoals.

On Monday 30th, at 0430 *Furious*, escorted by *Fearless, Legion* and *Lance,* was detached

The famous aircraft-carrier HMS Ark Royal, *with an oiler alongside, moored bow-to-bow with HMS* Faulknor *at Gibraltar in the summer of 1941. Force 'H', with the battle-cruiser* Renown, *the* Ark, *the light cruiser* Sheffield *and* Faulknor *and the 8th Flotilla, became world-famous for outfacing the numerically overwhelming Italian Navy in the western Mediterranean.* (Bill Silltow.)

to take station some five miles south of the rest of the force and the first Blenheim was picked up on radar at 0515, the Hurricanes starting to fly off at 0557. *Ark Royal* managed to launch twenty-six fighters but *Furious* only got nine into the air before a serious deck accident halted all further launching and she had to be escorted back to Gibraltar with eight others still aboard. Force 'H' then combined once more and returned to Gibraltar on 1 July.

Even before they had secured alongside new orders awaited them. The big ships might rest, but not the destroyers, and most certainly not *Faulknor*. Admiral Somerville was instructed to sail every available destroyer to join and escort convoy OG.66 to Gibraltar. The only destroyers available were *Faulknor*, *Fearless*, *Forester*, *Lance* and *Legion* and they left at 1620.

The Admiralty had Ultra decrypts, revealing U-boats concentrating against convoy OG.66 which had been sighted by Fw.200 'Condor' long-range aircraft. Homing broadcasts had been intercepted on 29 June and 1 July and at least thirteen U-boats were known to be in the vicinity. Thanks to good anticipation and the arrival of the five destroyers, these vultures were frustrated and scored no successes at all. It proved a long, slow slog for *Faulknor* as she developed engine defects. At 2018/5 July Captain De Salis signalled:

Faulknor E.T.A. Ponta Delgada 1030B/6/7

Porta Delgada is the main port of the island of Sao Miguel, Azores, and, on 6 July, they arrived in this neutral port to carry out temporary repairs. This was allowed under International Law, provided they did not outstay their welcome and sometimes both British and German ships shared Portuguese harbours!

On this occasion, they had a few pleasant hours ashore while some of the officers and men were most hospitably entertained by the crew of the Portuguese destroyer *Douro*, before sailing to rejoin the convoy and escort *Furious* part way back to the UK. Bad weather in the Bay delayed the squadron and the rendezvous with battleship *Royal Sovereign* was missed. *Faulknor* therefore continued on as escort until, eventually, the battleship was sighted. The 'Tiddley Quid' took off their mail by heaving line, and also took over the protection of *Furious* leaving the two destroyers to return to the Rock, *Faulknor* and *Fury* duly arrived back at Gibraltar at 0700/13 July. *Faulknor* went straight into dock for repairs to leaking fuel tanks and it was not until 1130/20th that she was undocked.

Plans had already been completed for the next big convoy, Operation 'Substance', whose object was the reinforcement of Malta and which involved the passing through the Western Mediterranean of six 15-knot freighters and a personnel ship. Carried out 21/27 July, 1941, this was the largest Malta supply operation to date.

The Home Fleet bolstered Force 'H's fighting strength with battleship *Nelson*, light cruisers *Arethusa*, *Edinburgh* and *Manchester*, minelayer *Manxman*, and destroyers *Avon Vale*, *Cossack*, *Eridge*, *Farndale*, *Lightning*, *Maori*, *Nestor* and *Sikh*. Force 'H' itself, plus *Nelson*, was to comprise the covering force, with fleet oiler *Brown Ranger* to ensure that those destroyers going right through the narrows would do so with full fuel tanks. Destroyer *Encounter*, returning with six empty freighters from previous convoys plus the naval auxiliary *Breconshire*, was also to bombard Pantellaria harbour should the opportunity occur. The convoy comprised *City of Pretoria*, *Deucalion*, *Durham*, *Port Chalmers*, *Melbourne Star* and *Sydney Star*, to which the naval personnel ship *Leinster* was added as troopship with 1,000 reinforcement for the Malta garrison embarked, with almost 4,000 others taking passage in the cruisers of Force 'X'. As if this were not complex enough, opportunity was to be taken for *Ark Royal* to fly off more Swordfish to be based at Malta.

The bulk of Force 'X' and the convoy sailed direct from the UK and passed through the Straits of Gibraltar on the night of 20th/21 July, sending in the short-legged 'Hunt' class destroyers to refuel as they did so while some of the cruisers embarked their cargo of troops from the liner *Pasteur* there. The oiler left the same night, escorted by destroyer *Beverley*, and finally Force 'H' sailed just before dawn.

Thick fog fortunately shielded these movements through the Straits but *Leinster* ran aground and had to be left behind. Force 'H' with *Renown, Nelson, Ark Royal, Hermione, Faulknor, Fearless, Firedrake, Foxhound, Foresight, Forester, Fury* and *Duncan,* moved into their covering position ahead and north of the convoy on the 21st, Admiral Somerville readjusted the destroyer screen to facilitate oiling, keeping *Nestor, Foxhound, Firedrake* and the three 'Tribals' and sending the others to join the convoy. He instructed Captain De Salis in *Faulknor* to transfer further orders to each ship, and then took the rest of the force north-east. The first day thus passed without incident.

Dawn on the 22nd found the destroyers taking it in turns to refuel from *Brown Ranger*. *Faulknor* was coupled up to the oiler for an hour, an unpleasant position in hostile territory, closely astern a fully-laden tanker; but at 1640, she cast off, resuming her position on the screen, her place immediately being taken by another. It was 1500 before all the escorts had so competed oiling.

On the Italian side Rome still remained unaware of 'Substance'. They knew Force 'H' had left Gibraltar, they always did, but assumed this was another air reinforcement sortie and took no major steps to press home reconnaissance until the 23rd.

It was when sighting reports started flooding in of both the convoy, Force 'H' and Force 'X' that the Italian Naval Command, belatedly decided that it too late for the fleet to sail, but despatched extra submarines, readied MAS squadrons in the Narrows for night attacks and placed their air force on full alert.

Having been granted two days respite, Somerville had all his forces concentrated by 0800 and the carrier had seven Fulmars in the air when the first wave of bombers came in at 0945. The high-level bombing failed, as usual, to score any hits, but it did achieve its secondary purpose of breaking up the rigid lines of the convoy and escort thus allowing the torpedo-bombers to penetrate closer in than usual and pick their targets, launching their missiles from both sides and making avoiding action difficult. Two selected the destroyer screen and launched against *Fearless* at ranges of 800 and 1,500 yards and heights of 70 feet. She managed to side-step one torpedo and then the second, but it came to the surface, changed course suddenly and hit her aft jamming her rudder and setting her oil tanks on fire. Although *Faulknor* and *Forester* both closed her and fought the fires, Somerville ordered that unless *Fearless* could steam she was to be abandoned and sunk. As a long tow was the only hope for *Fearless* this decision sealed her fate. Taking off survivors she was torpedoed by her flotilla mate and sent to the bottom, the first loss that the flotilla had suffered in two years all-out war.

Another group of torpedo-bombers penetrated the barrage, losing three of their number in the process, and launched against *Manchester*. One torpedo hit, causing heavy damage and putting three of her four engines out of action. She could still make eight knots, and did not share *Fearless's* fate, being sent back with *Avon Vale* as escort and brought safely in.

The convoy pushed on eastward under a clear blue sky, drawing ever nearer the Skerki Channel. Another raid developed at 1010, and a third at 1645, but both fared badly against barrage and fighters and no hits were made on any ship. Thus, despite their casualties, the fleet had got all their charges safely to the edge of the Skerki Channel by dusk on 23rd. At 1615, *Faulknor* reversed course with the bulk of Force 'H', but *Hermione* was sent to join Force 'X' replacing *Manchester,* and *Firedrake* and *Foxhound* steered to lead the convoy columns, with their minesweeps out.

Although Force 'H' remained unmolested in their waiting position, their flotilla mates had less luck. Further air attacks broke over the convoy at 1900 and *Firedrake*, forced to keep a straight, slow and steady course, made an easy target. Bracketed by a bomb salvo a near-miss amidships disabled her. *Eridge* managed to get a towline aboard and, after a long and fraught passage, she reached Gibraltar intact. E-boat attacks followed, *Sydney Star* taking a torpedo hit but surviving. Heavy attacks the next morning were also beaten off and all the convoy arrived at Malta. Force X landed their troops, refuelled and, with the exception of *Farndale* which had condenser trouble, left to begin the return journey.

Faulknor led Somerville's force eastward at 18 knots as far east as 8° 30′ E before reversing course on the afternoon of 24th to cover all these various homeward movements. At 0100 next day, in

... less typical Mediterranean weather it was hard to imagine ... (Crown Copyright.)

37° 42′ N, 7° 17′ E, six Swordfish were flown off for Malta. At 0323 the beams of searchlights were sighted from *Faulknor's* bridge, but their source was never discovered. At 0815 they joined forces with Force 'X' and course was again set to the west.

At 0900/26th torpedo tracks were sighted and the heavy ships made an emergency turn at 24 knots, followed soon after by another. *Forester* and *Cossack* steamed down the torpedo tracks to deliver a counter-attack. Nothing resulted, so they rejoined. Enemy air formations, both altitude and torpedo bomber were plotted, as expected, around 1100, but neither group got through to the ships.

At 1530, they caught up with the crippled *Firedrake* in tow of *Eridge*. As *Faulknor* and her companions overtook them, the ships' companies cleared lower deck and cheered ship. That same evening they arrived back at the Rock.

Faulknor refuelled on 27 July and secured alongside at the Tower inboard of *Foxhound*. It was here that crippled *Firedrake* came alongside outboard of *Foxhound* and her Lieutenant (E) went in search of his opposite number to connect power lines and give his ship lighting. *Foxhound's* engineer was not aboard but 'next door' so the 'Chief' crossed over again to find him.

> As he went in through the lobby and down the ladder to *Faulknor's* wardroom, he heard a cheerful roar. The wardroom was full of people, very full, so crowded they could hardly make room for him. But as he shouldered in they recognised him and shouted. He was not feeling 'much like parties' but he asked the reason for the festivity. This was the 'Million Miles' party. *Firedrake* with her voyage had completed the flotilla's million miles at sea.'[3]

This was an outstanding achievement, the 8th easily beating any other flotilla in reaching this milestone. One million sea miles, yet the war was only two years old. One million miles, *Fearless* had been lost; both *Fame* and *Firedrake* badly damaged but surviving. One million miles, but there were many more miles yet to go for *Faulknor* and the rest of the 'Fs'. They had hardly started yet!

For Captain De Salis next day was the more serious side of the war, interviews with his two captains whose ships had suffered so grievously: Pugsley of *Fearless* and Norris of *Firedrake*, and Boards of Enquiry to arrange, but already plans were in train for another sortie eastward. On 27 July *Firedrake* went into dockyard hands for initial repairs, but *Faulknor* sailed from Gibraltar at 0700 with *Forester* and *Fury* to augment the escort of OG.69, but she was later recalled for Operation 'Style' [Signal ST 1320B/27 from FOCNA- '*Faulknor* has been recalled to Gibraltar'] and all arrived back at the Rock again in the early hours of the morning.

This sortie eastward again, was necessary because the troops aboard the stranded *Leinster*, plus those that had returned aboard damaged vessels had to be transported to Malta. Thus 70 officers and 1,676 Army and RAF passengers embarked in *Arethusa*, *Hermione* and *Manxman* and destroyers *Sikh* and *Lightning*, which left Gibraltar on 31 July for Operation 'Style'. Force 'H' provided cover with *Renown*, *Nelson*, *Ark Royal* and destroyers *Faulknor*, *Foresight*, *Forester*, *Foxhound*, *Fury*, *Encounter*, *Cossack* and *Maori*. Oiler *Brown Ranger* also sailed escorted by destroyer *Avon Vale*, who later joined the main force, handing her charge over to *Eridge*.

The operation proceeded with hardly any interference from the enemy whatsoever. During the night of 31 July/1 August *Cossack* and *Maori* were detached, the former to operate off Alghero, Sardinia, which nine Swordfish bombed the next day, the latter to bombard Porto Conte, Sardinia at 0200 on 1st. The troops were conveyed through to Malta under cover without loss, while the main body of Force 'H' showed themselves near the Balearic Islands. The cruisers and destroyers reached Malta at 0900/2 August and sailed again at 1600 for Gibraltar.

On 3 August Force 'H' was 75 miles W.N.W. of Galita Island when, at 0835, Force 'X' from Malta was sighted six miles distant. Course was altered to 270° as the cruisers joined and the whole fleet withdrew to the westward at twenty knots as visibility gradually improved.

At daylight the fleet was divided into three groups to facilitate berthing arrangements at Gibraltar; Group One comprised *Ark Royal*, *Hermione*, *Lightning*, *Sikh*, *Encounter* and *Forester*, which proceeded ahead at 27 knots and entered harbour at 2030 that evening. Group Two comprised *Nelson*, *Arethusa*, *Manxman*, *Faulknor*, *Fury*, *Foxhound* and *Foresight*, at twenty knots, reached harbour at 2230, while the *Renown* limped in at eighteen knots, escorted by *Avon Vale*, *Cossack*, *Maori* and *Nestor* arriving at midnight. *Renown* was not the only ship of Force 'H' feeling the effects of so much sea-time. Somerville wrote:

> The people at home never seem to realise the *practical* difficulties of operations out here. My destroyers, from constant running, are in a poor way; *Hermione* has damage from ramming the U-boat. A party of crocks and yet here we are operating on the enemy's doorstep with an inferior Force and hundreds of miles from our own base.

Two years non-stop running was *indeed* taking the toll of the destroyers engines and, on the return journey, *Faulknor* had a complete breakdown. Finally they managed to get one engine working again and limped back to Gibraltar, going straight into dock for a full inspection. On 7 August serious defects were discovered in the starboard turbine, the blades of which were damaged.

The ADNI had earlier indicated concern at possible sabotage being carried out in Gibraltar dockyard, [Signal 2065/41/3842 of the 16 September] and Admiral Somerville signalled to Captain De Salis on 23 October:

> DNI is to be informed whether there were any grounds for suspicion of sabotage in connection with damage to *Faulknor's* turbines.

According to one publication, the findings were that this damage was not accidental, but the results of deliberate sabotage.[4] This is hotly disputed by former engine-room staff who were on duty at the time. Harry Stapleton first gives a general overview:

Accidental damage of the kind described cannot easily occur, there are too many safeguards and regulations to be observed whenever boilers, steam pipes or turbines are opened up for inspection.

During wartime I cannot see why main turbines would be opened up for inspection unless some special reason was put forward and permission obtained. This work would require dockyard assistance with specialist jacking equipment for raising casings. Foreign dockyard workers would not be left unattended and all operations would be carefully supervised by the ship's company.

Main steam pipes are not accessible as to break a joint is a major operation. A foreign body (nut or bolt etc.) might be introduced into the main steam system during boiler cleaning but there are 'steam strainers' in-line to protect the turbine blades.

Somewhere, either in the turbines or the condenser, some evidence of a 'foreign body' might have been found. This would be conclusive, but the chances are that such a particle would be deformed beyond recognition and no longer recognisable as having been introduced, after contact with very high-speed turbine blading. I cannot imagine that a member of the ship's company was in any way involved.

Even more specific is the eyewitness evidence of Vernon Coles, DSM who was an ERA aboard *Faulknor* at this time. He is quite adamant that:

> ... it very definitely was not sabotage which caused the problem and I find it very surprising that such a rumour exists. I happened to have been on the watch in the engine room main steaming.
>
> We were steaming at quite high power when metallic noises appeared in our starboard set of main engines, at the same time severe vibrations set in which caused us to slow down and put back into Gibraltar.
>
> Our Chief ERA, Horace Pead, voiced his opinion that we had lost turbine blades. The first engine we opened up was the starboard Low Power (LP) Turbine and after engaging the turning gear, slowly revolved the engine by hand and it was indeed discovered that we had lost blades on the LP ahead rotor. As such it is impossible to steer on the Starboard set without causing irreparable damage to the set. Therefore we had to come home on the Port set only. The cause was given as the hard steaming we had done since the last major refit, plus the near misses in the bombing which rather shook the ship.
>
> It is utterly impossible to cause that type of defect by sabotage. There is just *no way* to get solid objects in the steam tract from boilers to main engines. At 340 propeller revs the LP Turbine rotor is revolving at something like 2,400 revs per minute and as they weighed approximately two tons they are very finely balanced and, having lost a number of blades in one section of the rotor it necessarily follows that severe vibration ensues, with the rotor out of balance.

The problem was compounded in the case of *Faulknor* in that there was no heavy lifting gear or spare turbine blading available at Gibraltar and Somerville therefore proposed that she be sent home forthwith to undergo a complete refit, a suggestion which Their Lordships sanctioned. It was therefore agreed to sail *Faulknor* back to the UK on her one good engine with the next homeward-bound convoy. Somerville pointed out that this would leave the 8th Flotilla with but three operational ships, too few to screen *Nelson* and *Ark Royal* and the Admiralty approved his suggestion of retaining destroyers *Encounter* and *Nestor*, due to join Cunningham's fleet, until such time as two of the damaged 'Fs' could rejoin Somerville's flag.

Thus, on 9 August, they left for home and essential repairs, but no British warship sailed anywhere without being put to good use and *Faulknor* was made Senior Officer of the escort of convoy HG.

70, which consisted of destroyer *Avon Vale* and, for the first part of the journey, *Encounter* and *Nestor*. After *Encounter* and *Westor* had turned back to Gibraltar, this convoy was set upon by a wolf-pack consisting of the Italian submarines *Da Vinci, Morosini, Torelli* and *Malaspina,* reinforced by the German *U-69, U-94, U-95, U-98, U-557, U-561* and *U-565*. Eleven U-boats against two destroyers, one of them, *Faulknor*, a cripple.

Faulknor was forced by her condition to jog along at eighteen knots, operating as a kind of 'back stop' every time a contact was reported. But Captain De Salis was wise and experienced in the art of U-boat warfare and, although the odds were high against them, so well did *Faulknor's* captain handle his small team, that not one of the convoy was lost to the enemy.

At 1402 /10th, *Faulknor* was stationed ahead of the convoy when *Avon Vale*, on the port side of the merchantmen, reported a surfaced U-boat on her port bow at a range of six miles. *Avon Vale* dashed off to investigate leaving *Faulknor* limping along behind on her one shaft. The submarine dived soon after it had been sighted, but the exhaust from her main vents was plainly visible. At 1437, *Avon Vale* gained Asdic contact at 700 yards and she made two depth-charge attacks. *Faulknor* also gained a contact, which her own operator classified as 'doubtful', but she made a depth-charge attack with six charges set to explode at 150, 250 and 350 feet. *Avon Vale* acted as directing ship for this attack and reported that bubbles and disturbance in the water was seen for a considerable time after *Faulknor* had fired and it was thought for a time that a U-boat was about to surface as a result. *Avon Vale* then dropped another pattern by eye in the position where the bubbles were still rising but did not regain contact. Captain De Salis regarded this contact as a 'non-sub' but he organised a proper search.

At 1605, both destroyers gained a firm contact ahead, although again *Faulknor's* operators stated there was no hydrophone effect or appreciable Doppler, and that the extent of the target was 15° at a range of 800 yards. *Avon Vale* attacked with a full pattern at 1613 while *Faulknor* carried out three deliberate attacks, in the first of which five charges were dropped set to 250 and 500 feet, and in the second and third attacks six charges were dropped set to 150 and 350 feet. Contact remained firm throughout but the extent of the target became increasingly large and it proved difficult to distinguish the contact attacked from the many other disturbances due to the detonations, and the echo was again lost. Due to the vulnerability of his convoy Captain De Salis decided they had been away too long and reluctantly abandoned the hunt, setting course to catch up with the transports, now some way ahead. Their attack was later classified as a definite U-boat, but with insufficient evidence of damage.

They rejoined their charges soon after 2300 and resumed their screening positions, and just before midnight Cape St. Vincent was brought abeam. Then the irrepressible *Avon Vale* claimed another contact and soon U-boats seemed to be everywhere – the wolf pack had homed in on them. Dawn broke, and *Avon Vale* reported a submarine signalling – obviously calling up her comrades to join the party. Sending her out to investigate Captain De Salis took *Faulknor* out ahead of the convoy to a position where he would have more time for manoeuvring against any further such contacts. Skirmishing continued throughout the afternoon and night and the Admiralty, evidently alarmed by the enemy's concentrations, reinforced the convoy with two destroyers from Plymouth, *Boreas* and *Wild Swan*.[5]

The ominous forms of Focke-Wulf Kondor four-engined bombers circling on the horizon did nothing to alleviate their foreboding; the planes were again in sight at sunrise on the 13th and soon the pace began to quicken again. *Faulknor* herself, still out ahead of the convoy, spotted a U-Boat on the surface at 0630, and worked up her shaky engines to twenty-two knots in an attempt to ram her, but, when she was still some way off, the German sighted her and crash-dived. *Wild Swan* joined *Faulknor* and they searched the area to try to flush out the enemy before the convoy came up.

Almost at once both destroyers gained contact and there followed a long, grim, three-hour hunt: again and again the destroyers stormed in, sending down crushing patterns of depth-charges, while below the U-boat desperately twisted and turned, rocked by concussions. The first attack was made in 40° 19′ N, 15° 46′ W. A Focke-Wulf Kondor aircraft was seen signalling and immediately after *Faulknor* sighted the submarine on the horizon approximately seven miles' distant. Three attacks were delivered by *Wild Swan* and two by *Faulknor*. Towards 1000 after the sixth attack, a large and slowly spreading pool of oil was seen on the surface and they stopped to investigate. The Germans were in the habit of discharging oil to give the impression that they had been mortally wounded, so Captain De Salis remained in the area for a further two hours to await developments; but it was then decided that the enemy must have indeed succumbed and once more the two destroyers hastened to rejoin the plodding convoy.

This enemy submarine was considered to have been badly damaged. Subsequent examination of war records confirmed that she had sadly not been sunk, but must have been severely shaken, for the convoy received no further attention from the U-boats. No cargo ships had been lost despite the enemy's best efforts and *Faulknor* had shown that, although lame, she could still pack a punch.

On 16th the welcome sight of a Lockheed Hudson of Coastal Command appeared overhead and *Faulknor* put on her best speed, and drawing away from the convoy put into Plymouth, refuelled and rejoined the convoy for the passage up the Irish Sea. She escorted them safely into Londonderry, anchoring at 1345/16 August. A signal, timed at 1525 from the C-in-C, Western Approaches read:

> Londonderry sail *Faulknor* to Southampton when ready.

They duly retraced their passage next day, arriving at Portsmouth on 18 August 1941, where she de-ammunitioned ship before sailing round to Southampton for a very extensive refit. For many of her veteran crew this was their last glimpse of the ship.

Griff Fanthorpe recalled:

> When we returned to the UK in August, 1941, *Faulknor* was in urgent need of a refit – having been operational non-stop for nearly two years.

This she now underwent.

CHAPTER V

Arctic Battleground

At John I. Thornycroft's Southampton yard, *Faulknor* was docked and the crew dispersed on long leave during the major refit. The substantial modifications included the fitting of a High-Frequency Direction Finding ('Huff-Duff'); surface-warning radar set and increased depth-charge stowage and racks.

To compensate for the additional weight, one or two guns from the destroyer's main armaments were sacrificed; in the North Atlantic gun actions were rare, so this risk was accepted. Unfortunately, the new route to Murmansk, Russia, *increased* the risk of surface actions, for Germany's fleet was concentrated in Norway. *Faulknor* still retained her full Fleet Destroyer role, unlike *Fame,* who became a fast convoy-escort.

Faulknor thus retained full main armament, supplemented by 20-mm Oerlikon AA cannon. Firepower of her 4.7-inch weapons was increased to 250 rounds-per-gun reserve ammunition carried, while depth-charges stowage increased to thirty-eight. She was fitted out for Arctic conditions, and was to retain her Leader roles as escort group commander, fleet escort, convoy protector, escort group leader or striking force senior officer.

Engines repair proved far more extensive than at first thought and her completion date was continually postponed, *viz* this sequence of signals.

1857/20 August, from Flag Officer, Southampton:

> *Faulknor* taken in hand by Thornycrofts 20/8. Probable time required for repairs eight weeks.

From DoD 25 August:

> *Faulknor* completes 15 September.

From DoD 8 September:

> *Faulknor* completes 15 October.

1457 22 September, from FOIC Southampton:

> *Faulknor* completes 20 November.

1527 6 October, from FOIC, Southampton.

> *Faulknor* D/C is now 7 November.

Early in November, *Faulknor* was undocked and began sea trials in Southampton Water to test her reconditioned engines. Harry Stapleton:

Following major refits or repairs, speed trials are undertaken. The ship puts to sea and all boilers are connected and gradually maximum fuel burning capacity is reached, this is concurrent with 'full speed' nozzles on the high-pressure turbines being opened. This is the maximum power situation and the ship is timed over a measured mile. The object is to achieve satisfactory and trouble-free performance – not to try to break records. Wind and tide naturally influence speed so results will vary according to prevailing conditions, age of ship, state of machinery and, very important, a clean bottom!'

Faulknor, now seven years old, had been run very hard; was carrying a larger crew, extra equipment, armament, electronics and much else. Not surprisingly, she could no longer achieve her original trial speed.

I cannot recall this speed ever being officially achieved although we probably managed close to it when dire emergency demanded. On reflection I would give the possibility of 32–33 knots perhaps, with following wind and tide!

On 11 November, Inclining Experiments were conducted by DOD covering three different conditions following a letter from Captain De Salis on overloading and extensive top weight affecting stability. The figures produced make interesting reading:

	A	B	C
Maximum Stability	44°	46°	36°
Vanishes at	80°	90°+	66°,

Trials completed, *Faulknor* re-ammunitioned, re-stored and refuelled at Portsmouth, commissioning with a large percentage of fresh crew members, although Captain De Salis was still there, wise and solid, to guide them.

C-in-C, Portsmouth signalled 1343/9 November:

Faulknor will be sailed on 13 November.

War Complement for *Faulknor,* on 19 November, was 131 officers and men, broken down as Captain (D); one each Lieutenant-Commanders (G), (T), (N), (S) and (A/S); one Sub-Lieutenant, two Commander Gunners (DF) and (T); One Commander Boatswain (A/S); one Chief Petty Officer, six Petty Officers; twelve Leading and eighty Able and Ordinary Seamen; one Chief Yeoman; three Yeomen, four Leading Signalmen; four Signalmen; one Commander Telegraphist; three CPO Telegraphists; three Leading Telegraphists and three Telegraphists.

Faulknor finally left Portsmouth at 0900/15th, reaching Greenock via the Irish Sea, at 1100 next day. D/F calibration trials for her new equipment and other exercises followed for three days. This done, *Faulknor* left Greenock at 1400/20 November for Londonderry, refuelled and, received her first assignment.

Faulknor sailed on 21 November for 55° N, 10° W to rendezvous with battleship *Nelson* returning home from Gibraltar with a torpedoe-damaged bow and survivors of *Ark Royal* aboard. *Faulknor,* with destroyers *Icarus* and *Norman,* from Scapa, took over screening duties.

They took *Nelson* into Scapa at 1030/22nd, refuelled, and then sailed for Rosyth with *Icarus* at 1839. *Faulknor's* new weapons soon found employment when, late the same afternoon, Asdic obtained a firm submarine echo off *Nelson's* starboard bow. They dropped a single charge to keep the submarine down, but did not conduct a prolonged hunt, proceeding to Rosyth. At 1100, *Nelson* entered the dockyard and the destroyers returned to Scapa in heavy weather.

They arrived1640/ 23rd, but the seas were rough and, while going alongside an oiler, *Faulknor* badly damaged her bows. This necessitated a few days alongside Destroyer Depot Ship *Tyne*. Once buckled plates had been made good, *Faulknor* spent the next few days escorting battle-cruiser *Renown*, battleship *Resolution* and light cruiser *Trinidad*, in exercises and night shoots. Iceland was a staging-post on the way to Murmansk and *Faulknor* was given the mail for those bases after which, the scuttlebutt asserted, they would return to Liverpool for a 'special' job. This voyage was delayed because of storms and gales and, on 8 December, while still waiting to sail, news came of the Japanese attack on Pearl Harbor. Immediately the Iceland mail was dumped ashore and, at 1600/9 December, *Faulknor*, *Foresight* and *Matabele* conducted an anti-submarine sweep ahead of new battleship *Duke of York* and heavy cruiser *Cumberland*, screening them from 1645. The weather remained terrible, and speed had to be reduced as they clawed their way around the top of Scotland and down the Minches. The squadron had just arrived off Greenock when they received the shocking news that both battleship *Prince of Wales* and battle-cruiser *Repulse* had been sunk by Japanese Navy torpedo-bombers off Malaya. At 1216, the operation was abruptly cancelled and the squadron was ordered back to Scapa, arriving 1015/11th. *Faulknor* refuelled and re-embarked the Iceland mail, but, within hours this was again cancelled and *Duke of York* and the three destroyers left Scapa at 1630, for the Clyde.

The *Duke of York* checked her Gyro with *Faulknor* at 0933 and, after another very dusty passage, the squadron anchored off Greenock at 1527/12th, where shore leave was given. This became a nightmare; the weather deteriorated so much that the men ashore were unable to rejoin. About two hundred stranded sailors from the four warships were given a blanket apiece and slept rough in the naval barracks. Next morning the weather moderated sufficiently for them to re-embark, and, at 1050/13th, so did a V.I.P. party from London.

This comprised Prime Minister Winston Churchill, Averell Harriman, and First Sir Lord, Admiral Sir Dudley Pound and their parties, who were taking passage aboard the battleship to meet with President Roosevelt at the 'Arcadia' Conference, resulting in what became the historic 'Atlantic Charter'.

The squadron weighed at 1214/13th, passing the Greenock boom at 1253. *Duke of York* was bound for Chesapeake Bay, but *Faulknor*, *Foresight* and *Matabele* found the going very hard immediately against the full force of a North Atlantic gale. The squadron speed was twenty-five knots, with a broad southerly sweep to avoid U-boat concentrations.

Coder Ted Newman recorded:

> Weather was bad and, owing to the high speed we had to maintain, we began leaking badly, the Messes, Holds and Stores were getting flooded and we had a hectic time pumping and baling out. Part of our guard rails were busted on the bows and, before they could be cut away, they had busted on the ports in our mess deck. We couldn't do anything about this and water simply poured in. What with this and our mess gear rolling all over the place, except for when we were on watch or pumping party, we lived in our hammocks.
>
> The thud of the waves was just like bombs dropping – it's a wonder we still kept afloat. Our speed had to be reduced to 12 knots putting us well behind schedule. The Head was once again in a terrible state and could not be used for natural purposes. The smell was awful and could not be eased as the pumps had broken down and there was no water.

On the 16 December, there was still a heavy swell but the gale had abated somewhat, although *Faulknor* was still rolling. Next day there were more gales and it was declared unsafe for anyone to venture onto the upper deck. At 0840/17th *Foresight* was forced to stop for five minutes with engine difficulties and, although she got underway again, within four minutes the squadron had to reduce speed again to seventeen knots, increasing at 0924 to nineteen knots. Even this proved too much for the little ships to maintain.

It was clearly impossible for the destroyers to maintain the speed in such conditions and at 1805, *Duke of York* released them and proceeded alone. A signal was received thanking them for keeping up the high-speed escort, at great risk to themselves, and expressing the hope that they were not too uncomfortable.

'If only they had been in our place,' wrote Ted Newman ruefully.

Speed could now be reduced but it was still no sinecure and during the night *Faulknor* was hit by a freak sea and almost capsized. Only skilful work by Captain De Salis in using Port and Starboard engines alternately kept them on an even keel. Soon after *Foresight's* steering gear broke down, and her companions circled her at a tedious ten knots, Asdics pinging away but all sound being lost in the swirling undercurrents. Eventually, steering by her engines only, *Foresight* managed to get under way and slowly struggle on.

The storms abated temporarily and they reached the haven of Punta Delgada, Azores at 1430/18 December, in bright sunshine. While fixing some of the structural damage, boatloads of friendly vendors brought pineapples, bananas and other exotic fruit out to the ship. At night, the port was ablaze with lights, a sight not seen in the UK for over two years. Even here, the destroyers found they were in great demand.

Ted Newman noted:

> This last two days we had been flooded with signals from groups of destroyers carrying out anti-U-boat sweeps.

U-boats had been concentrated west of Spain in mid-December, ambushing convoy HG.76 and fierce battles developed over a period of days.

Flag Officer, North Atlantic, signalled at 1642/18th that the three Home Fleet destroyers should, after refuelling, proceed to Scapa at best speed, endurance and weather permitting, passing through 37° 40′ N, 25° 10′ W and 45° N and 21° W, as they were urgently required. However, at 1706, as the fight around the convoy intensified, he signalled the Admiralty:

> As there appears to be five or six submarines hunting HG. 76 proposed *Faulknor* and *Foresight*, after fuelling at Punta Delgada, should join HG. 76 if they can be spared. *Exmoor* and *Blankney* have to leave convoy shortly for fuel.'

ACNS relied at 2323:

> Regret these ships cannot be spared. The three ships left Punta Delgada 0930/19.

They sailed at 0800, working up to 24 knots. However, *Foresight's* damage meant that she could not maintain that pace and so, on 20th, *Matabele* was detached to Scapa independently, while *Faulknor* remained with her crippled sister. The ether was full of the news of U-boat packs and counter-attacks by the escorts but their journey proved uneventful, reaching Scapa on 23 December, securing alongside *Tyne* at 0600.

Subsequently they conducted exercises with battleship *Resolution* and carrier *Victorious* and spent Christmas and Boxing Day at anchor, making up for previous disappointment. The 27th found

Faulknor and *Forester* exercising with *Resolution*, followed by lonely patrols off the islands, setting the pattern for the final days of 1941.

New Year 1942 arrived with gale warnings, bitter cold and snow. Exercises with *Victorious* and the Home Fleet flotillas took place on the 7/8 January, followed by a visit from Rear-Admiral, (D) who complimented the ship and then said he hoped soon to send them to Norway! On 12th lower-deck was cleared for the reading of a charge against a stoker who had misused a privilege envelope, hardly a hanging offence, and next day there was another storm during the afternoon. Many ashore again could not rejoin; one who tried by motorboat found himself stranded in the Flow when the engine broke down.

Next day signals poured into *Faulknor's* coding office regarding Russia convoy PQ. 8, which had been attacked by a wolf-pack. The Commodore's ship had been torpedoed, as had *Matabele* which sank off the Kola Inlet. *Tirpitz* and other German heavy ships were preparing to sortie, so *Faulknor* sailed with the Home Fleet in haste to Hvalfjord, Iceland, arriving midday 19th amidst snow flurries. *Tirpitz* did indeed leave Germany, reaching Trondheim, Norway, undetected on 16th. The C-in-C, Admiral Sir John Tovey, thought she might be on her way into the Atlantic, as *Bismarck*, *Scharnhorst* and *Gneisenau* before her, and assembled his main force to intercept any such move.

The operation planned for *Faulknor* and others off Norway was cancelled, the sailing of the next convoy to Murmansk postponed and air reconnaissance finally found *Tirpitz* at anchor in Aasfjord. Meanwhile, *Faulknor* oiled on 25 January and secured alongside heavy cruiser *Kent* to store ship.

At Hvalfjord they said good-bye to their much-respected Captain (D); Captain De Salis leaving the ship 26 January 1942. De Salis had been a popular but respected skipper, one of the old school; to some awesome and remote, but cool of judgement and clear of thought; to others a father figure, and, in general, the crew were sorry to lose him. Mr C. Watson remembered him as, '… a religious man. On Sundays at sea, even if we were rolling around, if he could get away from the bridge we would have a short service in the Forward Mess Deck. On Christmas Day, when the C.P.Os were invited down into the Wardroom for a drink, Captain De Salis would just have a small glass as a token and that would be all. He was a good captain, and a gentleman'.

His successor was to prove equally popular and was another very fine officer indeed, Captain Alan Kenneth Scott-Moncrieff, DSO, RN. This officer, from a well-known Scottish family, ('Scotty' [secretly] to the lower deck), had first joined the Royal Navy in 1917 and served aboard battleship *Orion* until 1919. A signals specialist, his earlier wartime career had been as captain of the escort sloop (former Admiralty Yacht) *Enchantress* in the North Atlantic

Mr Watson again:

> We all thought how lucky we were to have another such good Captain (D), which he was in every way, always ready to grant leave if possible and he treated everyone as an equal, it wasn't possible to have a better skipper. I think it is fair to describe HMS *Faulknor* at this time as a very happy ship, of course there were the usual moans, but that's all.

The next few months were to strain everyone's good nature to the limits and beyond. Captain Scott-Moncrieff came aboard on the 27 January, his new secretary Lieutenant R. P. Peters, with Lieutenants C. S. Battorsby and P. D. G. Mathers joining the Staff. Early next morning, they slipped, and, in company with destroyers *Echo, Escapade* and *Intrepid*, sailed for Reykjavik. As one Australian crew member recalls, the Captain was prepared for the cold if none of the others were.

> I remember when we were apparently due to go on the Russia run, Alfie Gardner told me he had to go to the Captain's tailor in London to get a full fur-coat.

It remained bitterly cold with snow. On 29th, a merchant ship was torpedoed off Shagi, and *Faulknor*, with every available British and American destroyer, was rushed to sea for an anti-submarine sweep lasting several days.

Between 31 January and 20 February 1942, *Faulknor* escorted convoy, PQ 9, from Hvalfjord, Iceland to Kola Inlet, North Russia. Included in the convoy were two 250-ton ex-Norwegian whalers, *Hav* (T-101) and *Shika* (T-102), fitted out as anti-magnetic minesweepers for the Royal Navy and transferred to the Soviets. These, having very short endurance, were to be towed by *Faulknor* and *Intrepid* through the 'safe' area, in order to conserve fuel. Elaborate plans were made aboard the two destroyers to carry out this hazardous duty.

At 1640/31 January, *Faulknor* embarked canteen stores and *Intrepid* took aboard a boat for *Shika*, sailing at 2030 and steering at twenty knots for Seidisfjord. By 1100 next day, they had a foretaste of what they were in for when a strong easterly wind forced them to reduce speed, finally arriving at 1930/1 February.

A heavy concentration of U-boats in the area delayed PQ.9's sailing while anti-submarine sweeps were conducted between the British defensive minefields and the coast, from ten miles south of the entrance to ten miles north. *Faulknor* obtained a long-range HF/DF bearing at 0120, but, other than sighting half-a-dozen floating British mines, the night was without incident and the two destroyers secured alongside an oiler at 0830/2nd. This delay saw PQ 9 merged with PQ.10, and the combined convoy, ten freighters with trawler escorts, sailed 3 February.

The whalers now informed Captain Scott-Moncrieff that they had been fitted with extra fuel stowage, enabling them to steam 2,300 miles at ten knots. The tow was aborted, the destroyers being prepared to refuel them should their new consumption figures prove illusory. This gave the destroyers freedom of action to attack the U-boats. The convoy sailing was delayed eight hours and, as the destroyers needed to husband every ton of oil, the four warships left 0700/3 February, the whalers steaming at ten knots, the destroyers zigzagging on their bows. *Hav* lost touch during the night but was later discovered by *Intrepid* three miles to port and led back; she was to prove unreliable throughout the voyage.

Leaving the whalers to make their best course to catch up with the convoy, the destroyers steered to overtake by dawn 4th, but, as it was steaming at nine knots instead of the eight reported, they did not join until 1015/5 February. They overtook Russian freighter *Ijora* at dawn, who informed Captain Scott-Moncrieff that her maximum speed was $8\frac{1}{2}$ knots flat-out. She was then eighteen miles astern of the convoy and never did rejoin.

HMS Faulknor *escorting a Russian convoy in the vicinity of Bear Island, February 1942.* (K. Timson.)

HMS Faulknor *escorting a Russian convoy in February 1942. Note the ready-use shells in racks, the single Oerlikon aft, dan buoy marker in foreground.* (K. Timson.)

The convoy proved to be nine merchant ships formed into two columns. *Faulknor* assumed Senior Officer of the escort, placing herself on the starboard bow during daylight and on the beam at night, zigzagging as necessary, while *Intrepid* took the port side and, when the two whalers finally joined at 1000/6 February, they were stationed on the beam of the rear ship of each column.

At 1134, the Admiralty ordered PQ.9 and PQ.10 to alter course forthwith, and this was done, but at 1550, a new route was signalled from London. Again Captain Scott-Moncrieff prepared to instruct the Convoy Commodore of this when light cruiser *Nigeria* appeared and signalled; ' I consider it imperative to try and pass between longitudes 18° 30' and 20° 00' during dark hours.' A modified version of the Admiralty's second course was therefore adopted, which meant it unnecessary to alter course in the failing light, with the resulting loss of cohesion.

The weather was excellent for the first two days of the convoy's passage, but at 0800/7th, 100 miles north of North Cape, a southerly gale and blizzard arose. This coincided with a change of course and three of the convoy, plus the wayward *Hav,* lost touch. Of these, *Atlantic* was finally found by *Faulknor* at 1500, steering for the next day's rendezvous point, but she never rejoined the convoy.

Conditions eased slightly after dark and, by dawn 8th, the Commodore still had the two destroyers, *Shika* and five other freighters in company. The tiny *Shika* was still stoutly maintaining her correct station and Captain Scott-Moncrieff recorded that; '… cheering signals were exchanged between her and *Faulknor*.'

He continued:

> Further blizzards with south-westerly winds of force 6 to 8 reduced the convoy's speed to four knots. The temperature fell to 28° F and all the ships were soon covered with ice from their truck to the bow waves.

Although German reconnaissance aircraft were sighted from 6 February, and *Faulknor* went to Action Stations, they quickly lost contact. Icy winds with the length of the Arctic Ocean behind them, tore through their thickest clothes, freezing their bodies, while great angry seas buffeted and corkscrewed them around mercilessly. Station-keeping proved impossible. Through the flying spindrift, the lookouts caught an occasional glimpse of the little trawlers bobbing up and down on the heaving ocean like corks, whilst *Intrepid's* mast cut a crazy arc through the leaden sky astern. All through the day and that night they clawed on toward the rendezvous, Captain Scott-Moncrieff taking *Faulknor* every so often in a tight sweep to check that all the little whalers were still present, and then resuming their shaky course again. The cold, miserable afternoon wore on, and then smoke was sighted on the convoy's bow. A quick check showed all the ships in company, so the smoke could very well be hostile. Alarm bells clanged Action Stations, gunners and torpedo men blundered up onto the treacherous decks and clustered around their freezing weapons, as *Faulknor* swung swiftly round toward that distant plume of smoke. As they drew nearer they could identify the ship as one of the 'Colony' Class light cruisers of their covering squadron and, when challenged, she revealed herself to be *Nigeria*. After a brief exchange, she slid back into the murk again, and soon afterwards the weather closed down once more.

By teatime there were squalls of thick snow and the wind was whipping up the crests of the long rolling seas into icy spray; the night was as bad as the previous one had been and there was little rest for anyone aboard. They took advantage of conditions to change the course of the convoy to keep the enemy off the scent and were largely successful. Morning revealed the convoy scattered far and wide, sitting ducks for any lurking submarine; fortunately the Germans were also feeling the weather and no sightings were made.

They pushed on through a heavy swell and icy conditions. Their spirits were not raised much by a signal received stating that, because of lack of Soviet air cover at Murmansk they should expect casualties to both convoy and escort! The gales returned during the first watch and the convoy again became scattered. The ship rolled heavily from side to side and it was impossible to have heated food or to wash or make tea. The upper deck, superstructure, boats, guns and stays were frozen solid. They took what precautions they could against cold-weather damage to the guns, but little could be done apart from spraying them with the ships steam hose. Men's hands, carelessly meeting frozen steel, left patches of 'burnt' skin behind when snatched away, while thickening ice on the decks made all movement hazardous.

The 9th dawned bleak and cold with occasional snow flurries. The remnants of the two convoys were spread over six miles, but *Faulknor* maintained touch with the Commodore and *Intrepid* with the main body of the stragglers. The escorts cast about and, at 0700, the mast of an unidentified merchantman were spotted. They closed her, flashing the challenge, and, after a laborious exchange she was identified as one of the Soviet ships from the convoy, so Captain Scott-Moncrieff, after tucking her under his wing, resumed the search. At 1000, the rest of the convoy hove into sight and *Faulknor* pushed in among them to count heads. Six ships were rounded up by noon, at which time the weather again began to moderate, although the temperature continued to fall.

Captain Scott-Moncrieff later commented on the question of top-weight in the destroyers in these conditions.

> On the outward voyage both destroyers were low in fuel during the last twenty-four hours and both ships carried an estimated top weight of 15 tons of ice above the upper deck. It is considered that destroyers should oil at sea if possible during voyages.

They again took up position ahead and began an anti-submarine sweep. Navigational fixes were obtained from Group R radio stations, and excellent bearings were obtained from Set Navolok and Napip Navolok at ranges of over fifty miles which enabled a firm plot to be established, but the Cape Teriberski signals were never more than second class, even at twenty miles.

The convoy was still more-or-less intact, though somewhat scattered. The destroyers fussed about them, shepherding them back into orderly lines, and pushed on. The wind had fallen overnight to force 3. At 0130/10th smoke was sighted bearing 171°, and *Intrepid* was sent off *post haste* to investigate, soon returning with four minesweepers from 6th Flotilla. Guns crews lashed by the freezing spray, stood down or huddled in the sparse shelter of their gun shields – to fight in those conditions would have been almost impossible; but the smoke from the whalers *might* just have been from German destroyers, or worse.

The convoy arrived at Kola Inlet at 0730. As the Australian crew member recalled, their first contact with their Russian ally.

> When we got to Kola Bay at Murmansk and hove to, I happened to be on the bridge and the First Lieutenant told me to go down to the iron deck and escort the Russian Pilot up to the bridge. When the Russian pilot boat came alongside, a fur-clad figure came over our guard rail and landed at my feet and I realised it was a woman just over 5 feet tall (She was a four-ringed Captain in the Soviet Navy). Not knowing if she spoke English or not I just beckoned to her and walked up the ladder to the bridge and she followed me up. Well – when I got to the Bridge and she followed, I said to No. 1, 'The Pilot, Sir.' He just stared at her, dumbfounded and then called Captain Scott-Moncrieff from out of his day cabin. He took one look at the Lady Pilot, turned on his heel and just said, 'Take over, No. 1' and left.

One of the 'stragglers' had arrived the previous evening, the other two, along with *Hav,* and even *Ijora*, all turned up safely during the course of the following two days, so PQ. 9/10 was a total success.

Nigeria had already arrived and had mail for them. They anchored mid-stream and their suspicious allies allowed no shore leave. Next day *Faulknor's* crew spent the day chipping ice off the ship and de-icing the guns with steam hoses. Fires were lit in the mess-decks for the first time in a week; the water temperature at Murmansk was a cosy –24° C.

The haven, reached after such a painful struggle, proved a strange one. Although they had come through storm and dangerous seas at great risk, laden with vital war material the UK could ill afford, and escorting many Soviet ships, the reception the Russians gave our these two convoys was as chilly as the weather. They received no thanks for the tanks, guns and ammunition thus delivered, nor were they, this time, allowed alongside the Polynaroe Naval Base.

The *Faulknors*, for the most part, felt no regrets as they watched the shores of the 'Peoples Paradise' slip away astern when they set course for Iceland again. They left at 1800/13 February, escorting homeward-bound convoy QP.7, eight freighters in two columns, escorted by *Faulknor*, *Intrepid*, and, initially, the minesweepers. The destroyers, the only escorts fitted with radar, took the central positions on the screen.

C-in-C's signal, timed 1709/13 February, read:

> When QP. 7 disperses *Faulknor* is to proceed Scapa refuelling Seidesfjord if required.

The convoy's initial speed was 8½ knots, but this had to be reduced by a knot as the Russian *Stalingrad* could not keep up. The convoy and escorts were sighted by German aircraft the following day. The weather on 14th was good, with a south-westerly wind of force 3 to 4, the temperature remaining above freezing point. *Hazard* and *Speedwell* left at 0900, while, at 1600, the destroyers went to Action Stations for an unidentified ship, which turned out to be the AA cruiser *Cairo* taking Soviet officials home. Then the gales reappeared. Ted Newman wrote:

> ... we were tossed all over the place and mess decks flooded with mess traps sliding all over the place. At home people could never believe such conditions possible. During the night it got worse and began freezing, all the guns being put out of action. Our Mess was a shambles, hardly a thing remaining in the racks.

The 16th was no better. 'Gale still blowing and crew trying to de-ice the guns. It is impossible to keep a seat on the locker and all one can do when off watch is turn-in your hammock. Very few can stomach food or drink.'

Despite the gales, the convoy somehow remained intact and was still together at dawn of 15th; only *Stalingrad* continuing to give trouble, her speed averaging three knots. However, gales and blizzards on the night of the 15th/16th finally caused the convoy to scatter.

At dawn 16th, the wind was force 7 to 8 from the west, and the Convoy Commodore was three miles ahead of *Faulknor* with freighters *Jutland* and *Empire Holly*. Another group of four were astern of them, with *Stalingrad* at least twenty miles farther back on her own. The Commodore turned back and the three leading ships were organised in one group, escorted by the two destroyers, while *Britomart* and *Sharpshooter* joined the rest, but *Stalingrad,* '... had to be left to her own devices.'

Things eased during the afternoon and the three leading ships made reasonable progress, reaching the dispersal point at 1130/17th, a day-and-a-half later than planned. The minesweepers turned back to Kola at dawn and, with the convoy in the 'safe' area, it was dispersed.

Their voyage back was uneventful, save for the sighting of a Dornier 215 at 1220/19th. Ted Newman recorded the resulting farce:

> Action Stations! Gunnery Officer dashes to his post and says to the Skipper, 'We'll get him!' All the officers yelling down the pipes to their various departments. G.O. yells 'Fire', but nothing happens, so Skipper says, 'What about it?' Meanwhile *Intrepid* opens up. Plane drops two Verey lights to bluff us he is friendly but they are the wrong colour for the day. Should have been Blue and White. G.O. yells 'Cease Fire' as the Dornier gets out of range, although so far we had not fired! Suddenly a big bang and one of our guns fired, the shell landing about fifty yards away. What a panic. Luckily the plane never attacked us!

They conducted starshell firing and a throw-off full-calibre shoot before reaching Scapa at dawn 20 February.

Faulknor was dry-docked next day so that her hull could be examined for structural damage following the pounding she had received during the previous few weeks. Three hours manoeuvring saw them safely inside, with the aerials being taken down for renewal. Then there came another panic. The Germans sailed Pocket Battleship *Admiral Scheer*, heavy cruiser *Prinz Eugen* and three destroyers from Germany to Bergen and the Home Fleet hurried to intercept.

Faulknor's refit was abandoned, aerials replaced and the ship placed at 15 minutes notice to steam. They hastily re-stored from *Tyne,* only for the order to be rescinded. It was decided to boiler-clean and the First Lieutenant accordingly arranged a day's leave for the bulk of the crew at Kirkwall during 22/23 February. On 24th *Faulknor* returned to dry-dock for a three-day refit.

Convoy PQ.12 left Reykjavik on 1 March and the Home Fleet sailed from Scapa 1630 on 28 February, to give distant cover with battleship *Duke of York*, battle-cruiser *Renown*, light cruiser *Kenya* and destroyers *Faulknor, Fury, Echo, Eclipse, Eskimo* and *Punjabi*.

They arrived Hvalfjord at 1330/2 March, after another rough passage. *Faulknor's* Gyro broke down *en route* and they only narrowly missed a collision. The fleet sailed at 0600 next morning proceeding northward, hugging the coastline to avoid the worst of the weather, to refuel at Seidesfjord. They were to concentrate with battleship *King George V*, carrier *Victorious*, heavy cruiser *Berwick* and destroyers *Ashanti, Bedouin, Icarus, Intrepid, Lookout* and *Onslow*.

Taking it green over her bows, HMS Faulknor *noses down in a heavy swell off Iceland while escorting the aircraft-carrier HMS* Victorious *in 1942.* (IWM, London.)

The night of 4/5 March was torn by a howling gale through which the 2nd Battle Squadron plunged doggedly northward. Things started to go awry almost at once and continued to do so throughout the operation. *Berwick* suffered engine failure and had to be sent back. Light cruiser *Sheffield* was sent to take her place, actually passing *Faulknor* on her way to join Admiral Tovey's flag as *Faulknor* entered Seidesfjord to refuel. Within a short while she too was in trouble. Scores of British mines from the vast fields off Iceland had broken adrift in the weeks of gales and *Sheffield* was unlucky enough to strike one of these, being heavily damaged. At first, she thought she had been torpedoed. Her distress signal was received at 2100 and *Faulknor* altered course, went to action stations and, with *Eskimo,* increased speed to twenty-five knots to go to her assistance.

The two destroyers located *Sheffield* at 2343, and provided a 'continuous chain'[1] anti-submarine patrol around her until she managed to haul round and set course back to Iceland. *Faulknor* proved to be in little better shape than the cruiser as the merciless sea had severely distorted No. 1 gun shield, bending the thick metal back onto the breech of the gun as if it were cardboard; fortunately it was unmanned at the time. One of the Ready-Use lockers had been washed over the side with all its ammunition, while below decks, the men stumbled, cursing, to and from their stations, knee-deep in the milling icy water – a black world of heaving misery.

Ted Newman recorded:

We were tossed all over the place, terrific waves pounding over the forecastle and bridge, everyone in exposed positions getting soaked and No. 1 and No. 2 gun crews were unable to reach their guns, owing to ammunition lockers being washed all over the place, some of the crew being injured by these. Even steel ladders got bent by the force of the impact of the waves. At 2145 [actually 2343 according to *Sheffield's* report] we met *Sheffield*, she could manage a speed of six knots and we escorted her back to Seidesfjord, arriving at 1000 (actually 1222). She had been hit aft, one Marine was killed and a few injured. Her rum store was wrecked; we had to send over some of ours!'

Looking more like floating wrecks the three warships staggered into Seidesfjord and secured to refuel and mop up. No matter how weary they might be the destroyer men had to keep on. This was just the start of the adventure. Next day, while momentous events were unfolding to the east, *Faulknor* and *Bedouin* were on local anti-submarine patrol, returning next day and giving leave ashore. From Ultra decrypts, reinforced by submarine sightings, Admiral Tovey knew that *Tirpitz* had sortied with four destroyers to attack PQ.12 and, despite the atrocious conditions, attempted to intercept her. Meanwhile, *Tirpitz* battle group had sailed on the 6th and just missed the convoy, sinking instead a straggler from the homeward group QP.8. The Home Fleet was unable, in turn, to find the *Tirpitz*.

Faulknor went to one hour's notice on the 7th and next day sailed from Seidesfjord with *Bedouin*, *Eskimo* and *Tartar*, proceeding northward at high speed to rendezvous with the Home Fleet, which was at this time without any destroyers. As they hurried east *Faulknor* took in various signals from

HMS Faulknor *entering Seidesfjord, Iceland, after escorting the damaged light cruiser HMS* Sheffield, *which had been mined off Iceland, 5 March 1942.* (L. E. Pepper.)

The 'Q' gun deck and after funnel encased in ice: HMS Faulknor *in arctic weather conditions off Iceland, 5 March 1942.* (L. E. Pepper.)

the game of blind man's bluff that was taking place some hundred miles beyond them. The Admiralty was tracking *Tirpitz's* moves and relaying them to the fleet, but bad weather and bad luck frustrated each move. *Victorious* flew off a striking force of Albacore torpedo bombers but all their torpedoes missed the target.

Faulknor's force joined the Fleet at 1840/9th for the return to Scapa, various detached squadrons joining up for a large-scale exercise, which was cancelled on arrival of German reconnaissance aircraft. They arrived at 2300/10 March, when *Faulknor* moved to the side of the dry-dock in readiness for more repairs, but, before these commenced, they again received urgent sailing orders.

There remained one last slim chance of bringing the German battleship to battle should she sail from Narvik (Vestfjord) for Trondheim. Admiral Tovey ordered Captain Scott-Moncrieff to lead a force of eight destroyers from Scapa on the 11th and sweep along the Norwegian coast south of Vestifjord in the early hours of 13 March for just such an eventuality. They were to assume action stations at 2300/12th and remain closed up all night. At 0100, the flotilla would sweep down the

Norwegian coast off Bodo in line abreast at fourteen knots. If the enemy were sighted the destroyers would immediately attack with torpedoes. Whatever happened, at 0330 they would turn for home at 30 knots to avoid enemy aircraft.

This was the plan, which Captain (D) explained to the crew. *Faulknor* led the *Bedouin*, *Eskimo*, *Fury*, *Icarus*, *Intrepid*, *Punjabi* and *Tartar* from the Flow that evening, sailing at 30 knots into calm seas. The light cruisers *Nigeria* and *Trinidad* sailed separately as a back-up force. Some fighter protection was initially laid on but, on the first arrival of the Luftwaffe overhead, at 1800 that day, they were initially taken for British, thereupon all the RAF planes vanished and were not seen again. The Germans did not attempt to attack the destroyer force but merely contented themselves by reporting its composition, course and speed. Not surprisingly, *Tirpitz* did not sail until 2300/12th.

According to one account[2], the plan was for the destroyers to make their high speed dash across to the Norwegian coast in two divisions of four ships each, *Faulknor*, *Fury*, *Icarus* and *Intrepid* as one division and the four 'Tribals' under Commander B. G. Scurfield, in *Bedouin*, as second-in-command, in the other. On reaching their position offshore they were to sweep up the coast at 14 knots, '… the highest speed at which the bow wave would not break and show a white flash.' If *Tirpitz* was sighted the destroyers were to conduct a 'Star Attack', with four sub-divisions of two ships each attacking from each point of the compass. This classic manoeuvre would mean that, no matter which way the enemy turned, *some* torpedoes should find their mark. It was a much-practised form of destroyer attack, but on this occasion, they were not to get the chance to prove its merits.

Just before zero hour, *Punjabi's* gyro broke down and she turned back, but the remaining seven destroyers continued to carry out their orders. Soon after 0100 they formed their line of search. Visibility was poor, misty and dull, and some of the crew, discussing their chances should they actually stumble across *Tirpitz* at close quarters, fervently hoped that it would stay that way – and it did.

For two-and-a-half hours they steamed in formation off the enemy coast but failed to sight anything at all. By 0330 they had not made contact and, with a watery daylight attempting to lighten the sky, it seemed unwise to tarry further, so Captain Scott-Moncrieff hauled round to the west again and set course back to Scapa, shadowed from 0700 by enemy bombers.

The flotilla experienced heavy and sustained bombing attacks from then until midday, without damage. The arrival of a snowstorm was welcomed as it shielded them from the enemy's attentions; despite their hearing their attackers calling for reinforcements. The weather caused them to reduce speed but all arrived safely back at Scapa at 1500/14 March.

On return, *Faulknor* was able to carry out the much-delayed repairs, which lasted until the 19th. There followed two days exercising with *Renown* before *Faulknor* sailed with the Home Fleet for Iceland, in splendid weather, on 21 March. The late Lieutenant-Commander Roger Hill, then the very green skipper of the destroyer *Ledbury*, has left us this splendid account of the Home Fleet flotillas putting to sea from Scapa:[3]

> The next day, 22 March, off we went with the Fleet. I was fourth, astern of Alan in *Faulknor* out of harbour. Alan came rushing past, leaning over his bridge furiously waving and shaking his fist at a boom boat towing some buoys, which was across the channel. I had not got the ship pointed round enough and very nearly was badly late. I was doing 300 revs through the boom, with Beaky Armstrong shouting at me through his loud hailer, ' *Ledbury*, *Ledbury*, close up, blast you, close up.' Round the corner we rushed for the Hoxa entrance and we saw the Great Beasts just leaving. Alan went from twenty to six knots and I hauled over, being the starboard wing ship, and stopped. Under my stern flashed *Onslow* with 'Beaky's' loud hailer going full blast. I caught something about, 'God may know what you are doing but He is the only one.'

Next to me was *Ashanti,* and then *Punjabi,* then Alan in *Faulknor.* I was pushed in against the cliff and the vast 'Fleets' left me very little sea room. Then we were away, *King George V, Duke of York, Victorious* and *Renown.* A fine sight if you had time to look at it; screening diagram this and then that, and eighteen knots all the time. Then a zig-zag on top of it.

So we went all that day, (Sunday), and into Monday. Monday afternoon off Iceland – bang, we went into a thick fog. We maintained strict radar silence. It was awful and the tense strain was terrific.

The Home Fleet refuelled at Seidesfjord and took up patrol position north-east of Iceland. Again, the idea was to act as distant cover for the next Russia convoy, PQ.13 that left Reykjavik on 20 March, while the homeward-bound QP. 9 left Kola Inlet a day later. The Germans had been reinforced with heavy cruiser *Admiral Hipper. Faulknor* and her companions sailed through fog throughout 22nd/23rd but, at 1800, '... the mist lifted and it was a grand sight to see the fleet coming into view and taking up their proper places on the screen.' They refuelled and sailed again at 0400/24th, having some near misses with floating mines. Ted Newman wrote:

During the morning we ran into one of the worst gales I have ever known, terrific seas, hammering away, woke me up. The mess once again becoming a shambles. One destroyer had her bow stove in and had to return to base. The weather continued during the forenoon. It was impossible to cook dinner and we had corn beef sandwiches (those of us who could eat). Great waves had overrun our 12-inch bulwark and were washing up and down the flats on to the mess decks. When off watch, the only dry place was your hammock.

Over the next two days, the temperature remained at $-35°$ C but save for a near collision, was largely uneventful and they reached Scapa on 28th. *Faulknor* sailed at 2130 with *Echo, Escapade, Eskimo* and *Icarus,* escorting *King George V* and *Victorious* to Rosyth arriving at 1100, granting all-night leave. The 'buzz' predicted a long stay and many sent for their wives to come up. But, alas for plans, on Wednesday 1 April they were recalled and *Faulknor* put to sea in a rush at 2330, leaving many of the crew ashore.

Faulknor was SO of a destroyer force comprising *Escapade, Eskimo, Valorous, Vanity* and *Wallace,* sent to meet and cover the passage of ten Norwegian merchant ships, sailing under British charter from Gothenburg, Sweden, to Rosyth, between 1 and 4 April; Operation 'Performance'. These ships, delayed by litigation since January, sailed 31 March/1 April, attempting to break through to Rosyth. The operation was a repeat of an earlier one, so the Germans were well prepared. It became an unmitigated disaster. Only two of the ships succeeded; two more, *Lionel* and *Dicto,* returned to Sweden and the remaining six were quickly sunk by air and surface attack or mines.

Faulknor had collected one of the lucky ones, *B. P. Newton,* before sighting *Rigmor* on 2 April, in 57° 27′ N, 03° 21′ E, five miles distant, under attack by He.111 torpedo-bombers.

Captain Scott-Moncrieff signalled at 1630:

Enemy aircraft are bombing.

Rigmor was torpedoed twice before they could get close enough to protect her. Fierce fires broke out and, despite attempts to bring her in, air attacks continued and promised fighter support failed to materialise. Her crew rescued by *Eskimo, Faulknor* finally sank *Rigmor* by torpedo and gunfire before withdrawing. They were under continual air attack until dark, but suffered no damage thanks to the superb ship-handling of Captain Scott-Moncrieff.

A signal from Rosyth timed 0032/2 April read:

> *Faulknor* return to Rosyth with all destroyers.

Faulknor was proceeding up the Clyde, when a further signal ordered them back to the area they had just left to patrol until 0800 next morning. This done, they were again almost home, when sent out again. That night they located *Lind,* without further action. *Rigmor's* survivors informed their rescuers that the British Government had promised them all £50 apiece if they managed to get the ships to England and equipped them all with new life-saving equipment. This somewhat obvious ploy had resulted in German patrol vessels and aircraft waiting for them in the North Sea (*No* U-boats were actually deployed) and it was a wonder any survived.

Faulknor departed Rosyth at 1830/5 April, reaching Scapa forenoon 6th. Having stored ship, they conducted three-days of exercises with U.S. Task Force 39, battleship *Washington*, carrier *Wasp*, cruisers *Wichita* and *Tuscaloosa* and destroyers *Lang, Madison, Plunkett, Sterrett, Wainwright* and *Wilson,* which reinforced the Home Fleet.

Despite protests, convoy PQ.14 was enlarged to twenty-four vessels when it sailed on 8 April. Thick ice caused a third of these ships to turn back and one more was torpedoed.

At 1300/10 April, *Faulknor* sailed to cover this convoy but the order was later cancelled. Instead, at 0600/11th they escorted battleships *King George V*, *Duke of York*, carrier *Victorious* and light cruiser *Nigeria*, with destroyers *Onslow, Offa, Middleton, Wheatland, Ledbury* and *Belvoir*. The weather was kind and without incident. *Faulknor, Onslow, Offa* and *Middleton* were detached to Skalfjord, arriving at the Faeroes 2300/12th, oiling then rejoining the fleet, which now included

Eric Prigmore (x) and friends astride the barrel of 'A' mounting aboard HMS Faulknor *at Hvalfjord, Iceland, 1942. The battle-cruiser HMS* Renown *can be seen in the background. Note the 4.7-inch gun mounting's well, formed by taking out the original 'removable deck plates', designed to give the gun extra elevation to a maximum of 40°.* (Eric Prigmore)

heavy cruiser *Kent*, at 0400. They provided distant cover for QP.10, (sixteen empty freighters, four of which were sunk by U-boats), until 16th when detached with destroyers *Somali, Bedouin* and *Matchless* to refuel at Seidesfjord, arriving at 0900, before the fleet returned to Scapa. They arrived at 2300/18th, with *Onslow, Somali, Bedouin, Matchless, Middleton, Lamerton, Ledbury* and *Hursley*. They oiled and *Faulknor* herself remained at anchor for the next few days. The only incident was the court martial of two crewmembers who had been left adrift.

The next Russian convoys were PQ.15 (twenty-five ships) sailing 26th; and QP.11 (thirteen ships) leaving Murmansk 28th. *Faulknor* left Scapa with *Eskimo* and *Escapade* on 22 April, escorting *Duke of York*, reaching Hvalfjord 1000/24th. Next day a fruitless search was conducted for a missing aircraft, before proceeding to Reykjavik. Shore leave was followed by exercises on 28th, smoke-screens, depth-charge attacks and salvage, during which, while towing *Escapade* the chain snapped and caught in her screws. They escorted *Duke of York* with *Escapade* to join the fleet at sea on 1 May, in 67° 32' N, 10° 25' W at 2359. They continued northward for two days, the ether being full of disasters occurring over the horizon. Light cruiser *Edinburgh* was sunk; QP. 11 lost one Soviet freighter and torpedo-bombers sank three of PQ.15's ships on 2 May.

Faulknor arrived back at Scapa 2100/5th with *Duke of York, Victorious*, light cruiser *Kenya*, and destroyers *Inglefield, Eskimo, Escapade, Martin, Marne* and *Oribi*, before proceeding to Rosyth to boiler clean until 12 May.

On completion it was back to Scapa, meeting rough weather on the way. A leaking port meant three inches of water in the messdecks by the time they arrived at 0400/13th. More fleet exercises followed, sailing at 0345/15th with *Duke of York, Victorious,* heavy cruiser *London*, and destroyers *Fury, Marne, Eclipse, Oribi, Blankney, Middleton, Lamerton* and *Wheatland*. They met the American squadron, *Washington*, heavy cruiser *Tuscaloosa* and three destroyers, the combined force arriving Iceland at 1530/17th, where *Faulknor* secured alongside depot ship *Blenheim*. On 20th *Faulknor* escorted *Victorious* during air exercises and also received fresh fruit and eggs from *Tuscaloosa* anchored nearby. The Americans had daily issues of such basics, which *Faulknor's* crew had not seen any for many weeks.

The good people of Stourbridge, Lye and Amblecote, Worcestershire, had adopted Faulknor, during 'Warship Weeks' 7/14 March 1942. In May, it was announced that the three towns had between them raised the sum of £315,477 in response to a £300,000 target. The Chairman, Councillor J. A . Mobberley, J.P, informed Captain Scott Moncrieff that therefore his ship had formerly been 'adopted'. Captain Scott Moncrieff replied that he was 'delighted', sending a photograph of the ship and a short account of her history to date, and promising to keep them updated.

The next Russian convoys PQ.16 (35 ships) and QP. 12 (15 ships) departed Reykjavik and Kola respectively on 21 May. Heavily attacked by submarines and bombers, seven ships were sunk and three more severely damaged. *Faulknor* led the Home Fleet screen from Hvalfjord on 23rd, battleships *Duke of York* and *Washington*, carrier *Victorious*, heavy cruisers *London* and *Wichita*, destroyers *Fury, Eclipse, Icarus, Intrepid, Blankney, Lamerton, Middleton* and *Wheatland*. She refuelled at Seidesfjord 24th, then continued to patrol in very rough weather and bitterly cold conditions for three days. On 28th, with *Fury* and *Eclipse*, *Faulknor* escorted *Victorious* to Hvalfjord, arriving 1045 next day, refuelling and then on to Reykjavik on 30th. They remained at Hvalfjord for a fortnight conducting exercises and taking some Army personnel to sea as a change from their dour surroundings ashore.

A large Malta convoy took place at this time and many Home Fleet destroyers were detached to supplement its escort. Futher destroyers were loaned to Western Approaches so those that remained were in demand. At 2230/14 June, *Faulknor* sailed with battle-cruiser *Renown, Victorious* and destroyers *Fury, Echo, Eclipse* and *Wheatland* for Scapa, investigating a submarine contact on the way before arriving at 1900/16th.

On 19 June, several senior officers embarked aboard *Faulknor*, headed by Rear-Admiral Robert Burnett, Rear Admiral (D) – together with a camera team from British Movietone News. They led

Fury, Eskimo, and other destroyers to sea to conduct exercises and give the filmmakers their photo opportunities. The stills that resulted from this exercise have adorned the jackets and insides of books on destroyers ever since, purporting to be many different ships, but they were *all* taken from aboard HMS *Faulknor*, no matter what labels other authors and publishers have put on them since! During this exercise, the flotilla crossed the path of the brand-new battleship *Anson*, who curtly ordered them out of her way. She obviously did not realise Admiral Burnett was flying his flag aboard *Faulknor*, and thus the little destroyer out-ranked the new leviathan! As Ted Newman wrote at the time, 'We took priority and told her where to get off.'

At the end of the month the next Russia convoy operation was ready. PQ.17 (36 ships) left Reykjavik and QP.13 Murmansk on 27 June. They had the usual close escort, (including *Fury* of the 8th Flotilla) plus a cruiser covering force. The bulk of the Home Fleet, battleships *Duke of York* and *Washington*, carrier *Victorious*, heavy cruiser *Cumberland*, light cruiser *Nigeria* and destroyers *Faulknor, Escapade, Marne, Martin, Onslaught, Middleton, Blankney* and *Wheatland*, slipped at 1613/29 June, passed Hoxa Gate at 1659 and were through the Pentland Firth by 1743, heading north.

The fleet was to patrol north-east of Jan Mayen Island in case the German heavy ships sortied. Dunnet Head was 180° and speed was increased to 15 knots and then 18 knots as the fleet zigzagged from 1800 onward. By 0640 they were in sight of the Faeroes and submarine alarms became common.

Looking aft from the bridge of HMS Faulknor, *as merchant ships of a Russian convoy anchor in the Kola Inlet, summer 1942.* (Imperial War Museum.)

On 1st, destroyers *Ashanti* and *Onslow* and American *Mayrant* and *Rhind* were sighted at 0640, releasing *Faulknor, Escapade, Marne, Martin* and *Onslaught* to refuel at Seidesfjord. They rejoined the fleet at 2248, steering north for the next two days as the temperature fell sharply. Submarine alarms continued throughout the 2nd, and, at 1033, the *Faulknor* herself obtained a firm contact. The fleet made an emergency turn to port but no attack followed and the contact was lost. Nor was the Luftwaffe far away; at 1951, *Duke of York* picked up a prowler on her radar.

At 0112/3 July, *Cumberland* reported enemy aircraft closing and at 0210, a Focke Wulfe Condor was sighted, *Victorious* flying off one of her Sea Hurricanes to intercept. Unfortunately, this fighter immediately crashed, but *Marne* picked up the pilot. The enemy persevered and at 0200, two German reconnaissance aircraft, which shadowed until 0430, sighted the fleet. They reported heavy naval forces, including an aircraft-carrier, some three hundred miles south-west of the convoy.

Admiralty intelligence informed Tovey that concentrations of U-boats were north-east of him, gathering to attack PQ.17. In order to ambush *Tirpitz* if she sailed, it was vital that the Home Fleet not be sighted by German submarines straggling from this pack, so they altered course at 1723, crossing well behind the convoy's track. At 2135, light cruiser *Manchester* and destroyer *Eclipse* joined.

On 4 July, off Spitzbergen, *Faulknor* again refuelled. Until then all had been going well, the convoy beating off strong air attacks with few losses, but during the course of the next two days, everything abruptly changed. The story of PQ.17 has been told and retold many times with varying degrees of accuracy. Suffice it to say that the Admiralty received Intelligence that the German battle-group had sailed. The fear that they were about to attack the convoy led to a decision being made to scatter it. The destroyers of the escort and the cruiser covering force united to offer a forlorn battle to delay the worst. Instead, the German squadron returned to harbour, and left the U-boats and bombers to deal with the now defenceless merchant ships.

Faulknor and her companions, after steering to intercept the *Tirpitz* earlier, were too far away to help. The Home Fleet cruised north-west of Bear Island, running into fog, turning back towards Scapa on 5th. Signals poured in as the freighters went down; reports that a Russian submarine had torpedoed *Tirpitz* were received, but were total fiction.

At 2345, *Ashanti* returned with destroyer *Douglas* escorting fleet oiler *Grey Ranger* and, at 0028/6 July, *Faulknor* and *Escapade* refuelled. *Ashanti, Faulknor* and *Escapade* then rejoined the screen between 0035 and 0725. Shortly afterwards one of the shadowing aircraft got too close and was engaged by *Duke of York's* 5.25-inch battery, which forced it to keep its distance but it remained in touch. At 1035, they sighted the covering cruiser force and destroyers, which joined the Home Fleet's slender screen reinforcing *Faulknor, Eclipse, Escapade, Ashanti* and *Onslaught*. Just before midnight on 6 July the fleet separated, *Washington, Ashanti, Somali, Rowan* and *Wainwright* leaving for Hvalfjord. Next day, at 1840, fresh destroyers, *Inglefield, Icarus, Intrepid, Foresight, Blankney, Middleton* and *Wheatland* came out to take over the escort. *Faulknor* and *Keppel* were released so Commander Jack Broome could give the C-in-C the details of what had occurred to PQ.17, and they arrived at Scapa 1600/8 July.

Overdue for a major refit, *Faulknor* left Scapa on 12 July, arriving in the Humber the following day. The repairs, carried out by Messers Amos and Smith, were major ones, and she was to remain docked until 27 August, the crew being sent on leave.

The continued threat of German battleship attack made the torpedo again a very desirable weapon for destroyers, and the after bank of quadruple torpedo tubes, so hastily landed and stored two years earlier, was now re-installed. The 3-inch HA gun was resited in place of 'X' 4.7-inch mounting aft, a position giving a far larger sky arc. In this *Faulknor* was probably unique; the 'Tribals' had their 'X' twin 4.7-inch replaced by a twin 4-inch HA in the same way, but all the other 'A' to 'I' class survivors either retained the 3-inch in place of the after tubes or had it completely removed. The two quadruple 0.5-inch machine-guns, inaccurate and ineffective, were replaced by two more single 20-mm Oerlikons – a vast improvement.

Scapa flow 1942: the Destroyer Depot Ship HMS Blenheim *(left) with the destroyers HMS* Ashanti *and, outboard of her, HMS* Faulknor, *alongside, with a tug outboard of her.* (Imperial War Museum.)

Another addition was an improved mark of HF/DF, a development in the continuing electronic struggle for mastery over the U-boats. With several escorts equipped with this new apparatus, many different radio frequencies used by the Wolf-Packs could be picked up, and cross-bearings taken, which could fix the position of a signalling, submarine. Skilful operators were required to make the best use of it, but once a seasoned team had been trained in its use, it became a vital part of any destroyer's armoury. The number of depth-charges carried was also increased to enable her to fire the new 10-charge patterns being adopted as standard. The charges themselves were improved, including the fitting of new firing pistols so they could be set to detonate at greater depths. A depth-charge sinking to 100 fathoms took two minutes to do so, during which time the target submarine could have moved a considerable distance along her predicted track. *Faulknor's* earlier Arctic fittings, that had not proved up to the job in practice, were improved; $3/4$-inch Sprayed Limpet Asbestos was used for lagging vital pipe work and electric radiators were installed in the steering flat and at every gun and torpedo crew shelter, with steam coils under the weapons themselves and the compass platform. Her much-tested hull was full of leaks, which were supposed to have been attended to. She was also repainted, emerging resplendent in her new 'Peter Scott' colour scheme of pale green and blue.

A unique aerial view of HMS Faulknor *on 27 August 1942, in the River Humber after leaving Grimsby dock following her extensive refit. The after bank of quadruple 21-inch torpedo tubes has been replaced to deal with the German heavy ships on the Arctic convoy route; the 3-inch HA gun has been resited in 'X' gun position on the after deckhouse to give it the clearest arc of fire aft, the most common approach from German dive-bombers; two single 20 mm Oerlikon AA guns have been added in gun tubs at the forward end of the after deckhouse.* (Crown Copyright.)

Even so, when she left Hull on 28 August, the signs were that some work had been rushed. The turbine bearings ran so hot on the voyage back up the east coast that a guard had to be left permanently on watch in the magazine. In addition, the steering gear failed *en route* and the ship had to be conned from the after steering position. *Faulknor* eventually limped into the Flow at nine knots that evening.

It had been intended for her to join an air operation on her arrival but she was useless for anything in her condition and was promptly sent back to Hull to have the job done properly. All the way back their portholes leaked, causing the pumps to be manned the whole time, but on docking on 30 August, the mess decks were knee-deep in water. They went straight back into dry-dock without de-ammunitioning. DoD signalling that:

> Extension from 27.8 due to defects developing in steam tube bearing.

They left Hull again 2 September, arriving at Scapa the next morning. During *Faulknor's* absence the Home Fleet had been fully extended in providing strong reinforcements to help fight through the vital August convoy to Malta, then on the brink of starvation. They succeeded with Operation Pedestal, the greatest convoy battle of the Second World War.[4]

New tactics were being planned to fight through the next Russia convoy, PQ.18, mounted after pressure from President Roosevelt and Marshal Stalin. The Germans had drawn the wrong conclusions from their July victory, the submarines and aircraft taking all the credit when, in truth, it was the threat of *Tirpitz* and scattering of the convoy, which had led to the disaster for the Allies.

Admiral Tovey decided that the best substitute for a Battle Squadron would be the strongest possible force of torpedo-armed destroyers. These, with enhanced AA capabilities and strong A/S potential, would meet all threats during the most crucial period of the convoy's passage. By drawing on all four Home Fleet flotillas, sixteen fleet destroyers were mustered, *Milne, Marne, Martin* and *Meteor* of 3rd Flotilla; *Ashanti, Eskimo, Somali* and *Tartar* of 6th; *Faulknor, Fury, Intrepid* and *Impulsive* of 8th and *Onslow, Onslaught, Offa* and *Opportune* of 17th.

These formed the 'Fighting Destroyer Escort' under the command of Rear-Admiral (D), Bob Burnett, who would fly his flag in the new anti-aircraft cruiser *Scylla*.

The whole squadron was divided into two groups, under overall command of Captain Alan Scott-Moncrieff in *Faulknor*; Force 'A', under Captain H. T. 'Beaky' Armstrong in *Onslow*, and Force 'B', under Captain Ian Campbell in *Milne*. This arrangement allowed the destroyers to break off for refuelling in batches during the convoy's passage, using fleet oilers *Black Ranger* and *Grey Ranger*, or the Spitzbergen Fuelling Force (oilers *Blue Ranger* and *Oilgarth*, protected by heavy cruiser *Cumberland*, light cruiser *Sheffield* and destroyer *Eclipse*). During the most dangerous stage of the convoy's passage, all concentrated to provide maximum protection of all sixteen destroyers to bolster the close escort.

This latter included three Western Approaches destroyers, *Achates, Amazon* and *Malcolm*; two anti-aircraft ships, *Alynbank* and *Ulster Queen*; four corvettes, *Bergamot, Bluebell, Bryony* and *Camellia*; three minesweepers, *Harrier, Gleaner* and *Sharpshooter*; four trawlers and three motor

Destroyer exercises with the Home Fleet in preparation for the PQ.18 operation. Here Faulknor *is seen laying down a dense smoke-screen from both funnels to shield her while she closes to attack with torpedoes.* (British Movietone News.)

Destroyer exercises with the Home Fleet in preparation for the PQ.18 operation. The 'Fighting Destroyer Escort' of sixteen fleet destroyers, with four squadrons of four destroyers from each of the flotillas based at Scapa, was utilised to ward off any attack by German battleships. Their attack methods with smoke-screens and torpedoes, similar to that used in the Mediterranean at the Battles of Sirte, were practised intensively in the summer of 1942. Here Rear-Admiral Robert 'Bob' Burnett, Rear-Admiral (D), Home Fleet (left), chatting to Captain A. K. Scott-Moncrieff (Centre) on the bridge of HMS Faulknor *during one such exercise.* (British Movietone News.)

minesweepers. In addition, in case the *Tirpitz*, despite all, did break through, two submarines, *P. 614* and *P. 615*, travelled with the convoy, to carry out submerged attacks if all else failed. Finally, this convoy was to have its own air cover to counter the expected Luftwaffe attacks. The escort carrier *Avenger*, one of the new 'Jeep' carriers building on mercantile hulls in the USA, was added to the escort. She could carry twelve Sea Hurricane fighters and three Swordfish biplanes for anti-submarine work and was provided with her own 'personal' destroyer escorts for AA work, *Wheatland* and *Wilton,* for a total of twenty-one destroyers.

The covering force was heavy cruisers *London*, *Norfolk* and *Suffolk*, with destroyers *Bulldog* and *Venomous*; while the Battle Fleet – battleships *Anson* and *Duke of York*, light cruiser *Jamaica* and destroyers *Bramham, Broke, Campbell, Keppel, Mackay* and *Montrose* sailed from Iceland as Distant Cover.

The Luftwaffe had concentrated on Norwegian airfields to dispute the PQ.18's passage, and 133 German aircraft were available, and *Avenger* was their priority target.

The convoy left Loch Ewe 2 September, and on 4th, *Faulknor*, refit completed at the second attempt, left Scapa for Seidesfjord with the main escort, running through a full gale on the way and reaching Iceland on 5th. At Seidesfjord they anchored until 9th, then they sailed to join the convoy.

I have recorded this operation in depth elsewhere[5]; PQ.18 comprised 39 freighters, a fleet oiler and a rescue ship. *Faulknor* picked up the convoy at 2130/9 September, escorting it northward for two days before being sighted by the Luftwaffe on the afternoon of the 12th. Aircraft and U-boats began homing in and *Faulknor's* H/F and M/F D/F operators confirmed frequent bearings. Depth-charge attacks were made by several destroyers and the convoy made an emergency turn of 40° to port.

At 2103, in 75° 04′ N, 04° 49′ E, *Faulknor* was steaming to reinforce the starboard screen, when her Asdic obtained a solid contact, classified as 'Submarine', bearing 345°, 1,200 yards, which the bridge repeater confirmed. Captain Scott-Moncrieff altered course, increasing *Faulknor's* speed to 18 knots, as range reduced to 800 yards. The echo was 'moderate low' indicating that the enemy was steering away from them with a slight zigzag. Over the estimated point of contact at 2009, *Faulknor* fired a five-charge pattern, with the first and last depth-charges set to 250 feet, the outside thrown charges to 150 feet and the centre pattern charge to 100 feet. This attack proved perfect and the enemy never knew what hit them. Fifteen seconds after the five charges detonated astern, *Faulknor* picked up a very loud noise of submarine tanks being blown or vented.

This indicated that the U-boat had been very badly damaged and was attempting to surface. *Faulknor* turned for a second attack, but the echo was now far from clear (the target was breaking up) and, at 1016, just a single depth-charge was dropped, with a 100 ft setting. 'A tremendous patch of oil came to the surface' and *Faulknor* steamed around in this 'strong-smelling' and ever-widening patch for a fifteen minutes. A bucket was lowered to gather samples, which was confirmed to be diesel oil. The Asdic recorder paper showed a firm trace, having all the characteristics of a genuine submarine echo and, in the second attack, double echoes were obtained at the later stage. The tank venting noises were also clearly shown on the recorder paper but an attempt to obtain the depth of the wreck with the Type 760 echo sounding set was unsuccessful. There was no further echo and so Captain Scott-Moncrieff rejoined the screen leaving the large, and still spreading, slick of oil as the grave marker of forty German sailors.

The enemy so deftly annihilated was *U-88* commanded by Lieutenant-Commander Bohmann, and there were no survivors. As in the destruction of *U-138*, *Faulknor's* first attack had sufficed to do the job.

By 0930 next day two ships had been torpedoed, Russian *Stalingrad* and American *Oliver Ellsworth*, the former sank within five minutes, but the larger American 'Liberty' ship remained afloat after her crew had abandoned her, sinking very slowly by the stern. *Faulknor* hastened her on her way with a few 4.7-inch shells along the waterline and *Ellsworth* went to the bottom with her cargo of aircraft and ammunition an hour after being hit. Captain Scott-Moncrieff reported these losses to Admiral Burnett who was reinforcing the convoy with the rest of the escorts. At 1216, *Faulknor* obtained another confirmed Asdic contact, which *Onslaught* attacked without result.

The remaining escorts joined just in time for the enemy's principal air effort, a massed torpedo-bomber strike. These aircraft came in over the outer starboard screen and almost wiped out two columns of merchant ships there, eight ships being sunk. One victim, *Empire Beaumont*, was *not* on the starboard side of the convoy, nor was she hit, as were all the others, on her starboard but to port. The Captain of *Malcolm,* one of the nearest destroyers to her, believed that she had been torpedoed by a U-boat at this time, a view with which this author concurs, although the sinking has always been credited to the Luftwaffe. (See Diagram page 138).

Faulknor's captain gave an eyewitness view of the torpedo-bombers attack.

> It was a most marvellous sight – they flew in, forty of them in line abreast, thirty feet above the water. They went straight into our barrage, and although shaken still they carried on, and some got into the convoy causing inevitable losses. That was not the end of the attack, however, because they had to get away again.

Captain Scott-Moncrieff still had *Faulknor* in her usual position out ahead of the convoy, as further enemy aircraft sought an opening in the defences. At 1730, they sighted an aircraft apparently laying mines in the path of the convoy, and all ships made an emergency turn. Twenty-one minutes later, a floating mine was seen from *Faulknor* and reported. That night a U-boat sank the oiler *Atheltemplar*.

Contingency plans had been drawn up in case of an appearance by the German battle fleet. The destroyers were formed into eight divisions from 2 September for just this eventuality, *Faulknor* and *Fury* forming the 15th Division. As soon as the enemy heavy ships were to appear these divisions

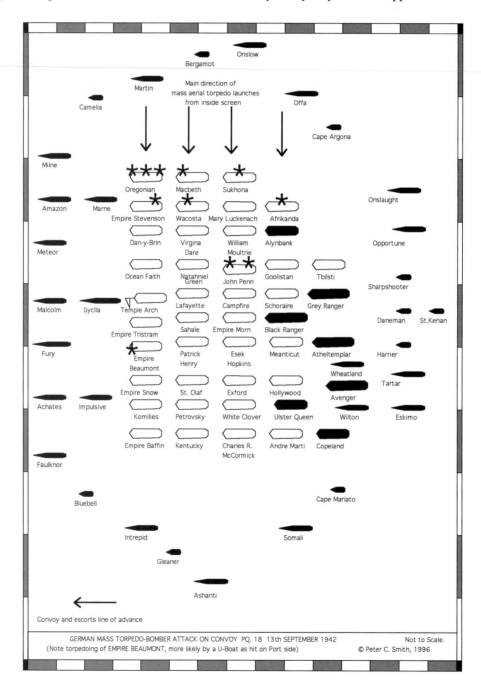

GERMAN MASS TORPEDO-BOMBER ATTACK ON CONVOY PQ. 18 13th SEPTEMBER 1942   Not to Scale.
(Note torpedoing of EMPIRE BEAUMONT, more likely by a U-Boat as hit on Port side)   © Peter C. Smith, 1996

would concentrate upon their respective Captains (D) in their flotilla leaders on the signal 'Strike'. The screen would immediately adopt a pre-arranged formation. *Faulknor* and *Milne* would lead outward to port and starboard of the screen and, once clear, their divisions would form on them. *Ashanti* and *Onslow* would remain in position on the wings of the convoy where their respective divisions would form on them. As the enemy attack developed Rear-Admiral Burnett would take *Scylla* out to make smoke and the nearest flotilla to the enemy would form up to attack under this veil, the remaining flotillas coming across to support them.

Should the enemy make an enveloping attack from two sides of the convoy, the nearest flotilla to each bearing was to make smoke and the remaining two flotillas would form up for the attack. In such a case it was accepted that there would be no supporting flotilla unless it was found necessary to employ *Achates*, *Amazon* and *Malcolm* in that role, (these three retained some torpedo tubes). Any German heavy ship trying to reach the convoy would have to run the gauntlet of seventy-six torpedoes backed up by a mixture of 4.7, 4.5 and 4-inch guns. But 'Strike' was never signalled. Although the Pocket Battleship *Admiral Scheer*, heavy cruiser *Admiral Hipper*, light cruiser *Köln* and destroyers *Richard Beitzen*, *Z.23*, *Z.20*, *Z.27*, *Z.29* and *Z.30* did sortie briefly, nothing came of it.

On 14th further air attacks took place, on a smaller scale than the first. The torpedo-bombers of K.G 26 made a wave-crest approach from ahead, passing between the leading escorts at close-range, corvette *Bluebell* for example reported two torpedo-bombers passing between her and *Intrepid* on one side and three more on the other side between her and *Faulknor,* all at less than three hundred yards distance!

This assault was made at 1410 by K.G 26 torpedo bombers. *Faulknor* was, at this time the port-wing destroyer of the leading screen with the *Malcolm* and *Achates*, and the German airmen had to cross this line first. Three Sea Hurricanes, which followed the enemy aircraft into the convoy's barrage, were all shot down and, at 1415, *Faulknor* steamed over to where one had gone in and rescued the pilot, *Wheatland* and *Tartar* saved the others.

The young pilot concerned, Sub-Lieutenant Gavin Torrance, was rescued by *Faulknor* intact and with his fighting spirit by no means dampened by his narrow brush with death. As Captain Scott-Moncrieff recalled;

> As soon as we had got him aboard he was begging me to send him back to his aircraft-carrier, which, he though of, might be running short of pilots. I managed to do so and he was soon fighting – and fighting successfully – again.

Air attacks continued that afternoon, but they scored no more hits although there were many near misses. *Bluebell* reported an attack at 1432 by a Junkers Ju.88 dive-bomber on the *Faulknor* thus:

> One dive-bombing attack was apparently commenced on the ship and seemed fairly determined, but when the aircraft was engaged by the close-range weapons it turned away and dropped its bombs fairly near HMS *Faulknor,* three-quarters of a mile away on our starboard bow.

Ted Newman recorded:

> We were very lucky, one bomb from high level landed just off our bows and twice we were dive-bombed. One being so near, the splash soaked our torpedo crew. Later, I was in the mess making tea and heard the drone of a Junkers diving. The terrific vibration of the bomb explosion shook and lifted the ship. It was the nearest to us so far. One of the gun crew said it was so close you could almost read the name of the maker of the bomb. There were many narrow escapes this day, but we didn't do so badly.

Faulknor herself contributed to the enemy's discomfiture for she bagged an enemy bomber at this time to add to her submarine kill, Able Seaman Thomas William West, manning one of the bridge Oerlikons, doing the job. He was credited with destroying one certain and confirmed Junkers Ju.88 torpedo-bomber and was later awarded the DSM in recognition of his excellent shooting.

Further torpedo-bomber attacks were made subsequently.

Captain Scott-Moncrieff recalled:

> I was then ahead of the convoy and, looking back, I could see a mass of tracer bullets and balls of fire – I have never seen anything like it. It was a real 'Brock's Benefit' night. One torpedo-bomber crashed and burst into flames behind the convoy. It silhouetted the entire fleet against the sky.

At noon the next day, 14 September, the Junkers and Heinkels of K.G 26 returned, but in smaller numbers. Captain Scott-Moncrieff described this graphically.

> At noon next day twenty-five torpedo bombers arrived in line abreast, attacking from ahead. One flew along my starboard side so low that I could look down on him. I counted twelve shells go into him and he crashed on my port quarter. Another passed along my side to drop his torpedo, but it bounced on the water and somersaulted, instead of running properly.
>
> Then the enemy carried out a 70 degree dive attack on the escorting ships, one large bomb – I could see the colour of it, fell abreast of my ship, nine feet from the engine room, but did no damage. Other ships at times disappeared behind the clouds of spray from near misses.
>
> Then the next wave of torpedo-bombers arrived, but practically all of them were dispersed by our gunfire, and that was when Admiral Burnett made the signal, 'Well done the forwards and halves.'

Submarine attacks alternated with the bombing, but *Onslow* sank *U-589*. The weather closed in on the 15th and 16th, with snow and mist while attacks petered out after *U-457* was sunk by *Impulsive*. Thirteen ships of this convoy were lost. *Faulknor* stayed with them until 076° N, 047° E, when the 'Fighting Destroyer Escort' left and joined the homeward bound convoy, QP.14 (15 ships) on 17 September.

This convoy contained survivors from the ill-fated PQ. 17 and the destroyers determined to try to give them extra special protection on the homeward voyage after the great trials they had experienced. Usually the enemy did not attack home convoys with as much vigour as outward ones, so they hoped for an easier passage – but it was not to be.

Weather conditions initially remained poor until the 20th, then cleared up, allowing the enemy to strike. Heavy U-boat concentrations kept the escorts fully stretched. Refuelling was again carried out by the destroyers at sea, the oiler from Spitzbergen joining the convoy on 18th. A diversion on 19th failed to throw the enemy off the scent; the convoy meeting a heavy concentration of submarines that same evening. Minesweeper *Leda* and freighter *Silver Sword* were both torpedoed and sunk, and destroyer *Somali* was torpedoed, sinking in tow of *Ashanti* on the 24th.

Avenger and *Scylla* left for Scapa on the evening of 22nd, leaving *Faulknor* as SO of a much-reduced escort force with orders to take them to the Butt of Lewis. The U-boats took advantage and, at dawn on 23rd, three more ships were torpedoed and sunk, *Bellingham*, *Ocean Voice* and oiler *Grey Ranger*. The first (and only) sight of RAF help came with the appearance of a lone Catalina, which was promptly shot down by a U-boat. This did not stop the BBC putting out their usual rubbish praising the 'massive' air support the RAF had given the convoy. The sailors were scathing of this constant misreporting. '*One* plane, and *that* was shot down!', recorded Ted Newman.

Conditions aboard *Faulknor* were deteriorating. They had no potatoes, meat or bread after the 22nd. Many ships were bulging at the seams with survivors. Two days of steady plodding at eight knots followed, with continual submarine alerts. On 25 September, *Faulknor* was relieved, handing over to local escorts off Cape Wrath, and entering the Flow on 26th for a three-day respite.

On 29 September they escorted *Victorious* for flying exercises, but spent the next day at their buoy with all available hands employed in painting ship and cleaning up in readiness for a publicity engagement due at Newcastle. With the paint still wet, *Faulknor* escorted battleships *King George V* and *Duke of York* during gunnery exercises. This duty lasted all night and they returned to Scapa at 0830 next morning. The following day Rear-Admiral (D) again came aboard and gave a speech to the ship's company in which he told them, '... the old story – how good we were, what traditions we had to uphold and hoped we had a good time at Newcastle.'

They sailed at 2100, arriving in the Tyne on 4 October, spending three days moored at Town Quay showing the flag. Marring their visit was the death of A.B. Robert Alexander (P/SSX 28421) from Mossend, Lanarkshire. Eric Prigmore said:

> Naturally we went ashore. One of my messmates, 'Jock' Alexander, while coming back aboard, unbeknown to anyone, fell between the ship and the jetty and was drowned.

Faulknor sailed at 1900/7th, returning to Scapa at 1000/8th to prepare for another 'Special Duty'.

This was the visit to the Home Fleet of Premier Winston Churchill on 9 September. *Faulknor* was assigned as despatch vessel for this occasion, a special and distinguished role that was to become commonplace for her as the war continued. The first guest to come aboard was royalty, King Peter of Yugoslavia embarking for the trip to Scrabster where, at 1000 he disembarked. Later fresh VIPs came aboard *Faulknor*, the Prime Minister, his son Randolph Churchill and Sir Stafford Cripps. They duly conveyed these across the Flow, securing alongside *King George V,* where the guests transhipped.

Ted Newman again:

> There was the usual 'flannel', everybody in rig of the day, but worse was to follow. Seamen had to wash the ship and everything had to be polished, no smoking on duty, etc. The Prime Minister, his son and Sir Stafford Cripps came aboard at 1600 – and we took them to Scapa. It was raining most of the time and, before leaving us, he inspected some of the crew, but didn't say much.

Captain Scott-Moncrieff, by contrast, wrote:

> We were honoured to be chosen to take the Prime Minister for a short trip when he came to visit the Fleet and he was, as usual, in great form.

Eric Prigmore tells a more humorous story: -

> Not very many people can say that they have seen Winston Churchill without his cigar. When we picked him up at Thurso to take him to Scapa Flow we went through the Pentland Firth at thirty knots in very choppy seas! As we approached the gate to Scapa Churchill left the wardroom for the bridge, holding hard onto anything that was stable. He was not a good sailor. Of course, there always has to be one smart-alec and, as the Prime Minster staggered his way past the torpedo tubes, a voice was heard from the 3-inch gundeck shouting, ' Where's your cigar, Winnie!' He didn't answer and looked very pale indeed! Anyway, by the time we entered the Flow and things got calmer he

recovered his composure a bit more and was up on the bridge with 'Scotty' Moncrieff, cigar still unlit but brandished, waving to the various ships companies as they cheered him in.

On 16 October, *Faulknor* led destroyers *Panther, Marne, Escapade* and *Middleton* escorting battleship *Nelson* and carrier *Formidable* from Rosyth to Scapa Flow. The sailing of the next Russian convoy, PQ.19 was postponed because the Home Fleet provided much of the naval cover for the Allied landings in French North Africa.

Faulknor was employed mainly on exercises, patrols and as Admiral Tovey's despatch boat over the next fortnight. On 15 October, they sailed with *Escapade, Marne* and *Middleton* to Rosyth escorting *Nelson* and *Formidable* with destroyer *Panther* back to Scapa. At 2215/17th, with *Middleton, Echo* and *Impulsive*, she escorted *Anson* to Iceland, arriving Hvalfjord at 0800/19th, before going alongside depot ship *Blenheim*. Two days exercising with *Anson* followed, the destroyers had to stop heavy cruiser *London* breaking through to Hvalfjord, an exercise that was deemed 'successful'.

On 23rd, shore leave at Reykjavik was followed by a return to Scapa with *Anson, Onslaught* and *Middleton* through very rough weather, arriving at 1100/26th before boiler-cleaning alongside *Tyne* until 30th. On 31st they conveyed Rear-Admiral (D) from Thurso to Scapa.

The publication of the honours and awards for the success of PQ.18, brought congratulations to the ship from the towns of Stourbridge, Amblecote and Lye in Worcestershire, which had adopted her during 'Warship Week'. In a letter of 5 November, thanking them, Captain Scott-Moncrieff stated:

I am afraid a great deal of fuss was made over the whole business of the Russian convoy.

However modest the skipper may have been about their role, Captain Scott-Moncrieff gained a well-merited DSO, and among those also honoured, other than officers and in addition to Gunner West, were Leading Seaman Frank Jackson, who also received the DSM, Chief Yeoman of Signals Archibald Colborne, Petty Officer Charles Edward Thomas Poole, Petty Officer George Compton Pert, Petty Officer Telegraphist William Henry Page Knight, Stoker Petty Officer Charles Hinde Watson, and E.R.A. Edwain Thomas, all of whom were Mentioned in Despatches for their general conduct, attention to duty, and example to others. Albeit the Captain's Secretary, Paymaster Lieutenant Rex Peter, was having to write to Miss Joan Moody on 9 January, that Captain Scott-Moncrieff, '… would not be able to send you an account of *Faulknor's* activities after all. For reasons of security and censorship he thinks it is better to leave it all unsaid.'

Essential RAF and other personnel with specialist equipment were required for various units operating in Russia and it was also decided to bring home from Murmansk twenty-eight empty freighters from earlier convoys which were laying idle, as convoy QP.15. The voyage would be made by the northern route, and take place under cover of almost continual darkness to give them some immunity.

On 4 November, *Faulknor* embarked several RAF pilots, officers and six W/T ratings with special sets from *Tyne*. They sailed at 1745, with *Echo* and *Intrepid*. With these extra personnel aboard there were 32 men packed into a mess built for 20. They reached Seidesfjord on Saturday 7th, refuelling from tanker *San Ambrosio*, and remaining alongside as the weather was calm.

Faulknor's crew took the opportunity for rest and recreation ashore. The American Army and the Red Cross made them very welcome at their canteen and sports hall, offering free food and entertainment. Captain Scott-Moncrieff with his officers, enjoyed the hospitality of the US tanker, envying the modern equipment with which she was fitted. They were especially impressed with the buoyant hose method of oiling she utilised, although Captain Scott-Moncrieff himself thought that the ends of the lines not being equipped with floats was still a problem. Picking up the tow and hose without such floats in his considerable experience, took three times as long.

At 0900 Thursday 12 November, they were joined by destroyers, *Icarus* and *Impulsive* at Seidesfjord and, at 1300, all five sailed north at eighteen knots in reasonably good weather. An Asdic sweep was conducted with ships spread one mile distant from each other until through the danger area. As they progressed, the weather worsened and soon they were plunging through a 90-knot gale.

During Friday 13th, the storm gradually abated, having given them a taste of what was to come, and they were able to increase speed. Captain Scott-Moncrieff meanwhile explained the plan, which was to pass between Spitzbergen and Bear Island, reach Murmansk to unload their specialised cargo and then, after re-oiling, help escort home convoy QP.15, due to sail from Kola Inlet on 17th. The fact that the German 8-inch cruiser *Admiral Hipper*, light cruiser *Köln* and five big destroyers, as well as the usual hordes of U-Boats, were ready for action in north Norwegian ports was also mentioned. However, nothing untoward happened that day or the next.

Having had no proper sun sightings since leaving Iceland, Captain Scott-Moncrieff requested three D/F beacons from 0001 on the 16th to guide him in but, in the event, the Soviet Authorities switched on only one beacon. Nonetheless, the destroyers made a good landfall and arrived at the Kola Inlet, picking up their pilots at 0630.

The pilots brought with them a hand message from the SBNO North Russia, Rear-Admiral D. B. Fisher, containing detailed berthing instructions. *Faulknor* anchored in Vaenga Bay and Soviet tanker *Ukagir* came alongside. She had two women stewardesses aboard, who were the objects of all attention. Later, British naval trawler *Chiltern* came alongside with messages. Fuelling completed, berth was shifted on the 17th to alongside the Russian Naval base at Polyarnoe, where they discharged their passengers and stores. Here they remained for the duration of their visit. Those that ventured ashore found that there was nothing to see or to buy, no money could be spent and no bartering was allowed. Civilian women were not permitted to talk to British sailors. It was bitterly cold; the front-line was only fifteen miles away and the sound of German and Russian guns could be heard.

Jack Banner recalled:

> I well remember the jetty at Polyarnoe and the chanting of the Russian children which went as follows- 'British ship very good, British sailor No Bloody Good! You got some chocolate Mister?' After receiving the chocolate that 'Jack' always handed out, the chant changed to, ' British sailor, him Very Fine Man' Obviously this doggerel had been taught to them by some of our lot on earlier visits.

Captain Scott-Moncrieff was taken by Admiral Fisher to meet the Soviet Commander of their Northern Fleet, Admiral Golovko, and, on Wednesday 18th, the Admiral with his Chief of Staff and Captain Rigerman, the Liaison Officer, returned the call aboard *Faulknor*.

'It would appear', Captain Scott-Moncrieff wrote later, 'that the average Russian, including the Russian Naval Officer, has no idea of the difficulties of the Russian Convoys.'

The Russians organised a dance at their Naval Club, which many of the lower-deck attended. On the 18th a Russian destroyer secured alongside and, for the first time, fraternisation took place between the Allied Navies, with vodka being widely spread about with dire results to both hosts and guests, including the Russian officers.

Heads were quickly cleared for, on 19th they went back alongside *Ukagir* in Vaenga Bay again to top with ten tons of extra oil fuel for the return voyage. They sailed at 1300 with *Echo, Icarus, Intrepid* and *Impulsive*, steering for 75° 06′N, 40° 36′E, to catch homeward-bound convoy, QP. 15 which had left Kola two days earlier.

Captain Scott-Moncrieff was Senior Officer [*Faulknor's* code name for this operations was 'Father', the escort as a whole, 'Boys' and the 8th Flotilla itself, 'Dogs' betraying no lack of humour on Captain (D) 8's part]. In general, the escorts were to zigzag at twelve knots, and only the destroyers were to leave the screen to conduct submarine hunts. 'Should a minesweeper or corvette obtain a contact the nearest destroyer is to take over the contact and hunt for a maximum of two hours before rejoining …' If a reasonable 'Huff-Duff' bearing and cut was obtained, one destroyer was to hunt but, because of the critical fuel situation, no destroyer was to rejoin the convoy after a hunt at speeds in excess of 23 knots. On daytime torpedo attacks being made on the convoy the destroyers on the attacked side were to carry out 'Artichoke', immediate attack, without further orders, and *all* the remaining escorts were to drop one depth charge set to fifty feet on the order 'Bang'. At night, the destroyers would carry out 'Raspberry', a limited response, only on receipt of orders while again on the signal 'Bang' all the other escorts would drop a single charge. Should any ship of the convoy be sunk the rescue ship was to be screened by the corvettes at the rear of the convoy.

Should the German fleet make an appearance all the destroyers were to concentrate and lay a smoke-screen between the enemy and the convoy. The destroyers would then engage and buy time for the convoy to withdraw on a reciprocal bearing while the minesweepers laid further smoke astern of them.

The 8th Flotilla was to join in the Barents Sea but, alas for the plans, the usual foul weather descended. The convoy and searching warships alike suffered a succession of very severe gales and, in almost continuous darkness, the ships soon became widely dispersed. Soviet destroyer *Baku* had whole sections of her superstructure washed away by the sea and her hull plates strained and opened, so that she only just managed to struggle back to harbour. Her companion was even less fortunate, *Sokrushitelny* breaking in half in the gale on 22 November, with her 187 survivors being rescued by Soviet destroyers *Kuibyshev*, *Razumny* and *Uritski*.

The British destroyers just had to carry on. No stranger to bad weather, *Faulknor* received a nasty shaking. All hope of finding the convoy was temporarily abandoned, the struggle was to stay afloat! Next day, sometime between 0900 and 1100, they lost another crewmember when Ordinary Seaman George Albert Cosham (P/JX 325561) from Eastbourne, Sussex, was washed overboard and drowned; no trace of him was ever found. It proved impossible to go topside in those storms and the guns' crews could not be relieved.

By 1330, the destroyers had clawed their way to the rendezvous position but found nothing and could see little. They searched all day, but, as W/T silence was being maintained, in vain. Captain Scott-Moncrieff planned to turn down the convoy's intended route on opposite course until he located them, but, as he recorded, '… the weather was so bad that the risk of collision was too great a possibility. The situation was such that I greatly doubted whether the turning signal to the convoy could have been passed due to poor visibility and the strong easterly gale.'

The minesweepers later informed him that only the leading ships of some of the columns received the turning signal; the remainder carried on northward, thus splitting the convoy. Conditions were so appalling that, in the Captain's own words, '… I turned the Flotilla to the west and ran before the gale until 0500 on the 21st. Great difficulty was experienced with steering and I found that revolutions for 15 knots on the weather engine with the lee propeller trailing enabled me to steer reasonably well and make good some 12 knots.'

During this hideous night both *Icarus* and *Intrepid* lost touch. At 0500, *Faulknor*, *Echo* and *Impulsive* altered course to 090° at eight knots and searched up the course of the convoy. Next day was, if anything, worse. The wind had backed to the north-east, Force 8, with very poor visibility and heavy sea and swell, as Ted Newman related:

> Never have we been in such bad weather – impossible to get about on deck, owing to heavy seas and ice. The convoy has been spread out and we went almost back to Murmansk before making contact. Continuous heavy seas breaking over have flooded the mess deck – the galley is out of action – also some of the sets in the Wireless office.

Just how bad things were aboard *Faulknor* at this time can be understood by a study of Captain Scott-Moncrieff's more sober and calm assessments made in his later report.

Moving all working parts of the armament every half hour was entirely adequate to keep the guns in action – *provided the guns not manned could be reached*.[6] This was not possible for considerable periods of the operation due to the rough weather and icing of the decks, which prevented a secure foothold. The combination of iced decks and the ship rolling moderately rendered access to the forecastle and quarter-deck guns unnecessarily dangerous at times when it should have been reasonably safe. It is suggested that a 3-inch stanchion in rear of gun wells (4.7-inch mountings) to which a guard-rail or lifeline could be rigged, would do much to improve matters in this respect, without necessarily interfering with the working of the guns.[7]

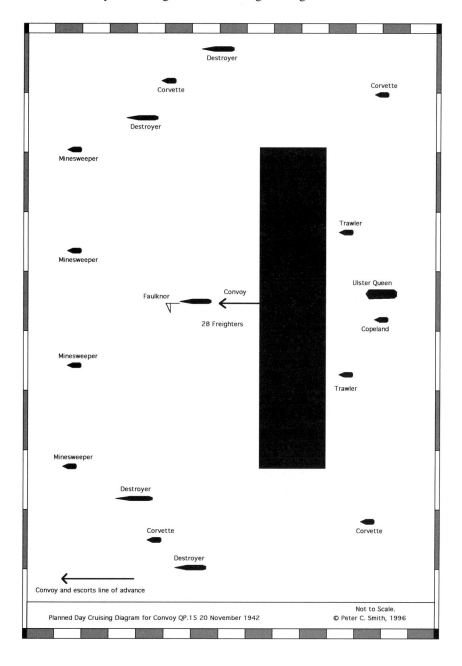

Planned Day Cruising Diagram for Convoy QP.15 20 November 1942

Not to Scale.
© Peter C. Smith, 1996

HMS Faulknor, *seen on the horizon (left background) guards another Russian convoy through 'Sludge Ice' in the Kola Inlet, 1942.* (Author's collection.)

There is a necessity for efficient breach covers in order to prevent spray working up inside and forming 'sludge ice' which may jam firing mechanisms, tray interlocking gear etc. The 3-inch HA gun with an overall cover was found to be perfectly serviceable after weather conditions had prevented access to it for a period of approximately 30 hours.

The use of 'Kill-frost' paste to all the ready-use shells and the hinges and clips of the 'ready-use' lockers before starting the operation was '… entirely successful, ice and snow being readily removable from anything which had been coated with it at all times.

He reported that Numbers Two and Three 4-7-inch guns and the two bridge-wing Oerlikons remained in action for the whole operation, that the 3-inch HA and after two Oerlikons were fit for use, but were not accessible for about thirty hours, while Numbers One and Four 4.7-inch guns became inaccessible and froze up a.m. Saturday 21 November. Number Four gun was brought into action a.m. on Sunday, and Number One gun was in action a.m. on Monday. In addition, Number One gun was out of action also for one night during the passage to Kola Inlet because of spray ice getting into the breach block and jamming the firing mechanism.

While the torpedoes themselves remained effective throughout thanks to the lagging and tube heaters and that their propellers were found to move freely on opening the rear doors to the tubes, the air pressure in the air vessel was found to drop 400 lb per square inch during three days of cold weather. However, had German battleships had to be taken under torpedo attack at this time things would have been dire, for the torpedo mountings themselves became inoperative because of the freezing of the firing levers, tube-ready switches, setting gear, breech blocks and firing mechanisms (despite canvas covers) and all access pockets. The firing pistols froze up on the after set of mountings despite the fact that the lip covers were intact and the tubes were trained fore and aft. The foremost set of tubes was not so affected because they were situated directly over the engine room.

As for the depth-charge equipment, the hydraulic system was rendered inoperative because of the glycerine and water freezing in the tank and at the trap and throwers, while the weather made it unsafe for their crews to work in any case. Primers had been unshipped to prevent accidents.

The Type 286 kept working throughout and, 'In a full gale and heavy seas echoes of merchant ships at six miles and destroyers at four miles were obtained, and what little success was achieved in intercepting ships was entirely due to RDF'.

At 0955/21st *Echo* sighted minesweeper *Bryony* who reported that she had radar contacts at 080° and 150° and fifteen minutes later those on *Faulknor's* bridge caught sight of freighters *St. Olaf* and *White Clover* in 75° 07' N, 30° 42' E. *Bryony* was ordered to remain with them but Captain Scott-Moncrieff hoped that these ships were the forerunners of the convoy and continued eastward. At 1125, two more freighters hove into view, *Esek Hopkins* and *Goolestan,* about a mile apart steaming determinedly onward at eight knots in 75° 02' N, 30° 57' E. After searching yet further eastward until 1400, Captain Scott-Moncrieff came to the conclusion that the convoy must have scattered and so turned back to regain touch with those already located.

They soon overhauled them and, at 1700, the *Impulsive* was ordered to take them along a new route, passing south of Bear Island instead of north, as ordered by a signal from the C-in-C timed at 1343. Unfortunately, unknown to Captain Scott-Moncrieff, *Impulsive's* radar was temporally out of order because of flooding of its cabinet and she never did establish visual contact with either merchant ship. *Faulknor* had been able to visually signal the new course to *Esek Hopkins*, but *Goolestan* had been left to *Impulsive's* care and so, unfortunately, did not get the message. Captain Scott-Moncrieff pressed on to overtake *Bryony* and her two charges to make sure that they had got the new course but, despite searching all through the night, failed to find them.

Drawing a blank, Captain Scott-Moncrieff therefore decided that the majority of the merchant ships were either to the north or had received the new route and had passed to the southward. Course was therefore set for the best estimated position of the convoy at 0900/22nd by *Faulknor* and *Echo.*

The following day the wind was Force 7 from the north, with poor visibility, and a moderate sea and swell. Ted Newman recorded:

> Conditions have not improved and there is still no news of the main body of the convoy. We are now near Bear Island and intend to hang around until tonight but, after that, we must get on our way as fuel is getting very low. Galley out of action – no bread can be baked, or dinner cooked.

They contacted *Intrepid* at 0505, but from 0510 until noon the three destroyers remained 'Hove to' spread across the line of the route of the convoy. Only one freighter was intercepted, the Vice-Commodore's *Dan-Y-Bryn*, located in 73° 57' N, 20° 51' E, and *Intrepid* was sent to escort her. The Vice-Commodore advised them that some ships of the convoy were to the north-westward but a search in that direction proved fruitless. They did manage to get soundings, which gave them a reasonable check on their position, then swept down the convoy route to the longitude of 8° E and commenced a north and south patrol on that longitude about latitude 73° 42' N.

By 23rd the weather eased up a trifle and, at 0600 they sighted freighter *Exford* escorted by corvette *Camellia* in 73° 44' N, 08° 10' E and, at 1025 they got radar contacts which turned out to be *Dan-Y-Bryn* and *Intrepid*. Just before noon, they were joined by four of the relief destroyers from Iceland,

Musketeer, Middleton, Oakley and *Orwell* in 73° 50′ N, 08° 00′ E (the other destroyer, *Ledbury*, had lost touch with her flotilla in the appalling conditions). The CO of *Orwell* wrote:

> At 1150 we suddenly ran into D8. Thought he was with the convoy but apparently not.

They also knew heavy cruisers *London* and *Suffolk* were just over the horizon. Captain Scott-Moncrieff set up a north and south patrol. At 1045 *Faulknor* sighted *Empire Snow* plodding along alone and signalled her the route, informing her that destroyers were ahead and astern of her. They also heard via short-range W/T from *Impulsive*, but as her fuel situation was critical, she was allowed to continue.

With the weather moderating it was deemed vital to gather the far-flung ships into escorted groups before U-Boats would pick off stragglers. The Luftwaffe failed to locate the convoy but two enemy submarines did find isolated targets, *U-625* torpedoing *Goolestan* in 75° 30′ N, 08° 00′ E at 0110. *Musketeer* did not pick up her distress signal until 1415 and Captain Scott-Moncrieff detached *Orwell* to hunt for survivors. *U-601* torpedoed and sank the Soviet *Kusnec Lesov* in 75° 30′ N, 08° 00′ E.

On Tuesday 24th, having encountered no more merchantmen, Captain Scott-Moncrieff decided that none were east of his force and, at 0700, the destroyers were split up to search some fifteen miles both port [*Faulknor* and *Echo*] and starboard [*Musketeer*, *Middleton* and *Oakley*] of the convoy route. As they steered south a very considerable set to the south-eastward was experienced, dead-reckoning positions differing by as much as one hundred miles from subsequent fixes after 72 hours without sights. At 1030, Captain Scott-Moncrieff decided to break wireless silence and inform the C-in-C of the position. That night and the whole of Wednesday 25th passed uneventfully, save for the sighting of the first Luftwaffe reconnaissance aircraft. *Faulknor* and *Echo* were conducting a range and inclination exercise at 1128 when the Type 285 radar picked up a second echo at range 120. The HA/LA guns were left in primary control in the hope of opening controlled fire, should the aircraft become visible between the clouds, which were 8/10th cover at 1,500 feet. This echo was lost during the initial approach and when the aircraft broke cloud cover temporarily about one mile off the port beam the DCT was unable to get on the target. A solitary Junkers Ju.88 passed overhead in 68° 45′ N, 05° 48′ W at about 1,000 ft. This aircraft obviously sighted them for it flew out to about three-and-a-half miles on the starboard bow, banked, turned and flew back before circling in low cloud over the two destroyers. *Faulknor* loosed off four rounds at this aircraft with her 3-inch gun as they glimpsed it through the murk. The order for local control barrage had in the meanwhile been passed to the 4.7-inch guns, but they were unable to get on to the target in time to open fire in the intervals when it was visible. The Junkers, not liking this reception, departed in the direction of Trondheim.

Captain Scott-Moncrieff commented:

> The fact that though fuse-prediction was possible from the FKC (Fuze Keeping Clock) while 285 ranges were being obtained, Director controlled fire could not be opened, bears out, once again, the importance of being well prepared for locally controlled barrages, particularly where the director is a DCT with comparatively limited AA visibility.

At 0255 Thursday, minesweeper *Sharpshooter* was sighted four miles off and ordered to join them. She reported to Captain Scott-Moncrieff that she had lost touch with the convoy in the awful weather of the 20th, and had since then taken the old route north of Bear Island and searched down the new route without locating any of them. At 0800 /24th, they gave up the hunt because of their fuel situations and headed for Iceland at best economical speed. At 0310 the Langanes Light, was sighted and, at 0830, *Onslaught*, the sixth destroyer of the relief group, was seen escorting freighter *William Moultrie* toward Seidisfjord. *Faulknor* arrived Seidesfjord at 0920/26 November and refuelled from *San Ambrosio*. They found *Impulsive* had arrived earlier that day having sighted no ships at all, and *Icarus* had arrived the previous night, again having had no contacts since losing touch on the night of the 20th/21st. Later, *Faulknor* secured alongside US tanker *Culpepper*.

Captain Scott-Moncrieff, with his own experience fresh in his mind, was afraid that some of the convoy might be so far out in their reckoning that they might be in grave danger of straying into the extensive Allied minefields off the east coast of Iceland. Accordingly, at 1300, he sailed *Icarus*, which had the longest time to recuperate from their ordeal, to patrol north of the field to intercept any strays. Likewise *Forester* and *Impulsive* were despatched at 1330 when minesweeper *Salamander* reported that she had bad condenser trouble, was only capable of four knots and required help. At 1700, *Intrepid* and *Ledbury* came in and were followed by *Middleton*, corvette *Camellia*, freighters *Exford*, *Esek Hopkins* and *Lafayette* and, finally, minesweeper *Halcyon*.

Further stragglers gradually arrived, the Commodore's ship, *Temple Arch*, *William Moultrie*, *Charles McCormick*, *Empire Morn*, *Empire Snow*, *Belomorkanal* and rescue ship *Copeland*. All were sent to an assembly point escorted by *Intrepid*, *Icarus* and *Ledbury*, corvettes *Bluebell* and *Camellia* and minesweeper *Sharpshooter*.

The weather suddenly worsened again on Friday 27th and violent gales blew up. Captain Scott-Moncrieff reported that:

> ... Under such circumstances at Seidesfjord in winter the only safe place is the open sea and most ships put to sea until the weather moderated. Some precarious moments were endured by all though the only collision occurred between *Sharpshooter* and *Empire Snow*.

HMS *Faulknor leaving Seidesfjord, Iceland, November 1942, with the rest of the flotilla astern.* (K. Timson.)

Reading between the lines it was quite a scramble. On the same day, they were informed that there were fourteen stragglers from the convoy at Akureyri. Next day Captain Scott-Moncrieff anticipated that a further convoy would be required for these ships and this he organised.

At midday on Saturday 28 November, Captain Scott-Moncrieff took *Faulknor* out to sea, steering east of the minefield and setting course back to Scapa at 26 knots. Their journey took 24 hours, which averaged out at 25 knots and took the record from one of the new 'O' class destroyers. On the way, a service was held for their lost colleague by a Chaplain taking passage with them. At Scapa where they arrived at 1430 on Sunday afternoon, they were allowed to swing round No 28 buoy in Gutter Sound for a week, but no shore leave was possible.

Captain Scott-Moncrieff summarised lessons of this operation:

'The weather conditions obtaining during the winter months in the Arctic and Barents Sea make interception of convoys at sea a matter of chance.' He continued,

> ... it is unlikely that any visual signals from the Commodore will get further than the leading ships of columns unless the weather happens to be calm. The visibility on the Northern part of the route was rarely more than 5 cables during passage of QP.15.
>
> With a following gale it must be realised that escorts are not able to proceed slowly enough to keep with the convoy and since zigzagging is not possible under these conditions there will be times when the convoy is unescorted. From experience last winter with PQ.9 and 10 and QP.7, and from the accounts of what happened to QP.15, the merchant ships will not be able to keep together in any heavy weather and they are bound to become scattered. This means there is no chance of collecting together again since there is no daylight for this operation to be possible, thus a gale early in the passage of a convoy results in the convoy scattering with no chance of reassemble.

These wise and experienced words from sea fell on stony ground in Whitehall. On the wider world stage the news from North Africa was good and various elements of the Home Fleet's strength were gradually able to return to Scapa, and, at 0120/ 8 December *Faulknor* and *Eclipse* escorted *Duke of York* to Rosyth, arrived at noon and were granted leave. They sailed on 10th for Scapa, but, at 1500, were detached to search for an aircraft, which had crashed in the sea off Peterhead, on a bearing of 082°, 110 miles away.

A signal, timed 1811 on 10th, from C-in-C, Rosyth instructed:

> If nothing found abandon search and arrive Scapa before dark tomorrow Friday.

They made 30 knots to the scene and arrived in the area at 2000 through choppy seas. They paid the usual penalty of flooded mess decks and chaos below decks. At 2015 they commenced a search firing star-shells and illuminating their searchlight all night, but in vain. Eventually the C-in-C Rosyth cancelled the search because of the bad weather and they returned to Scapa at 1000/11th.

Meanwhile a letter and a parcel, dated 12 December, from Chief Yeoman of Signals A. L. Colborne, to Stourbridge, enclosed photographs of the ship from the Chiefs' and Petty Officers' Mess, along with good wishes to the towns for the coming festive season. The parcel contained a 2-inch black-painted anti-aircraft shell container, dented and worn, the silvery metal showing through the paint. The cap was sealed with adhesive tape and when this was removed, the shell case was found to contain two large photographs of HMS *Faulknor,* attended by an escorting plane. There was also a covering letter and two neat brass-plates worded 'Presented by Chief and Petty Officers of HMS *Faulknor,* Christmas 1942.' The letter concluded: 'The best wishes for the coming season to the *Faulknor* Fund Committee and the good people of Stourbridge, and also our sincere thanks for the many kindnesses shown to us. A. T. Colborne, Chief Yeoman of Signals.' The photographs were framed and one photograph and one plate was sent to Amblecote and displayed in both towns' libraries. Captain Moncrieff also sent a Calendar and another photograph of the ship.

The politicians decided to resume the Russian convoys for a great many ships, laden with American war material of all kinds destined for the Soviet Army and Air Force, had accumulated at Loch Ewe and Iceland. They suggested that another large convoy should be fought through in the same manner as PQ.18. Admiral Tovey, the C-in-C, had other ideas. He considered that the conditions which prevailing during the summer months were now vastly different. Citing the case of QP.15, he argued that, in bad weather a large convoy would be far more easily scattered than a small one, opening up the prospect of another PQ.17 disaster, with the storms doing the job of *Tirpitz*. His views temporarily prevailed, as did his plan to send the covering cruisers right into the Kola Inlet.

Therefore, the thirty merchant ships ready were divided into two separate convoys, which, under the new numbering system, became JW.51 A and B. The first fifteen freighters and a fleet oiler, were to sail on 15 December 1942, escorted by destroyers *Beagle* and *Boadicea*, corvettes *Honeysuckle* and *Oxslip*, minesweeper *Seagull* and trawlers *Northern Whale* and *Lady Madeline*. Reinforcing from Seidesfjord would be *Faulknor, Fury, Echo, Eclipse* and *Inglefield*.

In preliminary moves *Faulknor* sailed on 13th with *Eclipse, Fury, Inglefield, Blankney* and *Ledbury* escorting light cruiser *Sheffield* flying the flag of Rear-Admiral, Destroyers, arriving Loch Ewe 14th and staying overnight. *Faulknor* and *Echo* left in a hurry the next day for Seidesfjord at 25 knots, arriving at 1600/16th, refuelling. At 2100 they left with *Beagle, Boadicea, Echo, Eclipse, Fury* and *Inglefield,* meeting JW.51A at 0800 on 18 December.

This convoy comprised *Briarwood*, (Convoy Commodore), *Empire Meteor, Gateway City, El Oceano, West Gotomska, Beauregard, Richard Bassett, San Cipriano, Greylock, Oremar, Dynastic,*

HMS Faulknor *alongside at the Soviet Navy's base at Poynaroe, with a Russian destroyer moored astern, Christmas Day 1942.* (Jack Banner.)

J. L. M. Curry, *Richard Bland*, *El Amirante*, *Windrush* and oiler *Oilgarch*, with corvettes *Honeysuckle* and *Oxlip*, minesweeper *Seagull* and trawlers *Lady Madeliane* and *Northern Whale*. These had sailed from Loch Ewe with destroyers *Blankney*, *Chiddingfold* and *Ledbury*, the latter three ships turning back in 66° N, 10° W on relief by *Faulknor's* flotilla. Captain Scott-Moncrieff then assumed SO of the total escort. In support were light cruisers *Jamaica* and *Sheffield* and destroyers, *Matchless* and *Opportune*.

They passed south of Bear Island because of the ice barrier, and the enemy failed to sight them. In these bleak climes, around Latitude 73°, there were only four hours of sunlight in every twenty-four where there were clear conditions. On 19th, *Faulknor's* oil fuel tanks were found to be leaking, and, because water was getting into two of her boilers the third boiler was also not working at full efficiency, reducing their maximum speed to 12 knots; adequate to escort the convoy but not to fight an action. They continued nonetheless; with only three to four hours of daylight they were well covered. As Ted Newman noted:

> It is strange to see the stars at 10 o'clock in the morning and the moon up at 3 o'clock in the afternoon. Although the moon has been very bright, there has been plenty of mist, so we have been well covered. Even the weather has not been so cold and we've been able to get some fresh air daily. The only incident of note being a ship sighted two miles away. She veered off and we did not investigate, possibly a Russian as we've heard no more.

By 23 December they were in 73° N, 38° E, steering to arrive at Kola Inlet and passing the outward convoy, to reach Polynaroe at 0900 on Christmas Day itself. Christmas, the Captain announced, would be celebrated on Boxing Day. This plan was duly kept to and they reached Kola Inlet on 25th, going alongside *Sheffield* at Polyamo at 0830.

Jack Barrett noted in his diary:

> We should have been met by two Russian destroyers last night, but it was too rough for them to come out, so the part of the convoy for the White Sea had to go on their own. We went alongside *Sheffield*, which was part of the covering force with *Jamaica* for this convoy. Christmas will be celebrated by the destroyers tomorrow.

As part of the celebrations, they entertained visitors from the cruiser and attended a concert laid on by the Russian Northern Fleet.

Ron Smith recalls Christmas in Murmansk. 'Do not leave a cooked turkey available on a

Happier times in Russia. Christmas Day 1942: celebrations aboard HMS Faulknor *with the visiting crew from a Soviet destroyer in the ship's messdeck.* (Raymond Johnson.)

mess shelf. Christmas in Murmansk, a seaman's' mess deck. Fur covered Russian comes aboard, a flurry, a commotion, a flash on the gangplank! Result. One seaman's' mess deck minus one turkey, one happy Russian dog.'

They anchored upstream finding German air-raids both regular and effective, five of the convoy being lost by dive-bombing. They were glad to secure alongside again on the 27th. Another concert was held aboard *Faulknor* next day and again Soviet sailors were entertained aboard.

On the 29th, *Faulknor* took her turn acting as despatch boat, taking passengers upstream, the flotilla's whalers having been left behind at Scapa. A strong storm blew up at this time with snow and temperatures plummeted to −30° C. and it took them three hours to secure alongside in these conditions. The water tanks aboard froze-up solid so drinking water was rationed.

They sailed 30 December escorting return convoy RA. 51 into the full force of the gale, which did not abate until that night. This convoy was not attacked although German bombers were observed searching for them at 1030/31st. By 3 December, they were south of Bear Island in clear weather steaming at eight knots and on 7 January, they were relieved, steaming for Seidesfjord at 25 knots and arriving at 2000.

While they had experienced an easy passage, JW.51. B had not, being set upon by Pocket Battleship *Lützow* and heavy cruiser *Admiral Hipper*. This led to the famous New Year's Eve battle when a small force of seven British destroyers defeated the German heavy ships sending Hitler into a towering rage.

Faulknor and her convoy was unscathed while this action was taking place south of them, and, by skirting the pack ice, they avoided all contact with the enemy. They left Iceland at 1000/8th for one of their 25-knot runs to Scapa, which they reached on the 9th, conducting a practice shoot *en route*.

HMS Faulknor *leads the 8th Destroyer Flotilla through rough seas off Iceland, January 1943.* Fury, Eclipse *and* Echo *are somewhere astern!* (Bill Silltow.)

HMS Faulknor *leading the 8th Destroyer Flotilla to sea from Seidesjord in moderate seas, January 1943.* (K. Timson.)

The Captain informed the crew they would be sailing south to boiler clean but, on the evening of 10th, Rear Admiral (D) came aboard and *Faulknor* raised steam ready to go to sea leading seven other destroyers on yet another 'suicide' mission off the Norwegian coast. Intelligence reported battle-cruiser *Scharnhorst*, heavy cruiser *Prinz Eugen* and destroyers *Friedrich Ihn*, *Paul Jacobi* and *Z.24* were on their way from the Baltic to reinforce the German fleet in Norway. *Faulknor's* task was to lead her scratch flotilla, made up of whatever destroyers were ready, and sweep along the Norwegian coast off Stadlandet, to intercept and attack with torpedoes, a repeat of the earlier operation.

They sailed into a howling gale, the flotilla reduced to seven ships when one destroyer broke down in harbour, which left *Faulknor, Inglefield, Onslaught, Queenborough, Echo, Vivacious* and Polish *Piorun*. Because of the high speed required the ships again took a pounding once outside the gate. Their numbers continued to be steadily reduced as the 11th wore on and the gale continued unabated. *Piorun* lost touch, then *Vivacious* broke down; then there were five. The weather conditions worsened further, so that it would have been impossible for the destroyers to fire their torpedoes, even if they had located the enemy. Captain Scott-Moncrieff decided the mission was hopeless and, at 2300, it was cancelled. Two destroyers were sent to stand by *Vivacious,* who eventually managed to raise enough steam for three knots and struggle back to Dundee. *Faulknor* took the other two back to Scapa, arriving at 1800/12 January. It had all been for nothing as the German fleet had reversed course on being sighted by aircraft the day before.

It was during this passage that *Faulknor* lost yet another of her crew overboard in a similar manner to earlier tragedies, this time it was Acting Petty Officer (Ty) D. G. Goodyear (P/SSX 20796), just 23 years old.

Bill Silltow recalled this tragedy.

> Goodyear was an outstanding Leading Seaman, obviously officer material and was made Acting Petty Officer. He was down for a course for full Petty Officer and was always on top of every situation. The weather was appalling that night, so bad that even a bolted down Ready-Use ammunition locker was lifted up by the seas right out of the ship and over the side. Ready-use shells from this were hurled about topside and some were heard above the gale rolling about outside the bulkhead of the Petty Officers' mess. Goodyear

promptly went out to secure these despite the conditions. He was never seen again. I always remember that when his effects were auctioned off to raise money for his family, I was struck by the immaculate condition of his kit and clothing. All were beautifully kept and cleaned, and they really did him credit. He was a great loss.

Between 14th and 20th *Faulknor* boiler cleaned at Rosyth and gave leave. They rejoined the fleet at 1000/21st, sailing at 2200 escorting *Anson* and *Sheffield* to Iceland, with destroyers *Eclipse, Inglefield* and *Montrose,* until 22nd when *Faulknor* and *Eclipse* returned to Scapa. They arrived 0945/ 24th going alongside *Tyne* for four days, repairing defects. This done, they escorted battleship *Howe* on her working-up exercises from 1st until 12 February. Another refit was on the cards and clearly required, as, when dropping the new powerful depth-charges, pipes were burst, bulwarks cracked and a stove smashed to pieces. Ted Newman wrote:

> Our Skipper is tearing his hair out over things which just won't work at the crucial moment. Each time we have an A/S exercise the Asdics fall over – even depth charges and torpedoes let us down. At present it's like being at a circus. We only hope that we don't have to join in with the operation which is now starting. A few words about our mess – at present we have 30, although it was built for 20 men only. Hammocks are slung in every conceivable place and then some have to sleep on the lockers. The air is foul by morning. During the afternoon it is a recognised thing for those off watch to get their heads down. By the time the forenoon watch comes down, there isn't even a place to sit – the lockers are filled and most of the deck is covered with bodies – not even room to walk around. They say that, after our refit, some of them are being shifted to their proper vessels – thank goodness!

On 13 February there was a conference held with Rear-Admiral (D), indicating that yet another Russian convoy was in the offing and much of the fleet had

HMS Faulknor *leading the 8th Destroyer Flotilla to sea from Seidesjord in moderate seas, January 1943. Note the ready-use shells in their racks, and the gun pit of 'Y' mounting aft.* (K. Timson)

HMS Faulknor *leading the 8th Destroyer Flotilla to sea from Seidesjord in moderate seas, January 1943. Note the depth-charge stowage and the smoke-making apparatus aft, as well as the barrel of 'X' mounting with weather covering secured.* (K. Timson)

Captain (D) A. K. Scott-Moncrieff, RN, seated at his desk and in his cabin aboard HMS Faulknor, *10 February 1943.* (Lady Scott-Moncrieff.)

already departed for Iceland in readiness. The captain lectured the crew on the situation and, after another delay because of an 80-knot gale sweeping the harbour, they departed 16th.

Jack Barrett wrote:

> *Faulknor* proceeded out of Scapa with *Inglefield, Obdurate, Obedient, Opportune* and *Orwell* in company at 1800. Sailing was delayed until last possible moment because of heavy gale, but we had to go out. We are now proceeding to Seidesfjord at ten knots, which is all we can do in this weather. After such a long spell in harbour (five days) most of us seem to be feeling it.

Ted Newman told the same story:

> Gale getting worse and we are having a most uncomfortable time. Besides seas washing over, we have our usual leaks. Met CS.10 [Admiral Burnett with the heavy cruiser *Cumberland* and light cruisers *Belfast* and *Sheffield*] and, for a time, we joined company. After a while he left us, as our speed was not high enough. Gradually we had to ease down as the gale got worse, and, late last night, we had to heave-to. This is the worst sea we have ever been in – the messes are in a terrible state – the only safe place being our hammocks. This has been the worst three days that we have ever had, and, at one time, 75% of the ship's company were sick.

Jack continued:

> We have been hove-to practically all day, but now we seem to have drifted towards the land, headway seems probable and we are hoping to arrive at Seidesfjord about 2100. At 2130, we at last get up harbour and proceed alongside oiler to refuel, as we shall be off again at an early hour tomorrow. Already the decks are covered with ice and in the messes too, where the bulkheads are sweating a thin layer of ice has formed, such pretty patterns, nevertheless very uncomfortable. The mountains around us are covered with snow, and several glaciers are clearly visible in the moonlight. It seems so much like peacetime up here, no blackout restrictions.

In his report, Captain Campbell recorded that, during 17/19 February 1943:

> Very heavy weather was experienced on passage north, and on arrival at Seidesfjord conditions in the fjord would not permit of either anchoring or fuelling until 2000 on 19 February. During this night *Milne, Faulknor, Obedient, Opportune, Orwell, Obdurate, Inglefield* and *Orkan* were fuelled.

At 0630, *Milne, Faulknor, Boadicea, Obedient, Opportune, Orwell, Obdurate* and *Inglefield* weighed and steered to rendezvous with the convoy, whose progress could only be estimated from a 48-hour old aircraft report. A signal, timed 0812, pinpointed the merchantmen and enabled contact to be made at 0805/21 January, in 67° 59′ N, 07° 33′ W.

Jack Barrett again:

> We were called at 0400 and left Seidesfjord. Passed through the mine barrier, hundreds have been cut adrift by the storms. At 0600 altered course to search for the convoy, which will be hidden in a fog bank. Carried out search all day and night. The gale has slackened and eased so now ships have opened up to five miles apart thus covering a search width of 35 miles. Dawn has just broken and we cannot see the convoy.

Convoy JW 53, with 22 ships left out of a planned 30 due to the weather, had as close escort destroyers *Meynell, Middleton* and *Pytchley,* minesweepers *Jason* and *Halycon*, corvettes *Bergamot, Dianella* and *Poppy* and trawler *Lord Austin*. Corvettes, *Bryony, Dianella* and trawler *Lord Middleton,* were missing. A return was made to the 'Fighting Destroyer Escort' concept, because of the lengthening hours of daylight. AA cruiser *Scylla,* again acted as flagship, while escort carrier *Dasher* provided air cover. The destroyer force was commanded by Captain Ian Campbell, Captain (D3) in *Milne* with the Polish *Orkan* 3rd Flotilla, *Obedient, Obdurate, Orwell* and *Opportune* 17th Flotilla and *Faulknor, Fury, Eclipse Intrepid, Boadicea, Inglefield* and *Impulsive* 8th Flotilla.

After two relatively easy voyages, *Faulknor's* more experienced hands sucked their teeth as the wind increased and counselled their newer 'oppos': 'We're in for it this trip, m'lad – mark my words!' – Indeed they were. Seemingly angry, the Sea Gods determined to prove once more, who really ruled these lonely waters.

For four nightmare days and nights the convoy clawed its way across the roof of the world beset by a gale of unparalleled violence. The seas were the worst most aboard could remember, and ships soon began to report themselves in trouble while others were driven hopelessly out of station. Liberty ships with heavy tanks in their holds found their cargoes shifting and took on hair-raising lists. Six of the convoy had to return to port before the operation had hardly commenced. The smaller warships of their escort fared no better. The destroyers thrust their slender hulls through the roaring cataracts of foam-flecked waves, plunging into troughs with a crash and a shudder, thin plating whipping with the tension, the men cowering behind whatever flimsy cover they could find, deluged by stinging spray and spindrift. The muffled lookouts, soaked and chilled to the bone, kept their isolated vigils, eyes straining to penetrate the murk as they silently mouthed to themselves the old destroyer ditty:

> This is my story, this is my song,
> We've been in commission, too bloody long,
> Roll on the *Nelson, Rodney, Renown*,
> This two-funnelled Bastard is getting me down

– and wishing they had taken that cushy shore billet at Rosyth after all.

Jack Barrett's diary recorded:

> 0800 and dawn has just broken and we can see at last the convoy escorted by *Jason, Poppy, Dianella, Bergamot, Camellia* and *Lord Austin*. Five ships of the convoy have got lost in the gale but we are not hanging back for them. At 1000 we take up our screening positions, we are in the rear. It is expected that *Dasher* with *Scylla* and four destroyers, will join up at dawn. Heavy blizzards are frequent now, and it's quite impossible to see the convoy at times.

Unfortunately *Dasher,* along with *Sheffield* and yet another merchant ship, had to return to Iceland with heavy storm damage, taking some of the destroyers with them as escorts. The rest of the 'Fighting Destroyer Escort' were now joined by *Scylla*, destroyers *Orkan* (Polish), *Fury, Intrepid, Eclipse* and *Impulsive*, the latter without her Asdic Dome and oscillator but with her skipper being determined to take part. This group had been fuelling at Akureyri and had also been delayed by heavy weather. The cruiser covering force was finally reduced to heavy cruiser *Cumberland* and light cruiser *Belfast.*

Jack Barrett wrote:

'*Dasher* has done the dirty on us and broken down, so now we have got no air protection as we cannot possibly believe that the RAF will be with us in this weather.' Later: '*Scylla* had taken up her position inside the convoy as AA barrage ship. Weather has calmed now but snow blizzards are still quite frequent.'

The 23 February was largely uneventful save for the fact that they were sighted by the Luftwaffe, a shadower remaining in the vicinity of the convoy until dusk and sending back detailed reports to his HQ in Norway.

Jack Barrett wrote:

> As expected, we have been spotted and reported by German aircraft, this is where *Dasher* would have been useful, so tomorrow we expect the works. At 1150 a Blohm and Voss 138 was sighted but the darned thing won't come within gun range, we have heard her homing in the U-boats. Our covering force consisting of the *Belfast*, *Cumberland* and *Sheffield* have also been spotted, they are only fifty miles from us, also the battlefleet, *King George V* and *Howe* are within calling distance, but they come no further than Bear Island, they may get cold poor things!

Eventually the storm's tempo decreased, the destroyers busied themselves hunting down the strays from the convoy, nudging them back into the fold. Chaos gave way to some semblance of order and they proceeded on at a good pace. With the bulk of the convoy rounded up, they made good progress over the next three days. The first indications of enemy submarines homing in came through the vigilance of *Faulknor's* HF/DF team. The Director of Anti-Submarine Warfare noted:

> Three destroyers were fitted with H/FD/F and the plot was maintained in *Faulknor* (Captain D.8). That the losses were not heavier was due to the accuracy of the appreciations, based on the H/FD/F plot that were made by Captain (D8).

Captain Campbell put on record that:

> Captain D8 in *Faulknor* with his own experience and his team of experts was a tower of strength to whose suggestions and appreciation's full effect and consideration were given on every occasion.

At 1600/24th HF/DF indications of a U-boat on the surface off the convoy's starboard bow resulted in *Faulknor* and *Obedient* being ordered to 'Scram' to find and sink it, at 1706 but, two minutes later, the latter ship reported a surface radar contact. Captain Campbell realised that this might not be an enemy surface craft, but when a check was asked for, *Obedient* repeated her report. Campbell considered that there was no time to delay in the gathering dusk if indeed the contact was the enemy and ordered 'Strike' at 1727. The destroyers moved out to attack but, before they had got far, *Obedient* clarified her report by informing them that the radar contact was a U-boat and the destroyers resumed their places on the screen.

By 1800, Captain Scott-Moncrieff was able to confirm to Captain Campbell that two, if not three, U-boats were evidently in the vicinity of the convoy. We now know that the *U-622* made torpedo attacks on *Faulknor* and *Obedient* as they moved out to her position, but missed both targets. She evaded further detection by diving. *U-255*, was also in contact and both tried repeatedly to get through to the convoy, but prolonged attacks with the new-style, more powerful depth-charges kept her at bay, with 'Grab', 'Tipple', 'Trade' and 'Scram' deterrent operations being freely employed over the next few days. *Faulknor* was placed at the rear of the convoy to better detect the submarines transmissions, which was no sinecure. Ted Newman noted:

For the first time I can ever remember, we are in the screen, astern of the convoy. It's not an enviable position, as most of the U-boats try to come in there and we have been very busy – *Somali* was in this position when she got hers.

Jack continues:

We have heard aircraft flying around but they haven't seen us in this weather, although at 1140 the snow cleared for about ten minutes and we saw two Junkers Ju.88s and heard them homing. It seems funny not to have been attacked yet. We seem to be keeping the submarines down, whenever we hear one on the surface starshell is fired and destroyers are detailed to drop a pattern of depth charges. These new charges we have been issued with are deadly, 70% more effective than the old ones, we can feel the blast of them eight miles away.

Once today two submarines were reported under the convoy and all the escorts dropped two depth charges each, they nearly lifted us all out of water and nothing further was heard of the U-boats!

On 25th he wrote:

Today we have been closed up at action stations for nearly nine hours. At lunch time fourteen Ju.88s attacked us splattering bombs all round but no one was hit, the barrage made them keep up too high. Then, again, twenty-five Ju.88s came over and dropped everything they could, but they seemed scared, just jettisoned their bombs anywhere, although some of them jumped on us out of the clouds and machine-gunned us. Only one casualty in the merchant vessels, a man with a shrapnel splinter in his leg, he has been transferred, with some difficulty, to *Scylla*. Just as dusk was falling another ten Ju.88s came over but no hits although several near misses were registered.

Again, numerous 'Huff-Duff' indications of submarines were received but no attack developed.
Jack Barrett recorded:

And so the night goes on, snowing like the devil and we can hear the U-boats making their sighting reports and homing other U-boats. Signal came through that all the escorts are to drop two depth charges. This done, again nothing more was heard of the U-boats so we have obviously made them keep well below the surface, whether any hits have been registered on them we cannot say as it's too dark.

A recent German reference book, printed in the U.K. [and accepted by its publishers as gospel] states that a bombing attack by ten Ju.88s damaged one ship, which is untrue, and also that the convoy *avoided* the U-boats by HF/DF. Jack Barrett's diary of the time reveals the truth.

0415 we are again called to Action Stations as now is the time when ships are most vulnerable to attack from the U-boats. Several are again reported under the convoy, a few depth charges soon put paid to them, an area for miles around must have been shaken by the explosions, they were even heard by our covering force *Belfast, Cumberland* and *Norfolk*, thirty miles away. This seems to be the most effective method of keeping them down.

The 'new' depth-charges to which both diaries refer at this time were of two types. The most lethal was the recently introduced Mark X type, packed with one ton of Minol, which were fired from torpedo tubes and contained as much explosive as a whole conventional ten-charge pattern. These monsters were about 17 feet long. Set shallow they would have blown the firing ships hull in underwater, so the destroyer had to steam at much higher speeds than normal during attacks. Settings up to 800 feet were possible for use against deep-diving opponents. The other was the newly developed 'heavy charge', the Minol Mark VII, fired in the conventional way from traps and throwers.

Jack Barrett continued:

> The visibility is rotten, snow blizzards and rain most of the time and when it clears for about half an hour at a time we can always see two Blöhm and Voss 138s flying around and homing the submarines. At 0900 we go back to normal routine, we spot a submarine on the surface and give chase, but the snow comes down and we lost contact.

The White Sea section was detached at 2345, while the rest of the convoy proceeded towards Bolshoi Oleni in fair weather, where Russian pilots boarded at 0645/27th. All twenty-two vessels reached Russia safely. Only after they had entered the 'security' of Soviet waters at Murmansk did enemy aircraft return with a determined attack by the Stuka dive-bombers of I/St.G 5.

Jack Barrett observed:

> 1200. Eighteen Ju.87s sighted and an attack by dive-bombing commences three minutes later. Several near-misses but no hits on the convoy. The second attack is made by twelve He.111 torpedo bombers, six of which are shot down before releasing torpedoes, the others dropped their circling torpedoes but again there were no hits.

Faulknor remained at Kola Inlet for several days, secured alongside cruiser *Belfast* where they attended church service on 28th. It was bitterly cold, with ice forming on the sea. There were continuous German air attacks, and eventually Ju.87 Stukas hit and sank *Ocean Freedom* and damaged four other of cargo ships as they lay at anchor in the 'safe haven' of Murmansk.

Faulknor left Kola Inlet 1600/1 March, escorting convoy, RA.53 (thirty freighters). On 2nd they sailed through a dead calm sea at eight knots with the convoy, frequent snow showers shielding them for the moment from the enemy. It was bitterly cold as they steamed into the Barents Sea, and again the ships' upperworks became ghostly phantoms of gleaming ice which neither steam hose nor pick could keep at bay for long. The pack ice was abundant and farther south than usual, forcing the convoy closer to the Norwegian coast than they generally chose to do. The sea was freezing, and from time-to-time the frail plates of *Faulknor* crunched as they sliced their way through patches of ice. By 4 March, the ship was iced up with 25° of frost.

This convoy was to make *Faulknor's* last passage through these bitter waters a memorable one, for both weather and enemy combined to give her a rousing farewell. The wolf-pack closed in and the next few days and nights heard an almost continuous roar of depth-charge attacks. The convoy was constantly shadowed by U-boats, and the time taken for the passage was increased by strong head-winds, giving the enemy more opportunity to press home attacks. Seven sightings were made of surfaced U-boats and there were three radar contacts, but the first attack did not occur until 5 March.

As they entered the Gulf Stream, the ice began to melt and the whole ocean appeared to be steaming. That day *U-255* torpedoed *Executive* and *Richard Bland* claiming to have sunk them both. In fact, she sank neither, for the latter, which took a torpedo in her forefoot, kept going with the convoy. Captain Scott-Moncrieff took *Faulknor* alongside the crippled American *Executive*, which had stopped but had no appreciable list. Her 53 crew had quickly abandoned her in the ship's boats, being picked up by escorting trawlers The cripple proved too badly damaged to salvage and it fell to *Faulknor* to finish her off.

They first dropped a Minol depth charge set to detonate at 50 feet beneath the ship, and it exploded under her bridge. *Faulknor* followed this up with six 4.7-inch fuzed HE shells spaced along the waterline. *Executive* 'heaved' after the depth-charge explosion and she started to settle at an accelerated rate with a broken back. Fires broke out on her bridge and upperworks. Captain Scott-Moncrieff added the final touch by loosening another Minol depth-charge, set to 50 feet, which, when fired from the thrower, landed in the after hold where it duly detonated. The freighter was left slowly sinking and heavily on fire; they did not linger for her cargo was chloride; and *Faulknor* rejoined the convoy.

Another proud ship had gone and this time the submarine had escaped scot-free. Later the same day the Luftwaffe's I/K.G 30, with twelve aircraft, carried out another desultory attack without result.

The full force of the gale struck the convoy on Saturday 6th and it was not long before the lightly-laden freighters, high out of the water and ungainly, were being flung about in wild disorder. With the storm came snow, a thick, swirling blanket which shut down visibility completely around the pummelled and buffeted ships, so that all sense of time and purpose was lost; the whole world soon consisted solely of one's own vessel, the skin-flaying wind, the heaving ocean and stinging sleet and hail. Again, the appalling conditions led to the breaking up of the convoy.

Aboard *Faulknor* there were lots of breakage's and the usual chaos below decks, but more worrying was the state of the fuel supply. It being far too rough to oil at sea and with the convoy spread far and wide, with much herding using up what fuel they did have, there became no alternative but for the destroyers to break off in groups, steer for Seidesfjord, refuel and then rejoin the convoy. The first group was detached at 1800/6th, *Faulknor*, *Eclipse*, *Impulsive* and *Opportune*, but the

Busy scene at Vaenga, Russia, after the arrival of Convoy JW.53. HMS Faulknor *can be seen alongside the light cruiser HMS* Belfast *(extreme right). Astern of them is the destroyer HMS* Onslow*, while in the foreground another destroyer, HMS* Obdurate*, is steaming out of the inlet and passing the heavy cruiser HMS* Cumberland *(extreme left).* (Imperial War Museum.)

weather was ghastly and little headway was made. They were instructed to search for some of the missing merchant ships *en route*, and carried out a patrol of an area forty miles wide by day and night, but nothing was seen.

With the wind abeam, they found the going fearful, their fragile plates groaning in torment at the endless pounding to which they were subjected. *Faulknor's* thrice-strained hull was shaken and tossed as if by giant hands; already overworked, there was a limit to what delicate machinery could stand, and they suffered severe damage while Seidesfjord still lay far to the north of them. Their fuel endurance was based on making good seven knots to Seidesfjord, but, in the conditions prevailing, it was not considered prudent to allow a larger margin, and, in the event, the destroyers were practically hove-to throughout Sunday 7 March.

They were hit by a severe southwesterly gale with winds of Hurricane force being registered and 'precipitous seas'. The destroyers speed was reduced to the minimum required to maintain steerage way and the ships were just about stationary.

The climax of this ghastly day came when *Faulknor*, in the words of Stan Hollett, 'fell off' a mountainous wave. The heart-wrenching plunge which resulted broke the Gyro's suspension, so the steering had to be done by means of a standard magnetic compass for the rest of the journey – a very tedious job for the Quartermaster in comparison with the relative ease of following a gyro-repeater. In those conditions, it demanded still further concentration from tired and exhausted men.

Ted Newman recorded:

> Heavy seas as high as mountains were thudding against us and we were flooded in many parts of the ship. In fact, water was everywhere except in the taps. The convoy was by now spread all over the place and most of them having trouble with their steering, owing to being so light.

Laymen, who have no concept or idea of what the sea is capable of, often accuse sailors of exaggeration. However, in the calm words of his official report, Captain Scott-Moncrieff confirmed these statements in full:

> *Faulknor* fell from a height into one trough which broke the gyro suspension and sprang many rivets.

He later elaborated exactly what it was like to ride out this Arctic storm in a small destroyer:

> The weather on 18 and 19 February to the south of Iceland and that on the 7 March to the north-east of Iceland was the worst I have ever experienced even when compared to a full Atlantic winter gale or Chinese Typhoon. The seas were very high and precipitous with a very short trough, which made an occasional bump a certainty. It was extremely unpleasant to be going down one wave with the oncoming wave high and threatening, seemingly about to

A 'touch of roughers', and there goes the motor boat yet again! HMS Faulknor *off Scapa Flow, March 1943.* (Charlie Lee.)

fall on the compass. The *Faulknor* is a magnificent sea boat, and rode out all weather without major damage except for the motor boat and davits which invariably get smashed each winter and will continue to do so whilst sited in their present position. It had been my intention to leave the motor boat behind and the Eighth Flotilla have orders to do so on all Russian convoys, but on this occasion it was blowing a Scapa gale when we left.

Even in these appalling conditions *Faulknor* never forgot her main duty to her merchant ships. Two or three U-boats were indicated on her HF/DF plot in the vicinity of the convoy. However, no attacks developed.

Ted Newman again:

> 7 March: Our Gyro compass has fallen over and none of the four destroyers can agree on our position. In spite of the Engineer's efforts, there was no drinking water all day until 2000 and no washing etc. We certainly looked rough. Four more destroyers left the convoy.

On Monday 8 March at 1800, *Faulknor's* force sighted Force 'R' and exchanged signals with *Cumberland* and *Belfast.* On reaching the barren coast of Iceland, the four little ships had struggled round it until they found temporary shelter in Seidesfjord at 2015, thankfully securing alongside the Panamanian tanker *Matincock.* They replenished almost bone-dry tanks, but all was not well with the oiler. In fact they found barely enough fuel to top all the ships, as Captain Scott-Moncrieff reported:

> It was not until oiling was nearly completed that I discovered the serious lack of fuel remaining in the tanker.

In fact, only 2,300 tons were available, which restricted the second groups fuelling dramatically when they arrived five hours later. All eight destroyers refuelled and were available by 0600. As the situation with the remaining escorts left with the convoy was desperate, they sailed once more out into the storm to try to relieve them. Their mission was for Captain Scott-Moncrieff to take charge of the escorts and attempt to round up the many stragglers into some semblance of order, *Faulknor* leaving at 1430 with *Eclipse, Impulsive* and *Opportune.*

They located the main group of twenty-one merchant ships at 1930 in 66° 38' N, 11° 24' W, steering 260° at six knots and took their places on the remaining screen, destroyers *Fury, Vivacious, Meynell* and *Pytchley,* and corvettes *Bergamot, Lotus, Poppy* and *Starwort.* The weather having moderated, U-boat transmissions began to fill the ether once more. The Liberty Ship *J L M Curry* had developed a split, which progressively cracked her hull forward and aft of number three hatch. Eventually her crew were taken off and she was sent to the bottom by shells from trawler *St. Elstan.* Another of the stragglers, freighter *Yorkmar,* was sending distress signals at 1708 reporting a 'suspicious vessel'.

At 2218 an SOS was received by another of the four, freighter *Puerto Rican,* which was torpedoed by *U-255* in 66° 44' N, 10° 41' W, 33 miles astern of the convoy. Her crew had abandoned ship but her boats were swamped in the heavy seas and later sank. Although *Eclipse* and *Impulsive* were immediately detached to pick up any survivors, and trawler *St. Elstan,* laden with the survivors from the *Curry* was also diverted to search, none of the crew were ever found, only a large oil patch, and the enemy chalked up another 'Axis Submarine Success'. The fourth straggler, *Cornelius Harnett,* was being escorted by destroyer *Ledbury* and at midnight, *Faulknor's* HF/DF plot indicated that a U-boat was also stalking them. *Ledbury* was duly warned and advised to carry out 'Tipple' and 'Grab' operations. Happily, both ships survived.

A torpedoed and burning Russian merchant ship, seen from HMS Faulknor, Arctic 1943. (Bill Silltow.)

During the next three days *Faulknor* was here, there and everywhere, their searches and hunting being assisted by the Fleet flagship which was now in the area. The superior radar of *King George V* was successfully used to help round up many of freighters. Some had their steering gear out of order and were adrift, and these had to be taken in tow as the weather moderated. By 10th nineteen of the original convoy had been brought together in a group. At 0248 that morning they were reinforced by *Inglefield* and this enabled *Vivacious* to be sent back to fuel, as were *Meynell* and *Pytchley* at 0940.

The weather was still very thick and Captain Scott-Moncrieff suggested to the Convoy Commodore that they should hold on until noon to see if conditions improved, but that, should visibility not get any better, they alter course to the Northward and await better conditions before attempting the hazardous East Coast passage off Iceland. He wrote:

> The need for an additional MF/DF beacon at Langanes in order to obtain a fix for position has been pointed out before and it was urgently required on this occasion and the following day. We had been without sights for 48 hours and it was not possible to get an accurate fix by RDF Dalatangi MF/DF beacon because it was only working on very reduced power due to storm damage.

He added:

> Luckily the gale was offshore otherwise I shudder to think what would have happened.

By 1000 visibility improved for a short period to one mile and the Commodore tried to organise the convoy into two columns, without very much success, '… as most of the merchant ships refuse to do anything in bad visibility.'

By 1330, Captain Scott-Moncrieff, out ahead of the convoy in *Faulknor*, had decided that it was too dangerous for convoy and escort to retain their south-westerly course any longer and course was altered via W/T to the north. Only freighter *San Cipriano* failed to make the turn and she was later heard to be signalling 'Land Ahead'. She survived this and was later found by *Scylla* off the Butt of Lewis just before midnight two days later!

Less fortunate was *Richard Bland*. Having survived one torpedo and weathered the storm despite her damage, she had been gamely limping on as the stern-most ship. Fate was unkind for she was thus a sitting duck and a very easy target for *U-255* which slammed a second torpedo into her at 1700 in 66° 53′ N, 14° 10′ W. She split in half just forward of her bridge, the stern part sinking quickly, the fore part staying afloat for a while. *Eclipse* and *Impulsive*, returning from their fruitless hunt for other survivors, were now directed to her last known position. *Impulsive* later rescued twenty-seven survivors from one lifeboat, *Eclipse* eight others, but the captain and other survivors in another lifeboat were never found. By 1830, clearing weather finally enabled the convoy to form into the two columns but they continued to steer north. Another freighter, *J H Latrobe,* developed steering defects and *St. Elstan* stood by while *Opportune* was sent to assist.

Captain Scott-Moncrieff recorded:

> I was seriously short of escorts by this time as the local escort had been unable to fuel quickly due to contaminated oil at Seidesfjord; escort was *Faulknor*, *Fury* and four corvettes. I was happy however, in the knowledge that there were probably no enemy submarines nearer than *Richard Bland's* position some 50 miles to the northward. The Admiralty informed me that a submarine was probably still in touch with RA. 53, but it was obvious from the HF/DF plot that the submarine concerned was with *Richard Bland.*

Thursday 11 March found the convoy in calm weather with up to two miles visibility but, at 0500, bearing of Dalstangi 160° showed Captain Scott-Moncrieff that his worst fears had come about and that the convoy was out of reckoning. He immediately signalled by lamp to the Commodore to get a turn to the southward initiated when, in his own words; '… visibility suddenly lifted and we found we were in position 343°, Glettinganes four miles, with the mountains over our heads and the convoy proceeding straight into the land. A nasty moment.'

The Commodore altered course by coloured light signal and led round and, almost immediately afterwards the visibility shut down again to one mile, with snow squalls and sleet showers. By what divine providence the murk had been lifted for that one brief glimpse of their imminent danger who can say, but *Faulknor* and her companions where thereby saved to fight another day.

They managed to keep the Glettinganes light in sight through the driving snow as the Vice Commodore led down the swept channel through the minefields, but again Captain Scott-Moncrieff wrote:

> … during a temporary gap I noticed there was no other ship of the convoy in sight. The captain of *Fury*, who was in charge of the rear, reported that he was sorting the situation. I turned the Commodore to the northward again and went back to see what was happening. *Fury* had done excellent work and was bringing down the main body in some order, which was most creditable considering the visibility rarely improved to more than two miles and was usually two cables.

The escort was reinforced at 0600 by *Pytchley* and *Vivacious* who were sent back to patrol the north end of the minefield and keep any merchant ships clear, while *Fury* was detached to Seidesfjord to collect *Oligarch* which had arrived with 700 tons of vital oil fuel and escort her in safely, while *Boadicea* performed a similar duty for *Cornelius Harnett*. Later *Eclipse* joined. By 1800 the situation was that RA.53 had nineteen merchant ships in company escorted by eight destroyers and was in 064° 25′ N, 013° 36′ W steaming at seven knots. During the evening first *Opportune,* then *Eclipse* and *Orwell* and finally *Fury* all joined, and two more stragglers were located safely.

Friday 12th saw this mass of shipping steering through strong westerly winds and a heavy swell and during the day various changes in the escorts composition took place as refuelled destroyers and corvettes joined and others were detached. By 2000 on the 12th *Faulknor's* work was done, and she received orders from Admiral Tovey to hand over the escort to *Vivacious* and return to Scapa with *Eclipse, Fury* and *Orwell, Inglefield* having been despatched earlier with defects. At 2000, they left the convoy steering for the Butt of Lewis at seven knots. then on to Scapa, *Faulknor* securing to No. 19 buoy, Gutter Sound at 1330 on Saturday 13 March.

Later they entered floating dock for examination. Not surprisingly this recommended that they be sent for another refit. Although they did not realise it at the time, this was to prove their last Russian convoy. However, *Faulknor* always seemed to be where the action was, and this was to remain the story of her life as the next phase opened.

CHAPTER VI

The Fight Avails

Asurvey by Scapa's Floating Dock revealed that *Faulknor's* damage necessitated another complete overhaul. They again sailed for the Hull yard and ship of Amos & Smith, for a month-long refit, from 17 March until 16 April. On return to Scapa Flow, *Faulknor* carried her Pendant Number (H. 62) painted in large white characters on either side of her hull abreast her bridge. Almost immediately a small leak was found in the forward mess. A full gale overnight as they headed north soon exposed other faults with water pouring into the seamen's and stoker's mess deck. They returned to Scapa in a worse state internally than a month before!

Next day the calibration tests were undertaken and, while the new motorboat was out, a gale blew up. Attempts to get it back inboard failed when, before they could fix the tackles, the heavy sea overturned it and the crew had to hang on for their lives. By the time the boat was finally recovered most of the upper works had been smashed. They were soon moving on to pastures new.

* * *

Heavy losses were being sustained by merchant ships in the Atlantic battle in March 1943. Every available destroyer and escort carrier was transferred from the Home Fleet to Western Approaches command where they were formed into Support Groups able to reinforce the escorts of hard-pressed convoys as required.

From February 1943, the anti-submarine war gradually built up to a crescendo. This was predominantly an electronics and Intelligence battle. Pinpointing the U-boat groups and re-routing convoys to avoid them, or rushing extra escorts to their defence, became very good ways to reduce the toll. Providing convoys with their own air cover was another vital step now that the small escort-carriers were joining the fleet in increased numbers. But first the correct methods of utilising all these facets had to be learnt and could only be learnt by application in combat conditions. In this *Faulknor,* with her enhanced 'Huff-Duff' capability became one of the trailblazers.[1]

Fleet destroyers withdrawn from the Home Fleet formed no less than five of these Support Groups. They were to operate independently, keeping at sea in the mid-North Atlantic for as long as possible, returning to base merely to refuel and rearm. The bulk of the 3rd, 8th and 17th Destroyer Flotillas were flung into this battle for a decisive six-week period. Captain Scott-Moncrieff was appointed Senior Officer of one such team, the 4th Escort Group, in mid-April, and, as soon as *Faulknor* had refitted, he joined her and they were thrown pell-mell into the action.

Faulknor sailed for Liverpool on 19 April, arriving at that grimy place next day. They refuelled and left for Gourock on 22nd, refuelled again and, on 23 April were ordered to cancel a planned exercise and proceed at top speed on the first of these sorties. This proved the prototype of such operations, during which the scale of merchant ship losses decreased and the U-boats suffered a decisive defeat – a period termed by Captain S. W. Roskill, 'The Triumph of the Escorts.'

Captain Scott-Moncrieff took, *Faulknor, Fury, Eclipse* and *Icarus,* at 25 knots to the aid of a convoy in bad trouble. Traversing heavy seas they soon reached the scene of combat and, two days out from Greenock, they sighted the mastheads of convoy HX.234, homeward-bound for Liverpool from New York. Because of a heavy attack on a previous convoy, HX.234 was routed well to the north of its usual track, but even so the U-boats had found it, the powerful 'Meise' wolf-pack of eleven submarines homing in. They sank two freighters, one of them a straggler. This convoy was escorted by the B4 Group from the Western Approaches and the convoy consisted of fifty heavily-laden cargo ships. Heavy rain, hail and snow blanketed the convoy during the night of the 23rd/24 April and this weather, combined with a number of route alterations, had helped ease the situation.

Faulknor arrived 0800/25 April, and remaining until 2000, when redirected to join another convoy to the south-west. This was SC.127, Liverpool-bound, escorted by the Canadian C1 Group. It had been the target of the seventeen-strong 'Specht' group of U-boats, but was skilfully re-routed to avoid both this and the 'Meise' pack, and then north to avoid yet another concentration, the 'Star' group. The 4th Escort Group sighted this convoy at 0940, relieving the 1st Escort Group. Fuel was running low when they joined this convoy of 56 freighters, '… which made for a grand sight', early on Tuesday 27 April, but they were able to refuel from one of its tankers.[2]

Thanks to Admiralty Intelligence the convoy suffered no loss and *Faulknor's* group consolidated as the five U-boats of the 'Amsel' pack sought them. Throughout the next two days, they maintained vigilance and, on 28th, obtained a submarine contact, which led to an indecisive hunt. For the next three days they were almost continually at Action Stations, few watches passing without incident.

By Thursday 29th, the convoy was considered safely through the danger zone. At 0430/30 April, *Faulknor* left for Greenock, arriving late on 1 May after a rough passage through a severe gale. They replenished and went to their buoys; as they were not officially based there so were not permitted to draw stores.

On 3 May they sailed from the Clyde with destroyers *Onslaught* and *Sabre* screening escort carrier *Archer* to Hvalfjord with a deck load of aircraft. These little escort carriers were soon to become

HMS Faulknor *entering Hvalfjord, Iceland 1943..* (Stilltow.)

indispensable to the Atlantic convoys. From PQ.18 Captain Scott-Moncrieff knew their value with their Swordfish and Albacore anti-submarine aircraft combating U-boats and their Grumman Martlet fighters deterring the *Kondors*. There were, as yet, still very few of them available, but the addition of one to 4th Escort Group was a real bonus when they sailed to renew the struggle. They hit another gale on their first day out and this got progressively worse. By the 5th it was so bad that the little squadron was forced to heave-to most of the day.

They finally reached Hvalford on 6th and secured alongside depot ship *Blenheim*. They were due to sail to Reykjavik and remain there for a few days but, at 2100, this move was abruptly cancelled and *Archer*, *Faulknor*, *Impulsive,* and *Onslaught*, left at 0800/7 May. There was a sixteen-knot north-east wind and the little carrier was pitching very quickly, which was not conducive for flying operations

Eventually the sea calmed, the day warmed and flying commenced when another emergency blew up. At 1600 they sighted a large four-engined bomber approaching, which was soon identified as a B-17 Flying Fortress with American markings. This aircraft flew around the squadron for two hours. Initially it was thought she was some sort of escort, but it transpired that the bomber was in trouble. Captain Alan Scott-Moncrieff recorded:

> This aircraft had been previously observed flying round us but visual communication with *Faulknor* had not been established. It was seen to fire Verey lights on first being sighted but these were not taken to be distress signals as they were assumed to be the incorrect recognition signal for the day (Two red and one green). The aircraft continued to fly round for some time and I assumed she was watching *Archer* operate her aircraft.
>
> However, I noticed the Fortress suddenly coming from astern low down and realised it was going to crash land. *Onslaught* was nearest and was at the scene of the crash within 6^1/$_2$ minutes. I led round and stopped to windward of *Onslaught* and managed to pick up three men who had not been picked up by her.

Lieutenant-Commander W. H. Selby of *Onslaught* added:

> Nine survivors were seen in the water of which five, including the pilot, Lieutenant Musser, were picked up by HMS *Onslaught*. Of the other four seen at first, one sank before the remainder were picked up by HMS *Faulknor*.

They learnt that the aircraft had been on the way from Canada to Iceland, but its navigator had 'lost' his radio fix on Iceland, and they began to run out of fuel. Finally, their options ran out with their fuel, and the bomber quite suddenly crashed into the sea, quickly breaking-up and sinking.

Stan Hollett, who watched the whole incident from *Faulknor's* bridge, remembered:

> We thought, in fact, that the crew were tempted to land on the flight deck of the carrier, which was little bigger than their giant aircraft, but realised in time that this was impracticable and pancaked in the sea. *Faulknor* picked up some of the crew – unfortunately one of their number was killed – and these friendly Americans formed part of the Chiefs' and Petty Officers' mess complement for several days and brought a complete change of topics of conversation – a welcome diversion.

At 2010 *Faulknor* signalled *Archer* requesting one Swordfish fly off to locate the convoy whose exact position was not accurately known. The Swordfish located the ships forty miles away, staying with them for half-an-hour, finally returning at 2345.

The Group joined convoy ONS.6, bound for Halifax, and protected by the B6 Escort Group at 0700/9 May, in 58° 48′ N, 38° 50′ W. *Faulknor* refuelled from the oiler while the carrier zigzagged astern of the convoy with the other two destroyers and operated her aircraft. Single anti-submarine patrols were maintained from 0500 onward despite the hazardous conditions, but found no indications of U-boats adjacent the convoy.

The sea conditions were very bad with heavy swell, sea 63, wind East 29 knots. At 1700 Sub-Lieutenant Martin took off on a test flight in an aircraft that had been repaired after an earlier accident. As he touched down, the carrier paid off very rapidly to starboard and, as he tried to go round again, his starboard wing hit No. 5 starboard Oerlikon gun tipping the Swordfish into the sea.

From *Faulknor* one of the crew was seen scrambling up a ladder. The other crewman was thrown a life-buoy, which he caught. The carrier's deck party then attempted to haul him up the side of the ship. He got halfway up and then slipped and fell back into the sea. He was still alive and managed to keep afloat; *Archer* immediately stopping her engines to prevent him being sucked into the screw.

Captain Scott-Moncrieff immediately manoeuvred *Faulknor* very gingerly towards him, taking the utmost care as he was being tossed up and down in the seas and there was danger from the destroyer's screws. The Captain shouted to the young airman from the bridge encouraging him to hang on and he managed a feeble wave back. Some of the crew then volunteered to go over the side to pull him in and he was soon safely aboard. This left the pilot of the Swordfish unaccounted for, but almost at once somebody spotted Martin floating by, apparently unconscious. A volunteer was ready to go in after him but was stopped from doing so and, before the order could be rescinded, the pilot drifted by and washed underneath the *Faulknor* and was not seen again. It was a sad end to a gallant rescue effort. By 1900, conditions were too bad for flying, *Archer* took station in the convoy and the three destroyers joined the screen.

The early hours of 10 May proved to be busy ones, with seven HF/DF bearings being obtained by *Faulknor* and *Archer* on the series 1 band between 0500 and 0235 but neither *Viscount* nor *Deveron* were able to obtain bearings on this series. *Faulknor*, *Impulsive* and *Acanthus* duly investigated the bearings respectively but without any positive sightings. There was an easterly gale blowing and it remained unfit for flying operations.

Communications between the ships and the aircraft were excellent, the carrier's T.R. 1304 set's performance increasing considerably over the open sea and when well clear of land. Good communication was maintained by both *Archer* and *Faulknor* with the patrolling Swordfish at a range of 80 miles. On the other hand, it was found that the convoy R/T Wave was very congested, especially when the Escort Group was in the vicinity of the convoy which it was supporting. The Swordfish's own transmitters were not powerful enough to break through this mush with the result that vital sighting reports could be delayed, or missed completely. It was considered that a second channel should be available to clear the aircraft from the convoy R/T Wave for normal working.

On the 11th *Faulknor* made her third rescue attempt in as many days when, at 1747, in 55° 17′ N, 44° 15′ W, they sighted wreckage and a ship's lifeboat so 'hands to boat stations' was piped again. They rapidly drew alongside the drifting boat, but they were too late. Inside was the pitiful evidence of another part of the human cost of this endless battle as Ted Newman poignantly recorded:

> Two men were found in it – one wearing just a thin pair of overalls, lying with his head over the side of the boat (which was practically full of water). The other, wearing only a shirt, was lying back over an oar – looked as though he had pulled until he was exhausted. Both were dead, although they didn't look as if they had been so for very long. Nothing could be done, so we left them. By the way they were dressed, it looked as if their ship had been sunk during the night.'[3]

As the weather was unfavourable the boat was left. The weather worsened and all flying operations ceased. The wolf pack took advantage of this to close with the convoy again and submarine alarms

HMS Faulknor *with a Fairey Albacore carrier-based anti-submarine aircraft flying overhead in the spring of 1943 this combination, combining the High Frequency Direction Finding (HF/DF) radio equipment of the destroyers and the range of the naval aircraft, closed the gap in the Mid-Atlantic and defeated the U-boat packs decisively.* (Imperial War Museum.)

were many that night but nothing transpired. On 11 May, at 0700 in 53° 45′ N, 44° 38′ W, *Faulknor, Impulsive* and *Onslaught* left the convoy and *Archer*, and proceeded to reinforce convoy ON.182.

This convoy was bound for New York and was sighted at 1300 on 12 May, in 59° 23′ N, 40° 434′ W. Its Canadian escort [the C5 Group], reported an easy passage thus far, although they welcomed the additions to their strength.

The three destroyers of the 4th Escort Group were spread as an Asdic screen ahead and on each bow by day, and stationed astern in positions Q, S and G, at night. When they met the new convoy off Cape Farewell, the sea was calm but there were many icebergs. They refuelled and continued towards St. John's. There was lots of wireless activity from the wolf-packs all around but *Faulknor* evidently brought her own luck with her, for there were no attacks; perhaps the enemy considered two escort groups too tough a nut to crack.

Faulknor certainly contributed in making the pack keep its distance. At 0155 on the 13th, in 58° 30′ N, 44° 00′ W, she obtained a High Frequency D/F bearing 160°, depth 15 ft and conducted a search, but with no result.

At 1945 on the 14th, in 53° 05′ N, 49° 01′ W, *Faulknor* and her two companions were detached from the convoy and proceeded to Argentina, Newfoundland, passing through heavy concentrations of icebergs off Cape Race. At 0830/16th they secured alongside an American tanker to replenish, which was refused because it was Sunday![4] With the memory of the death of the young pilot and the two merchant seamen fresh in their minds *Faulknor's* crew wondered whether some US citizens realised just what was occurring just miles from their safe and secure anchorage! The crew of the Flying Fortress were landed, and leave was granted, and each man had a miserly $5 allowance.

Ted Newman recorded his impressions:

> We went to a naval canteen and managed to squander our five dollars on goods to bring home. The Yanks leave us miles behind for organisation of benefits to the Forces. It didn't cost us a cent for food – we asked where we could eat and were told to eat with

the boys in the Yank barracks. We went in and joined the queue and it was a case of picking up a tray and visiting the various chefs, who gave us whatever we wanted – all slapped on the tray. We had sausage roll, veal, Russian salad, potatoes, cheese biscuits, jam, peaches and a cup of cocoa- no limit to what you could eat. It's surprising what they do eat. I saw one Yank eating baked beans and bread and jam together -everything is mixed up. After this we went to another place and had free coffee and then back to the barracks for a concert. It was a grand show and by the looks of the place it's a pleasure to be in their Navy. Nowhere in England could anyone walk into a Naval barracks and have things *ad lib* like that. It makes you wonder how they feel when they come to places like Scapa and England. Owing to one of the quartermasters going on watch drunk, on bottled rum, and trying to assault an officer, besides endangering the ship, our rum ration is now given out two and one. This makes nearly a cupful each and nobody likes it.

Then it was back to the war.

Archer, Faulknor, Impulsive and *Onslaught* sailed at 0830/19th, to overtake convoy HX. 239 of 43 ships. The sloop *Pelican* joined them from St. Johns at 1900 and they steered west passing intermittent icebergs. Captain Scott Moncrieff recalled:

> We had a number of excitements in the Atlantic, not only with U-boats, but with those eternal enemies, rough weather, fogs and icebergs. The iceberg region was particularly exciting and we spent two or three days wending our way through icebergs that varied in size from a teacup to a small island.

At 0800, Friday 21 May, they joined the convoy in 49° 15′ N, 40° 08′ W and *Archer* was placed in among the merchant ships until such time as flying operations were required, while the four escorts extended the screen with B3 Escort Group, (destroyers *Keppel, Escapade, Garland,* frigate *Towey* and corvettes *Orchis, Narcissus, Roselys, Lobelia* and *Renoncule)*

The convoy's 42 vessels included liner *Star of Australia*, with 750 passengers aboard, including many women, quite a responsibility. The weather was again rough but the buzz went round that they were due for leave on reaching the UK. Admiral Dönitz had other ideas and ordered the 'Mosel' pack of twenty-one U-boats into the area.

From 21st, their convoy and another quite close to them, ON.184 with an American Support Group in attendance, were subjected to heavy submarine assault. There were estimated to be at least twelve U-boats in the vicinity at one time, of which the escorts sank *U-569* and damaged *U-305, U-468, U-68* and *U-218.*

On Saturday 22nd Captain Scott-Moncrieff reported, '… considerable U-boat activity round ON.184 to the Northward of HX.239' and because of this *Archer* commenced her Swordfish patrols again. At 1410 one of these reported a U-boat 28 miles off the port bow. The aircraft attacked this U-boat and *Faulknor* and *Onslaught* carried out a square search until 1830, but without result. The two destroyers rejoined the convoy at 2300 and no British merchant ships had yet been sunk.

At dawn 22nd *Faulknor* and *Onslaught* swept astern of the convoy and on its quarters to a depth of twenty miles, and, at 0700 *Impulsive* and *Garland* investigated a 'Huff-Duff' fix on a U-boat on the convoy's port beam. During the next few hours Swordfish attacked U-boats at 38 and 34 miles off the convoys port quarter as the pack was kept at a distance, *Escapade, Garland* and *Impulsive* searching in their vicinity to keep them down. At 1030, a Swordfish from *Archer* damaged *U-752* with a rocket attack, the first success of this new weapon, the U-boat being finished off by the destroyers *Escapade* and *Keppel*. They found eleven survivors, who confirmed that the pack had not yet actually sighted the convoy.

Impulsive reduced speed to fourteen knots because of a defective starboard shaft and was placed astern of the convoy and during the afternoon *Faulknor* and *Onslaught* oiled. This was a classic case of active defence by surface escorts and carrier-based aircraft keeping the wolf-packs so far away from the convoy that they proved impotent. As well HF/DF and carrier aircraft, another factor was the escorts mobility, enabling high-speed dashes into 'outer field'. The fleet oiler was a fourth unsung winning facet in the 1943 victory of the escorts.

How fuelling dominated a destroyer's ability to fight, and fight again, can be seen by *Faulknor's* record.

HMS *Faulknor* – Oiling at Sea 7 May to 26 May 1943

Period	Distance in miles	Percentage of Fuel remaining	Percentage of fuel after oiling
7 May to 9 May	758	73	95
9 May to 12 May	995	63	95
12 May to 14 May	606	74.6	94
14 May to 16 May	746	55	–
19 May to 23 May	1532.5	50	95
23 May to 26 May	986	63.7	–

By 25th they had shaken off the U-boats and, at 1300, *Faulknor* left the convoy taking with her *Archer, Onslaught* and *Pelican*, while *Impulsive* was detached direct to Scapa as she had sufficient fuel to steam safely at fourteen knots. The escort-carrier flew off four Swordfish to conduct searches to the maximum range but one crashed three miles from the carrier, *Onslaught* rescuing the crew.

The failure of the wolf-pack to even sight HX.239 illustrates how great a victory had been achieved at this period. It marked *the* turning point of the Atlantic Battle.

Captain Scott-Moncrieff's summary of Support Groups, from his experience with HX.239 and other convoys, stated:

I am sure there is no difficulty in operating Aircraft Carriers within the convoy screen, especially the modern Escort Carriers which have a small turning circle. Under the worst conditions of light *Archer* had no difficulty in operating aircraft and still remaining within the convoy screen. He added that;

I would like to place on record my admiration for the manner in which HMS *Archer* was operated and handled. On the many occasions when heavy weather and bad visibility occurred, all that the patrols asked for was always forthcoming.

HMS Faulknor *fuelling at sea astern of an RFA fleet oiler during North Atlantic Convoy Support Group operations, May 1943.* (K. Timson.)

With regard the responsibility of the surface forces he wrote:

> Control of the screen by 'Senior Officer, Close Escort' although 'Senior Officer, Support Group' is the Senior Officer present, offered no difficulties and in all cases the Group Commanders were most efficient and helpful to me.
> Control of communications on the convoy R/T wave is essential.

Captain Scott-Moncrieff continued.

> With the added communications now present, due to the larger number of aircraft operating, this matter is becoming most important.' It was with communications that Captain Scott-Moncrieff was most critical.
> A noticeable feature in all the five Escort Groups that we worked with was the lack of 'R/T discipline'. This was particularly the case whenever the convoy became threatened and the volume of traffic increased. It seemed that the ship of the SO Escort rarely exercised any control; this resulted in a number of indiscriminate, and often unnecessary, transmissions. It is strongly suggested that if proper control is to be exercised an Officer (preferably a qualified Signal Officer) must be allocated for group signal duties. It is also essential that the SO Escort himself should at all times be fully aware of the R/T situation. (It seemed on at least one occasion that the S.O. Escort did not have his bridge loudspeaker switched on, as traffic at one time was so chaotic that no Senior Officer should have ever allowed such a state of affairs to continue).

He regarded as bad practice the use of convoy R/T to pass on all D/F reports so that all escorts not so fitted could get a picture of the situation. 'SO Escorts is the only person who can really appreciate the situation and ordinary D/F reports, in themselves, can often be very misleading to non-HF/DF ships.' His strong recommendation was that H.T.11 frequencies, 'which did not appear to be very popular in most of the groups' should be 'adhered to rigidly.'

Finally, Captain Scott-Moncrieff considered that it had proved that if R/T was to give the best results rigid control had to be exercised, and furthermore, exercised by an Officer who had *all* the local operational information. 'It does not appear adequate to leave this matter to a CPO Telegraphist. R/T signals can be made and received in half the present time if the group is well trained and well controlled and uses the correct procedures.'

Faulknor entered the Clyde, docked and underwent a boiler clean, giving leave until 2 June, when they left Greenock for Scapa, arriving next day.

They nosed in among the treeless islands of the familiar anchorage and went to her buoy in Gutter Sound as she had done so often before. Nothing seemed to have changed. Those on deck instinctively looked over at the main fleet anchorage where they saw, in addition to the great hunched shapes of the Home Fleet 'King George V' Class battleships and *Renown,* other silhouettes they had not seen for some time, the battleships *Warspite, Valiant, Nelson* and *Rodney* for example, aircraft-carriers *Formidable* and *Indomitable,* plus many cruisers. The Flow looked uncomfortably full. Where were they going, these powerful squadrons, and, more to the point, would they be in on it? Past form told them that such an assembly meant trouble, and trouble meant- *Faulknor!*

On 10th they carried out a shore bombardment, the first of many such exercises, *Faulknor* landing a small party ashore in the North Shetlands to note the fall of shot. Because of fog, the 4.7's shooting, when it finally took place, was, '... lousy – one shell nearly hitting a farmhouse. The party ashore had to console the farmer. W/T communications broke down and, on the whole, it was a wasted day.'

Faulknor's main armament guns remained the standard 4.7-inch Quick Firer type, which fired a 50-lb shell and had a maximum range of 17,000 yards. They carried 125 rounds of Semi-Armour Piercing, (S.A.P.), fifty rounds of H.E.D.A and fifty rounds of H.E.T.F. per gun. Eric Prigmore remembered:

Not only was I gunner on the 4.7-inch, I was also responsible for the care and maintenance of the guns under the Ordnance Artificer. I can say that at *no time* during my three years aboard *Faulknor* did we ever use the removable deck plates for altering the elevation of the guns, which was the standard 40°. In action we had to be ready in a few minutes.' In fact, as can been clearly seen from photographs taken at the time, the circle of plates around each mounting was kept permanently open to enable the guns to be used at maximum elevation *all the time.*

This gun had a crew of seven. Number One, on the left, was the Gun layer, who fired in independent, and trained the gun up and down. Number Two, was the Captain of the Gun, responsible for the breach in either independent or automatic firing. For automatic or salvo firing by all the guns together, he made an interceptor switch, which told the Director above the bridge that our gun was ready, and they fired. Number Three, that was me. I stood by a tray with a lever by my left hand. Number Four and Five placed Shell and Cordite Charge on the tray. I then depressed the lever, pushed the tray over in line with the breach and, with my right fist, punched them into the breach, which closed automatically. I may add that this was very tiring after about thirty or forty rounds. The shell weighed about 50 lb and the cordite 30 lb.

Number Four, the trainer of the gun, tracked the target left to right and worked with Number One through telescopic sight and crosswires set on the target. Number Seven sat in the gun-shield alongside me, Number Three and behind Number One. They had earphones on to take messages from the bridge and Director, what ammunition to use for surface action (S.A.P.) or High Explosive (H.E.), which exploded on contact. In the event of anti-aircraft firing he had a fuse key which set the distance to explode, which information was passed down the headphones, i.e 'Barrage Fuse 014', to set the barrage at one thousand four hundred yards range.

For Director Controlled firing, which was the most frequent form, the Gun layer and Trainer just followed the pointers in front of them on a machine and the two senior ratings in the Director fired the guns.

These exercises enabled the lower-deck 'buzz' to predict another major amphibious assault in the offing. On 13th, *Faulknor's* crew got another hint of their destination when they were issued with tropical kit. Next day they sailed in company with a battleship and cruisers with whom they conducted miniature battles and firing exercises until the 16th. All this training was, of course, for the planned invasion of

HMS Faulknor *at Scapa Flow, 1943, with HMS* Inglefield *seen astern.* (K. Timson.)

Sicily, Operation 'Husky'. A large percentage of the Home Fleet was to be transferred to the Mediterranean including battleships *King George V* and *Howe*, (Force 'C') and the reconstituted 8th Destroyer Flotilla, led by *Faulknor*.

Faulknor sailed from Scapa for Gibraltar with the two battleships, aircraft-carrier *Indomitable*, and destroyers *Fury, Echo, Eclipse, Intrepid, Inglefield, Offa, Piorun, Blankney, Brecon* and *Brissenden*, in good weather on 17 June. Leading this array to sea *Faulknor* passed the brand-new destroyer *Grenville*, which was working up and whose steering had broken down. Her skipper, Roger Hill, signalled to Alan Scott-Moncrieff:

> Good luck – once again we are Cinderella.

Faulknor flashed back a very accurate prediction:

> Don't fret, you will have your bellyful before the war is over.

The weather changed and the next three days saw rough conditions as they proceeded through the Bay of Biscay, and other ships joined them. Aboard *Faulknor* the ship's doctor began the processes of inoculating the whole crew against the more exotic diseases, even those who were aboard her back in 1941 when she was last in the Mediterranean.

On the evening of Sunday 20 June, a four-engined RAF Liberator bomber, 'J', from 86 Squadron, based at Aldegrove, had been giving long-range anti-submarine protection to the fleet. According to its skipper, Flying Officer ACI Samuel, RAFVR, they had been airborne since 1300 on 20 June and had expected to land back at base about 0500 on 21st. One engine had suddenly cut out but was re-started on the auxiliary fuel pump. However, it required an abnormally wide throttle setting in order to maintain the aircraft's height using up fuel. Samuel decided to ditch ahead of the destroyer screen

HMS *Faulknor taking aboard survivors from a crashed RAF Liberator bomber in the Bay of Biscay, 21 June 1943.* (Bill Silltow.)

where they would have a good chance of being picked up very quickly. Unfortunately, there was the usual heavy Biscay swell running, and when they touched down at about 130 mph, they smashed straight into a large wave, which swamped the Liberator sinking her very quickly.

The ditching occurred at 2320, some 3,000 yards, Red 30° from *Faulknor*, which was in her usual place at the head of the screen as Leader of the Fleet in position 'M', and speed was immediately increased to close the wreckage. They found Samuel and three of his crew in their rubber dinghy and hauled them aboard. *Faulknor*'s ship's whaler plucked three further members of the aircrew from the sea; unfortunately one of them, Flight Sergeant Fast, was found to be dead on arrival aboard. Another man was missing and presumed to have gone down with the aircraft. The survivors were placed under the care of the ship's Medical Officer in Captain Scott-Moncrieff's after cabin, and, despite two very severe injuries, all survived to be landed at Gibraltar.

At 0830 Monday 21st, the sad ceremony of burial at sea was conducted for Flight Sergeant Fast before *Faulknor* resumed her station. None of his fellow aircrew was in a fit enough state to attend. The battle squadrons exercised again as the weather eased and the climate got very much warmer. White bodies more used to Arctic ice fields and snowstorms in the Kola Inlet, now began to burn and blister in the unaccustomed sunshine.

Faulknor docked at Gibraltar on 23 June with battleships *Nelson*, *Rodney* (Force 'A') *Valiant* and *Warspite*, (Force 'B'), carriers *Formidable* and *Indomitable*, and destroyers *Fury*, *Echo*, *Ilex*, *Inglefield*, *Intrepid*, *Offa*, *Piorun*, *Panther*, *Pathfinder*, *Penn*, *Quail*, *Queenborough*, *Quilliam* and *Troubridge*; others arriving later.

Four days of AA exercises and such followed, before they left abruptly at 1630/28th, with destroyers *Fury*, *Echo*, *Eclipse*, *Inglefield*, *Intrepid*, *Ilex*, *Raider* and Greek *Queen Olga*, escorting *Warspite*, *Valiant* and *Formidable*, and light cruisers *Aurora* and *Penelope*. They initially sailed, for Algiers, going to Action Stations twice on that short leg, arriving 30th, and leaving early that same evening for Alexandria. The passage through the length of the Mediterranean was made without any challenge whatsoever from the Axis, the only incident being yet another aircrew recovery by *Faulknor* on 2 July. A keen-eyed lookout saw a Fleet Air Arm Albacore crash and they quickly closed the scene. Amid the usual debris they found and hauled aboard the three crew, the captain, Sub-Lieutenant (A) 'Jack' F. Harvey, RNVR, the Observer, Lieutenant (A) Philip Spademan, RN and the TAG, Leading Airman Bob 'Spike' Hughes, all unharmed save for bruises. Their aircraft, N4242 of 815 Bombardment Flight, had been on its way from Tripoli to Malta when it crashed. The ships[5] anchored off Ras-el-Tin lighthouse at 0630 on 5 July.

While at Alexandria and conducting exercises prior to the invasion of Sicily Ted Slinger recalls an incident, which almost terminated the career of Captain D8 and several of his flotilla captains there and then.

> I was on No. 1 gun as we exercised and we were put through extensive shoots. As we returned to harbour I was told by the coxswain that the 'skimmer', the small run-about boat used by the ship, was to be astern soon after anchoring at Alex.
>
> The Captain, A.K. Scott-Moncrieff, and two other captains we had on board as observers, wished to be taken to the depot ship *Blenheim*. As I was the coxswain I requested my opposite number to lower the boat and take it astern to the after gangway, while I showered and changed into the rig of the day.
>
> On boarding the boat I was just in time to observe the three captains talking to the officer of the watch, and was envious of the rest of the crew who were enjoying the pipe, 'hands to bathe'. The three captains then came aboard the skimmer, and, as it was only a small craft, some eight feet long, they stood on the back seat and held on to the rear canopy. As I slowly eased my way through the swimming crew, A.K. said, 'All right Slinger, Let her go!' so I opened the throttle. As we were somewhat overloaded she

seemed a bit sluggish, but suddenly, to my utter amazement, the boat shot forward at a great rate of knots. Realising something was not quite right I turned around and again to my chagrin, found I was the only one still onboard! Astern I glimpsed my canopy with 24 gold rings clinging to it!

You may well ask what did I do? Well, I first checked the petrol tank to see if there was enough petrol for me to make it back to England, which obviously was out of the question. So, with a feeling of this being my last day on earth, I returned to pick up the officers, and my canopy. My offer of a lift was refused as all preferred to swim the short distance to the gangway. I picked up my canopy and, to the sounds of the crew saying to the fully-clothed officers 'you'll find it easier if you were in swimming trunks, Sir', and other sarcastic comments that I felt would do my case *no* good at all, I returned to the ship's boom to investigate the cause of the disaster. I found that my opposite number had failed to fix the canopy with the four securing bolts after lowering the skimmer.

Quickly putting the bolts into the canopy and putting my foot against the beading, I broke the timber across the holes, which should have held the canopy down safely, only to look up and see the officer of the watch looking down on me and requesting an explanation. Luckily, he realised I was innocent and, probably not wishing to witness the only hanging at sea since Nelson's days, he went along with the idea, and I am pleased to say that all ended very well as my oppo forfeited his tot for the next two days in penance at his carelessness!

The Admiralty sent *Faulknor's* adopted towns a copy of the ship's badge, which was presented at the beginning of August 1943 by Vice-Admiral Sir Robert Hornell, KBE, DSO, RN at a ceremony at the Council Chamber. The plaque from Faulknor was set up in the entrance lobby to the then Council Officers in Mary Stevens Park. [This plaque still exists and is now mounted in a glass case in the foyer of the modern Stourbridge Library where it was photographed by the Author in May, 1996.] In

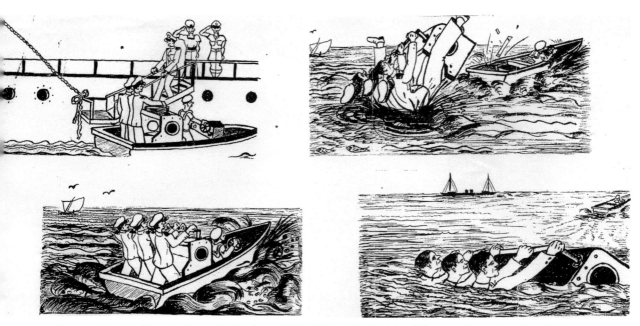

Cartoons from the Captain, Alexandria Harbour, 1943. AS-M and his Divisional Commanders going ashore. Driver opened full throttle – too much for the launch's canopy. We disappeared over the back of the boat to the huge delight of the ship's company, who were bathing at the time! (Allan Scott-Moncrieff, courtesy of Lady Scot-Moncrieff.)

return the councils sent a plaque, in chocolate painted metal with white lettering and the Borough's Coat of Arms picked out in coloured relief, back to the ship, which at that date had steamed 160,000 miles in action since the war began.

It was about this time they found themselves writing a monthly news bulletin, which was published in the local paper, the 'County Express'. This kept the folks at home informed of their doings, (as far as the censor would permit) and of their well-being, as well as thanking them for the numerous gifts of books, cigarettes and comforts, which they showered upon the crew.

Mrs Watson, wife of the headmaster of the local grammar school was Chairwoman of the 'Comforts Committee' and Miss Eileen Moody was the secretary. Another young lady dear to their hearts was Miss Joan Moody, a PTI and Skipper of the local Sea Rangers of Stourbridge who named their training headquarters SRS *Faulknor*. A cul-de-sac in the town, off Hill Street, was also named in the ship's honour. Faulknor Close was adopted in March 1970. There is also a Faulknor Drive, another cul-de-sac off Tarry Holloway, Shut End, Presnett, which was named in May 1978, also after HMS *Faulknor*, and is, appropriately enough, near Dreadnought Road. Books and magazines were sent to the crew and a Crew Fund was established. Among the gifts the crew sent back to the town was a scale model of the ship and various toys made by crew members for the children in the local Corbett Hospital, including a pony and trap and such like. They also sent the town the ship's Battle Ensign.

The local newspaper, *The County Express,* ran a story 'Pen Friends Ahoy!' in 1943, asking for locals girls to write to the forty or so *Faulknors* (from the South African Naval Forces) looking for news from home, and whose ages varied from eighteen to thirty-five, although the vast majority were in the range nineteen to twenty-two. One lasting result of this was the pen friendship between eighteen-year-old Yeoman Raymond Matthews from Bedford, and an Amblecote lass named Dayrell. Raymond had been called up that year and trained as an electrician. He recalled, 'I trained with 33 other sailors at Portsmouth. Only four of them survived the war.' The luck of the *Faulknor* again. This couple wrote to each other every day during the remainder of the war, and met each other at New Street Station in Birmingham when Able Seaman Matthews was on leave. The pair married at Holy Trinity church, Amblecote in 1946 and celebrated their 50th Wedding Anniversary on 26 January 1996.

They sailed again for 'Husky' at 1045 on 7 July, *Warspite* and *Valiant* with *Faulknor, Fury, Echo, Eclipse, Inglefield, Intrepid, Ilex, Raider* and *Queen Olga*, heading west. They concentrated with the 'First Eleven', *Nelson, Rodney, Formidable,* and *Indomitable,* light cruisers *Aurora, Penelope, Cleopatra, Euryalus,* and destroyers *Quilliam, Quail, Queenborough, Isis, Troubridge, Tumult, Tyrian, Offa* and *Piorun* from Oran, two days later 240 miles south-east of Malta. That night Force 'H' made a feint to the east until dusk, then, under cover of darkness, steered for a position off Cape Passero from where they could intercept any moves by the Italian Fleet. The first assault on the southern Sicilian beaches was due at 0245/10 July; and if the Italians were *ever* going to use their battle fleet to defend their country, this was surely that time. Force 'H' was there to deal with any such attempt. At 0520 the force overtook PQWS 37, the second of the slow invasion convoys, on their way to the beaches.

At 0800/8 July, there were several yellow and one red air raid warning during the forenoon but no sightings of aircraft. At 0615/9th, *Faulknor* sighted the oiler force, '…a terrible mess and mass of oilers and scrambling signals eventually sorted out…' wrote Captain Scott-Moncrieff. Eventually all but two destroyers managed to oil by 1400 when the force altered course 340° at eighteen knots. Force 'Q', *Aurora, Penelope, Inglefield* and *Offa*, parted company to carry out shore bombardments, Operation 'Arsenal'. Aboard *Faulknor* Captain Scott-Moncrieff cleared the lower deck and spoke to the ship's company before reading out Admiral Andrew Cunningham's message to the fleet. The points that *Faulknor's* crew were given by their captain were concise but pertinent. He told them that the Allies were landing in Sicily that night; that the operation would be carried out by the largest number of troops to date, with the biggest LCTs etc. They might meet the Italian fleet, but possible bombing would be their worst enemy next day. He emphasised that everyone must think clearly and calmly and that the main mission was to consolidate the landing and follow-up operations. If the Italians did show up it was his intention to '…go right in and endeavour to close to close quarters, but I think we stand little chance at big targets.' Finally he emphasised, 'Everyone is to remember that when called upon they must rush to get the guns into action in the minimum time. No Fatheads!'

'H' Hour was 0245/10 July, with moon set at 0730. A nasty sea got up at midnight but all the eastern landings were successful, and *Faulknor* led the fleet patrolling about 40 miles offshore, but there were no alarms. They spent all that day and the next cruising backward and forward, exactly 360°–180° but with no excitement whatsoever.

Captain Scott Moncrieffe recorded:

> July 10th, a great day in our history, found us taking part in the invasion of Sicily. Our activities were various and ranged from providing seaward cover for the landings to bombarding bridges, railways and towns on the coast of Sicily and Italy. Perhaps the thing we appreciated most of all was the glorious Mediterranean weather, with its succession of cloudless days and the calm blue sea. It was a very welcome change after our long periods in northern waters. Several of us suffered initially from sunburn, but we soon got over that, and now most of us are as brown as berries.

After two days patrolling up and down off Cape Passero, listening in to the bombarding ships making their contributions, but with nothing to disturb them but false air raid alerts, the Second Eleven went into Malta to refuel, *Warspite* and *Valiant* being the first battleships to do so since December, 1940. There was no time to go ashore, but Captain Scott-Moncrieff noted that, 'Malta does not look too bad, considering.'

Ted Newman recorded his different impression:

> This place has changed a lot since I saw it last. Nearly every building is damaged and the harbours are a mass of wreck buoys.

They sailed again at 1245/12 July, after refuelling, to resume their patrol. The force was due to show themselves off the beaches but the U-boat threat was considered too great a risk. They screened the first division to Malta in turn. They were called upon to bombard Catania airfield at 2200 but, as they could not arrive before 0100, they were unable to comply.

Faulknor and the 1st division did not arrive at Malta again until 1400/14 July, following a scare report that two Italian battleships had sailed from La Spezia, which proved false. *Faulknor* was nonetheless held out at sea until the 16th before berthing at Cautica wharf outside *Intrepid*.

By 15 July, Force 'H' was at full strength again but was not called into action, much to the frustration of Admiral Willis. *Indomitable* had been struck by an aerial torpedo on the 16th and returned damaged to Malta with *Warspite* and *Valiant* escorted by *Faulknor, Fury, Eclipse, Inglefield, Intrepid, Petard, Raider* and *Queen Olga*.

On 17 July, *Faulknor's* crew were taking a well-earned rest, swimming and sailing in the bay of Marsa Sirocco, when the two battleships and the flotilla were ordered to raise steam with all despatch and sail at once to conduct a bombardment of the Catania defences at 1830, prior to an attack by the army. The timing was obviously important.

Warspite and *Valiant* sailed at 1230 with *Faulknor* leading the screen; *Fury, Eclipse, Inglefield, Raider, Petard* and *Queen Olga*. However, *Valiant* fouled the boom and 'The Old Lady' continued on her own with monitor *Erebus*. Time, 1430; distance to cover, approximately one hundred miles. *Warspite* was no longer a speedy vessel, and the billowing black clouds of smoke pouring from her funnel indicated just how hard she was being pushed. *En route,* she did her usual party piece when her steering gear failed (as it had at the Battle of Jutland, twenty-seven years earlier!) and she careered round in circles creating chaos for her destroyer escorts that had to dash around in all directions to cover her. Eventually she was brought under control again. At 1545, they went to action stations and, at 1840, they took position about $10\frac{1}{2}$ miles from the Cape Molini lighthouse, *Warspite*, steaming at fifteen knots, with the destroyers stationed on either side of her. Four minutes later the battleship opened fire when some 13,000 yards from the Sciara Biscari lighthouse, her target area being a triangular area around the main military barracks 1,000 x 800 yards. Initially she fired eight two-gun salvoes from her 'A' and 'B' turrets, then six minutes later, she altered course 020° and 'X' and 'Y' turrets fired six further two gun salvoes each. Thirteen minutes later it was all over; *Warspite* had fired 57 rounds of 15-inch shell into Catania. An eyewitness reported how:

> A great mass of smoke and dust rose up out of the town.

Faulknor, leading the landward side of the destroyer screen, contributed her quota with her little 4.7s, along with *Intrepid* and *Queen Olga* as they duelled with shore batteries, whose return fire fell close to *Intrepid* but no ship was hit. At 1910, the enemy air force was stung into action and an attack took place on the screen, one bomber being shot down, crashing directly in *Faulknor's* wake. More danger came from their own side for *Faulknor* was nearly hit by barrage fire! An attack by three German FW. 190 fighter-bombers also missed but almost indirectly caused the *Faulknor's* demise. The cruiser *Euryalus* was close by and opened fire with her main batteries of 5.25 inch guns, pumping out rapid salvoes at almost sea-level against one of the sea-skimming aircraft as it passed low across *Faulknor's* bows, these salvoes almost sinking her. There were two blind barrages fired off by the fleet during the night but no aircraft were actually seen.

Cable party on the ships fo'c'sle as the flotilla puts to sea, Alexandria, 1943. (Imperial War Museum.)

During the return to Malta torpedo-bombers also attacked, again without success, and *Warspite, Euryalus, Faulknor, Fury, Inglefield, Intrepid, Eclipse, Petard, Raider, Exmoor* and *Queen Olga* arrived back at their buoys in Valetta harbour safely that night.

They sailed on 19th to join *Fury, Eclipse, Inglefield, Intrepid, Raider, Whaddon* and *Queen Olga* in an anti-submarine sweep as far as the Messina Straits. Allied aircraft, which were supposed to co-operate, failed to materialise but nothing was sighted save for two calcium flares and one Ju.88, which came over at very high speed but did not attack. The flotilla returned to Malta next day, but on 20th initiated another hunt at 0810, after an aircraft had reported sighting a periscope. No submarines were found, only an upturned lifeboat, which was sunk by *Eclipse*. They returned to Malta at 1740, *Faulknor* securing alongside *Warspite* and oiling from her.

They were off once more at 1300/21st sailing at 1300 and conducting another sweep towards Bizerta with *Eclipse, Inglefield, Ilex, Raider, Oakley, Eggesford, Lauderdale* and *Whaddon*. This hunt continued throughout the night, but without results, although they dropped delayed action 'Snowflake', some floats and depth charges. The former 'fell over' and failed to work, but the depth-charges worked all right. *Faulknor's* D/F team got a good fix and informed the 'Hunts' who were detached in the area of Capo Murro di Porco. Captain Scott-Moncrieff recorded that he was '..bored stiff and very tired..' at this fruitless exercise, but they continued the patient search on into the following day.

Meanwhile, at 1338, light cruiser *Newfoundland* was hit aft by a torpedo from Italian submarine *Ascianghi*. Captain Hutton, aboard destroyer *Laforey*, in his own words, '… altered course back to the northward informing the Rear-Admiral [CHJ Harcourt] that I intended to search for the submarine, leaving *Loyal* (whose Asdics were broken down) and *Lookout* to screen the cruisers. At the same time I ordered the 8th Destroyer Flotilla, who I knew were close, to join me with all despatch.'

On receipt of Captain Hutton's signal, Captain Scott-Moncrieff left the 'Hunts' and rushed to the scene with *Faulknor, Eclipse, Inglefield, Ilex* and *Raider*. On the arrival of the 8th Flotilla at 1440, Captain Scott-Moncrieff found that *Laforey* had already attacked a 'non-sub' contact at 1428. He now organised a full sweep of the area with four of his destroyers: *Faulknor, Inglefield, Ilex*, and *Raider* while *Eclipse* (Captain E. Mack) was sent to join *Laforey* in conducting a box-search, Captain Hutton recording that:

> I had suspected that *Newfoundland* had been hit from the port side and that the submarine was to seawards and to the northwards, so I started the search with *Eclipse* in that direction. At 1541 the U-boat had the temerity to fire two torpedoes at *Laforey* which missed astern.

Turning up the tracks the two destroyers soon obtained a good contact. *Laforey* then dropped eight depth-charges and *Eclipse* five depth-charges with instant results, for the submarine surfaced and, at 1623, was enthusiastically taken under gunfire by *Faulknor, Laforey, Eclipse* and *Raider*, although only *Laforey* actually scored any hits. *Laforey* picked up one survivor who informed them that their victim was the Italian submarine *Ascianghi*.

Ted Newman wrote:

> We soon got a 'ping' and, after dropping a few charges, brought the sub up. He showed fight, firing torpedoes and his gun – we then opened up on him and he finally sank. We picked up survivors.

These were duly landed at Grand Harbour on the flotilla's return to Malta on the 23rd. Both *Echo* and *Raider* then went to boiler clean, while *Faulknor* relieved *Ilex* as emergency destroyer.

The 8th Flotilla spent the 24 July in Valetta harbour, Captain Scott-Moncrieff inspected the *Ilex* which had '… a very groggy tube, but quite clean below', and the flotilla (*Faulknor, Inglefield, Eclipse* and *Ilex*), sailed at 1300 to carry out Operation 'Broom' a patrol close off the coast of Sicily again during the night of 25th/26th. They could plainly hear the sound of the fighting ashore, but they located no enemy shipping. Some Junkers Ju.88's on their way south were engaged during the night but, on being relieved by Polish destroyer *Piorun,* the flotilla returned to harbour with *Offa* and *Petard,* finding Malta had again been heavily bombed. They spent that day and most of the 27th at anchor. 'A dull day', wrote Captain Scott-Moncrieff, 'nothing doing.' They oiled and then went on operational alert owing to a scare that Italian limpeters would be making an attack on the assembled fleet that night. All destroyers came to half-an-hours notice to steam at 2330, but no attacks materialised.

On 28 July 1943, Captain Scott-Moncrieff left for a meeting aboard *Aurora* concerning the night's operation. They sailed at 1420, with *Inglefield, Ilex* and *Intrepid* as part of Force 'Q', under Commodore W. G. Agnew, meeting light cruisers *Aurora* and *Penelope* and destroyers *Laforey* and *Lookout* at 1500. Their mission was to conduct a close-range shore bombardment of vital enemy communications to the south of Locri, south-east of Cape Spartivento, on the toe of Italy. The force proceeded to within ten miles of the coast of Sicily to the latitude of Augusta, carrying out an anti-submarine sweep as they went. At 2030 that evening, they increased speed to 22 knots, and, at 2100, altered course to pass five miles off Cape Spartivento.

By 0100/29 July, the force was in 38° 08′ N, 16° 16.5′ E, and formed into single line ahead in the order *Aurora, Laforey, Lookout, Intrepid, Penelope, Faulknor, Inglefield, Ilex*, on a course of 040°. The two cruisers then opened fire with star-shell and 6-inch gunfire, the destroyers joining in with their 4.7-inch guns as soon as the star-shell had burst over the target. The first four warships targeted rail and road bridges in 38° 12′ N, 16° 13.8′ E, while the second quartet, *Faulknor's* group, bombarded rail and road bridges at 38° 11.3′ N, 16° 13.2′ E.

After eight minutes all shifted fire to road and rail bridges at 38° 13.4′ N, 16° 15.3′ E, each ship engaging in turn as they passed at ranges that varied between 9,000 and 8,000 yards. The bridges could not be identified individually and so shelling was concentrated along the foreshore in the hope of hitting the railway and the road. The only visible result was a small fire in the vicinity of the first four bridges. The only enemy reaction was firing of a green Verey light from Locri at 0018 and a fixed green light at Marina di Siderno at 0019.

At 0025, *Aurora* led round to 060° and the force carried out a sweep up the coast as far as Point di Stilo without result, although a solitary searchlight from Locri swept continuously to seaward for 0100 for half-an-hour or more without locating the British squadron. At 0136, Force 'Q' turned to 180° and the destroyers resumed normal screening positions, course being again altered at 0500 to 270° and speed reduced to 17 knots. An anti-submarine sweep was then conducted to a position some five miles off Augusta at which point *Faulknor, Intrepid, Inglefield* and *Ilex* were detached to carry out Operation 'Broom' an unrewarded anti-submarine sweep, before returning to Valetta at 1900. *Faulknor* and *Offa* oiled and, on 30 July, shifted berth to Sliema Creek.

At 0710, *Faulknor* returned to No. 10 buoy and Captain Scott-Moncrieff visited *Nelson* and later dined and bathed. Another air raid took place that night but it was not serious. Following discussions aboard cruiser *Mauritius*, another bombardment was planned for the night of 31 July/1 August. *Faulknor, Inglefield, Loyal* and *Raider* left Malta meeting light cruisers *Aurora* and *Penelope* and destroyers *Laforey* and *Lookout* from Augusta, to bombard Cotrone, on mainland Italy. Zero hour was at 0200 and the operation was almost identical to that of the 29th. Two enemy patrol craft, encountered off the coast were quickly despatched and only a solitary shore battery responded, firing three fairly accurate rounds. After the bombardment the destroyers conducted another Operation 'Broom' anti-submarine sweep until 1530/3 August, off Pantellaria, when relieved by other destroyers and returned to Malta to refuel. Anchoring at Marsa Sirocco a faulty distilling pump caused *Faulknor* to be *hors de combat* and they remained inactive for several days. On 3 August they were in Grand Harbour with *Warspite, Valiant, Inglefield, Raider* and *Queen Olga,* with *Faulknor* oiling alongside *Aurora,* when air raid yellow alert sounded. They cast off while still only three-quarters full, but no air raid took place. On 4th, Captain Scott-Moncrieff reported, 'Meeting of COs in *Nelson,* discussed old and new problems. Very tedious and long-winded.'

At 0900/5 August they left with *Intrepid, Inglefield, Ilex, Echo, Tyrian, Raider* and *Offa* to conduct exercises with *Nelson, Rodney* and *Formidable,* returning to Sliema the following day when news of the fall of Catania and Palermo was received.

Faulknor then went to Sliema creek before undertaking a boiler clean at Boat Hanger Wharf until 15 August. Captain Scott-Moncrieff was occupied with the finalising of an intricate new destroyer screen with the C-in-C, to be adopted for future operations. On 16 August *Faulknor* sailed to Augusta with *Intrepid* and *Piorun* and from there swept towards Cape Murro di Porco in the Messina Straits where an MTB force was operating. At 2200, they sailed again with *Quilliam, Queenborough, Quail, Ledbury, Wheatland* and *Brocklesby,* to patrol off the Straits of Messina and then escorted monitor *Roberts* and Dutch Gunboat *Flores,* plus a flotilla of MGBs, to cover the landing of 40 Royal Marine Commando fifteen miles north of Taormina. This force, embarked in two LSIs, *Prince Charles* and *Princess Beatrix*, and five LCTs, attempting to put out of action a German 9.7-inch gun battery and cut enemy communications ashore. At 2355, *Faulknor* engaged searchlights and a gun battery at Pallerto Point and at Reggio. Return fire caused some near misses, but both her targets were shut down.

Ted Newman recorded:

> It was a bright moonlit night and we went in so close inshore that I could have thrown a stone into Italy. Only one 9.7 opened up. It was very inaccurate and the monitor [*sic*] finished it off. Four landing craft were sighted; the MGBs attacked and scored one hit. We then went in and found that they were ours and had lost their way. We escorted them to their destination in case they were attacked again. At times we were so close in, you could have practically jumped ashore.

Raymond Johnson remembered:

> We covered the landings and carried a few of the commandos who had photographs all stuck together, which, when opened up, showed all the coast line, the same as you can buy nowadays at the seaside.

They saw MTBs engaging surface targets, which turned out to be four of our own landing craft which were miles out of position, so *Faulknor* herded them back to their correct landing place. 'There were no further excitements,' wrote Captain Scott-Moncrieff, 'and we all got home safely this Tuesday morning without mishap.'

They returned to Augusta, at 0700, leaving that night escorting Allied landing craft from Catania up to Messina, which proved to be a dreary job, plugging backwards and forwards all night. They anchored at Augusta at 0800, refuelled and then escorted light cruiser *Mauritius* to Malta, arriving noon on 19 August.

Next day *Faulknor* sailed for Algiers, with most of Admiral Sir Andrew Cunningham's staff and gear embarked. A conference with the Supreme Commander, General Eisenhower and the Service Chiefs, had set the date for the Salerno landings, Operation 'Avalanche', for 9 September and it had been decided that all the various staffs would concentrate their HQ in North Africa for this combined operation instead of being spread around the Mediterranean. Admiral Cunningham complained that communications at Bizerta were quite inadequate to deal with the vast amount of signal traffic and the telephone system was likewise insufficient. The solution was to have an HQ ship at Bizerta for the C-in-C and operations staff, while the routine staff work would be carried out at Algiers, hence *Faulknor's* mission.

Weighed down with brass (not for the first time, and certainly not for the last) *Faulknor* left Malta and arrived at Algiers at 1700/21st, where their guests were disembarked without mishap. They were then assigned the task of escorting a French ship along the coast to Tunis where they arrived next day. Brief shore leave was given while a party of soldiers were embarked and these were then ferried across to Syracuse between the 23rd and 25th. Once the troops had been off-loaded *Faulknor* returned to Malta once more, had one day inside the harbour and sailed again on the 27th. They met *Nelson* and *Rodney*, screening them during exercises all day and through the night, meeting carrier *Illustrious* next day and continuing the exercises. They finally returned to Malta on 30th.

On 1 September they sailed with *Fury*, *Inglefield*, *Intrepid*, *Eclipse* and *Raider* screening *Warspite* and *Valiant* and light cruisers *Mauritius* and *Orion,* for the bombardment of Reggio in support of 8th Army's crossing of the Messina Straits, Operation 'Baytown'. Bad weather cancelled a planned exercise on the way and the squadron arrived off their target area next day. The battleships commenced firing at 1000, the Italian gunners taking to their heels on the arrival of the first 15-inch salvoes! *Faulknor* and *Loyal* pushed right in to within a mile of the coast seeking targets and their 4.7s were soon hitting enemy positions at Cape Ali to good effect. After an hour, they pulled out and patrolled offshore all through the night covering the landings. When the Canadian troops went ashore at 0400 they met with no opposition; the operation became known as the 'Messina Regatta' thanks to the Royal Navy. *Faulknor* refuelled at Augusta, leaving for Malta at 1305 and immediately entering dock for urgent repairs, which took three days, from 4th to 7th.

The Salerno landings, Operation 'Avalanche', took place on 9 September 1943. Prior to that, however, the Italians threw in the towel. *Faulknor* was in the midst of all this action, having sailed with Force 'H' from Marsaxlokk, Malta, at 1715 Tuesday 7 September with battleships *Warspite* and *Valiant*, leading *Fury*, *Inglefield*, *Intrepid* and *Raider*. They were joined in the Swept Channel at 1820 by carrier *Formidable* and destroyers *Echo*, *Ilex* and *Queen Olga*. These formed the 2nd Division under Rear-Admiral A. W. La T. Bissett. Ten miles ahead were the 1st Division, under Rear-Admiral J. W. Rivett-Carnac, with battleships *Nelson* and *Rodney* and carrier *Illustrious* escorted by destroyers from the 4th and 24th flotillas, later joined by the French Destroyers *Le Fantasque* and *Le Terrible* who had changed sides from the Vichy to join Force 'H', under the overall command of Vice-Admiral Sir Algernon Willis. Again opinion was that, if the Italian battle fleet was *ever* going to fight, this was the last opportunity, but it was not to be, they chose surrender instead. The British fleet kept south of Malta to divert the Germans, and then steered west of Sicily, passing north of the island of Pantellaria, the Second Division being stationed approximately ten miles astern of the First.

Jack Barrett wrote:

> All forces are proceeding westward until midnight then we turn to the north and steam towards Naples where the Anglo-US troops are going to make landings at 0300 on Thursday morning, 2100. Joined forces with First Division.
>
> We got lost during the night owing to the sparker missing a signal but we have joined up again and are off Palermo in Sicily. At 2200 tonight we shall be 150 miles to the west of Naples steaming towards it, we are hoping that the Italian Fleet will finally come out. Two of the invasion convoys have been spotted but not attacked yet.
>
> News came that the Italians had accepted the terms of the unconditional surrender but we are still carrying on with the landing but it doesn't look as if we shall have opposition now.

So the Battle Fleet cruised and waited for action. They got it, but from the Luftwaffe. At 0545 on Wednesday, 8 September, low-flying aircraft, obviously torpedo -bombers, were detected some eight miles from the fleet. These were tracked to within four miles of the fleet and were met by a blind barrage, which they would not face, and they made off astern.

At 0730 the Second Division closed up the gap with the First and the whole fleet stayed concentrated ready for battle. By 1000 they had Maratimo Island in sight off which they cruised until 1730, when *Faulknor* and her companions were detached to operate independently in a position approximately fifteen miles, 330° from the First Division. As dusk closed, so did the enemy aircraft and, at 2100, they witnessed *Nelson* and *Rodney* over the horizon, opening up with Blind Barrage fire with all weapons, including 16-inch main batteries in a 'splash barrage'. Ten minutes later aircraft were located eleven miles out and gradually working their way round to 120° and closing to four miles, dropping clusters of red flares as sighting signals to their companions. At 2117 all the ships laid down a second blind barrage to deter these aircraft.

During the night of 8/9 September, about thirty German torpedo bombers repeatedly tried to get through to the invasion convoys but instead ran into the battlefleet and were defeated by enormous radar-controlled barrages, losing several aircraft. Off *Faulknor's* port quarter *Valiant* put up an impressive barrage from her multiple 4.5-inch gun batteries, deafening all aboard as they crashed out. *Faulknor* contributed a controlled barrage from her 4.7s, while her puny 3-inch 'Goose-gun' of course lacked any radar control, but it was comforting to hear the sustained roar from the big ships astern.

From 2120 until 0041 the Second Division was attacked at frequent intervals by enemy planes, which dropped both bombs and torpedoes. The sea was calm, there was no wind and a half moon gave good surface visibility. There was frequently more than one hostile aircraft on the radar screens fifteen miles from the Force, but all the attacks were conducted by individual aircraft. These individual attackers approached the fleet from the northward and retired in the same direction, while others hovered, awaiting their turn to approach.

One determined attack was made on *Warspite,* the aircraft pressing in to within 800 yards before dropping its torpedo. The drop was seen and the missile avoided by a turn to comb its track. The majority of these attacks were not pressed home and instead the enemy airmen seemed content to concentrate on the destroyers of the screen rather than try to penetrate through the barrage.

The nine destroyers were placed in a circular, all-round, screen. This, Rear-Admiral Bissett commented, '... was invaluable. On several occasions warning of attack was given by a destroyer opening fire, and as far as can be ascertained, few of the enemy aircraft were determined enough to pass over the screen, a number of them making their attacks on the destroyers. While this may be unpleasant for the destroyers, it achieves the object.'

At a Tactical Committee meeting held in the First Lord's War Room to analyse the operation later, he repeated:

> The disadvantages from the anti-submarine point of view of the circular screen are recognised. A screen for carriers has been designed giving destroyers equally placed at 2,000 yards from carrier. This is admittedly unpleasant for the destroyers during A.A. fire, especially barrages, but is flexible and is ideal for thwarting torpedo and dive-bombing attack.

It was certainly that. Several destroyers reported sighting torpedo tracks and *Ilex* reported being singled out for bombing attacks on two occasions. In return, at least one enemy aircraft was shot down by *Inglefield*, confirmed by the next on the screen, *Intrepid*. Several unexplained underwater explosions were felt in the big ships between 2130 and 2230, thought to be torpedoes exploding at the end of their runs.

The course adopted by the fleet during the night hours had as its aim, the object of keeping the ships as far as possible end-on to the moon to present the Axis airmen with as small a target as possible. Stationed ahead, *Faulknor* was not troubled by this but had to conform to the general movements of the squadron of course, and this sometimes placed her in a position were she was fully silhouetted and vulnerable. However, as Admiral Bissett later commented, '... from conversations with the Commanding Officers of the heavy ships and Captain (D) 8th Flotilla, the Second Division, as a result of this encounter with enemy aircraft at night, are full of confidence that their training has been on the right lines.'

At 0455 attacks resumed, and another blind barrage was fired at aircraft four miles distant, this proving to be the final enemy probe before dawn on the 9 September. At 0645, the Second Division once more concentrated with the First as a united fleet. At 1100 they made a depth-charge attack on a contact, and later *Raider* was detached to pick up a shot down enemy bomber crew sighted in a rubber boat off the fleet's port beam.

At 1330, *Warspite, Valiant, Faulknor, Fury, Intrepid, Echo, Raider, Queen Olga* and *Le Terrible* were detached for Operation 'Gibbon', the submission of the Italian Fleet.

Jack Barrett's diary recalls the momentous events of the invasion of Italy and of the surrender of the Italian battle-fleet to the Royal Navy thus:

> Thursday 9 September 1943: No opposition or not much. All night long we have been blazing away at German aircraft and as daylight comes, we are going to pick up the survivors of the six that were shot down. These worthies state that they did not know Italy had chucked it in, neither did they believe that we would be attacked during the daylight hours, so we may be able to sleep now!
>
> The landing went off successfully except that the airborne troops did not arrive – must have washed that part of the operation out. One man on destroyer *Offa* was killed by shrapnel from our own guns and three men were wounded on the destroyer *Raider* who has been detached to Palermo to land casualties.

Raider was detached at 1345 but later rejoined, while at 2130, the French *Le Terrible* was recalled to supplement the screen of Force 'H', parting company an hour later, and so she did not take part in the momentous events of the following day.[6]

The British squadron proceeded to rendezvous with the surrendering Italian ships in 360° Cape de Garde, 20 Miles, which was to take place at 0600/10th, in accordance with Admiral Andrew B. Cunningham's signals timed at 1029 and 1816 on 9th.

Jack Barrett wrote:

> We have just learned that we are being detached this afternoon to accept the surrender of three Italian battleships, six cruisers and eight destroyers who are coming down from Spezia. This will be a great occasion for us, never thought we should meet the Italian fleet this way, however it is much better this way.

Later. 'German aircraft are attacking the Italians and one battleship, *Roma* is burning but is still going strong. We expect to meet them about 0800 tomorrow.'

In fact, *Roma* was sunk in this attack by Dornier 217s armed with Glider Bombs. They mistook the German bombers for friendly escorts and took no avoiding action, nor did they open fire. Thus did the Axis allies part company!

Aboard *Faulknor* everybody had to be in rig of the day by 0700. Speed had been reduced to fifteen knots and, at 0802, *ML 443* came out with Captain Brownrigg and his staff as the official representatives of Admiral Cunningham, the little craft going alongside *Warspite* to transfer them.

At 0832/10 September, the rendezvous duly took place, and the men of *Faulknor* first sighted the Italian warships, looking clean and smart and obviously little affected by three years of war spent mainly in harbour. The British ships went to Action Stations at 0841 as the two fleets closed, reducing speed to 18 knots at 0903, to 15 knots 0909 and 12 knots at 0912. Three minutes later Captain T. M. Brownrigg, boarded the Italian Flagship, light cruiser *Eugenio di Savoia*, and, at 0916, the Italian fleet was ordered to 'Follow Astern', forming up behind the British squadron at 0930 and setting course for the Tunisian War Channel, the safe passage through the multitude of minefields that still lay athwart the central Mediterranean. The two British battleships, veterans of Calabria, Crete and Matapan, took the submission of their vanquished foes, while *Faulknor* and the *Fury,* victors of Spartivento and numerous convoy battles against the same opponents, steamed proudly ahead of the mixed force as it headed for Malta.

Jack Barrett again;

> Thursday 10 September 1943. 0600. We have arrived at the Rendezvous but cannot see anything in the dark, it is also raining. 0800. We sight the Italians and steam towards them at twenty knots, all our turrets are to remain fore-and-aft. They automatically form astern of the *Warspite* and *Valiant* and we advance at 15 knots towards Malta where we expect to arrive at 0900 tomorrow.

Thus did *Faulknor* take up her proud role as Leader of the Fleet and take the humiliated enemy in. At 1455 the following afternoon, off Malta, they were met by destroyer *Hambledon,* with the C-in-C, Admiral Andrew Cunningham, General Dwight D. Eisenhower and Commodore R. M. Dick, Chief of Staff, aboard. For 'Cuts' this must have been the proudest moment of his naval career, for all the brilliant actions he had waged against the superior numbers of the enemy during the grim days of 1940 to 1941 had laid the foundations for this triumph. The Italian squadron comprised battleships *Vittorio Veneto* and *Italia,* cruisers *Eugenio di Savoia, Duca D'Aosta, Montecuccoli, Duca degli Abruzzi, Garibaldi* and destroyers *Velite, Legionario, Oriani, Artigliere,* and *Grecale.* (See Diagram p. 191)

Captain Scott-Moncrieff duly received a signal from the C-in-C, Levant:

> I congratulate you and the six destroyers under your command on the excellent work done during an arduous week. Before you are called upon for further exploits I hope it may be possible for you to give shore leave at least once to each watch.

Signal flown by HMS Faulknor *at the surrender of the Italian Battle Fleet to the Royal Navy, 10 September 1943.* (K. Timson.)

Nothing else happened that day. 'The news bulletin on the BBC says fighter cover has been given to the ships but we have not seen anything of them (as usual!)'

Larry Chandler recalled:

> It was a lovely sight when we went out to meet the whole Italian Fleet and took their surrender. We escorted them to Malta to de-ammunition then took them to Alexandria for the remainder of the war.

At 1938 they left the War Channel, increasing speed to 15 knots once more. That evening Admiral Cunningham was able to signal that the Italian fleet had finally been laid, '… under the guns of the fortress of Malta'.

Ted Newman recorded:

> In spite of BBC reports to the contrary, there were very few people to greet us when we arrived. Signals were sent and cancelled immediately. One minute we were going out, the next we were staying in – nobody seems to know what's happening. Our Signals' Officer was sent to the Italian Flagship as Liaison Officer and it was quite a treat to see him taken around in an Italian motor boat.

The surrender of the Italian Battle Fleet, 10 September 1943. TOP PICTURE: HMS Faulknor *shown centre and closest to the camera, leading the Italian battleship and cruiser line on their way to Malta. PHOTOS 2–8. Various ships of the Italian fleet pass by. PHOTO 9 – The destroyer HMS* Hambledon, *with Admiral Sir Andrew Cunningham and General Dwight Eisenhower aboard, meets the surrendering Italian fleet.* (Imperial War Museum.)

As was recorded in the newsletter they sent to Stourbridge on 10 October, Captain Scott-Moncrieff had seen the surrender of the German High Seas Fleet at the end of the First World War and it was felt that it was something of a record to have seen two enemy fleets surrender in the course of one life time – '… and if he sees the Japanese Fleet surrender too, it will be an even better record!'

> We saw a lot of Malta and noted the immense bomb damage that the island has suffered. It was a great day for all the people who had been through that historic siege when they woke up to find the entire Italian Fleet in our hands …
>
> Captain Scott-Moncrieff later told how: – … the Italians were delighted to surrender. They told us it was the longest sea journey that they had ever undertaken, and seemed thrilled that their engines had stood the strain without breaking down!

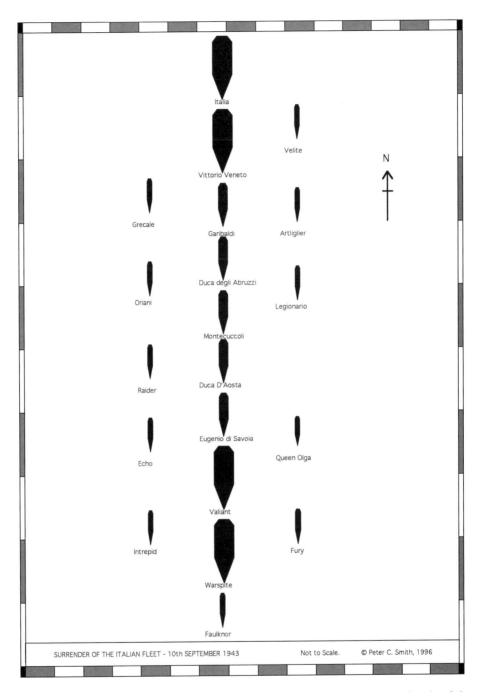

SURRENDER OF THE ITALIAN FLEET - 10th SEPTEMBER 1943   Not to Scale.   © Peter C. Smith, 1996

Our ship has now just completed 250,000 miles of steaming since the outbreak of the War. There are still two or three sailors in the ship's company who have been in the *Faulknor* all that time, and in the course of it they have been to a wide variety of places that range from the Western shores of Africa to Newfoundland, and from the Levantine Coast to the Northern Regions of Russia.

Captain Scott-Moncrieff added:

We all hope to come home one of these days, and in any case I am being relieved by Captain M. Somerset Thomas, DSO, Royal Navy, in the near future. I will come up to Stourbridge to thank your Committee personally for all they have done for us. I will bring photographs of the Ship for Brian Dangerfield of Brook Street, Stourbridge, and for Mrs Matthews of the Crispin Inn, and I should like to thank them personally for their kindness and help. My address at home is Black Fox Cottage, Prinsted, Emsworth, Hants, and I hope to be there by the beginning of next month.

He proved as good as his word.

On the 11th *Faulknor* and *Fury* left Malta for the Bay where the rest of the Italian fleet was gradually coming in from various ports.

Mr Barrett's diary continued:

> Sunday 12 September 1943: There are two more Italian battleships, (*Andrea Doria* and *Caio Duilio*), two cruisers (*Cadorna* and *Pompeo Magno*), and a destroyer (*Da Recco*) in the bay. These were brought in by *Howe* and *King George V*. Surrendered submarines are arriving very frequently. At Malta gave leave in the afternoon but had to recall libertymen as it was thought we were sailing with Italian fleet to Alexandria, then it was cancelled as another Italian battleship (*Giulio Cesare*) and two auxiliaries were coming in. Even then we gave leave but went out in the bay and went over to *Howe* at 2100 and back in morning by about 0600.

King George V and *Howe*, with *Faulknor, Fury, Echo, Eclipse, Intrepid* and *Queen Olga* (Greek), then escorted nine of the major units of the Italian fleet to Alexandria, arriving there at 0700/17th where they went alongside an oiler and gave overnight leave.

'Each destroyer has been detailed to take an Italian destroyer and anchor with the others outside the harbour itself,' Jack recorded. Next morning he rejoined *Faulknor* to find that, '… they had been waiting for us as we were going to sea with *Fury* and *Queen Olga*, proceeding to Haifa where we arrive tonight. (I wonder what we are going there for?)'

* * *

Jack was soon to find out, for this trip marked the beginning of the disastrous Aegean Campaign.[7] When Italy surrendered Churchill demanded that their main bases in the Aegean, Rhodes (now called Rodhos), Leros, Cos (now Kos) and Samos, could be quickly occupied by British forces and used as levers to get Turkey to join the war on the Allied side. Unfortunately, the Americans totally refused to release the necessary landing craft or long-range fighters, and were generally obstructive. Churchill, ignoring Norway, Greece or Malaya, tried to do it on the cheap. The Germans reacted quickly, seized Rhodes and flew in numerous bombers. The Premier ordered the local British commander to 'Improvise and Dare', so Cos, Leros and Samos were all hastily occupied. Their garrisons were then left to fend for themselves with support and supplies from the Royal Navy, and a token RAF contribution. It was the old, old story.

For *Faulknor,* at least*,* the campaign began with a victory. At 0800/17 September, they sailed with *Eclipse* and *Queen Olga* to carry out, Operation 'Rump', following C-in-C Levant orders of 2142/16th, to proceed through 035° 00′ N, 027° 54′ E and then through the Scarpento Strait (now Karpathos Strait) arriving at Position 'Q', 036° 17.5′ N, 2° 17′ E, at 2300/17th, thence conduct an anti-shipping sweep westward to intercept enemy shipping approaching Rhodes from Greece. The sweep was toward Stampalia island (now Astipalaia) unless updated reconnaissance indicated otherwise. Should they fail to sight the enemy they were to be clear of the area by dawn, returning to Haifa, Palestine. This was essential, for effective air cover was lacking, as so often before.

Captain Scott-Moncrieff was also informed that destroyers *Croome* and *Hurworth*, having supplied Leros, would be leaving that port at 2045 on the evening of the 17th for Alexandria and that any submarines encountered were not to be attacked as only Allied submarines were thought to be in the Aegean at this time. Both destroyer forces were told to keep at least ten miles clear of Cape Prasonisi, Rhodes.

The destroyers left Alexandria harbour and steamed north, but, at 1725 that evening, *Faulknor* sighted an enemy aircraft bearing 295°, twelve miles. Captain Scott-Moncrieff recorded he:

> … assumed that force had been sighted and would be reported, this was most unfortunate and I imagined the convoy would undoubtedly be turned back. In the event, apparently nothing was done and I assume the aircraft failed to sight us.

At 1850 the three ships increased speed to 28 knots to reach Position 'Q' as early as possible and, at 1930 they received a signal from one of the searching aircraft, timed 1600.

'Emergency: Position, course and speed 1 tanker 3,000 tons, 1 merchant vessel 1,000 tons, 1 E boat, 36° 45′ N, 25° 50′ E, 110° 6 (knots)'

On *Faulknor's* bridge calculations were made and this course and speed would place the enemy convoy between Stampalia and Kandeliusa between midnight and 0100, depending on their real speed. In order to avoid the Hunts course was altered to 310° at 2120 in order to pass ten miles northeast of Tria Nisia island (now Nisiros) and to 010° at 2245. This placed the flotilla athwart the expected line of advance of the convoy at 2305, when course would be altered to 295° and speed reduced to twenty knots.

At 2245 a Wellington bomber was sighted crossing *Faulknor's* bow and, at 2320 and at 0015, false radar reports raised their hopes of sighting the enemy. However, these both proved to be aircraft.

By 0015 the three destroyers were past the north point of Stampalia and Captain Scott-Moncrieff considered the enemy was west of him. He assumed the convoy had detoured to pass south of the island, so increased speed to 28 knots, steering 260° with the intention of circling Stampalia to approach the convoy from astern. However, at 0017, three ships were sighted on *Faulknor's* port bow at four miles range.

The enemy ships were shown by radar, bunched together and hugging Stampalia shoreline. *Faulknor* caught them shortly after dawn, with the advantages of surprise, speed and firepower.

By 0039 they were within 2,000 yards of the port wing ship of the German convoy undetected, making the final approach up-moon on the port quarter. The destroyers were in line ahead and reduced speed from 28 to 20 knots after gaining contact, in accordance with Clause 21 of the Fighting Instructions, to ensure maximum hitting time.

Faulknor and *Eclipse* opened fire on the port wing ship while *Queen Olga* engaged the starboard wing ship. Radar Range Control was used throughout the action by the two British ships, (except at the point-blank 'Fixed Sight Range' and below), the RTUs in the Type 285 office having been modified to give Range Transmissions down to 010 to permit this. Captain Scott-Moncrieff acknowledged:

> Type 285 Ranges were invaluable in giving immediate hitting results with the minimum of delay when shifting target. No difficulty was experienced in distinguishing the echo of the present target, and on only one occasion did the GCO have to pass an estimated range to enable the 285 operator to select the right echo.

Faulknor scored hits with her opening salvo. Her target was the *PLM.12,* also known as the *Paula,* but she was not a tanker, as reported throughout, but an ex-Vichy French freighter with machinery aft. After three salvoes into this ship, fire was shifted to the escort, *UJ 2104* (a converted whale-catcher, ex- *Darvik)* that was also hit with the first salvo. Meanwhile *Eclipse* continued hitting *Paula* consistently. All the destroyers used Direct Action fuzed HE shell, with a proportion of SAP (Semi-Armour Piercing) fitted with Night Tracer. In addition, fifty of the HE shell fired by *Faulknor* were also fitted with tracer. The tracers were most useful, both as an aid to spotting and in enabling individual ships to distinguish their own fall of shot. Flashless cordite was used for the forward guns, and again proved its efficiency in saving bridge personnel from blinding effect.

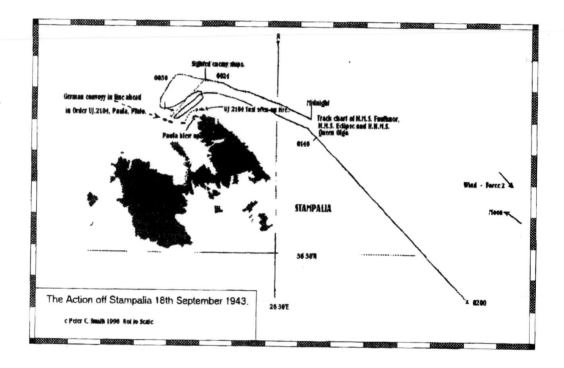

UJ 2104, having been hit severely by three salvoes from *Faulknor,* was soon heavily down by the stern, so *Faulknor* shifted her fire back into *Paula*. Meanwhile *Queen Olga* was enthusiastically pumping shells into the other merchant ship, the *Pluto* (ex-Italian *Trieste*).

The first run completed at 0050, course was altered in succession to starboard and fire was continued on both vessels. *Paula* was now stopped with two small fires forward and aft and her side was 'like a pepper pot', with a list to starboard. *Pluto* was heavily on fire. In total *Faulknor* fired 115 rounds of 4.7-inch H.E. fuzed No. 230 and 44 rounds of 4.7-inch SAP with Night Tracer.

At 0100 course was altered 180° in succession. As the torpedo officer was always complaining about the neglect of his cherished weapons ('a destroyer's main armament!'), the Captain gave him the job of finishing off the enemy. *Faulknor* made a perfect run up, parallel to the target; the sea was calm, everything seemed ideal. There was a hiss and a splash, and a 21-inch 'fish' sped swiftly towards its victim. There was a hush of expectancy while, in the distance, they could hear their companions finishing off the other vessel.

Hours seemed to pass, then there was a terrific explosion – *ashore*! Rock and debris erupted in a shower; they had missed the sitting duck and scored a direct hit on the island! Red-faced, they made a complete circle round the unhappy coaster, halving the distance between them as they did so; this time with a second launch there was no mistake, the second torpedo from *Faulknor* hitting the coaster amidships at 0115/18th. Five minutes later *Pluto* was seen astern to blow up 'satisfactorily.'

It took the torpedo-tube crew a long while to live this incident down, even if they did claim to be the only department aboard *Faulknor* to have recorded '50 Per Cent Hits for all firings!'

Course was then shaped for Scarpanto Strait and speed increased to 29 knots. However, at 0108 they received another aircraft sighting report from Wellington 'E' timed 2145:

> Position, course and speed 1 Merchant Vessel 2,000 tons, 1 Merchant Vessel 1,000 tons, 1 Merchant Vessel 500 tons, 1 Merchant Vessel of 300 tons.

Faulknor examined the east coast of Stampalia in case the two ships mentioned in the report had left Port Maltezana. They found only a small caique at 0215, which was ignored, and the flotilla cleared the danger area by dawn.

UJ 2104 was subsequently beached on Stampalia; her crew were made prisoner and shipped to Alexandria. Captain Thomas recalled:

> … we so badly damaged an enemy escort vessel that it went aground and the crew were made prisoner and it was *Faulknor* that had the pleasant job of taking them back into captivity. Under interrogation the prisoners revealed that among the personnel carried aboard was a German Naval Officer-in-Charge's party with specialist personnel embarked and stores for the German garrison at Rhodes, and that the ships were to have evacuated 6,000 Italian POWs on their return voyage.

Jack Barrett recorded:

> During the course of last evening we received orders to proceed up the Aegean Sea and annihilate a small German convoy of three merchant vessels and one escorting destroyer which were proceeding from Cos to Samos (*sic*) in the Dodecanese. Several times during the night we got surface radar echoes but they turned out to be 'ghosts'. An aircraft is supposed to be shadowing the enemy to home us on to them but the darn thing cannot find them!
>
> At 0200 we sighted the convoy along the path of the moon. We closed to about half a mile range and then we all opened fire, hitting with our first salvoes and taking the enemy by surprise. For about an hour we banged away at them and we saw boats pulling away from one of them. Fire was redirected at one of the others, our Oerlikon guns also opening up on them. The captain then decided to sink them with torpedoes, which in these ships is supposed to be our main armament, but we don't believe it. Anyway we had been gabbling on to the TGM all day that if we fired torpedoes they would miss. Anyway we fired one at about 500 yards range. We were only doing about seven knots and the merchant vessel target was stopped, so we thought that this couldn't miss, but then it was seen to pass just across the stern of the tanker. We all smiled to ourselves and wondered what the control officer was thinking about, to miss at that range. The *Queen Olga,* being Greek, was in her element, being in her own waters, and was letting them have it with all she had got, firing torpedoes which they know nothing about, and missing with the lot. Her captain well may be in for it when this is all over.
>
> We then steamed round still firing all the guns. All the enemy ships are now on fire but we are still enjoying shooting them up as they are full up with German troops. We fired another torpedo, this time it hit and it blew the ship sky high, debris falling all around us. This was practically the end, only one enemy ship had not yet sunk so we

turned away and as we rounded the island the last ship was seen to sink. Another good job done. We turn away at thirty knots and were now on our way back to Haifa, where we expected to arrive the next day.

Homeward bound through choppy waters, their torpedoes nearly found an unintentional target when a rating, reeling aft, lurched against the release lever which, combined with the ship's roll, caused one TNT-packed monster to slither smoothly from its mounting and, as the tubes were still trained outboard, slide over the ship's side. The guardrails were up and the torpedo's propellers fouled on them; the missile hung up, rolling sickeningly with the motion of the ship, threatening to detonate with every slap against her frail hull.

The swiftest movements ever witnessed aboard *Faulknor* followed, according to Stan Hollett. In record time a fire-axe was found, retaining wires hacked through and, with a final lurch, the offending torpedo plopped overboard as everyone hit the deck. Astern of them *Queen Olga* did a smart side-step at twenty-five knots and all awaited the bang, but, once again, nothing happened. The *Queen Olga's* crew were quite funny at *Faulknor's* expense during the return, all three arriving Haifa at 1945.

Alexandria was so distant from the theatre of operations that it became customary for the destroyers to lay up in Leros harbour by daylight under the protection *(sic)* of the Italian-manned anti-aircraft batteries. This policy soon led to disaster.

Between 20th and 23 September *Faulknor* ran troops and supplies from Haifa to Leros. At 2000/20th they embarked stores, Bofors guns and vehicles.

Mr Barrett's diary read:

HMS Faulknor *alongside the destroyer HMS* Fury *at Leros naval base, taking aboard evacuees, September 1943.* (Charlie Lee.)

Went ashore at Haifa. At 2000 arrived back on board to find that we have loaded up with vehicles, Bofors guns and jeeps, also 300 soldiers. *Fury* and *Queen Olga* also have the same. We sail at 0700.

The captain recorded:

> I understood that we were required to embark 20 tons of stores and 300 personnel per ship, but in the event the following amounts of stores were embarked – *Faulknor* 60 tons, *Eclipse* 52 tons, *Fury* 53 tons, *Queen Olga* 36 tons. *Intrepid* and *Echo* had proceeded 48 hours previously and I had heard that the Army would probably bring more gear than authorised and in consequence in *Faulknor* and *Queen Olga* two torpedoes previously expended were not replaced. Also the weather at this time of year allows a certain amount of latitude to be taken with top-weight, but we had embarked too much and the ships were, in consequence, very tender and unhandy.

At 0600/21st, a battalion of the Royal West Kent Regiment embarked, *Faulknor* taking 313 officers and men, *Eclipse* 305, *Fury* 340 and *Queen Olga* 300. These troops were accommodated aboard with great difficulty. There was barely enough space to move about *Faulknor's* decks during the day and at night the soldiers squeezed into her already over-crowded mess-decks. Destroyers were designed for speed and action, and were probably the least suitable type of warship to be utilised as troop-transports. However their most vital asset, high speed, made them the obvious choice, no other warship could get in and out of the Luftwaffe-dominated islands overnight.

They sailed at 0700, proceeding at 23 knots and they did not appear to have been sighted by the enemy. At 1830, *Faulknor* received a report from Wellington 'N' timed at 1352:

> IMMEDIATE. Position, course and speed 1 merchant vessel 2,500 tons 1 destroyer 2 planes 35° 33′ N, 25° 50′ E – 110 – 6

Captain Scott-Moncrieff plotted this and concluded that he could only intercept it if its true speed was between nine and ten knots. He considered increasing his own speed and arriving at the north end of the channel at 0200 and patrolling east and west until 0300, but, after consultation with Commodore P. Todd, CBE, DSO, RN, it was decided, in view of their primary object of getting the soldiers to Leros, and the unhandy state of the ships with so much deck cargo and troops aboard, that the flotilla should continue with its original mission and only engage the convoy if met.

They pressed on and dusk became night. Mr Barrett wrote:

> We are taking troops up to occupy the Italian-controlled island of Leros in the Dodecanese. We have to go past the German controlled islands during the dark hours and we are at Action Stations all night.

At 0227/22nd came another Wellington sighting:

> Position, course and speed 085° Promotion 24

The enemy ships had passed ahead of the flotilla being routed south of Rhodes. Any hope of interception had gone. There were no further reports or incidents and the destroyers arrived off Leros harbour boom at 0630, securing to buoys in the harbour three-quarters of an hour later.

Mr Barrett recorded:

> Arrived at Leros harbour entrance. We didn't know if there were any Germans left on the island and whether flying the Italian flag would enable us to pass the boom but we were soon relieved of our anxiety when an Italian motor-boat came out to meet us and lead us in. We then went to the buoys and disembarked the troops. Several air raid warnings but nothing actually happened. There is quite a good AA defence here (sic).

They made their recognition signals and the Shore Signal Station fired two white flares, indicating 'Boom open'. Once inside Commander R.A. Villiers, RN, came aboard *Faulknor*, small craft and barges were immediately sent out to all four destroyers and disembarkation of troops and stores commenced. By noon the Bofors guns remained to be hoisted out by Floating Crane. In addition a dumb-lighter collected a total of 265 tons of oil from all the ships and 27 tons of fresh water were left in the local water-boat, such was the state of the island's own supply. All was not finally completed until 1800, an anxious period for the ships to be exposed.

Faulknor kept her own radar watch throughout, using her Type 291 which was considered efficient, outside the land-echoes, from five to thirty miles, but Captain Scott-Moncrieff believed the local shore authorities had their own very comprehensive scheme of observation posts, which appeared efficient. On two occasions radar contacts caused the destroyers to go to Action Stations, but the aircraft turned out to be Spitfires from Cos Island who were not using their IFF (Identification, Friend or Foe) beacons. Captain Scott-Moncrieff therefore decided only to close up on receipt of shore authority's warnings, '..the harbour being apparently well protected by AA guns (sic)'

The destroyers next embarked 136 German prisoners from Stampalia, survivors from the convoy *Faulknor* had annihilated a few nights earlier. Captain Scott Moncrieff wrote:

> ... as accommodation was impossible in Leros we brought them to Alexandria in *Faulknor, Eclipse* and *Fury*. I thought it was safer not to give any to *Queen Olga* as they might not have survived the journey.

These POWs were put in the mess deck. Meanwhile C-in-C, Levant instructed the flotilla to make a diligent search on their return, for the two enemy convoys reported the previous night. Captain Scott Moncrieff considered that the Rhodes group would proceed south-about, but placed his ships to cover all eventualities. *Eclipse* patrolled the south end of Scarpanto Strait, the most obvious route, while *Fury* covered the north end. *Faulknor* and *Queen Olga* were available to reinforce either from 36° N, 26° E, should the eastern convoy be reported again. They were to proceed west of Stampalia departing via Kasos Strait. All four destroyers were to rendezvous, without fail, in 34° N, 28° 30 E at 0600/23rd.

At 2000, *Faulknor* and *Queen Olga* proceeded as planned, sighting nothing other than a white shore-light flashing 'SK' near Cape Sidheros, taken to be an aircraft beacon. Aircraft were reported in the vicinity several times but never approached the two ships.

Again Jack Barrett:

> We embarked a number of enemy prisoners, mainly Italians loyal to Mussolini. They had not seen butter for four years or meat for two. They seem glad now to be out of it, now they know some of the truth, but there is a Gestapo agent aboard here who is a perfect devil, he gave the Fascist salute when he arrived on board but that was soon knocked out of him. We are now proceeding back to Alexandria.

The four destroyers rendezvoused at 0600, *Faulknor* reaching Alexandria at 1415/23 September, securing alongside depot ship *Resource* for repairs.

They were still at Alexandria on 26 September, when *Intrepid* and *Queen Olga* sailed on another mission and put into Port Laki, Leros, at 0700. Barely two hours later Junkers Ju.88s attacked the harbour, sinking both the destroyers with heavy loss of life; an ominous lesson.

On 30th a German convoy was reported on the move in the islands, and, although repairs were far from complete, (portholes had not been repaired and the flooding continued), *Faulknor* and *Echo* were sailed to locate and destroy it. They left Alexandria at 0800/30 September, heading north, but, at 1430, the operation was cancelled. During their return they were signalled to carry out the mission again, but, on arrival at Alexandria, three 'Hunt' class destroyers were despatched instead. The reason for this was that battleships *King George V* and *Howe* were needed at home and required a destroyer escort to take them to Malta. The date of the battleships' sailing proved unfortunate, for *Faulknor* and her three companions were the only 'Fleets' at Alexandria with satisfactory endurance; the 'Hunts' had better HA armaments but shorter range.

Jack Barrett again:

> Thursday 1 October 1943: 0800. Got underway with *Howe, King George V, Fury, Echo* and *Eclipse* and proceeded to Malta where we arrived Sunday morning. The buzz is that we are going home, I wonder.

The *Faulknors* got their answer; the situation in the Aegean was going from bad to worse: with Cos fallen and Leros threatened the 8th flotilla was urgently needed to maintain nightly patrols. They left Malta 4 October, sailing east, not west. They obtained an Asdic contact and carried out a fruitless hunt which delayed them, finally securing at Alexandria at 2030 the following day. Jack recalled:

> In harbour all day, *Penelope, Aurora, Dido* and *Sirius* are expected in tonight. Only *Sirius* and *Penelope* managed it, the other two have collided with each other, not much damage from all the reports.

At 1130/6 October 1943, cruisers *Sirius* and *Penelope*, and destroyers *Faulknor, Fury* and *Eclipse* sailed from Alexandria for Scarpanto Strait at 26 knots, ready to act on any sighting reports. At 2245 the squadron ceased zigzagging and three destroyers were ordered by *Sirius* to change from their screening positions to prolong the line astern and, in complying, *Eclipse* reported her helm had jammed. She had to return to Alexandria on her own, steering by her main engines only.

As Jack recorded:

> Left harbour with *Eclipse, Fury, Penelope* and *Sirius* for the usual 'Club Run' up the Aegean, several enemy convoys are under weigh between the islands and an invasion of Leros or Samos is likely to come off. *Eclipse* turned back to pick up the crew of a Beaufighter that we had seen crash in the sea, so she won't catch up with us until tonight. For three hours we have been passing dead bodies, hundreds of them. We think they come from the convoy we sank a few days ago. *Eclipse* broke down at 2100 and had to steam back to Alexandria, she knows when she is well off!

The others pressed on, increasing speed to 28 knots at 2300. Reports of heavy concentrations of enemy shipping on the move in the Aegean had been coming in for some days now.

At 2300, in 'A' (35° 34′ N, 27° 40′ E), speed was increased to 28 knots until 0130, when they reached position 'B' (36° 30′ N, 26° 55′ E). If they received 'no worthwhile information' they were instructed to reverse course to position 'A'. They received no enemy sighting reports up to that time, and indeed *no* information regarding air reconnaissance arrangements was *ever* given by 201 Naval

Co-operation Group and they never knew if Wellington ASV aircraft were in the area. This explains a lot about why the Aegean Campaign ultimately ended the way it did!

At 0144, an 'Emergency' signal was received by *Sirius* but, because of an original ciphering error when it was sent, could not be read. A repetition was urgently requested, but not received until 0221. C-in-C, Levant instructed the squadron to proceed north again as the enemy invasion convoy was definitely in the area and thought ready for to assault. Position 'B' was reached for a second time at 0400. Course was adjusted west of Leros, closing the coast at first light. There was no evidence of any shipping or enemy military activity other than, at 0605, the sighting and illuminating by star-shell of two small craft, both of which were engaged when they did not answer the challenge. These were allowed to proceed as soon as they turned away, as they were assumed to be the British *Fairmile* and accompanying Italian MAS boat known to be at sea. No communication could be obtained with Leros via the W/T and this raised the spectre that the invasion might have already begun, or the enemy invasion fleet diverted to Samos.

Jack Barrett again:

> We passed Rhodes and Scarpanto at 30 knots as the moon was just coming up and we want to be well up the Dodecanese before midnight. The submarines kept reporting these convoys but they didn't seem to come out.
>
> Dawn, and still we had got nothing although now we were off Leros looking for invasion forces. A contact was picked up by *Sirius* who fired star-shell and opened up at the same time. It turned out to be one of our own patrol boats of which we knew nothing. However, they were quick in identifying themselves and luckily none of them were hit.

The squadron decided to make a circuit round to the eastern side of Leros at first light, to confirm the state of the garrison, and then move to Samos to check there also. The first part was done and all seemed quiet ashore. At 0645, when again steering away from the eastern Leros, *Penelope* received a sighting report on 4205 Kc/s, timed at 0415. No other ship in the squadron picked up this report but its result was electric. It was from the submarine *Unruly*, reporting seven tank-landing craft south of Amorgos Island at 0415, steering 060° at six knots.

Aboard *Sirius* the very courageous decision was taken to intercept, despite the danger of remaining deep in Luftwaffe-dominated waters at dawn. The squadron altered course to 245° at 25 knots at 0645. At 0715, off the north-east coast of Stampalia, two small ships were sighted bearing Green 45° and, simultaneously, another enemy ship was sighted five miles north-west of the landing-craft group.

Jack Barrett wrote:

> We then turned north toward Samos as daylight came, circling the island in case the invasion force had been diverted there, and, sure enough, when we get round to the west side of the island we saw a large convoy, a landing craft and small merchant vessels nearly inshore.

The British squadron came upon them south of Levita, like avenging angels out of the dawn horizon, and the action that followed was both brief and annihilating. While the two cruisers closed the convoy, *Faulknor* and *Fury* dealt with the merchant ship. As was recalled by Captain Thomas; 'The other ships of our force went for the barges and left the troopship to us.'

Their target was the freighter *Olympus* full of ammunition and, apparently, some two or three-hundred German soldiers. Both destroyers commenced firing at 0725. She was soon hit, quickly exploded and sank. Jack Barrett:

> We opened up on them at seven miles range, aircraft were attacking us but all their bombs missed. Our orders were 'Sink and destroy the enemy at all costs', and this is what we did. As we got within six miles of the enemy convoy another ship was seen on our starboard beam and *Faulknor* turned towards it. The blasted thing immediately hoisted the White Flag of surrender and fires distress rockets. We follow our orders and sink it anyway, the troops taking to the water but we stir them up a bit by going in amongst them zigzagging at thirty knots. Those that survived that churning up had five miles to swim.

The convoy consisted of one escort-vessel, *UJ 2111,* an armed trawler, mounting two 12-pounders; six large landing barges [*Siebel Ferries*] and a small motor launch. They were carrying a full of battalion of German troops and their battle equipment. These targets were engaged by *Sirius* and *Penelope* at ranges varying from 6,000 to 500 yards, and then later, *Faulknor* and the *Fury*, having disposed of their target, joined in the mêlée.

While the action was in progress sporadic attacks were made on the cruisers by Junkers Ju.88 bombers. Although not on a serious scale, they proved irritating for *Sirius* with her 5.25-inch main armament, to have to frequently shift one group onto HA targets. An enemy gun battery from a hill on Stampalia also fired on the British ships, without effect.

Fire also came from one of the barges, possibly from an embarked tank, but the British ships suffered neither damage nor casualties. Every single German ship was sunk save for one of the barges, over 400 Germans were drowned, 1,027 more were later rescued but without their equipment. It was a vicious scrap and the sea was littered with masses of shouting, struggling German soldiers. By 0810 all enemy craft were judged either sunk or sinking, so course was shaped southward at 24 knots.

Jack Barrett:

> In the meantime *Penelope* and *Sirius,* with *Fury,* are playing havoc with the others, most of them have been sunk or are burning badly. We got there in time to sink two more of them, then we all went in among them. Not many survived that, especially as German aircraft are dropping bombs on them, evidently meant for us! We then withdrew at 31 knots, we expect to get bombed for the next few hours.

They were!

Meanwhile it was known that two Hunt class destroyers, *Rockwood* and the Greek *Miaoulis*, on the way to Leros from north of Rhodes, must be close by and they were instructed to steer for Scarpanto Strait at best speed, reporting their position. They were later found to be fifteen miles astern of the squadron which, at 1000, turned back to provide mutual support. The addition of the two Hunts unfortunately reduced the squadron speed to 22 knots, but they could not have been left to face the wrath of the Luftwaffe alone.

While still deep in the Strait, the expected blips of a big bomber formation were picked up on the air-warning radar screens. Guns, which had recently blasted the enemy convoy to shreds, now swiftly elevated, high-angle ammunition was stacked as the low-angle shells were cleared away, tin hats adjusted by cursing sailors, as over the horizon rose the first of many swarms of Ju.87s and Ju.88s. As another of *Faulknor's* crew remembered – '… it was an extremely nerve-wracking morning'. With the sky never clear for long, wave upon wave of black-crossed dive-bombers screamed down on the twisting ships.

Sirius reported: 'The most dangerous was the attack by twelve Stukas (Ju.87s) at 1215. This was carried out in a very determined manner and resulted in *Penelope* being hit and near-missed and *Sirius* and *Rockwood* being near-missed.'

'We literally screamed for air support on the W/T', wrote Stan Hollett, 'and eventually our pleas were answered by American Lightnings who swept the enemy from the sky in a glorious few minutes,

Action in the Aegean. Series of photographs taken from on board HMS Faulknor, *showing the heavy air attacks made on the British naval squadron as it left the Aegean after wiping out a German troop convoy, 8 October 1943. A stick of bombs explodes close astern of HMS* Faulknor. (Jack Banner)

The 'Hunt' class destroyer HMS Rockwood *is seen close astern of HMS* Faulknor *at high speed laying a smoke-screen to sheild the squadron.* (Jack Banner.)

wheeled away with apologies for their short stay and disappeared southwards. They had flown all the way from Bizerta to render their invaluable aid at the extreme length of their operational range.'

Jack Barrett:

> 0900. Six Junkers Ju.88s are sighted but they scram when they are opened fire on. An air escort of eight USAAF Lightnings then arrived on the scene, a funny sight, never known us to get air cover before when we shout for it, anyway they send one Ju.88 down into the sea and probably destroyed another. They cannot catch up with the Me. 109s though, and cannot stay with us more than an hour owing to fuel, their reliefs didn't arrive so off they went, and the Jerries came over in force, ten Ju.87 Stukas, fourteen Ju. 88s and six Me.109s then attacked us. No hits in the first wave, but they certainly had some near misses on us. The second wave, which was the Ju.87 Stukas, as usual, did better; gunfire is not much use against them. They hit *Penelope* aft and had a near-miss on *Rockwood*.

Aboard *Faulknor* they had thought the *Penelope* 'was a goner', but it looked worse than it was as one of the cruisers smoke-floats had ignited producing a dense pall of smoke.

> The Ju.88s came over three more times before we got out of range but only succeeded in swamping us with water. None of our fighter protection arrived on the scene until it was all over, then only two Beaufighters came and they got shot down; we had to go back and pick up the crews. We are now making our way back to Alexandria, *Rockwood* and *Miaoulis* have been detached to Cyprus.

The squadron remained united until clear of the Rhodes-Crete area and not until 1700, when in position 'Z' (34° 05′ N, 28° 16′ E) were the Hunts detached to Limassol. The rest of the battered squadron steamed thankfully into Alexandria with blistered gun barrels and exhausted crews at 0130/8 October.

Faulknor and her companions certainly staved off the invasion of Leros for a time, but such sporadic successes could not keep the determined enemy at bay forever, and two days later another British squadron underwent a similar ordeal.

Again Jack Barrett:

> Arrived at Alexandria where we get the usual signal, 'Good work by all; you will be required again at 0630 tomorrow.

Jack Barrett recorded:

> Saturday 9 October 1943: Our sailing is cancelled as there is no one left but us to go out. Early this morning the Huns found *Carlisle* and company and bombed them to hell, *Panther* was sunk, 90 % of her crew were saved by *Petard*. *Carlisle* was badly damaged aft, two turrets out of action and her engines damaged so she couldn't steer. *Phoebe* arrived in Alexandria in the morning as reinforcement, as there is only the *Sirius*, *Fury* and us left operational. *Penelope*, *Aurora*, *Dido* and *Carlisle* are in dock, *Echo* and *Eclipse* have got condenseritis.

Faulknor had the luxury of a short period 'off duty'. This was needed for her crew were exhausted. They had some compensation in the shapely forms of a detachment of WRNS from the Alexandria Naval Base, invited aboard one sunny afternoon for 'a trip round the harbour'. They were a very welcome sight. 'Imagine', writes Stan Hollett, 'this bevy of beauties in light white uniforms standing on the ship's deck as she manoeuvred at speed – a delightful spectacle to a hundred or more deprived matelots!' Such thoughts in today's Politically-Correct, enforced mixed-crewed warships, would now

Leaving Alexandria harbour after her refit, with a party of WRENS on the quarterdeck, October 1943. This gives a good view of the HF/DF arrangement and the resited 3-inch H gun in 'X' position. The rear of the destroyer HMS Eclipse, *(H08) can be seen to the right.* (Imperial War Museum.)

Leaving Alexandria harbour after her refit, with a party of WRENS on the quarterdeck, October 1943. Another good close-up view of the gun pit around 'X' gun is to be had from this photograph. (Imperial War Museum.)

be considered 'offensive' but in those far-off days when men and women were considered different from each other, they were normal and without harm.

They were soon back among the islands and bombs again. Two days later they said farewell to their much-respected Commanding Officer as Captain Scott-Moncrieff left the ship. Before he went he addressed the ships company after church parade. He told them that, on completion of the present operation, which he estimated would be about another month, *Faulknor* would probably be going home.

Captain Scott-Moncrieff was highly respected. Eric Prigmore's view is typical:

> Our best captain, in my eyes anyway. I'm sure he saved the ship during the PQ.18 battle. He seemed aloof, yet fair. I always remember when we sank *U-88*. After the pattern of depth-charges went off and we went back over the spot to double-check. I was on the fo'c'sle at Action Stations on 'A' gun, and nosing over the guardrail. We all gave a great cheer when we saw the huge patch of oil bubbling up. Immediately we got an icy blasting from the bridge to 'be quiet', making us realise that men were dying very horribly down there.
>
> I also remember him the time we went to pick up the pilot from *Avenger* who was spotted floating down by parachute. We managed to get him inboard when a Junkers Ju.88 dived out of the clouds at us. All we could do, was to sit in the gun well and watch the plane drop his 500-lb bomb and observe it coming down. The Skipper, cool as anything, turned the ship's bows to meet the attack and the bomb missed us but the men at the amidships gun got a good soaking!

That evening Captain Scott-Moncrieff disembarked. His further service was distinguished and he retired in 1958 as Admiral Sir Alan Scott-Moncreiff, KCB, CBE, DSO, finally passing away on 25 November 1980. He always retained his affection for *Faulknor;* in December 1945, he wrote:

> She was a happy ship. I steamed over 100,000 miles in her during my period of command.

Their new CO, Captain Mervyn S. Thomas, DSO, RN, came to them with a fine reputation as a destroyer skipper. Captain Thomas wrote, on 17 December:

> You may wish to know how I felt when I was told by the Admiralty that I was to leave the Naval Air Station I commanded at Yeovilton, Somerset, for HMS *Faulknor*. Naturally I felt very proud at being given command of a ship with such a fine war record.

Despite the brave language, it was an awkward time to take command, in the middle of a desperate situation, with morale low at the heavy (and to most, pointless) losses being taken. Nor was there any time to settle down for next day, 12 October, they were on their way into the Aegean death-trap again.

The sea was quite rough and some of the new members of Captain Thomas's staff were sick. The weather eased as the night wore on and there was bright moonlight by 2200 when they went to Action Stations. In the end the 'suicide run' proved an anti-climax for nothing was seen but our own patrolling MTBs. They returned to Alexandria on 13th, refuelled and hastily sailed next day as Jack Barrett noted:

Captain M.S. Thomas, DSO, DSC, RN. He had a great record as a fighting destroyer skipper when he took over command of the Faulknor *during the difficult days of the disastrous Aegean Campaign in the autumn of 1943. Ill health forced him to relinquish command after only a short period.* (Imperial War Museum.)

> Thursday 14 October 1943: 0800. Left harbour with *Fury* and *Phoebe*, we rendezvoused with *Rockwood* and *Miaoulis* at 1600, then go through the narrows at 2100. The Hunts were detached to attack shipping in the harbour at Rhodes, they get away OK, otherwise nothing happened.
>
> Friday 15 October 1943. We are making our way along the Turkish coast towards Casteloriso, where we are going to stop until 1700 and oil off *Phoebe*. Later. It turned out a very difficult problem though as we could find nowhere to anchor, so we had to go alongside *Phoebe* while under weigh.
>
> 1730 Left Casteloriso and passed through the narrows at 2100. At 2200 we sighted two unknown vessels and challenged them. No reply so we opened fire on them. After a couple of minutes they managed to identify themselves and turned out to be two of our MTBs who had been damaged by bombing. One of them was in a bad way as a result of this and our gunfire and had to be sunk.

The squadron returned to harbour unscathed and *Faulknor* remained alongside 16th/19th undergoing urgent repairs. As Jack Barrett recorded, their numbers continued to dwindle.

> Sunday 18 October 1943. In harbour. *Sirius* got caught last night, a large bomb through her stern, fourteen killed, thirty wounded. She will be in dock for a while to come. That only leaves *Phoebe* in running order.

Despite their best efforts and occasional victories, the enemy continued to build up his strength; the islands and channels were many, the British warships available to scour them few – they simply could not plug every bolthole. The Levant destroyers were also employed in carrying reinforcements to our own garrison on Leros by night. The routine was that the ships refuelled and stored at Alexandria or

Haifa, loaded cargo or soldiers, and sailed during the morning to reach the island at dusk. Usually a cruiser, while they lasted, was stationed to the south to give support. Once amongst the islands the destroyers either landed their cargoes or patrolled overnight to prevent the Germans doing likewise, returning to base next day. Invariably they were sighted about mid-afternoon by the vigilant Luftwaffe, and continually bombed until blessed darkness hid them. These 'tramline excursions', as they became known, were far from popular, for the enemy always seemed well prepared.

This routine was eventually found uneconomic in both time and fuel and changed, the destroyers retreating into Turkish territorial waters during daylight. This produced feverish activity from local Turkish officials who boarded whenever *Faulknor* anchored, to ensure their neutrality was not being too blatantly infringed and to placate the Germans, of whom they were in dread. An enormous problem was that the Italian charts, which purported to show the positions of minefields laid by them earlier in the war, were extremely inaccurate. It was very unpleasant operating in waters in which mines were thickly strewed in indeterminate positions. This is how destroyers *Eclipse, Hurworth* and Greek *Adrias,* were all lost or damaged.

These patrols, always full of danger from mines below and bombers above, were never dull affairs and often quite bizarre. Once *Faulknor* picked up a lone operator from the Long Range Desert Group who was actually swimming from island to island after completing a sabotage mission on the Greek mainland, on his way back to his base somewhere in North Africa – he was very pleased to get a lift!

At 0530/20 October, *Faulknor*, *Petard*, *Dulverton* and *Miaoulis* sailed from Alexandria with cruiser *Aurora*. They proceeded through 310° to 35° 18′ N, 28° 48′ E at 20 knots, the force being code-named 'Nettle'. They were sighted by enemy aircraft three times between 1700 and 1830 so the enemy had them firmly plotted. At 1900, the force altered course for Scarpanto Strait, but, at 1930, *Aurora* and *Miaoulis* parted company to carry out a diversionary bombardment of Rhodes harbour.

Routine harbour duties, a sentry alongside HMS Faulknor *at Alexandria, autumn 1943. (Author's collection.)*

Meanwhile *Faulknor* and *Petard*, code-named 'Naval', proceeded at 27 knots to Leros disembarking stores, and *Dulverton,* code-named 'Nursemaid,' joined them in Turkish waters later.

Faulknor and *Petard* passed through the strait at 2200 at 29 knots, ready to unload at Parthani Bay, Leros. Near Levitha Island, shortly after midnight, aircraft were detected and, after course was altered toward Leros, flares were dropped to westward, whereupon the ships turned to starboard. They observed groups of flares being dropped ten miles astern of them. Unfortunately the enemy was *not* deceived, and, on entering Pharios Channel at 0135/21st, '… a string of brilliant flares were laid across the entrance, which lit up the harbour like daylight.' Both destroyers passed the boom into Parthani Bay at 0142. More flares were dropped closer astern of them; things were looking bad and worse was to come. Aircraft were heard approaching from astern and blind fire was opened. Three minutes later *Faulknor* embarked STO from her Motorboat and ordered *Petard* 'Follow me'.

Captain Thomas described these attacks:

> *Faulknor*, with *Petard* in company astern, arrived Partheni Bay, Leros, from the west at 0145 on 21st. Almost at once aircraft flares were dropped overhead, and the first attack was made from astern, while both ships were still in the bay and brilliantly illuminated; one bomb, (about 250 Kg) falling on *Petard's* port side. *Petard* engaged and *Faulknor* fired two rounds of 3-inch.
>
> *Faulknor* then turned 180° and led out of the bay, On arrival outside, course was set for the general direction of Turkish territorial waters, passing north and east of Leros. Almost at once further flares were dropped overhead and attacks made from astern, down moon. These attacks were countered by blind 3-inch fire on Type 291 bearing; or else ahead of the sound of the attacking aircraft. Violent evasive action was also taken.
>
> On arriving north-east of Leros, blind 4.7-inch barrages at maximum elevation (40°) were fired in addition to the 3-inch whenever the director could bear. The MLA (Mean Line of Advance) was then altered to the southward and attacks appeared to come from the starboard quarter (i.e. down moon).
>
> The aircraft were twice sighted during these later attacks. They appeared to be Ju.88s flying between 2–3,000 ft. When sighted they were also engaged by Oerlikon fire. A feature of these attacks was the skilful and accurate flare-dropping employed by the enemy; which gave him the advantage of visual attack over blind defence. (See Diagram)

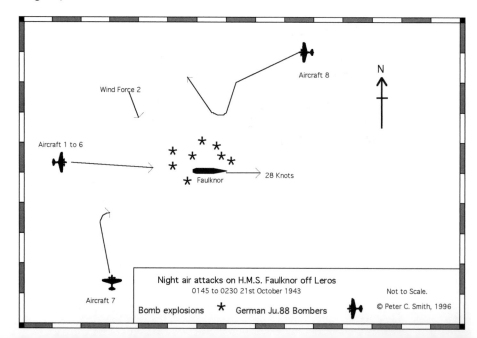

Night air attacks on H.M.S. Faulknor off Leros
0145 to 0230 21st October 1943
Not to Scale.

Wind Force 2
Aircraft 8
N
Aircraft 1 to 6
Faulknor
28 Knots
Aircraft 7
Bomb explosions ✶ German Ju.88 Bombers
© Peter C. Smith, 1996

Lieutenant Commander Rupert Eagen of *Petard,* reported: -

> Meanwhile both ships entered Parthani Bay and I saw that *Faulknor* was turning round. Captain D 8 then signalled me to go out again ahead of him, but as it was too narrow, I proceeded past *Faulknor* to turn and then follow her out. As I was groping for the gate, a brilliant string of flares were laid across the entrance, which helped enormously although the aircraft could be heard coming in. A good barrage was put up by the forward guns and the Oerlikons on the Flag deck; a good many bombs fell ahead of the ship and to the northward of Pharios Island, which I realised later were probably meant for *Faulknor.*

More flares were dropped at 0149, which lit the ship up clear as day, but, at 27 knots, *Faulknor* passed back through the boom and headed for Turkish Territorial waters via the Lipso channel. Captain Thomas wrote:

> From 0150 to 0240 I was illuminated by aircraft dropping groups of up to 8 flares at a time. The flares were followed by a low-level attack by one aircraft at a time. Bombs were observed to drop on 9 occasions. Two smoke floats were dropped about 0230.

Jack Barrett recounted:

> Just as we are passing the second boom into Leros harbour and after the pilot had got aboard we were lit up by about two dozen flares from aircraft, so we shot back out of harbour at 25 knots, flares following us all the time. *Petard* had gone off to starboard to try and dodge the bombs while we were weaving about like a trapped rat but each time we managed to dodge them. We even got 36 knots out of the old lady. The bombing went on for an hour, several near misses, two chaps hurt by shrapnel. Everybody was practically crazy, even the Skipper was getting fed up with it, we didn't care then if we got wiped out or not. In the end we found refuge in Turkish territorial waters and told the *Petard* to join us if she could find the way. A Turkish diplomat came aboard and wanted to know what we were doing there. Our excuse was that bombs damaged our steam joints. He told us we should have to move away from the town in case there was any more firing to be done.

Ted Newman recorded:

> Just as we crossed the boom (at Leros) Jerry came over and lit the place with flares. Five minutes later and we would have been caught tied up and certainly sunk. Great praise is due to our Skipper, who immediately turned round and got out of the harbour, giving us room to manoeuvre. For over an hour we were bombed and many were too near for comfort, people on deck getting soaked by the splashes. Our guns, being old-fashioned, could not be trained high enough once the aircraft got in close.

Captain Thomas had ordered *Petard* to keep her original rendezvous at Turk Berku in the Mandalya Korfegi. Because of the close attention of the enemy bombers he considered it inadvisable to lie up in the Gulf of Cos as ordered by the C-in-C. At 0310 *Petard* was ordered not to enter harbour but to join *Faulknor* and at 0346 *Faulknor* dropped anchor in Turk Berku, 37° 08′ N, 27° 25′ E.

At 0445, they were boarded by a Turkish official and told they must move by 1000 but might return later. At 0545 *Petard* arrived and at 0700, they were joined by *Dulverton*. Enemy aircraft watched the three destroyers at 0852 but nothing untoward happened. To pacify the Turks, *Faulknor's* flotilla weighed at 0935 and proceeded to Guvercinlik Bay remaining until 1910. *Faulknor's* force then proceeded at 22 knots, north of Pharmako and Arkoi Islands, then south to Levitha, leaving Patmos to starboard. Again the Luftwaffe was waiting for them; between 2250 and 2330 both destroyers were illuminated with flares and dummy attacks were made, despite more smoke-floats being dropped astern.

Ted Newman again:

> We managed to get to the sanctuary of a bay in Turkish waters, but were stopped and a Turkish official came aboard. Our Skipper spun him a yarn and brought out the whisky bottle. We were allowed to stay six hours. After the six hours were up, we went round the harbour a couple of times, and then anchored again. Having ascertained from the pilot that there was plenty of food on Leros, our Skipper decided not to risk the ship for the sake of a few jeeps and firewood (a plucky decision). When it was dark, we slipped and had to make our way back through the islands. *Dulverton*, having no stores, was detailed off to bombard. All went well until 2300, Jerry was there, as usual, and we had another couple of hours of bombing, but did not get hit.

Jack Barrett continues:

> Weighed and proceeded to Turk Birko which is still within territorial waters. 1915 Proceeded with *Petard* to Leros. But when we get there we are again attacked, although this time for not quite as long, but long enough to give us all the jitters.

Captain Thomas described:

> ...aircraft were detected by Type 291 approaching from ahead. Flares were dropped overhead; evasive action was taken and blind barrage fire was opened.
>
> The aircraft then circled and made several approaches as if to attack from ahead and either bow. Evasive action was taken and blind barrage fire was opened on each occasion, fire being continued until the range was reported as opening. After about ten minutes the aircraft worked down the side and made off astern. They were tracked by Type 291 waiting over the position where the smoke-floats had been dropped.

After passing through the Scarpanto Strait, they were joined by *Dulverton* at 0700/22nd and, at 0720, *Aurora* and *Miaoulis* arrived. At midday *Faulknor* and *Petard* were detached, returning ahead to Alexandria at 25 knots, arriving at 1730.

Jack Barrett again:

> Orders from C-in-C, Levant to detach *Petard* and *Faulknor* to Alexandria at best speed, so off we go at 32 knots – with long faces wondering what we are wanted for now.
>
> Arrived at Alexandria, *Faulknor* alongside to oil, *Petard* to jetty to discharge her jeeps and stores. *Petard* has orders to sail at 0100. *Faulknor* also, but as we had to fill two of our fuel tanks with water to balance the ship we can't go until they have been dried out, although we still have our cargo on board. This causes much anxiety and a gloom club has been formed in the mess.

Jack Barrett's diary entry read:

Sunday 25 October 1943: Left Alexandria at 0400 with *Beaufort* and *Belvoir* for Aegean. 0600 rendezvous with *Phoebe* proceeded at 26 knots.

1600. We were reported by German aircraft.

0830. Parted company with *Phoebe* and proceeded along Turkish coast at 15 knots.

Monday 26 October 1943: After seeing nothing all night except a few flares we proceeded up the Gulf of Cos to lay up until tonight, unless anything happens to bring us out.

Nothing did and they returned once more to Alexandria. *Faulknor* remained in harbour from 26 October until 2 November, having various defects made good.

Daily the BBC blared out how the Allies ruled the skies and the Luftwaffe was no longer a factor; daily and nightly the men of *Faulknor*, her companion ships and the soldiers on Leros were bombed, bombed and bombed and never saw an Allied aircraft. The deadly Stukas had been written off as 'failures' by the RAF during as the Battle of Britain, but three years later, the Allied airmen proved totally incapable of dealing with them.

Between 2nd and 6 November 1943, *Faulknor*, *Echo*, *Penn* and *Pathfinder* ran stores and troops to Leros by night. On 3 November troops of the King's Own embarked aboard *Faulknor*, *Echo*, *Penn* and *Pathfinder* who sailed just before midnight. The soldiers had only their light weapons, plus 80-tons of stores; all motor transport, anti-tank guns and carriers were left ashore.

Faulknor, *Penn* and *Pathfinder* embarked stores from 20 and 38 quays respectively, each taking about twenty tons of stores and 250 soldiers each. *Echo* received four tons of naval stores; the rest did not arrive alongside until about 2315. Captain Thomas recorded:

> Judging from the stores already loaded in *Faulknor*, *Penn* and *Pathfinder* it was thought these stores were in addition to those catered for. The delay for embarkation was not considered acceptable …

Larry Chandler remembered:

> We picked up soldiers from Alexandria and Palestine to help out the defence of Leros. They consisted of cooks, carpenters and other army tradesmen.

The four laden destroyers left Alexandria, meeting light cruiser *Phoebe* outside, the combined squadron proceeding at 2312 to Limassol, Cyprus, passing through position 309 at 2359 at 24 knots. On 3 November they met a surfaced submarine, which proved friendly, and also sighted a large number of waterspouts before running into an exceptionally heavy thunderstorm with large hailstones during the forenoon. On arrival at Limassol at 1115/3 November all destroyers fuelled from *Phoebe*, and the destroyers each took the opportunity to shift 6-tons of their deck cargo to *Echo*. All five ships slipped at 1445 and proceeded at 25 knots, passing twenty-five miles from Cape Khelidonia until 1745, when the destroyers were detached.

They steered north of Rhodes into the Gulf of Doris, laying up in Turkish waters during daylight on 4th. The original intention was to proceed to Arineh Bay but this was switched to Yedi Atala, anchoring in the western bay at 0620. An unidentified aircraft passed overhead at 0930 and two others were sighted at 1100 and 1715, so the Germans were fully aware of their presence. At 1930, they proceeded at 15 knots keeping close to the Turkish coast. The day passed quietly, at 2130 off Mordala Island, and again at 2140, they sighted caiques under sail, but as both vessels were in Territorial waters they could take no action. They passed south of Cape Krio and proceeded west, increasing speed at 2300 to twenty knots steering north of Piskopi and Kandeliusa and south of Nisiros. The sky remained overcast with low and heavy cloud.

At 0130, *Penn* and *Echo* were detached to Partheni Bay with orders to rejoin *Faulknor* at Guvercinlik at 0615. *Faulknor* and *Pathfinder* reached Leros without hindrance, passing the Porto Lago boom at 0155/5th. Lights had been placed on the mooring buoys but Captain Thomas wisely decided not to secure but to keep both ships moving. Caiques, motor launches and an 'F' lighter came alongside and the soldiers were slowly disembarked, along with the limited stores. This was completed by 0325.

Bill Silltow remembered how tense everyone was at Leros where any delay could prove fatal.

> We lay in the harbour for what seemed an age waiting for something to happen. In the end Captain Thomas decided enough was enough, he took the loud hailer and across the black and silent harbour his voice rang out, 'Where the hell is my Lighter?' We all felt much the same way.

Ted Newman:

> It took over an hour to disembark the troops and supplies, owing to bad organisation. Troops weren't ready and were chasing around looking for their packs, when they should have been off, while our lads had to do all the unloading. Fortunately, we hadn't been spotted. A boatload of civilians came alongside, trying to leave the island, but our Skipper had not time for them. We brought back four saboteurs, who had set fire to a petrol dump, destroying six months supply of petrol.

At 0327, the destroyers proceeded at twenty knots through Lipsoi Channel, north of Pharmako, thence to Guvercinlik Bay. *Echo* and *Penn* having discharged in turn, duly joined them off the channel between Tarandakia Island and Salih Adasi at 0550 and, ten minutes later, three boats of the 10th MTB flotilla joined from astern. The destroyers anchored in the bay with the MTBs secured alongside until 1800.

Faulknor and *Echo* then proceeded at 17 knots, passing north of Pharmako and Patmos and west of Amorgos, increasing to 25 knots at 2130 and 26 knots at 2359; searching among the islands for enemy convoys, without success. In the early hours of Saturday 6th they dropped delay-action smoke floats, snowflake and depth-charges off Port Vathi, Amorgos and Stampalia to cause a diversion, before heading south and were met in position 495 by *Phoebe* at 0605/6 November, reaching Alexandria at 1600.

They sailed again at 1530/8 November with 'Hunt' class destroyers *Beaufort* and *Pindos* (Greek), each with fifty soldiers embarked. On arrival at Limassol next day they fuelled from oiler *Cherryleaf* then anchored. C-in-C's signal, timed 0939, ordered:

> Proceed at 1130 ninth through 474 479 and 482 speed of advance 20 knots. Orders follow.

At 1130, the three destroyers sailed and half an hour later were joined by *Penelope*, but were recalled again by a signal timed 1314:

> Return to Limassol and complete with fuel.

At 1350 they entered Episkopi Bay and, while one destroyer maintained an anti-submarine patrol, each ship replenished. At 1925, further detailed instructions were received.

> *Faulknor, Beaufort, Pindos* proceed 474 479 482 to 035° 30′ N, 030° 35′ E (Rpt) at 1730/10th code word Naval priority high. 2. Then proceed close to Casteloriso and

Turkish coast, south of Symi to Cape Krio about 0200/11th speed of advance 22 knots.
3. Lie up in Gulf Cos. You may be required to bombard Cos harbour as you pass.

Yet further instructions were received in a signal timed 0914.

> Be prepared to bombard Cos harbour and roadstead tonight where it is expected there
> will be a concentration of landing craft. Suggest Hunts should close in and deal with
> anything in the roadstead while *Faulknor* plasters the inner harbour and surroundings.
> Further signal will be made.

The enemy force had reached Port Kalimnos and Cos, and was expected to make the final part of its
journey after refuelling. The fate of Leros was now finely balanced and the night of 10th/11
November saw the Royal Navy making a last-ditch attempt to intercept the German invasion fleet.

Two destroyer striking forces were despatched. The first, *Petard*, *Rockwood* and the Polish
Krakowiak, had fuel remaining for one night's operations. The second, *Faulknor*, *Beaufort* and the
Greek *Pindos*, entered the Aegean during the night of the 10th/11th, bombarding Port Kalimnos and
Cos harbour and roadstead respectively. *Petard's* force was ordered to withdraw from the Aegean on
completion, and *Faulknor's* force to lie up in Mandalya Gulf.

At 1100/10 November, they joined *Penelope* until she turned back. Further instructions from C-in-
C arrived in a signal timed 1324.

> Comply with my 0914. On completion withdraw into Gulf of Cos for a time, and then
> proceed to Guvercinlik Bay. Chart 1546 to lie up keeping close to Turkish mainland
> repeat mainland after passing close Cos Channel. Orders for disembarkation of troops
> follow.

At 2330, they passed a small sailing vessel thirteen miles east of Cape Marmarice, and, at 0500 on
the morning of Thursday 11th, in 36° 57′ N, 27° 28′ E, while approaching Cos from the north-west
to carry out their bombardment, three or four bombs were dropped on the force by aircraft who did
not use flares. Undeterred, the destroyers duly conducted a bombardment of Cos.

Captain Thomas decided to retain the two Hunts astern of *Faulknor*, and not detach them as C-in-
C Levant's suggestion, '.. in order to maintain cohesion and prevent the possibility of their fouling
Faulknor's range while operating close inshore.' The ships formed into line-ahead at 22 knots three
cables apart at 1930. He selected a bombarding course that gave a mean range to the inner harbour
of 060°, this range being selected as giving the best compromise between close action and allowing
sufficient angle of descent to allow *Faulknor's* salvoes to fall in the inner harbour while firing over
the castle on the east flank of the harbour. The squadron passed south of Symi to position A, two miles
from Mordala Island by 0240, then through position B, C and D, respectively bearings and distances
from Kum Point light, 080° 10.4 miles, 055° 6 miles and 055°, 3 miles.

The destroyers reached position Baker at 0258, but before they reached position Charlie, an enemy
aircraft made an undetected approach from astern and carried out an attack on the rear ship. A stick
of bombs exploded wide of the *Beaufort's* port quarter, the assailant escaping without a shot being
fired. The British ships were in Turkish territorial waters at the time and soon intercepted an enemy
R/T report of 'Three units in sight'. Captain Thomas turned his squadron to the west in order to
remain in territorial waters a little longer.

At 0342, they assumed bombarding profile and reduced speed to 15 knots on course 150. Targets
were assigned; *Faulknor* the inner harbour, *Pindos* and *Beaufort* any craft anchored in the Roads.
Beaufort was to be responsible for any counter-battery fire, while the two 'Hunts' were to join in
Faulknor's target if no shipping was found in the Roads.

In her prime! A splendid view of HMS Faulknor *at speed in the Mediterranean in 1943. Her second bank of torpedo tubes has been re-shipped to increase her offensive power once more, while the 3-inch HA gun has been repositioned on 'X' gun's location to give a high field of fire astern, covering the favourite attack line of the Junkers Ju.87 Stuka dive-bombers. Single 20 mm Oerlikons are mounted abreast the bridge and at the forward end of the after superstructure. Dark hull and light upperworks of the Mediterranean Fleet are again carried.*
(author's collection, Crown Copyright.)

Captain Thomas recorded:

> The castle itself, the right-hand edge of which had been chosen as *Faulknor's* aiming mark, was clearly visible in the moonlight, and a good Type 285 echo was obtained from it. The 3-inch gun opened fire with starshell at 0345 and 4.7-inch fire, (range 063°) was opened. Fifteen seconds later, in order to coincide the first star shell burst with the first splash, 4.7-inch was opened with an 'up-ladder'; A and B were observed to fall short in the water, two bursts from C were observed in the town behind the castle. 'No correction Zigzag' was therefore ordered, while the enemy very promptly started to lay a smoke screen over the harbour.
>
> The Zigzag group appeared to fall mostly in the town; a down correction was therefore ordered of 400 yards before firing the next zigzag group. Salvo A of this group was observed to hit the castle, the bursts of the remainder of the group as seen through the smoke screen appeared to be about right for range, and accordingly, zigzag groups were continued until the end of the bombarding course had been reached at 0349, without making any further range correction. All these latter salvoes appeared to fall in the target area.

Faulknor fired 56 rounds of 4.7-inch HE and 15 rounds of 3-inch star shell; *Beaufort* 50 rounds of 4-inch HE and 12 rounds of 4-inch star shell and *Pindos* 36 rounds of 4-inch HE. But, as Admiral Willis later related: – 'Cos harbour and Roads were apparently empty.' *Faulknor* then led round towards Kara Ada and speed was increased to 20 knots.

Meanwhile *Petard's* group had attacked Port Kalymnos, the already damaged *Trapani*, was hit again and capsized, but the enemy invasion barges present were, in Willis's words, '… probably behind the Mole and escaped damage.' On receiving Petard's report Captain Thomas decided, on completion of his own bombardment, to lie up at Port Deremen at the head of the Gulf of Cos, so as to be in a position to assist *Petard*. Captain Thomas informed Levant HQ at 0355/11th:

Bombardment completed. Intend lying up in Port Deremen in view of *Petard's* 0336.

Course was set for Port Dereman where they duly anchored. At 1022, Captain Thomas signalled Admiral Willis.

> Evident territorial waters not respected when ships under way. Grave risk moving without cloud cover. Fuel remaining 0800/11 *Faulknor* 68.3 %; *Beaufort* 67 %; *Pindos* 69%. Position observed 1003.

Air reconnaissance during 11 November revealed considerable movement of landing-craft between Cos and Kalymnos, and appeared final preparations for the assault on Leros from the northern bays of Kalymnos were being made. A reconnaissance of Cos harbour in the afternoon showed a concentration of enemy landing-craft. The British ships were kept under close observation and, at 1003 a single Ju.88 flew over the harbour and another at 1708.

Captain Thomas signalled at 1714/11th:

> Observed by one Ju.88 at 1705. Intend remaining at Port Deremen unless otherwise ordered.

Initially, Levant Command agreed with his decision to stay put. A signal, timed at 1714, read:

> Unless I get further information intend you stay where you are tonight.

Admiral Willis recorded: -

> The enemy's intentions were still not clear. It was necessary to conserve fuel, in Captain (D), Eight Destroyer Flotilla's force, since his Hunts had only enough fuel for one night's operations and the next force of destroyers could not arrive in the area until late on the night 12th/13th. After dark Captain (D) Eighth Destroyer Flotilla was therefore ordered to move his force to a bay nearer the area.

Then orders were given by C-in-C Levant to Thomas to move his three destroyers closer to Cos Channel, and send his two Hunts into the Roads to attack enemy shipping reported by our aircraft at 0120 and 0122. Captain Thomas received these instructions in two signals timed at 2153 and 2215/11th respectively:

> Shift your force to Nassilika Bay 036° 59' N, 027° 30' E or Alakishli Bay preferably latter by 0100 12th. 2. A Wellington is reconnoitring Cos Roads about 0100 12th. If any shipping or lights are located there send Hunts to destroy them with gunfire and report result. Suggest good time for this 0230 to 0300. 3. Keep additional watch 3450 K/Cs from 2300 until 0400.
>
> My 2153. Stay in one or other of these bays tomorrow 12th and give the Hunts fuel. Port Dereman is too far away in present situation.

At 0100 on Friday 12 November, in compliance to his new instructions, Captain Thomas proceeded to Alakishli Bay, twenty miles from Cos Roads, arriving at 0157 on 12 November.

Captain Thomas was instructed to send his two 'Hunts' in to destroy any shipping that the aircraft might locate at Cos. Even as the three destroyers were shifting their berths from Port Deremen to Alakishli, British aircraft were sending in sighting reports, at 0120 and 0122, of two groups of eight and seven landing barges respectively, at sea and steering north-west from Kappari Island, well inside the minefields east of Kalymnos.

It was the German invasion fleet carrying the crack troops of 22nd Infantry Division under Lieutenant-General Frederick Mueller to carry out Operation 'Typhoon', the invasion of Leros.

The Germans had hitherto been reported as two groups of eight and seven landing craft steering north-west from Pserimos Island, well *outside* those deadly minefields east of Kalymnos. That these craft turned out to be much more than this was *not* appreciated by the Operations Room at Alexandria, who first were in receipt of the reconnaissance reports, nor by Captain Thomas who got them later.

The optimum time to destroy these forces was while they were at sea between the aerial sighting at 0120 and the landing at 0500/12 November. The only ships available to do so were the two destroyer forces. Why were they not sailed? Admiral Willis stated:

> It had always been expected that the enemy would launch his assault in daylight from the cover of the minefields at the northern end of Kalymnos. Captain (D) Eighth Destroyer Flotilla appreciated that the forces now reported were *moving up* to these bays and that he would be unable to interfere with them on account of the minefield.

Admiral Willis went on to clearly state: -

> *Due to an erroneous appreciation in the Commander-in-Chief's Operations Room,* it was not believed that these might in fact be the assaulting forces until it was too late *to order* Captain (D), Eighth Destroyer Flotilla, to intercept.

This passage indicates plainly two points. 1) The fault lay with C-in-C, Levant's shore staff, and, 2) Captain Thomas was under *direct* orders from them. Admiral Willis continued:

> It now appears that one group made for the islands north of Leros and attacked from this direction, while the second group approached from the cover of the minefield. There is no doubt that, had Captain (D) Eighth Destroyer Flotilla been ordered to intercept at once, the northern assault force might have been destroyed. However, it is easy to be wise after the event and as the enemy maintained a continual night air-reconnaissance in the vicinity of the destroyers wherever they were, and were thus able to direct their own surface forces clear of them, it is very far from certain that any of the invasion flotilla would have been intercepted.

Accordingly, the destroyers did not sail to intercept these until after dark on 12th, by which time it was too late. Captain S. W. Roskill, in the Official History, stated:

> Even though the senior officer of the destroyers was troubled by shortage of fuel, and knew that more destroyers could not arrive until the next night, it now seems that he should have taken his ships on patrol earlier.

Captain Thomas was *ordered* to shift berth, and he complied. He was *ordered* to send in his ships *after dusk*, and he complied. He did not send them in earlier, *nor* was he advised to. Roskill also stated:

> Nor did the naval Commander-in-Chief's operation room, where the air reports had also been received, deduce that the invasion forces were approaching the threatened island, and order the destroyers to sea.

Even if *Faulknor* and her companions *had* sailed earlier there was every chance they would have been quickly spotted by the Luftwaffe, as they had on every previous occasion. Although this had never before deterred them from pressing home their attacks, the enemy would have been forewarned and taken avoiding action. Thus success would not have *automatically* been assured.

In view of the fierce criticism made of Captain Thomas's decision, it should be clearly put on record in his defence that *Faulknor* and her companions were short on fuel and when aerial reconnaissance revealed heavy movements of enemy vessels between Cos and Kalymnos, it was considered vital that *Faulknor's* force should conserve what fuel it had for the *next nights* operations as the relieve force could not reach the area until late on the night of 12th/13th.

Not until 1800/12th, did Captain Thomas take *Faulknor, Beaufort* and *Pindos* on a sweep around the disputed island, sweeping close inshore to seek out reinforcing landing ships.

The Senior British Naval Officer ashore had reported to Wellington V10 that the squadron might not arrive off the island until 2100, so Captain Thomas signalled that he would in fact arrive at 2000 and this fact was repeated to V10 by Leros WT. The destroyers then swept up the east coast of Leros and star-shells were fired over Alinda Bay, but no sign of any shipping, hostile or otherwise, was seen. Searchlights from the Italian defence positions ashore illuminated the squadron on several occasions. As it was understood that all these were 'friendly' the SBNO was requested, at 2155, to have these lights kept off the force. They were taken under searchlight illumination by the Italians on the Crusader Castle, as was described by war correspondent L. Marsland Gander.

> … it illuminated for a brief moment a beautiful sight – two grey streamlined shapes of British destroyers steaming silently in line ahead. There was a spontaneous low cheer from the little group outside the tunnel.[8]

Not surprisingly after that, the destroyers located no enemycraft. A report was also received from Wellington V10 north of the island, that he could see no shipping, so Captain Thomas took his ships through Lipso Channel to search the west coast of both Leros and Kalymnos. Still nothing was seen in the bays on this coast, he considered examining Levitha. But as enemy reports of shipping proceeding to Levitha were old, it was decided to return nearer to the vicinity of Leros and course was set for the Lipso Channel again.

At 2130, they received a request from the Army ashore to carry out a bombardment of the Clidi Battery, then in enemy hands. A map reference to the peak of Mount Clidi was given but Captain Thomas asked from which side the bombardment could be safely given without endangering friendly forces. While waiting a response, course was shaped to a position north-east of the island. Shell bursts could be seen on the eastern flanks of the island, near the top of the mountain, and since these were assumed to be from friendly artillery ashore directed at the enemy, the DCT was ordered to keep laid and trained on the position of these explosions.

At 2210, no answer to their question having been received, they commenced firing on a navigational range of 078°. Captain Thomas reported:

> The first salvo was unobserved but, on the assumption that it had fallen in a depression short of the peak, 'Up 800' was ordered, and the second salvo fell right on top of the peak. 'Down 200' was then ordered and two salvoes were fired, both fell just short and slightly below the peak slightly above the position where the artillery bursts had been observed. Assuming that the peak was in enemy hands, and that the battery would be slightly below it, it was not considered that our own troops would be endangered by continuing fire at the same range, while even if the salvoes were not actually hitting the battery, they were falling in a position where they would embarrass the enemy.

Accordingly, a rapid group was then fired, all three salvoes of which fell in the same position as salvoes three and four.

The two Hunts then joined in, and their 4-inch bursts were seen on the shoulder of the mountain, north of *Faulknor's* bursts. After eight minutes, at 2218, they received the order to cease firing from the SBNO and fire was checked. In total *Faulknor* fired 28 rounds of 4.7-inch HE, *Beaufort* 26 rounds of 4-inch HE and *Pindos* just three rounds of 4-inch HE.

Because the opposing lines were very close together, indeed almost mingled in that confused terrain, the destroyers had to stop firing in case they endangered their own men, but it did give the beleaguered Tommies ashore a brief boost to the morale; the Royal Navy had not forgotten them.

At 2230, *Faulknor* altered course northward to pass through the Lipso Channel and, on receipt of another signal from SBNO, proceeded to examine the southern coast of Levitha. They observed the harbour from one miles range but again, no shipping was seen. The only sign of life was a light flashing a succession of 'As' from a small hut ashore.

Accordingly, the destroyers proceeded to Turk Berku to lie up in accordance with instructions. By 0810 on Saturday 13th, a southerly gale had blown up, hampering all seaborne movement and *Faulknor* withdrew her squadron to the anchorage.

Throughout the 13th fierce fighting continued ashore, but the British garrison was outfought by the German paratroops. Signals, 'late, contradictory and confused', kept arriving on *Faulknor's* bridge, reflecting the imperspicuity ashore and back at Levant HQ. It was left for Captain Thomas to interpret and act on these as best he could.

Timed 1209/13th Admiral Willis signalled:

> Leave lie-up at dark tonight 13th. Proceed at best speed through Cos Channel north of Rhodes to Alexandria if fuel permits otherwise to Limasol. 2. *Echo* and *Belvoir* passing Cos Channel to westward about 2100 13th 3. Your code word Naval high. 4. Report intentions and estimated PC and S for 0600 14th.

This was clear enough but Captain Thomas estimated his ships had just about enough fuel to reach Cyprus. Preparations began but at 1551/13th Captain Thomas received yet another set of instructions from the C-in-C.

> Army urgently require bombardment between line joining (A) 08 7422 to 32 077414 (B) 08 3 430 to 06 6 419 gridded chart F. 0368, from 2045 to 2100B tonight 13th as preparation for counter-attack. 2. Carry out this bombardment before withdrawing in accordance with my 131209. 3. Maximum volume of fire and precise time of ceasing fire are major considerations. Bombard from eastward.

Eighteen minutes after despatching this to *Faulknor*, Levant had second thoughts and hedged their bet.

> Army may not want bombardment of area in my 131551. It should not, repeat not, be carried out until receipt of further orders. 2. In any case Army most anxious bombardment eastern slope Mount Appecitici. It would be invaluable if *Faulknor* could carry this out from northward. Own troops west of 026° 52′ E.

A further signal followed from Admiral Willis, timed 1831:

> My 131809 that bombardment of area in my 131551 *is required, repeat is required.* 2. Carry out bombardment in my 131809 immediately afterwards.

This was followed at 2030 by yet another change:

> Cancel paragraph 1 of my 131831 Paragraph 2 stands about 2100.

In the space of the day therefore, *Faulknor* had been ordered:

> (a) to withdraw to base.
> (b) to carry out a bombardment.
> (c) not to carry out the bombardment but to carry out another one.
> (d) to carry out both bombardments.
> (e) to cancel one bombardment and carry out the other!

Meanwhile, in view of the fuel situation, Captain Thomas had also been trying to clarify things with the Senior British Naval Officer ashore on the embattled island, firstly whether the bombardment was required or not and secondly, could it be advanced in order that the destroyers could be clear of the Aegean and well away from the dive-bombers before daylight. If not, then the force might have to lie up again in Turkish waters for yet another night, and, should that be the case, '... I would not have had fuel enough to get away at all.'

Accordingly, *Faulknor* signalled SBNO Aegean at 1837:

> Can you please advance time from 2045 to 1945.

No reply being received to this signal Captain Thomas was forced to advice Leros of his position. This he did at 1918:

> Cannot afford to wait. Am going on my way.

Therefore *Faulknor's* force withdraw to Alexandria and, while steaming hard to the east, finally received a much-delayed response from Leros, time of origin of 1928:

> Please plaster following area from 19 SW, repeat SW Circle centre 037° 09.6', 026° 49.8'

It was too late. As Captain Thomas reported later:

> I had every intention of bombarding Alinda vicinity in accordance with Commander-in-Chief, Levant's 131551 but Leros did not ask for this or reply to my signal. Even though this would have delayed my leaving the Aegean by 2 to 3 hours I would have stayed to bombard and chanced my getting away but Leros apparently no longer wanted it. (This was confirmed later).
>
> Great confusion of signals, their late receipt and conflicting orders from the Commander-in-Chief and Leros were a primary cause of my abandoning bombardment.

During the night the relieving force, *Echo, Dulverton* and *Belvoir,* were arriving in the area and Captain Thomas therefore signalled to Leros at 1955:

> Have had to go on, my reliefs will be there in accordance with C-in-C's 131311.

Admiral Willis commented:

It was unfortunate that late and corrupt signals and general doubt as to what was required led Captain (D) Eighth Destroyer Flotilla to withdraw without bombarding on night 13th/14th. *I do not consider, however, that he could well have acted otherwise.*

For *Faulknor* and her companions the ordeal was over. At 0600 on Sunday 14 November they met light cruiser *Phoebe* and proceeded to Limasol, arriving at 1600 their fuel tanks almost bone dry. *Faulknor* oiled from *Cherryleaf* and left at 1800 arriving Alexandria 0900 Monday 15 November.

How did these momentous and complex events appear to *Faulknor's* lower-deck at the time? As usual, they saw things more clearly than some 'experts' later on. Ted Newman's diary read:

> Jerry began the invasion of Leros at night under a full moon. We went in to prevent any further sea landings. We circled the island until 0400, searching for enemy craft, and bombarded the Jerries from out of a gun position they had taken. At daylight we had to hide up as no fighter cover could be given. Our fuel was very low and it was imperative that we got away on the 12th. Things looked grim on Leros. We were asked to bombard again at 2100 on our way back, but fuel wouldn't allow it, so we asked to advance the time to 1945. No answer was received, so we asked *Echo* to take over. Everyone seemed to be in a panic, signals flying right and left, with nothing definite being done. We made our way to Limassol and *only just had enough oil to get there*. We arrived back at Alexandria on the 15th and went in for a refit. We couldn't keep at sea any longer, having over 1500 hours on each boiler and many defects.
>
> 16 November, 1943. End of Leros: a badly managed affair. Some troops were evacuated by MTBs and various small craft, *Petard* and *Echo* helped. It's a horrible thought when you think of all those lads we had only just taken up. Lack of air support again.

This proved to be *Faulknor's* last involvement in the unhappy Aegean campaign. But, when Leros finally fell, *Faulknor* left behind one of her own who died a heroes death ashore. Lieutenant Phipps, Signals Officer, had volunteered to act as Army/Navy Liaison Officer ashore at Army HQ. He became a close friend of Major The Earl Jellicoe. In his capacity as Flag Lieutenant to Senior British Naval Officer, Alan Phipps was killed at 0600 helping to defend Fortress Brigade HQ. Captain Jimmy James, CB, MC Intelligence Officer, Royal West Kents, described this brave young man's last moments to Jeffrey Holland:

> This naval specialist dropped into a slit trench occupied by Lieutenant James, and promptly commenced firing his revolver at the enemy. Phipps remarked: 'I always wanted a shore posting but never imagined it would be like this!' Then came a burst from a Schmeisser and he was killed instantly. Immediately after the British surrender, Major The Earl Jellicoe, gave his parole to *Leutnantgeneral* Mueller in order to search for the body of Alan Phipps, who was his close friend.

Lieutenant Philips's lonely grave now stands on the island he gave his life for in vain. He typified the spirit and ideals of *Faulknor*. Phipps and Broadbent were the only two members of *Faulknor's* crew to lose their lives in combat, even though their ship served continuously in the front line of battle from Day One of the war right through to the very last day. True, several of her crew had lost their lives by being swept overboard, three in all over the six years, and a further two had been killed in accidents at Newcastle and Gibraltar, but overall the luck of *Faulknor* was phenomenal. Among the awards for outstanding service during the Aegean Campaign awarded to *Faulknor* were DSCs to Lieutenant-Commander E. G. May; Lieutenant Dalrymple-Hamilton; Lieutenant N. A. McNeile and Lieutenant (E) Halliday.

RECORD OF MOVEMENTS OF HM SHIPS TAKING PART IN THE AEGEAN OPERATION

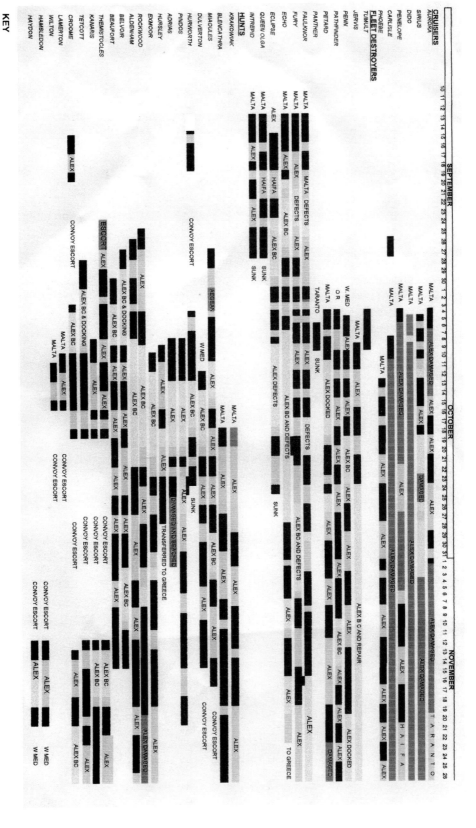

KEY

■ = AT SEA

▨ = IN HARBOUR

▩ = IN DOCKYARD

▦ = DAMAGED

BC = Boiler Clean

A DofD signal of 22nd confirmed *Faulknor* was:

Taken in hand 16.11 Alexandria. Short refit. Completes 24.11.

Actually *Faulknor* remained docked at Alexandria until 27 November, and even so, there still remained many jobs undone. Their first assignment was to escort light cruiser *Dido* to Malta and she left Alexandria at 0730 on 28th with destroyers *Aldenham* and *Exmoor.* They were scheduled to fully refit at Malta. *En route* the four ships conducted a bombardment exercise and had just completed this when an urgent signal informed them that light cruiser *Birmingham* had been torpedoed and *Faulknor* was immediately detached to her assistance.

HMS *Faulknor* *firing a torpedo during an exercise in the Mediterranean in 1943. In the action off Stampalia one Nazi troop ship was finished off in this manner – eventually!* (Bill Silltow.)

Birmingham had been torpedoed at 1118 by *U-407,* off Cyrenaica, while on passage through the Mediterranean from Gibraltar to Alexandria. Incredibly, she was unescorted, steaming a zigzag at 25 knots. The torpedo struck under the forecastle and the explosion threw water right over her bridge, so severe was the impact. She suffered 27 killed and 27 more badly wounded, her speed dropped to ten knots and she took on a list to port of 8 degrees. The hit being well forward, her main machinery remained intact and she could answer her helm.[9]

Birmingham was in a highly dangerous situation, damaged and alone, with the U-boat unmolested and able to take time to deliver the *coup-de-grace*. Captain Williams took his crippled ship closer inshore and then steered toward Alexandria at her best speed of 15 knots signalling her dilemma. C-in-C, Levant immediately sent two 'Hunt' Class destroyers, the Greek *Themistocles* and Polish *Krakowiak* as an anti-submarine screen. Other ships despatched were tug *Brigand* and minesweeper *Romney* from Tobruk. At 1316 *Faulknor* received this signal:

Emergency Secret Cipher. Captain (D). 8 Proceed at best speed to join *Birmingham* torpedoed in position 33° 05′ N, 21° 43′ E course 080° 12 knots. Hunts follow you. *Krakowiak* ORP and *Themistocles* searching.

They duly pulled out the stops, and, while the rest of the exercising group returned to harbour, *Faulknor* sped off alone westward, duly sighting the damaged cruiser at 2155.

Captain Williams must therefore have been very relieved when, at 2155, *Faulknor* was sighted approaching at high speed. On arrival they were stationed one mile ahead for the night and in this position they escorted her through to the dark hours. The two ships overtook and joined a convoy at 0750/29th and, at 1020 the same morning, *Fury* and *Pathfinder* joined the escort and took her safely on to Alexandria.

Her duty done, *Faulknor* again reversed course toward Malta, arriving early 30 November.

At 1510, *Faulknor* undertook an anti-submarine patrol, returning the next day without incident. Although due to refit, after two days 'swinging round the buoy' they were allocated fresh tasks due to preparations for Operation 'Shingle', the proposed landing at Anzio in the rear of the German defence line in Italy.

Among the unsung members of HMS *Faulknor's* ship's crew at this time were several of the four-footed variety. Captain Thomas gave this account:

> You may be interested to learn that we have four pets on board. They are *Mishka*, *Sally*, *Leros* and *Rocket*. *Mishka, Sally* and *Leros* are dogs, or rather 'she-dogs', while *Rocket* is a Tomcat. *Rocket* we got from the destroyer *Rocket*. He spends most of his time sleeping in the Accountant Officer, Paymaster Sub-Lieutenant, F. G. Chilcott, RNVR's cabin. He finds the Mediterranean weather rather too warm for him. *Leros* belongs to the Stoker's Mess deck. A soldier gave her to Stoker Harry Hoyle just before he was landed at Leros in the middle of the night. She is a smooth-haired terrier. *Sally* is a Springbok, a rough-haired terrier, born at sea in the destroyer *Quilliam* of a South African mother and father. She has never been ashore in her life and is a proper young 'sea dog'. She is the property of the Petty Officers' Mess but her personal guardian is Petty Officer Frederick Ryder. *Mishka*, which means in Russian 'Little Bear', belongs to the Torpedo Officer and lives in the Ward Room. She is a Polyarnoe husky acquired when *Faulknor* was in North Russia.

Paymaster Sub-Lieutenant Chilcott himself amplified *Rockets* role aboard, and also told of her full title, being '… the proud owner of 'Paymaster Cat *Rocket*' – so-called because he spends a large part of his time fast asleep, and that is the chief occupation of Paymasters, according to the Executives!'

Faulknor embarked the Flag Officer, Mediterranean, Admiral Sir John H. D. Cunningham, and his staff at Malta on 3 December and transferred them to Augusta before sailing on to Naples through rain and rough seas. Having refuelled they conducted a series of patrols off that port between the 4th and 19 December. On the latter date Captain Thomas announced to the crew that 8th *Faulknor* was now officially part of the Mediterranean Fleet and would serve two years and three months in this theatre. There were also some changes in personnel around this time; the new Flotilla Secretary, Paymaster Lieutenant H.J.C. Cotter joined in November, and Lieutenant J. E. Scollick, RANVR joined in December.

A very *rare photograph showing HMS* Faulknor *with her Pendant numbers (H62) painted up on her hull, never done with flotilla leaders, during her very brief period as a 'private ship'. This photograph was taken from the aircraft-carrier HMS* Formidable *in the Mediterranean in the summer of 1943.* (Ken Timson.)

The Operation 'PWB' was scheduled next. The original object of this operation was to make the enemy believe that a major landing was about to take place in the Gaeta area. The front-line of the 46th (British) Division was held on the line of the River Garigliano and it was hoped that such a ruse would draw in German army reserves away from the area where the Fifth Army intended to attack. A force of LSIs, LCIs and LCTs, along with a naval Bombarding Force was to assemble in Pozzuoli Bay on 12 December and simulate a landing near Gaeta. The landing ships were to be escorted by destroyers *Loyal* and *Paladin* and light forces; Bombarding Force 'A' [light cruiser *Orion* and destroyers *Echo*, *Wheatland* and *Whaddon*] and Force 'B', [Dutch gunboat *Flores*, and destroyers *Faulknor* and *Ilex*]. 'H' Hour was originally fixed for 0200/13 December, and *Faulknor* was put on alert. Tough going ashore led to a postponement, and they remained at Naples while the plan was re-thought.

Next day *Faulknor* and *Echo* sailed as escorts for an Augusta-bound convoy. This proved uneventful and they anchored at Malta on the 22nd. They sailed for Naples on Christmas Day arriving Boxing Day. They celebrated Christmas on the 27th and the officers gave a concert.

As customary, the Chiefs and Petty Officers were invited for drinks in the wardroom and Torpedo Officer Moore was given permission by the Captain to unveil his party piece. This turned out be a beautifully made miniature scale model of one of the *Victory's* cannon, complete with a six-inch brass barrel and wooden truck. The whole thing was fired electrically and loaded with a ball-bearing. Amidst scenes of traditional ceremony and in strict accordance with the loading and firing instructions laid down in old Admiralty manuals, the trigger was pulled and the cannon fired. There was a sharp crack and a smell of burning, and the ball-bearing went straight through the wardroom plating! A repeat performance, although eagerly clamoured for, was vetoed!

On night 29th /30 December, 1943, it was business as usual, conducting the replanned simulation attack, now renamed as Operation 'PWG'.

Faulknor and *Laforey* sailed from Pozzuoli Bay with the American *PT.201* and *PT.202*, at 1800/29th, escorting two LSI's *Royal Ulsterman* and *Princess Beatrix* carrying 9 Commando who were to mount a raid behind the enemy's front at the mouth of the river Garigliano river, 35 miles north of Naples. The force, Force 'B', passed through the Ischia Channel and steered towards their beaches. Because of a navigation error by the radar-equipped American PT boats leading the LCAs, they made landfall south of the river, but this mistake was rectified and they landed at 0025.

Unopposed, the troops completed the modified plans, withdrawing after inflicting casualties and damage on the enemy. Meanwhile the LCAs returned safely to their parent ships. *Faulknor*, *Laforey* and the Dutch gunboat *Flores* bombarded Scauri, Gaeta and Itri as a diversion, *Faulknor's* targets being a machine-gun position at Map reference 673957, a road and a railway running from 705956 to 720958 and the area between those and the beach, as well as the north-east corner of square 6897. *Faulknor* fired 120 rounds of 4.7-inch shell before retiring, with no reply. The Commandos reported that supporting fire came down about fifty yards ahead of Group 'Z' and broke up a German counter-attack. Their mission was later reported as successful, many of them making their way back across the river to Allied lines.

Faulknor was on anti-submarine patrol on 31st in company with the destroyers *Loyal* and *Ilex* and minesweepers *Acute*, *Albacore*, *Circe* and *Fly*, covering troop convoy NSF 11 returning to Naples on New Year's Eve. Routine patrols and exercising followed, as 'Shingle' was rescheduled for 22 January 1944.

Meanwhile, on 5 January 1944, Captain Thomas had been taken into hospital and Lieutenant-Commander E. G. May took over command of the ship. Lieutenant-Commander May was to write in a letter dated 1 March 1944 that:

> I have been First Lieutenant of HMS *Faulknor* for the past eighteen months. Captain M. S. Thomas left the ship and will be going to a shore job. He was very sorry to leave but not as sorry as we were to lose him.

Captain Thomas later recovered and continued his war service on a shore appointment in the Mediterranean, continuing in the Navy post-war, but died, whilst still on active service, on 21 August 1947.

Lieutenant-Commander May had strong connections with Stourbridge, which he listed at this time. 'My father, who now lies buried at Cofton Hackett near Barnt Green came from West Heath and my mother from Hopwood, all these places lying within a very small Worcestershire radius. Before joining the Navy I lived for many years at Edgbaston and I have stayed in several places around Barnt Green with my relations, who all live thereabouts.'

He added that he was enclosing a list of 36 young Sailors who would be very pleased to have 'pen friends' of Stourbridge girls and all were indeed subsequently found such partners by the two enterprising Miss Moodys.

On 6 January 1944, *Faulknor* and *Laforey* returning from an exercise that was cancelled halfway through owing to bad weather, was despatched *post haste* to aid two freighters, which had strayed into the extensive Allied minefield off the small island of Ischia in the Gulf of Naples. One of these, *Largs Bay* detonated two mines and was in serious trouble, being well ablaze. *Faulknor* was unable to close her while she was still inside the mined area, but stood by and waited for her to drift clear. After two hours the crew were forced to give up the fire-fighting and abandon ship, being picked up by motor-launches.

Because of their new CO's rank *Faulknor* was now 'junior' boat and, in the words of one of the crew, 'was pushed and shoved around by everybody now, doing continual patrols.' The extra staff carried while Captain (D) were expected to be redrafted to another flotilla leader, *Inglefield*, (Acting-Commander C. F. H. Churchill) or sent into the pool, but nothing occurred immediately and patrolling and exercising continued. It was at Malta at this time that Raymond Johnson was drafted to *Faulknor* from *Echo*. He gave the author these impressions of life aboard from the lower-deck viewpoint.

> The Captain at that time was Lieutenant-Commander E.G. May, and he promoted me from Ordinary Seaman to Able Seaman. My action station was on 'B' gun deck, at the 4.7-inch gun, which had a lot of use. My duty station was on the iron deck where the torpedoes were located.
>
> We had to supply and prepare our own food and the cook in the galley used to cook it for us. Then we had to collect it and serve it out to our messmates. We used to do this on a rota basis. My specials were shepherds pie – Bulley Beef with potatoes spread over the top – and rice pudding. I never had any complaints! I looked forward to the end of the month, when a tally of all the food used was accounted for. If you did not use all your allowance you would be given paste cards to purchase from the NAAFI cigarettes, soap etc. A few times we had to use one bucket of water daily for washing our clothes and ourselves. Our mess used to have a food locker fixed to the bulkhead near the anchor chain, and where we used to sling our hammocks.

Between 13th and 15th *Faulknor* embarked some soldiers for a day trip and exercise, and these were still aboard when she was diverted to take part in an anti-submarine sweep later in the day. This lasted for two days, the soldiers quite enjoying their extended outing, before they returned to Naples on the 16th. The same day they sailed to Madelaena before returning to Naples on the 17th.

To aid the Army's crossing of the Garigliano on the night of the 17th/18th, prior to 'Shingle', the Royal Navy conducted a series of bombardments of the German positions around Gaeta and Terracina. On 17 January *Faulknor* with the light cruisers *Orion* and *Spartan* and destroyers *Janus*, *Jervis*, *Laforey* and *Urchin* conducted such attack. They arrived in position at 0630 the following morning and commenced firing in support of 5th Army guns ashore. Targets included Mount Scauri, Castellonorato a road junction east of Formia and several others. At 1630 there was an ineffective sortie by German torpedo-bombers. A solitary enemy shore battery opened up but *Laforey* silenced it. Meantime, *Faulknor* accompanied *Spartan* further up the coast where they made a diversionary bombardment. Progress ashore was slow and Mintermo had to be demolished before the troops could make any headway and supporting tanks put ashore. *Faulknor* continued to give what was called 'useful fire support' throughout the day off the Garigliano River and enemy mobile batteries replied with accurate fire.

During the night of the 18th/19th, *Spartan* and *Orion* bombarded Terracina area and both cruisers, with *Laforey*, *Jervis*, *Janus* and *Faulknor* again provided fire support for 10th Army Corps. Smoke screens delayed fresh bombardment, but at 1600 the job was completed, the warships returning to Naples at 2000, to re-ammunition and refuel in readiness for the big landing

At Anzio, the naval bombarding and screening force comprised light cruisers *Orion* and *Spartan*, destroyers *Faulknor*, *Inglefield*, *Grenville*, *Janus*, *Jervis*, *Laforey*, *Loyal*, *Ulster*, *Urchin*, *Beaufort*, *Brecon*, *Tetcott*, and AA Ship *Palomares*. It was not expected that any warships would be retained long, indeed *Faulknor*, *Grenville* and *Janus* were due to return to Malta for escort duties. It did not turn out quite like that!

The British Assault force sailed in several groups. Force 'D' consisted of *Bulolo*, *Glengyle*, *Derbyshire*, and *Sobieski*, *Boxer* and *Bruiser*, LCIs *147*, *175*, *219*, *303*, *307* and *308*, escorted by the AA Ship *Palomares*, and destroyers *Laforey* (Captain D 19), *Loyal*, *Faulknor* and *Grenville*, who sailed from Pozzuoli at 1230 on D minus 1, 21 February 1944, to rendezvous with *Bulolo* from Naples. Lieutenant-Commander May recalled:

> We were one of the units in the initial assault which, as you will have read, took the enemy completely by surprise. A fine and inspiring touch to the landing was added by the Senior Officer of the Force who, as the invasion fleet steamed steadily towards Anzio, ordered one minute's silence to ask God's blessing on our cause and to make our peace with God.

The bombarding ships took up their positions, while the patrol destroyers, which included *Faulknor*, guarded against E-boats and U-boats offshore. At 0001/ 22nd, *Buolo* led them to position N B and when the signal to stop engines was executed *Glengyle* led her column to a position on the port beam of column two and they veered their anchors to the bottom. By 0220 *Faulknor* was conducting anti-submarine patrols out to sea, to protect Admiral Troubridge's Northern Attack Force.

Although not originally assigned as one of the bombarding destroyers *Faulknor* was assigned the W/T Call sign J1G for communications in case required. At 2217 the signal 'E boat attack likely tonight', added to rumours that German destroyers might also sortie. In response *Grenville* signalled *Faulknor*, 'Take station astern, 5 cables', but, after spending all night closed up, nothing had happened, and there were no air attacks either. It all seemed an anti-climax.

At 0815/22nd, *Faulknor*, *Grenville*, *Tetcott* and *Beaufort* were ordered to conduct anti-submarine patrols in Area Two, but this continued only briefly before, at 0902, *Grenville* and *Faulknor* were ordered by *Ulster* to anchor. Desultory shelling of the anchorage by German artillery commenced at 1110 with little effect.

By evening the unladen LSTs formed a combined return convoy, MAN 10, which sailed for Naples at 1800 escorted by *Faulknor* and minesweepers *Rinaldo* (SO), *Bude*, *Cadmus*, *Rothesay* and danlayer *Waterwitch*, arriving at *0930*/24 January. Back at the beachhead things took a more sinister turn with the arrival in force of the Luftwaffe.

Having refuelled at Naples *Faulknor* returned to Anzio at 1130, into a rising storm, escorting Landing Ship, Tank, (LST) *Thruster*, which had embarked soldiers and motor transport at Niaida. Her refuelling made them late for the main convoy, leaving the Bay of Naples at 15 knots for 'X-Ray' beach where they arrived at position 'W' in the middle of an air raid at 1730. A torpedo-bomber attacked *Thruster* from the starboard beam, and was engaged by *Faulknor*. Only a very prompt reaction of 'full speed ahead and hard-a-starboard' saved the two torpedoes hitting. The storm wrecked the British sectors pontoon causeways, so *Peter* beach was closed and Admiral Troubridge embarked aboard HQ ship *Bulolo,* which *Faulknor* escorted back to Naples. Further heavy air-attacks broke over the anchorage as they sailed down the swept channel but they came through unscathed, *Faulknor* finally anchoring at Naples 0700/25th.

At midday 25 January, *Faulknor* took two transports, *Empire Austin* and *Fort Meductic,* up to Anzio but the storms were so severe they were instructed to abort. They put about and had almost reached Naples again when told to told reverse course! The seas eased slightly during the night but, just before they reached the beaches, a third signal came ordering them back to Naples. Again they reversed course, and again, at 1000 when that harbour was again in sight, the staff signalled them to return to Anzio! Back again for the third time they plodded with the two merchantmen, arriving at 1800. Nobody wanted them; the limited capacity of the remaining pontoons meant they still could not be unloaded. After a frustrating night *Faulknor* returned to anti-submarine patrol.

During middle watch on 30th two terrific explosions were heard aboard *Faulknor*, thought to be ammunition dumps exploding ashore. Actually the Ammunition Ship *Samuel Huntingdon,* hit by a glider-bomb earlier, had caught fire and finally blew up. During the forenoon they closed a Liberty ship and took off the pitifully few survivors from cruiser *Spartan*, also sunk by a glider-bomb, just 35 men, whom some genius had transferred to a vessel laden with ammunition! Not surprisingly their nerves were shot and they were glad to transfer to *Faulknor* who conveyed them to Naples on 31 January. After two hours in harbour they joined a three-day anti-submarine hunt with destroyers *Cleveland* and *Hambledon* in 40° 50′ N, 12° E. *Faulknor* and *Kempenfelt* reinforced them, and continued searching throughout the evening, next day and night.

More destroyers arrived while others left to refuel. By dawn of 2nd, *Faulknor, Kempenfelt, Ulster, Blencathra* and *Cleveland*, later joined by *Grenville*, were patiently scouring the area to no avail. They continued to hunt all night but, on 3 February, *Faulknor, Grenville* and *Ulster* left for Naples unrewarded.

Gunnery rating A Pavey recalls joining *Faulknor* at Malta on 2 February 1944.

> I was on the Tank Landing Ship *Thruster* at Sicily, Salerno and Anzio but joined *Faulknor* and went straight back to the latter beachhead, much to my dismay! We carried on anti-submarine sweeps; bombarding enemy positions ashore at the request of one of the Guards' Regiments who were having a sticky time; and dodging about in general.

The rumour mill speculated they were not getting a Captain (D) back again and that many of The Staff were to be drafted once they reached Malta, a stop on their way to Haifa for their expected refit. However, as this refit also involved changes to her armament, it was finally considered too big a job for Haifa to manage and the destroyer *Liddesdale* was sailed there in their place. *Faulknor* was then scheduled to be refitted at Gibraltar, once that Dockyard had finished work on *Fury*, meantime *Faulknor* had to continue.

The weather continued poor on 4th when they sailed with *Grenville* and the AA ship *Ulster Queen*, escorting convoy NV.18A, mainly LSTs, to Augusta. Conditions were such that the ships could not get into that port and were diverted to Bizerta. Another pounding followed and on 6th they were now told to try Tunis. At dusk the following day the convoy anchored in the Gulf of Tunis and the destroyers sailed for Malta, arriving during the forenoon of 8 February 1944. *Faulknor* went into dock to boiler clean until 14th.

While here, on 11 February, the SS *Riverton*, broke adrift in Torre Annunciata harbour and drifted down on the destroyer berths, ramming and damaging both *Kempenfelt* and *Ulster*. *Faulknor* and *Grenville*, both refitting at Malta, replaced them thus, on 14 February *Faulknor* left Sliema Creek for Naples carrying fifty passengers, and many of them were seasick.

They reached Naples on 16th with destroyer *Zetland*, but, on entering harbour, were ordered to Anzio without delay. They were at the beachhead at 1800/17th implementing AA and A/S patrols that same night. Next day they were ordered to provide Anti-aircraft cover for the cruisers on bombardment duty. At that date *Faulknor* and the anti-aircraft cruisers *Colombo* and *Delhi*, were the only British warships fitted with some form of jamming apparatus to block the enemy radio-controlled bombing. The three were to be officially known as 'J (for Jamming) ships'.

17 February saw the German counter-attack against the defensive perimeter and, for a time, the Allies' position was tenuous. Light cruisers *Dido* and *Penelope* maintained continuous fire support while *Faulknor* screened them; this support being given to light cruiser *Mauritius* next day when she carried out three bombardments of Formia.

On 19 February *Faulknor* with destroyers USS *Hilary P. Jones (DD427)*, and *Madison (DD.425)* laid a smoke screen to cover American light cruiser *Philadelphia (CL 41)* while she took her turn in the Fire Support Area, at 41° 21′ N, 12° 34′ E, shelling targets in the Formia area. Return fire from German guns at Cape Circe south of them, aimed at *Philadelphia*, pitched in the water closer to *Faulknor* than their actual target, close enough to give *Faulknor's* crew, 'some nasty shocks.'

As Carl Heuer remembers:

> ... the Yank cruiser disappeared after we had gone in and lain a smoke screen close inshore to shield her so she could carry on with the bombardment. After we had taken our chances and laid the screen we came round from behind it only to see them going hard back to Naples! The destroyers ended up doing the bombardment themselves!

Philadelphia later manned ship and cheered *Faulknor* on her return to Naples harbour to thank them for their action in covering their retreat from a perceived submarine threat, but the *Faulknors* themselves thought she had run from German gunfire and resented being left in the lurch, and so this well-meant gesture badly misfired.

Raymond Johnson recalled:

> I was down on the iron deck at the Anzio beach head, where we were laying smoke screens for a bombarding cruiser so they could fire over us at the enemy positions ashore. Strangely, we were not at Action Stations at the time, so there most of us stood behind the spud locker made of canvas and chicken-wire. Suddenly the enemy got our range and fired a salvo of large shells some of which fell rather close. We instinctively ducked behind the nearest cover, the canvas spud locker! What a stupid thing to do – a near miss and fragments of shell could have wiped out the lot of us. I have never seen a ship move so fast, as we did then, our stern was tucked well down and we were away from there.
>
> On our return to Naples we moored close to this American cruiser, all her crew cheering, flag-waving, the works. They thought they had done wonderfully well. In reply, and in contrast, our lot on the iron deck stuck two fingers up as a rude gesture because while they had high-tailed it when the guns went off we had been left behind at the beachhead to help the Army.

By the 20th *Faulknor*, low on fuel, returned to Naples. Commander Churchill thought it opportune to transfer all Flotilla papers from *Faulknor* to *Inglefield* and, with these aboard, sailed back to the beachhead. All the Staff were drafted to other flotilla leaders and it was announced that, from 14 February 1944, *Faulknor* was no longer a leader but a 'private boat'.

Thus ended, if only for a brief time, a great tradition, dating back to her first day of commissioning, 24 May 1935, almost nine years before. In post-war reference books it became standard for historians to claim repeatedly that *Faulknor* and *Jervis* were the only two Flotilla Leaders to spend the *entire* war in that role. In truth neither did. The error came about because of the mis-reading of an earlier Admiralty Press Release, printed in several British newspapers thus:

> *Faulknor*, a nine-year old destroyer, has now served continuously as a flotilla-leader for longer than any other destroyer afloat. She has steamed 250,000 miles on active service.

This, repeated by Derisley Trimmingham of Bermuda in *The Navy* magazine in the mid-1950s was adopted unquestionly by other 'historians' who failed to check the facts. These two ships *did* carry out that role for longer than many others, but *Jervis* had already become a private boat, leaving *Faulknor* easily holding the record for she had been a Leader four years *before Jervis* and three years *before Inglefield* had commissioned. (Another destroyer that served as a Leader from the outbreak of the war for a long period was *Duncan).* Moreover, *Faulknor's* days of leading the 8th Flotilla were far from over.

At Naples they too endured a drifting merchant ship careering around the anchorage. This menace started to drift down on *Faulknor*. Warnings were duly shouted for her own cable to be slipped, but the officer of the watch failed to take action until the warning had been repeated again, with the merchant vessel now dangerously close. The renegade hit *Faulknor* a glancing blow, adding yet another dent to her hull. The captain later held an enquiry on the matter, the OOW admitting he had failed to take action fast enough.

For *Faulknor* these strenuous days were relieved by short rests at Capri, where some of the crew took the opportunity to visit Gracie Fields' villa and the Blue Grotto, while others swam and lazed in the sun. They also managed to get ashore for short periods in Naples.

Bob Parham recalls *Faulknor's* three-day visit to Capri:

> During odd periods of rest from the bedlam of the Anzio beachhead they anchored off Capri. On one occasion they secured alongside a very large and shiny new American destroyer, all gleaming paintwork and bristling with guns. The US sailors looked down at *Faulknor's* rusty paint and peeling gun barrels and made continuous derogatory remarks about a rust bucket, which did not endear our Allies to the crew one little bit. Of course *Faulknor* had been fighting this war for five years non-stop so far and had probably seen more sea time in any *one month* of that time than the Yankee boat would see in her entire career, so it rankled a good bit.

A different side of the coin was expressed at the same place when, by an amazing coincidence, the crew of the Fortress bomber that *Faulknor* had plucked out of the sea in mid-Atlantic, turned up and made themselves known. They recognised her pendant numbers and a great time was had by all. It was pure luck that *Faulknor* actually had her pendants painted up on her hull at both brief periods.

C-in-C Levant's War Diary for 24 February stated Acting Commander W. F. H. Churchill was to become Captain D8 in *Faulknor*. Whether the C-in-C was blessed with second sight or not, this prediction was made the day *before* Commander Churchill's existing command, *Inglefield*, with the flotilla papers now aboard, was sunk off Anzio on 25 February, making it inevitable that *Faulknor* should resume her former status with the minimum break in continuity!

Also on 24 February, they joined a submarine hunt off Ischia and Ponza off the Gulf of Gaeta, in rough weather. At 2127/ 26th *Laforey* and *Faulknor* were sweeping the south-west approaches to Anzio anchorage, when a submarine contact was made in 41° 07' N, 12° 03' E. *Laforey* made five depth charge attacks and *Faulknor* one before the ships returned to Naples to refuel. They observed oil aplenty but no definite kill. They resumed hunting that night being joined by destroyers *Urchin, Lamerton* and *Wheatland*, concentrating in the area of their first contact. This 'flooding' of the probable U-boat contacts was standard practice in the Mediterranean and was known as 'Swamp' operations.

The 'Luck of the *Faulknor*' manifested itself again that night. While anchored offshore a drifting mine was carried into the ship by the prevailing wind before any avoiding action could be taken. Witnesses watched with hearts in their mouths as it bumped down *Faulknor's* starboard hull until it reached the stern. One last bump and it carried clear. Once at a safe distance it was fired on with the ship's rifles, even though many thought it must have been a dud, until it detonated with a huge explosion and a tall column of dirty water!

Carl Heuer recalled:

> … *Faulknor* had one of her lucky days. A loose mine drifted down the side of the ship. The ship's engines were stopped, but nothing could be done until it drifted slowly alongside and passed safely astern, then it was fired on and blown up. As they used to say, it's good to serve on a lucky ship!

The patrols continued, an added backdrop being the sight of Vesuvius in eruption, although the resulting thick layers of fine ash were a considerable problem. Although rumour of an impending change of scenery was rife aboard, *Faulknor* continued to lead a charmed life in the hell of the Anzio beachhead.

Faulknor left Naples for Capri on 28 February, but was recalled to Naples by Captain (D 14), then, at 1730, left again for Capri, remaining until 4 March. Their next job was to escort the LSI *Thruster* to Ajaccio on the west coast of Corsica. It proved another rough voyage. Those that went ashore soon found that the French still harboured deep hatred for anything British. They apparently could not forgive us for humiliating their local lad Napoleon in 1815.

'No welcome for Englishmen here', recorded Ted Newman.

On 6 March they moved to Calvi on the north-west coast, granting leave again, but few bothered to take up the offer. *Faulknor* was again Flotilla Leader and would again become D8's command, having been a 'Private Ship' for exactly less than a month! The 8th Flotilla at this date comprised *Fury*, *Isis*, *Echo* and *Garland*. Of these, *Garland* had been serving with a Polish crew since 1940 and *Echo*, refitting at Malta, was transferred to the Greek Navy on 5 April being renamed *Navarino*.

At Naples on 8 March their new skipper joined. As related, Commander C.G.H. Churchill's, command, *Inglefield*, had been sunk off the Anzio beaches on 25 February, by a radio-controlled bomb. Ginger-bearded Commander Churchill was a 'character' in the full sense of the word, in the days when the Royal Navy, and especially the destroyer service, was full of such. He had a long background in destroyers and flung *Faulknor* around with great panache and verve. When *Inglefield* had sunk she had taken with her all the flotilla files and documents so laboriously compiled over the years and so recently carelessly transferred from *Faulknor* just a few days before! Their replacement subsequently involved the reduced writing staff several months' very hard work.

The two destroyers were very similar in design and age so Commander Churchill was soon at home. 9 March found them back at Capri, and next day, they received a confirmation of the Gibraltar refit, due to commence on 22nd. On 13th they were suddenly ordered to sea for Gaicio, but this was cancelled and instead they escorted LSTs to Bizerta as convoy NV26. They left Capri on 14 March meeting bad weather, which reduced speed to five knots.

Faulknor reached Bizerta on 16th and was due to sail west later escorting convoy MKS 43 to Gibraltar and that refit, but news was received that two ships, *Maiden Creek* and troopship *Dempo*, had been torpedoed in westbound convoy SNF.17, and they were hurried off to take charge of the sub-hunt off Bougie. At 0943 on 17 March, in 37° 05'N, 05° 28'E, the convoy was steering a course of 241° and zigzagging, when a torpedo struck the leading ship of the starboard column, another ship, diagonally in line in the next column was also hit on the starboard side. The attacker was *U-371* (Lt-Commander Mehl). Counter-attacks were launched and continued for many hours.

Faulknor reached, 37° 23′ N, 05° 53′ E, at 0600 on 18th, Commander Churchill taking over co-ordination of the operations, *Catterick* being ordered to join, while the *Mendip* was detached to Algiers. Ted Newman recorded that the whole episode resulted in considerable panic communications-wise. 'I had the busiest time of my life.'

They continued to search around 37° 35′ N, 6° E, for 48 hours. By midday 19th *Faulknor* and her companions had worked their way very close to the enemy. Mehl recorded three destroyers were tracking him, making methodical sweeps up and down their search pattern, occasionally coming very near indeed. He wrote;

> Towards evening they separated from each other. One [*Faulknor*, co-ordinating the box search] stayed to the north, on an east to west patrol, the other two were placed to my east and west on north and south courses.

The destroyers were joined by aircraft, not always helpfully. For example, on the night of the 19th/20th, *Faulknor* had to undergo an aerial attack by one of their own aircraft, so surely becoming the only destroyer to be depth-charged from above!

As Ted Newman succinctly recorded in his diary:

> During the night, one of our own aircraft dropped his depth-charges nearly on us by mistake. Hunt still on, but no sign of the sub.

Carl Heuer also recalled the event vividly:

> I well remember this. I was in the wheelhouse as Quartermaster at the time. It caused quite a stir as they were dropped not far off and shook the ship. There was a lot of shouting down voice pipes to increase the revs and alter course. We could hear Commander Churchill on the bridge going mad and telling the pilot of the aircraft, in no uncertain terms, where to go via the radio contact they had on the bridge to contact aircraft. I have always understood it was the Yanks and not the RAF; I can remember all the lads saying, 'Bloody Yanks again!' and remembering the Anzio incident.

The U.S. Navy's Patrol Squadron VP-63 was certainly operating in the Western Mediterranean in spring of 1944, but it is equally possible that the attack was made by No. 458 Squadron, R.A.F, who certainly made several sightings and attacks during this hunt. This squadron had twenty Canadian officers on its strength and Commander Churchill may have been conversing with one of them. There is no confirmation from either unit's war diary, however.

This air blunder proved a temporary distraction, and did little to alleviate *U-371's* increasingly precarious position. Above her the 'Swamp' operation continued, moving steadily north-west. By 0445 Mehl was recording: – 'The destroyer steering a westerly course [*Faulknor*] has stopped close to our boat' *U-371* was still at Square CH 6858 and Mehl wrote despairingly, ' The destroyer is now above me. I am at 70-metres depth and I cannot go any deeper.'

A tense period of waiting and listening by both hunter and hunted followed. This was shattered at 0512, Mehl reporting that the destroyer had dropped three depth-charges, but they did no great damage. By 0630 Mehl decided it was safe to edge his way out of the trap, steering a course of 270 degrees away from the western edge of the destroyer box above him.

> During the course of the day the three destroyers moved the hunt farther away towards the east and the south.

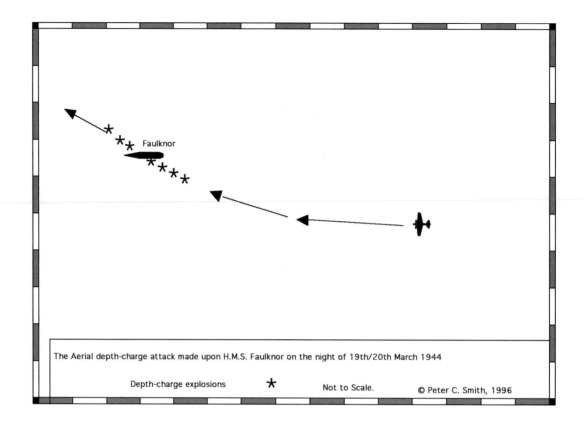

The Aerial depth-charge attack made upon H.M.S. Faulknor on the night of 19th/20th March 1944

Depth-charge explosions ✱ Not to Scale. © Peter C. Smith, 1996

At 1600, *Faulknor* was relieved by *Farndale* who took over while *Catterick* was sent in to refuel. Mehl watched as this took place, '… the three destroyers reunited themselves close by my position, steering course 290° towards the Balearics, exactly as I wished to go. They were at the limit of my detection equipment. If they do not locate me by nightfall I intend to lose myself by steering slowly to the south.'

The hunt was called off at noon, and *Faulknor*, *Farndale*, *Cleveland* and *Cadmus* found an oiler at Algiers before proceeding to Gibraltar, arriving on Wednesday 22 March 1944. It was the end of another chapter and marked the termination of her long and proud career in the Mediterranean.

CHAPTER VII

D-Day to End Game

F*aulknor* lay alongside the dockyard wall in the destroyer pens at Gibraltar until 27 March when her much-heralded refit commenced. A signal dated 2014/25 March stated:

> *Faulknor* taken in hand 27/3. D/C 29/4

On 15 March, Commander Churchill recorded Lieutenant Commander May had, '… returned home for course, to be followed, I hope, by a permanent command. How long I shall stay, I do not know. Some time I hope. The job suits me and *Faulknor* has suffered enough changes lately.'

The crew were not impressed by Gibraltar dockyard, for, although there seemed ample local labour with little or nothing to occupy their time the ship's crew had to undertake most of the work themselves, even when they went into dry-dock on the 22nd. Many of the ship's officers were applying for drafts to other ships, but Churchill refused to allow many ratings to leave the ship. They were not allowed to visit the rest camp and arrangements were made for them to live aboard a troopship in dock close by. They slept aboard her and returned to their ship each day to do the work. Among those who did leave was Sub-Lieutenant Chilcott. Fresh officers joining the ship around this time were Lieutenant R. Stark in December; Lieutenant W. R. Wells, DSC, Lieutenant J. D. L. Scholfield, Lieutenant F. R. Coombes and Lieutenant P. J. Van der Weld, all in January, Temporary Surgeon-Lieutenant T. Smith in April, while Surgeon Lieutenant D. M. Nelson, MB., Bch, RNVR joined in May and Lieutenant B. G. Bond joined at the end of June.

Mr Pavey again:

> Later, when things started to get quiet in the Mediterranean, we were sent to Gibraltar to have a quadruple Pom-Pom put in, which replaced 'Q' 4.7-inch mounting in between the funnels. This conversion took six weeks to complete, lifting the old gun out and installing the new mounting, because the mounting of the 4.7 was utilised for the pom-pom and had to be chiselled down for a few days, in order that the quadruple mounting would fit.
>
> When the great day came to test the pom-pom we went to sea and tested it with blank ammunition. Everything was going well until we elevated the gun and half a blank shell fell on the mounting, luckily missing the gun's crew. What had happened was that a 2 lb shell had hit the wireless aerials, because they had not installed a safety bearing for the new mounting! Anyway, everything was sorted out in the end.
>
> The captain's steward, a dour Scot, was a butler in peace time. The captain had to go ashore to live while the ship had all the jobs done at the Rock. Trouble was that the steward had not had any inoculations done and would *not* have any either! So he remained on board *Faulknor* for this whole period and Commander Churchill had to fend for himself.

The Coat of Arms of the Borough of Stourbridge arrived aboard in February and was fixed to the bulkhead just inside the Quarter Deck lobby. Another welcome present at this time from the same source was a parcel of 1,000 cigarettes.

The refit ended 2 May and three days of sea trials of the new equipment followed. *Faulknor* now carried an impressive array of Naval equipment for such a small ship: in addition to Asdic and Torpedo Tubes, she carried the Type 86 VHF, R/T; M/F D/F plus the new type HF/DF; a Type 650 Jammer (JIG); a Type 285 GA Radar with Yaggi (fishbone) array, a 50 cm wavelength with an $8^1/_2$ mile range for long-range AA gunnery; Type 291 Radar (W.C.) [Combined Air/Surface] with $1^1/_2$ metres wavelength, manually rotated, with 35 miles range, 10,000 ft altitude for air warning and 8/9 miles range surface warning; and the Type 242M Interrogator (IFF) fitted to WC Set S/A Type 'C' Mark II. Her depth charge stowage was now 60.

Again, shore-based personnel were taken to sea during these outings, WRNS, Army and RAF among them. On 5th the local Admiral came aboard *Faulknor* for inspection. He would not deny the buzz that they were headed for home but four hours' privilege leave was granted before they put to sea from the Rock, on 7 May escorting a troopship. Thus *Faulknor* said a final farewell to the Mediterranean Sea whose waters she had known so well in peace and adversity.

Next morning they left the troopships for Scapa with destroyers *Fury*, *Isis* and *Urania*. Commander Churchill was determined to make the trip in record time. The Engine-room staff were ordered to steam the maximum possible speed with the oil fuel available. This was done with precision, but, in the Pentland Firth, they were down to the last thimbleful. With the ship so light, the tumultuous waters of the Firth made the last few miles memorable for *Faulknor* rolled considerably.

HMS Faulknor, *approaching the Rock after trial shoots.* (Author's collection.)

Anchoring at 1800/11 May, they became part of the Home Fleet Destroyer Command. An inspection of the fleet by H.M. King George VI next day saw a party from *Faulknor* told off for the ceremony. This occurred at 1600 aboard Destroyer Depot Ship, *Tyne*. The King graciously insisted that, as they had been away from home for a year, they be given four days leave to see their families before their next great task, widely tipped as the 'Second Front'.

This was the best-organised leave ever. *Faulknor* left Scapa and arrived Rosyth 0800/13 May. A maintenance crew took over while the entire ship's company embarked in a special train from Inverkeithing to Edinburgh, then onward.

Carl Heuer remembers;

> The King asked why our ship's company were wearing white hats. On being told that they had only just returned from the Med, he said, 'See they are given leave'. It must have been an unusual thing for him to do.

Mr Pavey recalled:

> In the end, on conclusion of this work, we sailed for the UK where we were sent to Methyl on the east coast of Scotland where all the ship's company were given four days leave each. On returning to Methyl after our leave we sailed straight away for Scapa Flow. After a few days working up trials we were sent south to Portsmouth.

Leave concluded at midnight 17th and, by 0730 next day, *Faulknor* was back at Scapa conducting a night exercise. A week of training followed, close-range bombarding fire-support predominating. Individually, in company with the flotilla, and with battleships and cruisers of the bombarding force, they trained hard until they were highly proficient. Pinpoint accuracy was the only acceptable standard for which they strove.

Forty-four Home Fleet destroyers were allocated to Operation 'Neptune', twenty-eight being attached to ANCXF (Allied Naval Commander Expeditionary Force – Admiral Sir Bertram Ramsey) as bombarding ships. Between 20 and 30 May, all these destroyers sailed, at first in singles and then in groups, from Scapa Flow south.

Newcomer Surgeon-Lieutenant I. D. M. Nelson, recalled:

> I boarded *Faulknor* on 20 May, 1944. My predecessor Surgeon Lieutenant Rooke had already left. I only read his Journal (quarterly reports to the medical department of the Admiralty) and saw his capable management of the wine cellar of the ship. He had bought Tio-Pepe Sherry at Gibraltar for 2/6d a bottle and we had fifty bottles!
> I was 'hijacked' into helping to paint the ship overall from light Mediterranean camouflage to a different, darker temperate design, all equipment, including old dungarees, being supplied. It was cool work to start with, but I soon warmed with work. I only painted at deck level, ratings were hanging from a plank over the side doing likewise.

With *Fury*, *Isis*, *Undaunted*, *Urania* and *Ursa*, *Faulknor* left Scapa at noon on 24 May, for Portsmouth. Passing Land's End early 26th, they headed up-Channel in thick weather, reducing to ten knots, anchoring off Bembridge, Isle of Wight that evening in warm weather.

On 29th, Commander Churchill wrote to Stourbridge thanking them for the gifts received; books, playing-cards, tobacco and magazines; although a piano accordion, sent to the ship's band at Malta the year before, hadn't arrived. He advised:

I have made the first move towards sending you two old Ensigns that have been flown in battle, and I hope I shall have some luck in that direction.

Exercises continued at heightened pace, 'Abandon Ship' being practised so much by Commander Churchill that many became convinced *Faulknor* was certain to be sunk! Gas masks had to be taken to Action and Abandon-Ship Stations. Churchill recorded how, after mooring in St.Helen's Roads on 30 May, the following six days were fully occupied with meetings aboard *Kempenfelt* with Captain D26, and in correcting and reading nine complete volumes of orders, and these, '.. did not include various odd pamphlets and sets to provide for contingencies that might or might not occur. Nor did it include navigational data and intelligence dope'

Even as late as 2 June, she was listed as 'Attached from the Mediterranean'. Simultaneously they were referred to as 'detached from the Home Fleet ' to Admiral Ramsey's Invasion fleet, a somewhat confused state of affairs. *Faulknor* remained listed as Flotilla Leader, D8, in all the documents.

Surgeon-Lieutenant Nelson noted:

> From one large collection of naval vessels in Scapa Flow, we arrived amidst another vast fleet at Spithead. We were anchored off the Isle of Wight between Seaview and Ryde Pier where we awaited the start of D-Day.
>
> Two memories of those waiting days were interesting. I could not find my naval cap after I had been ashore to HMS *Victory* to replenish medicines. There were so many officers at the buffet for lunch that it got taken by someone else. I could not find one to fit me, so, much to the disgust of the Captain, I arrived back in the ship without one. The Captain quickly sent me ashore again to buy a new one at Gieves in Portsmouth!!
>
> Among the officers of HMS *Faulknor* at this time were Captain C. H. F. Churchill, DSC, RN, Captain; Lieutenant J.B. Burfield, RN, First Lieutenant; Lieutenant Coombes RNVR; Lieutenant Nelson, RNVR; Surgeon Lieutenant I. D. M. Nelson, Medical Officer; Engineer Lieutenant Peter J. Van de Weld RN (a South African); Sub-Lieutenant G. D. L. Scholfield, RN, Navigator; Sub-Lieutenant Grist, RNVR; Midshipmen, De Pass and Mr Knight, the Gunner (a Warrant Officer).
>
> In a ship of destroyer size (160–180 men) an officer or man who was incapacitated for more than a day or two had to be replaced by a healthier one from ashore if that was possible, so my medical duties were not very onerous (excepting casualties from enemy action). So the MO was usually the wine caterer for the twelve officers. This meant seeing that there was adequate spirits and wine for the officers' mess. There was no wine available and in any case then HM Ships seldom drank wine at sea, it was not a national habit then and a small ship had no storage space for it. So it was sherry, port, gin, whisky, brandy and beer with the usual mixtures. Oh, yes, we had lemons and ice!!
>
> The ship was adopted by Trowbridge in Worcestershire and the good ladies of that town sent us knitted scarves, mittens and socks and I got the job of replying for the ratings who had these items given to them, as many of the sailors could really not write the appropriate letter which the Captain felt every man should write, so I helped the poorer spellers.
>
> We were all ready to move off on the night of 4–5 June, but the move was called off because of rough seas and bad weather, so it was postponed 24 hours. For three days previous to departure, no one was allowed ashore and there were strict instructions about letter writing, all the ratings letters were constantly censored by the officers and no hint or suggestion of where we were or what we were doing was countenanced.
>
> The postponement of D-Day by twenty-four hours found *Faulknor*, *Fury* and *Isis* left outside the torpedo nets, and they anchored of Nodes Point, hard by St. Heliers Fort, before we moved across to the beachhead.

Just before we left, the Captain did tell us we were part of the invasion fleet, it had been pretty obvious ever since I joined the ship and he told us that, if necessary, we were expendable!! That news seemed to worry no one as far as I could see.

I went 'to the ready' for dealing with possible casualties. My Sick Berth Attendant remained in the sick bay under the port side of the bridge and I went aft to the wardroom. The sick bay had two berths (bunks) one above the other, a small desk and chair for me to see anyone requiring advice, storage for medicines and a tap and sink. The SBA lived in the sick bay where all the medicines and medical equipment was stored, except for a bag of emergency drugs that I carried with me when in action.

The principal Naval dispositions on the Naval side for D-Day involved landings between St. Vaast la Hougie in the west and River Orne in the east. *Faulknor* was assigned to 'Juno' Beach; part of Bombarding Force E, the sector covering the Courseulles area, centre of British assaults. These beaches were dominated by two large German gun-batteries, Ver sur Mer and Molineaux. Both 'Juno' assault groups, J1 and J2, [3rd (Canadian) Division, and No. 48 Royal Marine Commando, with the 7th and 8th (Canadian) Infantry Groups], were loaded and assembled at Portsmouth and the Solent.

The bombarding ships for 'Juno' were light cruisers *Belfast* and *Diadem*, destroyers, *Faulknor*, *Fury*, *Kempenfelt*, *Venus*, *Vigilant, Bleasdale, Stevenstone, Glaisdale, Alonquin* (Canadian), *Sioux (*Canadian) and *La Combatante* (Free French). Cruisers were allocated the heavy batteries as targets, destroyers assigned the coastal defence positions, each ship also being allocated a set group of targets to be engaged initially from a fixed position approximately two-and-a-half miles offshore. Targets were to be reduced while the landing craft formed up and closed the beaches. The destroyers, each preceded by a minesweeper, were then to weigh anchor close, saturating the beachhead until the troops were safely ashore. They were then to withdraw to protect offshore shipping against expected enemy counter-attacks from sea and air. They were also required to engage selected targets ashore if called upon.

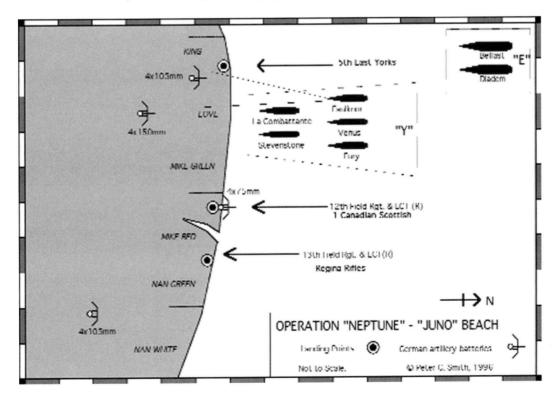

Faulknor was chosen to be the *very first* surface ship[1] in the Invasion of Europe. This enormous honour (*totally* ignored by the many books, TV films, press and media coverage of the 60th Anniversary) fell to her as she was selected to act as guide to the minesweepers to the beachhead to clear the way for the rest of the invasion fleet. She and *Fury* sailed from the Solent on 5 June, 'H-Hour' Minus 18 hours 45 minutes, leading convoy J1, a Minesweeping group, which comprised 9th Minesweeping Flotilla, dan layers and smaller motor minesweepers, whose vital mission was to clear No. 7 Channel southward to the beaches, one of ten such channels from the assembly point Z south-east of the Isle of Wight, known as 'Piccadilly Circus', down 'the Spout' and to the actual assault beaches.

Exact positioning was vital to the success of the whole invasion, so *Faulknor's* navigation was crucial. Having positioned the minesweeping forces exactly as required at H-Hour minus seven hours ten minutes, *Faulknor*, *Sioux* and *Vigilant* reversed course and returned to the Solent, picking up Assault Convoy J3, the leading group of Assault Force 'J' and led them across. Then *Faulknor* and *Fury*, as Group J.10 (b), with the Code Word 'Baronet', reduced speed to five knots on reaching position 'QQ' ready to be led into their bombarding position.

The BYMS each streamed their double-Oropesa sweeps and *BYMS 2052* took station ahead of *Stevenstone* and *La Combattante*, while *BYMS 2055* led in *Venus*, *Faulknor* (Bombarding Ship G. 11) and *Fury*, (Bombarding Ship G.12), sweeping them to position 'LP1', clear of the approach routes, from the lowering position to the ten-fathom line.

On arrival near LP1, *Stevenstone* took station 090° three cables from *La Combattante* with *Venus*, *Faulknor* and *Fury* 1,000 yards astern of them and, at 0640, proceeded at 8 knots towards the beach on a mean course of 210°.

Faulknor's particular target and responsibility were German beach defences west of La Riviere, in the Courseulles sector of 'Neptune'. So, although allocated to 'Juno' beach, *Faulknor* was also instrumental in assisting with her gunfire, the 5th East Yorks ashore in the 'Gold' sector, on 'King' beach.

Faulknor slipped into her firing position and anchored broadside to the coast. At every gun the men stood ready, gun muzzles elevated, locked onto their targets. Ashore there was an absolute, uncanny,

In this photograph, taken from the bridge of HMS Faulknor *at first light on 6 June 1944, British landing-craft can be seen in the background steaming past to land on the Normandy beaches on D-Day. In the centre of the picture is the destroyer HMS* Fury, *while to her left and astern can be seen the 'Hunt' class destroyer HMS* Stevenstone, *with, just visible beyond her bow, the destroyer HMS* Venus. (Dr I.D.M. Nelson.)

silence. The light crept up over the scene, the coastline sprang to life – it was exactly as depicted on the sand models they had been studying for weeks.

At H Hour for Juno beach, 0655, the guns of the bombarding squadron crashed out in one long, unending drum-roll of fire, to which the harsh bark of their own 4.7-inch was duly added. From behind them came the deeper roar of the two cruisers and, farther out, the mighty crashing of the 15-inch guns of battleships *Warspite* and *Ramillies* pounding the Seine batteries.

The Official Report on Juno beach recorded that the naval bombardment, '… proceeded with clockwork precision, in complete accordance with the assault fire plan. Batteries at Beny-sur-Mer and behind Nan White were engaged by *Diadem* and the *Kempenfelt* respectively. On the right *Venus*, *Faulknor*, *Fury*, *Stevenstone* and *La Combattante* engaged beach Sector targets on Mike and Nan Green with direct fire at ranges down to 3,000 yards.'

Surgeon-Lieutenant Nelson recalled:

> …the deep throated roar of the shells from the battleships *Warspite* and *Ramillies* passing overhead towards their targets, the German heavy gun batteries ashore. The memory of the rocket-firing LCTs (long landing craft fitted with up to one hundred rockets) will never be forgotten. The rockets were released together in salvoes and seemed as if they would fall backward, but in a roar and explosive flash, they sped toward France to carpet the shore with high explosive ready for the touchdown of the troops.

Briefly, *Faulknor's* T/S broke down, but all guns continued firing in local control. By then it was quite light and they were able to home in on their targets using a railway station as a guide.

Alfie Pavey, serving as AA II on the new pom-pom between the funnels, recalled that they were anchored close enough for his gun to be allocated its own specific target:

> Our orders were to lay 2,000 yards offshore and to get rid of our ammo by 0800. On our port side lay Free French destroyer *La Combattante*, a Hunt class ship smaller than us, and she was anchored closer in than we were. Our pom-pom was given a specific target, which was some woods near the shore, and we smothered it. It was not long before we were given the order 'Cease Fire'. We were then under order to return at once to Portsmouth and re-ammunition ship.

At 0705, they moved in closer, continually firing. The 'Hunts' with their shallower drafts, were able to proceed 1,000 yards ahead of the 'Fleets' down to within 3,000 yards of the shore, but *Venus* ordered the movements of all five destroyers as he found it necessary for the engaging of requested targets. Four minutes later, *La Combattante*, just ahead of them, reported going aground and both the 'Hunts' went astern until they were some 3,000 yards from the beach, with the 'Fleets' just behind them. Commander Churchill had freedom to shift *Faulknor's* firepower to other targets; provided this assisted the assault, did not endanger our own forces and expenditure of shell was profitable. They had been told, 'The assault will only succeed if the attack is pressed home boldly and resolutely.' All destroyers had been told of the importance of keeping within the limits of the Fire Support Area itself to avoid hampering the movements of the incoming landing-craft or obscuring the view of destroyers in adjacent areas like 'Gold'.

They were to restrict average rate of ammunition expenditure to two rounds-per-gun per-minute until H Minus 40, when the rate of fire increased to four rounds-per-gun per-minute as they engaged the pre-arranged targets during the final stage of the Assault. While the other destroyers could only expend 40% of their ammunition during the Assault, with the remaining 60% being then available for indirect fire support later, *Faulknor* had a special mission and dispensation to leave early, so she could fire off as much as she wished.

Thus, they continued to fire into allocated targets until the first wave of landing-craft touched down, before shifting to strong-points on the flanks. The enemy batteries replied with 'intermittent fire' from 0735, doing no damage. Close Liaison with the troops ashore was absolutely essential. The safety of the soldiers, (which, in *Faulknor's* own particular case, were the 5th East Yorks and the 'K' Canadian Scottish, of the 3rd (Canadian) Division, landing on 'Mike Green' beach at H plus 45) depended on the effectiveness of the destroyers 'Drenching Fire' in obliterating as many defence positions as possible.

To ensure this went smoothly *Faulknor* had the Bombardment Liaison Officer (BLO) Number 66, aboard, Captain F. W. Sharman, R.A. He operated on 3796 Kc/s (Jig 3). *Faulknor's* W/T Call Sign on BCW and FOB Waves, was 'YEM', while her R/T Call Sign on the VHF Wave was 'Morbid'. At her closest point *Faulknor* was able to engage targets up to 15,000 yards inland, sufficient to cover the initial invasion waves. Although heavy enemy fire initially pinned down the 5th East Yorks, they took their primary objectives 'with the judicial use of naval gun-fire'. La Riviere had fallen by 0900.

Faulknor then transferred her fire to aid her Canadians. Initial direct fire was at 3,000 yards range to cover the advance to 'Yew' line. Force Commander signalled the bombardments were, 'carried out in complete accordance with the fire plan'.

At 0739, the destroyers shifted target to 'Love' beach, again with good results, ceasing fire at 0803. Commander Churchill stated:

> We were lucky enough to have a front seat in the stalls at the landing on the Normandy coast on 'D' Day and to take part in the preliminary bombardment. A very spectacular and enjoyable entertainment. The more so because it was about 99$\frac{1}{2}$ % safe as far as we were concerned.

This vital job complete, *Faulknor* moved out to sea, picking her way carefully through the swarms of incoming vessels and floating debris. At 1000 they went alongside HQ ship *Hilary* embarking both Official Naval and BBC's correspondents' despatches for home.

At noon they secured alongside at Portsmouth, re-ammunitioning and cleaning up the ship in readiness for a V.I.P. of the highest order.

Seen from HMS Faulknor *off 'Juno' Beach at Normandy on D-Day, 6 June 1944. LCIs (in foreground) circle under guard of an MTB, while behind them more LCTs arrive off the beaches.* (Raymond Johnson.)

How did D-Day appear to *Faulknor's* crew?
Carl Heuer:

> We left Scapa sailing down the North Sea and arriving at Portsmouth on 2 June, making our way through the masses of shipping to anchor off Seaview. We sailed on the evening of the 4 June, but as the weather was so rough, were recalled. On the evening of the 5th we sailed with minesweepers acting as their escort and guide to the areas off the invasion beaches to be swept. On arriving we left the minesweepers to their dangerous job and steamed to meet the main invasion convoys. So many ships – an amazing sight. Arriving off the beaches we were in the line nearest to the shore, broadside to the beach. At 0530 the bombardment commenced. All our 4.7-inch guns were firing – the noise was terrific as all the cruisers and battleships lying further offshore opened up. Having been in the Italian landings we were used to bombarding but this was something out of this world. It continued for an hour after which we moved further out to sea. As the masses of landing craft came in loaded with troops – what a sight – some of them came under heavy fire. At about 1000 we proceeded to the command ship, picking up BBC and newspapers' war correspondents' reports. We were ordered to Portsmouth.

Raymond Johnson:

> Our sighting points at Normandy were water towers and church steeples at Courseulles (Calvados) and nearby. We hit anything that moved.

Mr Pavey:

> When the time came for the invasion of France we were sent to lie off the Isle of Wight until the time came for us to get under weigh. We sailed the night before escorting the mine sweepers and when we were over the other side our orders were to lie 200 yards offshore and get rid of our ammo by 0700.
>
> Our new pom-pom was given a target, which was some woods near the shoreline and it was not long before we had dealt with that and the order was given 'Cease Fire'. Another part of our duties was to proceed back to Pompey on completion of firing where we were told a party from the barracks would be sent aboard to re-ammunition the ship.
>
> On our way back to Portsmouth we were closed up on the pom-pom and, looking down the starboard side there was a party of ratings and officers carrying out the task of burying bodies at sea. After getting back to Portsmouth the ship was got ready to return to France as soon as possible, but then we were told to hang on for a while as we were having some passengers aboard.

The burial party was consigning to the deep the bodies of Stoker J. Holmes, of *LCT 517* and Signalman S. A. Setchell, of HMS *Mickleburg*, two injured men from damaged warships with no MOs of their own, transferred to *Faulknor* for urgent medical treatment, but who had died aboard despite all efforts. Surgeon-Lieutenant Nelson remembered:

> I had to deal with two badly wounded sailors brought aboard from a landing craft that had been hit during the invasion, both had multiple shrapnel wounds. Holmes was practically dead and died on being brought aboard and I worked on the other for two

hours including putting up a saline drip, but he too died of shock and multiple wounds. They were both buried at sea in the English Channel.

Carl Heuer told me:

> Under special orders we threaded our way through the massive armada of ships. One landing craft with two wounded ratings came alongside and asked if we could take them aboard as we carried an MO. This was quickly done and we were soon gathering speed on our way to Pompey. Sorry to say both ratings died and about noon hands not on duty were piped aft for burial at sea. A sad occasion but once more we were soon on our way and in the early afternoon Pompey came in sight. As we entered harbour a group of Wrens stood on the breakwater waving.

There was not much time to spare as Surgeon-Lieutenant Nelson recalled:

> We arrived in Pompey about midday re-ammunitioned and cleaned ship. We were met by various Senior Officers wanting news. One Surgeon Captain and two Surgeon Commanders came to me, expecting dire news of heavy casualties, and I remember they were amazed at how few we had taken. We were all tired. I retired to my cabin soon after dinner and was practically asleep when I was awakened by the Sick Berth Attendant knocking on my cabin door (it was of sliding mahogany wood). All he said was the Captain wished me to close the bar as some VIPs were coming aboard.
>
> Lieutenant-General B. L. Montgomery and his staff came aboard and he occupied the Captain's day cabin, and his staff took over the wardroom. I remember there was a Brigadier and other senior Army officers, as well as an American and British Signalman, complete with 'back pack' signal equipment with antennae waving in the breeze. These latter stayed on deck – fortunately the weather was fine.

Montgomery was piped aboard *Faulknor* by A.B. Raymond Matthews. At 1730, they sailed back to the beachhead. It was a calm night and 'Monty' spent time on the bridge chatting to the Captain. After a quiet crossing they arrived off the French coast.

Carl Huer:

> We proceeded up harbour to our buoy, the first warship to return from the invasion beaches to the UK. As soon as we were secured to the buoy the oiler and ammunition lighters came alongside to replenish our depleted tanks and magazines. The ship was cleaned when I came on duty at six. As Duty Quartermaster I was told by the Officer of the Watch to report as soon as a barge appeared from shore, which I did, wondering who was in it. The Captain appeared on the quarterdeck. As the barge came alongside I was amazed to see the famous beret of Field Marshal Montgomery with his staff. They quickly came aboard. As the last one disappeared below I was ordered to pipe special sea duty men to their stations and duty watch prepare for sea. I filled in details in the log and took it with me to the wheelhouse.
>
> The cable was slipped from the buoy and as the motor boat was hoisted in on the davits we were under weigh, gathering speed to leave harbour on our way back to the beaches. On the way the ship was closed up to action stations. My job was action quartermaster. On having been relieved on the wheel by the coxswain I was asked to get cocoa for the bridge. On taking it to the bridge. Monty was there and he was initiated to Navy Kai! On

being handed it he asked, 'What do you do – eat or drink it?' as, by tradition, it is made so thick.

Surgeon-Lieutenant Nelson remembered:

> I was very busy the whole time Montgomery was aboard, deciphering signals mainly for the General and repeated to *Faulknor*. The signals were almost all about firepower required along the beachhead and I delivered some of them to the bridge where the Captain and the General were. Also on the bridge was Captain Wolgan, RA a fleet bombardment army officer that we carried at this time, as well as the Officer of the Watch, yeoman of signals and a signalman.
>
> I carried the signal form on a clipboard and was required to let the Captain see it first of all. He slowly brought out his half-moon spectacles and read it and then passed it to Montgomery with the remark – 'It's for you.' I was only called to aid the deciphering staff of a rating and a Sub-Lieutenant because of their heavy workload. It was the only time the decipher staff was overloaded although I helped them at a more leisurely pace at other times.

One post-war historian gives a very different account of this journey across the Channel. According to Alistair Horne.[2]

> Monty promptly retired to his bunk, giving Henderson [Captain Johnny Henderson, Montgomery's *Aide-de-Camp*] the instruction, 'Wake me up at 6 a.m. – report on the battle'. Early the next morning an extremely anxious destroyer captain called Churchill, described by Ray BonDurant [Captain Ray BonDurant, an American, another of Montgomery's ADCs] as a 'red-bearded young man who looked pretty rugged', confessed to Henderson that in the huge mêlée of ships, he was lost and drifting. Suddenly an American battleship loomed up: the *Faulknor* had floated down right off Cherbourg Peninsular!

'Drifting' and 'floating' to most people would indicate loss of engine power in which case *Faulknor* would have been in serious trouble, and would certainly explain her being out of position. BonDurant, and also, seemingly, Horne, obviously had not the remotest idea that *Faulknor* had been one of the key navigation ships for the whole vast operation the day before and would not normally have got 'lost' without there being a serious reason.

Neither Montgomery, nor crewmembers that were present make any mention of such an incident. Mr Pavey:

> That was when Monty and all his Staff took passage. On arriving on the other side again, all Monty's Staff went ashore by landing craft and he stayed aboard for a couple of days. We used to steam up and down the beachhead, Monty strolling up and down the port side. Then we closed the minelayer *Apollo* where Ike was aboard and Monty went aboard to talk to him, staying awhile before returning to *Faulknor*.

Carl Huer, who was on the bridge that night, states that these stories were nonsense:

> Monty did not retire 'immediately', it was almost midnight. Captain Churchill did not 'get lost', we were never 'adrift' and there was **NO** American battleship in sight from our bridge.

Montgomery recorded events thus:

> I sailed at 9.30 that evening in the destroyer HMS *Faulknor* (Captain C. F. H. Churchill, RN) which was standing by to take me across. On the morning of June 7th, 1944, which was D+1, HMS *Faulknor* arrived with me off the beaches and then proceeded westwards into the American area … we located USS *Augusta* in which was General Bradley … HMS *Faulknor* then returned to the British sector and we located HMS *Scylla* and HMS *Bulolo*. General Dempsey and Admiral Vian came on board the *Faulknor*. Then Eisenhower and Admiral Ramsey arrived in the latter's flagship, and I went on board and had a talk with them.

Surgeon-Lieutenant Nelson confirmed:

> Various senior officers were around in various ships so *Faulknor* went over to the American sector where General Omar Bradley was aboard the US cruiser *Augusta*. Monty went aboard the cruiser for a talk and *Faulknor* then returned to the British sector where the HQ ships *Scylla* and *Bulolo* were lying, and from them General Miles Dempsey and Admiral Philip Vian came aboard *Faulknor*. Vian was always a rude man, he practically pushed me off the deck as he sped along to see Montgomery.

Lt. General Bernard Montgomery (centre) talking to Commander Churchill (left) on the bridge of HMS Faulknor *off the Normandy beachhead, 6.30 to 7 a.m, 8 June 1944.* (R.E. Fairweather.)

While Monty was aboard he shared 'Kai', navy cocoa, in the wheelhouse with the OOW. Monty said it was 'Marvellous Stuff'. He could not understand the Yeoman's Semaphore as the Navy worked at twice the speed of army signallers. At one time they had Admiral Ramsey aboard as well. Eventually they found the LCT with Monty's caravan on board.

Faulknor had been placed at Monty's disposal and, at his request; they sailed westward at first light on 7 June, to the American sector where General Bradley was afloat in the heavy cruiser *Augusta*. Monty went aboard the US ship, while the *Faulknors* exchanged insults and jokes with their opposite numbers. The waters of the beaches resembled an upturned anthill, full of small craft, and farther out some American destroyers were busy shelling a target inland. Everyone seemed in good spirits and the weather was fair.

After a long discussion, the General re-boarded *Faulknor* and they returned to the British sector, securing alongside AA cruiser *Scylla* which was acting as Admiral Philip Vian's flagship. From her, and from HQ ship *Bulolo* close-by, Admiral Vian and General Dempsey co-ordinated operations afloat and ashore; both men came aboard *Faulknor* for talks in her wardroom. The crew, who felt that their small destroyer was gradually becoming a floating Whitehall, swore that she would eventually sink under the sheer weight of brass embarked. But there was much more to come.

Montgomery wrote that the round-the-Fleet trips aboard *Faulknor*:

> … were delightful; there was plenty to look at, ships everywhere, and blockships and artificial harbours starting to arrive.

Things were still going well ashore, initial gains being briskly consolidated, and with the departure of Vian and Dempsey, Monty was transferred to minelayer *Apollo* to confer with General Dwight Eisenhower and Admiral Sir Bertram Ramsey. This was followed by a quick trip back to *Augusta,* where General Omar Bradley and his Chief of Staff came aboard for further discussions. These concluded, they returned alongside *Scylla* at 2030.

> Some time later the American General Omar Bradley had a meeting with Monty. On another occasion Admiral Vian came aboard to see him. As you know, we ran aground; Monty wanted to get nearer to the beach and he couldn't have got nearer than that! He didn't hang about after that, requesting to go ashore. Having lost our Asdic dome, we were sent to Southampton to have a patch put over the hole until we could be fitted with another.

Another eyewitness recalled:

> We arrived off the beaches in the early hours of the 7 June. As soon as it was light, and the ship was at Monty's disposal, we started the rounds of the command ships. There was so much top brass aboard it was unbelievable. On the 8th at about 0630 Monty wanted to go closer inshore. The Captain took us very close and unfortunately we ran aground. There we were, a sitting duck! A landing craft was signalled to come alongside to take Monty and his staff ashore and we were left to be towed off by another landing craft. Upon inspection it was found that the Asdic dome was torn off. We were ordered back to Pompey for repairs, dry-docked and given leave, but it didn't last.

Field-Marshal Montgomery and his aides leave the temporarily grounded HMS Faulknor *aboard the American landing-craft 3T9-4 G to land on the Normandy beaches on D+2.* (Dr. I.D.M. Nelson.)

Monty was obviously itching to join his troops, giving instructions that he would like to be put ashore at 0700 the following morning. Therefore, at 0600, Captain Churchill began edging *Faulknor* toward the beach, Monty having insisted on getting as close to *terra firma* as possible before disembarking. Despite the utmost care *Faulknor* went aground with a shudder about two cables from the beach. They could have hardly got any closer and the General, undismayed, signalled for a landing craft to come and fetch him, jauntily waving farewell as he clambered unaided into it, his poor ADC, laden down with maps and gear, following more precariously in his wake.[3]

Their guest safely ashore, they concentrated on getting afloat again, being hard fast. A tug was signalled for and duly arrived, only to run aground herself. Evidently the charts for the area were not as accurate as thought. Captain Churchill was still pondering his next move when he was hailed by the crew of an American landing craft which, with a couple of companions, bobbed up alongside, asking if they could, '…get you out of a hole, bud?' This cheerful bunch was as good as their word and, while the stranded tug's crew looked on, soon had *Faulknor's* stern pulled round until she floated off.

After thanking them, a damage control party was sent below and later reported that, once more, *Faulknor* had lost her Asdic dome – this was becoming almost a traditional result of helping the Army! The damage to the hull meant constant monitoring and they had to keep the pumps going day and night while on patrol.

Just before midnight they found the upturned hull of a capsized 'Chant' petrol carrier in Area 'Pike' which was an obvious danger to the congested shipping lanes. After reporting their intentions, *Faulknor* proceeded to shell it. Pumping 4.7-inch salvoes into the wreck resulted in a satisfactory eruption of flame and fire as her cargo duly ignited. While thus engaged, at 2324, Captain (D.26) in *Kempenfelt*, who had just assumed the duties of Captain Patrols, Eastern Task Force, relieving Captain (D.23) observed them.

Kempenfelt had been busy re-organising patrols when, at 0251, reports started to come in of an enemy destroyer flotilla trying to break through to the beachhead. Four German destroyers from Brest, *Z.32*, *Z.24*, *ZH.1* and *T.24*, had indeed sortied out after nightfall.

What followed was, in the words of *Kempenfelt's* CO, '… not clear, owing to the confused enemy reports and congestion on the patrol waves. It was plain at the time and from subsequent reports, that ships were missing many signals …' This led to another meeting between the two destroyers at 0302, as *Venus* and *Stevenstone* moved out to the west at high speed to intercept the enemy and *Kempenfelt* also retraced her course to do likewise. *Faulknor*, having despatched the wreck, had anchored to make another check on her leaking plates. What happened next in the darkness and the confusion are best described in the words of *Kempenfelt's* report:

> I moved out to engage the enemy, and, finding an unexpected destroyer *with two funnels* [All the German ships were two funnelled ships, most of the more modern British destroyers from the J Class onward, were singled-funnelled], *Kempenfelt* was on the verge of engaging her when she was identified as *Faulknor*. She was then ordered to follow, and was found to be at anchor in this curious and unauthorised position. No explanation has been obtained for this unorthodox and tiresome action.

Obviously *Kempenfelt* was unaware of *Faulknor's* damaged state. Despite her condition, Commander Churchill duly complied, taking station astern and steering to reinforce the other two destroyers, ordered at 0311 by the Naval Commander, Eastern Task Force, to counter-attack in Area Tunny. Two minutes later Vian signalled to the British destroyers that all coastal forces were clearing the area to give destroyers free rein to engage any targets encountered. At 0320 HQ ship *Largs* reported an unidentified destroyer north of Sword beach steering north-west and, two minutes later tension continued to rise when *Largs* reported a surface craft five miles north-east of Sword beach. *Kempenfelt* and *Faulknor* altered course to 110° at 0332 and went to twenty knots.

At 0334, the enemy flotilla's position was reported as 227° Cap D'Antifer, nineteen miles, steering east. *Kempenfelt* ordered *Venus* not to enter Area Tunny South but, at 0340, they obtained radar contact on a bearing of 075°, range 11,200 yards. At 0344, *Venus* was ordered to counter-attack ignoring the earlier signal not to enter the area. One minute later they achieved radar contact down to 5,900 yards from *inside* the minefield and *Venus* requested position of the enemy and of *Stevenstone*. At 0351, *Kempenfelt* and *Faulknor* had *Venus* in sight to the north-west and proceeded to her support. It all ended in an anti-climax, for, in the glare of searchlights from *Venus* and star-shells from *Kempenfelt*, all they could see were three radar balloons, laid out by 2nd Cruiser Squadron earlier to assist bombarding ships. Captain D. 26 reported. 'No enemy destroyers in area. Position 226°, CAF 19, course 250° 20 knots, *Venus, Faulknor* and *Stevenstone* in company. Enemy, three barrage balloons.'

The flotilla was now on the very edge of the Scallops minefield, and so, in the absence of the enemy, *Kempenfelt* and *Faulknor* returned to their original holding position, anchoring in 49° 26' N, 0° 29' W, while *Venus* and *Stevenstone* resumed their patrols.

The German destroyers got nowhere near the beaches, being intercepted off Ile de Bas by the 10th Flotilla, who sank, *Z.32* and *ZH.1*, and badly damaged *Z.24*.

Faulknor returned to Portsmouth on Friday 9 June, with *Fury, Vigilant, Urchin, Scourge* and Norwegian *Stord*, the first three ships re-ammunitioning and returning to the assault area with *Kelvin, Undaunted* and *Undine*.

On Saturday 10th, *Faulknor* returned to Portsmouth with *Fury, Kelvin, Ulster, Undine, Undaunted, Venus, Vigilant* and Canadian *Alonquin*. *Faulknor's* hull was examined and, on 11th, repaired by the dockyard. The dockers cut off the damaged Asdic dome, plating over the hole as a temporary measure, pending full replacement later. Her propellers also needed attention. The crew were given leave while this was done. They later learned they had been scheduled to take Winston Churchill to France, but he had to switch to destroyer *Kelvin*. It was a pity but, after all, he had already taken passage aboard *Faulknor* once.

Faulknor could not initially play her full part as a Fleet Destroyer until her Asdic dome was replaced; but temporarily she could not be spared; nor could a suitable dockyard be found, for the South Coasts yards were full, repairing damaged landing-craft. Therefore duringg the following weeks they continued with evening and night patrols, and, in between, acted as 'Despatch Boat' for VIPs visiting the beaches.

Faulknor's routine was to leave her anchorage off Lee Tower up-harbour, embarking her distinguished passengers off Clarence Pier around 1400. They sailed to the beachhead, cruised up and down for a time, returning to Pompey late afternoon. Defensive patrols were different; the Luftwaffe would sneak in at dusk, hiding amidst the streams of Allied aircraft constantly criss-crossing the area, to make torpedo-bomber and dive-bombing attacks. Because the many friendly aircraft swamped the radar screens, this type of attack proved difficult to counter.

> We were then used as a despatch boat, taking all types of officers over to France, returning each evening to Pompey and then following the same routine the next day. On one trip we took about eleven admirals or senior officers who were responsible for various stores. We also took over a crowd of Free French officers where they remained.

On Friday 16 June *Faulknor* went alongside *Tyne* at Portsmouth, to effect repairs to her training receiver and, next day Admiral Sir Charles Little, C-in-C Portsmouth, embarked for passage to the Assault Area, returning the same day. The weather was good and so mild that the Admiral fell asleep in a deck-chair on the quarterdeck!

On 18 June a large party of VIPs embarked; four Admirals, headed by Admiral Sir Bertram H. Ramsay, ANCXF, and his staff, two Vice-Admirals (including William James of the famous Pear

Soap 'Bubbles' advert) and Lord Reith, Head of the BBC. They were conveyed to France, *Faulknor* returning to her anchorage the same evening. Next day *Faulknor* was taken in hand for defects, her No. 1 boiler room and port fan being examined. Yet more top brass arrived aboard, Admiral Sir Bruce Fraser and his staff taking passage. *Faulknor* was back in Portsmouth next day. Another sortie due on the 20th was postponed because of severe storms in the Channel, C-in-C Portsmouth's signal timed 0741/20 June confirming:

> Sailing postponed four hours.

On 21 June, *Fury*, faithful companion in so many hard-fought battles, was mined off the beaches, but *Faulknor's* own amazing luck continued to hold out, and her charmed life in the front line continued. Off the storm-wracked beaches Captain D.26 aboard *Kempenfelt* signalled to Admiral Vian aboard *Scylla*:

> Please let me know in good time if you are going to move. I must go to patrol anchorage to look after my trawlers, who have no anchors, no coal, no water, no food, no instructions. Situation impossible.

Vian replied:

> Avoid being eaten, help is coming. We shall remain here as far as I know until arrival of COs in *Faulknor*.

That same morning, the Chief of Staff to ANCFX, Commodore J. ('Jock') Hughes-Hallett, embarked in *Faulknor* with his entourage. The weather was still very rough and the great man was very sick, as indeed were a number of naval ratings. At 1230 *Faulknor* went alongside *Scylla*, the Commodore transferring for a conference, returning aboard at 1555 when they returned to Portsmouth. Another brief visit to the dockyard for yet more repairs, this time to the ships ladders, followed.

On 24 June, D + 18, the assault phase ended, control of the British Assault Area being transferred ashore. At 0830, the First Lord of the Admiralty, The Rt. Hon. Albert Alexander, the Second Sea Lord, Vice-Admiral Sir Algernon Willis, Naval Secretary, Lord Bruntisfield and Lord Beaverbrook, all embarked in *Faulknor* at Portsmouth. Surgeon-Lieutenant Nelson recorded:

> I was aft in the wardroom (my station when at sea), when the phone rang and it was the Captain. – ' Doc, could you come to the bridge'. Without knowledge of why I was requested, I reported to the bridge – Alexander had a smut in his eye! He was a man of approximately sixty years of age with large sagging, lower eyelids. I was just about to bung a clean handkerchief out of my battledress pocket to extract the 'foreign body' and I pulled down his lower eyelid and a piece of grit fell out onto his cheek. Much relief for Alexander and from the Captain, 'Good Show, Doc!' How well you remember details when 'operating' in public!

Their visitors transferred to HQ ship *Hilary* before inspecting Arromanches and the various British beach sectors. Whilst they were aboard, *Faulknor* had the rare distinction of flying the Flag of the Board of Admiralty at her masthead. The party returned to Portsmouth, *Faulknor* securing alongside at 2215.

Faulknor spent that night and next day at anchor, but closed up because V-1 'Doodlebugs' were being aimed at Portsmouth and Spithead to disrupt the Allied supply flow, ineffectively. That same night German E-boats from Alderney tried to attack the anchorage but were intercepted by Canadian destroyers *Chaudiere* and *Gatineau*. *Faulknor* went to Action Stations and prepared to intercept, but was not, in the end, required. She sailed for the beaches again on 26th, returning to Portsmouth on 30th.

Faulknor remained the sole representative of the flotilla, [and was still listed as D.8 on 3 July] and, on 7 July embarked the Free-French General Joseph Koenig, the defender of Bir Hakeim; together with his staff, for passage to Cherbourg. Captain Churchill wrote of General Koenig:

> When one recalls his light heartedness and laughter, one realises he can have had no doubts as the successes that his forces were upon the eve of achieving.

This view was reinforced by Surgeon-Lieutenant Nelson who remembered that, in strict contrast to Vian, Koenig was, '…polite and saluted me. When he repeated the salute I spoke to him and asked why he had saluted me? He said 'You are a Staff Officer (the red Medical Officer's tab on my shoulders denoting Surgeon Lieutenant were slightly akin to the red tabs worn by senior Army staff officers). 'No, Sir, I am the ship's doctor', I replied. 'Better still' was Koenig's instant response!

To replace the Asdic dome and affect other repairs, *Faulknor* sailed for the Humber on Saturday 8 July arriving at Grimsby 10th, the crew receiving fourteen days leave. *Faulknor* was beginning to show the effects of five years of almost non-stop running; no longer the sleek, purring flotilla leader of 1939, but a salt-caked, rust-speckled veteran with more than one honourable scar. However, as Commander Churchill noted when writing to Miss Eileen Moody on 19 June:

> I hope we ain't dead yet!!

The occasion was the enclosing of two of *Faulknor's* Battle-Ensigns flown in battle, as tokens of thanks to the people of Stourbridge. Churchill added:

> I wish they were not quite so old and grubby but you cannot have it both ways. They must be either Ensigns that have been flown in battle, in which case they will be old and worn and dirty from funnel smoke, or else they would be comparatively new ones that have probably only been flown in harbour on Sundays, if at all!

Requests for photographs of the ship foundered on the wall of Civil Service immobility.

> All such things have to be acquired 'officially' these days. A bit of a farce with an old destroyer. It wouldn't make two pennyworth of difference to the war if I took out a camera now and sent a photo of her straight to Hitler …

Fortunately for posterity a photograph *was* taken of *Faulknor* a few months later, and, after a forty-year hunt, made available to the author by Surgeon-Lieutenant Nelson, so we know her exact appearance in the last year of the war.

Rowland Fairweather recalled:

> I joined HMS *Faulknor* on 13 July, 1944 when the ship was in dry-dock at Grimsby. When I arrived aboard *Faulknor* only a skeleton crew was on board, most of the men were on leave.

Ginger-bearded Captain Churchill frequently conned his ship in or out of dockyards unaided, using his engines and ringing down the revs to the engine room, which drove them frantic. Unfamiliar with Grimsby, his attempt to back *Faulknor* out of dock resulted in the propeller striking some submerged obstruction. The damage was not considered serious, but subsequently a marked vibration and shaking occurred around eighteen knots; below or above that, it was not noticeable.

Faulknor reached Portsmouth on 22 July, sailing again on 23rd escorting monitor *Erebus* to her firing position off Caen where she conducted bombardments with the Dutch gunboat *Flores*. *Faulknor* patrolled off the beaches overnight as Senior Officer of the various 'Sturgeon' patrols, designed to protect the Inner 'Trout Line' of armed landing craft protecting the exposed northern flank of the landing area in Seine Bay against German human torpedo ['Marders'], explosive motor boats and E-boats

Between 2315/23rd and 0515/24 July, *Faulknor*, as Captain Patrols, had destroyer *Cottesmore* with her on one leg of the patrol, while *Goathland* and *Quorn* took the other, each pair patrolling a four-mile line, at a speed of eleven knots, three cables apart between 49° 37.6′ N and 00° 17′ W. At 0423, in 49° 36.5′ N, 00° 19′ W. While altering course under her zigzag, *Goathland* set off a ground mine that detonated under her quarterdeck and lifted the ship several feet. Both the engines and the W/T were put out of action, as was most of her electrical equipment. Fortunately her hull remained intact and there was no loss of life. *Quorn* took her in tow, while *Faulknor* protected them until daylight and, before returning to Portsmouth, signalled *Goathland* at 0527:

> Am leaving *Cottesmore* to escort you.

Faulknor was back on 'Sturgeon' patrol again next night, coupled with AA watch by day, on the 24/25 July and 25th/26th. Supply Petty-Officer Corrigan left this poetic reflection on *Faulknor's* patrol duties off the beachhead.

Normandy Patrol

> The darkened ship glides slowly through the night,
> Dull grey, lean, panther-like –
> Her weary crew, grows sleepy as the hours creep by.
> From east to west, from darkness into light,
> A vigilance she keeps, 'Patrolling Area Two'
> And all is calm and stars laugh in the sky,
> And red-rimmed lids commence to droop over bloodshot eyes,
>
> Down to the south, on land, men fight and die,
> But here, detached and quiet, the hours creep by.

Surgeon-Lieutenant Nelson remembered:

> On July 24th we were over to the beachhead again. The artificial harbour was in good shape and equipment was regularly going ashore and some ships' officers were also allowed to go ashore. Lieutenant Nelson RNVR (a Londoner) and I went ashore at Courseulles in the afternoon. Walking up a street from the shore at Courseulles-sur-mer we were approached by a jeep with a Marine driver and a Royal Marines Major. The Major was a local Provost Marshal and through his megaphone shouted, 'Will the naval officers *not* walk in the middle of the road!' It turned out to be Sid Hill who, as a Captain R.M., I had known in the Middle East. 'Hello Doc', he said on recognising me, 'what are you doing here?' I replied I was a ship's doctor from a destroyer offshore. At once he said, 'Have you got any booze then?' 'Yes, what do you want?' It was arranged that I return to the ship bring some alcoholic supplies and 'dine' with the Marine Provost

Artist William McDowell's impression of HMS Faulknor's *Ju.88 kill off the Normandy beaches, 26 July 1944.* (*Sphere*, via Bill Silltow.)

Officers in their 'Mess' – a tent in a nearby field'. He gave us a quick run amongst the Normandy hedgerows, breached where our tanks had crashed through. I remember seeing a large bloated cow lying dead in a field, but no Germans. So we returned to the *Faulknor* and I duly went ashore later, was collect by Sid with a kitbag of whisky, gin and sherry for his mess. This was paid for at *Faulknor's* Mess prices and the R.M. Provost Mess was delighted! I was the only officer of my ship to 'dine' in Normandy.

Sid Sibley recalled one occasion when *Faulknor* dropped anchor in the Solent without the cable! Sub-Lieutenant F. Grist (who had joined the crew from *Echo* on 14 February 1944) insisted that Sid had knocked the slip too late, then looked over the side to see if he could see it! What the Skipper called the Lieutenant cannot be repeated! The old lady was also beginning to feel her age and hard-running a bit by now. On one AA patrol there was too much weigh on the ship and she refused to answer her helm. The captain had to be called and Robby Robinson had to be sent to the after steering position to rectify the situation.

Just before sunset on 26 July, the Luftwaffe mounted a determined torpedo-bomber attack against patrolling warships with twelve Junkers Ju.88s. They scored no hits and two were lost. One fell to *Faulknor's* guns, her second *confirmed* Junkers Ju 88 kill of the war. This plane deliberately selected *Faulknor* as a target, but fortunately the ship's lookouts were alert. Captain Churchill brought *Faulknor's* bows head-on to the Ju.88 in the usual manner and the bombs all exploded in the sea clear of the ship. The aircraft, in pulling out of its attack dive, had to cross low over the ship, and was duly engaged by the starboard short-range weapons and one round from the 4.7-inch gun. As the Junkers pulled up over the ship's mast he was raked all along the length of his belly by a double burst from both the bridge-wing Oerlikon gunners, who could hardly have missed. As the sun went down, the German bomber followed it, hard hit and on fire, and was clearly seen to crash half a mile away in an extremely satisfying manner. *Faulknor's* sole casualty from this splendid little action was the

Captain, who, in his eagerness to congratulate his gunners, leaned over the bridge and grabbed the hot barrel of the Oerlikon for support!

During a lull in attacks they steered toward the wreckage looking for survivors. They had got one man inboard when another bomber attacked them and they had to get under weigh in a hurry, leaving the rest in the water. After the second attack had been avoided, another survivor firing his pistol to attract their attention drew them back. They lowered the ship's whaler, shone lights and eventually he was found and dragged aboard.

'We managed to shoot down a Junkers Ju.88', recalled Mr Fairweather, 'and we took the pilot and his navigator prisoners during one of our sorties over there'.

Commander Churchill related:

> It happened during a torpedo attack on our patrols one moonlight night. One bird so misjudged his attack that he failed to get his torpedo off and in his manoeuvring got close enough to give our short-range weapons a chance. He crashed in the sea about half a mile away and we picked up two rather objectionable Nazis.
>
> As a result of this attack we suffered one slight casualty. About twenty minutes after the incident one very stupid man, who is quite old enough to know better – to wit the Captain – put his hand on the hot muzzle of the starboard foremost Oerlikon and burnt himself. He has kept the fact discreetly to himself until this moment but feels the joke is too good to let pass altogether.

Surgeon-Lieutenant Nelson related:

> The aircraft went down in flames and at the command, 'Away sea boat's crew' off went the motor boat to bring back two Germans. One was tall, one was small, the latter with a severe laceration of his skull. As the motorboat was being hoisted inboard the Chief Engine Room Artificer (a Chief Petty Officer) quietly reached down and took the revolver from the pouch of one of the Germans. I was near him – I had been alerted because of the head wound, and said, 'You did that neatly, Chief.' His reply was, 'Got to keep your eyes open, Sir!'
>
> The injured German was Uffz Horst Winkler from Leipzig. (He had originally been in the fur trade pre-war). The other German was truculent (a true Nazi). He was stripped off and locked in the officer's bathroom and a guard was mounted outside the door. After I was finished dealing with the injured German I was asked to see this worthy and try and get him to put on some naval issue kit. One of the midshipmen spoke German and it was thought the man was cold and should be given a warm bath. The snag about this was the hot water tap which had long since ceased to function and had been replaced with a flexible lead from the steam supply aft. One filled the bath with cold water and turned on the steam valve – hot steam brought the bath to required temperature – you had to be very careful that the very flexible hot pipe did not scald you before you achieved the right temperature!
>
> When this was explained to the German he would not co-operate, but eventually he towelled down and put on the rescue kit. He completely refused food and drink, I gather he thought he was going to be doped! We later transferred them to the HQ Ship. It should be noted that Leading-Seaman Cocking, the starboard Oerlikon gunner, was mentioned in despatches for his shooting, but the more important factor in 'our win' was the captain's seamanship.

The patrols continued to the end of July, Raymond Johnson recalling:

> I was put on the pom-pom's gun crew. We were a bit restricted for aiming because we were sited between the two funnels, but we did help to bring down a German aircraft at Normandy and it was announced on the BBC.
>
> When on watch between going to the bridge for lookout duty, we would spread ourselves out on top of the ammunition boxes, around which was a screen. It was very cold during the nights but during daylight hours it was not too bad. At least you could clean the pom-pom. I remember we used to have several misfire shells failing or faulty, and exploding before time.

Between 1 and 3 August opportunity was taken to give leave as the ship was docked for further minor repairs. On completion, they sailed for Cherbourg on 4 August, to operate from there with destroyer *Grenville*. Journey time to the beaches was shorter but the patrolling remained much the same. While on patrol on 7 August their new Asdic packed up and specialist officers from *Grenville* had to come aboard to repair it.

They remained working from Cherbourg until 8 August when *Faulknor* received orders to sail to Plymouth. Battleship *Rodney* was to use her nine 16-inch guns to shake up the strong German coastal batteries in the Channel Islands, and they sailed with *Jervis* as escort, arriving at Portland at 2020/10 August. They left at 0600 next morning, proceeding to the Western Assault Area and thence to bombard Alderney, and, at 0726, were joined by destroyer *Saumarez* from Portsmouth. At 0905, when almost in position, the bombardment was cancelled because of the weather conditions, and *Faulknor* returned to Portland with *Rodney* at 1200.

At Portland *Faulknor* and *Rodney* were joined by *Urania* during the early hours, the latter having been detached from the patrol at 0200 on the 11th but the operation was again cancelled at 1330.

The attempt was repeated next day, *Jervis* sailing from Portsmouth to Portland where she, *Faulknor* and *Rodney* proceeded at 0742/12th. From a position off Cap de la Seine *Rodney* shelled German 305-mm gun positions on Alderney. The bombardment lasted two hours 31 minutes, seventy-five 16-inch shells being fired. Air reconnaissance two days later showed it to have been very successful, with probable damage to three out of the four guns. Roger Hill of *Jervis,* wrote:

> On 12 August we went to Portland and joined two old friends – one was *Rodney* and the other *Faulknor* with Bill Churchill still in command. We screened *Rodney* to Cherbourg, where she anchored near the peninsula and bombarded the twelve-inch guns, which were on Alderney. A Spitfire flew over the top as the shells arrived and a lot of flak went up. The range was about eighteen miles and *Rodney* signalled: 'Spotting aircraft reported shots mostly centred on three Western guns, including direct hits. Fourth gun received near misses. No round more than four hundred yards from centre of target. Seventy-five rounds fired.

They escorted *Rodney* back to Portland, arriving at 2200 hours, both destroyers sailing to Cherbourg immediately to resume patrols. Next day Churchill and Hill were summoned to the HQ of Rear-Admiral J. W. Wilkes, USN Commander Western Area, to whom they were temporary attached.

He ordered them to intercept German shipping using the safe routes in-between the islands under the protection of the heavy guns. The Americans 'plan' was for *Jervis* to run the gauntlet of all these batteries and penetrate the channel between Alderney and the Cherbourg peninsular, sinking any shipping she located plying between Jersey and Guernsey. Any she flushed out would be picked off by *Faulknor,* blocking the channel by patrolling off Guernsey. Roger Hill later recorded:

It seemed crazy to me; Bill told me he would make a diversion to draw the attention of the coastal guns; but we knew they had an excellent radar network, guns of all sizes – three-inch, four-inch, eighty-eight millimetre, and the twelve-inch guns at Guernsey, and also unlimited ammunition, which they would be delighted to fire it away before they surrendered.

Bill Churchill and I agreed there was no need to take risks, since the Channel Islands were cut off completely and must fall in due course. Our crews and ships had survived five long years of war and we were now winning, the light was growing at the end of the tunnel, and it seemed pointless to attack this most heavily gunned area for the sake of some newspaper report. Not so the American Admiral, banging the chart for emphasis, 'I want *ree-sults*', he said, his cigar jutting upwards aggressively...

They duly carried out the mission, *Jervis* steaming through the Alderney race flat-out at 36 knots, dropping a smoke-float decoy and, under a hail of heavy shells, fortunately unscathed, was met by a highly-relieved *Faulknor* on the other side. Of enemy shipping there had been absolutely no trace at all. Hill signalled to Churchill:

This passage too warm, joining you.

Churchill replied:

I have not enjoyed the last thirty-six minutes one little bit. Could not make them take any notice of me. Please confirm it is not you burning in the middle or did you catch a Hun ship?

The reply was:

Regret, no. It is my decoy, which they ignored.

On 18 August, *Faulknor* and *Jervis* were off Roches d'Oeuvres island where, among the twisted rusty girders of some defence works, they had seen some radio equipment. Hill was granted permission by Commander Churchill to land a shore party and, after *Jervis* had fired a few salvoes, both whalers were towed in and the landing party prepared to go ashore. Meanwhile *Faulknor's* ship's doctor had reported seeing enemy troops and ordered *Jervis* to soften up the islet a bit more. This was done but the landing party found the island deserted with all equipment already destroyed.

Hill signalled Churchill:

At your age never trust a Doctor's diagnosis!

Having liberated at least one speck of the Channel Islands both destroyers returned to Cherbourg on 19th. They continued working from that port, with *Grenville, Saumarez* and *Jervis,* a unique combination of four Flotilla Leaders operating as one squadron. They bombarded shore targets on the Brest Peninsular, until forced to retire out of range by the heavier German return shelling. Next day they returned to Portsmouth with *Jervis,* anchoring off Spithead before entering the dockyard for refit and repairs between 21st and 27 August.

Ashore, the 1st Canadian Army prepared to assault Le Havre and the Allied navies initiated a close blockade of that port to prevent Germans warships from escaping or evacuating the garrison. This led to repeated clashes. On the night of 13th/14th destroyers *Onslaught* and *Saumarez* tangled with the German 24th Minesweeping flotilla. *Saumarez* was slightly damaged, *Faulknor* replacing her. Patrols alternated between Le Havre and Alderney and Guernsey, where another flotilla of enemy minesweepers was trapped.

On 28th/29th they left Portsmouth with *Saumarez* to patrol off the Channel Islands. At 2335 a surface vessel plot appeared and they steered to intercept. At 0200/30th they made radar contact with a ship where no ship was supposed to be. Alarm bells rang and *Faulknor* went to Action Stations and prepared to open fire. The target was steering 191° at 6½ knots. Captain Churchill ordered the gunners to illuminate and *Faulknor* fired six star-shells at 0203. The mystery ship was slow to react and, when she did, gave the wrong identification code. She was the American escort *Maloy* (DDE 791), well outside her patrol area, and *Faulknor* almost sank her before she was correctly identified. The whole affair caused a flap at the US Naval HQ at Cherbourg. However, *Maloy* turned 090° away from *Faulknor,* who continued her patrol without further complications.

Commander Churchill tested German reactions on these patrols, but they never caught them napping, Carl Huer remembers:

> The skipper used to go in close, to within the German batteries gun range to see if they were awake. We never failed to get a couple of rounds dropped near us, upon which we would move back out.

By end of August Le Havre was empty of enemy shipping and *Faulknor* returned to Portsmouth. They prepared to take part in the planned Operation 'Fusilier', supporting the army assault on Le Havre, but this was cancelled at the last minute.

Battleship *Malaya* from Portland, escorted by destroyers *Grenville* and *Offa*, conducted a 15-inch gun shoot at 1100/31 August against the coastal batteries on the Isle de Cezembre. *Faulknor* and *Ulysses* patrolled respectively north of Alderney and south of Guernsey guarding against possible E-boat or submarine attacks. The bombardment scored hits on battery positions and in the barrack area, before *Malaya* was escorted to Portsmouth.

Further bombardments by battleship *Warspite* and monitor *Erebus* followed, but when Le Havre fell on the latter date there remained little left to do but blockade the Channel Islands. Rowland Fairweather:

> We were detailed to act as escort to one or two of our bombarding battleships. We would do a sweep while they bombarded near Le Havre or the Channel Islands where there were German 'M' Class minesweepers, which carried a large gun each. They were trying to break out under cover of darkness and reach safety. This patrolling carried on each evening when we used to rendezvous with one or the other of the battleships.

At 2209/3 September, Captain D17, instructed *Faulknor* to sail on 5th to relieve *Jervis* in the Western Assault Area, and they returned to Cherbourg in very bad weather. Halfway across they came across motor minesweeper *MMS 302* whose engines had given up and, with great difficulty, *Faulknor* got a line across, managing to hold her steady until a rescue tug arrived. They continued patrolling with *Saumarez*, she north of Alderney, *Faulknor* north of Guernsey, protecting the Cherbourg to Morlaix convoy route. They received a signal from the US Commander of Task Force 125, at 0907/6th, which detached the two ships at 1115.

This proved to be the end of their work in support of the Army ashore and the beginning of yet another new phase in *Faulknor's* long career.

* * *

On 18 September *Faulknor* and Canadian corvette *Port Arthur* escorted convoy SL.169 of 24 ships through the Channel as far as Tilbury, returning to Portsmouth at 2100. Between 22 and 9 October,

Faulknor underwent boiler cleaning. The 8th Flotilla, reduced to one effective ship, was temporarily disbanded. Western Approaches Command, signalled 0518/24th, that *Faulknor* join 14th Escort Group in the South-Western Approaches and English Channel, and she sailed for Larne. Before leaving Portsmouth they welcomed Captain A. K. Scott-Moncrieff aboard at Commander Churchill's invitation. Needless to say 'Scotty' was delighted at the chance to visit his much-loved former command. He wrote to Miss Moody on 10 October:

> I dined on board *our* ship the other night and a great thing it was for me. I met many of my friends in the ship's company, but only one officer was left who was with me in 1943.

Faulknor left Portsmouth 9 October for Milford Haven, arriving 10th; leaving next day with destroyer *Impulsive* and reaching Larne, Northern Ireland 1630/12th. They found 14th Escort Group, destroyers *Duncan*, *Forester*, *Havelock* and *Hotspur*, and carried out an intensive three-day exercise with this experienced anti-submarine unit. *Faulknor* was to screen *Malaya* from the Clyde to Scapa between the 16 and 17 October, but *Faulknor* and *Impulsive* were instead sent to assist urgently some Russian submarine-chasers caught in a storm in the Bay of Biscay, almost out of fuel.

They left at high speed, refuelling at Milford Haven between 0700 and 2145, then continuing south as the weather moderated. By evening 14th, they were in radio contact with the Soviet ships. They found that these had already received succour from frigate *Pitcairn* who had fuelled them, after beating off a U-boat attack, so they were no longer in danger of capsizing. *Faulknor* and *Impulsive* therefore returned to Milford Haven before sailing as escorts to troopship USS *Mount Vernon*, with 6,001 US Army personnel aboard, and the Hospital Ship *Aba*, with 241 Invalids embarked. They guarded these through the Irish Sea to Liverpool, leaving them at 1000/16th and refuelled from an oiler off Moville at the entrance to Lough Foyle, near Londonderry. They reached Scapa 1300/17th, oiling on arrival, but found that the screening of *Malaya* had been cancelled and the battleship remained anchored in Loch Striven.

Faulknor and *Impulsive* were then to escort battleship *King George V* during gunnery exercises on 19 October, but, again, this was cancelled at the last minute.

Far away in the sleepy Midlands countryside, Sub-Lieutenant R. B. Botwood, RNVR, substituting for Commander Churchill, was taking part in a ceremony in which the ship's Battle Ensign, which she had flown at Anzio, was presented to Colonel E. F. DuSautoy, TD, DL, the Sector Commandant, Staffordshire Home Guard, in the Methodist Hall at Amblecote. The Chairman of the Council, A. Watson, received the Ensign stating, 'the flag would be given a proud place among their possessions. They would always value the spirit in which it was presented by the ship's company.' He displayed the Ensign and said it had, '… obviously braved the battle and the breeze'.[4]

In 1949, Councillor C. E. Hammersley, a former Lieutenant-Commander in the Indian Naval Reserve during the war, decided that the Anzio Ensign was more worthy of a dignified notice than the scrap of paper attached to the wall alongside where it was displayed. He therefore had an oaken plaque bearing the ship's crest and details of her career made and presented it to the town. Captain Scott-Moncrieff was invited to unveil it, but was on the way to the Far East at the time in light cruiser *Superb*, and could not do so. He did send his warm regards. It was noted that boys from Oldswinford Hospital would shortly be going for naval training aboard *Superb* so the connection continued.

Alas, the towns more recent successors seem to have not kept faith with the sentiments and actions of those days, and, in June, 1996, nobody in Dudley Metropolitan Council knew of the present-day whereabouts of either Ensign.

At 1900, Sunday 22 October, *Faulknor* left Scapa with *Impulsive*, for Milford Haven, for Western Approaches duty, arriving at 0800/24th. They began to escort the 'Monster' liners transporting troops across the Atlantic Ocean, the euphemism for this being 'Special Escort Duty'.

Rowland Fairweather wrote:

Most of our time based at Milford Haven was spent taking large troopers into the Atlantic. Mostly we picked them up just outside Liverpool and escorted them six hundred miles out to clear U-boat alley, two destroyers and one fast liner, which included famous ships like *Andes, Queen Mary,* Polish *Batory,* French *Pasteur, Ille de France,* etc. After six hundred miles they went on without escort, relying on their speed. Not a lot of action but the weather was terrible. One trip with *Queen Mary* we could not even change gun's crews without turning into the weather. It took two of us on the wheel to keep on course. In the end the captain of *Queen Mary* signalled to us, 'You have my heartfelt sympathy. I am proceeding. Good Luck', and she was gone. There was no way we could keep up with her thirty plus knots so we turned into weather and waited for the next one coming in. We brought one of the Queens in on one trip and our Captain told us she had aboard the largest number of Yanks brought over in one ship, I forget how many thousand there were aboard her.

The first of the 'Monsters' escorted was the famous *Mauritania, Faulknor* and *Impulsive* sailing from Milford Haven at 2320/25 October to meet then escort her out toward the Azores, until 2000 the next evening. The weather was dirty and they were hard-pressed to keep pace with her despite her age. Ted Newman related that *Faulknor,* '… did everything except turn over.' It was no better on the return leg, when they picked up *Aquitania* at 1230/27th and brought her back in. The ship's motorboat was stove in by the mountainous seas and they had to stop to clear the wreckage. The liner plunged on into the night and they never caught them, reaching Milford Haven, much the worse for wear, at 1030/ 28th.

Carl Huer recalled:

> I well remember when we were based at Milford Haven it always seemed to be raining and it got pretty rough in the harbour, even when we were at anchor. I remember a Sunderland flying boat sinking at its moorings close to us due to the bad weather.

Faulknor and *Impulsive* were hurried to sea at 1659 on the last day of the month to join Force 27 from Plymouth hunting a U-boat off the Scilly Islands. *Faulknor* made several determined depth-charge attacks on a contact, but when this later proved to be a 'non-sub', Commander Churchill stopped the ship in the middle of the resulting shoals of floating dead fish and buckets were lowered over the side. Sufficient were got inboard to give everybody a good fish supper.

On 2 November, *Faulknor* and *Impulsive* were joined by *Brissenden,* and the hunt continued with the three destroyers carrying out a zigzag search between 49° 45′ N, 04° 50′ W and 50° 00′ N, 03° 30′ W. Next day they met convoy HX.315 off the Lizard at 0500, and escorted them east until 1623, safely past Portland Bill. The destroyers carried out a zigzag sub-hunt between 50° 15′ N, 02° 42′ W and 49° 54′ N, 03° 50′ W.

On 4th, in position 203, Start Point nineteen miles, they were relieved by the 'Hunts' *Albrighton* and *Tanatside* from Plymouth, as *Faulknor* and her companion were urgently required for a special escort duty. After refuelling at Plymouth they escorted US troopship *General William Black.* After investigating an aircraft contact on the 5th, they rendezvoused with convoy SL.174 as a support force, transferring the next day to convoy UC.44A for similar duties, between Portland Bill and the Eddystone Light, then entered Plymouth for storm damage repairs.

On 6 November Plymouth Command reformed the 8th Destroyer Flotilla, with *Faulknor* as (Senior Officer), *Impulsive,* Canadian Tribals *Iroquois, Haida* and *Huron* and Polish *Blyskawica* and *Piorun.* Surgeon-Lieutenant Nelson recalled:

> I well remember a return drinks party while in port aboard the *Blyskawica* where it appeared the Polish officers drank neat Vodka like water! I had never seen such spirit drinkers.

Faulknor and *Impulsive* returned to Milford Haven at 0830/ 8th, sailing again next morning. The weather was ghastly, so much so that the two destroyers could not keep up with the liner and had to return to Milford Haven at 0800/13th. They left on Special Escort Duty at 1600/15 November, catching another dusting.

On 15 November Ted Newman wrote:

> Went out in the worst weather we have experienced since being on Russian Convoys. Mess decks are flooded and, once again, we had to let the convoy carry on. It's impossible for submarines to operate anyway. Returned to Milford on the 17th. Went out again on the 18th to escort *Empress of Scotland.* Not much rest for us these days. Weather still bad, mess decks flooded and lockers floating around.

Raymond Johnson wrote:

> The thing I hated most was being in rough seas, which we frequently were at this time. The ship used to pitch and roll and, now and then, we used to have seawater on the mess decks. The water would slosh back and forth, which was bad luck for us because our lockers with our kit in would become soaked through. It's a good job we had an Engineering Chief who would allow the crew to dry-out their kit in the boiler room.
>
> On off-duty leisure time after meals, we cleared away the tables and card-playing was favourite – Solo, Brag, Poker, Pontoon, playing most for stakes which consisted of cigarettes, Victory 'Vs' and the like, made especially for the Navy. I didn't mind losing because we honestly believed they were made from camel-dung!

Faulknor and *Impulsive* had returned to Milford Haven at 1300/17th to refuel. At 2000 next day *Faulknor* sailed with destroyer *Nubian,* on another 'Monster' run. Their charge was *Empress of Scotland*, with 3,443 Royal Navy personnel embarked, bound for Sydney, NSW At 1415/17 November, 1944, C-in-C, Western Approaches, Admiral Sir Max K. Horton, KCB, DSO, signalled the NOIC (Naval Office in Charge) Milford Haven:

> Request you will sail PS *Blyskawica* and HMS *Nubian* to rendezvous SS *Empress of Scotland.* Radio distinguishing group SS *Empress of Scotland* – PETER WILLIAM. On crossing 11° West, escort detach to Milford Haven.

This was followed, at 1714, by a correction:

> For *Blyskawica* read *Faulknor*.

FOIC Milford Haven replied at 2120/18th:

> Sailed HMS *Faulknor* and HMS *Nubian* to rendezvous SS *Empress of Scotland.*

On completion, they anchored at Milford Haven 0800/ 20th, sailing at 1000/23rd, still in very bad weather, which forced them to reduce speed. They escorted the American troopship *Wakefield* from Liverpool down the Irish Sea with 543 US Army personnel embarked, returning to Milford Haven 1330/24th. This was repeated on the 26th, sailing at 0800 with *Blyskawica*, meeting and escorting liner *Aquitania* out and bringing back *Andes* from Halifax with 271 Royal Navy, 503 RAF and 3,387 Canadian Army personnel aboard. On 27th they could not get into Milford and *Faulknor* instead anchored overnight at Cardiff. A boiler clean was overdue and, on 28th, they escorted American hospital ships *Chateau Thierry* and *St. Mihiel* to Weymouth before entering Plymouth.

On 8 November, Commander Churchill wrote:

> We have been steaming pretty hard lately, and, either through the stinking weather we have been having, or through the job requiring all my attention most of the time, I have been unable to write while at sea. The days are getting mighty short too and I don't have artificial light on at sea for the sake of night blindness.

Rowland Fairweather recalled:

> Going back to the Plymouth period I now recall we were in dry-dock for a while. The reason for this I'm not quite sure but I well remember carrying out repairs to the W/T aerials. Another Sparker and I were sitting each end of the yardarm when it suddenly tilted to one side. This indicates we had experienced some rough weather and we were docked for general repairs.
>
> When we operated out of Plymouth for some reason we didn't seem to be liked as we were always Duty Destroyer or out on the buoy rather than alongside.

Bob Parham told me:

> The C-in-C Plymouth had a dislike of us for some unknown reason and we were always given the worst jobs and never allowed much time to ourselves. On one occasion the captain celebrated our return after yet another rough trip by playing 'Here we are again' on the ships tannoy as we entered harbour. The C-in-C (Admiral Sir Ralph Leatham) was *not* amused and we were sent to the duty destroyer buoy off Drake's Island immediately ready for the next dirty job that came along. When picking up the shackle on this buoy once it kept spinning and threw our seaman off. The captain reported a faulty buoy but was told that nobody else had reported a problem with it. Commander Churchill replied that we were the only ones ever asked to secure to it but that got us nowhere either!
>
> Our captain had a bit of a name for denting the old girl mind you, he was nick-named 'Clanger' Churchill by the engine room staff after the noise of the repeater there which continually clanged '300 Ahead, 300 Astern' as he manoeuvred the ship in and out of harbour.

Lieutenant Nelson's opinion differed:

> Commander Churchill was a square man of average height with a gingery, wispy beard. He was just over forty years old and had his previous command, the destroyer *Inglefield,* sunk under him in the Mediterranean before being transferred to the *Faulknor*. He was excellent seaman and an adept 'driver' of a destroyer, capable in all weathers. I judged him a capable assessor of seamen and most of the ship's company were happy to serve with him.
>
> Dogs are not usually allowed in RN ships, except by permission of the Captain. I was amazed one day to find he had allowed a largish mongrel bitch to be brought into one of the messdecks. He asked me to 'vet' the dog for disease. I said I was a medical doctor, not a vet. He gaily replied animals and humans are all much the same! The bitch had been roaming round the dockyard at Portsmouth and had been befriended by some of the seamen. It had the audacity to defecate on the quarterdeck, the holy of holies. The captain

called for me to inspect the 'heap'. He judged it normal, I countered that I would only be sure if I examined it bacteriorlogically! However the problem solved itself when seven pups were born, two died at birth and the rest, and mother, had to be drafted ashore.

We had an RN Midshipman, Robert de Pass, son of Commodore de Pass, RN, Chief-of-Staff to the C-in-C, Eastern Fleet. His family were reasonably well off and well connected and after the war he played polo with Prince Philip. However, he was always seasick although in rough weather he did try to stand his watch on the bridge. I remember in one bad patch I was also on the bridge and he looked terrible. The Captain came up the ladder to the bridge in sou-wester gear hat and cape, for heavy sea-spray was regularly coming over our open bridge. Just as his head appeared at bridge level, the midshipman turned and vomited over the 'old man'. 'Bloody Hell' yelled the Captain, 'Wash me down', which was promptly done by throwing a bucket of sea water over him, and then, 'Get that bloody mid-shite-man out of here!' Exit Midshipman de Pass until the weather improved! I think the Captain had little time for such a poor 'sea-dog'. He and all the officers never let the midshipmen (we had two) away with anything – it was all part and parcel of their apprenticeship.

On 17 December *Faulknor* undocked, sailing to Falmouth for calibrations before steering for Milford Haven. In the middle of this essential work a signal came that a U-boat was on the rocks off Land's End and Commander Churchill broke off trials and took *Faulknor* out of Falmouth pell-mell to the scene of the incident.

Lieutenant Nelson remembers, '…sailing up the English Channel at top speed (about thirty knots) on a beautiful moonlight night – we had alerted for a U-boat scare in the Channel. Ahead of us we saw a flying bomb (V-1) being shot down by an RAF fighter – a great explosion in the dark sky. Yet I remember that evening for the exhilaration of a fast ship in calm waters on a lovely night with me walking the quarter deck and watching the bow wave, higher than the deck of the ship, pounding out in white foam astern of us.'

On arrival, they found that it was all over and that the Canadian frigates *Montreal* and *Ribble* had picked up 43 survivors and four bodies from U-1209, which had rammed Wolf Rock and sunk. *Faulknor* set course for Milford Haven but, *en route,* another submarine contact was reported off Dodworth Point and *Faulknor* was put in charge of the hunting operation.

U-486 had attacked convoy BTC 10 off Dodman Point on the 18th, torpedoing *Silver Laurel*. A swamp operation followed. Commander Churchill reached Dodman at 1735 to organise the hunt, with destroyers *Melbreak, Impulsive, Sardonyx* and Polish *Piorun*, which he disposed to enclose the Dodman roughly in a semi-circle and a three-day hunt ensued. *U-485*, reported firing torpedoes at a hunting destroyer but missed, the *Faulknor's* luck had held out yet again!

Destroyers *Farndale* and *Haydon*, on their way to Sheerness, made a good Asdic contact in position 158° Dodman Point six miles and attacked. Both *Faulknor* and *Melbreak*, [now known as Force 29 for the operation] joined in the search, without result and, at 1443, the contact was declared a 'non-sub'. Force 29 continued to hunt in a ten-mile radius circle 166°, Eddystone Light twenty-seven miles until, at 1711, *Faulknor* returned to Plymouth to refuel. They then met and escorted in liner *Queen Elizabeth,* before returning to Milford Haven.

Commander Churchill's relief arrived next day and he handed *Faulknor* over to Commander Deric E. ('Pinky') Holland-Martin, DSO, DFC, RN. The newly-promoted Captain C.F.H. Churchill, DSC, RN, managed to visit the Stourbridge area on Saturday and Sunday 13/14 January 1945, when he addressed the Stourbridge Sea Cadets after Church Parade at St. Mary's Church, Oldswinford. Although promoted to full Captain and given a new ship, the move was not to Churchill's liking:

The girls of Sea Rangers Ship Faulknor *at Stourbridge, 1944. Their training ship was named in honour of HMS* Faulknor, *which had been 'adopted' by the town during 'Warship Week' in 1942.* (Mrs J.M.H. Braithwaite.)

I turned over command to Commander Holland-Martin in rather a hurry and the ship sailed only about five hours after he came aboard. I am sad at leaving her and at leaving destroyers in which ships I have served (anyway nothing bigger) since 1917. Now I have an appointment to an old Flat Iron (monitor *Abercrombie* destined for the invasion of Japan) abroad.

Marriage to Miss Dorothy Tregoining, of Ferryside, Carmarthenshire, followed in December, 1945, and his Naval career continued, Captain Churchill finally passing away in 1990, aged 91.

Admiral Holland-Martin confided, '… the old lady's glory days were over when I took over', but there was still valuable work to perform. Lieutenant J. D. L. Scholfield, First Lieutenant since January, 1944, replacing Lieutenant-Commander May, remained. Under their new skipper they were immediately back into the fray, sailing on 20 December to rendezvous with liner *Andes* which had sailed from Liverpool with Dutch destroyer *Van Galen* for Freetown and Cape Town. Commander Holland-Martin recorded:

> When we met we exchanged the usual official signals and were then surprised to get a private one flashed to us from the signalman. It read 'I come from Stourbridge'.

They escorted *Andes* out into the Atlantic, then both destroyers met and returned with *Mauritania*, whom they took back to Liverpool. They secured in Gladstone Dock, remaining for Christmas and Boxing Day.

Rowland Fairweather:

> We spent Christmas 1944 in Liverpool. What a run ashore that was. A couple of chaps went home to Birmingham and never made it back in time as we sailed the day after Boxing Day after waiting out at the bar for Polish liner *Batory* to come out. As she finally appeared through the evening dusk her tannoy was playing 'We'll meet again' by Vera Lynn, and all the troops were lining the ship's rails, something I'll never forget.

Faulknor then met *Aquitania* and escorted her back to the Clyde before arriving Plymouth on 30 December.

New Year's Eve saw many of the crew able to celebrate with a run ashore. Any that celebrated too well probably regretted it as they were rushed to sea on New Year's Day to escort another convoy, which they brought up-Channel as far as Portland before returning to Plymouth on 3 January, entering the dockyard on 5th.

They left with Dutch destroyers, *Van Galen* and *Tjerk Hiddes* at 0600/10 January to rendezvous with 15th Escort Group, *Javanese Prince*, submarine *Telemachus* and motor-ships *Durham* and *New Zealand Star*, in 49° 37' N, 07° 00' W. The latter were detached with frigate *Narborough* for the Irish Sea. *Faulknor* shepherded the remainder through the Channel until relieved off Portland Bill by destroyer *Vanoc* and frigate *Spragge*.

On 13th, *Faulknor* and *Van Galen* rendezvoused with the English Channel section of convoy CU 53 in 48° 40' N, 07° 01' W at 2345, providing additional escort as far as the Isle of Wight, The OIC had predicted in August that the Germans with their new technology would switch U-boats '... close inshore in the Bristol Channel and St. George's Channel and near Lands End.' And so it proved.

Captain D.E. Holland-Martin, DSC DSC, RN. another destroyer skipper wi a great war record, mainly in 'Triba class ships, he took over command Faulknor in the closing stage of the wa (Imperial War Museum.)

Rare photograph of HMS Faulknor *showing her last wartime configuration and paint scheme, on 3 January 1945, entering the Hamoaze, Plymouth, at the end of another patrol. taken from* Royal Ulsterman. (Dr I.D.M. Nelson.)

The underseas threat was far from over and *Faulknor's* diligent vigilance was as necessary in 1945 as it had been throughout the previous six years. Moreover, many of the ships they escorted through the Channel at this period were vital troopship or hospital ships, packed with American and Canadian troops from the hard land-fighting ashore. These charges were deserving of the best protection that *Faulknor* could offer them. *Faulknor's* work then, right up to the end of the war, was both vital and important.

On 15 January *Faulknor* and *Van Galen* met escort carrier *Activity en route* to Belfast, prior to her sailing to the Indian Ocean. They relieved her Portsmouth escorts in 180°, Start Point fourteen miles, and remaining with her until the Milford Haven buoy, returning to Plymouth on the 18th.

Cruising watch on the 'tween-funnels quadruple 2-pdr pom-pom gun platform, winter 1944–5. (Ted Slinger.)

Faulknor was off again at 1200 next day, with *Blyskawica*, meeting convoy UC 53A at H2 buoy. The transport *Cheshire* was detached off the Lizard, and they escorted her as far as Lundy, handing her over to destroyer *Whitehall* and frigate *Loring*.

On 21 January 1945, *Faulknor* sailed at 0900 to meet *Clan Chattan,* independently bound for Falmouth, in 48° 30′ N, 05° 40′ W at 0200. At 2143 in 063°, the Lizard 7.7 miles, *Faulknor* got a good Asdic contact. After a short hunt she handed over to destroyer *Icarus. Faulknor* escorted her charge until 1500, off Trevose Head, she was relieved by destroyers *Duncan* and Canadian *Assiniboine.*

On 22 January their boilers were washed through to keep them going for a little while longer before a much-needed boiler clean and refit. They sailed for Londonderry on 27th but, when almost there, were suddenly recalled and their move of base cancelled. They arrived back at Plymouth at 0800/29th and next day, at 1318, left with *Van Galen* to escort battleship *Valiant* returning damaged from the Indian Ocean on the last lap of her long journey home for repairs, reaching Plymouth 1 February.

The routine continued, *Faulknor* sailing at 1800/3 February, with destroyers *Tanatside* and *Van Galen* as Force 26, proceeding via QZS.601 to meet the English Channel section of convoy CU.56 in latitude 48° N. They endured heavy seas, and, at 1209/4th, the convoy was ordered to zigzag on receipt of an Admiralty Intelligence message reporting a U-boat within 60 miles of 49° 00′ N, 05° 30′ W. On reaching Portland Bill, the Plymouth ships were relieved by Portsmouth escorts and *Faulknor* returned to base with *Tanatside.*

Both ships left at 2305/5th to meet convoy TBC.59 which included Landing Ship, Dock *Eastway,* escorted by destroyer *Croome,* bound for Barnstaple Bay, and transport *St. Albans Victory,* escorted by corvette *Kingcup,* whose destination was Mumbles. *Faulknor* was due to relieve *Croome* but when three other large merchant ships failed to sail, *Faulknor* was recalled at daylight.

At 0130/9 February, with destroyer *Brissenden,* they relieved destroyers *Havelock* and *Inconstant* escorting American troopship *General George O. Squires* and *Mormacmoon* from St. Helens. *Faulknor* was detached with the former at Eddystone and brought her into Plymouth.

On 10th, *Faulknor* escorted French Armed Transport Ship *Barfleur* to Brest, again encountering heavy weather. She left her charge there and returned to Plymouth on 12 February, refuelled and at 1900 with *Tanatside,* left to relieve corvettes *Alisma* and *Delphinium,* escorting the *Midnight* and *Antenor* to Mumbles and Barry respectively. These were met 180 Start Point, twelve miles, at 2200, continuing in company until *Faulknor* took *Antenor* on as far as Scarweather, under orders of FOIC Cardiff, then guided LSI *Isle of Thanet,* from Cardiff, returning to Plymouth with her at 0800/14th.

At 2130/14 February, as Force 26, *Faulknor*, *Tantatside*, *Brissenden* and Canadian *Iroquois*, joined the English Channel section of convoy CU.57 and, at 1300 next day, they had reached 47° 10′ N, 06° 48′ W. There was no interference from the enemy but at 0409 on 16th two merchantmen, *Java* and *Westerly Victory* collided eight miles off Start Point, *Tanatside,* who with *Faulknor,* stood by them, reported that they were completely locked together. *Java* had her steering gear and port quarter badly damaged losing four men killed and two severely injured. She was towed in, while *Westerly Victory,* with damaged bow, reached Plymouth under her own steam, with *Faulknor* and *Tanatside* on the 16th.

Faulknor sailed at 1000, despite thick fog, to meet combined convoys ONA.285, OS 11 and KMS 85 at the seaward end of minefield QZS. 601. Carl Heuer remembers.

> We were escorting this convoy off Lands End, with *Faulknor,* as usual, the senior escort and in her normal position out ahead. Two American destroyer escorts came out to strengthen the escort and immediately took station ahead of us. I was on the wheel, and I heard down the voice-pipe a very upset Commander tell the signalman to make to them, 'I am a senior commander of His Majesty's Navy and whilst I am in command of this escort you will take station astern!' Which they duly did!

Faulknor later extracted freighters *Frederick Victory* and *Golden Fleece* proceeding ahead with them to Mumbles. The fog worsened as the day wore on and they anchored at Falmouth overnight.

On 21/22 February, with *Impulsive*, *Faulknor* met the English Channel section of CU. 58 in 47° 46′ N, 06° 34′ W at 1400 providing additional escort to Portland Bill, returning at 1000 next morning to Plymouth dockyard to boiler clean.

They resumed work on 2 March, *Faulknor* sailing at 1300 (Force 26) with destroyers *Bulldog*, and Canadian *Iroquois* and *Huron,* plus frigate *Barbados*. They met troop convoy UC. 58B off Portland as additional escorts until the Lizard, when they were detached and, with American escort *Ramsden*, escorted Mumbles-bound ships to position 'B' at minefield QZS. 432. The destroyers then proceeded past minefield QZS. 668 to rendezvous with battleship *Malaya* and freighter *Antenor,* bound for Plymouth and Southampton respectively.

Malaya was to pay off into reserve after almost thirty years' service, and *Faulknor* guarded her overnight, arriving at 0916/4th. While boiler-cleaning on 9 March, *Faulknor* received a touch of fame in a *News Item* Broadcast put out by the BBC at 1700. (Perhaps Lord Reith had remembered his trip to Normandy the previous year!) This listed the achievements of the 'Fighting Fs', as they called them, and told listeners that:

> *Faulknor*, *Fame* and *Forester* are still serving with the Fleet. The Flotilla exists no more, (which caused a few wry faces in the 8th Flotillas wardrooms at Plymouth) but their records still stand. First Destroyer Flotilla to steam one million miles in this war. First U-boat sinking of the war. Escorting of every east-bound Malta Convoy. HMS *Faulknor* – longest continuous service as Flotilla Leader of any destroyer afloat.

On 9 March, *Faulknor* conducted exercises before sailing at 2200 with Canadian destroyer *Huron*, meeting convoy CU. 90, in 46° 44′ N, 06° 55′ W at 1600. *Faulknor* continued with the English Channel section to Portland Bill, returning to Plymouth next morning. They patched some leaks sprung on the return leg and remained until the 12th, going out briefly on convoy duty, returning next day.

Strong remnants of German destroyer and minesweeper flotillas remained in the Channel Island and French Biscay ports. The Nazis even mounted their own amphibious assault on the French port of Granville, Gulf of St. Malo, on the night of 8/9 March. This raid inflicted considerable damage, blowing up the harbour installations and the freighters, *Kyle Castle*, *Nephrite,* and *Parkwood*, and capturing the collier *Eskwood*, towing her away in a splendid act of defiance that humiliated an over-confident Allied Command.

In a classic case of 'Shutting the Stable Door' *Faulknor* was sailed at 1915/14th, and with *Huron*, patrolled between The Lizard and Start. At 2030 the two destroyers shifted patrol to between 49° 23' N, 03° 55' W and 49° 06' N, 03° 49' W, later covering convoy COC.104.

After an uneventful night spent at Action Stations, they arrived Falmouth at 0843, repeating the operation from 1700 until 0500/16th.

With destroyers *Huron* and *Bulldog* and frigate *Narborough*, (Force 26) *Faulknor* sailed at 1700 for the same patrol but later joined convoy CU.61 in 48° 05' N, 06° 04' W. They escorted the English Channel section of this group from 0800 to Portland, returning Plymouth at 2346.

Further defects appeared; Number Three boiler had to be closed down and sealed off completely, and Number Two was unreliable, restricting them to a top speed of 31-knots in fair weather only, until a proper refit.

Surgeon-Lieutenant Nelson recalls one incident.

> We were lying in the Sound, at half hour's notice to steam, when a pinnace acting as a harbour supply boat came alongside to deliver mail. As the boat turned away after casting off from us, the Wren coming from aft to rejoin the coxswain in the bow of the boat, missed her hold and was flung into the sea as the boat heeled over. The sea was very cold, the Wren was not wearing a life jacket and the Sound was deep. Many things happen in a destroyer in an emergency, what happened was:
> 1) An immediate call out of lifeboat crew.
> 2) The tannoy alerts everyone.
> 3) The Chief Stoker (E.R.A.) quickly picked up a nearby lifebelt and flung it to land beside the Wren in the water.
> 4) The Captain (Holland-Martin) and First Lieutenant appear on the quarterdeck.
> 5) The pinnace turns in a tight circle to recover the Wren.
>
> The Captain ordered the coxswain of the pinnace (a PO Wren) to come alongside again, the First Lieutenant says, 'Doc, you can deal with the frozen Wren. Use my cabin.' It was next to the officer's bathroom. So I am presented with a 'drowned' Wren who was nearly all right but very cold indeed. I went and prepared a hot bath for her, the same old problem of the flexible steam pipe. I left the Wren in a hot bath and went to the Wardroom to let the Captain know she was OK, who naturally signalled ashore that she was safe and sound. It was a bright cold day and the entire episode had been closely watched from the Signal Tower ashore and from the other ships. We kitted the Wren out in survivor's kit and she returned in her own boat ashore. It was left to me to return the brassiere and panties to their owner, but only after A. B. Morgan (a peacetime laundry man) had washed and ironed them for her. He left them neatly folded on my bunk!

He also remembered some of the other 'characters' of *Faulknor's* ships company at this period.

> The Captain's steward, Bruce, had been the valet of Lord Lovat, Commando leader of the Lovat Scouts. He did not wish to accompany his master into the army so naturally was selected as a steward in the Royal Navy. I often used to see him at sea taking the Captains lunch along the deck in rough weather holding on to the safety rope with one hand, the other holding the lunch in a knotted napkin! But our most interesting meeting was at the requestmen and defaulters table where the Captain heard requests and punished defaulters.
> The Master-at-Arms, a Chief Petty Officer, in our case the coxswain, instructed the ratings at the table and read out the requests or defaults. The Captain was supported by

the First Lieutenant and other ship's officers, sometimes I was asked to be present, especially if there was a medical point involved.

Bruce appeared at the captain's table as a defaulter. He had not applied for his three-year 'Good Conduct Badge', which was each ratings responsibility, for which he got a few pence per day extra. When asked why he was not interested in having more pay, he quietly replied in his lovely Scottish voice, ' You see it does not matter to me, for His Lordship (Lord Lovat) kindly makes up my pay.' Holland-Martin gave him two days stoppage of pay for defaulting anyway!

The Gunners' Mate, Chief Petty Officer Pert, was a fine senior rating. I used to talk to him at sea in his office/den on the starboard side of the ship, where he always offered me a sip of rum. I don't like the stuff unless it is suitably diluted. He had a great insight into how the get the best out of his men. I was later, in the fifties, to meet him again, as an instructor aboard HMS *Sussex* when I was in the RNVR division there and was pleased to help him get his aged mother into a local old persons' home in Brighton when I was deputy MOH there.

The Chief Stoker was an excellent seaman, it was he who threw the lifebelt to the Wren in the cold water of Plymouth Sound. He was an excellent engineer too, I gather. He need to be for the South African Engineering Officer was scared in action and always hovered in the deck hatchway leading to the engine room. He admitted to me he hated to be down in the engine room if there was any possibility of action!

A.B. Lister, my part-time Steward, was a pleasant Londoner, who had been in a laundry in peacetime. The finish of my shirts, collars and handkerchiefs was always excellent, no matter what the weather.

I was always amazed by the Petty Office Yeoman of Signals, who always spotted things at sea before anyone else on the bridge where I was allowed to be at any time except when in action or on entering or leaving harbour. I liked the way his proficiency was always expected but always acknowledged by all the officers of the watch.

On the evening of 20 March, *Faulknor* joined Force 27, destroyer *Bulldog* and frigate *Thornborough*, escorting convoy UC. 61A which was under U-boat threat. Nothing occurred and, at 1900/ 22nd, *Faulknor* was detached in 50° 30′ N, 08° 00′ W, along with American escort destroyer *Rinehart*, arriving Plymouth at 0800.

At 1430/25 March, *Faulknor* sailed with frigates *Narborough* and *Thornborough,* (Force 26), escorting LSD *Eastway en route* for Gibraltar with sloop *Weston*. They left her on crossing 48 North, joining the screen of convoy CU. 62 at 0800/ 26th, which they escorted up Channel to Portland Bill.

Commander Holland-Martin was notified that the Admiralty had cancelled the major refit scheduled for his ship, long overdue and much needed. *Faulknor* had to carry on as best she could and, at the end of the European War was to be paid off to refit at leisure, before recommissioning as the Leader of the anti-submarine training flotilla with *Fame, Hotspur* and similar veterans. So they continued, sailing at 1300/27 March to join American destroyer escort *Clarence L. Evans* escorting liner *Vienna* in position 'B' of minefield QZS. 432, as additional escort as far as Portland Bill.

In April 1945, *Faulknor's* routine changed to assisting enforce the blockade of the German forces in the Bay of Biscay ports. The enemy were surrounded in Bordeaux, La Pallice, La Rochelle, Lorient and Nantes. The Allies had two aims; preventing any German warships escaping to neutral Spain, and assisting the Free French Navy liberate those ports from Nazi occupation. French naval forces at Plymouth under command of Rear-Admiral G. S. Rue, included battleship *Lorraine*, heavy cruiser *Duquesne*, destroyers *Le Fortune, L'Aventure, L'Alcyon* and five escort vessels, ready for Operation 'Venerable', the bombardment of the Gironde area.

The Allied blockade was commenced on 7 April, in the Bay of Biscay, with operational control by CFNTF, under the general direction of Admiral Leatham at Plymouth. The forces included destroyers *Faulknor*, *Beagle* and *Bulldog*, French destroyers *Basque, Le Fortune* and *L' Alcyon,* frigates *L'Aventure*, *La Decouverte*, *La Surprise,* and destroyer escort *Hova*.

'I well remember', wrote Surgeon Lieutenant Nelson, 'in stormy weather escorting the old French battleship *Lorraine* to Cherbourg and the British battleship HMS *Ramillies* through the Bay of Biscay in better weather. We were warned to be careful in the Bay of Biscay about fishing boats who might report our position to the Germans, so we stopped some French fishing boats to see if they were authentic fishermen. They were so we gave them cigarettes in return for fresh fish. Once, in the Bay of Biscay, we dropped a depth charge to get fresh fish. (This practice was officially frowned upon for, apart from alerting the enemy by the noise, it was an expensive waste of high explosive). But we did trawl with buckets and nets some lovely fresh fish which pleased the whole ships company.'

The first of these forces put to sea from Plymouth at 1600 on 1 May, *Faulknor*, *L'Aventure*, *La Surprise* and *La Decouverte*, as Force 27, to conduct Operation 'Assault' off the Biscay coast between 47° 35' N and 45° N.

On 2nd, they encountered heavy seas, which yet again knocked out their Asdic and revealed more leaks. After passing 47° 50' N, 05° 32' W, they stopped several suspect ships before continuing the designated patrol area. That evening they established a night patrol between 46° 42' N, 02° 43' W and 47° 27' N, 02° 022' W.

Next day the weather moderated and became sunny. *La Decouverte* left for Brest at 0400, but the remainder commenced a sweep south-east and south, stopping and searching a few fishing vessels, without sign of fleeing Germans. Patrols continued on 4 April, with *La Decouverte* rejoining at 1158. Eight Spanish trawlers were sighted at 45° 16' N, 02° 22' W in illegal waters and ordered to return home. They patrolled overnight but, at 1100/5 April, *Faulknor* handed over to *La Surprise*, returning to Plymouth.

On 6 May Commander Holland-Martin left for a new appointment in London, and the following day a new skipper, Commander C. E. Fardell, R.N, came aboard. Continuing his distinguished career in the service, Admiral Sir Deric Holland-Martin, GCB, DSO, DSC, RN, wrote, on 13 May, 1945, from the office of the Second Sea Lord in Queen Anne's Mansions, London, that:

> I have recently left *Faulknor* for a job up here.

He later became Second Sea Lord and Chief of Naval Personnel 1957-60, C-in-C Mediterranean and C-in-C Allied Forces, Mediterranean 1961-64, commanding the Imperial Defence College in 1964. Promoted to Admiral in 1961 he retired in 1966, having been made a CB in 1958, KCB in 1960 and GCB in 1964

Commander Fardell joined *Faulknor* after a two-and-a-half year spell in shore jobs, with the Naval Staff in Washington D.C. and at the Admiralty, which had been followed by a three-month period during the D-Day period when he was sent down to help with the Mulberry Harbour project, '..unfortunately never further than in the Solent, in other words, the despatching end.' He wrote that he found the command of a destroyer after all this, '… a pleasant change.'

Faulknor sailed at 2200 on 10 April, 1945, with frigates *Narborough* and *Thornborough,* as Force 26, to bring in the English Channel portion of convoy CU. 64 which they met in 48° 40' N, 05° 45' W at 0700 the following morning. Frigate *Holmes* later supplemented the squadron. After an uneventful passage *Faulknor* returned late on 11th. Further defects resulted in running repairs over three days. On 14th Commander Fardell announced that, after one more trip, they *would* get a full boiler clean.

Opportunity was taken on 14th to mount the ship's concert, '*Faulknor Fanfare*'. Among the many talented members of the crew involved in 'The Musical Maniacs' was able seaman H. C. Benson, brother of the famous all-girl band's Ivy Benson. Stan Hollett was the compere; Lieutenant H.D.

Jackman played accordion, Telegraphist H. Gray the Mandolin. Among the many delights on the bill that night were Harry Parsons, 'The Popular Yorkshire Comedian', Tansy Lee, 'The Personality Singer', and Charles ('George Formby') Keefe.

At 0700/16th they sailed with *Narborough* as additional escorts to the American LST convoy Number 4. Fog soon closed in, but this was the only hazard and, on crossing 48° 30′ N, *Faulknor* returned to Plymouth arriving on the afternoon of 17 April. They de-ammunitioned ship and went into dock for their full boiler-clean and refit.

In May came the unconditional surrender of the German Armed Forces in Europe. It also saw the liberation of the Channel Islands, the only part of the United Kingdom to be occupied by the enemy, yet among the last to be freed. The Germans were not easily persuaded to disarm. On 6 May, a signal to the Commander German Forces in the Channel Islands, informed him that GOC, Southern Command, Lieutenant-General Kirkman, was authorised to accept his unconditional surrender. The German replied he, '… received orders only from his own Government!'

Another signal was sent via C-in-C Plymouth, ordering him to send a representative to meet British representatives in a British destroyer in a position south of Les Hanois Light, to sign a surrender document. A guaranteed safe passage for destroyer and escort was also required. The destroyer selected was HMS *Faulknor*.

Alas for their plans, six years of warfare against the Axis had not stopped the old ship, but British dockers were another matter! VE Day arrived and *Faulknor* was still not ready to comply. The dockers earmarked to complete the job and get her to sea for the great occasion, simply failed to turn up for work, they just downed-tools. While destroyer *Bulldog* substituted for them, *Faulknor's* crew were painting ship and re-ammunitioning until 1700, and were unable to celebrate Germany's downfall. The following day saw the same routine.

The reoccupation of the Channel Islands followed, and first priority was supplying food and basics, Operation 'Nutmeg'. *Faulknor* finally undocked and was got ready for sea for this final act. On 11 May, they escorted a supply convoy for Guernsey, *Empire Rapier*, *Empire Lance*, *St. Helier*, *LCH. 167*, six LSTs, *Gulnare*, and tugs *Gresillion* and *Growler*, the latter towing Lighter *C. 86*. *Faulknor* was Senior Officer of the escort, with Polish-manned destroyer *Garland*, American destroyer escorts *Borum* and *Malloy*, tug *Dochet* and *HDML 910*. That same afternoon the *Faulknor* received aboard Vice-Admiral Huffmeier, German Commander in the Channel Islands, and Major-General Wolff, OC German Troops, with their two batmen, for passage back to Plymouth. They sailed at 1845, with the four men confined to the Captain's quarters under armed guard.

Raymond Johnson:

> We brought back the German commandant and his assistant aboard *Faulknor* and I was one of the sentries placed over the pair of them.[5] I was armed with a rifle and fixed bayonet and we had an interpreter with us. My orders were to shoot if they went anywhere near the guardrails on the quarterdeck. Our interpreter was a German-hater, I cannot recall his nationality, but he was embittered and he made me very nervous indeed. I was glad when we got back to Plymouth.

They arrived back at that port at 2330, where the prisoners were handed over to the Military authorities. *Faulknor* and frigate *Cosby* sailed at 0600/14 May, to take up anti-submarine patrol between Lizard and Start. An Admiralty order of 8 May instructed all surrendering U-boats to proceed to their nearest collecting areas, which for the English Channel was Weymouth Bay, and, while this was generally being complied with, no chances were being taken.

They returned to harbour at 0200, sailing to meet convoy HX.353 in 180° Bishops Rock, twelve miles, at 1940. They rendezvoused at 0800 and two hours later, on relief by *Narborough*, returned at

0700/15th. Commander Fardell went home on compassionate leave following his wife's death after a long illness, and a junior officer from the Devonport pool, served as temporary captain until he returned.

At 1000 next day, *Faulknor* and *Narborough* left Plymouth for St. Peter Port, Guernsey, to bring in the surrendered German 24th Minesweeping flotilla, Operation 'Nestegg'. As soon as they stuck their bows outside the boom they received the recall signal but were sent out again to complete their mission at 1400.

They found the enemy ships awaiting them and, while anchored at Guernsey, the harbour was full of small boats full of gleeful islanders viewing the beaten enemy and their captors. *Faulknor*, *Narborough* and the tug *Growler*, duly sailed with the enemy ships, five Minesweeping trawlers, Auxiliary minesweeper *FL-13* and two patrol vessels, with their own crews on board, at 0700/19 May. They were cheered into harbour at Plymouth at 2130. Although hardly as impressive as the surrender of the Italian fleet two years earlier, this was an equally symbolic end of German naval ambitions, and once again *Faulknor* led them in.

They remained at Plymouth undisturbed for four days, celebrating *Faulknor's* Tenth Birthday. The normal life span for destroyers was fifteen years, but wartime running counted double and *Faulknor* had been run as hard as any warship in the preceding six years. She was feeling her age, but she still a kick in her. Commander Fardell resumed command on 25 May and they sailed for Guernsey at 1200, returning next day. On 29th the C-in-C, Admiral Sir Ralph Leatham, came aboard *Faulknor* with his staff and she conveyed them to the Channel Islands, arriving at St. Helier, Jersey, 1200. They acted as his despatch vessel as he toured the various islands with his entourage, sailing to St. Peter Port, Guernsey at 1620, and returning to Plymouth late on 30th.

At 1500/1 June they sailed with destroyer *Garland*, escorting liners *Pasteur* (which had sailed from Southampton on 1 June, escorted by frigates *Hargood* and *Waldegrave*) and *Mariposa*, which had sailed from Le Havre on 31 May escorted by destroyer *Watchman*. These were on the first leg of their voyages to Halifax and New York respectively, with 972 and 1,651 repatriated American and Canadian POWs, veterans of Dieppe among the latter, as well as many war-brides. *Faulknor* and *Garland* met these off Portland at 2000, and escorted them out to 12° West. True to form, the weather proved foul. Great seas found all the old leaks, the mess decks were flooded once again and many of the crew were seasick. At 0400 the destroyers were released to Plymouth, arriving 0800/3 June.

Over the next two days the damage was repaired, the ship cleaned and tidied then painted throughout in readiness for the planned visit by Their Majesties the King and Queen to the Channel Islands. On 5 June *Faulknor* sailed with frigate *Cosby* at 1438 to act as despatch ships, reaching St. Peter's Port at 1950, only to find a 24-hour postponement due to bad weather. The Royal visit was to have been made by air, but it was decided that a sea crossing would prove much safer.

There followed a hasty rescheduling; *Faulknor* receiving an urgent signal to proceed to Portsmouth at best speed, sailing at 1235. It was assumed that the Royal Party would embark aboard *Faulknor* and a further spate of cleaning and polishing ensued during the high-speed run back across the Channel. It all proved fruitless for, in another change of plan, Their Majesties finally sailed aboard light cruiser *Jamaica* at 1100/6 June. It was a year to the day since *Faulknor* had led the invasion ships to Normandy and now the Sovereign, wearing the uniform of Admiral-of–the-Fleet, was to meet his freshly-liberated subjects.

Jamaica, flying the flag of the C-in-C, Admiral Sir Geoffrey Layton, at fore, the Union Flag at the topmost yardarm and the Royal Standard at the mainmast, sailed from Portsmouth being met in Spithead by her four destroyer escorts, *Faulknor*, *Brilliant*, *Impulsive* and *Caesar,* in drizzling rain. On arrival off Jersey at 1015/7 June, the squadron was given the order 'Splice the Mainbrace'.

Because the Royal Party was to fly from Jersey to Guernsey and then later from Guernsey to Portsmouth, the four destroyers and *Cosby* took up Air-Sea Rescue positions along their route, in case the aircraft ditched. On completion of this final duty for the Monarch and the country, *Faulknor* returned

At Dartmouth. Warships laid up in the River Dart in late 1945. Leading the line are three destroyers, HMS Beagle *(H30), with, inside her, HMS* Faulknor *and, outboard of her, HMS* Bulldog. (H.G. Casserley collection, via Friends of Dartmouth Museum.)

to St.Peter Port at 1515. At 0800/8 June, she left with *Cosby,* reaching Plymouth at 1150. On arrival it was announced to the ship's company that she was to decommission and pay off to the Reserve Fleet.

The final voyage for most of HMS *Faulknor's* wartime crew was made on 12 June, 1945, when, at 1600, she sailed from Plymouth for the last time as an active warship, reaching Dartmouth at 1700 where she was to lay up as in Category 'B' Reserve.

Dartmouth had been long preparing to cope with an influx of such warships who were no longer needed in the active fleet but were thought likely to be worth preserving for future use. Famous ships and not so-famous ships, they all joined *Faulknor* in a sad, growing band at the mouth of that beautiful river. It was the end of a magnificent naval war record without peer.

However, it was *not* yet quite the end of her story... ...

* * *

On 22 June, Commander E. G. Fardell left the ship, having been appointed to command destroyer *Racehorse* in the East Indies Fleet. The First Lieutenant, Lieutenant F. R. Coombes, RNVR, took over his duties for the next ten days.

Faulknor's associations with Stourbridge continued, the pen-friendships sometimes resulting in something deeper. An example of this was the marriage in July, of Able Seaman C. Kendall, formerly of the ship, and Miss S. Shilvock of Wollaston. Nor was this the only such union to take place. In August Able Seaman Raymond Herbert Matthews, from Gifford Road, Bedford, announced his engagement to Miss Dayrell Inscker and were married at Holy Trinity Church, Amblecote. A/B Matthews had served aboard *Faulknor* for several years. He had been drafted to the brand-new destroyer HMS *Croziers*[6] [built by Yarrows on the same slip as *Faulknor*], but wrote that:

> I'm serving aboard another destroyer since my last letter to you, which is just off the stocks from Glasgow and is a little over two months old, but I would rather be aboard *Faulknor* if I had my time over again. She was a fine ship with a splendid war record, and was loved by all who manned her during her war service.

Others remembered *Faulknor* still with affection. The Rev. Brian Bond, formerly Lieutenant Bond, Signals' Officer aboard *Faulknor,* in October, 1945, at the Methodist Theological College near Birmingham, stated on a visit to Stourbridge New Road Methodist Church that, during the war, '… everybody on the ship knew of the generosity of the Stourbridge people which made the other ships green with envy.'

Captain Holland-Martin himself wrote that he, '… knew of no ship which had been so well looked after by those who adopted her.'

Leading Signalman Eric G. Wingrove, from Chesham, was another visitor to the adoption towns. He had served for two-and-a-half years aboard *Faulknor* and visited Amblecote to meet his pen friend and say thank you for all they had done for him and his shipmates. Able Seaman Eric Coffey, of Tamworth was another. It was far from a one-sided connection however, and the Corbett Hospital, already the beneficiary of numerous toys from the crew, was among worthy local causes to benefit from donation from the ships company sent in by Lieutenant F. R. Coombes and the surviving Wardroom Officers also donated the balance of their funds to the same good destination. [The '*Faulknor*' Fund' was not finally wound up until 2 March 1946, terminating this very successful adoption scheme after four years.]

But *Faulknor* was not yet among the dead and departed! As Sub-Lieutenant A. Macdonald wrote to Joan Moody on 24 September:

> At first it was the intention for the ship to pay off completely, but, far from being paid off, *Faulknor* is still in commission in the Reserve Fleet. Very few of the original complement are still on board but the ship still has a complement of 125 ratings. She is now the ship of the Senior Officer, Reserve Fleet, Dartmouth.

By September 1945, *Faulknor* was under the care of Temporary Commander (Eng) L. A. Wynn. It was intended that she lead the A/S training flotilla, with proven submarine-killer destroyers, including *Fame* and *Hotspur,* to keep the hard-earned expertise alive in the peacetime fleet, but, alas, this excellent idea also fell through. Faced with a sudden excess of many hundreds of warships, and a Government dedicated to immediate disarmament, the Admiralty decided to scrap arbitrarily every ship over five-years old. If a ship had been laid down prior to 1940, no matter what her condition, she was to go. There were a few exceptions to this, their old companion, *Fame*, for example, survived a few more years before being sold abroad, but this ruling sounded the death-knell for *Faulknor* and most destroyers from the pre-war fleet.

'The war was over', recalled Ronald Fairweather to the author, 'and we proceeded to Dartmouth and were laid up mid-stream in the harbour with many other vessels lying astern of us. Most of the crew were paid off and returned to shore bases, but I remained on board as part of the 'Care and Maintenance' party in charge of the W/T office. I was a Telegraphist and had other duties that included collecting mail from Dartmouth Post Office and signals from a shore base which I had to pass to all ships lying astern of HMS *Faulknor.*'

> After that we went to Dartmouth where we had three weeks to de-ammunition ship and get her ready for paying off. I carried our last captain's luggage over to Kingswear. The time came when we all had to do the same and it is a sad feeling being on a railway platform watching your shipmates going to their various barracks on different trains. I was a Chatham rating and my messmates were from Pompey and some from Guz. My shipmates Bill James and Tich, left before I did and I felt very lonely when their train left. Anyway that was my recollection of the *Faulknor*.

The Requiem for *Faulknor* and other proud fighting ships thus relegated to retirement, was poignantly written by Captain S.W. Roskill:

A watchful and experienced Admiralty knew that those that were not too worn-out or too old might yet be needed again, in a sudden emergency which gave no time to build. And so, before many months had passed the creeks and estuaries of Britain's rivers began to receive groups of salt-rimed, rust-stained little ships. Their fragile and valuable equipment removed or protected by sealed 'cocoons', funnel covers laced on, and gun tampions driven hard home. Moored bow to stern they could not even swing to the tides they had known so well, but as the ripples ebbed and flowed could only gently nudge each other, and pass through the group the mumbling mutters of their memories.

He might almost have had *Faulknor* in his mind when he wrote:

> This one, the leader, had carried a famous Escort Group Commander, and with him on the bridge had fought through convoy after convoy; her depth charge racks and throwers had loosed death on many a lurking U-boat, detected by the relentless probing of the Asdic in her bottom…'[7]

Here she lay, forgotten by the majority of her crew and an uncaring nation. But not all!

On Friday, 14 September, during Regatta Week on the River Dart, a party consisting of Mrs H. T. Marsh, Mrs A. L. Hansford her daughter Sylvia, visitors from Stourbridge, viewed the ships and went aboard some laid up there. While aboard one of the Steam Gunboats Mrs Hansford saw the nameplate 'HMS *Faulknor*' alongside and told the Petty Officer showing them round that Stourbridge had adopted her during the war.

They were duly invited aboard, even though *Faulknor* was not officially open to the public but acting as the 'Mother' ship to the other vessels, providing accommodation for sleeping quarters etc., and Sub-Lieutenant A. Macdonald escorted them on a tour of the ship. Mrs Hansford was presented with a certificate on the ships notepaper, which read:

> This is to certify that the bearer visited HMS *Faulknor* during Regatta Week at Dartmouth and expressed complete satisfaction with the ship.

Petty Officer Frederick Lister gave them an old pass of his as a souvenir, and this pass still exists, having been handed over to Stourbridge Library by Mrs Hansford's husband Arthur, in July, 1987. This party was not the only representatives from their adoption towns to visit *Faulknor* during her final days, however.

Other visitors that *Faulknor* received at this time, weretwo young sisters who had 'adopted' her three years earlier. Mrs Joan Braithwaite recalled how:

> My sister and I (then the Misses Joan and Eileen Moody) and a party of five WVS ladies went down to Dartmouth to see her – she was by then out of commission in the river Dart. The 'powers-that-be' would not let us take any souvenirs from off 'our' ship, but I believe they promised the ship's bell to Stourbridge Council. However, I managed to 'acquire' the Ships seal which, just like her White Ensign, seems to have got lost!

The party of seven ladies was taken out to the ship aboard a landing craft, and sang sea shanties in the wardroom aboard. They also visited *Bulldog* alongside and later the Royal Navy College, Dartmouth. The Admiralty later presented the Borough Plaque, which had been presented to the ship, back to the Sea Rangers in 1948 and loaned the White Ensign to them.

Soon after the visit of the Moody sisters Sub-Lieutenant Macdonald was writing, on 27 November:

We've been very busy yesterday and today. Yesterday *Beagle* and *Bulldog* sailed and we had to tidy up after they had gone. Today two corvettes came alongside. The outlook from the upper deck is entirely different now and it will take us quite some time to get used to the fact that we no longer have two destroyers alongside.

Larry Verdun Chandler recalls the grand old ship's last days also:

I was the senior SPO when we took her to the scrap yard after spending a year in the mouth of the Dart on the Reserve Fleet. I served aboard *Faulknor* from the day war was declared to the very end. In all the old girl steamed a total of 310,000 sea miles, the hardest-working destroyer in the entire Royal Navy.

Faulknor was moored at the mouth of the river Dart and, as Dartmouth had no railway station, the ferry from Kingswear used to pass our bows every time a train came in. The name of the ferry was the *Mew,* and when the lads had a few pints and missed the last boat to come aboard they used to 'Crash Down' on the *Mew.*

One of my SPOs married a local widow and when he had finished his watch down below asked me if he could go ashore, but he said he would swim ashore, so I let him go. We did not de-fuel because we were the 'Living Ship' for all three vessels. I used to take a party of men up the Dart to get coal for the galley – and just before we went to Milford Haven, I fuelled ship ready for that passage. A couple of days before we left the Dart I spent all the money left in the canteen fund on a grand party ashore in a room above a pub where the RAOB Lodge had their meetings. The landlord brought the beer upstairs by the bucketful – I did take a few bottles back on board for the chaps on duty.

On 27 December 1945, *Faulknor* was reduced from Category 'B' to Category 'C' Reserve, another nail in her coffin. On 22 January 1946, she sailed from Dartmouth for the last time. She entered Devonport dockyard for her armament to be removed prior her final voyage to Milford Haven. The final official statement concerning HMS *Faulknor* came that same day when it was announced she had been sold to BISC (Salvage) for scrapping at Thomas W. Ward's, Shipbreakers, Sheffield, and would, in due course, be demolished at their Milford Haven depot.

In a signal of 1747 30 January 1946 from C-in-C, Portsmouth, confirmed that:

British Iron and Steel Corporation state that *Faulknor* is to be made available to them at Dartmouth for breaking up. *Faulknor* sails Plymouth 4/2

Harry Stapleton noted that:

Any ship in the Reserve Fleet would not be in first class sea-going order and to expect to exceed previous full power speed is most unlikely. This in particularly must apply to the *Faulknor* as she had restricted speed performance due to a defective port-unit extraction pump, and although a spare unit had been ordered around the time of the Anzio landings, this item, although desperately awaited, never materialised in my time and I left the ship after VE Day. At a guess, a top speed of 31 knots would be an extremely good result.

From the engine room viewpoint, the *Faulknor* did not in my time of nearly four years, with the one exception referred to above, suffer any major defects beyond ordinary maintenance, these being mostly concerned with steam leaks from glands and joints. Depth-charging severely tests any mechanical item and pipe work and gunfire helps to find a few minor items requiring attention.

Faulknor was a very well-constructed ship and made of good pre-war steel plate. She took some frightful poundings from the elements, particularly in the North Atlantic, Icelandic and Norwegian waters and on one occasion, the worst I ever was to experience, the Barents Sea. We worked hard, watch keeping round the clock, sometimes for several weeks on end and when chance offered while in harbour we all attended to routine maintenance and defects requiring attention.

Boiler cleaning periods gave opportunity for a few days respite and time to attend to larger jobs on pumps, generators and evaporation equipment for the distillation of sea water required for boilers and domestic purposes. Sometimes dockyard assistance was made available if possible, or from a parent Destroyer Depot ship.

Once *Faulknor* was alongside in the dockyard in Devonport, cranes lifted all her surviving guns and torpedo tubes out of her. This took longer than expected. D-of-D signalled Admiral Superintendent, Devonport on 13 March concerning the *Faulknor*:

Request Inclining Experiment before steaming to breaking-up yard.

However, Mr Tennyson of Section 20 of the DNC at Bath replied at 1727/15 March, to both parties:

Stability of *Faulknor* in condition ready for steaming to breaking-up yard with guns, torpedo tubes etc. removed has been investigated and found satisfactory. Inclining experiments not necessary.

The engineering room staff could indeed be proud of their work in keeping the ship going for so long through such extremes. The proof of their dedication came in March 1946, when *Faulknor* sailed from Devonport dockyard for the last time. Larry Chandler recalled:

On the way up to Milford Haven we connected up all three boilers and still managed to get *over 30 knots* out of her.

We all left her a few days later from the same place where we secured her, and the day before we returned to Royal Navy Barracks, Portsmouth, I ordered my stokers to collect

HMS Faulknor's *ship's nameplate used as the house nameplate for a cottage in Little Milford, 1996.* (Tim Hart.)

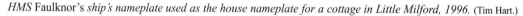

all the fire extinguishers in the ship, bring them to the upper deck and discharge them. You can well imagine what happened to the foam, the lads had the time of their lives spraying anyone that came near.

When she arrived at the Welsh port her draft forward was 11 feet, and aft was 12 feet. *Faulknor* was officially handed over to the ship-breakers, Thomas W. Ward, at their Castle Works at Milford Haven, on 4 April 1946 and work to dismantle her commenced on 10th. Her epitaph was written in a Milford Haven newspaper report early in 1946:

> A sorry sight at Messrs. T. W. Ward's ship-breaking yard today is HMS *Faulknor*, laid bare by oxy-acetylene. One of Britain's famous destroyers, she has sailed her last voyage. She took part in five invasions and was leader for the first two years of the war of the 'Fighting F' flotilla, which has been credited with the first U-boat sinking of the 1939–45 war. Now the *Faulknor*, adopted by Stourbridge during the war, has come to rest, twelve years after launching, twelve years of glorious and valiant service to Britain.

The sad story continued. By 26 July, 1946, the record book of the Yard Superintendent at Ward's office was recording the various small tools being utilised on board her by the breaking crew, five blow lamps, 5 oxygen regulators, and so on, and by September 2nd was also recording the final selling off of various equipment from *Faulknor*, a sorry itinerary which included six single beds at

Lady Scott-Moncrieff with some of the veterans of HMS Faulknor *at the annual reunion at Portsmouth of the* Faulknor *Association, May 1992.* (H.R. Parham.)

ten shillings each, fifteen blankets, pillows, various items of cutlery and finally one kettle for eight shillings and nine pence! Later records show a total of 1,099 tons of Out-Turn Material being salvaged, which included steel scrap (846 tons), Cast Iron (52 tons), Armour (48 tons), Copper (11 tons), Gun Metal (23 tons), Yellow Metal (62 tons), Lead and Zinc (6 tons) and other sundries, which realised the sum of £9,132, against which the Demolition Costs totalled just under £8,483, or a cost per ton of £7.75 in today's money. The book finally closed on 31 March 1948 and *Faulknor* was no more. The ship's bell, subject to a long search by the author and the Association alike, vanished into limbo with the ship. It would be nice to think that somewhere it still survives, the last memento to an illustrious career.

* * *

Her passing was swift, abrupt, but typical. This country, supposedly so steeped in its heritage of tradition, failed to preserve one of those hundreds of little ships which for six years had fought the grim but so vital Battle of the Atlantic, the outcome of which, had it been reversed, would have meant starvation, surrender and goodness knows what other horrors for the population at the hands of the

Nazis. Perhaps it was not strange that, in the immediate aftermath, the natural concern of the nation was to rebuild all that had been shattered. How sad that *Faulknor* was not preserved; few ships fought in so many naval actions: Norway, Malta Convoys, hunting the *Bismarck*, *Tirpitz*, *Scharnhorst* and *Gneisenau*, Russia convoys, and invasions, Narvik, Dakar, Sicily, Italy, and Normandy. In between all these actions and battles she still found time to sink three U-boats and assist in crippling others, more than most escorts which spent their entire careers in the North Atlantic.

It was not to be. Some years after this book was first published two ships *were* saved from the Second World War Royal Navy, light cruiser *Belfast* and destroyer *Cavalier*. This gave the author much satisfaction, even though the latter only joined the fleet in 1944 and saw little action, but at least she was a Fleet destroyer, even her beautiful lines were hideously marred by a hideous 'Seacat' deckhouse.

One thing from HMS *Faulknor* that could have lived on, as it had before from year to year, was her name; but even this also faded away with her passing. A much reduced Navy, fighting reluctant and blind Governments year-upon-year for every penny of dwindling funds, turned to the people, naming ships after cities, towns and even villages, until, by the mid-1950s the Navy List looked liked

HMS Faulknor's *Memorial Tree at the National Memorial Arboretum, Burton on Trent, 2002.* (Carl Hueur.)

a Railway Timetable. One small group of frigates was a welcome exception to this dreary catalogue and fitting successor to naval traditions being named after famous sailors – but there proved few stirring names among those selected; one looked in vain for *Grenville*, *Inglefield*, or perhaps *Faulknor*. Recently, more traditional names are once again reappearing. However, with the entire surface Navy reduced to a pitiful *thirty* surface ships and an average of only two destroyers a year being built, it is doubtful if we shall ever see her name afloat again.

HMS *Faulknor's* achievements remain, however; she and the others of her breed who, for a brief period, brought an extra touch of dash and glamour to the history of the Royal Navy – the Destroyers..

Appendix I

STATISTICAL DETAILS HMS *Faulknor*

1932 Estimates; Ordered 17 March 1933; Laid Down 31 July 1933; Launched 12 June 1934; and Completed 24 May 1936.

Builders:	Messrs. Yarrow & Co., Limited, Scotstoun, Glasgow.
Job Number:	1640.
Displacement:	1,458 tons standard (1,505 tons calculated); 2,009 tons full load* (Actual at Launch: 1,792.25 tons Gross, 681.05 Net.
Dimensions:	332 feet (between perpendiculars); 343 feet overall x 33′ 8″ beam x 19′ 10½″ feet (Moulded Amidships Depth); 10½ feet (mean) draught.
Deck Camber:	Upper Deck – 9″ on 32′ 3″; Fo'c'sle – 10″ on 32′.
Machinery:	Parsons Geared Turbines, two shafts, 38,000 shaft-horse power, giving 36 knots (designed), 36.648 knots (on trials). Three Yarrow Water tube boilers, 300 lb psi; Total HS 27.300; Combustion Space total 2,850. Twin screws, with 10 feet diameter 3-bladed propellers, with a pitch of 12′ 10″ and an area of 8,856 square inches.
Trial Figures:	At 5,000 SHP, 12 hours at 20.76 knots. Oil Burnt 24.93 tons = 0.929 lbs/SHP/hour. SHP = 5004. Radius of Action on 430.6 tons of oil, i.e. 85% full capacity was 4304 knots.
Armament:	Five 4.7-inch Quick Firing, Low Angle (maximum elevation 40°) Guns in single mountings with open shields. Maximum range 16,700 yards. 200 rpg carried.
	Eight 0.5 inch Anti-Aircraft Machine Guns in two quadruple mountings.
	Four Lewis Guns.
	Thirty-five rifles.
	Eight 21-inch Torpedo Tubes in two quadruple mountings.
	Eight Mark 9 Depth Charge Release Gears, one Rail, two Depth Charge Throwers; twenty Depth Charges carried.

Complement:	Peace	War	Accommodation
Captain (D) and Officers	12	12	11
Gunroom Officer no cabin	–	–	1
Warrant Officers	4	4	4
Petty Officers	37	37	42
Seamen, Stokers etc.	126	133	134
Total	179	187	192

Oil Fuel:	490 tons giving 6,000 miles radius of action at 15 knots.
Costs:	£330,239 (total); £271,886 (excluding main armament), of which hull £118,300; machinery & boilers £145,351; auxiliary machinery £8,235.
Other Details:	One 24-inch Searchlight on 'amidships platform.
	One 10-foot Range Finder and a Director Control Tower (Low Angle) on bridge.

*When inclined in March 1935 the ship was 55 tons light on design, 34 tons being on machinery, 10 tons on hull and the remainder on equipment.

Endurance figures in 1939

1,270 miles endurance at $31\frac{1}{2}$ knots speed
1,400 " " $30\frac{1}{2}$ " "
1,830 " " 27 " "
2,240 " " $24\frac{1}{2}$ " "
3,120 " " $20\frac{1}{2}$ " "
5,210 " " 13 " "

Appendix II

Wartime Alterations

1935–39   None.

1940   (a) After bank of torpedo tubes replaced by a single 3-inch High Angle Gun and shield.

(b) After funnel cut down by seven feet in height

(c) Stump Mast (fitted before the searchlight platform replaced tall mainmast.

Both (b) and (c) were to increase the sky arcs of the 3-inch Gun (a).

1942   (a) 'X' Gun removed, after bank of torpedo tubes replaced and the 3-inch HA Gun remounted in 'X' position. Single 20 mm Oerlikon guns added port and starboard at fore end of the after shelter deck, and also port and starboard abreast the bridge, replacing the 0.5 Machine Guns.

(b) The original L.A. Range Finder on the bridge replaced by HA Director with Type 285 Radar. Under this arrangement the main armament was controlled by the HA Director and was ranged by the HA Director, although for barrage fire only the guns could also be controlled by the HA Director.

(c) Type 286 PQ General Warning Radar fitted, with aerial at head of foremast. High Frequency Direction Finder Outfit FH4, added, aerial on as pole mast aft. 'Huff-Duff' MF/DF Outfit PM12, fitted, aerial on forward side of the of bridge.

1943   Type 291 Radar replaced Type 286 PQ.

1944   'X' Mounting landed replaced by Quadruple 2-pdr Pom-Pom on rebuilt deck.

Twin Oerlikons replaced single abreast bridge to give new total of six.

1945   Final armament:

Three 4.7-inch QF LA Guns in single mountings, 'A', 'B', 'Y'.

One 3-inch HA Gun 'X'.

Four 2-pdr pom-poms in one quadruple mounting 'Q'.

Six 20-mm Oerlikon AA guns, in two double mountings abreast bridge, and two single mountings aft

Two Lewis Guns.

35 Rifles.

Eight 21-inch Torpedo Tubes (The original after bank of four tubes having been replaced) Eight Mark 9 Depth Charge Release Gears, one Rail, two Depth Charge Throwers, Depth Charge stowage increased to 39. Ballast carried to counter top weight, 40 tons.

Full War Complement 201 Officers and Men.

Displacement slightly reduced by wartime alterations; in 1946 it was 1,355 tons standard and 1,880 tons full load.

TOTAL Miles steamed 3 September 1939 to 12 June 1945: 310,000.

Appendix III

Battle Honours
Atlantic 1939-43
Norway 1940
Spartivento 1940
Malta Convoys 1941
Arctic 1942-43
Sicily 1943
Salerno 1943
Aegean 1943
Anzio 1944
Mediterranean 1943-44
Normandy 1944

Appendix IV

Commanding Officers
Date of Appointment

May 1935	Captain M. L. Clarke, DSC
March 1936	Captain V.H. Danckwerts, CMG
April 1938	Captain C. S. Daniel
February 1940	Captain A.F. De Salis
January 1942	Captain A.K. Scott-Moncrieff, DSO
September 1943	Captain M. S. Thomas, DSO
December 1943	Lieutenant-Commander E. G. May
April 1944	Commander C.F.H. Churchill
December 1944	Commander D.E. Holland-Martin, DSO, DSC
May 1945	Commander G. E. Fardell

Appendix V

Distinguished Personages aboard HMS *Faulknor*

Date	*Personality*	*Occasion*
23/25 July 1935	HRH Prince of Wales	Visit to the Channel Islands
9 June 1942	HRH King Peter of Yugoslavia	Visit to the Home Fleet at Scapa Flow
9 June 1942	Prime Minister, Winston S. Churchill, Sir Stafford Cripps, Randolph Churchill	Visit to the Home Fleet at Scapa Flow
19 June 1942	Rear Admiral Sir Robert Burnett, Rear-Admiral (D) Home Fleet	Home Fleet Destroyer exercises and British Movietone News filming
October 1942	Admiral Sir John Tovey, C-in-C, Home Fleet	Despatch Boat duties Scapa Flow
18 November 1942	Admiral Golovko, C-in-C Soviet Northern Fleet	Polyarnoe Naval Base, Murmansk
3 December 1943	Admiral Sir John H. D. Cunningham, C-in-C Mediterranean and staff	Conveyed from Malta to Augusta
6/8 June 1944	Field-Marshal Sir Bernard Montgomery and staff	Visiting beaches & HQ Ships off Normandy beaches
7 June 1944	General Dempsey, Admiral Sir Philip Vian	Conference with Montgomery
7 June 1944	US General Omah Bradley, C-in-C. US Troops	Conference with Montgomery
18 June 1944	Admiral Sir Bertram Ramsey, ANCXF, Lord Reith, Head of the BBC, three Admirals and two Vice Admirals	Visiting D-Day beaches
19 June 1944	Admiral Sir Bruce Fraser, C-in-C, British Pacific Fleet	Visiting D-Day beaches
21 June 1944	Commodore J Hughes-Hallett, COS, ANCXF	Visiting D-Day beaches
24 June 1944	Albert Alexander, M.P., First Lord of the Admiralty, Naval Secretary Lord Bruntisfield, Lord Beaverbrook, Sir Algernon Willis, 2nd Sea Lord	Visiting D Day beaches
9 July 1944	French General Koenig and staff	Transported to France
11/12 May 1945	Vice-Admiral Huffmeir, German C-in-C, Channel Islands; Major General Wolff, German OC Troops Channel Islands	Taken into captivity from Guernsey to Plymouth on Liberation of Channel Islands
29/30 May 1945	Vice Admiral Sir Ralph Leatham, C-in-C, Plymouth	Inspection of Channel Islands

Appendix VI

THOSE WHO DID NOT RETURN
'WE WILL REMEMBER THEM'

Rank, Name	Date of Loss	Area and circumstance
A.B. John W. Spanner	28-11-39	Lost overboard in heavy seas off Norway
Ord/Smn Thomas Broadbent	16-4-40	Killed by German sniper fire at Narvik
Petty Officer (Supply)	25-12-40	Killed by broken neck in Idris William Wirtz accidental fall aboard due to bad weather on leaving Gibraltar
A.B. Robert 'Jock' Alexander	5-10-42	Killed in accidental fall at Town Quay, Newcastle
Ord Smn George Albert Cosham	23-11-42	Lost overboard in heavy seas off North Cape
Acting Petty Officer D. G. Goodyear	12-1-43	Lost overboard in heavy weather off Norway
Lt. (S) Alan Phipps	16-11-43	Killed by Germans in final assault on British Army HQ at Leros

Appendix VII

Prime Sources, References and Secondary Material
Files on HMS FAULKNOR to view at PRO
ADM1/10633 – Includes rescue of survivors from Swedish merchant vessel *Grania*
ADM1/12827 – Messages relating to Surrender of Italian Fleet, 1943
ADM 53/103155-103176 – Logs of HMS *Faulknor* 1937–38
ADM 53/108648-108658 – Logs of HMS *Faulknor* Jan-Nov 1939
ADM 53/117057 – Log of HMS *Birmingham* 28-30 November 1944
ADM 53/117381 – Log of HMS *Dido* 28-30 November 1944
ADM 53/118676 – Log of HMS *Valiant* 8-12 September 1943
ADM 53/118717 – Log of HMS *Warspite* 8-12 September 1943
ADM 53/15831/2 – Logs of HMS *Duke of York* June/July 1942
ADM104/ 106-107 – Index to Register of Deaths
ADM104/112-113 – Register of Deaths (Naval Ratings) 1919-1948
ADM 104/127-139 – Reports of Deaths (Naval Ratings) September 1939 – June 1948
ADM 116/2468 – China Station Piracy in Hong King waters 1925/28
ADM 116/2502 – Piracy in Hong Kong waters 1926/28
ADM 116/2547 – China Station R of Ps 1926/28
ADM 116/2624 – China Station R of Ps 1928/29
ADM 116/2509 – China Station R of Ps 1926/28
ADM 116/3076 – Home Fleet Diary 1935/36
ADM 179/431 – List of Daily Sailings 'Neptune'
ADM 179/502 – Operation 'Neptune' defensive Destroyer patrols
ADM 179/506 – Operation 'Neptune', R of P Force 'J'.
ADM 179/516 – Eastern Task Force Reports
ADM 187/1-49 – Pink Lists September Various Dates 1939/1944
ADM 199/17 – Convoy TC. 1 and TC. 3 R of P
ADM 199/24 – 1939-40 ON & HN Convoy Reports 39/40
ADM 199/73 – North Russia convoys JW./RA Reports 1943
ADM 199/83-4 – Naval support of land forces Mediterranean 1943/44
ADM 199/126 – 1939/40 Anti-U-Boat attacks Reports
ADM 199/190-1 – Daily State of Mediterranean Fleet 1942-4
ADM 199/237/114 – Convoy ONS 6
ADM 199/258 – Naval Ops Med. Aegean, HMS *Faulknor's* R o P 17/18-9-43
ADM 199/376 – Home Fleet Destroyer Command War Diary 1940
ADM 199/393 – Home Fleet War Diary 1939-40
ADM 199/452 – Italian Armistice 1943
ADM 199/464 – Convoy SNF.17 R o P Anti-Submarine attacks by escorts.
ADM 199/475 – Norway- Narvik R of P HMS *Faulknor*
ADM 199/485/490 inclusive – Operations at, Capture of, Evacuation from Narvik April/June 1940
ADM 199/575, 576, 2920 – Convoy HX.234
ADM 199/577 – 1943/44. – HX. Convoy Reports
ADM 199/578 – Convoy HX.239
ADM 199/579, 580 – Convoy SC.127

ADM 199/617 – 1941/43. R of P *Faulknor* 31-1-42 – 20-2-42 PQ 9 & QP 10

ADM 199/686 – -Convoy SNF.17 R o P Commodore

ADM 199/721 – 1942 PQ/QP Convoy Reports

ADM 199/757 – Arctic Convoys PQ.17

ADM 199/758 – 1942-43 PQ/QP Convoy Reports Gearbox II

ADM 199/805-6 – Naval Operations Mediterranean 1944

ADM 199/817, 906, 907 – Operation 'Menace'

ADM 199/863 – Operations 'Avalanche' and 'PWB' 1943 R of Ps

ADM 199/873 – Operation 'Shingle', C-in-Cs R of P

ADM 199/946 – Avalanche/Husky R of P

ADM 199/1007 – 'Monster' Liner Convoys – Signals.

ADM 199/1040 – 1943-45 HM & Greek Reports Aegean. R of P *Faulknor*

ADM 199/1049 – Battle of Spartivento, R of Ps

ADM 199/1392 – Milford Haven Oct-Nov 1944

ADM 199/1393/1394 – Plymouth Command War Diary Jan-Dec 1944

ADM 199/1397 – R of P Normandy War Diary

ADM 199/1430/1 – Levant Command War Diaries Jan/March 1944

ADM 199/1442 – Western Approaches Command War Diary May/June, 1944

ADM 199/1559 – Original plans for 'Neptune'

ADM 199/1645 – Operation 'Neptune' Destroyers R o Ps

ADM 199/1654- 6 – Assault Area Reports 'Neptune'

ADM 199/1664-1689 – Normandy Signals

ADM 199/1970 – Anti-U-Boat attacks analysis 1940-45

ADM 199/1973 – Anti-U-Boat attacks analysis 1939

ADM 199/1782 – 1940-42. Proceedings of U-Boat assessment committee 18-6-41 13-8-41 10-8-41 (1752)

ADM 199/1783 – Anti-U-Boat attacks analysis 1942

ADM 199/1790 -1940-45 U-Boat committee

ADM 199/2058 – 1941 Monthly A/S Reports (*U-138)*

ADM 199/2067 – Mining of HMS *Goathland*, R of P; Torpedoing of HMS *Birmingham* R of P's; Mining of HMS *Sheffield*, R of P

ADM 217/688 – 691 – Milford Haven War Diary November/December 1944

ADM 217/185 – R of P *Faulknor* rescue of Liberator crew dated 5 July 1943

ADM239/60-77 Particulars of War Vessels

AIR 27/384 – Squadron Combat Diary No. 36 Squadron RAF

Log Book of Sub-Lieutenant (A) 'Jack' F Harvey, RNVR, July-August, 1943. (Courtesy of Stephen Harvey, Mildenhall).

Log Books of HMS *Faulknor* December, 1939 to June, 1941 inclusive. (Viewed in 1967, since destroyed by M.o.D.).

Admiralty Ship Movement Binder for HMS *Faulknor* 1938-46. Preliminary Narrative of The History of the Canadian Military Forces Overseas 1939-1940, Chapter One, Copy supplied by Directorate Of History, National Defence Headquarters, Ottawa, Canada.

History of HMCS Ottawa II; Copy supplied by Directorate of History, National Defence Headquarters, Ottawa, Canada.

Report of Proceedings 5th Canadian Escort Group with Convoy ON 182; Copy supplied by Directorate of History, National Defence Headquarters, Ottawa, Canada.

Ships Cover (519) HMS *Faulknor,* National Maritime Museum, Brass Foundry, Woolwich Arsenal, London.

Ships Cover (515) *Fearless* Class destroyers and Leader, National Maritime Museum, Brass Foundry, Woolwich Arsenal, London.

Ships Cover (492), HMS *Exmouth*, National Maritime Museum, Brass Foundry, Woolwich Arsenal, London.

Log Book of *U-371* 17–21 March, 1944. *Bundesarchiv-Militararchiv* Case 10.30432.

Log Book of USS *Philadelphia* 18/20 February, 1944, National Archives, Washington, D.C.

Log Book of USS *Maloy,* 27/30 August, 1944.

Building Record and Trials Record Books for HMS *Faulknor,* Job Number 1640, Yarrow & Company, Scotstoun, Glasgow.

List of Westbound Troopship Sailings 1945 – Directorate of History document, Ottawa.

Lloyd's Register of Shipping, 1944-45.

T. W. Ward & Co, Shipbreakers, Milford Haven Depot, Breaking Up Record and Sales Book for HMS *Faulknor*, 1946.

Record Cards for Ledger, T. W. Ward & Co, Shipbreakers, Milford Haven Depot. Department of Marine Technology, University of Newcastle.

Letters written to Miss Moody of the *Faulknor* Fund Committee, Stourbridge by Captain A.K. Scott-Moncrieff; Captain M.S. Thomas; Lieutenant -Commander E.G. May; Commander C.F.H. Churchill; Commander D.E. Holland-Martin; Commander G.E. Fardell; Paymaster Lieutenant Rex P. Peter; Paymaster Sub-Lieutenant Chilcott; Sub-Lieutenant Macdonald; Chief Yeoman of Signals A.L. Colborne; Able-Seaman H. Matthews and Able Seaman Charles Frederick Lister, held in Case 15, Reference Section, Stourbridge Library.

Notes

Introduction

1. And not only books: on the web sites set up in recent years by former matelots, who if anyone, *should* know better, and who only had to glance at any reference book, schoolboy howlers continue. For example on the HMS *Hood* web site, *Faulknor*, even when copied from the ships logbook, is misspelt as *Faulkenor* throughout!

Chapter I

1. It has become a 'fashionable' trend in many post-war books to lump the Leaders in with their classes as if they were one and the same. This is at best sloppy and at worst, factually inaccurate.
2. Hodges, *Destroyer Weapons,* Conway, 1979.
3. *Flotillas* by Lionel Dawson, Rich & Cowan, 1933. The author de-rates destroyers and favours large cruiser types.
4. *Asdic* came from the initials of the Allied Submarine Detection Investigation Committee, set up in 1917, but post-1948 was replaced by Sonar, just as Flotilla was replaced by Squadron, as part of the general subordination of the Royal Navy to the Americans that took place in NATO.
5. All figures from original data held by Yarrow and kindly supplied to the Author. They differ from most previously inaccurate quoted and published figures.
6. Note the spelling- with *OR* at the end. Frequently in book after book of post-war 'histories' and thrown-together reference books, the name is misspelt as Faulkn*er,* more examples of sloppy writing, researching and authorship. Nor are modern writers alone in this. At the first reunion of the HMS *Faulknor* Survivors' Association at which the author was guest, 'Aggie Weston's' in Queen Street advertised her on their announcement board as *Falconer*! The book *Fighting Ships in the Age of Steam*, Len Ortzen, London, 1978, features *Destroyer Leader* in its Chapter Eight, copying almost word-for-word, but still misspells her as *Faulkner*, thus being doubly inept!
7. The numbers in square brackets indicate the composition after reorganisation as the 8th Flotilla, which took place in May, 1939. It should be stressed that *Fearless* and *Fortune* were *built* as Divisional Leaders. CSA smoke laying apparatus was only built into *Fame, Foresight, Forester* and *Fury.*

Chapter 2

1. See *Naval Electronic Warfare,* by Dr. D. G. Kiely, Brassey Defence Publishers, 1988.
2. See *Life Line*, Charles Graves, William Heinemann, London, 1941
3. See *Make a Signal!* Jack Broome, Putnam, 1955

Chapter 3

1. It is often forgotten that the only reason why Japanese aircraft were able to sink *Prince of Wales* and *Repulse* in December 1941, was because they were operating from French airfields in Indo-China giving them the range required, and that the French on these fields toasted this Japanese victory enthusiastically. Treatment of the unfortunate survivors of light cruiser *Manchester* and destroyer *Havock,* interned in French North Africa, was *worse* than in Nazi POW camps. French Glenn Martin bombers frequently attacked Gibraltar and inflicted damage on our warships off Syria. When the Vichy apologists present their case, as they have done often and shrilly, such facts are usually forgotten or glossed over.

2. See *Engage the Enemy more Closely*, by Correlli Barnett, Hodder & Stoughton, 1991)

3. See, *Action Imminent* by Peter C Smith, William Kimber, London, 1980, for the full and complete account of this fiasco.

4 See *Action Imminent*, William Kimber, London, 1980 and *Hit First, Hit Hard*, William Kimber, London, 1979).

5 See *Destroyer's War*, A. D. Divine, Faber & Faber, London, 1942.

Chapter 4

1. *The Somerville Papers*, Document 169.

2. In addition to *Foresight* at Malta, and damage to *Fortune*, the *Firedrake* had run aground off Malaga, Spain at the end of March and had to be sent home to refit and repair, she did not join until July; *Fame* which had run aground off Whitburn, Tyne, in November 1940 and burnt out, had to be virtually rebuilt which took almost a year, and never did join Force 'H'.

3. *Destroyer's War, op cit.*

4. *Amazon to Ivanhoe* by John English, World Ship Society, 1993.

5. See HMS *Wild Swan* by Peter C Smith, William Kimber, London, 1985.

Chapter 5

1. Report of Proceedings damage to HMS *Sheffield,* (ADM 199/2067).

2. See HMS *Bedouin and the Long March Home,* by Percy Hagger, Navigator Books, 1994.

3. See *Destroyer Captain* by Roger Hill, DSO, DSC, RN (London, 1975). This author was privileged to both recommend and edit for publication this very revealing book.

4. For the definitive account see, Peter C Smith, *Pedestal; the convoy that saved Malta* (Goodall, 2002).

5. See: Peter C Smith, *Arctic Victory*, Crecy Books, 1994.

6. Italics in original.

7. A note by the Director of Armaments added that this was 'Only applicable to E & F Class plus *Garland*', presumably because these ships being those destroyers originally fitted [or in the latter case, subsequently re-equipped] with the removable deck plates, now left permanently removed with the gun wells exposed.

Chapter 6

1. The media and modern historians credit radar and air cover as the winning factors in the U-boat war. In truth it was W/T and the surface escorts that won this battle. See letters from R.A. Laws and especially H.H. Ogilvy to *IEE News*, 4 November 1993.

2. The passage of this convoy is described in *Seizing the Enigma*, by David Kahn, but he omits any reference whatsoever to 4th Escort Group's part.

3. The 4,962 ton *Nailsea Meadow* had been torpedoed and sunk in 40° 30′ N, 32° 30′ W the night before.

4. Until it was pointed out to the American captain, that Pearl Harbor had taken place on a Sunday also!

5. The minelayer *Abdiel* and destroyers *Faulknor, Fury, Echo, Eclipse, Inglefield, Intrepid, Ilex, Raider, Queen Olga* and *Witherington.*

6. Most histories incorrectly state that *Le Terrible* was present at the surrender but the actual Reports of Proceedings of Admiral Bissett make it clear that she was *not*. See C-in-C, Mediterranean's Signal timed at 1806 of 9 September 1943. In fact, *Le Terrible* joined *Le Fantasque* also detached from Force 'H' and both ships arrived at Algiers on 12 September.

7. For the complete account of this campaign, see *War in the Aegean,* Peter C. Smith & Edwin R. Walker, London, 1974.

8. See – *Long Road to Leros*, by L Marsland Gander, London, 1945.
9. In the book *U-Boat Fact File*, by Peter Sharpe (Midland 1998), it is stated on page 93 that HMS *Birmingham* was sunk in this attack! This is complete nonsense, for, after repairs she remained in service with the Royal Navy until 1960. On reflection, it is very strange indeed that the *U-407* failed to finish off such a sitting duck and this has never been explained. Also, that the Admiralty sailed *Birmingham* through such dangerous waters without any destroyer escort beggar's belief.

Chapter 7

1. The honour of the *first* warships at the D-Day landings goes to midget submarines *X.20* and the *X.23,* which had been lying submerged off Juno and Sword beaches ready to shine green guiding lights.
2. See *The Lonely Leader; Monty 1944-45*, by Alistair Horne, Macmillan, London, 1994.
3. Again, in a footnote, Alastair Horne comments that *Faulknor* grounded, '… in apparently so amateurish a fashion, so close to enemy guns.' He also stated that, '… the unfortunate Churchill, having now committed two solecisms, doubtless feared for his future.' Like the 'drifting' account, such comments betray a starting lack of understanding of close-in coastal navigation off a hostile shoreline, especially when the Senior British Army officer makes a 'request'! Carl Huer states firmly: – 'The reason we went aground was due to Monty's insistence we go in closer!' Surgeon-Lieutenant Nelson, the senior surviving officer of *Faulknor* and actual eyewitness stated:

> Montgomery had asked if he might be first ashore early next morning so the Captain cautiously moved closer, cautious because all the beach marks were unseen and the coast had changed in four years and had not yet been re-charted and sounded. So we went aground and sheared off our Asdic dome.

4. In 1948 the Council had the plaque they presented to the ship returned to them and they passed it on to the local Sea Rangers. These, it was recorded, already had in their possession the second Ship's Ensign, which had been flown when the Channel Islands were liberated. When the Sea Rangers were disbanded this also disappeared.
5. Although Ted Newman recorded – 'During the forenoon a German Admiral and an Army Officer came aboard to sign the surrender terms' – and many others remember it like that, this is *not* what really happened, for the surrender had *already* been signed aboard the *Bulldog* previously. Because of the rank of their prisoners, – 'Everybody had to be in the Rig of the Day and much ceremony was made of it all' – *is* correct. As Ronald Fairweather correctly told me: – 'When we had left the harbour after our boiler clean, we went over the Channel Islands and we brought back all the German Generals and Admirals who were in command there and I was detailed as one of the Guard of Honour for them. Royal Marines armed to the teeth. But what really caused the German officers much amazement was the crew of the landing craft, WRNS – quite unthinkable!
6. Alas poor *Croziers,* completed 30 November, 1945, she was only to grace the Royal Navy for a brief year before the Government sold her to Norway and, on 10 October, 1946, she became RNN *Trondheim.*
7. Captain S.W. Roskill, *The War at Sea*, Vol.4, Pt 2, London, 1963.

Glossary of Naval Terms

AA	Anti-aircraft
AB	Able seaman
ACNS	Assistant Chief of Naval Staff
ADO	Air Defence Officer
AFCC	Admiralty Fire Control Clock
A-K Line	Cruiser squadron ship positions ahead of fleet in naval battle
AMC	Armed Merchant Cruiser
AP	Armour Piercing
A' Arc	Position of ship relative to target when all main armament will bear
A/S	Anti-submarine
Asdic	Allied Submarine Detection Information Committee.
AT	Admiralty Telegram
ASV	Aircraft/Surface Vessel - radar detecting both
BCS	Battle-cruiser Squadron
CAFO	Confidential Admiralty Fleet Order
Capital Ships	Battleships and Battle-Cruisers as defined by Washington
Captain (D)	Senior Captain in control of a Destroyer Flotilla
CG	Centre of Gravity
C-in-C	Commander-in-Chief
CNS	Chief of Naval Staff
Controller	Controller of the Royal Navy
CPO	Chief Petty Officer
CS	Cruiser Squadron
CSA	Chloro-Sulphonic Smoke Apparatus
DC	Depth Charge
DCT	Director Control Tower
DCNS	Deputy Chief of Naval Staff
DDNO	Deputy Director of Naval Ordnance
D/F	Direction Finding
D of C	Director of Contracts
DG	De-gaussing (protection from magnetic mines)
DOD	Director of Operations Division
D of P	Director of Plans
DNAD	Director Naval Air Division
DNC	Director of Naval Construction
DNO	Director of Naval Ordnance
DP	Dual Purpose, guns which could engage air and surface targets
Deep	Deep Displacement - warship tonnage fully laden for war
DSD	Director of Signal Division
DTD	Director of Tactical Division
DTM	Director of Torpedoes and Mining
DTSD	Director of Training and Staff Duties
EC	Endless Chain (patrol pattern in figure-of-eight configuration)
E-in-C	Engineer-in-Chief of the Navy
ERA	Engine Room Artificer
Flotilla	Collective noun for small ship squadrons in Royal Navy until 1947
FMO	Flotilla Medical Officer
FKC	Fuze Keeping Clock

FS	Fuze Setter
FP	Full Power
G	See C. G.
GM	Metacentric Height
GZ	Righting Lever
HA	High Angle guns for engaging aircraft targets
HE	High Explosive
HF/DF	'HuffDuff' High Frequency Direction Finding
Hogging	Condition of ships hull stress when centrally supported by waves
HP	Horse Power or High Pressure
HCP	Hydraulic Control Power
IHP	Indicated Horse Power
IO	Illumination Officer
kw	Kilowatt
LA	Low Angle guns for engaging surface targets only
LKBP	Last Known Bearing Position
LNT	London Naval Treaties
MTB	Motor Torpedo Boat (German = E-boat; Italian - MAS-boat; american = PT boat
mg	machine gun
MF/DF	Medium Frequency/Direction Finding
MV	Muzzle Velocity
OA	Overall (Total length of ship)
OD	Ordinary Seaman
OOW	Officer of the Watch
OT	Oil tight
PC	Propulsion Coefficient
	Pdr-Pounder
PIL	Position in Line
PO	Petty Officer
PO Tel	Petty Officer Telegraphist
PPI	Plan Position Indicator
QF	Quick Firing
QR	Quadruple Revolving (Torpedo Tubes)
R/F	Range Finder
RDF	Reflection Direction Finding (Radar)
RPM	revs per minute
RU	Ready Use (ammunition stowed close to guns for quick usage)
SHP	Shaft Horse Power
Standard	Standard Displacement of ship as defined by Washington
SAP	Semi- armour piercing shells
Sagging	Condition of ships hull stress when both end are supported with hull in wave trough
SO	Senior Officer
TT	Torpedo Tubes
TSDS	Two Speed Destroyer Sweep (for minesweeping)
TBI	Target Bearing Indicator
TDS	Torpedo Deflection Sight
TSDS	Transmitting Station
TDS	Torpedo Deflection Sight
VC/VF	Auto-recognition system (Visual Contact/Verification)
V/S	Visual Signal
W/T	Wireless Telegraphy
VCG	Vertical Centre of Gravity

Index

Aba, Hospital ship 256
Abdiel, H M minelayer 90
Abercrombie, HM monitor 261
Acanthus, HM corvette 171
Acasta, HM destroyer 49, 82
Achates, HM destroyer 135, 138
Active, HM destroyer 58, 61
Activity, HM escort carrier 263
Acute, HM minesweeper 224
Admiral Hipper, German heavy cruiser 42, 77–8, 85, 128, 139, 143, 153
Admiral Scheer, German pocket-battleship 68, 123, 139
Adrias, Greek destroyer 207
Agnew, Comodore, W G 184
Albacore, HM minesweeper 224
Albrighton, HM destroyer 257
Aldenham, HM destroyer 222
Aldersdale, oiler 48–9, 57
Alexander, A/B Robert 141
Alexander, Rt. Hon Albert, First Lord 248
Alisma, HM corvette 263
Alonquin, HM Canadian destroyer 237, 247
Alsey, ss 80
Altmark, German prison ship 36, 41, 103
Alynbank, HM AA ship 135
Alysse, Free French corvette 99
Alstertor, German supply ship 102–5
Amazon, HM destroyer 3, 55–6, 135, 138
Ambuscade, H M destroyer 3
Anadgum, SS 65
Andes, liner 257–8, 261
Anson, HM battleship 130, 135, 142, 155
Antenor, ss 263–4
Apollo, HM minelayer 243–4
Aquitania, RMS 35, 257–8, 262
Archer, HM escort carrier 169, 171–3
Ardent, HM destroyer 48–9, 51
Arethusa, HM light cruiser 58, 60–1, 63, 81, 107, 110
Argus, HM aircraft-carrier 63–4, 69, 77–8, 89, 98, 100
Ark Royal, HM aircraft-carrier 17, 19–21, 24, 27, 57, 60–71,

76–8, 86–7, 89–92, 95–7, 99, 102, 106–8, 110–1, 115
Armstrong, Captain H T "Beaky" 127, 135
Arsenal, Operation 180
Artigliere, Italian destroyer 189
Ascianghi, Italian submarine 183
Ashanti, HM destroyer 29–30, 32, 42, 123, 128, 132, 135, 138, 140
Asphodel, H M corvette 81–2, 85
Assault, Operation 267
Assiniboine, HM Canadian destroyer 263
Atheltemplar, oiler 135
Athenia, liner 19–20
Atlantic, SS 120
Atlantis, ss 103, 105
Augusta. US heavy cruiser 244–5
Aurora, HM light cruiser 19, 27, 30, 39, 42, 47–9, 51–5, 178, 180, 184–5, 199, 204, 207, 210
Australia, HMAS heavy cruiser 65–7, 79
Avalanche, Operation 185–6
Avenger, HM escort-carrier 136, 140, 205
Avon Vale, HM destroyer 107–8, 110, 112

Bacon, Petty Offier 77
B P Newton, blockade-runner 128
Baku, Soviet destroyer 144
Balteaks, RFA 52
Bankok, Vichy ss 86
Banner, Jack 102, 143
Bantemps, Hans 105
Barbados, HM frigate 264
Barfleur, French armed transport 263
Barham, HM battleship 35, 65–8
Barrett, Jack 152, 157–61, 186, 188–9, 192, 195–6, 198–200, 203–4, 206, 209–10
Basque, French destroyer 267
Batory, Polish liner 43, 257, 262
Battorsby, Lt C S 118
Baytown, Operation 186

Beacon Street, ss 85
Beagle, HM destroyer 151, 267, 273
Beaufort, HM destroyer 211–5, 21–8, 226
Beauregard, ss 151
Bedouin, HM destroyer 19–20, 24, 27–31, 42–3, 48–54,64, 123, 125, 127, 130
Belfast, HM light cruiser 157–61, 164, 237, 276
Belgol, oiler 28
Belgravian, ss 55, 65
Bellingham, SS 140
Belomorkanal, ss 149
Belvoir, HM destroyer 129, 211, 218–9
Benson, A/B H C 267
Bergamot, HM corvette 135, 158, 164
Berwick, HM heavy cruiser 67, 70, 75–7, 123–4
Bethouart, French General 48
Beveerley, H M destroyer 107
Bianca, ss 89
Bideford, H M sloop 99
Birmingham, HM light cruiser 222
Bismarck, German battleship 97, 118, 276
Bissett, R/Adm 186–8
Black Ranger, oiler 135
Blankney, HM destroyer 117, 130–2, 151–2,177
Bleasdale, HM destroyer 237
Blencathra.HM destroyer 227
Blenheim. HM depot ship 130, 142, 169, 178
Blue Ranger, oiler 135
Bluebell, HM corvette 135, 139, 149
Blyskawica, Polish destroyer 49, 54, 257–8, 263
Boadicea, HM destroyer 151, 157–8, 167
Bohmann, Lt-Cdr 137
Bonaventure, H M light cruiser 77–8
Bond Lt B G (Rev Brian) 233, 271
BonDurant, US Cpt Ray 243
Boreas, H M destroyer 112–3

Borum, US destroyer escort 268

Botwood, Sub-Lt R B 256

Boxer, HM LSI 226

Bradley, US Gen Omar 244

Braithwaite, Mrs Joan 272

Bramham, HM destroyer 136

Brecon, HM destroyer 177, 226

Breconshire, RAF 107

Breda, SS 39

Bremen, German liner 19

Bresnan, Jack 79–80

Bretagne, French battleship 58, 60

Briarwood, ss 151

Bridgewater, HM sloop 65

Brigand, tug 222

Brilliant, HM destroyer 96–7, 269

Brissenden, HM destroyer 177, 257, 263–4

British Hope, oiler 85

British Lady, oiler 43

British Lord, oiler 55

British Premier, oiler 79

British yeoman, oiler 99

Britomart, HM minesweeper 123

Broadbent, A/B Thomas Robert 45–6, 220

Brocklesby, HM destroyer 185

Broke, HM destroyer 136

Broom, Operation 184

Broomdale, oiler 24

Broome, Cdr. J 132

Brown Ranger, oiler 107–8, 110

Brownrigg, Capt T M 188–9

Bruce, Captains steward 265–6

Bruiser, HM LSI 226

Brummage, Petty Officer 36

Bruntisfield, Lord 248

Bryony, HM corvette 135, 147

Budd, Rodney "Rosie" 45–6, 48, 50, 52, 55

Bude, HM minesweeper 226

Bulldog, HM destroyer 135, 2648, 272–3

Bulolo, HM HQ ship 226–7, 244

Burfield, Lt J B 135, 236

Burnett, Rear-Admiral Robert 130, 138, 157

C-86, Lighter 268

Cadmus, HM minesweeper 226, 232

Caesar, HM destroyer 269

Caio Duilio, Italian battleship 192

Cairndale, oiler 99

Cairo, HM AA cruiser 39, 122

Calcutta, HM AA cruiser 33, 64, 91, 93

Camellia, HM corvette 135, 147, 149

Campbell, HM destroyer 11

Campioni, Admiral 70, 75

Cap Contin,ss 91

Capetown Castle, ss 79

Cardonrna, Italian light cruiser 192

Carlisle, HM AA cruiser 91, 93, 204

Casanance, SS 65

Catterick, HM destroyer 231–2

Cavalier, HM destroyer 276

Chandler, Larry Verdun 190, 211, 273–4

Charles McCormick, ss 149

Charles Plumier, French blockade-runner 69

Chateau Thierry, US hospital ship 259

Chaudiere, HMC destroyer 249

Cherryleaf, oiler 212, 220

Cheshire, ss 263

Chiddingfold, HM destroyer 152

Chilcott, Paymaster Sub-Lt F G 223, 233

Chiltern, H M trawler 143

Chroby, Polish liner 35, 42

Churchill, Cdr C F H 225, 228–31, 233–4, 236, 240, 2434, 246, 249, 251–2, 254–7, 259

Churchill, Randolph 141

Churchill, Winston S 37, 41, 90, 116, 192, 247

Cilicia, AMC 81

Circe, HM minesweeper 224

City of Nagdapur, ss 81, 85

City of Pretoria, ss 107

Clan Campbell, ss 91

Clan Chattan, ss 91, 263

Clan Cumming, ss 78

Clan Forbes, ss 69, 77

Clan Fraser, ss 69, 77

Clan Lamont, ss 91

Clan McDonald, ss 78

Clarence L Evans, US destroyer escort 266

Clarke, "Nobby" 51

Clematis, H M corvette 79

Clerke, Captain Marshal L 13

Cleopatra, HM light cruiser 180

Cleveland, HM destroyer 227, 232

Coat, Operation 68

Cocking, Ldg Seaman 252

Codrington, HM destroyer 48–9

Coffey, a/b Eric 271

Colborne, Chief Yeoman A L 142, 250

Cole, A P 4

Coles, Vernon 37, 45, 50, 76–7, 79–80, 82, 111

Collar, Operation 69

Colombo, HM AA cruiser 228

Commandant Domine, Free-French sloop 65

Commandant Duboc, Free-French sloop 65

Commandant Teste, French seaplane-carrier 58

Coombes, lt F R 233, 236, 270–1

Copeland, rescue ship 149

Cork & Orrery, Adm of the Fleet, The Earl 43, 47–8

Coreopsis, H M corvette 99

Cornelius Harnett, ss 164, 167

Cornwall, HM heavy cruiser 65

Corrigan, Supply PO 250

Cosby, HM frigate 268–70

Cosham, Ord/Smn George Albert 144

Cosack, H M destroyer 37, 90, 102, 107, 109–110

Cotter, Paymaster Lt. H J C 223

Cottesmore, HM destroyer 250

Courageous, HM aircraft-carrier 20, 26, 33

Coventry, HM AA cruiser 64, 70, 91, 93

Cripps, Sir Stafford 141

Crisp, AB "Crippo" 102

Croome, HM destroyer 192, 263

Croziers, HM destroyer 270

Culpepper, US oiler 149

Cumberland, HM heavy cruiser 65–6, 116, 131–2, 135, 157–160, 164

Cunningham, Admiral A B 60, 68, 78, 90–1, 93, 96, 180, 185, 188–90

Cunningham, Vice-Ad Sir John 223

Cyclamen, H M corvette 79

Da Recco, Italian destroyer 192

Daglish, Lt J S 36

Dalrymple-Hamilton, Lt 220

Danemann, HM trawler

Dangerfield, Brian 192

Daniel, Captain C S 19, 21, 24–6, 29, 33, 36

Dan-y-Bryn, SS 147

Daring, HM destroyer 35

Darlan, French Admiral 58

Dasher, HM escort carrier 158–9

Da Vinci, It sub 112

Defender, H M destroyre 70, 72, 74

De Gaulle, French General Charles 65, 67

de Pass, Midshipman Robert 236, 260

De Salis, Captain Anthony Fane 19, 27, 36–401, 43–9, 50–1, 54–5, 58, 61–2, 70–5, 79, 82, 86, 92–4, 96–9, 102–3, 105–8, 110, 112, 115

Delhi, HM AA cruiser 61, 65, 228

Delight, HM destroyer 35, 42

Delphinium, HM corvette 263

Dempsey, Gen Miles 244–5

Demro, ss 230

Derbyshire, ss 57, 226

Despatch, H M light cruiser 69–70

Deutschland, German pocket-battleship 32

Deveron, HM frigate 171

Deucalion, ss 107

Devonshire, HM heavy cruiser 32–3, 65–7

Diaspro, Italian submarine 97

DeWinton, Captain 58

Diadem, HM light cruiser 237, 239

Diana, HM destroyer 35

Dianella, HM corvette 158

Dick, Commander R M 189

Dicto, blockade-runner 128

Dido, HM light cruiser 90, 93, 199, 204, 222, 228

Dietl, German General 47

Divine, David, journalist 72

Dochet, tig 268

Doenitz, German Admiral Carl 173

Dorsetshire, H M heavy cruiser 80, 98

Douro, ortugese destroyer 107

Douglas, HM destroyer 58, 61, 132

Dracula, Operation 69

Dragon, HM light cruiser 66–7

Dragoon, Operation 69

Du Sautoy, Col, E F 256

Duca degli Abruzzi, Italian light cruiser 189

Duke of York, HM battleship 116–7, 123, 128132, 135, 140, 150

Dulverton, HM destroyer 207–10, 219

Duncan, HM destroyer 68–71, 76–9, 108, 229, 256, 263

Dunedin, HM light cruiser 77, 87

Dunkerque, French battle-cruiser 58, 60, 86, 99

Dunlop, Opeation 90

Duquesne, French heavy cruiser 266

Durham, ss 107, 262

Dynastic, ss 151

Eagen Lt-Cdr Rupert 209

Eastway, HM landing ship dock 263, 266

Echo, HM destroyer 65–6, 118, 123, 128, 130, 142–3, 145, 151, 154, 177–8, 180, 185–6, 188, 192, 197, 199, 204, 211–2, 218–9, 224–5, 230, 251

Eclipse, HM destroyer 5, 42, 65, 78, 123, 130, 132, 135, 150–1, 155, 158, 163–4, 166, 168, 177–8, 180–1, 183–4, 192, 194, 197–8, 204, 207

Edinburgh, HM light cruiser 107, 130

Effingham, HM light cruiser 47, 49

Eggesford, HM destroyer 183

Eisenhower, US General Dwight D 185, 189, 244–5

El Almirante, ss 151

El Oceano, ss 151

El Oro, ss 34

Electra, HM destroyer 39, 43, 49

Empire Auston, ss 227

Empire Beaumont, SS 137

Empire Holly, SS 123

Empire Lance, ss 268

Empire Meteor, ss 151

Empire Morn, ss 149

Empire Rapier, ss 268

Empire Snow, SS 148–9

Empire Song, ss 78, 91–3

Empire Trooper, ss 77

Empress of Australia, liner 35, 56

Empress of Britain, liner 35

Empress of Scotland, liner 258

Enchantress, HM sloop 118

Encounter, HM destroyer 39,47–9, 63–4, 68, 70–3, 76–7, 107, 110–2

Enterprise, HM light cruiser 35, 48–9, 58, 60–4

Erebus, HM monitor 181, 250, 255

Eridge, H M destroyer 107–110

Escapade, HM destroyer 39–14, 43, 47, 49, 57, 63, 65–7, 118, 128, 130–2, 142, 173

Escort, HM destroyer 49, 58, 61

Esk, H M destroyer 43

Eskimo, HM destroyer 20, 24–5, 27–8, 30, 42

Eskwood, ss 265

Essex, ss 78

Ettrick, ss 65–6

Eugenio di Savoia, Italian light cruiser 189

Euryalus, HM light cruiser 180, 182–3

Evans, Admiral 42

Excess, Operation 78

Executive, ss 161–2

Exford, SS 147, 149

Exmoor, HM destroyer 117, 183, 222

Exmouth, H M destroyer 3–5, 8

Express, H M destroyer 43

Fairweather, Rowland 249, 252, 255–6, 259, 261, 271

Fame, HM destroyer 3, 13, 15, 19, 27–8, 307, 51, 55

Fanad Head, SS 20, 24

Fanthorpe, Griff 90, 105, 113

Fardell, Cdr. C E 267, 269–70

Farndale, HM destroyer 107–8, 232, 260
Fast, Flt-Sgt 178
Faulknor, Captain Robert 13
Faulknor, HM destroyer (1914) 13
Faulknor, HM river launch 13
Faulknor, SRS 180
Fearless, HM destroyer 13, 15, 19, 24–9, 57–8, 61, 63–4, 79, 86–91, 93–6, 99, 102–3, 106–8, 110
Fender, Operation 86
Fields, Gracie 229
Fiji, HM light cruiser 65, 86–7, 90–1
Firby, SS
Firedrake, HM destroyer 19–22, 24, 27–8, 30–1, 35–7, 64, 67–70, 72, 75, 77–8, 108–110
Fisher, R/Adm D B 143
Fiume, Italian heavy cruiser 76
Fleur de Lys, H M corvette 99
Flores, Dutch gunboat 185, 224, 250
Fly, HM minesweeper 224
Flying Wing, drifter 64
Forbes, Admiral Sir Charles 17, 27, 30–1, 42
Foresight, HM destroyer 13, 15, 19, 27, 29–32, 34–6, 58, 61–7, 86–7, 904, 96–9, 102, 108, 110
Forester, HM destroyer 13, 15, 24, 27, 29, 31–7, 42–3, 58, 61–72, 76–86, 91, 94–102, 107–110
Formidable, HM aircraft-carrier 175, 178, 180, 185–6
Fort Lamy, ss 65
Fort Meductic, ss 227
Fortune, HM destroyer 13, 15, 19–20, 24–7, 30–8, 42, 51, 64–9, 77–8, 86, 89–92, 94–6
Fougueux, French destroyer
Foxhound, HM destroyer 13, 15, 20–2, 24, 27, 29, 32–7, 42–3, 49, 57–9, 61–2, 69, 77–8, 97, 99, 100, 102–3, 106, 108, 110
Franz, Lt-Cdr Johannes 26
Fraser, Admiral Sir Bruce 248
Frederick Victory, ss 264
Friedrich Ihn, German destroyer 154
Fricke, Lt 102

Furious, HM aircraft-carrier 30, 42, 77–9, 86–7, 96–101, 106–7
Fury, HM destroyer 13, 15, 19, 24–5, 29–33, 35–6, 58, 64–72, 75–9, 86, 90–1, 94–100, 102, 106, 108,110, 123, 126, 130–1, 135, 138, 151, 158, 164, 166–7, 168, 177–8, 180–1, 183, 186, 188–9, 192, 198, 201, 204, 206, 222, 227, 230, 234–9, 247–8
Fusilier, Operation 255

Gairdner, Cpt J O G 65
Gallant, HM destroyer 63–4, 67–8
Gardner, Alfie 118
Garibaldi, Italian light cruiser 189
Garland, Polish manned destroyer 173, 230, 269
Gateway City ss 151
Gatineau, HM Canadian destroyer 249
General George O Squires, US troopship 263
General William Black, US troopship 257
Gensoul, French Admiral 58–9
George VI, King 30, 235, 269
Gibbon, Operation 188
Giulio Cesare, Italian battleship 70, 192
Glaisdale, HM destroyer 237
Glasgow, HM light cruiser 63
Gleaner, HM minesweeper 135
Glen Farg, SS 29–30
Glengyle, HM LSI 226
Gloire, French light cruiser 65
Gloucester, HM light cruiser 78
Glorious, H M aircraft carrier 77, 84
Gloxinia, H M corvette 70, 92
Gneisenau, German battle-cruiser 30, 32, 83–5, 87, 98, 118, 276
Goathland, HM destroyer 250
Golden Fleece, ss 264
Golovko, Soviet Adm 143
Goodyear, Actg P/O D G 154
Goolestan, SS 147–8
Graves, Charles 50–1
Gray, Tgst H 265
Grecale, Italian destroyer 189

Grenade, HM destroyer 47–8
Grenville, HM destroyer 177, 226–7, 253, 255, 277
Gresillion, Tug 268
Greylock, ss 151
Grey Ranger, oiler 132, 135, 140
Greyhound, HM destroyer 63–8, 70, 72, 74
Griffin, HM destroyer 64, 67–8, 70, 72, 74
Grist, Sub-Lt F 236, 251
Grom, Polish destroyer 48–9, 52–5
Growler, Tug 268–9
Guglielmo Marconi, It, submarine 59, 61, 99
Guido, ss 82
Gulnare, armed yacht 268
Gurkha, HM destroyer 37

Haida, HM Canadian destroyer 257
Halcyon, HM minesweeper 149, 158
Haliday, Lt (E) 220
Hambledon, H M destroyer 189
Hammersley, C E 256
Hansford, Mrs A L 272
Hansford, Sylvia 272
Harcourt, R/Adm C H J 183
Hardy, HM destroyer 36–7, 44, 47
Hargood, HM frigate 269
Harrier, HM minesweeper 135
Harriman, Averell 116
Harmodius, ss 81
Harvester, HM destroyer 91, 96–7
Harvey, Sub-Lt Jack F 178
Hats, Operation 64–5
Hav, Soviet whale-catcher 119–120, 122
Havelock, HM destroyer 91, 96–7, 256, 263
Havock, H M destroyer (1898) 4
Havock, H M destroyer (1937) 49
Haydon, HM destroyer 260
Hazard, HM minesweeper 122
HDML-309, HMS 268
Henderson, Lady 9
Henderson, Rear Admiral Sir Reginald 9
Henderson, Captain Johnny 243

Hereward, H M destroyer 70, 72, 74, 77–8

Hermann Kunne, German destroyer 45–6

Hermione, H M light cruiser 106–7, 110

Heuer, Carl 228, 230–1, 235, 241–3, 257, 264

Hero, HM destroyer 43, 49, 77–8

Hesperus, HM destroyer 42, 55, 91, 96–7, 99–100, 102

Hide, Opeation 77

Hilary P Jones, US destroyer 228

Hilary, HM HQ ship 248

Hill, Lt-Cdr R P 127, 177, 253, 234

Hill, Marine Major S 250

Hindpool, ss 81

Hitler, Adolf 106, 153

Holland, Captain C S 59

Holland, Jeffrey 70, 220

Holland-Martin, Cdr. Deric E 'Pinky' 260–1, 265–7, 271

Hollett, Stan 201, 204, 207

Holmes, HM frigate 267

Holmes, Stoker J 241

Hood, HM battle-cruiser 17, 27, 31–2, 36–7, 57, 60–1, 63–4, 87, 97

Horne, Alastair 243

Hornell, V/Adm Sir Robert 179

Honeysuckle, H M corvette 151–2

Horton, Adm Sir Max 258

Hostile, HM destroyer 37, 43, 49

Hotspur, HM destroyer 63–4, 70–1, 256, 266, 271

Hova, French destroyer escort 267

Howe, HM battleship 155, 159, 175, 192, 199

Hoyle, Harry 223

Huffmier, German V/Adm 268

Hughes, Ldg-Acftsmn Bob 'Spike' 178

Hughes-Hallett, Cpt John 248

Hunter, HM destroyer

Huron, HM Canadian destroyer 257, 264–5

Hurry, Operation 63

Hursley, HM destroyer 130

Hurworth, H M destroyer 192, 207

Husky, Operation 69, 177

Hutton, Cpt R M J 183

Hyacinth, H M corvette 70

Hyperion, HM destroyer

Icarus, H M destroyer 31–2, 43, 115, 123, 126, 128, 132, 143, 148, 168, 263

Ijora, SS 199, 122

Ile de France, French liner 257

Ilex. HM destroyer 37, 78, 178, 180, 183–6, 224

Illingwoth, Commodore 81–2

Illustrious, HM aircraft-carrier 64, 78, 186

Ilsenstein, SS 34

Imogen HM destroyer 32, 37, 55–6

Imperial, HM destroyer 32

Imperialist, H M trawler 99

Implacable, HM aircraft carrier

Impulsive, HM destroyer 31–2, 34, 135, 140, 142–3, 147, 149, 158, 163–4, 166, 170–4, 256–8, 260, 264, 269

Inconstant, H M destroyer 163

Indomitable, H M aircraft carrier 175, 177–8, 180–1

Inglefield, HM destroyer 37, 65–7, 130, 132, 151, 154–5, 157–8, 165, 177–8, 180–1, 183–7, 223, 226, 228–30, 259, 276

Inscker, Miss Dayrell 270

Intrepid, HM destroyer 31, 177–8, 180–2, 184–8, 192, 197, 199

Iron Duke, training ship 9

Ironside, Lord 48

Iroquois, HM Canadian destroyer 257, 264

Isis, HM destroyer 34, 76–7, 180, 230, 234–6

Isle of Thanet, HM LSI 263

Italia, Italian battleship 189

Ivanhoe, HM destroyer 31–2, 43

'J' Ships 228

J H Latrobe, ss 166

J L M Curry, ss 151, 164

Jack, Lt W G 36

Jackal, H M destroyer 90

Jackman, Lt H D 268

Jackson, L/S Frank 142

Jaguar, H M destroeyr 70, 77–8

Jaguar, Operation 96

Jamaica, HM light cruiser 135, 152, 261

James Captain A B D 71

James, Captain Jimmy 220

Jaems, Vice-Adm Sir Williams 247

Janus, HM destroyer 64, 78, 225–6

Jason, HM minesweeper 158

Java, ss 264

Javanese Prince, ss 262

Jean Bart, French battleship 58

Jellicoe, Major The Earl 220

Jenkins, W S D 3

Jersey, H M destroyer 90–1, 93

Jervis, HM destroyer 225–6, 228–9, 253, 255

Johnson, Raymond 185, 225, 228, 241, 253, 258, 268

Jupiter, HM destroyer 42, 47

Jutland, SS 123

Karanja, ss 65

Kashmir, HM destroyer 39, 42, 90–1

Keefe, Charles 268

Kelly, HM destroyer 37, 90

Kelvin, HM destroyer 35, 42, 70–1, 247

Kempenfelt.HM destroyer 227, 236–7, 239, 246–8

Kendall, ab C 270

Kent, HM heavy cruiser 130

Kenya, HM light cruiser 81, 123, 130

Kenya, ss 65

Keppel, HM destroyer 58–9, 61, 132, 173

Kersaint, French destroyer 58

Kiely, Dr. David 28

Kimberley, HM destroyer 37, 39, 42–3

Kingcup, HM corvette 263

King George V, H M battleship 78, 87, 98, 123, 128–9, 141, 159, 165

Kingston, HM destroyer 32, 35

Kipling, HM destroyer 90–1

Kirby,.ss 20

Kirriemoor, ss 80

Kirkman, Lt-Gen 268

Knight, W/O Gunner, Henry Page 142, 236

Koenig, French Gen. Joseph 249

Koln, German light cruiser 30, 39, 139, 143

Konigsberg, German light cruiser 39

Kormoran, German raider 103

Krakowiak, Polish destroyer 213, 222

Kuibyshev, Soviet destroyer 143

Kusnec Lesov, SS 148

Kyle Castle, ss 264

La Combatante, Free French destroyer 237–9

La Decouverte, French frigate 267

La Surprise, French frigate 267

Lady Madeline, HM trawler 151–2

Lafayette, ss 149

Laforey, HM destroyer 183–4, 224–6, 229

L'Alcyon, French destroyer 266–7

Lahore, ss 81

Lamerton, HM destroyer 130, 229

Lance, H M destroyer 106–7

Lancier, Italian destroyer 76

Lang, US destroyer 129

Largs Bay, ss 225

Largs, HM HQ ship 69, 246

Lauderdale, HM destroyer 183

Laval, Pierre

Layon, Admiral Sir Geoffrey 269

L'Aventure, French destroyer 266–7, 269

LCH-167, HMS 268

LCI-147, HM landing craft infantry 268

LCI-175, HM landing craft infantry 226

LCI-219, HM landing craft infantry 226

LCI-303, HM landing craft infantry 226

LCI-307, HM landing craft infantry 226

LCI-308, HM landing craft infantry 226

LCT-517 241

Le Fantasque, French destroyer 186

Le Fortune, French destroyer 266–7

Legion, H M destroyer 106–7

Legionario, Italian destroyer 189

Leinster, ss 107–8, 110

Le Terrible, French destroyer 58, 186, 188

Leatham, Adm. Sir Ralph 259, 267, 269

Leda, HM minesweeper 140

Ledbury, HM destroyer 127, 129, 148–9, 151–2, 164, 185

Lee, Tansy 268

Leros, ships dog 223

Lever, Operation 60

Liddesdale, HM destroyer 227

Lightning, H M destroyer 107, 110

Lionel, blockade-runner 128

Lister, P/O Frederick 266, 272

Little Orme, HM drifter 30

Little, Adm Sir Charles 247

Lobelia, HM corvette 173

Loch Shin, HM trawler 52

London, HM heavy cruiser 97, 130, 135, 142, 148

Lookout, HM destroyer 123, 183–4

Loring, HM frigate 263

Lorraine, French battleship 266–7

Lotus, HM minesweeper 164

Lovat, Lord 265–6

Loyal, HM destroyer 183–4, 186, 224, 226

Lutjens, Admiral 84

Lutzow, German pocket-battleship 153

Lynn, Vera 262

Lynx, French destroyer 58

Lyster, Rear-Admiral A L St.G 37

MacDonald, Sub-Lt A 271–2

Mack, Cpt E 183

Mackay, HM destroyer 136

Mackesy, Major-General, P J 43, 47, 54

Madden, Captain A 29

Madierense, Portuguese ss 97

Madison, US destroyer 129, 228

Maiden Creek, ss 230

Malaspina, Italian submarine 112

Malaya, HM battleship 35–6, 76–8, 81–6, 255–6, 264

Malcolm, HM destroyer 135, 137–8

Malloy, US destroyer 255, 268

Maori, H M destroyer 42, 107, 110

Manchester, HM light cruiser 70–1, 75, 107–8, 132

Manxman, H M minelayer 107, 110

Mariposa, ss 269

Marne, HM destroyer 130–2, 135, 142

Marsh, Miss H T 272

Marsdale, Armed Boarding Vessel 102

Marsland Gander, L, journalist 217

Martin, HM destroyer 130–2, 135

Martin, Sub-Lt 171

Mashona, HM destroyer 19, 29–30, 32–3, 40, 42, 64

Matabele, HM destroyer 24, 29, 40, 42, 116–8

Matchless, HM destroyer 130, 152

Mather, Lt P D G 36

Matthers, Lt P D G 118

Matthews, a/b Raymond Herbert 180, 242, 270

Matthews, Mrs 192

Mauretania, RMS 257, 261

Mauritius, HM light cruiser 184–6, 228

May, Lt-Cdr E G 220, 224–6, 233, 261

Mayrant, US destroyer 132

McCoy, Cdr. J A 50

McNeile, Lt N A 220

Mehl, Lt-Cdr 230–2

Melbreak, HM destroyer 260

Melbourne Star, ss 107

Menace, Operation 64–6

Mendip, HM destroyer 231

Meteor, HM destroyer 135

Mew, ferry 273

Meynell, HM destroyer 158, 164–5

Miaoulis, Greek destroyer 201, 203, 206, 210

Mickleburg, HMS 241

Middleton, HM destroyer 129–32, 142, 147–9, 157

Midnight, ss 263

Milford, H M sloop 65, 79

Milne, H M destroyer 135, 138, 157–8

Miska, ships dog 223

ML-443, HM motor launch 188

MMS-302, HM motor minesweeper 255

Mobberley, Councillor 130

Mogador, French destroyer 58, 60

Mohawk, HM destroyer 36, 64

Monarch of Bermuda, liner 35, 43, 56 79

Montecuccoli, Italian light cruiser 189

Montenol, oiler 32

Montgomery, Lieut-Gen Bernard L 242, 244, 246

Montreal, HM Canadian frigate 260

Montrose, HM destroyer 136, 154

Moody, Miss Eileen 180, 249, 256, 272

Moody, Miss Joan 142, 180, 271–2

Moore, Torpedo Officer 224

Morgan, Lt-Cdr E V 73

Morgan, ab 265

Moresby, HM destroyer 36

Mormacmoon, US transport 263

Morosini, Italian submarine 112

Moss, Lt R L 36

Mount Vernon, US troopship 256

Mueller, German Lt-Gen Frederick 216, 220

Musketeer, H M destroyer 148

Naiad, H M light cruiser 79, 107–8, 111–2

Napier, H M destroyer 86

Narborough, HM frigate 262, 265–9

Narcissus, HM corvette 173

Nardana, ss 81

Navarino. Greek destroyer 230

Nelson, HM battleship 17,19, 27, 30–4, 58, 107–8, 110–1, 115–6, 142, 175, 178, 180, 184–7

Nelson, Surgeon-Lt DM, MB, Bch, RBVR 233, 235–6, 239, 241–4, 248–50, 252, 257, 259, 265, 262

Nephrite, ss 264

Neptune, Operation 235

Nestegg, Operation 269

Nevada, ss 65

Newman, Coder Ted 89, 106, 116–7, 123–4, 128, 131, 139–41, 144, 152, 155, 157, 159, 163–4, 171–2, 181, 183, 185, 190, 209–10, 212, 220, 230–1, 258

New Zealand Star, ss 69, 91–2, 262

Newcastle, HM light cruiser 30, 32, 70, 76

Newfoundland, HM light cruiser 183

Nicholson, Capain Gresham 24, 29

Nigeria, HM light cruiser 120–2, 129, 131

Nizam, H M destroyer 86

Norfolk, HM heavy cruiser 97, 135, 160

Norman, HM destroyer 115

Norris, Lt-Cdr Stephen 72, 75

North Devon, SS 38

North, Rear/Adm Sir Dudley 65

Northern Prince, ss 78

Northern Spray, HM trawler 49

Northern Whale, HM trawler 151–2

Nova, Norwegian Puffer 49

Nubian, HM destroyer 37, 64, 258

Nutmeg, Operation 268

O-21, Dutch submarine 90–1

Oakley, H M destroyer 147–8, 183

Obdurate, H M destroyer 157–8

Obedient, H M destroyer 157–9

Ocean Coast, ss 65

Ocean Freedom, SS 161

Ocean Voice, SS 140

Offa, HM destroyer 129, 135, 177–8, 180, 184, 255

Oilgarth, oiler 135, 152, 167

Oliver Ellsworth, SS 137

Olliver, Captain R D 37

Olympus, German troopship 200

Onslaught, HM destroyer 131–2, 135, 137, 142, 148, 154, 169–70, 172–4, 254

Onslow, HM destroyer 123, 127, 130, 132, 135, 138, 140

Opportune, HM destroyer 129, 135, 152, 157–8, 163–4, 166–7

Orchis, HM corvette 173

Oram, Syoker 82

Orania, ss 36

Oremar, ss 152

Oriani, Italian destroyer

Oribi, HM destroyer 130

Orion, HM battleship 118

Orion, HM light cruiser 186, 224–6

Orkan, Polish destroyer 157–8,

Orwell, HM destroyer 147–8, 157–8, 167

Osprey, HM shore base 29

Ottawa, HM Canadian destroyer

Overlord, Operation

Oxlip, H M corvette 151–2

P 614, HM submarine 136

P 615, HM submarine 136

Page, P/O Tel William Henry

Paladin, HM destroyer 224

Palomares, HM AA ship 226–7

Pandora, HM submarine 62–3

Parham, Bob 229, 259

Panther, H M destroyer 142, 178, 204

Parkwood, ss 264

Parsons, Harry 268

Pasteur, French liner 107, 269

Pathfinder, HM destroyer 178, 211–2, 222

Paul Jacobi, German destroyer 154

Paula, German supply ship 194

Pavey, Alife 227, 235, 239, 241, 243

Pead, Chief ERA Horace 111

Pedestal, Operation

Pelican, HM sloop 173–4

Penelope, HM light cruiser 42–3, 51, 178, 180, 184, 199, 201, 203–4, 212–13, 228

Penn, HM destroyer 178, 211–2

Pennland, ss 65

Performance, Operation 128

Peony, H M corvette 70

Persee, French submarine

Pert, P/O George Compton 142, 266

Petain, Marshal 58

Petard, HM destroyer 181, 183–4, 204, 207–10, 213–4
Peter, King of Yugoslavia 142
Peter, Paymaster Lt Rex 142
Peters, Lt, R P 118
Philadelphia, US light cruiser 228
Phipps, Lt Alan 220
Phoebe, HM light cruiser 79, 91, 93, 204, 206, 211, 220
Pindos, Greek destroyer 212–5, 217–8
Pinguin, German raider 103
Piorun, Polish destroyer 154, 177–8, 180, 184–5, 257. 260
Pitcairn, HM frigate 256
Plunkett, US destroyer 129
Pluto, German supply ship 194–5
Poitiers, ss 65
Pompeo Magno, Italian light cruiser 192
Poole, P/O Charles Edward Thomas 142
Poppy, HM corvette 164
Port Arthur, HM Canadian corvette 255
Port Chalmers, ss 107
President Houducce, trawler 65
Prestol, oiler 27, 30
Prince Charles, HM LSI 185
Principle, Operation 86
Prigmore, Eric 141, 175–6, 205
Primauguet, Vichy French cruiser 65
Prince of Wales, HM battleship 97, 116
Princess Beatrix, HM LSI 185, 224
Prinz Eugen, German heavy cruiser 97–8, 123, 154
Proteus, HM submarine 62–3
Provence, French battleship 58, 60
PT-201– US motor torpedo boat 224
PT-202– US motor torpedo boat 224
Puerto Rican, ss 164
Pugsley, Cpt A F 110
Punjabi, HM destroyer 19–20, 24, 27, 29–32, 37, 42–3, 64, 123, 127–8
PWD, Operation 224
Pytchley, HM destroyer 158, 164–5, 167

Quail, HM destroyer 178, 180, 185
Queen Elizabeth, HM battleship 87, 89, 91–3
Queen Mary, RMS 37, 257
Queen Olga, Greek destroyer 180–3, 185–6, 188, 192, 194–9
Queenborough, HM destroyer 154, 178, 180, 185
Quilliam, HM destroyer 178, 180, 185, 223
Quisling, Vidkun 42
Quorn, HM destroyer 250

Rabaul, ss 103
Raeder, German Grand-Admiral 42
Raider, HM destroyer 178, 180–1, 183–8
Raikes, Admiral 81
Railway-I, Operation 106
Railway-II, Operation 106
Ramillies, HM battleship 17, 70, 76, 79, 239, 267
Ramsden, US destroyer escort 264
Ramsey, Admiral Sir Bernard 235, 244–5, 247
Ration, Operation 76
Rawlpindi, AMC 32
Razumny, Soviet destroyer 144
Reina del Pacifico, liner 43
Reith, Lord 248, 264
Rendall, David 33, 48, 51, 76
Renoncule (Free French corvette) 173
Renown, HM battle-cruiser 37–7, 64, 68–973, 75, 77–8, 85–92, 96–102, 106, 108, 110, 116, 123, 127–8, 130
Repulse, H M battle-cruiser 17, 19, 27, 33, 35, 37, 42, 86–7, 89, 91, 116
Resolution, HM battleship 54, 58, 60–1, 63, 65–7, 116–8
Rhind, US destroyer 132
Ribble, HM frigate 260
Richard Beitzen, German destroyer 139
Richard Bland, ss 151, 161, 166
Richelieu, French battleship 58, 60, 66
Rigerman, Soviet Cpt 143
Rigmor, blockade-runner 128–9

Rinaldo, HM minesweeper 226
Rinehart, US destroyer escort 266
Riverton, ss 227
Rivett-Carnac, R/Adm J W 186
Roberts, HM monitor 185
Robinson, Robby 51, 251
Robinson, Lt Cdr J C 72, 75
Rocket, Operation 96–99
Rocket, ships cat 223
Rockwood, HM destroyer 201, 203, 206, 213
Rodney, HM battleship 17, 19, 27, 30–2, 35–7, 42, 98, 175, 178, 180, 1857, 253
Roma, Italian battleship 188
Rommel, General Irwin 60
Romney, H M minesweeper 222
Rooke, Surg-Lt 235
Roosevelt, US President F D 116, 132
Roselys, HM corvette 173
Roskill, Cpt S W 4, 168, 216, 271
Rothesay, HM minesweeper 226
Rowan, US destroyer 132
Royal Oak, HM battleship 17, 33, 37
Royal Sovereign, HM battleship 17, 76, 107
Royal Ulsterman, HM LSI 224
Rue, Rear-Adm G S 266
Rump.Operation 192
Ryder, PO Frederick 223

Sabre, H M destroyer 169
Salamander, HM minesweeper 149
Salient, Operation 90
Sally, ships dog 223
Salvia, H M corvette 70
Samuel Huntingdon, ss 227
Samuel, F/O A C I 177–8
San Ambrosio, oiler 142, 148
San Casimiro, ss 89
San Cipriano, ss 151, 166
Sardonyx, HM destroyer 260
Savorgnan de Izrazza, Free French sloop 65–6
Saumarez, HM destroyer 253–7
Scharnhorst, German battle-cruiser 83, 85, 87, 98, 118, 154, 276
Scholfield, Lt G D L 233, 236, 261

Scollick, Lt J E   223

Scott, H M sloop   35

Scott-Moncrieff, Captain A K   118–122, 126, 128, 130, 135, 137–43, 147–52, 154, 159, 163–6, 168–78, 180–1,183–5, 189, 191, 193, 197–8, 205, 256

Scourge, HM destroyer   247

Scurfield, Cdr B G   127

Scylla, HM AA cruiser   1135, 138, 140, 158, 165, 244–5

Seek, Opeation   77

Selby, Lt-Cdr W H   169

Sharpshooter, HM minesweeper   123, 135, 148–9

Sharman, Captain F W , RA   240

Sheffield, HM light cruiser   19, 27, 30, 39, 42, 64, 68–70, 77–8, 86–7, 90–1, 96–100, 124–5, 135, 152, 154, 157–9

Shika, Soviet whale-catcher   119–20

Shivlock, Miss S   270

Shingle, Operation   222, 224–5

Sibley, Sid   251

Siggins, Ldg/Smn Joe   45

Sikh, HM destroyer   37, 102, 107, 110

Silltow, Bill   105, 154, 212

Silver Laurel, ss   260

Silver Sword, SS   140

Sioux, HM Canadian destroyer   237–8

Sirius, HM light cruiser   199–201, 206

Skeena, HMC destroyer   58

Slinger, Ted   178

Smith, Ron   152–3

Smith, Surgeon-Lt T   233

Sobieski, ss   65, 226

Sokrushiteny, Soviet destroyer   144

Solbin, SS   48

Somali, HM destroyer   19, 24, 29–30, 32–3, 40–2, 130, 132, 135, 140, 160

Somerville, Admiral Sir James   57–8, 60, 64, 69–71, 75, 77, 81, 86–7,, 89–91, 96–8, 102, 106–8, 110–1

Southampton, HM light cruiser   70, 78

Spademan, Lt Philip   178

Spanner, Ldg/Smn, John W   32

Spark, Operation   63

Spartan, HM light cruiser   225–7

Spearfish, H M submarine   27

Speedwell, HM minesweeper   122

Splice, Operation   96

Spragge, HM frigate   262

St. Albans Victory, ss   102, 263

Stalin, Marshal Josef   134

St Elstan, trawler   164, 166

St. Laurent, HMC destroyer   58

St. Mihiel, US troopship   259

St.Helier, ss   268

St.Olaf, SS   147

Stalingrad, Soviet freighter   122–3, 137

Stapleton, Harry   110, 114, 273

Stark, Lt R   223

Star of Australia, liner   173

Starwort, H M corvette   164

Sterrett, US destroyer   129

Stevenstone, HM destroyer   237–9, 246–7

Stileman, Ltd Cdr L H   36

Stord, Norwegian destroyer   247

Strasbourg, French battle-cruiser   60

Style, Operation   110

Substance, Operation   107–9

Suffolk, HM heavy cruiser   135, 147

Superb, HM light cruiser   256

Sussex, HM heavy cruiser   266

Swordfish, HM submarine   39

Sydney Star, ss   107–8

TA-24, German destroyer   246

Taku, H M submarine   94

Tanatside, HM destroyer   257, 263–4

Tancock, Lt-Cdr E B, DSC   72

Tartar, HM destroyer   19–20, 24–5, 40, 64

Taxiarorus, ss   85

Telemachus, HM submarine   262

Temple Arch, ss   149

Tennyson, Mr, DNC   274

Terre Neuve, Vichy ship   60

Tetcott, HM destroyer   226

Themistocles, Greek destroyer   222

Thomas, Captain Mervyn Somerset   192, 195, 200, 206, 208–219, 223–225

Thomas, ERA Edwain   142

Thornborough, HM frigate   266–7

Thruster, HM LSI   226–7, 230

Tielbank, ss   81

Tiger, HM battle-cruiser   36

Tiger, Operation   90–1

Tigre, French destroyer   58

Tirpitz, German battleship   118, 125–7, 132, 135–6, 151, 276

Tjerk Hiddes, Dutch destroyer   262

Todd, Commodore Peter   197

Todd, Lt-Col. R J F

Torelli, Italian submarine   112

Towy, HM frigate   173

Tracer, Operation   96, 99

Trafalgar, ss   103

Trapani, German troopship   214

Tregoining, Miss Dorothy   261

Trimmingham, Derisley   229

Trinidad, HM light cruiser   116

Triumph, H M submarine   76

Troubridge, HM destroyer   178, 180

Troubridge, R/Adm Tom   227

Tumult, HM destroyer   180

Tuscaloosa, US light cruiser   129–30

Tyne, HM depot ship   116–7, 123, 142, 155, 235, 247

Typhoon, Operation   216

Tyrian, HM destroyer   180, 185

U-27, German submarine   25

U-30, German submarine   33–4

U-31, German submarine   33

U-39, German submarine   24, 26

U-50, German submarine   36

U-88, German submarine   137, 205

U-94, German submarine   112

U-95, German submarine   91

U-98, German submarine   112

U-105, German submarine   81, 85

U-124, German submarine   81, 85

U-138, German submarine   101–2

U-218, German submarine   173

U-255, German submarine   159, 161, 166

U-305, German submarine   173

U-371, German submarine   230, 232

U-407, German submarine   222

U-457, German submarine   140
U-468, German submarine   173
U-486, German submarine   260
U-556, German submarine   98
U-557, German submarine   112
U-561, German submarine   112
U-565, German submarine   112
U-589, German submarine   140
U-601, German submarine   148
U-622, German submarine   159
U-625, German submarine   148
U-752, German submarine   173
U-1209, German submarine   260
UJ 2104, German escort vessel 194–5
UJ-2111, German escort vessel 201
Ukagir, Soviet oiler   143
Ulster Queen, HM AA ship 135, 229
Ulster, HM destroyer   226–7
Ulysses, H M destroyer   255
Undaunted, HM destroyer   235, 247
Undine, H M destroyer   247
Unruly, HM submarine   200
Urania, HM destroyer   234–5, 253
Urchin, HM destroyer   225–6, 229, 247
Uritski, Soviet destroyer   144
Ursa, HM destroyer   235

V-4, German destroyer   36
Valiant, HM battleship   35, 37, 42, 58, 61, 63–4, 175, 178, 180–1, 1869, 263
Valorous, HM destroyer   128
Van de Wald, Eng. Lt Peter J 233, 236
Van Galen, Dutch destroyer 261–3
Vanity, HM destroyer   128
Vanoc, HM destroyer   262
Vansittart, H M destroyer   100
Velite, Italian destroyer   189
Velox, H M destroyer   58, 61, 63–4, 81
Venerable, Operation   266
Venomous, HM destroyer   135
Venus, HM destroyer   237–9, 246–7
Vian, Adm Philip   244–5, 248
Victorious, HM aircraft-carrier 99–100, 102, 117–8, 123, 126, 128–32, 141

Victory, HMS   224, 236
Vidette, HM destroyer   58, 64, 81
Vienna, ss   266
Vigilant, HM destroyer   237–8, 247
Ville d'Alger, liner   56
Villiers, Cdr R A   198
Vimy, HM destroyer   34
Vindictive, HM repair ship 48–9, 61
Viscount, HM destroyer   171
Vittorio Veneto, Italian battleship   70, 189
Vivacious, HM destroyer   154, 164–5, 167
von Goertzke   24
Vortigern, HM destroyer
VP-63, US squadron   132, 231
Wainwright, US destroyer   129
Wakefield, US troopship   258
Waldegrave, HM frigate   269
Walker, HM destroyer   34
Wallace, HM destroyer   128
Walter, Cdr, P N   35
War Diwan, oiler   19, 27, 31–2, 36
War Pindari, oiler   32, 57
Warspite, HM battleship   36, 42–3, 47, 49, 51, 75, 175, 178, 180–2, 185–9, 239, 255
Washington, US battleship 129–32
Wasp, US aircraft-carrier   129
Watchman, HM destroyer   58, 269
Waterwitch, H M netlayer   226
Watson, A   118, 142
Watson, Mrs   180
Wells, Lt W R   233
Weser Exercise, Operation   39
West, A/B Thomas William 140, 142
Westenland, ss   65
Westeerly Victory, ss   264
West Gotomska, ss   151
Weston, HM sloop   266
Whaddon, HM destroyer   183, 223
Wheatland, HM destroyer 129–32, 135, 139, 185,224, 229
Whirlwind, HM destroyer 55–6
White Clover, SS   147
White, Operation   69

Whitehall, HM destroyer   263
Whitworth, Vice-Admn   42–3
Wichita, US light cruiser 129–30
Wild Swan, HM destroyer 100, 112–3
Wilfred, Operation   42
Wilkes, US R/Adm J W   253
William Moultrie, SS   148–9
Williams, Cpt   222
Willis, R/Adm Sir Algernon 181, 186, 214–6, 218–9, 248
Willmott, Lt. H N C   55
Wilson, US destroyer   129
Wilton, HM destroyer   135
Winch, Operation   86
Windrush, ss   151
Wingrove, LdgSeamn Eric G 271
Winkler, Uffz Horst   252
Wirtz, Idris Wiliam   77
Wishart, HM destroyer   58, 64, 68–9, 70–1, 80, 98, 100
Wivern, H M destroyer   100
Wolf, Maj-Gen   268
Wolgan, Cpt, RA   243
Woolwich, HM depot ship   35, 39, 57
Wren, HM destroyer   55
Wrestler, HM destroyer   58, 61, 67, 80, 89, 91–100
Wynn, Tmpy Cpt (Eng) L A 271

Yarrow, Sir Harold   3
York, HM heavy cruiser   64

Z-20, German destroyer   139
Z-23, German destroyer   139
Z-24, German destroyer   154, 246
Z-27, German destroyer   139
Z-29, German destroyer   139
Z-30, German destroyer   139
Z-32, German destroyer   246
ZH-1, German destroyer   246
Zetland, H M destroyer   228
Zulu, HM destroyer   39–41, 43–4, 46–7, 49, 51–2, 64